play the french

3rd edition

by John Watson

EVERYMAN CHESS

Gloucester Publishers plc   www.everymanchess.com

First published in 2003 by Gloucester Publishers plc (formerly Everyman Publishers plc), Gloucester Mansions, 140A Shaftesbury Avenue, London WC2H 8HD

British Library Cataloguing-in-Publication Data
A catalogue record for this book is available from the British Library.

ISBN 1 85744 337 3

Distributed in North America by The Globe Pequot Press, P.O Box 480, 246 Goose Lane, Guilford, CT 06437-0480.

All other sales enquiries should be directed to Everyman Chess, Gloucester Publishers plc, Gloucester Mansions, 140A Shaftesbury Avenue, London WC2H 8HD (tel: 020 7539 7600 fax: 020 7379 4060)
email: info@everymanchess.com; website: www.everymanchess.com

Everyman is the registered trade mark of Random House Inc. and is used in this work under license from Random House Inc.

EVERYMAN CHESS SERIES (formerly Cadogan Chess)
Chief advisor: Garry Kasparov
Commissioning editor: Byron Jacobs

Typeset and edited by First Rank Publishing, Brighton.
Cover design by Horatio Monteverde.
Production by Navigator Guides.
Printed in the United States by Versa Press.

Contents

Bibliography

Books
Advance French: Alternatives to 4 c3, Jim Bickford (Syzygy 2002)
Chess Informant 1-86, Chess Informant
C18-19 French Defence, Viktor Korchnoi (Chess Informant 1993)
Die Franzoesische Verteidigung 3.Sc3, Hagen Tiemann (Reinhold Dreier 1998)
Four Gambits To Beat the French, Tim Harding (Chess Digest 1998)
Franzoesisch Winawer: 7 Qg4 0-0, Stefan Kindermann & Ulrich Dirr (Chessgate 2001)
French Classical, Byron Jacobs (Everyman Chess 2001)
French Defence 3 Nd2, Lev Psakhis (Batsford 2003)
French Defence Main Line Winawer, John Moles (B T Batsford 1975)
French Defence, Alexander Kalinen (Russian Chess House 2002)
French Defence, Neil McDonald, (ChessPublishing.com)
French Defense 2, Nikolai Minev (Thinker's Press 1998)
French Winawer, Neil McDonald (Everyman Chess 2000)
New In Chess Magazine and Yearbook through 2003, New In Chess
The French Tarrasch, John Emms (B T Batsford 1998)
Encyclopaedia of Chess Openings C, 4th Edition, Chess Informant 2000
The Main Line French: 3 Nc3, Steffan Pedersen (Gambit 2001)
The Complete French, Lev Psakhis (Batsford 1992)

Databases and software
MegaBase2003
TWIC 1-457 (This Week in Chess, games)
Correspondence Database 2002; ChessBase, 2002
MegaCorr2; Tim Harding, 2001
ChessBase Magazine (CBM) through #89; CD-ROM; ChessBase

Introduction

It may surprise the reader that in my largest database, mostly consisting of games from the last 10 years, the French Defence has been played in about 6.75% of *all* chess games (the French Defence figure excludes King's Indian Attacks that can also be reached by a Sicilian Defence order). This is less than 1 e4 e5 and less than the always-popular Sicilian Defence, but more than the Najdorf, Dragon, Rauzer, Accelerated Fianchetto and Taimanov Sicilians combined! In correspondence chess, the percentage rises to 8.2%, quite a chunk of all games played. The popularity of the French derives from its flexible and double-edged character. One can play it safely or with the most aggressive intentions. Black's share of the centre is greater than in most other defences to 1 e4, arguably only less than that after 1...e5 (which tends to cede space early on anyway). Thus the risk of being overrun is small and at the same time White is hard-pressed to make his first-move advantage count at all. Finally, Black can achieve dynamic counterchances in every main line.

I associate today's modern French Defence with specialists and innovators such as Bareev, Morozevich, Radjabov, Mikhail Gurevich, Korchnoi, Lputjan, Psakhis, Khalifman, Dreev, Nikolic, Uhlmann, Chernin, Kiriakov, Djurhuus, Yusupov, Sergey Ivanov, Ulybin, Gulko and Kindermann. Other leading players like Shirov, Ivanchuk, and Anand also use the French from time to time. Only a very few openings are played with such regularity at the grandmaster level.

As with the first two editions of *Play the French*, this is a repertoire book that offers the reader two or more distinct variations to play against all important white systems. The idea is to provide maximum flexibility should some line of play prove unsatisfactory or in need of repair. As always, 8 years of practice since the last edition have drastically altered the theory on practically every variation. I have therefore thoroughly revised most older lines, but also presented new solutions. For example, I have added the Classical System (1 e4 e6 2 d4 d5 3 ♘c3 ♘f6), the Tarrasch Variation with 3...♗e7 (after 1 e4 e6 2 d4 d5 3 ♘d2), a set of new answers to the King's Indian Attack (1 e4 e6 2 d3), a new Main-Line Winawer Variation (3 ♘c3 ♝b4 leading to 7 ♕g4 0-0), and so forth. This is not to say that any major systems in the last edition are bad; on the contrary, none of them has been discredited. The inclusion of these new lines, however, provides some fresh air and illustrates the breadth of playable variations in the French Defence. Of special note: Chapter 12 expands upon the lines of the 6...♕c7 Winawer that were presented in the second edition. Full credit for this chapter goes to Norwegian FM Hans Olav Lahlum, who updated all of the variations therein. He used sources that I wouldn't have had access to and the insights of many strong players to put together a lucid exposition of that system. See also that chapter's introduction.

An opening book that tries to cover every useful byway will necessarily be dense and in some spots difficult to read. Thus one may want to skim over chapters before settling in to a closer examination. But I would urge the reader to pay particular attention to logical alternatives to what are (temporarily) the 'main lines'. This not only prepares one to meet moves that are likely to be played, but also informs one of key ideas that may not be explicitly re-described as the main line unfurls.

There are too many people to thank individually; I am in debt to the many, many players who sent me material and questions via email. I received by far the most help from the above-mentioned Hans Olav Lahlum, who apart from Chapter 12 sent me many games and ideas in numerous other variations. Hans Olav wants to thank his friends who helped with the chapter on 6...♕c7; they are cited in his exposition. Two players that were particularly helpful were my friend Joachim Wintzer, who made pertinent suggestions, and the insightful Antti Koponen who provided me with some excellent new ideas. French expert Stefan Kindermann nudged me in the right direction at the right time. Finally, my editor Byron Jacobs deserves credit for shaping a rough manuscript into a coherent and hopefully readable book.

John Watson,
September 2003

Chapter One

Advance Variation: Introduction

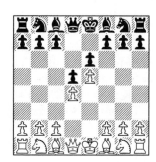

1 e4 e6 2 d4 d5 3 e5

Historically, the Advance Variation and the Exchange Variation were the first popular responses to the French Defence. The theory of 3 e5 was stimulated by the provocative ideas of Nimzowitsch but no leading advocate took his place and the Advance Variation was in remission for most of the modern era. In the last two decades, however, 3 e5 has taken a quantum leap in popularity. With the increasing number of top-level players using the French and with White's inability to find promising positions in many traditional lines with 3 ♘c3 and 3 ♘d2, leading grandmasters have employed 3 e5 to get a different type of central advantage. They have devised new strategies to support that centre, notably by flank advances on both wings. These innovations have enjoyed considerable success at the top levels; at the moment, the Advance Variation is so popular that it barely lags behind 3 ♘d2 in frequency (with 3 ♘c3 still very much the leading choice, of course).

3...c5

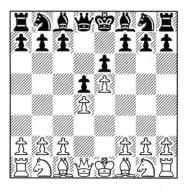

The principled continuation, attacking the centre at its base (d4). Now White has four main choices. 4 c3 is the main line and subject of Chapters 2 and 3. Here we look at:

1.1 4 dxc5
1.2 4 ♕g4
1.3 4 ♘f3

Others are either unchallenging or weak:

(a) 4 b4?! is a sort of Wing Gambit that is popular at lower levels (compare Chapter 15); Black continues 4...cxd4 5 a3 and now:

(a1) 5...♘c6 6 f4 (6 ♘f3 ♕c7 7 ♗f4

♘ge7 intending ...♘g6) 6...♘h6 (6...a5 7 b5 ♘ce7 8 ♘f3 ♘f5 9 ♗d3 ♘gh6∓ with the ideas ...♗c5 and ...♘e3 Frenkel-Rao, Boston 1988) 7 ♘f3 (7 b5 ♘e7 8 ♘f3 ♘ef5∓) 7...a5 8 b5 ♘e7 9 ♘xd4 ♘ef5∓ with multiple ideas including ...♕b6 and ...♗c5;

(a2) 5...a5!? is another good solution, e.g., 6 b5 ♘d7 7 ♘f3 (or 7 f4 ♘h6 8 ♘f3 ♘f5 9 ♗d3 ♘e3 and ...♗c5) 7...♕c7 8 ♗f4 ♘e7 9 ♗e2 ♘g6 10 ♗g3 ♗c5∓ Cherkasov-Nikolenko, Czestochowa 1992;

(b) 4 ♗e3 ♕b6 5 b3!? (5 dxc5 ♗xc5 6 ♗xc5 ♕xc5 is comfortable, e.g., 7 ♕g4?! ♕xc2! 8 ♕xg7 ♕c1+ 9 ♔e2 ♕xb2+ 10 ♘d2 ♕xa1 11 ♕xh8 ♔f8) 5...♘c6 6 ♘f3 cxd4 7 ♗xd4 ♘xd4 8 ♕xd4 ♗c5 9 ♕d2 ♘e7∓ Renaud-Hook, Dubai 1986;

(c) 4 f4 is probably the most interesting of these deviations, but it takes time and opens White's centre to attack after 4...♘c6 (or 4...cxd4 5 ♘f3 ♘c6 and 6 ♘xd4 ♕b6 or 6 ♘bd2 ♘h6 7 ♗d3 ♘g4 8 ♘b3 ♗b4+ 9 ♔e2 f6 10 h3 ♘e3 11 ♗xe3 dxe3 12 c3 ♗e7∓) 5 c3 ♕b6 6 ♘f3 ♘h6 7 b3 (two lines that leave Black with a pair of bishops and White with a miserable one are 7 ♕b3 cxd4 8 ♕xb6 axb6 9 cxd4 ♘f5 10 ♗b5 ♗d7 11 ♗xc6 bxc6 Pulnikov-Iljin, Togliatty 2001; and 7 ♗d3 ♗d7 8 ♕b3 ♕xb3 9 axb3 cxd4 10 ♘xd4 ♘xd4 Ozkan-Ozturk, Ankara 2002, when simplest was 11 cxd4 ♘f5 12 ♗xf5 exf5∓) 7...cxd4 8 cxd4 ♗b4+ 9 ♔f2 – analysis by Minev. At this point a cute and effective line is 9...♘g4+! 10 ♔g3 (10 ♔g1 ♗e1!, and 11 ♕xe1? ♘xd4 12 ♗e3 ♘xf3+ 13 gxf3 ♘xe3-+ or 11 g3 ♗f2+ 12 ♔g2 ♘xd4∓) 10...h5 11 h3 h4+! 12 ♘xh4 (12 ♔xg4 f5+ 13 exf6 e5+) 12...♖xh4! 13 ♗e2 (13 ♔xh4 ♘f2 14 ♕h5 ♕xd4!) 13...♘f2! 14 ♔xf2 ♘xd4∓;

(d) 4 ♘d2!? is the equivalent of the Tarrasch variation 3 ♘d2 c5 with the strange-looking 4 e5!?. Black can play 4...cxd4 (or 4...♘c6, e.g., 5 ♘gf3 ♕b6 6 dxc5 ♗xc5 7 ♕e2 Balogh-Rittner, corr 1958, and now the easiest move is 7...f6 8 ♘b3! fxe5 9 ♘xc5 ♕xc5 10 ♘xe5 ♘f6 with development and activity; Black even has the idea of ...♘xe5 and then ...♕xf2+) 5 ♘gf3 ♘c6 6 ♘b3 ♕c7 7 ♗b5 (7 ♗f4 ♗b4+) 7...♗d7 8 ♗xc6 (8 ♕e2 ♗b4+ 9 ♗d2 ♗xd2+ 10 ♘bxd2 ♘ge7∓) 8...bxc6 9 ♕xd4 c5 10 ♕f4 ♘e7 with the two bishops and intending 11 ♘g5 f6! 12 exf6 ♕xf4 13 ♗xf4 gxf6 with a massive centre;

(e) 4 ♗f4 cxd4 (4...♕b6 5 b3 ♘c6∓) 5 ♘d2 ♕b6 6 ♘b3 ♗b4+ (Harding). Then 7 ♗d2 ♘c6 8 ♘f3 f6 is good for Black;

(f) 4 ♗b5+ will trade White's 'good' bishop for Black's 'bad' one, but the real problem is that it helps Black to develop: 4...♗d7 (or 4...♘c6, since 5 ♘f3 ♕b6 gains a tempo unless White plays the depressing 6 ♗xc6+ bxc6) 5 ♗xd7+ ♘xd7 6 ♘f3 (6 c3 ♕b6 followed by ...♘e7-c6 and/or ...f6 depending upon White's plan) 6...cxd4 7 ♕xd4 ♗c5 8 ♕d3 f6! 9 ♗f4 ♕b6 10 0-0 ♘e7!? (10...g5!, e.g., 11 ♗g3 g4 12 ♘fd2 fxe5) 11 exf6 gxf6 12 ♕b3!? ♕c6 13 ♗e3 e5 and Black has his typical central advantage, T.Barnes-Sporn, email 1998.

1.1 4 dxc5

One of White's most popular options to 4 c3. Rather than defend d4, White shifts his attention to bolstering e5 and bringing his pieces to more active squares than in other lines. The drawbacks to 4 dxc5 are that White gives up the pillar of his centre and Black develops rapidly. I find this variation truly instructive in that one will see the combination of dxc5 and e5 throughout this book in re- markably many variations exhibiting similar strategies.

4...♘c6

Avoiding the awkward 4...♗xc5 5 ♕g4.

5 ♘f3!

White should avoid 5 ♗f4?! ♗xc5 6 ♗d3?, which practically loses after 6...♕b6! 7 ♘c3 (7 ♘f3 ♗xf2+ 8 ♔e2 ♕xb2∓) 7...♗xf2+! 8 ♔f1 ♗d4 and Black stands to win. Also not impres- sive are 6 c3 ♘ge7 7 ♘f3 ♘g6 8 ♗g3 f6! 9 b4 ♗b6 10 exf6 ♕xf6 11 ♗d3 0-0∓ and 6 ♕g4 ♘ge7! with the idea 7 ♕xg7 (7 ♗d3 ♕b6) 7...♖g8 8 ♕xh7 ♗xf2+! 9 ♔xf2 ♕b6+ 10 ♔e2 ♕xb2.

5...♗xc5

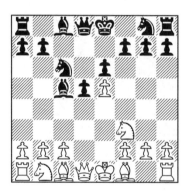

6 ♗d3

(a) 6 a3?! is too slow after 6...f6: 7 b4 ♗b6 8 b5!? (8 exf6 ♘xf6 9 ♗e2 0-0 10 0-0 e5! 11 b5 ♘d4) 8...♘xe5 9 ♘xe5 fxe5 10 ♕h5+ ♔f8 11 ♕xe5 ♗c7 and Black wins the centre again, e.g., 12 ♕e3 ♕f6 13 ♖a2 ♘e7 14 ♗b2 e5;

(b) 6 ♗f4?! allows 6...♕b6 (6...♘ge7 and 6...f6 are also fine) 7 ♗g3 ♕xb2 8 ♘bd2 ♘ge7 with White having insuf- ficient compensation for a pawn.

6...f6

The clearest course, since it liqui-

dates the centre. For those wishing for a game of a more closed nature, 6...♘ge7 is a good alternative:

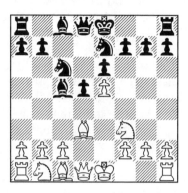

(a) 7 0-0 ♘g6 8 ♖e1 (a good plan for Black is illustrated by 8 ♕e2 0-0 [or 8...♗b6 9 c3 ♗c7 10 ♗g5 ♕d7 11 ♗xg6 fxg6] 9 c3 ♗b6 10 ♘a3 ♗c7 Avirovic-Subaric, Novi Sad 1945; now White should try 11 ♗xg6 fxg6, but Black has at least equal play, espe- cially since in many lines ...♖xf3 can give him a pawn, mobile centre, and attack for the exchange) 8...♕c7!? (8...0-0 may be the easiest course, intending ...♗b6, ...♗d7, ...♗c7 and responding to ♗xg6 with ...fxg6) 9 ♕e2 ♘d4 (Czerniak suggests 9...♗d7 followed by ...0-0-0) 10 ♘xd4 ♗xd4 11 ♗xg6 fxg6!? (the most interesting move) 12 c3 ♗b6 (12...♗c5! is more accurate; Black follows up as in the game, or by ...0-0, ...♗d7 and dou- bling on the f-file) 13 ♘d2 0-0 14 ♘f3 ♗c5 (a tempo down, but still satisfac- tory) 15 ♗e3 b6 16 ♗d4 a5 17 ♕e3 ♗a6 18 ♖ad1 h6 with interesting play, Westermeier-Reefschlaeger, Menden 1974. Black has the idea of ...g5 and again doubling rooks;

(b) 7 ♘c3 a6!? (to secure a7 for the bishop; 7...♘g6 is equal) 8 0-0 ♘g6 9 ♗xg6!? (9 ♖e1 0-0 and White lacks for a plan) 9...hxg6 10 ♘e2 ♕c7 11 ♗f4

Biti-Thi Thanh Houng, Moscow 1994, when 11...♗d7 12 ♕d2 0-0-0 was natural and good;

(c) 7 ♗f4 ♕b6 (the most ambitious; 7...♘g6 is also logical) 8 0-0 ♘g6 9 ♗g3 (9 ♕c1 ♘xf4 10 ♕xf4 – Keres, but Black can grab a pawn and reduce White's attacking possibilities by 10...♕xb2 11 ♘bd2 f5!; in P.Short-Heidenfeld, Castleconnell 2000, White tried the gambit 9 ♗xg6 fxg6 10 ♘c3, but Black can simply grab a pawn by 10...♕xb2, since 11 ♘a4 ♕b4 12 ♘xc5 ♕xf4 gives White very little) 9...♕xb2 10 ♘bd2 ♘gxe5! (10...♕a3 11 h4 ♕a4!? with the idea 12 h5 ♘f4 is also interesting) 11 ♘xe5 ♘xe5 12 ♖b1 ♕c3 13 ♖b3 ♕d4 14 ♗xe5 (14 ♗b5+ ♘d7 15 ♗xd7+ ♗xd7 16 ♖xb7 – Pachman, when 16...♗c6 17 ♖c7 ♕a4 consolidates the pawn) 14...♕xe5 15 ♗b5+. This keeps the king in the centre but Black has the bishop pair and mobile central pawns: 15...♔e7 16 ♖e1 ♕d4 17 ♖ee3 a6 18 ♗f1 ♖d8 19 ♖bd3 ♕h4 20 ♖g3 g6 21 c4 ♔f8 and White had no compensation, T.Johansson-E.Berg, Bergen 2001.

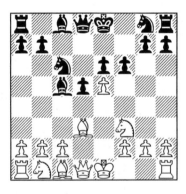

7 ♕e2

7 ♗b5? ♕b6 intending 8 ♕e2 ♗xf2+ is weak, and the others are fun for Black:

(a) 7 exf6?! ♘xf6 8 0-0 0-0 9 c4 (9 ♖e1 e5!; 9 ♕e2 e5! 10 ♘xe5 ♘xe5 11 ♕xe5 ♘g4 12 ♕h5 g6∓) 9...♕d6 (9...e5!? 10 cxd5 e4 11 dxc6 ♕xd3 12 ♕xd3 exd3∓ Van Scheltinga-Van der Tol, Netherlands 1946) 10 ♘c3 a6 11 ♗g5?! ♘g4!∓ intending ...♖xf3 Camilleri-Debarnot, Malta 1980;

(b) 7 ♗f4? practically loses by force: 7...fxe5 (or 7...♕b6) 8 ♗xe5 (8 ♘xe5? ♕f6∓, e.g., 9 ♘xc6 ♕xf4 10 ♕h5+ g6 11 ♗xg6+ ♔f8 12 ♘e5 ♘f6 13 ♕e2 ♕c1+ 14 ♕d1 ♕xd1+ 15 ♔xd1 ♗d4-+ Rohel-Keitlinghaus, Badenweiler 1990) 8...♘f6 (or 8...♘xe5! 9 ♘xe5 ♕g5) 9 0-0 0-0 (threatening ...♘g4) 10 h3 ♘e4! 11 ♕e2 ♖xf3! 12 gxf3 ♕g5+ 13 ♔h1 ♘xf2+, etc.

7...fxe5

Here Black can play ultra-dynamically by 7...♕c7!? 8 ♗f4 g5! 9 ♗g3 g4.

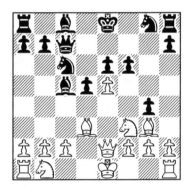

This wins a key central pawn at the cost of exposing Black's king. Thus far this move has done reasonably well and I see nothing wrong with it. Here are two examples: 10 ♘fd2 (10 ♘h4 ♘xe5 11 0-0 ♗d6 12 ♘c3 a6 was solid enough in Van der Nat-Van Oirschot, corr 1976) 10...♘xe5 11 ♗b5+ ♔f8!? (11...♗d7 12 ♗xd7+ ♔xd7 is also unclear. White wants to attack, Black to consolidate his extra pawn by, e.g., ...♖e8 and ...♔c8) 12 ♘c3 ♗d4 13 0-0 a6 14 ♗d3 h5 with the idea ...h4, Thomson-Caamano, corr 1988. Black's intended ...h4 will interfere with White's only dangerous plan of ♔h1 and f3. The game continued 15 ♖fe1 h4 16 ♗xe5 ♗xe5 17 ♕xg4 ♗xh2+ 18 ♔h1 ♗d6 19 ♕f3 ♗d7 and White didn't have enough for the pawn.

8 ♘xe5

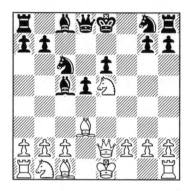

It's remarkable that this position might even turn out to be advantageous for Black. His central majority is very important and White cannot maintain his outpost on e5.

8...♘xe5

This leads to a degree of simplification, but there remains an imbalance in the position. Instead 8...♘f6 can be played in order to equalise or even win if Black is willing to take some risks. He threatens ...♘xe5 and ...♗xf2+, and play might go 9 ♗f4 (9 0-0?! ♘xe5 10 ♕xe5 0-0 11 c4 ♕b6 again threatens ...♗xf2+: 12 ♕e2 ♗d7 13 ♘d2 ♖ac8∓ Makropoulos-Hug, Nice 1974; 9 ♘xc6 bxc6 10 ♘d2 0-0 11 ♘f3 ♕c7! planning ...♗d6 and in some cases ...♘g4) and now:

(a) 9...0-0 heads for equality: 10 0-0 ♘e4 11 ♘xc6 bxc6 12 ♗e3 ♗xe3!? 13 ♕xe3 ♘f6 14 ♘d2 Becker-Maroczy, Karlsbad 1929; now Becker gives 14...♕b6! when a plausible line is 15

♕xb6 (15 ♕e5 ♕b8!? 16 ♘f3 ♘g4 17 ♕h5 ♘f6 18 ♕e5=) 15...axb6 16 ♘f3 c5 17 ♘e5 (17 c4 ♖a4!? 18 b3 ♖a3) 17...c4 18 ♗e2 ♘d7 19 ♘xd7 ♗xd7 20 f4 ♔f7= intending ...♗e7-d6.

(b) 9...♕b6!? is more ambitious and practically forces White to gambit by, for example, 10 0-0 (or 10 ♘xc6 ♕xb2 11 ♕e5 ♕b6) 10...♕xb2 11 ♘xc6 bxc6 12 ♘d2 ♕a3, when White has something for the pawn but I'm not sure that it's enough.

9 ♕xe5 ♕f6

This is Black's best chance for advantage: he tries to get to an ending that will be favourable to him by virtue of his central majority. Again 9...♘f6 suffices for easy equality and perhaps a tiny bit more. White must take care, e.g., 10 0-0 (10 ♗f4? ♗xf2+; 10 ♗b5+?! ♔f7 when ...♕b6 and ...♖f8 with ...♔g8 will follow: 11 0-0 ♕b6 12 ♗e2 – versus ...♗xf2+ with a ...♘g4+ fork in mind – 12...♖f8 13 ♘d2 ♔g8 14 ♕g3 e5!) 10...0-0 11 c4?! ♗d6 12 ♕e2 ♗d7 13 ♘c3 ♕c7 14 h3 ♖ac8!? 15 cxd5 exd5 16 ♗g5 ♖ce8 17 ♕d2 Gallego-Mawed, Bled 2002, and one course was 17...♗c6 18 ♗xf6 ♖xf6 19 ♖ae1 ♖ef8 with a small edge due to the bishops.

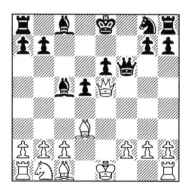

10 ♕e2

White needs take more care than

Black due to the latter's central majority and in fact he has few desirable moves:

(a) 10 ♕c7?! is speculative after 10...♕xf2+ 11 ♔d1 ♗d7! 12 ♖f1 ♖c8 13 ♕xb7 ♕xg2∓;

(b) 10 ♗f4 ♗d4!? 11 ♗b5+ ♔f7 12 ♕c7+ ♘e7 13 c3 ♗b6∓;

(c) 10 ♗b5+ ♗d7!? (or 10...♔f7 and 11 ♕g3 ♘e7 or 11 ♕c7+ ♕e7 12 ♕g3?! ♘f6 13 0-0 e5 or 13...♗d6, but White can doubtless play better) 11 ♗xd7+ ♔xd7 12 ♗f4?! (12 ♕e2! ♘e7 13 0-0 ♘c6 is unclear but Black has more activity) 12...♖c8 13 0-0 ♘e7 14 ♘d2 ♘g6 15 ♕xf6 gxf6∓. Thus the move 10 ♗b5+ yields approximate equality but the play remains complex in any case;

(d) 10 ♕g3 ♘e7 11 ♘c3 0-0 12 0-0 ♘f5 13 ♕h3 Heidsiek-T.Schmidt, corr 1988; and 13...♗d7 was solid and good;

(e) 10 ♕xf6 ♘xf6 threatens ...♘g4 and ...e5, e.g., 11 0-0 0-0 (or 11...♘g4 12 ♗f4 0-0 13 ♗g3 e5 14 h3 e4∓) 12 h3 e5∓.

10...♘e7 11 ♘d2

11 ♗b5+ ♘c6 runs into similar problems after ...0-0 with an early ...e5.

11...0-0 12 0-0

12 ♘f3 ♗b4+.

12...♘c6 13 c3 e5 14 ♗c2 ♗e6 15 ♘b3 ♗b6

Silman's suggestion 15...♗d6!? is quite good.

16 ♗e3 d4 17 ♗d2 ♖ad8

and Black was slightly better Zubarev-Grigoriev, Moscow 1923. It's enjoyable to see such an old game having relevance. Whether White even truly equalises after 4 dxc5 is not clear, which says a lot about the nature of central pawn play in the French.

1.2 4 ♕g4

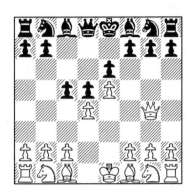

Nimzowitsch's radical idea. White abandons d4 and intends to overprotect e5 by means of ♘f3, ♕g3, and later ♗f4 and/or ♖e1. 4 ♕g4 is in some ways less of a challenge for Black than 4 dxc5. Bringing the queen out before the other pieces is not necessarily bad; but if she loses more time and fails to create weaknesses in the enemy camp such a foray can hardly be justified. In the previous edition I gave 4...♘c6 5 ♘f3 cxd4 6 ♗d3 ♕c7 (see the next note). Another popular and successful line is 4...cxd4 (or 4...f5 5 ♕g3 cxd4 6 ♘f3 ♘c6, often transposing) 5 ♘f3 f5 6 ♕g3 and 6...♘c6 or 6...♘e7 intending ...♘d7-c5. Here as my main line I will show a less tested and generally simpler response that solves Black's problems and creates ones for White. It was played by Botvinnik as far back as 1937 and has been revived to good effect in recent times:

4...♕a5+

Meeting a queen move with a queen move! Black's idea is to be sure that White's queen will lose time to ...♘h6 by diverting the c1 bishop from a potential capture on h6. At the right moment ...f5 can also be useful. The line 4...♘c6 5 ♘f3 cxd4 (note that here 5...♕a5+ 6 ♗d2 ♕b6 attacks b2, and otherwise 7 c3 cxd4 transposes to our 4...♕a5+ main line) 6 ♗d3 ♕c7 was analysed in detail in the second edition.

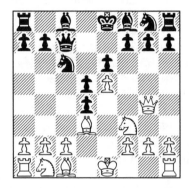

Here let me present a brief update for Black covering the main continuations:

(a) 7 ♗f4 ♘ge7 is fine for Black, but 7...♘b4 has scored 80% in my database! Of course things aren't really so bad for White, but Black is certainly content after 8 0-0 (8 ♘a3 ♘xd3+ 9 cxd3 ♕b6 10 ♗c1 ♘h6! 11 ♕xd4? ♗c5 is extremely strong, e.g., 12 ♕a4+ ♗d7 13 ♕c2 ♗b4+!? 14 ♗d2 ♖c8 15 ♕d1 ♗c5 16 ♗e3? ♗xe3 0-1, in view of 17 fxe3 ♕xb2, Cornelison-Dirr, email 1994; a well-known trick is 8 ♘xd4?! ♘xd3+ 9 cxd3 ♕b6 10 ♘b3 ♕b4+ 11 ♘1d2?? g5 winning a piece) 8...♘xd3 9 cxd3 ♕c2 10 ♘xd4 ♕xd3!? (10...♕xb2 is more likely to yield an advantage, when 11 ♘b3 h5! chases the queen to a square from which Black's development is not so hindered, for example, 12 ♕f3 ♗d7 13 ♘1d2 ♗a3!) 11 ♖d1! (if 11 ♘b3 h5! and the queen has no good square) 11...♕g6 (11...♕a6!?) 12 ♕e2 M.Pruess-Kummerow, Dortmund 1991; and now Black's best course was 12...♗d7!= with the idea 13 ♘b5 ♖c8;

(b) 7 ♕g3 f6 with:

(b1) 8 ♗xh7?! ♘xe5 9 ♗g6+ ♔d8 (9...♔d7! is even better) 10 ♘xd4 (10 ♘xe5 ♕xe5+ 11 ♕xe5 fxe5∓ with an extra pawn and huge centre) 10...♘e7 11 ♗d3 ♘xd3+ 12 ♕xd3 ♖xh2 13 0-0 ♖h8∓ Toth-Maillard, corr 1990;

(b2) 8 exf6 ♕xg3 9 f7+ ♔xf7 10 hxg3 ♘f6 11 ♘g5+ ♔g8 12 f4 ♘b4 (or 12...h6 13 ♘f3 ♘e4) 13 ♘d2 ♘xd3+ 14 cxd3 Linskens-Munoz Izcua, Montevideo 1954; and best was 14...♘g4! 15 ♘b3 e5!∓;

(c) 7 0-0 f6!? (7...♗d7 8 ♖e1 0-0-0 has also been successful) and:

(c1) 8 ♗xh7 ♘xe5 9 ♘xe5 fxe5 10 ♗g6+ (10 ♖e1 ♘f6 11 ♗g6+ ♔d7!) 10...♔d8 11 h3 (11 ♕g3 ♗d6) 11...♘f6 12 ♕d1 Smyslov-Lisitsin, Moscow 1942; 12...♗c5!∓ and Black will soon mobilise with ...e4;

(c2) 8 ♗f4 fxe5 9 ♘xe5?! (9 ♕h5+ ♕f7 10 ♕xf7+ ♔xf7 11 ♘xe5+ ♘xe5 12 ♗xe5 ♘e7!∓ intending ...♘c6 and ...♗c5) 9...♘f6! 10 ♗g6+ (10 ♘xc6 ♘xg4 11 ♗xc7 bxc6; 10 ♕g3 ♗d6) 10...hxg6 (or 10...♔d8 11 ♕g3 hxg6 12 ♘xg6 e5 etc.) 11 ♕xg6+ ♔e7∓.

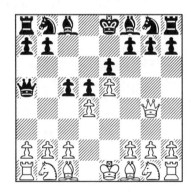

5 c3

The most popular reply. 4...♕a5+ is a pragmatic move that counts upon the drawbacks of each response. Much of what follows is analysis without examples, but the main ideas should be clear:

(a) 5 ♘d2 ♘c6 (5...♘h6 is also fine) 6 ♘gf3 (6 dxc5 ♘h6 7 ♕f4 ♗e7! 8 c3 [8 h4 f6! 9 exf6 ♗xf6 and ...0-0] 8...g5! 9 ♕e3 ♘f5 10 ♕e2 ♕xc5 with superior development) 6...♘h6

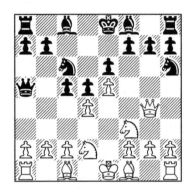

Here's the drawback to 5 ♘d2. Black exploits the fact that the c1 bishop no longer covers h6: 7 ♕f4 ♘b4 (forcing the king to move) 8 ♔d1 (8 ♘b3? ♕a4) 8...c4 9 a3 (after 9 ♘b1?! ♘xa2, there is no way to exploit the pin and Black threatens to play ...♘c3+; 9 c3 ♕a4+ 10 b3 cxb3 11 ♘xb3 ♘xa2 12 ♔c2 ♗d7 13 ♘fd2 ♖c8 14 ♗b2 ♗b4 15 ♔b1 ♗xc3 16 ♖xa2 ♗xd2 0-1 Nei-Gleizerov, Osterskars 1995; Black ends up with a couple of extra pawns, although White could have played on) 9...♗d7 10 b3 ♖c8! 11 ♗b2? (yet 11 bxc4 dxc4 12 ♘xc4 ♕a4 is also good for Black: 13 ♕d2 ♘g4! 14 ♘e1 ♘d5 15 ♘b2 – forced thus far – 15...♘xf2+! 16 ♕xf2 ♘c3+ 17 ♔d2 ♘e4+ 18 ♔e3 ♘xf2 19 ♘xa4 ♘xh1 20 ♘b2 g6-+) 11...♖xc2 12 ♔xc2 c3∓ 13 ♔b1? cxb2 0-1 Pusch-Kern, Recklinghausen 2000;

(b) 5 ♗d2 ♘h6! (5...♕b6 is less clear but still promising after 6 ♗c3 ♘h6 7 ♕f4 ♘f5 8 ♘f3 ♘c6 or 6 ♘c3 ♘h6, e.g., 7 ♗b5+ ♕xb5 8 ♘xb5 ♘xg4

9 ♘c7+ ♔d7 10 ♘xa8 cxd4 11 ♘f3 ♘c6 and ...b6; or, finally, 6 b3 cxd4 7 ♘f3 ♘c6 8 ♗d3 f5 9 exf6? ♘xf6 10 ♕g3 ♗d7 11 a4 ♘e4∓ Kaarne-Sisatto, Finland 1998) 6 ♕g3 (6 ♗xa5 ♘xg4 presents White the double problem of ...♘c6 and defending his centre, so 7 h3 ♘h6 8 ♘f3 ♘c6 9 ♗c3 ♘f5∓ could follow) 6...♕b6 (hitting b2 and d4) 7 ♕b3 ♕xb3 8 axb3 ♘c6 9 ♘f3 (9 ♗xh6?! gxh6 10 dxc5 ♗xc5!? 11 ♘f3 ♘d4!; here 10...♘xe5 or a move earlier 9...♘xd4! was also strong) 9...♘f5 10 dxc5 ♗xc5 with the freer play. Black is somewhat better.

5...cxd4 6 ♘f3!?

It seems odd, but trying to gambit a pawn may be best. The alternative 6 ♕xd4 ♘c6 is easy for Black to play, as in the stem game for 4...♕a5+, Rabinovich-Botvinnik, Moscow 1937: 7 ♕f4 ♘ge7 8 ♗d3 (8 ♘f3?! ♘g6 9 ♕g3 ♕c7 10 ♗f4 f6 11 ♗b5 fxe5 12 ♗xe5 ♘gxe5 13 ♕xe5 ♗d6∓) 8...♘g6!? (here 8...d4 9 ♘f3 ♘d5 is also interesting) 9 ♗xg6 hxg6 10 ♘f3 ♕a6 11 ♘g5 ♘d8 12 ♘d2 ♕d3!? 13 ♘b3 b6 14 ♗d2 ♗d7 15 0-0-0 ♖c8∓.

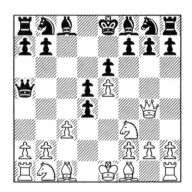

6...♘c6

Black could accept the gambit by 6...dxc3, but that isn't necessary, especially since he also has the option of 6...f5, for example, 7 ♕g3 ♘c6 8 b4

Buchnicek-P.Kucera, Mlada Boleslav 1993; and here 8...♕a4! was strong in view of 9 b5 ♕c2! 10 ♕f4 ♕e4+ 11 ♕xe4 fxe4 (or 11...dxe4 12 bxc6 exf3 13 cxd4 ♘e7!∓) 12 bxc6 exf3. Then White has serious difficulties, e.g., 13 cxb7 (13 ♗b5 ♔f7 14 cxb7 fxg2 15 ♖g1 ♗xb7 16 cxd4 ♘e7 17 ♖xg2 ♘f5∓) 13...♗xb7 14 cxd4 fxg2 15 ♗xg2 ♘e7 16 ♗h3 (versus ...♘f5) 16...♘c6 17 ♗b2 (17 ♗e3 ♘xe5!) 17...♘b4! 18 ♔d2 ♖c8 19 ♘a3 ♔d7 20 ♖hc1 ♗e7 threatening ...♗g5+ as well as ...♖hf8.

7 ♘xd4

7 ♗d3 would be a poorly-timed sacrifice due to 7...dxc3 8 ♘xc3 (8 bxc3 d4 9 0-0 dxc3 10 ♘a3 and now 10...h5 11 ♕g3 h4 12 ♕g4 h3! or 10...♘h6!? 11 ♗xh6 gxh6 12 ♘c4 ♕c5 13 ♖ab1 ♘b4! 14 ♖fd1 ♗d7∓, Jimenez Villena-Shabalov, Linares 2000) 8...d4!? (or 8...♕b4, since White cannot avoid the exchange of queens due to ...d4) 9 ♘xd4 ♘xe5 10 ♕g3 ♘xd3+ 11 ♕xd3 ♗d7 with a solid extra centre pawn.

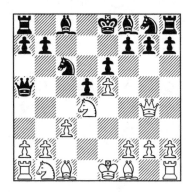

7...♘xe5!?

This wins a key central pawn at the risk of some attack by White. Black can also play effectively by 7...♕c7 8 ♗f4? (8 ♘xc6 is best, although 8...bxc6 strengthens Black's centre, e.g., 9 ♕g3 ♘e7 10 ♗d3 ♘g6

11 f4 ♕b6! preparing ...♗e7 and/or ...♗a6) 8...♘xd4 9 cxd4 ♕b6!, hitting b2 and d4. If 10 ♗c1, 10...♘h6 11 ♕f4 ♘f5 wins the d-pawn.

8 ♕g3

8 ♕h5?! ♘d7! 9 ♗d3 (not 9 ♘xe6? ♘gf6 winning a piece) 9...♘gf6 and White has nothing for the pawn.

8...♘g6

There's nothing wrong with 8...♘c4, and 8...f6 is promising. In the latter case Black intends to give the pawn back for development and dark squares after 9 ♗f4 (9 ♗e2 ♔f7 untangles and prepares ...♗d6) 9...♕b6 10 b3 (10 b4 ♕c7 11 ♗b5+ ♔f7 holds on to the extra pawn and mobile centre, for example, 12 0-0 a6 13 ♗e2 ♗d6∓) 10...♔f7!, preparing ...♗d6 and giving back the pawn for development and dark squares.

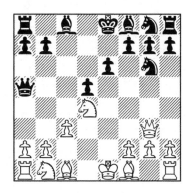

9 h4

White lacks compensation after 9 ♘b5 e5 10 ♗d3 f5! or 9 ♗d3 ♗d7 10 0-0 ♘f6.

9...♘f6 10 h5 ♘e4 11 ♕e3 ♘e7 12 ♘d2

12 ♗d3 e5 13 ♘f3 ♘c6! 14 ♗xe4 dxe4 15 ♕xe4 ♗e6 16 0-0 0-0-0 with space, two bishops and a clear advantage.

12...♘xd2

Or 12...♘d6 with ...♘ef5 in mind.

Then 13 ♗d3 ♛b6 14 ♘2f3 f6!∓ prepares ...e5.

13 ♗xd2 ♗d7 14 ♗d3 ♘c6 15 0-0 ♘xd4 16 ♛xd4 ♛c5 17 ♛e5 f6 18 ♛g3 ♛d6

and Black has consolidated the extra pawn with insufficient counterplay for White.

Notice the number of good options the second player had along the way. The whole 4...♛a5+ variation is only lightly tested, but appears to offer Black more than adequate chances.

1.3 4 ♘f3

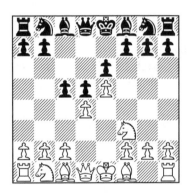

Of White's alternatives to 4 c3, this is the most common.

4...♘c6 5 ♗d3

5 dxc5 is 1.1 and 5 c3 is the subject of the next two chapters. The move 5 ♗b5?! has been played in over 200 database games, but loses time after either 5...♗d7 (threatening ...♘xe5), which has scored 73%, or 5...♛b6!? which has scored a cool 80% for Black, e.g., 6 ♘c3! (6 ♗xc6+ bxc6 7 0-0 – else ...♗a6 – 7...cxd4∓; 6 ♛e2 cxd4 7 0-0 ♗d7 – intending ...♘xe5 – 8 ♗d3 f6!∓) 6...♗d7 7 ♗xc6 bxc6 8 dxc5 ♗xc5 9 0-0 ♛c7 10 ♘a4 ♗b6 11 b4 ♘e7 12 c3 0-0 13 c4?! c5! 14 bxc5 ♗xa4 15 ♛xa4 (15 cxb6 axb6 16 ♛e2 dxc4∓) 15...♗xc5 16 cxd5 ♘xd5 17

♗d2 ♖fc8 18 ♔h1 ♖ab8∓ Brans-M.Nikolic, Dresden 2000.

5...cxd4 6 0-0 f6

An interesting juncture. 6...♗c5 was analysed in the last edition and is in good theoretical shape. 6...f6 immediately challenges e5. An obscure but promising alternative is 6...g6!?, as suggested in the last edition. There are few examples, but play might proceed 7 ♖e1 (7 a3?! ♗g7 8 ♗f4 of Kobelev-Lobach, USSR 1988 invites 8...f6! 9 ♖e1 fxe5 10 ♘xe5 ♘ge7 with an extra pawn and superior activity; 7 ♗f4 ♗g7 8 ♘bd2 f6 probably transposes but here 7...♛b6 is an option) 7...♗g7 8 ♗f4 (8 ♘bd2 f6 9 exf6 ♘xf6 10 ♘b3 0-0 with the idea 11 ♘bxd4 ♘xd4 12 ♘xd4 e5! 13 ♖xe5 ♘g4) 8...f6 9 ♘bd2 (9 ♗b5 ♘ge7 10 ♘xd4 0-0; 9 exf6 ♘xf6 10 ♗b5? 0-0 11 ♗xc6 bxc6 12 ♘xd4 ♛b6 or here 12...♘e4) 9...♘ge7! (or 9...fxe5 10 ♘xe5 ♘f6=) 10 exf6 (10 ♛e2 fxe5 11 ♗xe5 ♘xe5 12 ♘xe5 0-0 13 ♘df3 ♘c6∓) 10...♗xf6 11 ♘e5?! (11 ♗h6 ♛d6 and ...e5; 11 ♘b3 0-0 12 ♛d2∓) 11...♘xe5 12 ♗xe5 ♗xe5 13 ♖xe5 0-0 14 ♘f3 ♛d6 and White has nothing for the pawn.

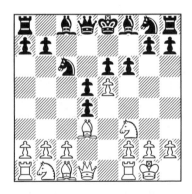

7 ♛e2

(a) 7 ♖e1? loses the centre to 7...fxe5 8 ♘xe5 ♘xe5 9 ♖xe5 ♘f6 10

♗b5+ (10 ♗g5 ♗d6 11 ♗b5+ ♔f7 12 ♖e1 h6 13 ♗h4 g5! 14 ♗g3 ♗xg3 15 hxg3 ♕b6∓) 10...♔f7 11 ♕xd4 ♗d6 12 ♖e3 (the best try) Kogan-Perez Garcia, Dos Hermanas 2000; now 12...♕c7! 13 ♕h4 g5! 14 ♕h6 ♕xc2 and White is in bad shape;

(b) 7 ♗f4? g5! (7...fxe5 8 ♘xe5 ♘f6 9 ♕e2 transposes to 7 ♕e2) 8 ♗g3 g4 9 ♘h4 (9 ♘xd4!? ♘xd4 10 ♕xg4 ♘c6 11 ♕h5+ ♔d7 12 ♘c3 ♕e8 and White has some attack, but not enough for a piece) 9...fxe5 10 ♕xg4 ♘f6∓ Black has a pawn and huge centre, and intends moves like ...♗d6, ...♕b6, and ...e4;

(c) 7 ♗b5 ♗d7 8 ♗xc6 bxc6 9 ♕xd4 c5 (or 9...f5 first, e.g., 10 ♕f4 ♘h6 11 ♘g5 ♗e7 12 ♕g3 ♘f7! 13 ♘xf7 ♔xf7 14 c4 d4 15 ♘d2 c5 16 ♘f3 h6 with two bishops and moves like ...♖b8, ...♗c6, and ...g5 in store, Gamback-Kiriakov, Skelleftea 2001) 10 ♕f4 f5 11 c4 (otherwise Black's two bishops and central majority give him the advantage) 11...d4 12 b4 (12 ♘bd2 a5! 13 b3 ♗e7 14 ♘e1 Arnason-J.Watson, Gausdal 1978; 14...♘h6!∓ and ...♘f7) 12...cxb4 13 ♘xd4 (13 ♕xd4 ♘e7 14 ♗f4 ♘c6 15 ♕e3 ♕b6 with the idea ...♗c5) 13...♘e7 14 ♕e3 ♘g6!? (or 14...♘c6 15 ♗b2 ♘xd4 16 ♗xd4 ♕c7) 15 f4 (15 ♘d2 ♕b8 16 ♘2f3 ♗c5 17 ♗b2 0-0) 15...♗c5 16 ♘d2 a5 (16...♗a4!?) 17 ♘2b3 ♗a7 18 a3 a4 19 axb4 axb3 20 c5 0-0 with the idea ...♘e7-d5, among others, Bickford-Pals, corr 1997/8.

7...♕c7

I use this as the main line because it is probably the best way to play for a win and also because there is less theory than after 7...fxe5 8 ♘xe5, when both 8...♘f6 and 8...♘xe5 were analysed in the second edition of this book. The former keeps more pieces

on the board; its main line goes 8...♘f6 9 ♗f4 (9 ♗g5 ♘xe5 10 ♕xe5 ♗d6 11 ♗b5+ ♔f7 12 ♕xd4 ♕c7∓; 9 f4 ♗d6, e.g., 10 ♘d2 0-0 11 ♘df3 ♕b6) 9...♗d6 10 ♘d2 0-0 11 ♘df3 ♕c7 (11...♕e8!? 12 ♗g3 is complex after Bickford's 12...♘h5= or 12...♗d7 13 ♘xc6 ♗xg3 14 ♘cxd4 ♗d6 15 ♖ae1 ♕h5 Hodgson-Speelman, Brighton 1984) 12 ♗g3 (a cute miniature followed 12 ♖ae1 ♘e4 13 ♘xc6 ♗xf4 14 ♘cxd4 e5 15 ♘b3 ♗g4 16 ♔h1?? ♘g5 0-1 Aagaard-McDonald, Budapest 1996). At this point I suggested 12...g6 unclear, with the idea ...♘h5; in practice, 12...♗d7 has also held the balance.

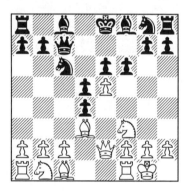

8 ♗f4!?

8 ♗b5 is safer, but Black has an easy time of it after 8...fxe5 9 ♘xe5 ♘f6 (9...♗d6!? 10 ♕h5+ g6 11 ♘xg6 ♕f7=) 10 ♘d2 (10 ♗g5 ♗d6 11 ♗xf6 0-0! is a nice trick; if White tries to win material by 12 ♗xg7 ♕xg7 13 ♘xc6 bxc6 14 ♗xc6, then the bishops and huge centre dominate following 14...♖b8, e.g., 15 ♗b5 ♖b6 16 ♘d2 e5) 10...♗d6 11 ♘df3 (11 f4 0-0 12 ♘df3 ♘e4) 11...0-0 with a pawn and active play; 12 ♖e1 falls short after 12...♘e4 13 ♘xc6 bxc6 14 ♗d3 ♘c5!.

8...g5! 9 ♗g3

9 ♗xg5!? fxg5 10 ♘xg5 is an enter-

prising piece sacrifice that falls short after 10...♕xe5 (or even 10...♕g7 11 ♕h5+ ♔e7 12 f4 h6 13 ♘f3 ♔d8!?) 11 ♕h5+ ♔d7 12 ♘d2 ♘f6 13 ♕f7+ ♗e7 14 ♘df3 ♕d6 and Black's position is safe enough.

9...g4 10 ♘h4

10 ♘fd2 f5 has the idea of ...h5-h4 and/or ...♗h6 and ...f4.

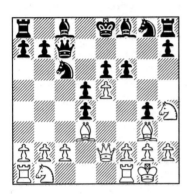

10...fxe5!

This takes over the centre (four pawns to none!). A safe alternative is 10...f5!? 11 ♘d2 (11 f3 ♘h6) 11...♘ge7!? (11...♘h6) 12 f4 ♘g6 13 ♘b3 ♗e7 14 ♘xg6 hxg6 and a well-timed ...g5 (probably after ...0-0-0) will keep the advantage.

11 ♕xg4

11 ♗b5 ♗g7 12 ♕xg4 ♘f6 13 ♕xd4 0-0! 14 ♗xc6 ♘e4! threatens the bishop on c6 and ...♘xg3.

11...♘f6 12 ♕e2 ♗d6 13 ♗b5 0-0 14 ♘d2

and 14...e4 or 14...♘a5!?, with the advantage in both instances. As in so many lines of the Advance Variation, Black's central pawn mass is the most important factor on the board.

Chapter Two

Advance Variation: 5...♗d7

1 e4 e6 2 d4 d5 3 e5 c5 4 c3

White maintains the pawn chain. This is played in over 85% of games after 3 e5.

4...♘c6 5 ♘f3

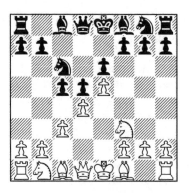

This is the main line of the Advance Variation. White supports d4 before undertaking operations. As we shall see, Black can attack either the 'base' of the pawn chain at d4 or its 'head' at e5, or both. I will recommend two systems, beginning with: 5...♗d7 (this chapter) and 5...♕b6 (Chapter 3).

White has some little-known deviations at this point, of which only one is moderately popular.

(a) 5 ♕g4? cxd4 6 cxd4 ♕b6 7 ♘f3 ♘h6! 8 ♕f4 (8 ♗xh6? ♕xb2) 8...♘f5∓ Weiss-Halberditz, corr 1933;

(b) 5 f4 ♕b6 6 ♘f3 ♘h6 transposes to 4 f4;

(c) 5 a3!? could transpose after 5...♕b6 6 ♘f3 to 3.1 6 a3. Black also has 5...a5!? (or 5...f6!? 6 ♘f3 ♕c7, e.g., 7 ♗f4 cxd4 8 cxd4 g5 9 ♗g3 g4 with the idea 10 exf6 ♕a5+ 11 ♘fd2 ♘xf6=) 6 ♘f3 cxd4 7 cxd4 ♘ge7 8 ♘c3 (8 ♗d3 ♘f5 9 ♗xf5 exf5 10 ♘c3 ♗e6 is a standard kind of position that tends to be okay for Black) 8...♘f5 9 ♗b5 (9 g4 ♘h4) 9...♗d7 10 ♗xc6 ♗xc6 11 0-0 ♗e7=;

(d) 5 ♘e2 ♕b6 (5...f6 6 f4 fxe5 7 dxe5 ♘h6 8 ♘g3 ♗d7 9 ♗e2 ♕b6 10 0-0 0-0-0 was comfortable for Black in Romero Holmes-Korchnoi, Pamplona 1990) 6 g3 (consistent, now that the knight on e2 blocks the bishop) 6...f6 7 exf6 (7 ♘f4?! g6 8 exf6 cxd4) 7...♘xf6 8 ♗g2 cxd4 9 cxd4 ♗d6 10 0-0 0-0 11 ♘bc3 ♗d7= Neretljak-Brynell, Rodeby 1998;

(e) 5 ♗e3!? is Kupreichik's move, to reinforce d4. It is the most popular of these options to 5 ♘f3 and leads to original play:

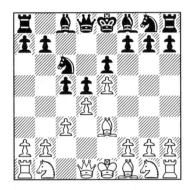

(e1) 5...♘h6 hasn't been played much, but I think that it is logical since White's bishop would have to move twice to capture on h6: 6 ♘f3 (6 ♗d3 ♕b6 7 ♕d2 ♘g4 8 ♘f3 ♘xe3 9 fxe3 ♗e7 10 0-0, and now 10...0-0 11 b3!? f6 12 exf6 ♗xf6= or 10...c4 11 ♗e2 0-0 12 ♔h1 f6 13 exf6 ♗xf6= Shaked-J.Watson, Los Angeles 1995) 6...♘f5 (6...♕b6 7 ♕d2 ♗d7 8 ♗e2 ♘f5 9 0-0 ♘xe3 10 fxe3 ♗e7 unclear, Sengupta-Barua, Calcutta 2002) 7 g4?! ♘xe3 8 fxe3 f6 9 exf6 gxf6 10 ♖g1 ♕b6 11 b3 cxd4 12 exd4 ♗d7 13 g5 ♗e7 14 ♗d3 0-0-0∓ B.Orton-J.Watson, Las Vegas 1998.

(e2) The normal move is 5...♕b6 6 ♕d2 f6 (two good options are 6...cxd4 7 cxd4 ♗d7 8 ♘c3 ♖c8 9 ♘f3 ♘a5 10 ♖c1 ♗b4 11 ♗d3 ♘c4 12 ♗xc4 ♖xc4= Starostits-Glek, Baden-Baden 2001, and 6...♗d7 7 ♘f3 f6 8 ♗d3 fxe5 9 ♘xe5 ♘f6 10 0-0 ♗d6 11 f4 0-0= – Ulibin and Lysenko) 7 ♘f3 (an instructive example was 7 f4 ♘h6!? 8 exf6 gxf6 9 ♗e2 ♘f5! 10 ♗h5+ ♔d8 11 ♗f2 cxd4 12 cxd4 ♘fxd4 13 ♘c3 ♗c5 14 0-0-0 ♗d7 15 ♔b1 ♘b3?! 16 axb3 ♗xf2= Filimonov-Shorokhov, Smolensk 2001) 7...fxe5 (or 7...♗d7 8 ♗d3 fxe5 9 dxe5 ♘h6 10 0-0 ♘f7 11 ♗f4 ♗e7 12 ♖e1 0-0-0∓ Westerinen-Ulibin, Benidorm 1993; here Ulibin

gives 9 ♘xe5 ♘f6 10 0-0 ♗d6 11 f4 0-0=) 8 ♘xe5 ♘f6 (8...♘xe5 9 dxe5 ♘e7!?) 9 ♗d3 ♗d6 10 dxc5 ♗xc5 11 ♗xc5 ♕xc5 12 ♘xc6 bxc6 13 0-0 0-0=.

5...♗d7

Sometimes called 'Euwe's move', 5...♗d7 was played by Greco in 1620(!), revived by Korchnoi in the 1970s, and is now a main line. It is a very flexible move that waits for White to commit to a plan. Black reasons that ...♗d7 will be part of almost any set-up. There are also several concrete move order advantages. If White plays 6 ♗d3, Black can play 6...cxd4 7 cxd4 ♕b6 with the Milner-Barry Gambit (a line that strong masters don't believe in). In the case of the move 6 ♗e2, there are many variations in which Black can hit the front of the pawn chain by ...f6 (generally that is a less effective move with a bishop on d3). The manoeuvre ...♘e7-f5 also has more effect after ♗e2 because White doesn't have the option of an immediate ♗xf5. We will also see the idea ...♘ge7-g6 become effective. Finally, Black can reply to 6 a3 with a more flexible strategy, e.g., the queen might go to c7 instead of b6. Playing ...f6 is a theme in every case; this contrasts with the old strategy of attacking the base at d4, and has become a normal way of proceeding. I should mention that 5...♘ge7, with similarly flexible ideas, has also been used with considerable success in the last decade. After 6 ♗d3, Black can play 6...♘g6, but a great amount of theory is now attached to 6...cxd4 7 cxd4 ♘f5. Another unique approach is 5...♘h6, which has done rather well in the past two years. I think that it's fair to say that all of these ideas without the traditional 5...♕b6 have taken some of the sting out of the Advance Variation, although both sides willingly enter this line for the unbalanced play that it produces.

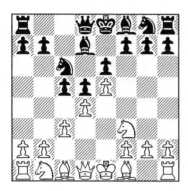

From the diagram we consider:

2.1 6 dxc5
2.2 6 a3
2.3 6 ♗e2

Of course White can play almost anything, but the following are also logical:

(a) As mentioned, 6 ♗d3 cxd4 7 cxd4 ♕b6 will generally lead to the Milner-Barry Gambit, discussed in Chapter 3 via 5...♕b6 6 ♗d3 cxd4 7 cxd4 ♗d7. Another response is 6...♕c7 with the idea 7 a3 c4 8 ♗c2 0-0-0, having in mind either ...f6 or ...f5/...h6/...g5. Also played is 6...♖c8, e.g., 7 a3 (better is 7 dxc5, although it hasn't achieved much after 7...♗xc5 8 0-0 ♘ge7 9 ♗g5 h6 10 ♗h4 g5 11 ♗g3 ♘f5= with the idea 12 ♗xf5?! exf5 13 ♕xd5 ♘e7 and ...f4; on 7 0-0, 7...cxd4 8 cxd4 ♘b4= wins the two bishops) 7...cxd4 8 cxd4 ♕b6 9 ♗c2 (9 0-0 ♘xd4 10 ♘xd4 ♕xd4 11 ♘c3 of Klausner-Rivas, Marbella 1982 compares very poorly for White with a main-line Milner-Barry gambit after 11...♕xe5 12 ♖e1 ♕b8) 9...♘xd4! 10

♘xd4 ♗c5 11 ♘e2 ♗xf2+ 12 ♔f1 f6 Bjornsson-M.Hansen, Gausdal 1994, with two pawns and a powerful attack for the piece;

(b) 6 ♘a3 f6 (or 6...cxd4 7 cxd4 ♗xa3 8 bxa3 unclear, e.g., 8...♕a5+ 9 ♕d2 ♖c8) 7 ♘c2 fxe5 (7...♕b6 with the idea ...0-0-0) 8 dxe5 ♕c7 9 ♗f4 0-0-0 (or 9...♘ge7 10 h4 h6 11 ♕e2 0-0-0 unclear, Balinas-Espig, Odessa 1976) 10 ♗e2 ♘h6 11 ♕d2 ♘f7 12 ♕e3 ♗e7 planning ...g5, Dominguez-Topalov, Zaragosa 1992;

(c) 6 ♗e3 is logical and related to the Kupreichik idea 5 ♗e3 above. There are several reasonable answers, including:

(c1) 6...cxd4 7 cxd4 ♘ge7 (7...f6!?) 8 ♘c3 ♘f5 9 ♗d3 ♘xe3 10 fxe3 ♕b6 (10...g6!? 11 0-0 ♗h6 12 ♕e2 0-0 intending ...f6) 11 ♕e2 ♗e7 12 0-0 0-0= Roeder-Weih, Bundesliga 1986;

(c2) A simple but previously neglected idea was 6...♘ge7 7 dxc5 ♘f5! 8 ♗d4 ♘fxd4 9 cxd4 b6! 10 cxb6!? (10 ♗b5 bxc5 11 ♕a4 ♕b6∓) 10...♕xb6 11 ♕d2 ♖b8 12 ♘c3 (12 b3 ♗b4 13 ♘c3 ♕a5) 12...♕xb2 13 ♖b1 ♕xd2+ 14 ♔xd2 ♗b4 15 ♗d3 ♔e7 16 ♖hc1 ♖hc8 17 ♔e3 ♗a3∓ O.Castro-Gulko, Cali 2001.

2.1 6 dxc5

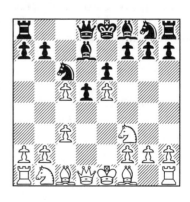

An important idea from Sveshnikov. 6 dxc5 used to be a main line after 5...♗d7 and helped to revive the Advance Variation, but it is doing rather poorly these days. Black develops quickly and White's positional idea of securing the centre (normally by b4-b5) is countered by queenside play and ...f6 ideas. This is crucial for understanding the apparently slow 5...♗d7, so I'll devote some attention to it.

6...♗xc5 7 b4

This thrust was the main reason for the popularity of 6 dxc5 in modern times. Since 7 ♗e2 instead concedes the centre after 7...f6, the alternative is 7 ♗d3, which is less weakening and probably sounder:

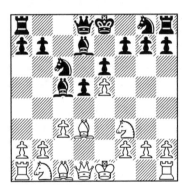

(a) 7...f6 8 b4 (8 ♗f4 g5!? intends ...g4 and provokes 9 ♘xg5!? fxg5 10 ♕h5+ ♔f8 11 ♗xg5 ♗e7! 12 ♗h6+?! ♘xh6 13 ♕xh6+ ♔g8∓; 8 ♕e2 fxe5 9 ♘xe5 ♘xe5 10 ♕xe5 ♘f6 11 0-0 0-0 and White has his usual problems with both Black's development and centre pawns: 12 ♗e3 ♗b6 13 ♗d4 ♗c7 14 ♕g5 h6 15 ♕h4 e5 16 ♗c5 e4 17 ♗e2 ♖f7 with a clear advantage, Campora-Speelman, Menor 1994) 8...♗b6 (8...♗e7 is also fully playable after 9 b5 ♘xe5 10 ♘xe5 fxe5 11 ♕h5+ ♔f8 12 ♕xe5 ♗f6 13 ♕d6+ ♘e7

14 0-0 e5= Sveshnikov-Savon, Lvov 1978) 9 b5 ♘xe5 10 ♘xe5 fxe5 11 ♕h5+ ♔f8 12 ♗a3+ ♘e7 13 ♕xe5 ♔g8 14 ♘d2 ♘g6 15 ♕g3 ♕f6!∓ with ideas like ...e5, ...♕xc3, and ...♘f4, Ciemniak-Schmidt, Bundesliga 1993;

(b) 7...♘ge7 8 0-0 (8 b4 ♗b6 9 b5 ♘a5 transposes to 7 b4; 8 ♗f4 ♘g6 9 ♗g3 f5!? 10 h4 ♕c7 11 b4 ♗b6 12 ♕e2 h5! 13 0-0 ♘ce7= – Knaak) 8...♘g6 9 ♕e2 (9 ♖e1 ♕c7 10 ♗xg6?! fxg6! 11 ♗f4 0-0 12 ♗g3 ♘e7 13 ♘bd2 ♘f5 14 ♘b3 ♗a4∓ Sveshnikov-Balashov, USSR Ch 1976; a good example of the ...fxg6 idea in the Advance Variation, very often effective if White's bishop ends up stranded on g3) 9...♕c7 10 ♖e1 0-0 (10...f6!? 11 exf6 gxf6 12 c4 d4 13 a3 Pachman-Voicelescu, Bucharest 1953, and 13...a5 is unclear) 11 ♗g5 (11 h4 f6!; 11 b4 ♗b6 12 a4 a5 13 b5 ♘ce7 14 ♗a3 ♗c5 with play against the White queenside) 11...f6 12 exf6 gxf6 13 ♗h6 ♘f4 14 ♗xf4 ♕xf4= Paredes-Goldschmidt, 1992.

7...♗b6 8 b5

8 ♗d3 is effectively answered by 8...♘ge7, but also good is the immediate liquidation of White's centre by 8...f6 9 b5 (9 ♗f4 fxe5 10 ♘xe5 ♕f6 11 ♘xd7 ♗xf2+ 12 ♔xf2 ♕xf4+∓ G.Lee-Cooper, Ayr 1978) 9...♘xe5 (9...♘a5 has also been played) 10 ♘xe5 fxe5 11 ♕h5+ ♔f8 12 ♗a3+ (12 ♕xe5 ♘f6 13 0-0 ♖c8 14 ♗g5 ♔f7= G.Wall-A.Summerscale, Torquay 2002) 12...♘e7 13 ♕xe5 ♔g8 (or 13...♔f7 14 ♕h5+ ♘g6 and Black with the centre and c-file stands well) 14 ♘d2 ♘g6 15 ♕g3 ♕f6 16 0-0 ♕xc3 17 ♘b3 ♕e5∓ Bastian-Luther, Binz 1995.

8...♘a5 9 ♗d3

(see following diagram)

9...♘e7

The main move, but not necessarily

best, since White has nothing special versus Black's alternatives, both emphasising the open c-file:

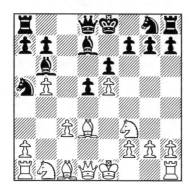

(a) 9...♘c4!? 10 a4 ♕c7 11 ♕e2 a6 12 bxa6 ♖xa6 13 0-0 ♘e7= Kharlov-Dreev, Moscow 1991;

(b) 9...♕c7! is a multi-purpose move, taking over the c-file, hitting e5, and preparing to castle queenside:

(b1) 10 ♕e2 ♘e7 11 h4!? was Kharlov-Kramnik, USSR 1991; but it's not clear what White's idea was after 11...♘c4, e.g., 12 h5!? (12 a4 a6! 13 bxa6 ♖xa6) 12...♗xb5 13 h6 gxh6! 14 ♗xh6 0-0-0 etc.;

(b2) 10 0-0!? ♘e7 (again, 10...♘c4! hits b5 and e5; since 11 ♗xc4 ♕xc4 seems good for Black and 11 a4 a6! takes the initiative, play might proceed 11 ♖e1!? ♗xb5 12 ♘d4 ♗d7, when 13 ♕h5 is unclear but 13 ♕g4?! ♘xe5! 14 ♕xg7 ♘xd3 15 ♕xh8 0-0-0 16 ♖d1 ♘xc1 17 ♖xc1 ♕f4 is too strong, e.g., 18 ♘a3 ♘f6 19 ♕g7 ♘g4) 11 a4 ♘g6 12 ♖e1 ♗c5!? (12...♘c4=; 12...f6!?) 13 ♖a2 0-0-0 14 ♗e3 ♗xe3 15 ♖xe3 f6 16 ♖ae2 ♔b8 unclear, Sveshnikov-Popovic, Palma de Mallorca 1989.

10 0-0 ♖c8

Crazy play followed 10...♘g6 11 ♖e1 (11 ♗a3) 11...0-0 12 ♗g5 ♕e8 13 a4!? ♖c8 14 h4 h6=, when White got

too ambitious with 15 h5? hxg5 16 hxg6 fxg6 17 ♖a2 ♕f7 18 ♕c2 ♕f4 19 ♗xg6 g4 20 ♘h4 g3! 21 ♗h7+ ♔f7 22 ♕g6+ ♔e7 23 ♕xg7+ ♔d8-+ Davies-Benson, Port Erin 1998.

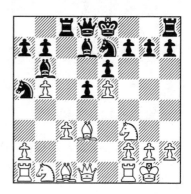

11 a4

Perhaps the most logical move is 11 ♕e2, to reinforce e5 while covering c4. But Black has no particular difficulties after 11...h6 (or 11...0-0, since 12 ♗xh7+?! ♔xh7 13 ♘g5+ ♔g6 14 ♕d3+ ♘f5 15 g4 ♖c4! 16 gxf5+ exf5 is fine, as given by Psakhis) 12 g3!? ♕c7 13 ♔g2?! ♘c4 14 a4 ♘g6! 15 ♖e1 (Psakhis gives 15 ♗xg6 fxg6 16 ♕c2 0-0! 17 ♗xh6!? ♖xf3! 18 ♔xf3 ♘xe5+ 19 ♔g2 gxh6 20 f4 ♘f7 21 ♕xg6+ ♔f8∓) 15...0-0= Giaccio-A.Rodriguez, Buenos Aires 2000.

11...♘g6 12 ♖e1

12 ♗a3 ♗c5= was the game Sveshnikov-Balashov, Lvov 1978. After 12 ♖e1, White intends ♖a2-e2 to reinforce e5.

12...♘c4 13 ♖a2 ♕c7 14 ♖ae2

Now 14...a6 15 bxa6 bxa6 has been tried several times, but it's also safe enough to play 14...0-0. Then 15 h4!? can be met by 15...f6! 16 ♗xg6 hxg6 17 exf6 (17 ♗f4 a6!? 18 bxa6 bxa6 19 g3 ♕c5=) 17...♖xf6 and Black has very active pieces which make up for his weakened pawn structure.

2.2 6 a3

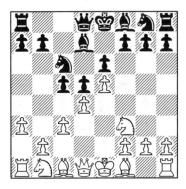

A very popular move. I think that it is less dangerous for Black than the analogous 5...♕b6 6 a3. For example, there are more immediate threats against d4 after 5...♕b6 6 a3, but Black's queen sometimes gets in the way and has to retreat to c7 or even d8. Also, 5...♗d7 is more flexible in lines like the one below where Black attacks e5 by ...f6. Then he might want to play ...♕c7 and perhaps ...0-0-0. Finally, after the continuation 5...♗d7 6 a3, the b6-square can be useful for a knight (i.e. ...♘ge7-c8-b6).

6...f6!?

A direct approach suggested in early editions. By attacking the centre, 6...f6 tries to prove that 6 a3 is too slow. It has been scoring well in master practice and offers double-edged play. Black has several other valid alternatives which have also gotten good results, including 6...c4 and 6...a5. Because it is instructive, I'll use 6...♘ge7 as a second recommendation.

This flexible move (reserving the choice between ...♘f5 and ...♘g6) can resemble a number of other Advance Variation lines. An abbreviated overview of the key lines:

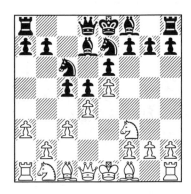

(a1) 7 ♗d3 cxd4 8 cxd4 ♘f5 (8...♕b6 9 ♗c2 ♘f5 10 ♗xf5 exf5 11 ♘c3 ♗e6 has also proven playable) 9 ♗xf5 exf5 10 ♘c3 ♗e6 11 b4 ♗e7 12 h4 h6 13 ♔f1 ♖c8 14 ♕d3 ♕d7 15 ♗f4 a6! 16 ♘d2 ♘a7 17 ♖h3 ♕c6 18 ♖c1 ♘b5 19 ♘db1 ♗d7 ½-½ Bruno-Minzer, Buenos Aires 1993;

(a2) 7 b4 is the consistent and most important try. Then 7...cxd4 8 cxd4 ♘f5 is a type of position that players on both sides of the Advance Variation should study. It is very similar to that with 5...♕b6, but the queen might want to stay on d8 to save a tempo and support moves like ...♘h4 or even ...♗e7 and ...g5. Here are some examples that illustrate the main themes in this often-arising structure. They show why Black has a relatively easy time with it:

(a21) 9 ♗b2 ♕b6 transposes to 5...♕b6 6 a3 lines, which is not bad but also unnecessary. The more logical 9...♗e7 and 9...♖c8 are considered equalisers, and the ambitious thrust 9...b5!?, intending ...a5, has done surprisingly well. On 10 ♗xb5, 10...♘xe5 11 dxe5 ♗xb5 12 ♘c3 ♗c4 is an effective course, for example, 13 g4!? ♘e7 14 h4 h5!? (14...♘g6) 15 ♘g5 ♕d7 16 gxh5 ♘f5∓ M.Petrov-Degraeve, Metz 2002;

(a22) Similarly, the line 9 ♗e3 b5!? (9...♘xe3 10 fxe3 g6!? might be considered, intending ...♗h6, ...0-0, and ...f6) 10 ♘c3 a5! 11 ♘xb5 axb4 12 a4 ♗e7 13 ♗d3 0-0 14 0-0 ♘a5 gave Black good play in Van der Hoeven-Michiels, Amsterdam 2001;

(a23) 9 g4!? is sometimes too loosening. Here 9...♘h4 (9...♘h6 is also fine, since 10 ♗xh6!? gxh6 leaves Black with two bishops and open lines; then ...♖c8 and in some cases ...♖g8 and ...h5 will follow) 10 ♘bd2 ♘xf3+ (10...♖c8!) 11 ♘xf3 ♕b6 12 ♗e2 ♗e7 13 ♗b2 ♖c8 was equal in Shmyrina-Paulet, Halkidiki 2001;

(a24) 9 ♘c3 ♖c8 (Black can also launch a standard kingside attack after, e.g., 9...♗e7 10 ♗b2 ♖c8 11 ♗e2 h5 12 0-0 g5!, Yilmaz-Dreev, Berlin 1991) 10 ♗b2 ♘h4! 11 ♘xh4 (11 ♘a4?! ♘xf3+ 12 ♕xf3 ♘xe5) 11...♕xh4 12 ♘a2 (12 ♘e2? ♘xb4−+) 12...♕e4+!? (or simply 12...♗e7) 13 ♕e2 ♕g6!? Illescas Cordoba-Speelman, Linares 1992. This is probably about equal, although White is rather disorganised.

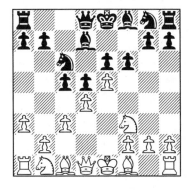

7 ♗d3
The most challenging move, trying to exploit the kingside looseness created by ...f6. Nevertheless there are a few other reasonable options:

(a) 7 b4!? follows up on White's 6th. Because a3 and b4 take time, however, Black is able to break up White's centre and to develop quickly: 7...fxe5 8 b5 (8 ♘xe5 ♘xe5 9 dxe5 ♕c7 and ...0-0-0; 8 bxc5?! e4 9 ♘g5 ♘f6∓; 8 dxc5?! e4 9 ♘d4 ♘f6∓ Popchev-Dolmatov, Polanica Zdroj 1987; finally, after 8 dxe5 ♕c7 9 ♗f4 ♘ge7 10 ♗d3, 10...g6!? is particularly attractive since Black's pieces come out smoothly, e.g., 11 ♕d2!? ♗g7 12 0-0 0-0 13 ♗g3?! cxb4 14 cxb4, and now 14...♖xf3! is obviously sound but Black took another effective route via 14...♘f5 15 ♖e1 ♘xg3 16 hxg3 ♖xf3! 17 gxf3 ♗xe5 18 ♖a2 ♘d4 19 ♕e3 ♖f8 0-1 in Castaneda-Morales, Guaymallen 2001) 8...♘xd4!

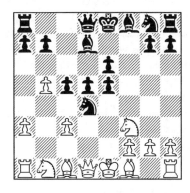

This sacrifice for three pawns has been played for over a decade and looks sound. Black gets a mobile central pawn mass after 9 cxd4 (9 ♘xe5 ♘f5 10 ♕h5+ g6 11 ♘xg6 ♘f6 12 ♕h3 ♖g8 13 ♘xf8 ♔xf8 14 ♗d3 ♘e4!? [better is simply 14...♕e8] 15 ♘d2? ♘g5 16 ♕h5 ♕f6 17 ♗b2 c4 18 ♗c2 ♕e5+ 19 ♕e2 ♕xe2+ 20 ♔xe2 ♗xb5 21 a4 ♗c6 22 h4 ♘e4 23 ♘xe4 dxe4 24 g3 ♖d8 ½-½ Movsesian-Luther, Cappelle la Grande 1998 – Black was a little better throughout) 9...exd4 with dynamic play, e.g., 10 ♗f4 ♘f6 11 ♘bd2

♕b6 (11...♕a5 12 ♗e2 ♘e4 13 0-0 ♘c3 14 ♕e1 ♗e7=) 12 ♘e5 ♕a5 13 g4 (13 ♘xd7 ♔xd7 14 ♕e2 ♗d6!) 13...♘e4 14 ♗g2?! g5 15 ♗g3 ♘xd2 16 ♕xd2 ♕xd2+ 17 ♔xd2 ♗xb5 with powerful passed pawns, Zawadzki-Sitnikov, Halkidiki 2000;

(b) 7 exf6 ♘xf6 (or 7...gxf6 8 ♘h4 ♕e7 9 ♕h5+ ♕f7 unclear – Dolmatov) 8 ♗d3 c4 9 ♗c2 ♗d6 10 0-0 0-0 11 ♕e2 ♕c7 12 ♖e1 ♕b6!? 13 ♘bd2 ♖ae8 14 ♘e5? ♗xe5 15 dxe5 ♘g4 with too many threats, Mekshi-Zhukova, Kavala 2002;

(c) 7 ♗f4?! ♕b6 8 b4 cxd4 9 cxd4 g5! 10 ♗e3 g4 11 ♘fd2 fxe5 12 ♘b3 exd4 13 ♘xd4 ♗h6! 14 ♕xg4 0-0-0 15 ♘c2 ♗xe3 16 fxe3 e5∓ Gramer-Djurhuus, Gausdal 1991;

(d) 7 ♗e2 fxe5 8 dxe5 puts Black an effective tempo up on the old line 5...♗d7 6 ♗e2 f6 7 0-0 fxe5 8 fxe5. One example went 8...♕c7 9 ♗f4 ♘h6 10 0-0 ♘f7 11 ♖e1 ♗e7 12 c4 d4 13 h4 (to stop ...g5) 13...0-0-0∓ 14 ♗d3 Saez-Sermier, Villeurbanne 2002, and among others 14...♖df8 15 ♘bd2 ♗xh4! was good.

7...fxe5

Black breaks up the centre and puts direct pressure on e5 There are two good alternatives, which only underscore the loss of time that a3 entails:

(a) The adventuresome 7...cxd4 8 cxd4 ♘h6! is a promising approach, with the idea of ...♘f7 furthering the attack on e5: 9 0-0 (the natural 9 ♗xh6 gxh6 10 ♘h4?! ♕b6 11 ♕h5+ ♔d8 strongly favours Black) 9...♘f7 10 ♖e1 Movsesian-Luther, Groningen 1998. Now I like simply 10...fxe5 11 ♘xe5 (11 dxe5 g5 intends both ...♗g7 and ...g4, e.g., 12 b4 ♗g7 13 ♗b2 g4 14 b5! gxf3 15 bxc6 ♗xc6 16 ♕xf3 ♕b6 and ...0-0 or ...0-0-0) 11...♘cxe5

12 dxe5 ♗c5 13 ♗f4 ♕b6! 14 ♖e2 ♗b5 and Black has an easy game;

(b) The most popular option is 7...♕c7: 8 0-0 (8 exf6?! ♘xf6 9 0-0 c4 10 ♗c2 ♗d6 11 ♖e1 0-0-0 12 ♕e2 ♖df8 13 ♘e5 ♗e8 14 f4 g5! 15 fxg5 ♗xe5 16 dxe5 ♗h5∓ Branford-Martin, Westergate 1992; 8 ♗f4 c4 9 ♗c2 0-0-0 10 ♘bd2 ♘h6 11 ♗g3 f5 12 ♗f4 ♘f7 13 h4 ♗e7 14 ♕e2 g6 15 g3 h6, preparing ...g5, Kodric-Soln, Bled 2001) 8...0-0-0 (or 8...fxe5!? 9 ♘xe5 ♘xe5, when 10 ♗f4?! ♕b6 11 ♗xe5 ♕xb2 12 ♕h5+ ♔d8 doesn't give White compensation).

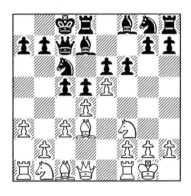

At this point White has three instructive continuations:

(b1) 9 ♖e1 c4 (9...h6!?) 10 ♗f1!? ♘ge7 11 ♘bd2 fxe5 (11...♘g6 12 exf6 gxf6 13 b3 cxb3 14 ♕xb3 was unclear in Afek-Schaefer, Budapest 1993) 12 ♘g5 (12 ♘xe5 ♘xe5 13 dxe5 ♘g6 14 ♘f3 ♗c5∓) 12...exd4! 13 ♘f7 dxc3 14 bxc3 ♘g6 15 ♘xh8 ♘xh8∓ Genin-Epishin, Leningrad 1980;

(b2) 9 ♗f4 c4 10 ♗c2 h6! 11 h4 (11 ♗g3 f5!∓, since 12 ♗xf5? exf5 13 e6 f4 14 exd7+ ♖xd7 15 ♗h4 g5 is decisive) 11...♗e8! (11...g5!? 12 ♗h2 f5 13 hxg5 ♗e8 with compensation, Buchal-Fischer, Germany 1997) 12 b3?! cxb3 13 ♗xb3 ♗h5 14 ♘bd2 fxe5 15 dxe5 ♗c5∓ Adams-Epishin, Ter Apel 1992;

(b3) 9 ♕e2 h6 10 b4 c4 11 ♗c2 f5 (intending ...g5) 12 ♘h4 ♗e8 13 f4 ♗e7 14 ♘xf5?! (overambitious, but 14 ♘f3 allows 14...♗h5 when Black will soon attack by ...g5, at least equalising) 14...exf5 15 ♗xf5+ ♚b8 16 ♕g4 g5! 17 fxg5 hxg5 18 ♗xg5 ♗h5 19 ♕g3 ♗xg5 20 ♕xg5 ♘ge7 (White has three pawns for the piece but Black has two open files aimed against the king) 21 ♘d2 ♖dg8 22 ♕e3 ♘xf5 23 ♖xf5 ♕h7 24 ♖f6 ♗e2! 25 h3 ♗d3 26 ♔h2 ♘e7 27 ♘f3 ♘f5 28 ♕f4 ♔a8 29 ♖g1?! ♕h5! 30 e6 ♗e4 31 ♖f1 ♖g3 32 ♖xf5? ♕xh3+! 0-1 Grischuk-Short, Reyjavik 2000.

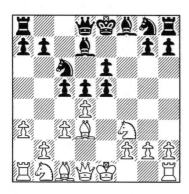

8 dxe5

8 ♘xe5 ♘xe5 (8...♘f6!? 9 ♗f4 ♕b6 10 ♘xc6 bxc6=) 9 dxe5 and now:

(a) 9...g6 10 c4 (10 0-0 ♕c7 11 f4 c4 12 ♗c2 ♗c5+ 13 ♔h1 ♘e7 14 ♘d2 0-0-0 15 b4 cxb3 16 ♘xb3 ♗b5= Afek-Hebert, Paris 1995) 10...♕c7 11 0-0 ♗g7 12 cxd5 ♗xe5 13 dxe6 ♗xe6 14 ♕a4+ ♗d7 15 ♗b5 0-0-0 16 ♘c3 a6 17 ♗xd7+ ♖xd7 ½-½ Charbonneau-Barsov, Montreal 2002;

(b) I suggested 9...♕h4!? in the previous edition but it remains untried. The queen move prevents ♕h5+ and prepares ...♘h6 and ....♗c6, or ...c4 with ....♗c5. For example, 10 ♘d2 (10 g3 ♕h3 11 ♗e2 h5) 10...♘e7 11

♘f3 ♕h5 (hardly clear, but Black looks well off) 12 ♗e2!? ♕f7! 13 ♘g5 ♕g8 planning ...h6, ...0-0-0, and ...♗e8-g6.

8...♕c7

This position has been extremely kind to Black. Also satisfactory are 8...c4 9 ♗c2 ♗c5 and 8...♘h6 9 0-0 ♘f7, when the strength of a knight on f7 shows itself, e.g., 10 ♖e1 g5 11 h3 ♗g7 12 ♘bd2?! (12 c4 tries to break up Black's centre, but would cost a critical tempo after 12...dxc4 13 ♗xc4 h5!) 12...♕e7 13 c4 0-0-0 14 ♖b1 h5 and Black's pressure on e5 and the kingside proved decisive in Druon-Boissel, corr 1993.

9 ♕e2

The idea of ...♘h6-f7 is a major theme since the king can escape via ...0-0-0, whereas ♗xh6 is awfully risky due to Black's attack down the g-file and pressure on e5:

(a) 9 0-0 0-0-0 (9...g6 is an increasingly popular idea in such positions, e.g., 10 ♖e1 ♗g7 11 ♕e2 ♘ge7 12 b4 c4 13 ♗c2 a6!? 14 a4 0-0 15 ♘a3 ♘f5 16 ♗g5 ♖f7∓ with doubling on the f-file, Ocampo-Munoz, Guiines 1998) 10 ♖e1 ♘h6 11 ♗xh6 gxh6 12 c4 d4 13 ♘bd2 Bosboom-Langeweg, Eindhoven 1988, and here 13...♗g7 14 ♕e2 ♗e8 intending ...♗h5 or ...♔b8 and ...♗g6 was fully satisfactory;

(b) 9 ♗f4 0-0-0 10 ♘bd2 ♘h6 11 ♕e2 ♘f7 12 0-0-0?! (12 0-0 ♗e7 13 h4 c4 14 ♗c2 ♖df8 and Black is at least equal) 12...c4 13 ♗c2 b5!? (13...♗c5! looks stronger) 14 ♖he1 a5 15 ♘g5 ♘xg5 16 ♗xg5 ♖e8 intending ...b4 with a meaningful attack, S.Lalic-King, London 1989.

9...♘h6

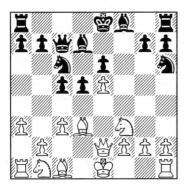

10 0-0

(a) 10 ♗f4 ♘f7 11 h4 (clamping down on ...g5) 11...0-0-0 12 ♘bd2 ♗e7 (12...c4 13 ♗c2 ♗c5 develops more smoothly) 13 b4 c4 14 ♗c2 ♖df8 15 g3 g6 16 0-0 ♖hg8! (the idea is ...h6 and ...g5) 17 b5 ♘a5 18 a4 Panagopoulos-Sigalas, Halkidiki 2002; now 18...h6! would have led to a clear advantage;

(b) 10 c4 is at best harmless, e.g., 10...dxc4 (or 10...♘f7 11 cxd5 ♘cxe5) 11 ♗xc4 ♘f5 12 ♗f4 (12 0-0 ♘cd4 13 ♘xd4 ♘xd4) 12...♘cd4 13 ♘xd4 ♘xd4 14 ♕d1 g6!? 15 0-0 ♗g7 16 ♖e1 0-0 17 ♗g3 ♗c6 with wonderful pieces and ...♖ad8 on the way.

After 10 0-0, Afek-Haak, Vlissingen 2002 continued 10...♘f7 11 ♖e1 c4 12 ♗c2 ♗e7 13 h4 0-0-0 (or simply 13...0-0, since the moves ...♗c5 and ...♕b6 will tie down White's pieces down) 14 ♗f4 ♖dg8!? 15 ♘bd2 ♕d8 (Now h4 is a target and every defence

has a drawback) 16 g3 (White has similar problems after 16 h5 g5 and 16 ♗g3 g5) 16...g5 17 hxg5 ♘xg5∓.

2.3 6 ♗e2

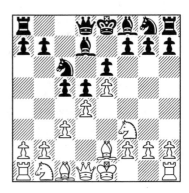

The main line. White develops quickly, planning 0-0 and ♖e1. I will propose two solutions:

2.31 6...♘ge7
2.32 6...f6

2.31 6...♘ge7

My favourite. This knight is flexibly placed to assist in various attacks on White's centre. We look at:

2.311 7 0-0
2.312 7 ♘a3

After 7 dxc5 ♘g6, Black will win back the pawn on e5 with a nice centre, e.g., 8 ♗e3 ♘cxe5 9 ♘xe5 ♘xe5 10 0-0 ♗e7 (10...♘c6!? with the idea 11 f4?! ♘c4!) 11 ♗d4 (11 f4 ♘g6!? 12 f5 exf5 13 ♕xd5 f4! 14 ♗xf4 ♘xf4 15 ♖xf4 0-0 with great compensation) 11...♕c7 12 f4 ♘g6 (or 12...♘c6) 13 f5 ♘f4!∓.

2.311 7 0-0 ♘g6

A move considered anti-positional

for a century or so, simply because it attacks the 'wrong' part of the chain, and because the knight is subject to harassment. It is now a favourite of M.Gurevich and P.Nikolic and has been very successful in recent years. The idea is simple: ...f6 and the destruction of White's pawn chain.

7...♘f5 is also played and worth considering if you don't like 7...♘g6. It intends ...cxd4 with a standard attack on the d4 square. White can try to exploit this move order by 8 ♗d3!?, e.g., 8...cxd4 (8...♘h4!? looks quite reasonable) 9 ♗xf5 exf5 10 ♘xd4 (10 cxd4 ♗e7 11 ♘c3 ♗e6 is a standard position that I consider equal) 10...♗e7 11 ♖e1 (11 ♕b3 ♕c7 12 ♕xd5 ♕xe5 13 ♕xe5 ♘xe5 with the bishop pair, Hendriks-M.Gurevich, Amsterdam 2001) 11...0-0 with the idea 12 ♕b3 ♕a5; Black has satisfactory play.

8 g3

A slightly unconventional move intending h2-h4; this already acknowledges that simple development won't prevent Black's plan from being realised, for example:

(a) 8 ♗e3 ♗e7 (Black has also scored very well after 8...cxd4 9 cxd4 f6) 9 ♘a3 (9 ♘bd2 is more common, when after 9...0-0 10 ♘b3 c4!? 11

♘bd2, Black has the normal 11...f6 or 11...b5) 9...0-0 10 ♘c2 cxd4 11 cxd4 f6 12 exf6 ♗xf6 with plenty of activity;

(b) 8 ♗d3 ♗e7 9 ♗e3 ♕b6 10 ♕d2 c4 11 ♗e2 0-0 12 g3 (12 ♕c2 ♕c7 13 ♘bd2 f6) 12...♕d8!? 13 ♘e1 f5 14 f4 (14 exf6 ♗xf6∓) 14...b5 15 ♘g2 ♖b8 (or 15...b4) 16 b4 a5 17 a3 ♖a8∓ Jonkman-Herbneck, Saint Vincent 2000.

8...f6

A fully playable option is 8...♗e7 9 h4 (the point of 8 g3, but...) 9...0-0! 10 h5 ♘h8

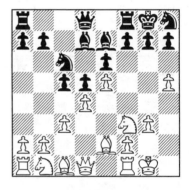

This offside knight (having no moves!) is now actually well placed in the corner, because it supports the attack against the head of the pawn chain by ...f6 and ...♘f7. Korchnoi first played a similar idea some years back via 9..cxd4 10 cxd4 0-0 11 h5 ♘h8 12 h6 g6 13 ♘bd2 f6. The interpolation of 9...cxd4 is perhaps inaccurate here because White gains the extra option of ♘c3, but that's not clear. From the diagram, play continues 11 h6 g6 (actually, 11...g5!? seems to work out well, with ideas like ...f6 and ...♘g6 or ...♘f7, e.g., 12 ♗e3 cxd4 13 cxd4 f6 14 exf6 ♗xf6 15 ♘c3 ♘f7) 12 dxc5 f6 (12...♗xc5 13 c4 f6 is another idea that looks fine, e.g., 14 cxd5 ♘xe5 15 ♘xe5 fxe5 16 ♘c3 ♕b6

17 ♘e4 ♗d4∓) 13 exf6 (trying to win a pawn; 13 c4 will probably transpose into the last note) 13...♗xc5 14 ♗g5 ♘f7 15 ♗h4 ♕c7. White is a pawn up, but Black is active with a potentially mobile centre: 16 ♕d2 (16 ♘bd2? g5! intending 17 ♘xg5 ♘xg5 18 ♗xg5? ♕xg3+) 16...♘ce5 17 ♘xe5 ♕xe5 18 ♔h2 Timman-P.Nikolic, Amsterdam 1999, and now 18...g5! would have been good for Black due to 19 f4 ♕xf6 (or 19...gxf4 20 gxf4 ♕f5) 20 fxg5 (20 ♗xg5? ♘xg5 21 fxg5 ♕xf1! 22 ♗xf1 ♖xf1 wins) 20...♕e5 21 ♗d3 ♕e3! 22 g6 ♘e5! 23 gxh7+ ♔h8 24 ♕xe3 ♗xe3 and Black will recover both pawns with advantage.

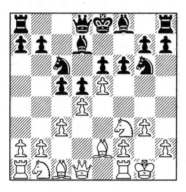

9 ♗d3

Black is able to break up the centre after 9 h4 fxe5 10 h5 e4! 11 ♘h2 (11 hxg6 exf3 and 12 ♗d3 ♕f6 13 gxh7 c4 14 ♗c2 0-0-0 15 ♘d2 g6 16 ♘xf3 ♖xh7 with good play, or 12 ♗xf3 hxg6 13 ♖e1 ♕f6 14 dxc5 ♗xc5 15 ♕xd5 0-0-0 16 ♕e4 e5 17 ♗e3 ♗f5 18 ♕a4 ♗xe3 19 ♖xe3 e4 20 ♗g2 ♕g5∓) 11...♘ge7 (threatening ...cxd4 and ...♘f5), e.g., 12 dxc5 ♘f5! (or 12...e5 with the idea 13 ♘g4 ♗e6 14 b4 d4!∓) 13 g4 (13 b4 ♗e7 14 ♘a3 0-0 15 ♗f4 a5 16 b5 ♘a7 17 b6 ♗xc5!∓) 13...♘h4 14 ♗e3 (14 b4 ♗e7 15 h6 g6∓ with ideas like ...0-0 and ...♘e5) 14...♕c7

15 ♘a3 a6 16 c4 d4 (16...♕e5∓) 17 ♗xd4 ♘xd4 18 ♕xd4 ♗xc5 19 ♕xe4 0-0-0 and Black is overwhelming White with the threats of ...♕g3+ and ...♗c6.

9...cxd4!?

Good, but 9...fxe5! looks very strong and is likely the best move:

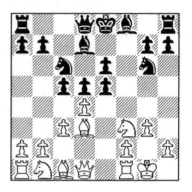

(a) 10 ♘xe5 ♘gxe5 11 dxe5 ♘xe5 (or 11...g6) 12 ♕h5+ ♘f7 13 ♖e1 (13 ♗xh7 ♕f6) 13...♕f6 with the idea ...0-0-0.

(b) 10 ♗xg6+ hxg6 11 dxe5 (11 ♘xe5 ♘xe5 12 dxe5 ♗b5 13 ♖e1 ♕d7 14 ♕c2 ♕f7; 11 ♕c2? e4) 11...♗e7!? (contemplating ...g5; the alternative is 11...♕c7 12 ♗f4 0-0-0 with the idea 13 ♘g5 ♗e7! 14 ♘f7 g5 15 ♘xd8 ♗xd8 16 ♗e3 ♘xe5 17 ♘a3 ♕b6!? 18 b4 g4!∓) 12 h4 (12 c4 dxc4 13 ♘bd2 ♘b4 14 ♘xc4 0-0; 12 ♕c2?! 0-0 13 ♔g2 g5 14 h3 ♗e8 15 ♘a3 d4; 12 ♘a3 g5 13 g4 0-0 14 ♔g2 ♗e8 15 ♕d3 d4∓) 12...0-0!? 13 ♗f4 (13 ♘bd2? ♖f5 14 ♕e2 ♕c7 15 ♖e1 ♖af8∓) 13...♖xf4!? (13...♕b6 14 ♕c2 ♖f5 15 ♘bd2 ♖af8∓ is easier, but less fun) 14 gxf4 ♕f8, e.g., 15 ♕d2 ♕f5 16 ♔h2 ♕h5! 17 ♔g3 ♗d8! with the idea ...♘e7-f5.

10 cxd4

Or 10 exf6 ♕xf6 11 cxd4 ♗d6 with good activity.

10...♘b4

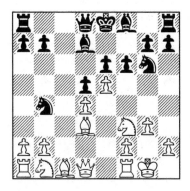

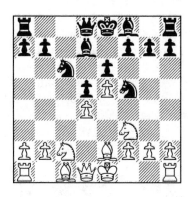

pawn chain. Black often plays the reasonable alternative 7...cxd4 8 cxd4 ♘f5 9 ♘c2

11 ♗e2!?

White has two moves that are probably better:

(a) 11 ♗xg6+ hxg6 12 a3 ♘c6 13 ♘h4!? (13 ♕d3 ♘e7!? 14 ♘c3!, when 14...g5 with the idea ...♕b6 is unclear) 13...♔f7 (13...g5!?) 14 ♕d3 g5!?. This is double edged, one idea being 15 ♕g6+ ♔g8 16 exf6 ♕xf6 17 ♗xg5 ♕xd4 with a wonderful centre;

(b) 11 ♘c3 ♘xd3 12 ♕xd3 fxe5 (12...♗e7!?) 13 dxe5 ♗c5 (13...♗e7) 14 ♗e3 ♗xe3 15 ♕xe3 0-0 is unclear.

11...fxe5 12 ♘xe5 ♘xe5 13 dxe5 ♗c5 14 a3

Or 14 ♗e3 d4!? 15 ♗d2 ♘d5=, with many options for both sides.

14...♘c6 15 ♗h5+ g6 16 ♗h6 ♕e7!?

Perhaps 16...♕b6 was more accurate. This is Meessen-M.Gurevich, Charleroi 2001. White blundered by 17 ♕c1?? with the idea 17...gxh5 18 ♗g5 ♕f8 19 ♗h6, but 19...♘d4! 20 ♗xf8 ♘e2+ 21 ♔g2 ♘xc1 won the game. Instead, the line 17 ♗e2 ♘xe5 (17...0-0-0!? 18 ♕c1!) 18 ♘c3 would have tried to keep Black's king in the centre, although I'd still prefer to be the second player after the move 18...♕f6.

2.312 7 ♘a3 ♘g6

Again aiming at the head of the

Note 5...cxd4 6 cxd4 ♘ge7 7 ♘a3 ♘f5 8 ♘c2 ♗d7 transposes if White plays 9 ♗e2, but with that order White also has 9 ♗d3, thinking about a capture on f5. Then Movsesian-Lyrberg, Neum 2000 showed one line: 9...♗e7 10 h4 ♕b6 11 ♔f1!? a5! 12 ♗xf5 exf5 13 h5 f4! 14 ♗xf4, and in ChessPublishing both 14...♗g4 and 14...♗f5! (intending 15 ♘e3 ♗e4) are recommended, with compensation.

From the diagram, there is a great deal of theory, but in general one should be wary of early simplification that favours White's centre. A brief overview of other ideas:

(a) 9...♕b6 and:

(a1) 10 0-0 a5 11 ♔h1 ♘b4 12 ♘e3 ♖c8 13 ♘xf5 exf5 14 ♗d2!? ♗e7 15 a3 ♘c6 16 ♗c3 0-0= Grischuk-M.Gurevich, Esbjerg 2000. Or 11...h5 12 b3, when 12...♖c8 is suggested by Cherniaev, and another method is 12...♗e7 13 ♕d3 f6!? 14 exf6 gxf6 15 ♗f4 ♔f7! with obscure prospects in Gwaze-N.Pert, Oxford 2003;

(a2) 10 g4?! ♘fe7 11 0-0 h5 12 h3 hxg4 13 hxg4 ♘g6 (McDonald) 'with ideas of ...♗e7 or ...♘h4' looks equal or better;

(a3) 10 h4 f6! 11 g4 ♘fxd4! (11...♘fe7 is unclear) 12 ♘cxd4 (12 ♘fxd4 ♘xe5 or 12...fxe5 13 ♘xc6 ♗xc6) 12...♘xe5 13 g5 ♗c5 14 0-0 ♘xf3+ 15 ♘xf3 ♕b4! 16 ♘e1!? (16 ♗e3 ♕g4+ 17 ♔h1 ♕h3+ is a draw) 16...♕xh4 17 ♘g2 ♕b4 18 ♗d3 0-0-0 and with 3 pawns for the piece and White's weakened kingside, Black can be quite happy, Movsesian-M.Gurevich, Bosna 2000.

(b) 9...♗e7 10 0-0 g5! (Black can play on the flank as well) 11 g4 ♘g7!?

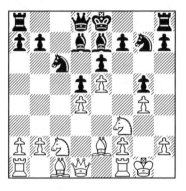

A fianchettoed knight, and without a square to move to! But it can be effective in supporting ...h5 and/or ...f5: 12 b4 a6 13 ♖b1 f5!? (this open more lines with unclear effects; 13...h5!?) 14 exf6 ♗xf6 15 a4 h6 16 ♘ce1!? 0-0 17 ♗e3 ♗e8 18 ♘d3 ♗g6= Dvoirys-Zakharevich, Elista 2001.

8 h4

Given time, Black will attack the centre with ...f6, for example, 8 ♘c2 ♗e7 9 g3 0-0 10 h4 cxd4 11 cxd4 f6! 12 h5 ♘h8 (now the idea is ...♘f7 to force the exchange of the e5 pawn) 13 h6 g6 14 exf6 ♗xf6 15 0-0 ♘f7 and Black has nice pressure on the centre with ideas of ...♘d6-f5/e4. White tried to free himself by 16 ♘e3?! ♘xh6 17 ♘xd5 exd5 18 ♗xh6 ♖e8 19 ♖e1, but 19...♗g4!∓ threatened ...♖xe2 in

Jonkman-I.Botvinnik, Tel Aviv 2000.
8...cxd4 9 cxd4 ♗b4+

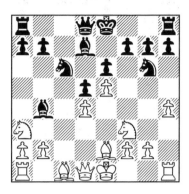

9...♗xa3!? 10 bxa3 weakens the white pawns but cedes the dark squares. Nevertheless, after 10...h6! 11 h5 ♘ge7 12 0-0 of Grischuk-Graf, Bled 2002, Black could have tried 12...0-0!? intending moves like ...♘f5, ...f6 and eventual play on the queenside. This is only for the brave.

10 ♔f1

The knight on g6 comes in handy in another way following 10 ♗d2 ♕b6 11 ♗xb4 ♕xb4+ 12 ♕d2 0-0 13 h5 ♘f4! 14 ♗f1 g6 15 hxg6 fxg6=.

10...h6!

Not only stopping h6, but preparing a reorganisation of the knight to f8 and then to h7!

11 ♘c2

11 h5 ♘f8 resembles the game.

11...♗e7 12 h5

(a) McDonald suggests 12 g3, although 12...0-0 13 ♔g2 ♘h8! and ...f6 is an effective idea seen in the note to White's 8th move;

(b) 12 ♗d3 has been played to discourage ...f6. Then Black can go in for 12...0-0 13 ♗e3 f5!? 14 exf6 ♖xf6.

12...♘f8 13 ♖h3! ♘h7!

The point. Now Black has the idea ...♘g5 in addition to the usual ...f6. This all looks odd, but White hasn't done much either, and in all these positions the pawn on h5 can eventually become a target.

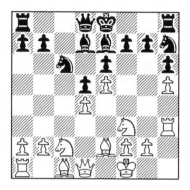

14 ♗d3

14 ♖g3 might be met by 14...♞g5 15 ♞xg5 hxg5 16 f4 ♛c7! with the idea 17 fxg5 f6! and otherwise ...0-0-0 with attack.

14...0-0 15 ♖g3 ♚h8 16 ♗f4 f5! 17 exf6

Instead, McDonald gives the line 17 ♛d2 ♗e8 18 ♖h3 ♞g5 with black advantage (the h-pawn has become a problem).

After 17 exf6, Movsesian-P.Nikolic, Istanbul 2000 continued 17...♞xf6 18 ♞e5 ♞xe5 19 ♗xe5 ♗e8 20 ♖h3 ♗d6!? 21 ♞e1!? (21 ♛e2 looks logical but allows 21...♗xe5 22 dxe5 ♞e4! 23 ♗xe4 dxe4 intending 24 ♛xe4 ♛d2) 21...♗xe5 22 dxe5 ♞e4! 23 ♞f3 ♖f5! 24 ♛e2 (24 g4? protects the h-pawn but loses all the key squares after 24...♖f4) 24...♖xh5 25 ♖xh5 ♗xh5 26 ♗xe4 dxe4 27 ♛xe4 ♛b6∓. Black's king is safer, his pieces are better, and ...♖f8 is coming.

2.32 6...f6

Some readers will not be comfortable with the ...♞ge7-g6 ideas shown above. As an alternative I present a repertoire with 6...f6, which was rec-

ommended in earlier editions. It contains many ideas which haven't yet been looked at by theory.

7 0-0

The only serious move. 7 exf6 ♞xf6 with the idea ...♗d6, ...0-0 is a standard idea but even better for Black with the bishop on e2. And 7 ♗f4? ♛b6! intending ...♛xb2 or ...g5-g4 allows of no good answer. Finally, 7 c4?! cxd4 8 cxd5 exd5 9 exf6 ♞xf6 10 ♞xd4 ♗c5∓ was Kupreichik-Dolmatov, USSR Ch 1980.

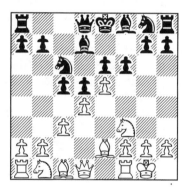

7...♛c7

6...♛c7 7 0-0 f6 reaches the same position. 7...♛c7 tries to exploit the fact that Black's queen is not yet committed to b6 and so can hit e5; this may also lure White's pieces to the wrong squares.

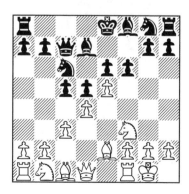

8 ♗f4

The most successful move thus far. 8 ♖e1 tries to defend e5 tactically, when Black has two effective responses:

(a) 8...fxe5 9 ♘xe5 ♘xe5 10 dxe5 0-0-0. This is a hard position to assess which McDonald thinks is 'dynamically equal': 11 ♗g4 ♘h6!? (11...g6!? is a logical idea, intending 12 ♗f4 h5 13 ♗h3 ♗h6=) 12 ♗xh6 (12 ♗g5 ♖e8 13 ♗h5 g6 14 ♗f6 ♖g8 15 ♗f3 maybe be slightly in White's favour) 12...gxh6 13 ♘d2 ♔b8 14 ♕e2 ♖g8 with unclear play, Strijbos-Hochstrauer, Rotterdam 1998;

(b) 8...0-0-0 is a promising alternative, e.g., 9 ♗f4 (9 ♗f1 fxe5 10 ♘xe5 ♘xe5 11 dxe5 g6!?; 9 ♗e3 fxe5 10 dxc5 ♘h6!?) 9...g5 (9...h6!?) 10 ♗e3?! (10 ♗g3 ♕b6! intends ...g4; There could follow 11 b4 cxb4 12 exf6 ♘xf6 13 ♘xg5 ♖g8 14 ♘f7 ♖e8 and ...♖g7 with a very slight white advantage) 10...g4 11 ♘fd2 cxd4 12 cxd4 Broekman-Kleinhenz, Triesen 2000; and the easiest course was 12...fxe5 13 dxe5 ♕xe5 14 ♗xg4 ♗d6 with an obvious advantage.

8...♘ge7

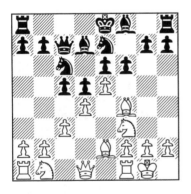

9 ♗g3

Other moves don't look dangerous:
(a) 9 ♗d3 f5! 10 ♖e1 c4 (10...♕b6!?)

11 ♗c2 ♘g6 12 ♗g3 (12 ♗e3 ♗e7) 12...♗e7 13 h4 0-0= Galdunts-Komarov, USSR 1991;

(b) 9 ♘a3 a6!? (9...♘g6! 10 ♗g3 fxe5 11 ♗d3 cxd4 12 cxd4 ♕b6 with plenty of activity) 10 ♗g3!? (10 ♗d3) Bastian-Lobron, Bundesliga 1990; now 10...♕b6 looks best, e.g., 11 ♕d2 cxd4 12 cxd4 ♘f5=.

9...♕b6!

Even though this whole system is relatively unexplored, it's surprising that such a simple more has only been tried a couple of times. Black tries to exploit the fact that the g3 bishop isn't able to defend the centre or queenside.

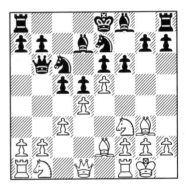

10 ♕d2!

(a) 10 exf6 gxf6 11 ♕b3 ♕xb3 12 axb3 cxd4 13 ♘xd4 ♘xd4 14 cxd4 ♘f5 15 ♖d1 ♘xg3 16 hxg3 ♗b4∓ with two bishops and the better pawn structure;

(b) 10 ♘a3 ♘f5! (or 10...cxd4 11 exf6 ♘f5!) 11 exf6 gxf6∓.

10...cxd4!?

10...♘f5! 11 exf6 gxf6 looks good.

11 exf6

11 cxd4? ♘f5 12 ♖d1 ♘xg3 13 hxg3 fxe5 14 ♘xe5 (14 dxe5 ♗c5 15 ♖f1 0-0 16 ♘c3 ♘d4 17 ♖ac1 ♖f5!∓) 14...♘xe5 15 dxe5 ♗c5 16 ♗h5+ g6 17 ♗f3 0-0 18 ♘c3 ♖f5 19 ♖e1 ♖af8∓ Montoro-De

Dovitiis, Buenos Aires 1998.
11...gxf6 12 ♘xd4 e5

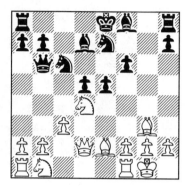

13 ♘b5

13 ♘xc6 ♗xc6 is at least equal for Black because of his centre.

13...♘a5! 14 ♘1a3!

Otherwise Black consolidates after 14 ♘5a3 ♗e6.

14...a6 15 ♕e3! d4 16 cxd4 ♘f5!

16...axb5? 17 dxe5 ♕xe3 18 fxe3±.

17 ♕e4 ♘xg3 18 hxg3 axb5 19 dxe5 0-0-0 with unclear complications. White might be a little short of compensation because Black's pieces are active. A lot of the above is pure analysis, but at this point 6...f6 and 7...♕c7 seems a good practical line with no major drawbacks.

Chapter Three

Advance Variation: 5...♛b6

1 e4 e6 2 d4 d5 3 e5 c5 4 c3 ♘c6 5 ♘f3 ♛b6

This introduces our alternate system against the Advance Variation. Black immediately attacks the centre and will tend to play more direct moves than with 5...♗d7. The systems have some overlap, since the line 5...♗d7 6 ♗d3 cxd4 7 cxd4 ♛b6 transposes to 5...♛b6 6 ♗d3 cxd4 7 cxd4 ♗d7 below.

Material divides into:

3.1 6 a3
3.2 6 ♗e2
3.3 6 ♗d3

Others:
(a) 6 dxc5?! ♗xc5 7 ♛c2 f6 destroys White's centre, e.g., 8 b4 (8 exf6 ♘xf6 9 ♗f4 0-0 10 ♗d3 e5!) 8...♗e7 9 ♗d3? fxe5 10 ♗xh7 e4 11 ♗g6+ ♔f8 12 ♘g5 ♗xg5 13 ♗xg5 ♘e5∓;
(b) 6 g3?! f6! 7 ♗g2 (7 ♘h4 g6!) 7...cxd4 8 cxd4 ♗b4+ 9 ♔f1 (9 ♘c3 fxe5 intending ...d4) 9...fxe5 10 dxe5 ♘ge7 11 ♛e2 ♘f5∓.

3.1 6 a3
Over the past 15 years or so, this move has been the hottest line in the Advance Variation and used heavily at the top levels of international play. In fact, my most comprehensive database has over 7000 games with 6 a3, considerably more than the traditional 6 ♗e2. Since most French players still use 5...♛b6, one could say that 6 a3 is the most critical line for modern Advance Variation theory.

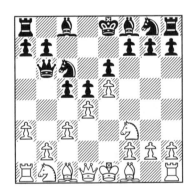

6...♘h6!?
There is an undeniable logic to developing rapidly versus the slow 6 a3. Black intends ...cxd4 and ...♘f5, winning a pawn. The main idea is to follow up with straightforward development (...♗d7, ...♗e7, ...♜c8, and an

eventual ...f6). In the second edition, I called the main move 6...♘h6 below a 'slightly irregular answer which I believe has been underestimated'. Now there are some 1250 games in my database, and practically every top French player has used it. Black has of course a wide variety of alternatives. 6...c4 is the oldest move and is holding up well, but it is also less flexible. And I have the impression that the enormously popular line with 6...♗d7 7 b4 cxd4 8 cxd4 ♖c8 is falling a little short against some precise move orders by White. Of course that could change, but it seems to me that 6...♘h6 isn't as dependent upon special tactics as 6...♗d7 is. However, I do think that Black has an excellent weapon that has only been lightly explored, i.e. 6...f6!?. This, a suggestion from the first edition, still strikes me as sound and worthwhile.

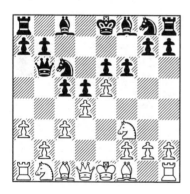

Black can (like his opponent) play on both wings here: on the queenside with ...0-0-0, ...♔b8, ...♘a5 and ...♖c8 or on the kingside with ideas like ...fxe5, ...♘h6-f7, ...g6 and ...♗g7. Let's look at the briefest of overviews: 7 ♗d3 (the most common reply; 7 b4 has been answered by 7...c4 and 7...cxb4 8 cxb4 fxe5, but the most interesting alternative was 7...fxe5!? 8

dxe5!? ♘h6! 9 ♗xh6 gxh6 10 ♗d3 ♗g7 11 0-0 0-0∓ Guigonis-Renaudin, Paris 2000) 7...c4 (also noteworthy are 7...g6!? 8 b4 [8 exf6 ♘xf6 9 ♕c2 ♕c7] 8...cxd4 9 cxd4 ♗g7; and 7...fxe5, e.g., 8 dxe5 ♘h6!? 9 0-0 c4 10 ♗c2 ♘f7, Afek-Murey, St Quentin 1999) 8 ♗c2 g6!? (or 8...♗d7 9 0-0 0-0-0) 9 0-0 fxe5 (9...♗g7 is also reasonable) 10 ♘xe5 (10 dxe5?! ♘h6 11 ♕e2 ♘f7∓) 10...♘xe5 11 dxe5 ♘h6 12 ♕e2 ♗g7 13 ♗e3 ♕c7 14 f4 0-0 and the play is balanced. Perhaps the 6...f6 variation should be seen more often.

7 b4

(a) 7 ♗xh6? ♕xb2 8 ♗c1 ♕xa1 9 ♕c2 is unsound: 9...c4! intending ...♘a5, ...♗d7, and ...♘b3;

(b) 7 ♗d3 doesn't go well with a3: 7...cxd4 8 cxd4 ♗d7 9 0-0?! (a strange form of Milner-Barry Attack, trading a3 for ...♘h6; this should favour Black) 9...♘xd4 10 ♘xd4 ♕xd4 11 ♘c3 a6 12 ♕e2 ♕g4!? 13 f3? ♗c5+ 14 ♔h1 ♕h4∓ 15 g3 ♕h3 16 ♕e1 ♗c6 17 ♗f4 0-0 with an extra pawn and active pieces, Dvoirys-Lputian, Istanbul 2003.

7...cxd4

Here two moves have been tested for White:

3.11 8 ♗xh6
3.12 8 cxd4

3.11 8 ♗xh6 gxh6 9 cxd4

This is a fascinating line with which White trades off his important c1 bishop to damage Black's pawn structure and secure his d4 pawn. Black gets two bishops and has good development in return for the broken pawn structure on his kingside. The plan is to play the moves ...♗g7, ...0-0, and ...f6.

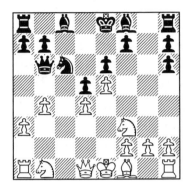

9...♗d7

I like the fact that this move prevents 10 ♗d3 (due to 10...♘xd4) and it probably needs to be played anyway. 9...♗d7 also clears the c-file, so that a move like 10 ♘c3 can be met by 10...♘xb4 11 axb4 ♗xb4 (see below, and note that the bishop hasn't gone to g7 in this case).

I recommended 9...♖g8!? in the last edition; but now we know that it gives White the advantage for positional reasons, which for completeness I should specify: 10 ♘c3! (10 b5 ♘a5 11 ♘c3 is not very convincing in view of White's queenside weaknesses; for example, 11...♗d7 12 ♘a4 ♕c7! is strong) 10...♗d7 (my main move in the second edition 10...♖g4? looks bad for several reasons, one of them being 11 h3 ♖f4 12 ♗b5 a5 13 0-0! axb4 14 axb4 ♖xa1 15 ♕xa1 ♖xf3 16 gxf3 ♕xd4 17 ♕a8± ♔d7? 18 ♘a4 ♗xb4 19 ♖c1 ♔c7 20 ♗xc6 1-0 Keitlinghaus-Blauert, Budapest 1998) 11 ♘a4! (11 ♖c1?! ♘xb4 12 axb4 ♗xb4 gave plenty of compensation in Kretschmer-Wrba, corr 1993; 11 g3? ♖g4! 12 ♗h3 ♖xd4 13 ♘xd4 ♕xd4 14 ♕xd4 ♘xd4 15 0-0-0 ♘f3 16 ♗g2 ♖c8 17 ♔b2 ♘xe5 18 ♗xd5 ♘g4!∓ Hakuc-Djabri, email 1999) 11...♕d8 12 g3! (12 ♘c5 ♗xc5 13 bxc5

f6 14 exf6 ♕xf6 15 ♖b1 ♖b8! 16 ♕d3 ♖g4 17 ♖d1 b6! with mutual chances) 12...♖g4? (12...f6; 12...f5!?) 13 ♗e2 (or 13 h3! ♖e4+ 14 ♗e2±) 13...a5 14 b5 ♘a7 15 ♕b3 ♖e4 16 ♘c3 a4 17 ♕b2 ♕a5 18 0-0± D.Olafsson-A.Karlsson, Reykjavik 2000.

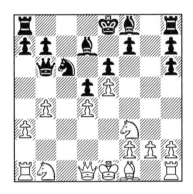

10 ♗e2

This solid move is best. 10 ♘c3 allows 10...♘xb4! 11 axb4 ♗xb4

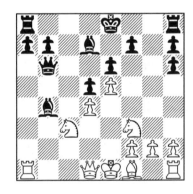

when Black's attack on c3 has no adequate answer, showing the value of delaying the f8 bishop's development. One line goes 12 ♕b3 ♖c8 13 ♖c1 0-0 (with the idea of doubling on the c-file, but also of ...f6) 14 ♔e2 ♕a6+ 15 ♔d2 (15 ♔e3? ♕a3) 15...♕a5 16 ♗d3 ♖c7 (or 16...♗a4 17 ♕b2 ♖c6) 17 ♘g1 ♗a4 18 ♕b2 f6! 19 exf6 ♖xf6 20 f3 e5! 21 ♘ge2 ♖fc6-+.

10...♖c8

Black again retains the ...♘xb4 idea while making a useful move. But 10...♗g7 is also fine, since 11 ♘c3?! (11 0-0 ♖c8 transposes) 11...f6 12 ♘a4 ♕d8 13 0-0 of Pisa-De la Villa Garcia, Spanish Ch 1993 should have been met by the simple capture 13...fxe5! 14 ♘xe5 ♘xe5 15 dxe5 ♗xe5 16 ♗h5+ ♔e7 etc.

11 0-0 ♗g7

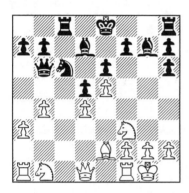

12 ♕d2!?

Surprisingly, this runs into trouble. Since moves by the b1 knight lose the d-pawn, here are the alternatives:

(a) 12 ♕d3 isn't really satisfactory after 12...f6! 13 b5? (13 exf6 ♗xf6 14 ♖d1 0-0∓) Degraeve-C.Bauer, Montpellier 1993, and now 13...♘xe5! 14 dxe5 fxe5∓, since the advance ...e4 is next;

(b) 12 b5 is probably best, although Black stood well after 12...♘e7 13 a4 f6 14 ♕d2!? fxe5 15 ♘xe5 ♘f5 16 ♗h5+ ♔e7 17 ♕b4+ ♕d6 18 ♕xd6+ ♘xd6∓ with a discernible advantage, Halwick-Barlow, corr 1998.

12...♘xd4!?

12...0-0 has been played quite a few times (e.g., by both Korchnoi and Lputian) and is also good, planning ...f6 and reserving the ...♘xd4 move (13 ♘c3? ♘xd4!). The text is perhaps

objectively no better, but doesn't give White any respite.

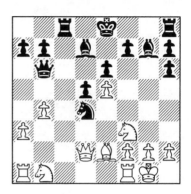

13 ♘xd4!

Better than 13 ♕xd4 ♕xd4 14 ♘xd4 ♗xe5 15 ♘b3 ♗xa1 16 ♘xa1 ♗a4 17 ♘d2 ♔e7∓. After 13 ♘xd4, the play might go 13...♗xe5 14 ♖d1 ♗a4 15 ♕e3! ♗xd1 16 ♕xe5 ♗e2! 17 ♘xe2 (17 ♕xh8+ ♔d7 18 ♕xc8+ ♔xc8 19 ♘xe2 a5 gives Black a bit too much material) 17...0-0∓, when Black's mobile centre and activity outweigh White's rather ineffective knights.

In general, the 8 ♗xh6 variation allows Black too much counterplay. White has to play carefully just to maintain the balance and can easily fall victim to tactical blows.

3.12 8 cxd4 ♘f5

and now:

3.121 9 ♗e3
3.122 9 ♗b2

3.121 9 ♗e3

This move was previously thought to frustrate winning attempts on Black's part. Current theory, however, indicates that he has several ways to create double-edged and promising play.

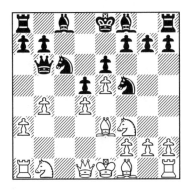

9...f6!

Right now this older line looks promising to me. It turns out that Black doesn't have to accede to a likely drawing line but can try for more, whereas White (in order to avoid that line), risks being left at a disadvantage.

(a) To enter into a closed manoeuvering game, Black may want to try to block the kingside. One way would begin with 9...♗e7:

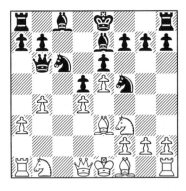

Play here has gone 10 ♗d3 (10 ♗e2 0-0 11 ♘c3 f6 12 ♘a4 ♕d8 13 exf6 ♗xf6 14 0-0 e5= Prang-Boehle, 1993; 10 ♘bd2 ♘xe3 11 fxe3 f5 12 exf6 ♗xf6 13 ♗d3 e5!∓; 10 g4 ♘xe3 11 fxe3 f6!∓; 10 b5 ♘a5 intending a quick ...♗d7 and ...♖c8) 10...♘xe3 11 fxe3, and now 11...f5! tries to set up a com-

plex manoeuvring struggle after 12 0-0 0-0 (threatening ...f4) 13 ♘c3 ♕d8! 14 ♘e2 ♗d7 15 ♘f4 a5! 16 b5 ♘a7 17 a4 ♘c8 intending ...♘b6, ...♖c8, ...♘c4. The two bishops are temporarily passive but where is White's play coming from?

Alternatively White could keep the position open: 12 exf6 ♗xf6 13 ♘c3 (13 ♘g5 ♗xd4!, e.g., 14 exd4 ♕xd4 15 ♕h5+ ♔e7! 16 ♕f7+ ♔d6–+; 13 0-0 0-0 14 ♘c3 ♗d7) 13...0-0 14 0-0 (14 ♕c2 g6 with the idea 15 ♗xg6!? hxg6 16 ♕xg6+ ♗g7 17 ♘g5 ♖f6 18 ♕h7+ ♔f8 19 ♕h5 ♔e7 20 ♕h7 ♔f8=) 14...g6 15 ♕c2 ♔g7?! (15...♘e7 followed by ...♗d7 and ...♖ac8 looks fine) 16 ♘a4 ♕d8 17 ♘c5± Carlsen-Lahlum, Gausdal 2001.

(b) Another blocking strategy is seen in 9...♗d7 10 ♘bd2 (10 ♗d3 could be answered by 10...♘xe3 11 fxe3 f5) 10...♘xe3 11 fxe3 f5 12 ♗d3 (12 exf6 gxf6 13 ♗d3 e5!? 14 b5 ♘a5!) H.Akopian-J.Watson, Los Angeles 1998; and Black's simplest course was something like 12...♗e7 13 0-0 0-0 14 ♘b3 ♕d8 with the idea 15 ♘c5 b6 16 ♘xd7 ♕xd7 17 ♖c1 (17 ♗b5 a6) 17...a6 18 b5 ♘b8 19 bxa6 ♘xa6=;

(c) 9...♘xe3 10 fxe3 g6 11 ♗d3 ♗h6 12 ♕e2 0-0 has been played a fair number of times; one idea for White might be 13 g4!? (13 0-0 f6 or 13...♗d7) 13...♗d7 14 h4 with ideas like 14...♖ac8 15 ♘bd2 ♘e7 (15...♗g7 16 h5 ♘e7 17 ♕h2) 16 h5 g5 17 ♘b3 etc.

10 ♗d3

Interesting and tactical. White may have difficulties in what used to be a drawing line:

(a) 10 b5 ♘xe5! 11 dxe5 ♘xe3 12 fxe3 ♕xe3+ 13 ♕e2 (13 ♗e2? fxe5 is bad, leaving Black with two bishops and the centre) 13...♕c1+!? ½-½ Romanishin-Lputian, Yerevan 1988, in view of 14 ♕d1 ♕e3+ 15 ♕e2 ♕c1+ etc. This verdict has been unchallenged but there are other possibilities. First, 14...♕b2!? 15 ♘bd2 fxe5 16 ♖b1 ♕xa3 17 ♘xe5 ♕e3+ 18 ♕e2 is analysis by Paul Cumbers, when Neil McDonald suggests 18...♗c5, 'though I still prefer White'. This should be looked at; perhaps White's grip on e5 slightly outweighs the two bishops.

It seems to me that Black has a better winning try than Cumbers' by playing 13...♕xe2+ 14 ♗xe2 fxe5 15 ♘xe5 ♗d6, since then he gets the centre but prevents the bind on e5. Something like 16 ♘f3 0-0 17 0-0 ♗d7 18 ♘bd2 ♖ac8 might follow, intending ...e5. Black only has two pawns for the piece but they are mobile passed central pawns and his bishop pair is powerful. There's also the immediate problem that White can't yet challenge the c-file. I think that this is worth playing and that therefore 10 b5 doesn't even necessarily secure a draw;

(b) 10 exf6 keeps the pieces on, although it has scored poorly after 10...gxf6 11 ♘c3 (11 ♗d3 ♘xe3 12 fxe3 e5 [or 12...♗d7] 13 ♘c3 ♗e6 14 ♕b3 0-0-0 15 ♘a4 ♕c7 16 0-0 ♔b8 17 ♗b5 e4 18 ♘d2 ♗d6∓ G.West-Barlow, CAPA email 1997) 11...♘xe3 12 fxe3 ♗h6 and:

(b1) 13 ♕d2 0-0 14 ♗d3 ♔h8 15 ♖d1 (15 0-0 ♘xd4!) 15...♗d7 16 0-0 ♗e8 17 ♔h1 ♘e7;

(b2) 13 ♔f2 0-0 14 ♗d3?! ♘e5 15 h3 ♗d7 16 ♖e1 ♖ac8 17 ♖c1 ♘xd3+ 18 ♕xd3 a6 19 ♔g1 ♖c7∓ Nilsson-Fernandez Romero, Dos Hermanas 2002;

(b3) 13 ♕d3 0-0 14 ♗e2 ♗d7 15 0-0 (15 ♘a4 ♘e5! 16 ♘xb6 ♘xd3+ 17 ♗xd3 axb6 18 ♔e2 Gruic-Arkhipov, Belgrade 1990, and simplest looks

18...e5∓) 15...♗e8!? (15...♘e7!) 16 ♔h1 (16 ♘a4 ♕d8 17 ♘c5 ♕e7=) 16...♗g6 17 ♕d2 ♘e7 18 ♘h4 ♗g5 19 ♘xg6 hxg6= Petrov-Fernandez Romero, Linares 2002.

10...♘xe3 11 fxe3

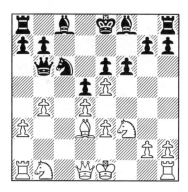

11...fxe5

Or 11...♗d7!?, e.g., 12 exf6 gxf6 13 ♘c3 ♗h6 14 ♕e2 ♘e7 (simpler seems 14...0-0 15 0-0 ♖f7 and ...♔h8 next) 15 0-0 (15 ♘e5 fxe5 16 ♕h5+ ♔d8 17 ♕xh6 ♖c8 was unclear in Jonkman-San Segundo Carrillo, Mondariz 2000) 15...0-0 16 ♔h1 ♖ac8 17 ♘d1?! ♗g7!? 18 ♘f2 e5 19 dxe5 fxe5 20 e4 d4∓ Morozevich-Bareev, Monaco 2002.

12 b5 ♘xd4!

Not 12...exd4!? 13 exd4! and White stands much better, nor 12...e4?! 13 bxc6 exd3? 14 ♘e5± Prie-De la Villa Garcia, Leon 1991.

13 exd4

13 ♘xe5? ♘f5 hits e3 and favours Black.

13...e4

This has become a well-known position: I think that Black is distinctly better.

14 ♗xe4!

Weak is 14 ♘e5? ♕xd4, and 14 0-0? exf3 leads to 15 ♕xf3 ♕xd4+ or 15 ♖f2 ♗d6 with a winning position.

14...dxe4 15 ♘e5

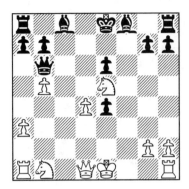

15...g6

This is good, but apparently simpler is the recent 15...♗d7! of Potkin-Filippov, Togliatti 2003, which intends 16 ♕h5+ g6 17 ♘xg6 hxg6 18 ♕xh8 0-0-0 with excellent play. So the game went 16 0-0 0-0-0 with Black better. This needs analysis and tests.

16 0-0

16 ♘c3 ♗g7 17 ♘xe4 0-0 and White can't castle, whereas 18 ♘f3 ♕xb5 is also bad.

16...♗g7 17 ♔h1 ♗xe5 18 dxe5 ♕xb5 19 ♘c3 ♕xe5 20 ♕b3 b6

Or perhaps 20...e3!?. After 20...b6, Hurley-T.Clarke, Ireland 1996 went 21 ♖ad1, and now Cumbers and McDonald have combined to produce the sample line 21...♗b7 22 ♘b5 (22 ♕a4+ b5 23 ♘xb5 ♗c6) 22...♖d8 23 ♖xd8+ ♔xd8 24 ♘xa7 ♕c5 25 ♕xe6 ♔c7 26 ♕f6 ♖e8 27 ♕f4+ ♕e5 28 ♕c1+ ♔b8 29 ♘c6+ ♗xc6 30 ♕xc6 ♕e6, a pawn up. This is all up for grabs, but it's hard to believe that Black isn't in general able to use his extra pawns to consolidate. And White has to contend with the newer 15...♗d7 as well.

3.122 9 ♗b2 ♗d7

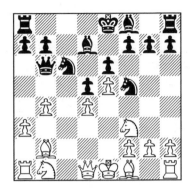

There are several move order issues here. The text prevents 10 ♗d3 in view of the hanging d-pawn. Although 9...♗e7 is played consistently as well (e.g., by Lputian), it doesn't prevent that move, and I also prefer to have the e7 square to retreat the knight to after White's g4. Still, 9...♗e7 has it's own advantages and my choice here is as much a matter of taste as an objective assessment.

10 g4

Whether or not this is the best move, it is the most critical, and the most frequent except for 10 ♗e2. White's space-gaining ideas like h4 and g4 are the most dangerous ones, and several of the alternatives show that White cannot develop slowly without affording his opponent good chances:

(a) 10 b5?! ♘a5 gives up the c4 square too easily: 11 ♘c3 (11 a4 a6 12 ♘c3 ♗b4 13 bxa6 bxa6 14 ♗e2 ♖c8∓ Hitzker-Kaland, Pinneberg 1992) 11...♖c8 12 ♘a4 ♕d8 13 ♖c1 ♖xc1 14 ♕xc1 a6 (14...♘c4! 15 ♗xc4 ♕a5+∓) 15 ♘c5? (15 ♘c3∓) 15...♗xb5 16 ♗xb5+ axb5 17 0-0 ♘c4∓ Marszalek-Beyen, Leningrad 1960;

(b) 10 ♕d3 ♖c8! threatens ...♗xb4, so a sample line might go 11 ♗c3 a5!? (best is probably 11...♗e7 12 ♗e2 0-0

13 0-0 f6) 12 b5 ♘a7 13 a4 ♗b4 with mutual chances;

(c) 10 h4 is a modern treatment, the idea being to play h5 and g4 to establish a large space advantage on the kingside. In the meantime, the Black knight is denied access to g6 after a retreat to e7. Nevertheless, Black has well-placed pieces and two options:

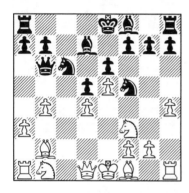

(c1) 10...h5 11 g3 ♗e7!? (11...♖c8 intending ...♘a5 may be even better, e.g., 12 ♕d2 ♗e7 13 ♗h3 ♕b5!? 14 ♘c3 ♕c4 with good play) 12 ♗h3 ♖c8 (12...a5!?) 13 ♕d2 (13 0-0 ♘a5) 13...a5 14 ♗xf5 exf5 15 ♘c3 ♘a7! 16 0-0 (16 ♘xd5? ♕c6) 16...♗e6 with approximate equality. Notice that in these lines all 7 White pawns are on the colour of his 'bad' bishop, but that this is more of an advantage than a problem for him!

(c2) 10...♖c8 (quick development is the cure for Black's problems here) 11 g4 and:

(c21) 11...♘h6 12 ♖g1 ♗e7 (12...♘a5!? 13 ♘fd2?! ♗e7 14 ♗c3 ♘c4 15 ♘xc4 dxc4 16 ♘d2 0-0! unclear, Kozak-Antonio, Las Vegas 1999, due to 17 ♘xc4? ♖xc4! 18 ♗xc4 ♕c7∓) 13 ♘c3 ♘a5 14 ♘a4 ♕c6 15 ♘c5 ♘c4 16 ♗c1 ♘g8! 17 ♗d3 ♗xc5 18 dxc5 b6 19 ♗xc4 dxc4 20 ♗e3

Sveshnikov-Dizdar, Dubai 2002, and 20...♘e7! 21 ♖c1 b5 was good, intending moves like ...♘d5 and ...♕a6 with ...♗c6.

(c22) 11...♘fe7!? 12 ♘c3 ♘a5! 13 ♘a4 ♕c6 14 ♘c5 ♘c4 15 ♗c1 h5! 16 gxh5 ♘f5 17 ♗h3 was Movsesian-Haimovich, Panormo 2001. Here Movsesian suggests 17...b6 'and Black shouldn't be worried about the future at all'.

(d) 10 ♗e2

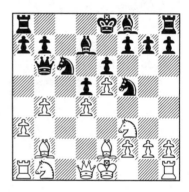

(d1) 10...♗e7 11 0-0 0-0 12 g4! (12 ♕d2?! f6 13 exf6 ♗xf6 14 ♘e5 ♗e8!∓ S.Lalic-N.Berry, Birmingham 2001) 12...♘h4 (or 12...♘h6 13 h3 f6) 13 ♘xh4 ♗xh4 14 f4 f6!? unclear;

(d2) 10...♖c8!? (with the idea ...♘a5) 11 0-0 ♗e7 12 ♕d2 h5 13 ♖d1!? g5! 14 ♘c3! (14 ♘xg5 ♘cxd4 15 ♗xd4 ♘xd4 16 ♕xd4 ♕xd4 17 ♖xd4 ♗xg5 18 f4 ♗d8! 'threatening ♗b6 when Black has the two bishops and control of the c-file' – McDonald) 14...g4 15 ♘e1 Grosar-Tukmakov, Bled 2001; and now simply 15...♘cxd4! (15...♕d8!? 16 ♘c2 ♗g5 17 ♕e1 ♘ce7 was played) 16 ♘xd5 ♘xe2+ 17 ♕xe2 exd5 was very strong, since White nearly has to enter the variation 18 e6 ♕xe6 19 ♕xe6 ♗xe6 20 ♗xh8 f6 21 ♖ac1 ♖b8! followed by ...♔f7 trapping the bishop.

10...♘h6

Also playable is 10...♘fe7

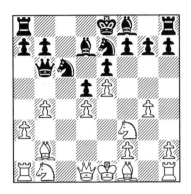

11 ♘c3! (11 ♗d3 h5 12 g5 g6 13 h4 ♘f5 14 ♗xf5 gxf5 15 ♘c3 ♘e7! 16 0-0 ♘g6∓ Ancheyta-Nogueiras, Santa Clara 2001; 11 h3 ♘a5 [or 11...h5] 12 ♘bd2 ♘g6 13 ♗c1 ♘c4! Novikova-Matlakov, St Petersburg 2002, intending 14 ♘xc4 dxc4 15 ♗xc4 ♖c8 16 ♗d3 ♗c6) 11...♘a5! 12 ♕d2 (12 ♘a4 ♕c6 13 b5 ♕c7 14 ♘d2 [14 ♖c1 ♘c4 15 ♕b3 ♕a5+∓] 14...♘c4 15 ♘xc4 dxc4 16 ♘c3 ♘d5∓ Lindfelt-P.H.Nielsen, Nyborg 2001) 12...♖c8 13 ♖c1 ♘g6 14 h4 ♗e7 15 g5 (15 h5 ♘f4 16 ♕f3 ♗g5= Grischuk-Kruppa, Elista 2000) 15...h6 (or simply 15...0-0! intending 16 h5 ♘f4 or even 16...♕xd4! 17 hxg6 fxg6, so Potkin-Hug, Istanbul 2003 continued 16 ♖g1!? ♘xh4 17 ♗d3, when 17...♘g6 18 ♕g4 ♖c7! 19 ♖h1 ♖fc8 20 ♕h5 ♔f8 21 ♕xh7 intending 21...♗xg5 would have been strong) 16 gxh6 Grischuk-Radjabov, Wijk aan Zee 2003, and here McDonald (and later Grischuk!) mentions 16...gxh6!? 17 h5 ♘h4 18 ♕g4 ♘f5, which looks okay.

11 h3

White loses a pawn after 11 ♗h3? a5!; and 11 ♖g1 allows 11...f6 (or 11...♗e7 and ...♖c8) 12 exf6 gxf6 13 ♘c3 ♘f7 (13...♗d6) 14 ♘a4 (14 ♖c1

♗h6! 15 ♖c2 ♘e7∓ Lautier-Bauer, Val d'Isere 2002) 14...♕c7 15 ♖c1 ♕f4! 16 ♘c5 ♗xc5 17 dxc5 ♘ce5 18 ♘xe5 Short-Lputian, Batumi 1999; and McDonald notes that 18...fxe5! is quite strong.

11...f6

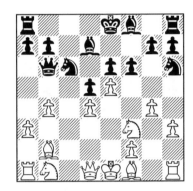

Shirov-Sadvakasov, Astana 2001 continued 11...♖c8 12 ♘c3 ♘a5 13 ♘a4 ♕c6 14 ♖c1 ♘c4=.

12 ♘c3

12 ♗d3 can as usual be met by 12...fxe5 13 ♘xe5 ♘xe5 14 dxe5 ♘f7: 15 0-0 g5!? (or 15...a5 16 b5 ♗c5) 16 ♘c3 ♗g7 17 ♖e1 0-0 18 ♕d2 ♘h8?! (18...♖ac8∓) 19 ♘d1 ♖f3 20 ♗d4 ♕d8± ½-½ Hollrigl-Van der Weide, Liechtenstein 1999.

12...fxe5 13 dxe5

13 ♘a4 is counterproductive after 13...♕d8 14 ♘xe5 ♘xe5 15 dxe5 ♗e7 with dark square control.

13...♗e7

Or 13...♘f7. After 13...♗e7, Sveshnikov-Lputian, Sochi 1993 continued 14 ♘a4 ♕d8 15 ♖c1 0-0 16 ♘c5 ♗xc5 17 ♖xc5. Apart from 17...♘f7, as played, Black had 17...♘e7! intending ...a5, when the second player has a slight edge, a risky line going 18 ♖c1?! (better is 18 ♖c3 ♘f7 19 ♖e3 ♘g5∓) 18...♘xb4! 19 g5! (19 axb4 ♕xb4+ 20 ♕d2 ♕e4+) 19...♘f5 20 axb4 ♘h4! 21 ♘xh4 ♕xb4+ 22 ♕d2 ♕e4+ 23 ♕e3 ♕xh1∓.

This has been lot of detail on one variation, but it has been the most important line of the Advance Variation for many years now.

3.2 6 ♗e2

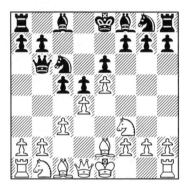

The traditional main line, somewhat superceded by 6 a3 but still very important and extremely complicated.

6...♘h6

After this flexible move, White must attend to the threat of ...cxd4 and ...♘f5. He can do so by:

3.21 7 b3
3.32 7 ♗xh6

Others:

(a) 7 dxc5? ♗xc5 8 0-0 ♘g4∓;

(b) 7 ♘a3? cxd4 8 ♗xh6 gxh6 9 cxd4 ♕xb2 10 ♘b5 ♕b4+ 11 ♔f1 ♕a5∓ Kestler-Uhlmann, Bundesliga 1991;

(c) 7 0-0? cxd4 8 cxd4 ♘f5∓.

(d) 7 ♔f1? cxd4 8 cxd4 ♘f5 9 ♘c3 and now Black can capture the pawn by 9...♘fxd4! 10 ♘a4 (10 ♗e3 ♕xb2 11 ♘xd5 exd5! 12 ♘xd4 ♗e7∓) 10...♕b4 11 ♗d2 ♕e7 12 ♗g5 f6 13 exf6 gxf6 14 ♘xd4 fxg5 15 ♗h5+ ♔d8

16 ♖c1 ♘xd4 17 ♕xd4 ♗g7 and Black is better – Boey;

(e) 7 ♗d3 tries to prove that in a Milner-Barry sort of position, the extra move ...♘h6 actually hurts Black: 7...cxd4 8 cxd4 ♗d7 (or 8...♘f5 9 ♗xf5 exf5 10 ♘c3 ♗e6 11 ♘e2 h6 12 h4 0-0-0= Benjamin-Shaked, Kona 1998) 9 ♗c2 (in view of the threat ...♘xd4) and Black can play simply 9...♘b4=, or more interestingly:

(e1) 9...f6 exploits Black's considerable lead in development to break down White's centre: 10 ♘c3 (10 ♗xh6? gxh6 11 b3 ♗b4+ 12 ♔f1 fxe5+) 10...♘f7 11 exf6 gxf6 12 a3 ♗d6 13 b4 0-0-0 14 ♗e3 ♔b8 15 ♕d3 ♘e7∓ 16 ♔e2? ♖c8 17 ♖hc1 ♘f5 18 ♗d2 ♖c4 19 ♗e3 ♖hc8 with irresistible pressure, Levin-J.Watson, Philadelphia 1997;

(e2) 9...♘f5! is the most straightforward. Then 10 ♗xf5 exf5 is the standard position from Benjamin-Shaked above (8...♘f5). White has played four moves with his bishop as opposed to the usual two (♗d3 and ♗xf5), whereas Black (potentially) loses one tempo when he plays ...♗e6. Thus he is a tempo up on normal lines and must stand satisfactorily.

3.21 7 b3 cxd4 8 cxd4 ♘f5

To my knowledge, my suggestion after 8...♗b4+ 9 ♔f1, 9...0-0!?, is still untried. This would preserve the option of playing the move ...♘g4 at some point.

9 ♗b2 ♗b4+ 10 ♔f1 0-0

The position after 10 ♔f1 has been outrageously favourable to the Black pieces in practice. Here 10...♗e7 has given Black a 60% winning percentage in my database with about a 100-point performance rating advantage; but 10...♗d7 is another effective alternative, as it has an amazing 500-

point performance rating advantage for Black in 55 games! (Of course, that is by no means proof of objective worth, and the sample sizes are reduced by unrated games, but still...) A typically entertaining line is 11 g3 0-0 12 ♔g2 f6 13 a3 ♗e7 and the white king still isn't safe: 14 b4 fxe5 15 dxe5 ♗c5! 16 g4 ♘fe7 17 ♘c3 ♗xf2! 18 ♘a4 ♕e3 19 ♖f1 ♘g6 20 ♖xf2 ♘f4+ 21 ♔f1 ♘h3! 22 ♕e1 ♘xe5 23 ♗xe5 ♗xa4 24 ♗d4 ♕e4 25 ♕d2 ♕g6? (25...♗xf2! 26 ♔xf2 ♖xf3+ 27 ♗xf3 ♖f8 with the idea 28 ♕e3 ♖xf3+ 29 ♕xf3 ♕xd4+) 26 ♕e3? 0-1 Martinovic-Pavlovic, Igalo 1994. White is lost after 26...♘xf2.

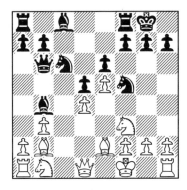

11 ♘c3

This developing move avoids weaknesses and is best. Alternatives:

(a) 11 ♗d3 f6! 12 ♗xf5 (12 a3 ♗e7 13 ♗xf5 exf5∓ leaves White with a stranded king and weaknesses) 12...fxe5!? ('!!' – Tsouros, but objectively better is 12...exf5!∓) 13 ♗c2? (13 ♗h3! e4 14 ♘e1 e5 15 ♗xc8 ♖axc8 – Tsouros; but here 14 ♘g5! improves) 13...e4 14 ♘e1 e5 15 a3 ♗d6 16 b4 exd4 17 ♗b3 ♗e6 18 f3 exf3 19 ♘xf3 ♖xf3+!-+ was Nicoleris-Tsouros, Greece 1973;

(b) 11 g4 is the old and most dangerous line, which deserves some

study:

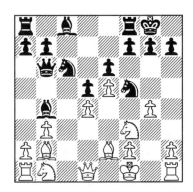

11...♘h6 and White has:

(b1) 12 h3?! f6 (or 12...♗d7 13 a3 ♗e7 14 b4 f6! 15 exf6 ♖xf6 16 g5? ♖xf3) 13 exf6 ♖xf6 14 a3 (for 14 g5 ♖xf3, compare 12 ♖g1) 14...♗d6 15 g5 ♖xf3 16 ♗xf3 ♘f5 17 ♘d2 ♗d7! 18 ♗g4 ♘cxd4 19 b4 ♖f8 20 ♗xd4 ♘xd4 21 ♘f3 ♗b5+ 22 ♔e1 ♖f4 23 ♘d2 ♘f5 24 f3 ♕e3+ 0-1 Gutierrez Castillo-Matamoros Franco, Malaga 2001.

(b2) 12 ♖g1 f6 13 exf6 (a beautiful game followed 13 a3 ♗e7 14 exf6 ♖xf6 15 g5 ♖xf3 16 gxh6 ♖f7 17 ♗d3 g5!! 18 ♕h5 ♗d7 19 ♘d2 ♖af8 20 f3 ♕c7 21 ♖e1 ♔h8 22 ♖e2 ♗f6 23 ♖eg2 ♕f4 24 ♖e2 ♗xd4-+ Kiselev-Bilokha, Kiev 1999) 13...♖xf6 14 g5 (the move 14 ♘c3 can be met conservatively by 14...♗xc3 15 ♗xc3 ♘f7, or by 14...♘f7 15 g5 ♖f4 16 ♘a4 ♕c7 17 ♗c1 e5! 18 ♗xf4 ♗h3+ 19 ♖g2 exf4∓) 14...♖xf3 and:

(b21) 15 gxh6?! .♖f7 16 ♗d3 e5 (or 16...g6! – Botterill) 17 ♕h5 e4 18 ♗e2 Botterill-Ligterink, London 1978, and here Botterill gives 18...g6!∓ which in fact looks winning.;

(b22) 15 ♗xf3 ♘f5 16 ♖g4 ♗d7 17 ♘c3 ♖f8, e.g., 18 ♘a4 ♕c7!? 19 ♔g1 ♗e8 20 ♘c5! (20 ♕e2 ♗h5! 21 ♕xe6+ ♔h8 22 ♕xd5 ♗xg4 23 ♗xg4 ♕f4 24 ♕g2 ♘cxd4 25 ♖d1 ♘h4∓) T.Reich-

P.Meister, Bayern 1988, and best was 20...♞fxd4∓;

(c) 11 a3 ♝e7 12 b4 f6 13 g3 fxe5 14 dxe5 a5! 15 b5 ♝c5 16 g4 ♞fd4–+ Campora Perez-Matamoros Franco, Seville 2001;

Returning to 11 ♞c3:

11...f6 12 ♞a4

12 g4 ♞h6 (or just 12...♞fe7 aiming at f4) 13 exf6 ♞xg4!? 14 fxg7 ♜f7 with complex play, Gudbrandsen-Lahlum, Oslo 2000.

After 12 ♞a4, the main line goes 12...♛d8 13 h4 (13 a3 ♝e7 14 b4 fxe5 15 dxe5 ♝d7∓ Sorokin-Sokolsky, USSR 1951) 13...fxe5 14 dxe5 ♝e7!? (or 14...♝d7 15 ♝d3 ♝e7! 16 h5 ♜c8) 15 ♝d3 ♝d7! with the idea ...♝e8-h5. This is advantageous, since 16 g4? ♞xh4 only exposes White, and if 16 ♜c1, 16...♝e8 17 h5 ♝g5 activates Black's pieces.

3.22 7 ♝xh6

This is the most critical line after 6 ♝e2 ♞h6. White gives up the bishop pair in order to inflict damage upon Black's pawns.

7...gxh6

Commentators have given a wide variety of conflicting analysis about 7...♛xb2?!; ultimately it seems inferior after 8 ♝e3! ♛xa1 9 ♛c2 cxd4 10 ♞xd4! ♝d7! 11 0-0! (11 ♞b3 ♞b4) 11...♞xe5 12 ♞d2 ♛xf1+ 13 ♝xf1± with the idea ♛b3 and ♞b5.

8 ♛d2

This is better than 8 b3? cxd4 9 cxd4 f6! 10 exf6 ♝b4+ 11 ♚f1 0-0 with attack down the f-file, Karlsson-Helmers, Reykjavik 1982: 12 a3 ♝d6 13 ♞c3 ♜xf6 14 ♞a4 ♛c7 15 b4 ♛f7!? (15...♛g7!∓) 16 ♜c1 e5!? (16...♝f4) 17 ♜xc6! (17 dxe5 ♞xe5 18 ♞c3 ♝e6∓) 17...bxc6 18 dxe5 ♜xf3 19 ♝xf3 ♝xe5∓.

8...♝g7 9 0-0 0-0 10 ♞a3

White has no other good way to develop his pieces.

10...cxd4

10...♝d7 11 ♞c2 ♜ac8 12 dxc5!? (12 b4! is the main line) 12...♛c7!?=.

11 cxd4 ♝d7

Noteworthy is the unique order 11...f6 12 exf6 ♜xf6 13 ♞c2 (13 ♜ad1 ♝d7 14 ♞c2 ♝e8 15 b4 a6 16 a4 ♝g6= Patience-Pye, Eastleigh 2001) 13...a5 (to prevent b4; compare 11...♝d7 12 ♞c2 a5). Here typical play might go 14 ♞e3! (14 ♜ab1 ♝d7 15 b4 axb4 16 ♞xb4 ♛a5=) 14...h5! (my idea in several lines, preventing ♞g4) 15 ♞c2 ♝d7 16 ♜ab1 ♝e8= and ...♝g6.

12 ♞c2

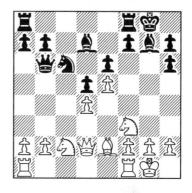

The basic position. White wants to

expand on the queenside by b4 and a4, and/or attack Black's kingside (e.g. by ♘e3-g4). Black will play ...f6, after which he hopes that the two bishops, f-file, and/or pressure on d4 will yield good play.

12...f6

The normal move. But a very important alternative is 12...a5!?, by which Black temporarily prevents b4:

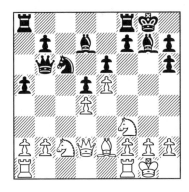

(a) 13 a4 f6 (13...♘b4 14 ♘e3 h5 15 ♖fd1 f6 with good counterplay) 14 exf6 ♖xf6 15 ♖fb1 ♗e8! 16 b4?! ♗g6 17 bxa5 ♕xa5 18 ♕d1 ♖f7 (18...♕a7!∓) 19 ♖b5?! Trygstad-Brynell, Gausdal 2001; and now 19...♕a7! leaves White no good defence against ...♗xc2 and/or ...♖af8.

(b) 13 ♖ab1 f6 14 exf6 ♖xf6 15 b4 axb4 16 ♘xb4 ♕a5=, as above;

(c) 13 ♘e3 h5! and:

(c1) 14 g4!? f6! 15 exf6 ♖xf6 16 gxh5 (16 g5? ♖f4 17 ♘g2 ♖f7∓) 16...♖af8 (16...♗e8=) 17 ♘e5 ♗e8 18 ♘xc6 (18 ♖ad1 ♖f4!∓) 18...bxc6 19 ♘c2 e5 20 dxe5 ♖f4!∓;

(c2) 14 a4 f6 15 ♗b5 fxe5 16 ♗xc6 bxc6 17 ♘xe5 ♗e8 18 f4 ♖b8 19 ♖f2 c5∓ D.Fernando-Brynell, Bled 2002;

(c3) 14 ♖ad1 f6 15 exf6 ♗xf6 (15...♖xf6 16 ♘e5 ♗e8 17 ♘xc6 bxc6=) 16 ♘e5 (16 ♘c2 ♗e8 and ...♗g6) Rajlich-J.Watson, Las Vegas

1998, and now the easiest course was 16...♗xe5 17 dxe5 ♘xe5 18 ♗xh5 ♗b5 19 ♗e2 ♗xe2 20 ♕xe2 ♖ae8=.

13 exf6

13 ♗d3 fxe5! 14 ♘xe5 (14 dxe5 ♖xf3 15 gxf3 ♘xe5∓) 14...♘xe5 15 dxe5 ♖f7∓ (or 15...♕xb2).

13...♖xf6 14 b4

White shouldn't allow Black to develop uninterrupted by ...♖af8 and ...♗e8-g6. The alternative is 14 ♘e3 ♖af8 15 ♖ad1 ♖f4 16 ♘c2 ♗e8!∓ Oll-Rohde, New York 1994.

14...♖af8

The standard move, but it leads to positions that are difficult to play. So close attention should be paid to 14...♗e8!?, a promising move that represents a new plan in the position: 15 b5 (15 a4 ♗g6 16 a5 ♕c7 17 ♖fc1 a6=) 15...♘d8! ('!' for originality: instead of heading for g6 or f5, Black envisions a knight on f7 that covers e5 and can look for greener pastures via d6).

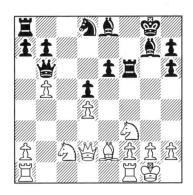

Now White has:

(a) 16 ♘e5 ♘f7 with these plausible continuations:

(a1) 17 f4? ♘xe5 18 fxe5 ♖xf1+ 19 ♖xf1 ♗xe5 with the idea 20 ♕xh6? ♗xd4+ 21 ♘xd4 ♕xd4+ 22 ♔h1 ♗g6∓;

(a2) 17 ♘xf7 ♖xf7! 18 a4 ♖c8 19 a5

♛d6 20 g3 (20 ♖fc1 ♖fc7∓) 20...e5=;

(a3) 17 ♞g4 ♖g6 18 a4 ♖c8! 19 ♖fc1 ♞d6! 20 ♞e5 ♞e4! (20...♝xe5 21 dxe5 ♞e4 22 ♛e3!?) 21 ♛e1 (21 ♛e3? ♖c3) 21...♖f6! 22 a5 ♛d6 23 ♞f3 ♞g5=;

(b) 16 a4 ♞f7 17 ♞e3 h5 18 ♖ac1 (18 ♝d3?! ♖xf3! 19 gxf3 ♛xd4) 18...♞d6! 19 ♛b4 (or 19 ♞e5 ♞e4 20 ♛d3 ♖f4!=) 19...♞e4 20 a5 ♛d8!? (20...♛d6!=) 21 b6 ♝f8 22 ♛b2 ♝d6 23 ♞e5 axb6 24 ♛xb6? (better is 24 f3 ♞g5 25 ♛xb6 ♛xb6 26 axb6 ♖f4=) 24...♛xb6 25 axb6 ♞d2 26 ♖a1 ♖b8 27 ♖fd1 ♞b3 28 ♖a7 ♞xd4 29 ♖xd4 ♝xe5∓ Fernando-Gdanski, Cappelle la Grande 2002.

The line with 14...♝e8 and the idea ...♞d8-f7 is a fun and little-investigated way to create counter-chances and avoid the theoretical 14...♖af8.

15 b5 ♞e7

This has been played in many games. Probably White is slightly better in a theoretical sense, but so far Black has more than held his own in terms of results. Another sound option is 15...♞a5!?, my suggestion from the second edition whose main drawback is that it can easily lead to a draw. It has now been tested: 16 ♞e5 (16 ♖ab1 ♖f4! keeps White tied down, and 16 ♛e3 ♖f4 [16...♖c8!?] intending 17 ♞e5 ♝xb5 18 ♖fb1? ♖e4 winning for Black) 16...♝xb5! 17 ♖ab1 (17 ♞g4 ♖f4 18 ♖ab1 ♞c4∓; 17 ♖fb1?? ♖xf2; 17 ♛e3 ♖f4!) 17...♝xe2 18 ♖xb6 ♝xf1 19 ♖b1 ♖xf2 20 ♛xf2 ♖xf2 21 ♔xf2 ♝a6 (thus far my analysis of 14...♞a5; Black has two bishops and two pawns to compensate for the exchange and his weak rook pawns) 22 ♖e1 (22 ♞b4 ♝xe5 23 dxe5 ♝c4, about equal and leading correctly to a draw, Jonkman-Tiggelman, Vlissingen 1999) 22...♝b5

23 ♖e3 a6 24 a3 ♝a4 25 ♞e1 Rajlich-Hummel, North Bay 1998; and although 25...♞b3 was still well inside the drawing range, simpler was 25...♞c4 26 ♞xc4 dxc4 27 ♞f3 ♔f7 28 ♞e5+ ♔e7=.

16 ♞e5 ♝e8

17 g3

(a) 17 ♝d3 ♞g6 18 ♝xg6 hxg6 19 a4 Thipsay-Konguvel, London 2001; and Black should try 19...g5! (versus f4, and clearing the way for a future ...♝g6) 20 ♖ae1 a6 21 bxa6 ♛xa6 with excellent play;

(b) 17 a4 (a popular move with the idea ♖a3-g3, but Black can challenge the centre first) 17...♞g6 18 ♞g4 ♖6f7 19 ♞xh6+?! (19 g3 h5 20 ♞h6+ ♝xh6 21 ♛xh6 ♞f4! 22 ♝xh5 [22 ♛g5+ ♖g7 23 ♛e5 ♝g6=] 22...♖f6 23 ♛g5+ ♖g6! 24 ♛e5 ♞xh5 0-1 Kun-Szuk, Budapest 2000) 19...♝xh6 20 ♛xh6 ♞f4 21 ♝f3 ♖g7 22 g3 ♛d8! (threatening ...♖g6) 23 ♔h1 ♖g6 24 ♛h4 ♛xh4 25 gxh4 ♞d3∓ Adams-Lobron, Amsterdam 1994.

17...h5 18 a4

Or 18 ♞e3, e.g., 18...♞f5!? 19 ♞xf5 ♖xf5 20 f4 ♝xb5!? 21 ♖fb1 ♖xe5! 22 fxe5 ♝xe5 23 ♔g2 ♛xd4 24 ♛xd4 ♝xd4 25 ♝xb5 ♖f2+ 26 ♔h3 ♝xa1 27 ♖xa1 ♔g7, perhaps with ...h4 next. Black's two passed central pawns look good enough to hold, but this demonstrates the marginal nature of Black playing this line past his 14th and 15th move options.

18...h4

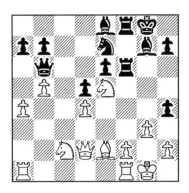

This position was drawn in Magem Badals-Vallejo Pons, Mondariz 2000, but Topalov-Bareev, Novgorod 1997 showed that White was somewhat better: 19 &d3 hxg3 20 hxg3 h5? (20...&g6! with only a small advantage for White and play for both sides) 21 &e3 &h6?! (21...&d8 22 &ac1 &g6‡) 22 a5 &d8 23 f4±. Overall, 15...&e7 is playable, but 15...&a5 should completely equalise.

Looking back over this variation for better winning chances, Black should strongly consider the promising alternatives 12...a5 and 15...&e8. I think that he can be happy with both of these more ambitious moves. Also interesting is the lesser-known 11...f6.

3.3 6 &d3

This normally leads into the Milner-Barry Gambit, in which White gives up a pawn for rapid development. This gambit has now been relegated to a rare sideline, but we must also look at new ideas, e.g., on White's 8th and 9th moves.

6...cxd4 7 cxd4

7 0-0 has been answered by 7...&d7 in several games, transposing after 8 cxd4 &xd4. Also possible is 7...dxc3 8 &xc3 &d7, 8...&ge7, 8...f6!?.

7...&d7

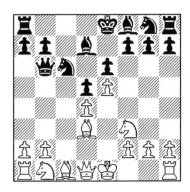

Not 7...&xd4?? 8 &xd4 &xd4?? 9 &b5+.

8 0-0

Gambiting the d-pawn is normal because the options are so dispiriting:

(a) 8 &e2?! is a full tempo down on older 6 &e2 lines after 8...&h6! 9 b3 &f5 10 &b2 &b4+‡ 11 &f1 0-0 12 &c3 f6 and Black will wreak havoc down the f-file;

(b) 8 &c2!? is slow. After 8...&b4, White has lost any chance for advantage (he has scored 22% in my database, although only weaker players are involved): 9 &c3 (9 &a4 &a6!‡ – Schwarz, e.g., 10 &xd7+ &xd7 and ...&d3+ follows; 9 0-0 &xc2 10 &xc2 &c8 11 &c3 transposes; 9 &b3? &b5 9...&xc2+ 10 &xc2 &c8 (or 10...&e7 11 &e3 &c6 12 0-0 &e7 intending ...0-0 and ...f6) 11 0-0 &e7 12 &e3 (12 &d3 &c6 13 a3 &a5 14 b4 &c4‡ Jonathan-Soln, Szeged 1994) 12...&c6 (or 12...&f5!) 13 &d2 (13 a3 &a5) 13...&b4! 14 a3 Stadler-Ilchmann, corr 1958-9; 14...&xc3! 15 bxc3 &a5‡ – Heemsoth;

(c) 8 ♘c3 ♘xd4. Now 9 ♘xd4 ♕xd4 is the main line gambit. White also has:

(c1) 9 ♘g5!? resembles the 9 0-0 ♘xd4 10 ♘g5 gambit line below. But this order may be flawed due to 9...♘c6!, since ♖e1 is not available, e.g. 10 0-0 (10 ♕e2 loses a pawn after 10...d4! 11 ♘b5 [11 ♘d1 ♕a5+ and ...♕xe5] 11...a6 12 ♘d6+ ♗xd6 13 exd6 ♕b4+ 14 ♗d2 ♕xd6∓) 10...♘xe5 11 ♖e1 (11 ♘xd5 ♕d6!) 11...♘xd3 12 ♕xd3 ♘f6∓ with the idea 13 ♘xd5 ♘xd5 14 ♕xd5 ♗b4 15 ♖e2 ♗b5;

(c2) 9 0-0 ♘xf3+ (9...♘c6∓) 10 ♕xf3 ♘e7 11 ♕g3 ♗c6! 12 a4 ♘f5 13 ♗xf5 exf5 14 ♕g5 d4∓ Sobolevsky-Enders, Muelhausen 2000.

8...♘xd4

Now:

3.31 9 ♘g5
3.32 9 ♘xd4

Other ways to gambit the pawn are tricky but insufficient:

(a) 9 ♘bd2 ♘c6 (9...♘xf3+ is not bad either) 10 ♘b3 ♘ge7 (or 10...f6!? with the idea 11 ♗f4 fxe5 12 ♘xe5 ♘f6) 11 ♗e3 (11 ♗f4 ♘g6 12 ♗g3 a5 13 a4 f5 14 exf6 gxf6 15 ♖e1 ♔f7) 11...♕c7 12 ♖c1 ♘g6 13 ♗c5!? (13 ♖e1 ♘gxe5!) 13...♗xc5 14 ♗xc5 ♘gxe5 15 ♖e1 ♖c8! 16 ♗a3 ♘xd3 17 ♕xd3 ♘e5!? 18 ♖xc7 (18 ♕e3!? ♘xf3+ 19 gxf3 ♕d8 20 ♖xc8 ♗xc8 21 ♕c5 f6) 18...♘xd3 19 ♖xc8+ ♗xc8 20 ♖d1 ♘f4 21 g3 ♘g6 22 ♖c1 ♔d7 23 ♘g5 f6 and Black was still two pawns up in Nun-Schmittdiel, Prague 1990;

(b) 9 ♘c3!? is mentioned by Bickford as a transpositional device, e.g. 9...a6 10 ♘xd4 ♕xd4. The alternatives are 9...♘c6 and 9...♘xf3+! 10 ♕xf3 ♘e7, e.g., 11 ♕g3 (11 ♔h1 ♘g6 12 ♕e2 ♗c5∓) 11...♗c6 12 a3 (12 a4

♘f5 13 ♗xf5 exf5 is Sobolevsky-Enders above; 12 ♖e1?! g6 13 ♗g5 ♗g7) 12...a6 13 b4 ♘g6∓ Maderna-Najdorf, Mar del Plata 1942.

3.31 9 ♘g5

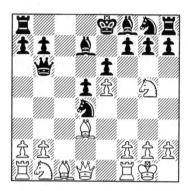

This is known as Sorensen's Gambit. It has undergone a spurt of popularity and White has enjoyed a number of nice attacking victories, but it is dubious at best if the opponent is prepared.

9...♘c6!

The simplest course, fighting for the initiative by attacking e5.

10 ♖e1

This is thought to be best and has been played almost exclusively. White's other plausible moves are:

(a) 10 ♕e2 ♘b4 (K.Krantz's solution) 11 ♗xh7 ♗b5 12 ♕f3 ♘h6 13 ♖e1 ♗e7 14 a3 ♘c6 15 ♗c2 ♘d4 16 ♕d1 ♘g4! and Black is winning. Black has also gotten a clear advantage after 10...g6 11 ♘c3 ♗g7, as in Wuttke-Lieb, Berlin 1998;

(b) 10 ♗f4? ♕xb2 (or 10...♗e7 11 ♕h5 g6 12 ♕e2 ♘b4!) 11 ♘d2 ♘xe5 12 ♖b1 ♕d4 13 ♗xe5 ♕xe5 14 ♘df3 ♕c7 15 ♕e2 ♗d6-+, e.g. 16 ♕b2 (16 ♖fc1 ♗c6 17 ♘d4 ♘e7-+ Storey-A.Whiteley, Newcastle 1995) 16...♘f6 17 ♕xb7 ♕xb7 18 ♖xb7 h6 19 ♘h3 g5!-+, winning a piece!

(c) The sacrificial try 10 ♘c3?! ♘xe5 11 ♘xd5 is met by 11...♕d6! (as given Krantz) with Black a clear pawn up after 12 ♘f4 ♘f6.

10...♗c5!

This is not the only solution, but it seems to virtually refute White's gambit. In my database, 10...♗c5 has scored 71% with a 3071 to 2106 Performance Rating advantage! Of course that's silly, but White really doesn't seem to have a thing for his pawn here.

11 ♕f3

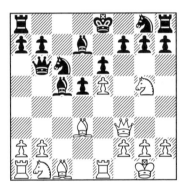

11...♘h6

The most common, but 11...0-0-0! looks even stronger: 12 ♘c3 (12 ♘xf7?? ♖f8-+) 12...f6! (12...♘h6 isn't bad either, with 13 ♗f4 ♘d4 or 13 h3 ♗d4) 13 exf6 (White blundered in one game by 13 ♘a4?? ♕a5; also bad is 13 ♘f7 ♘xe5! 14 ♖xe5 fxe5 15 ♘xh8 ♘f6 16 ♘f7 e4! 17 ♗xe4 ♖f8!∓) 13...♘xf6 14 ♘f7 ♘g4! (or 14...♘b4) 15 ♕xg4 (15 ♘d1 ♖hf8∓) 15...♗xf2+ 16 ♔f1 ♗xe1 17 ♔xe1 ♕g1+ 18 ♗f1 ♘d4-+.

12 ♘c3

12 h3? ♗d4! wins.

12...♘d4

Again 12...♗d4 is good: 13 ♗f4 (13 ♘xd5!? ♕a5! 14 ♘c3 ♘xe5 15 ♕e4 ♕c5∓; 13 ♘xh7 0-0-0 14 ♗g5 ♘xe5 15

♖xe5 ♗xe5 16 ♗xd8 ♖xd8-+ Calzolari-Poupar, Clichy 1999) 13...♘e7!? 14 ♘e2 ♘g6 15 ♗xg6 fxg6!? 16 ♘xd4 ♕xd4 17 ♖ad1 ♕xb2! (17...♕b6 18 ♕a3! is given by Sorenson expert Lennart Hansson) 18 ♖b1 ♕xa2 19 ♖xb7 ♘f5∓.

13 ♕f4

13 ♕d1 ♘hf5 14 ♕h5 g6 15 ♕d1 ♖c8∓ Bailen Canales-Barr, corr 1998, or 15...0-0!.

13...♘df5

Or 13...♘hf5 14 g4 h6∓. After 13...♘df5, Schmedders-Wilde, Sueder 1996 went 14 ♗d2 0-0 15 b4! ♗e7! 16 ♘xh7!? ♔xh7 17 g4 ♕xb4 18 ♘e4 ♕a3-+.

3.32 9 ♘xd4 ♕xd4

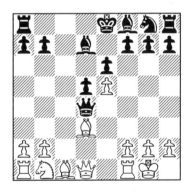

The Milner-Barry proper.

10 ♘c3

(a) Like most lines in this section, 10 ♕e2 has scored overwhelmingly for Black, e.g., 10...♘e7 (10...f6 is my suggestion; one line is 11 exf6 ♘xf6 12 ♖d1 ♕h4!∓, and not much better is 11 ♕h5+ ♔d8 12 ♕f7 ♘e7 13 exf6 ♕xf6 14 ♕h5 g6 15 ♕e2 ♘f5, when two central pawns and development outweigh king position) 11 ♔h1 (11 ♘c3 ♘c6 is normal, intending 12 ♘b5 ♕xe5!; unnecessary but fun was 11...♘g6 12 ♗e3 ♕xe5 13 f4 ♕b8 14 f5 ♗d6! 15 ♗b5 ♗c6 16 fxg6 ♗xh2+ 17 ♔h1 hxg6–+ Lemmers-Pliester, Amsterdam 1993) 11...♘c6 (11...♛h4 is also good) 12 f4 ♗c5!? 13 a3 a6 14 ♖a2 0-0 15 b4 ♗a7 16 ♘d2 ♛e3∓ J.Brown-Hummel, Las Vegas 1997;

(b) 10 ♖e1?! ♘e7 11 ♘c3 a6 12 ♗e3 (12 ♛f3 ♘c6 13 ♛g3 0-0-0 14 ♗f1 ♗e7!∓ Lundquist-Dijkstra, corr 1962) 12...♛xe5 13 ♛f3 ♘g6 (13...d4!?∓; 13...♗c6∓) 14 ♗xg6 hxg6 15 ♗f4 ♛h5∓ Parkyani-Anka, Budapest 1990.

10...a6

The main line: it rules out ♘b5 and clears the a7 square for the dark-squared bishop. Given the priority of other subjects I'm going to give only one solution here. I should mention that 10...♛xe5 is doing brilliantly theoretically but it is more difficult in practice than 10...a6.

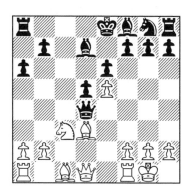

11 ♛e2

11 ♖e1 ♘e7 transposes to 10 ♖e1 above. Others:

(a) 11 ♔h1?! ♛xe5 12 f4 (12 ♖e1 ♛d6 13 ♛f3 ♗c6∓) 12...♛d6 13 ♗e3 ♗e7 14 ♛f3 ♗c6 15 ♗d4 ♘f6 16 ♖ae1 g6!∓ Eley-Whiteley, Great Britain 1978;

(b) 11 ♛f3 ♛xe5 12 ♗f4 ♛f6 13 ♛g3 ♘e7 and 14 ♗g5 ♘f5 or 14 ♖fe1 ♗c6.

11...♘e7

The traditional move although in fact 11...♛h4!? has scored 70% for Black in limited outings, e.g., 12 f4 ♗c5+ 13 ♔h1 h5!? 14 ♗e3 ♗xe3 15 ♛xe3 ♘h6 16 ♖f3 ♘g4 17 ♛g1 ♖c8∓ Duggan-Gunter, St Heliers 1997.

12 ♔h1

The older 12 ♖d1 isn't seen much. Black continues 12...♘c6 (12...♛h4!?) and:

(a) 13 ♗xa6 ♛xe5 14 ♛xe5!? (14 ♗xb7 ♛xe2 15 ♘xe2 ♖a7 16 ♗c6 ♗xc6 17 ♘d4 ♗d7 18 ♗e3 ♖b7 19 b3 ♗d6∓ McCann-Jestadt, California 1993) 14...♘xe5 15 ♗xb7 ♖a7 16 ♗xd5 exd5 17 ♖e1 f6 18 f4 ♗c5+ 19 ♔h1 d4∓ Mnatsakanian-Monin, USSR 1979 (and several later games).

(b) 13 ♗b5 ♛b6!? (or 13...♛h4 14 ♗xc6 ♗xc6 15 ♗e3 ♛c4!) 14 ♗a4 ♗c5!∓.

12...♘c6 13 f4

Unsound looks 13 ♗e3 ♛xe5 (13...♛h4 is good, threatening ...d4, e.g., 14 g3 ♛d8 15 ♗f4 ♗e7∓) 14 f4 ♛d6 15 f5 (15 ♖ad1 ♗e7 16 f5 ♛e5) 15...♛e5! 16 ♖ae1 ♗d6∓.

13...♗c5

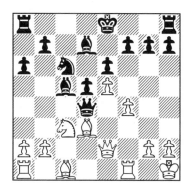

Yet another line with an overwhelming score (+350 performance rating points for Black). The reasoning behind ...♗c5 is to develop, prevent ♗e3, and allow ...♛f2 after

White's ♖d1.

14 ♗d2

This both discourages ...♕b4 and prepares 15 ♖f3 with the idea ♗e3 (14 ♖f3?? allows mate on g1). It's slow, but everything seems bad here:

(a) 14 ♖d1 isn't played much. After 14...♕f2 15 ♕g4 (15 ♕h5 ♘b4!), however, no one has tried my 15...0-0-0! with the idea ...h5, e.g., 16 ♗d2 h5 17 ♕h3 g5!. Instead, 15...g6 has led to even results in spite of some Black advantage;

(b) 14 a3 ♘a5! (not the only move; 14...♗a7 15 ♗d2 g6 16 ♖f3 ♕b6 is quite good) 15 ♗d2 (15 b4 ♕xc3! 16 ♗d2 ♕d4 17 bxc5 ♘b3 18 ♗e3 ♕c3 19 ♖ab1 d4!–+ L.Kristensen-Jorgensen, Esbjerg 1996) 15...♘b3 16 ♖ae1 ♗a7 17 ♖f3 ♘xd2 18 ♕xd2 g6 19 ♘e2 ♕b6 20 ♖c1 ♖c8 21 ♖xc8+ ♗xc8∓ Niccoli-Naumkin, Bergamo 2002.

14...♗a7

14...♘b4!? 15 ♗b1 ♗a7 16 a3 ♘c6 17 ♗d3 g6 18 ♖ac1 (18 ♖f3 ♕b6!; 18 b4 ♕b6 19 ♖ab1 ♘d4 20 ♕d1 ♖c8∓ Soylu-Lputian, Manila 1992) 18...♕b6 19 b4 ♘d4 20 ♕d1 ♘f5!? 21 ♘a4 ♕d8

22 ♘c5 ♗c6! 23 ♘xa6 ♘e3 24 ♗xe3 ♗xe3∓ with the bishop pair and queenside pressure, Golod-Barsov, Dieren 1998.

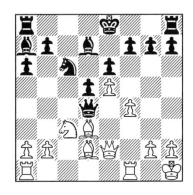

15 ♖ae1

15 ♖f3 ♘b4 16 ♖af1 (16 ♗b1?? ♕g1 mate; 16 a3 ♘xd3 17 ♖xd3 ♕f2) 16...♘xd3 17 ♖xd3 ♕c4∓, e.g., 18 f5 exf5 19 b3 ♕g4!.

15...g6 16 ♖f3 ♕b6 17 ♗e3 ♕a5 18 ♗xa7 ♘xa7 19 ♕f2 ♘c6 20 ♕h4 ♕d8 21 ♕h6 ♕e7∓. This is from the game L.Hansen-Jorgensen, Holbaek 2001. White has little if anything for the pawn.

Chapter Four

King's Indian Attack

1 e4 e6

This chapter will deal with the classical King's Indian Attack and its most popular offshoot. Hence:

4.1 2 d3
4.2 2 ♕e2

4.1 2 d3

This introduces the King's Indian Attack proper, so called because White sets up the same basic position as Black often does in the King's Indian Defence to 1 d4. The sequence of White moves tends to be e4/d3/♘d2/♘gf3/g3/♗g2/0-0, with ♖e1 and/or c3 to follow. Over the years, the 2 d3 system has been used by some leading players, notably Fischer (although he didn't stick with it long, preferring the more dynamic 2 d4 and 3 ♘c3). Pal Benko's creative practice of the opening should be noted; it was his games that inspired Fischer to take up the KIA. And although few leading players today employ it consistently, Lev Psakhis remains one of the KIA's high-level modern adherents, whereas Morozevich plays both it and the variant 2 ♕e2. And of course numerous strong players will occasionally dabble in 2 d3 when they wish to avoid a game with a lot of critical theory, as Short, Bareev, and Anand have done. In spite of its passive reputation, French players will be defending against the KIA a great deal of the time because it appeals to so many average players, not least because they can play their first 7 or 8 moves without thought. I proposed the same two systems against The King's Indian Attack in the first two editions. Those are still completely valid, but for fun I have added a few new set-ups and eliminated one of the old ones. Most black defences equalise against the KIA (accounting for its lack of popularity at the very top), but a reason for my new choices is to give the French player some ideas that are relatively unexplored and therefore difficult for your opponent to respond to automatically.

2...d5

Very often the line presented in 4.12 is entered by playing 2...c5, which is a personal favourite given in the previous editions, but some French players may not wish to play the Closed Sicilian positions arising from 3 ♘f3 ♘c6 4 g3 g6 5 ♗g2 ♗g7 6 0-0 ♘ge7 7 ♘c3, or those from 3 g3 ♘c6 4 ♗g2 g6 5 ♘c3 ♗g7 6 f4. Needless to say, those relatively harmless systems need not deter one from playing such a sound and unbalanced system as Black.

3 ♘d2

I'll discuss move order issues both here and after Black's 3rd moves, for example:

(a) 3 g3?!, trying to save the move ♘d2 and keep open ♕g4, has a couple of drawbacks, but the main one is 3...dxe4! (3...♗d6!? 4 ♕g4 g6 5 ♕e2 ♘c6= is not as strong but it is instructive, e.g., 6 ♘f3 dxe4 7 dxe4 e5 8 ♗g2 ♘f6 9 0-0 ♗g4 10 c3 h6 11 h3 ♗e6 and Black is at least equal) 4 dxe4 ♕xd1+ 5 ♔xd1 ♘f6! (5...♗c5 also leaves White short of equality, e.g., 6 f3 ♘c6 7 ♘d2 e5∓) 6 f3 (6 ♘c3 ♗b4!? 7 ♘b5 ♗a5 8 ♗d2 ♗b6 9 f3 0-0∓) 6...♘c6 (6...♗c5∓) 7 ♗e3 (7 ♗b5 ♗d7 8 ♗e3 0-0-0 9 ♘d2 a6 10 ♗e2 ♗e7 11 c3 e5 12 ♔c2 ♗e6∓) 7...b6!? 8 ♘d2 ♗b7 9 ♗b5 0-0-0∓;

(b) 3 ♕e2 will sometimes transpose into 2 ♕e2, but White must also deal with lines like 3...♗c5!? 4 exd5 (4 ♘f3 ♘e7 5 d4 ♗b6 would be experimental, e.g., 6 e5 0-0 7 g3 c5 8 dxc5 ♗xc5 9 ♗g2 b6! intending ...♗a6) 4...♘f6 5 dxe6 ♗xe6 (5...0-0!? 6 ♗e3!?) 6 ♗e3 ♗xe3 7 fxe3 ♘c6 8 ♘f3 ♕e7 with the idea ...0-0-0 and ...♖he8, soon forcing central concessions.

After 3 ♘d2, the play splits:

4.11 3...♘f6
4.12 3...c5

4.11 3...♘f6 4 ♘gf3

4 g3 again intends to leave White's options open, for example, 4...c5 5

♘gf3 (or 5 ♗g2 and 6 f4) takes Black out of the system he wants. Black could try 4...dxe4 5 dxe4 e5 here, but then the f1 bishop can still develop along the f1-a6 diagonal in conjunction with attacks of the e-pawn. That's a decent sequence, but Black has two more interesting ideas:

(a) 4...♘c6 5 ♗g2 (5 f4?! dxe4 6 dxe4 e5 and White has major weaknesses; 5 ♘gf3 dxe4 6 dxe4 ♗c5!; 5 c3 and Black has 5...e5= or 5...a5) 5...dxe4 6 dxe4 e5

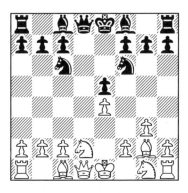

(a1) 7 ♘e2?! is rather passive because it takes the pressure off e5. Black can play directly by 7...♗c5 or try to force weaknesses by 7...♗g4 8 0-0 (8 f3 ♗e6 9 0-0 ♗c5+ 10 ♔h1 ♕e7 11 ♘b3 ♖d8∓) 8...♘d4 9 f3 ♗c5 10 ♔h1 ♗e6 11 c3 ♘c6 12 ♘b3 ♗b6∓;

(a2) 7 ♘gf3 is the position that Black has been looking for: White's bishop is passive on g2 while both of Black's bishops develop freely, and in the absence of ♗b5 his e-pawn is simple to defend. See the instructive example of this position below via the order 4 ♘gf3 ♘c6 5 g3 dxe4 6 dxe4 e5 7 ♗g2.

(b) 4...b6 intends to occupy the a6-f1 diagonal once White plays ♗g2, or to settle for ...♗b7 if White decides to play passively and waste the g3 move. One sequence would be 5 ♗g2 (5 ♘gf3 dxe4 6 dxe4 ♗c5) 5...♘c6 6 ♘gf3 dxe4 7 dxe4 ♗a6! 8 c3 (8 e5 ♘d7; 8 c4 ♗c5) 8...♕d7 9 ♕a4 ♗d3!∓.

After 4 ♘gf3 I will give no less than 3 systems:

4.111 4...♘c6
4.112 4...♗c5
4.113 4...b6

4.111 4...♘c6

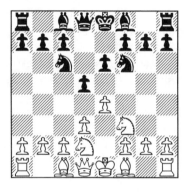

5 c3!
Called 'best' by nearly everyone over the last 5 years, 5 c3 is the only reason that 4...♘c6 has been somewhat under a cloud. But I think that Black has some original ideas in these lines. Against moves other than 5 c3, Black will usually play for ...dxe4 and ...e5:

(a) 5 ♗e2 ♗d6 (maybe an original idea? Black covers e5 and waits on ...e5; possible too is 5...♗c5!? 6 0-0 e5!? 7 exd5 ♕xd5=) 6 0-0 0-0 7 c3 a5 8 ♕c2 e5 9 exd5 ♘xd5 10 ♘c4 a4!? or 10...♗e6 11 ♘g5 ♗f5=;

(b) 5 g3 dxe4 6 dxe4 e5 (as mentioned above, the idea is that g3 weakens the light squares and loses a tempo if White plays ♗c4 or ♗b5. Compare this with the Philidor De-

fence; it is an example of how having a tempo less can mean getting more information about what the opponent is doing, in this case g3, and then putting it to use) 7 ♗g2 (this invites Black to try to occupy the a6-f1 diagonal by ...b6 and ...♗a6; on the other hand, putting the f1 bishop elsewhere would leave White's kingside light squares undefended, e.g., 7 ♗b5 ♗c5 and 8 0-0 ♗g4 or 8 ♗xc6+ bxc6 9 ♕e2 ♕e7 10 ♘c4 ♗a6 11 ♘fxe5 0-0 intending ...♗d4, or 12 c3 ♕e6 13 b3 ♗xc4 14 ♘xc4 ♘xe4 15 0-0 ♘xf2 16 ♕xe6 ♘e4+ 17 ♔h1 fxe6∓) 7...♗c5 8 0-0 0-0

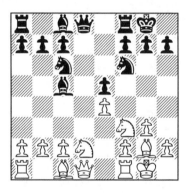

(b1) 9 c3 a5 10 ♕c2 b6 11 ♘c4 ♗a6∓ 12 ♖d1 ♕e7 13 ♘e3 ♖ad8! 14 ♘d5 ♘xd5 15 exd5 e4! 16 ♖e1? (16 ♘e1? ♘e5! 17 ♗xe4 ♘g4! – Fappas; 16 dxc6 is best) 16...♗d3 17 ♕b3 ♕f6 18 dxc6 (18 ♗g5 ♕f5 19 ♗xd8 exf3∓) 18...exf3 19 ♗h1 ♗e2-+ Fargags-Fappas, Germany 1979;

(b2) 9 ♕e2 a5 10 ♘c4 ♕e7 (10...♗g4 11 c3 ♕c8!?) 11 ♘e3 (11 ♗g5 ♗g4 12 c3 h6 13 ♗xf6 ♕xf6 14 h3 ♗e6; 11 c3 b6 and ...♗a6, when the queen is not happy on e2) 11...♘d4! (11...♖d8) 12 ♘xd4 exd4 13 ♘c4 ♗g4 14 ♕d3 ♘d7 (14...♖fe8 is mentioned by Wintzer; then 15 e5 ♘d7 16 ♗xb7 ♖ab8 17 ♗c6 ♕e6 18

♗xd7 ♕xd7 gives Black more than enough for a pawn) 15 a4 f6 16 ♗d2 b6 17 ♔h1 ♖ad8 18 ♗f4? (18 f4 ♖fe8∓) 18...♗b4! 19 f3 (19 ♕xd4?? ♘e5 19...♘c5 20 ♕e2 ♗e6 21 ♗c1 (21 ♖fd1 d3 22 cxd3 ♘xd3!∓) 21...d3 22 cxd3 ♖xd3-+ 23 ♘a3 ♖fd8 24 ♗f4 ♗b3 25 ♘b5 ♘e6 26 ♗e3 ♗c5! 27 ♗xc5 ♘xc5-+ Matthaei-Wintzer, Bundesliga West 1997;

(c) 5 e5 ♘d7 6 d4 f6 and because of the wasted d3-d4 Black is a whole tempo up on the Guimard Variation (2 d4 d5 3 ♘d2 ♘c6 4 ♘gf3 ♘f6 5 e5 ♘d7). Thus:

(c1) 7 exf6 ♕xf6 8 ♘b3 ♗d6 (or 8...e5 9 dxe5 ♘dxe5 10 ♘xe5 ♕xe5+ 11 ♗e2 ♗d6∓) 9 ♗b5 e5! 10 dxe5 ♘dxe5 11 ♕xd5 ♗e6 12 ♕e4 ♘xf3+ 13 ♕xf3 ♕xf3 14 gxf3 ♗d5 15 ♘d4 0-0 16 ♗xc6 bxc6 17 ♗e3 c5-+.

(c2) 7 ♗b5 fxe5!? 8 dxe5 ♗e7 9 ♗xc6 bxc6 10 ♘d4 (10 0-0 0-0∓ with the bishop pair and ...c5 to come) 10...♘xe5 11 ♕h5+ ♘f7 12 ♘xc6 ♕d6 13 ♘xe7 ♕xe7 14 0-0 0-0 15 ♘b3 e5!∓.

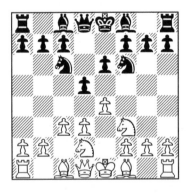

5...♗d6!?

This is one of those ideas that I thought I'd come up with myself but when I sat down to write this chapter I found 13 master games with it! It tries to address the dual issues of White's moves e5 and b4, and I have

supplied some analysis to indicate that it succeeds in doing so. Normally Black plays 5...a5 to stop b4, which is supposed to favour White but that's not clear either and deserves a close look: 6 e5! (in my opinion the only chance for an advantage; others include 6 ♕a4 ♗e7 7 e5 ♘d7 8 d4 0-0 9 ♗b5!? ♘a7 10 ♗d3 c5 11 h4!? f5 12 ♘f1 cxd4 13 cxd4 ♘b6 14 ♕d1 ♗d7∓ Friedman-Shulman, Connecticut 2003; and 6 ♗e2 ♗e7 7 0-0 0-0 8 ♕c2 e5 9 b3 b6 10 ♗b2 ♗a6 11 ♖fe1 ♕d7 12 ♖ad1 ♖ad8= was a typical reversed Philidor's Defence, Sergeev-Lipka, Czech Rep 2002; the typical Philidorian 6 ♕c2 e5 7 ♗e2 ♗e7 is equal, and has been played in many games; finally 7...g6!? is an interesting option) 6...♘d7 7 d4 f6 and:

(a) 8 ♗b5 is given '!' by McDonald and has done well, but may not do much: 8...fxe5 9 dxe5 (9 ♘xe5? ♘cxe5 10 dxe5 c6 11 ♗d3 ♘xe5∓) 9...♗e7 10 0-0 0-0 11 ♕e2 ♘c5?! (11...♕e8!? intending ...♕h5 – Kindermann; a good idea that should be tried!) 12 ♘b3 ♘xb3 13 axb3 ♗d7 14 ♗d3 with a small but definite advantage, Kindermann-Farago, Budapest 1988;

(b) 8 exf6 ♕xf6 9 ♗b5 ♗d6 10 ♘f1 0-0 11 ♘e3. This position has arisen many times in practical play. Black might try 11...♘b6!?, to guard d5 and prepare ...e5, e.g., 12 0-0 (12 ♗d3? e5) 12...♗d7 (12...e5?! 13 ♘xd5! ♘xd5 14 ♗c4 ♗e6 15 dxe5 ♘xe5 16 ♗xd5 ♘xf3+ 17 ♗xf3±) 13 ♗d3 (13 ♗xc6 ♗xc6 14 ♘g4?! ♕f5 15 ♘ge5 ♗xe5 16 ♘xe5 ♗b5∓) 13...e5 14 ♘xd5 ♘xd5 15 ♗c4 exd4 16 ♗xd5+ ♔h8 17 cxd4 ♗g4=.

6 ♕e2

Threatening e5. Black seems to consolidate his position in every case:

(a) 6 g3 0-0 7 ♗g2 e5 (7...dxe4 8

dxe4 e5 unclear, e.g., 9 ♕e2 ♗g4 10 ♘c4 a5 11 h3 ♗e6 12 ♘xd6 ♕xd6 13 0-0 ♖ad8) 8 0-0 ♗e6= with the idea 9 ♘g5 ♗g4 10 ♕b3 ♗e2;

(b) 6 b4 e5 (or 6...a6 7 ♗b2 e5, or 6...a5!? 7 b5 dxe4 8 dxe4 ♘e5 9 ♘xe5 ♗xe5 10 ♕c2 Portisch-Ljubojevic, Montreal 1979, and 10...♗d6 11 ♘c4 ♗c5± was best) 7 exd5 (7 b5 ♘e7 8 ♗b2 0-0=) 7...♘xd5 8 b5 (8 ♗b2 0-0 9 ♘c4 ♗g4=) 8...♘ce7 and Black has no problems;

(c) 6 d4 dxe4 7 ♘g5 e3!? 8 fxe3 0-0 9 ♗d3 e5=;

(d) 6 ♗e2 0-0 7 0-0 a5 8 ♖e1 ♖e8 (8...e5!?) 9 h3 h6 10 b3 b6 11 ♗f1 e5 12 a3 d4= Baklan-Gdanski, Magdeburg 2000.

6...e5

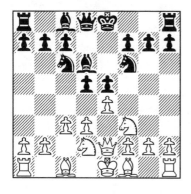

7 exd5?!

White should prefer either 7 b4 a6 (or 7...0-0 8 b5 ♘e7) 8 ♗b2 0-0= or 7 g3 0-0 8 ♗g2 ♗e6=.

7...♘xd5 8 ♘c4 0-0 9 ♘xd6?!

Best is 9 ♗d2 ♗g4 10 h3 ♗h5 11 0-0-0 ♕f6 12 g4 ♗g6∓.

9...♕xd6 10 ♗d2 ♗f5 11 0-0-0 ♖ad8∓ with excellent play against the backward d-pawn. It seems to me that Black has sufficient play after 4...♘c6, and in particular both 5...a5 and 5...♗d6 should hold their own against 5 c3.

4.112 4...♗c5

I have to admit that not so long ago when I first noticed a game with this move I thought it a very irregular one. But my database has over 110 games with 4...♗c5 and they don't show me any convincing reason not to recommend it. The idea is a provocative one: to lure White's central pawns forward in order to undermine them. Barring that, the bishop will be an aggressively placed piece on c5.

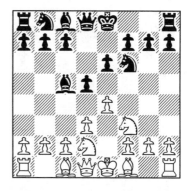

5 e5

By far the most important move, as seen from:

(a) 5 g3? dxe4 6 dxe4 (6 ♘xe4 ♘xe4 7 dxe4 ♗xf2+ 8 ♔xf2 ♕xd1 9 ♗b5+ ♕d7∓) 6...♘g4, and White (who has fallen for this trap more times than one could possibly imagine) is objectively lost;

(b) 5 ♗e2 dxe4 (5...♘c6!? 6 0-0 e5) 6 ♘xe4 (6 dxe4!? e5, or Black can try the funny Philidor-like 6...♘g4 7 0-0 ♗xf2+ 8 ♖xf2 ♘e3 9 ♕e1 ♘xc2 10 ♕d1 ♘xa1 11 b4! with very unclear play) 6...♘xe4 7 dxe4 ♕xd1+ 8 ♗xd1 ♘c6 9 ♗f4 ♗b6 (9...f6!? 10 ♗xc7?! e5) 10 0-0 f6 11 ♖e1?! (11 e5=) 11...e5 12 ♗e3 ♗e6∓ Gushpit-A.Ivanov, Barlinek 2002;

(c) 5 d4 is almost never played and may very well transpose to Chapter

7: 5...dxe4!? is an independent response (5...♗b6 6 ♗d3 c5 7 dxc5 ♗xc5 transposes to the 3...♗e7 Tarrasch chapter; 5...♗e7 is a direct transposition to that same chapter with an extra move on both sides, i.e. 2 d4 d5 3 ♘d2 ♗e7 4 ♘gf3 ♘f6) 6 dxc5 exf3 7 ♕xf3 ♘c6 and Black's free play makes this appear equal, e.g., after 8 ♘e4!? (8 ♗d3 ♘e5; 8 c3 0-0 9 ♗e2 e5) 8...♘xe4 9 ♕xe4 0-0 10 ♗e2 (10 ♗f4?! e5 11 ♗d3 f5 12 ♕c4+ ♔h8; 10 ♗d3 f5 11 ♕e3 e5) 10...e5 11 0-0 ♗e6=.

5...♘fd7 6 d4

(a) 6 g3!? isn't played, but demands some analysis: 6...♘c6 (maybe 6...♗b6 7 ♗g2 c5 is a good sequence, e.g., 8 0-0 ♘c6 9 ♖e1 ♗c7 10 ♘b3 ♘cxe5 11 ♘xe5 ♘xe5 12 ♘xc5 0-0=) 7 ♘b3 ♗e7 (a fascinating line would be 7...♗b6!? 8 d4 f6!? 9 c4! dxc4 10 ♗xc4 fxe5! 11 ♗g5 ♘f6 12 ♘xe5 ♘xd4 unclear) 8 d4 f6!? (8...0-0) 9 exf6 (9 ♗h3 fxe5! 10 ♗xe6 e4∓) 9...♘xf6 10 ♗b5 ♗d7 11 ♕e2 (11 0-0-0 0-0 12 ♗xc6 ♗xc6 13 ♘e5 ♕e8 14 ♗f4 ♗b5 15 ♖e1 ♗d6=) 11...0-0! 12 ♗xc6 ♗xc6 13 ♕xe6+ ♔h8 with at least sufficient compensation;

(b) 6 c3 is subtle: where does Black wish to put his pieces?

(b1) 6...0-0?! 7 d4 ♗e7 (7...♗b6 8 ♗d3 c5 9 ♘f1!? f5 10 ♘g3 ♘c6 11 ♘e2 cxd4 12 cxd4± Kasparov-Rendle, London 1998) 8 ♗d3 c5 9 0-0± Black has castled too early in this variation that can also arise in Chapter 7;

(b2) 6...♗b6! 7 g3?! (7 b4!? f6 8 d4 fxe5 9 ♘xe5 ♘xe5 10 dxe5 ♕h4!? 11 g3 ♕e7 12 ♗d3 0-0= Bruno-Playa, Buenos Aires 1994; for 7 d4 c5 see the main line with 6 d4 ♗b6) 7...f6 8 ♗h3?! (8 exf6 ♕xf6) 8...fxe5 9 ♗xe6 ♘c5! 10 ♗xc8 ♘xd3+ 11 ♔e2 ♘xc1+ 12 ♖xc1 ♕xc8∓.

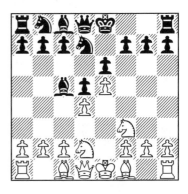

6...♗b6!?

That Black's system is fundamentally sound is shown by the fact that 6...♗e7 7 c3 (or 7 ♗d3 c5 8 c3) 7...c5 transposes to a Chapter 7 main line in which Black has equal chances! But 6...♗b6 is also full of interest.

7 ♘b3!

A logical move played in order to neutralise ...c5 and to get the knight out of the way of its own pieces. 7 ♗d3 c5 presents no problems for Black after 8 c3 (8 c4?! ♘c6 9 0-0 cxd4 10 cxd5 exd5 11 ♘b3 ♘f8?! [11...0-0 12 ♖e1 ♖e8 13 ♗f4 ♘f8!∓] 12 ♗g5 ♕c7 13 a4!? ♘e6 14 ♖e1 ♗d7!?= Ree-U.Geller, Netanya 1968) 8...♘c6 9 dxc5 ♗xc5 (or 9...♘xc5 10 ♗c2?! ♘d7 11 ♕e2 ♕c7 12 ♗a4 0-0 13 ♗xc6 bxc6∓) 10 ♘b3 ♗b6 11 ♕e2 ♕c7 12 ♗f4 (12 ♗b5 0-0 13 ♗xc6 bxc6 14 0-0 a5! 15 ♖e1 ♗a6∓ Orsagova-Kiss, Rimavska Sobota 1996) 12...f6! 13 0-0!? (13 exf6?! ♕xf4 14 fxg7 ♖g8 15 ♕xe6+ ♘e7; 13 ♘bd4! ♘dxe5 14 ♘xe5 fxe5 15 ♘xc6 exf4 16 ♘e5 0-0∓) 13...♘dxe5∓ Dulik-Wrba, email 1997.

7...c5 8 dxc5

8 c3 ♘c6 9 ♗e3 cxd4 (9...c4!? 10 ♘bd2 f6=) 10 cxd4 ♗a5+? (10...f6!) 11 ♘xa5 ♕xa5+ 12 ♗d2 ♕b6 13 ♗c3 0-0 14 ♗d3± Khalifeh-Kristinsdottir, Istanbul 2000.

8...♘xc5 9 ♗e3

9 ♗g5 ♕c7! – Kindermann.

9...♕c7 10 ♘xc5 ♗xc5 11 ♗xc5 ♕xc5 12 c3 ♗d7 13 ♕b3

To prevent ....♗b5. Kindermann analyses 13 ♗d3 ♗b5 14 0-0 ♗xd3 15 ♕xd3 ♘c6=.

13...♘c6 14 ♗d3 f6!?

During the game Kindermann expected 14...d4!, liquidating the centre; after 15 ♗e4 dxc3 16 ♕xc3 ♕xc3+ 17 bxc3 ♘a5 (17...♖c8 may be still better) 18 ♖b1 ♖b8 19 ♘d4 b6, Black has at least equalised.

15 exf6 gxf6 16 ♕xb7

16 ♕c2 0-0-0 17 0-0-0 e5 18 ♗f5 ♘e7 with the advantage – Kindermann.

16...♖b8 17 ♕c7 ♖xb2

Black could apparently have drawn by force following the move 17...e5!?, which cuts off the queen from the kingside after 18 0-0 (18 0-0-0 ♖c8 19 ♕b7 ♖b8 20 ♕a6 e4 21 ♖he1 ♗c8 22 ♕a4 0-0) 18...♖c8 (18...e4 19 ♖ae1) 19 ♕b7 ♖b8 20 ♕a6? (20 ♕c7 ♖c8=) 20...e4∓.

18 0-0 ♕xc3 19 ♖ad1

and White had significant but unclear compensation in Kindermann-Sarana-Hungeling, Bad Wiessee 2002. A cute idea is 19...♖xa2 20 ♘d4! ♕a5! 21 ♘xe6!.

4.113 4...b6

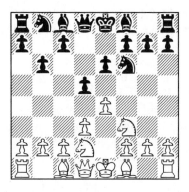

This is now a well-established solution to the KIA. Black's c8 bishop can go to b7 or a6 depending upon what White does, and in particular the desired g3/♗g2 set-up will encourage an early ....♗a6.

5 c3

(a) 5 g3 dxe4 6 dxe4 ♗c5! (Black has scored 58% with this move)

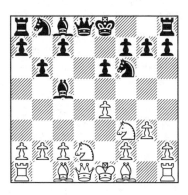

7 ♗b5+ (7 ♗g2 ♗a6 8 c4 ♕d3 9 ♕b3 ♕xb3 10 axb3 ♗b7 11 ♘e5 ♘c6! 12 ♘d3 ♗e7 13 e5 ♘d7 14 f4 a5 15 0-0 0-0-0 and Black had a solid grip on the position, Heinz-Germer, Willingen 2001; 7 ♗d3 e5 8 0-0 ♗h3 9 ♖e1 ♘g4 10 ♖e2 ♕f6 11 c3 g5! 12 ♕e1 a5 13 b3 h5 14 a4 h4∓ Rolletschek-Kindermann, Graz 2001) 7...♗d7 8 ♗d3 ♘c6 9 c3 (9 ♘b3 ♗d6 10 c3 0-0 11 h3 e5∓ Bhat-G.Rey, San Francisco

2000) 9...e5 10 b4 ♗d6 11 0-0 0-0 12
♕c2 ♗g4 13 ♗e2 a5 14 b5 ♘b8!? 15
♘c4 ♘bd7 16 ♖d1 ♕e7 17 ♘h4 ♗e6
18 ♘f5 ♗xf5 19 exf5 h6 20 ♘xd6 cxd6
21 c4 ♘c5 Morozevich-Dreev, Yalta
1995. In this battle of elite grandmasters, Black has achieved a powerful
knight outpost on the open c-file to
match up against the bishops. He
went on to win, but this position is
hard to assess;

(b) 5 e5 ♘fd7 6 g3 c5. This is a
standard ...b6 position that produces
interesting play based about the attack on e5. Black has done very well
here, mainly because the d2 knight
has no good squares to go to in order
to prepare ♗f4: 7 ♕e2 ♕c7 (7...♘c6 8
♘b3 ♕c7 9 ♗f4 c4!? [9...a5 was a good
choice] 10 dxc4 ♗a6 11 ♘bd4?! ♗xc4
12 ♕e3 ♗xf1 13 ♔xf1 ♘xd4 14 ♘xd4
♗c5 15 c3 0-0∓ R.Montgomery-
A.Shaw, corr 1983) 8 c4 ♗b7 9 ♗g2
dxc4!? 10 ♘xc4 b5 11 ♘a3 a6 12 0-0
♘c6 13 ♖e1 ♗e7 14 ♘c2 0-0 15 b3
♘b6∓ Lushnikov-Grishanovich, St
Petersburg 1999.

5...c5

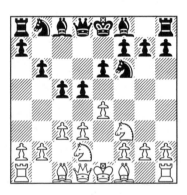

6 e5

(a) 6 ♕a4+ ♗d7 (6...♕d7 7 ♕c2
♕c7! 8 ♗e2 ♘c6 9 0-0 ♗d6 10 ♖e1
0-0∓ Bauer-Bareev, Cannes 2001) 7
♕c2 ♕c7 8 ♗e2 ♗e7 9 0-0 0-0 10 ♖e1

♘c6 11 ♗f1 ♖ac8= Van Delft-Hert-
neck, Tegernsee 2003;

(b) 6 g3 is cooperative, because
White cannot abandon d3: 6...♗a6!? 7
exd5 (7 c4!?) 7...♕xd5 (7...exd5 8 d4
♗xf1 9 ♘xf1 ♗e7=) 8 ♘c4 ♗xc4!? 9
dxc4 ♕xd1+ 10 ♔xd1 ♘c6 11 ♗g2
♖c8= or maybe a touch better for
White's bishop pair, Short-Bareev,
Sarajevo 1999.

6...♘fd7

A position contested by some top
players.

7 d4

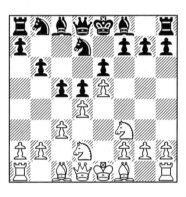

7...♗e7

Black has also played:

(a) 7...♗a6!? 8 ♗xa6 ♘xa6 9 0-0
♗e7 10 ♘e1 b5 (a battle of wing attacks begins) 11 ♕g4 g6 (11...0-0 12
♘df3 ♔h8=) 12 ♘df3 h6 13 h4!? ♕b6
14 ♗e3 c4= Van Weersel-De Jong,
Wijk aan Zee 2002;

(b) 7...♘c6 8 ♗b5 ♗b7 9 0-0 a6 10
♗a4 g5!? Chudnovsky-Bhat, Catons-
ville 2000. There should follow 11
♘b1! ♗e7 12 ♗e3± Objectively better
was 10...♖c8 intending ...b5, ...cxd4,
...♘b4, and ...♕c7.

8 ♗b5!? ♗a6!?

8...0-0 9 0-0 ♗a6 10 a4 ♗xb5 11
axb5 a5!=.

9 a4! ♗b7!

9...cxd4 10 cxd4 0-0 11 0-0 ♕c8 12

♖e1 ♘c6 13 ♖e3± Adams-Bareev, Frankfurt 2000.

After 9...♗b7!, Anand-Dreev, London [rapid] 1995 continued 10 0-0 ♘c6 11 ♖e1 ♖c8 (11...a6!?) 12 ♘f1 c4 13 ♘g3 h5! 14 b4! cxb3 15 ♕xb3 ♘a5 16 ♕c2 ♘c4!?=.

4.12 3...c5

This move introduces what is arguably the most solid counter to the King's Indian Attack that still retains great flexibility and ambition. Black wants to play ...♘c6/...♗d6/ ...♘ge7 and create a thoroughgoing imbalance in the position. He may play in the centre for ...e5 and/or ...d4 or on the queenside with ...b5. I have recommended this system for two editions and since it is a second (or really, fourth) system in this book I will present the basics without much detail, since the ideas are similar in most subsystems.

4 ♘gf3

4 g3 has independent significance:

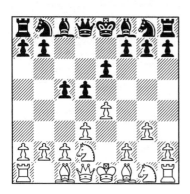

This has become a popular move order to prevent the ...♘c6, ...♗d6 move order by hitting d5 before ...♘ge7 can be played. It can lead to:

(a) 4...♗d6 (this is necessary if Black wants to play the ...♗d6, ...♘c6, ...♘ge7 set-up) and White has:

(a1) 5 ♗g2 ♘e7 6 f4 (6 ♕g4 0-0) 6...0-0 7 ♘gf3 ♘bc6 8 0-0 f6 9 ♕e2 ♗c7 10 ♘b3 b6 11 ♘h4 a5! (11...e5!?) 12 c3 a4 13 ♘d2 b5 (13...♖a7=) 14 f5 b4! 15 fxe6 ♗xe6 16 exd5 ♗xd5= was the game Sheremetieva-Fomina, Debrecen 1992.

(a2) 5 f4 ♘c6 6 ♘gf3 is similar, although 6...♘h6!? threatens ...♘g4 in some lines (after 7 ♗g2?!, for example) and supports ...e5, e.g., 7 h3 0-0 8 ♗g2 f5!? 9 e5 ♗c7 10 0-0 ♘f7 with a solid position and ideas of ...g5 and ...b5;

(a3) 5 ♕g4 is the consistent move, playing to weaken Black's kingside. Now there is another split:

(a31) 5...♘f6!? 6 ♕xg7 ♖g8 7 ♕h6 ♘c6 with a large lead in development and unclear compensation, e.g., 8 c3 ♗d7 9 ♘gf3 ♕e7 and ...0-0-0. The only practical example that I could find went 10 ♕e3 ♗c7 11 ♗g2 0-0-0 12 ♕e2 h5!? (White was doubtless somewhat better about here, but both sides' moves can be criticised) 13 b3 dxe4 14 dxe4 h4!? 15 ♘xh4 ♘g4 16 ♗b2 ♘ce5 17 c4?! ♗c6 18 ♗xe5 ♘xe5 19 ♘hf3? ♘d3+ 20 ♔f1 ♕f6 21 ♖d1 ♖d7 22 h4 ♖gd8 23 ♖b1 ♗a5 when the extra pawns mean little or nothing, Vlassov-Kobylkin, Yalta 1995;

(a32) 5...g6! looks weakening, but it can actually be useful in some positions and White's queen loses time because of the threat ...e5, e.g., 6 ♕e2 ♘c6 7 ♘gf3 ♘ge7 8 ♗g2 (8 h4!? could be met by 8...f6!? with the idea 9 h5?! g5; but also fine is the modest 8...♗c7 9 ♘b3 e5 10 h5?! ♗g4! 11 hxg6 fxg6 12 exd5 ♘xd5 13 ♗h3 ♗xh3 14 ♖xh3 ♕d7 15 ♖h4 0-0-0 16 ♗h6 ♘d4 with a solid edge, Vorobiov-S.Ivanov, St Petersburg 2003) 8...f6 (or 8...b6 9 exd5 exd5; or 8...♕c7 9 0-0 ♗d7 10 exd5 exd5 11 c4 0-0 12 cxd5 ♘xd5 13 ♘c4

罝fe8∓) 9 exd5 (9 0-0 0-0 10 exd5 exd5
11 c4) 9...exd5 10 0-0 0-0 and Black's
development is freer than White's.

(b) 4...公c6 5 鱼g2 dxe4! (White's
point is 5...鱼d6? 6 exd5 exd5 7 鱼xd5
公ge7 8 鱼g2±) 6 dxe4 b6 and Black's
bishop will be unopposed on the a6-f1
diagonal:

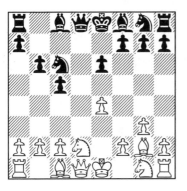

7 公e2 鱼a6 8 c3 (8 0-0 豐d7 9 c4 罝d8
10 豐a4 公b4 11 豐b3 公e7 12 a3 公d3
13 罝d1 公c6 with an edge) 8...豐d7 9
0-0 罝d8 10 f4 公ge7 11 豐e1 e5!? 12
豐f2 exf4 13 gxf4 公g6! 14 公f3 鱼e7 15
鱼e3 0-0 16 罝ae1 鱼d3 17 e5 f6∓
Dutschak-Fischer, Bundesliga 1998.
4...公c6 5 g3 鱼d6 6 鱼g2 公ge7 7 0-0

The basic position for this system,
which is solid but gives plenty of
winning chances. These appealing
aspects account for the roughly 1500

games with it in my database.
7...0-0

Black can try to benefit from doing
without this move:

(a) 7...豐c7 8 公h4 (8 罝e1 鱼d7 9
豐e2 f6 – compare 7...0-0 8 罝e1 豐c7; 8
公e1 0-0!? 9 f4 f6 10 公ef3 鱼d7 11 罝e1
罝ac8 12 公f1 b5= Rolletschek-Linn,
Dearborn 1991) 8...g5!? (or 8...鱼e5 9
f4 鱼f6 10 公hf3 g6) 9 公hf3 h6 intending ...鱼d7, ...0-0-0. 9...f6!? is also interesting;

(b) 7...b6 8 公h4 (8 罝e1 鱼c7 9 公f1
鱼b7 10 h4 h6 11 c3 dxe4 12 dxe4
豐xd1 13 罝xd1 罝d8= Lederer-
Ma.Tseitlin, Beersheva 1990) 8...鱼e5!?
9 f4 鱼f6 10 公hf3 g6 11 e5 鱼g7 seems
more effective than the 7...0-0 8 公h4
鱼e5 line below, because now 12 c3
鱼a6! prevents d4.

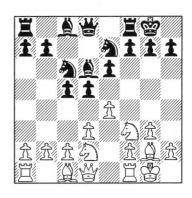

After 7...0-0, White usually plays:

4.121 8 罝e1
4.122 8 公h4

8 豐e2 and 8 c3 often transpose, but
8 豐e2 e5!? 9 exd5 公xd5 is an option
(10 公c4 鱼g4 11 c3 f6), and 8 c3 b6 9
罝e1 allows 9...dxe4 10 dxe4 鱼a6=.

4.121 8 罝e1

This is far and away the most
popular move. White eyes the possi-

bilities of c3 and e5.

8...♕c7

Here 8...b6 and 8...f6!? (rare but interesting because it's so flexible) are also played. But the main alternative is 8...♗c7 9 c3 (9 e5? ♘g6 10 ♘b3 b6 11 d4 cxd4∓; 9 exd5 ♘xd5 10 ♘e4 b6= or here 9...exd5; 9 ♘h4 e5!=; finally, 9 ♕e2 can be answered by 9...b6 intending the plan ...a5 and ...♗a6, or 9...e5!?)

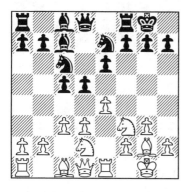

A popular position. Black has used some 7 different moves here, all of them playable! These are 9...d4, 9...f6, 9...dxe4 10 dxe4 b6, 9...♘g6, and:

(a) 9...b6 (easily the most frequently-played move) 10 e5 (10 exd5 ♘xd5 11 ♘c4 ♗b7=, or again 10...exd5=) 10...a5 (or 10...♔h8! with the idea ...f6) 11 ♘f1 (11 d4 ♗a6 [or 11...♘f5 12 ♘f1 f6 13 exf6 ♕xf6=] 12 ♘f1 cxd4 13 cxd4 ♕d7 14 h4 ♘b4 15 ♖e3 ♖fc8 16 a3 ♘bc6 17 b3 ♘f5∓ Dzhumaev-Saltaev, Abu Dhabi 2000) 11...♗a6 12 h4 d4 13 c4 ♕d7 14 ♘1h2 f5?! (14...f6!) 15 exf6? (15 a4±) 15...gxf6 16 ♘g4 (16 ♗h3 ♘f5 17 ♘g4 ♔h8 – Karpov) 16...e5 17 ♗h3 ♕e8 18 ♗h6 ♖f7 19 ♗d2 ♔h8∓ Sznapik-Karpov, Skopje 1972.

(b) 9...♖b8 10 a3 (10 e5 b6 11 d4 ♘f5 12 ♘f1 f6 13 exf6 ♕xf6= Ostojic-Pytel, Kikinda 1976; 10 ♕c2 b5 11

♘b3 c4! 12 dxc4 bxc4 13 ♘c5 ♖b5 14 ♗e3 ♗b6 15 b4 cxb3 16 ♘xb3 ♗xe3 17 ♖xe3 ♕c7=) 10...a5 11 a4 b6 12 ♕c2 ♗a6 13 ♗f1 ♕d7 14 ♘b1 ♘g6∓ intending ...f5, Makropoulos-Grivas, Athens 1989;

(c) 9...a5 10 a4 b6 11 exd5 exd5 12 ♘b1 (12 d4 ♗g4= Medina-Portisch, Palma de Mallorca 1967) 12...♗g4 13 ♘a3 d4= Vaganian-Sokolov, Minsk 1986.

9 c3

(a) 9 ♕e2 f6 10 c3 might transpose after 10...♗d7, but Black also has 10...d4 11 ♘c4 e5 12 ♗d2 (12 a4 ♗e6) 12...b5! 13 ♘xd6 ♕xd6∓ Rosenberg-Bukhman, USSR 1974;

(b) 9 b3 ♗d7 10 ♗b2 d4! 11 ♘c4 (11 c3 dxc3!? 12 ♗xc3 e5 13 ♘c4 f6, at least =, Pacis-Galego, Manila 1992) 11...e5 12 a4 b6 13 ♕d2 f6∓ Calvo-Karpov, Madrid 1973;

(c) 9 ♘h4 g5!? (9...♗d7 10 f4 f6=) 10 ♘hf3 f6 11 d4 ♘xd4 12 ♘xd4 cxd4 13 exd5 e5 Foygel-Serper, Seattle 2003; I prefer Black here.

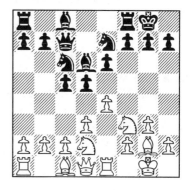

9...♗d7

Or 9...b5 10 ♕e2 f6, e.g., 11 a3?! ♖b8 12 d4 cxd4 13 cxd4 ♕b6 14 ♘b3 b4 15 e5? fxe5 16 dxe5 ♘xe5! 17 ♘xe5 bxa3∓ was V.Georgiev-Peev, Tsarevo 2001.

10 ♕e2 f6!

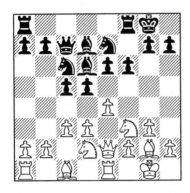

Now White can't play e5, whereas Black has several plans including ...b5 and ...d4 with ...e5. This position has done well for Black, for example, 11 ♘f1 (11 a3 can be met by 11...a5 12 a4 ♗e8!? intending ...♗f7 or 11...d4!? 12 cxd4 cxd4 13 b4 e5) 11...d4 (11...♗e8 12 ♘h4 ♗f7=) 12 ♗d2 (12 a4 e5 13 ♘3d2 a6 14 ♘c4 b5 15 ♘xd6 ♕xd6 16 axb5 axb5 17 ♖xa8 ♖xa8∓ Savic-Kalevic, Belgrade 2001) 12...e5 13 ♖ec1 ♖fc8!? 14 h3?! ♗e6 15 ♘1h2? (but these positions are notoriously hard to play) 15...♕d7 16 h4 b5 17 cxd4 cxd4 18 ♘e1 a5 19 f4 ♗b4∓ A.Zaitsev-Gufeld, USSR Ch 1969.

4.122 8 ♘h4 ♕c7

One option is 8...f5!? 9 f4 b5 10 c3 ♖b8 11 exf5 exf5 12 ♘df3 b4 13 c4 d4 14 ♖e1 h6 15 ♗d2 ♕c7= Meier-Boensch, Berlin 1992.

9 f4 f6

This position has discouraged players from 8 ♘h4. Now neither e5 nor f5 achieve anything, so the whole plan looks artificial.

10 c3

Black's manages to get both queenside expansion and central play after 10 ♘hf3 b5 11 c3 ♗d7 12 ♕e2 ♖ae8!? 13 ♖e1 ♘g6 14 ♘f1 a5 15 h4 c4 16

dxc4 bxc4 17 exd5 exd5 18 ♗e3 ♗f5∓ Mooses-Noroozi, Tehran 2001.

10...♗d7

Not the only move. Also effective was 10...d4 11 a4 ♗d7 12 ♘c4 e5 13 ♗d2 dxc3! 14 bxc3 ♗e6 15 ♖f2 ♖ad8 16 ♕f1 ♕d7 17 ♗e3 b6 18 f5 ♗f7∓ in Nicholson-Fernandez Romero, Seville 2003.

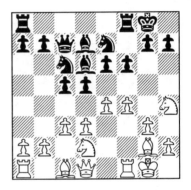

11 ♘b3!?

11 ♕h5!? ♗e8 12 ♕e2 ♗f7 13 ♘df3 ♖ae8!? (13...dxe4 14 dxe4 e5) 14 e5? (14 ♗e3 was about equal) 14...fxe5 15 fxe5 ♘xe5 16 ♘g5 ♘7c6 17 ♗h3 h6! 18 ♖xf7 ♘xf7 19 ♘xe6 ♘cd8!–+ Rigo-Sax, Magyarország 1976.

11...d4! 12 c4 a6 13 ♗d2 ♖ab8 14 ♖c1 ♗e8

A typical manoeuvre for Black, rerouting the bishop to eye the queenside.

15 ♕e2

Or 15 g4 ♗f7. After 15 ♕e2, Nevednichy-Horvath, Odorheiu Secuiesc 1993 continued 15...♗f7 16 ♘f3?! (16 ♔h1 e5!) 16...e5! 17 f5 b5∓ with the idea 18 cxb5 ♖xb5.

4.2 2 ♕e2

An old move, tried by Chigorin and revived in recent years by Morozevich and others. I don't really think that objectively 2 ♕e2 poses many problems for Black but it has scored brilliantly versus the unaware and you'll probably see it some time since there are over 5000 games with it in my database! The main point of 2 ♕e2 is to meet 2...d5?! with 3 exd5 ♕xd5 4 ♘c3. Otherwise White usually enters a King's Indian Attack set-up where the queen is oddly placed except for early e5 thrusts. One problem for White is that Black can choose systems in which e5 is either impossible or ineffective. Two of these are:

4.21 2...♘f6
4.22 2...c5

4.21 2...♘f6

I think that this has been underestimated. Black prepares ...d5 and de-

velops, so to make sense of 2 ♕e2 White has to commit his centre, arguably too early.

3 e5

Natural but not very challenging.

(a) After 3 d4, Black can of course play 3...d5, but I like 3...c5!

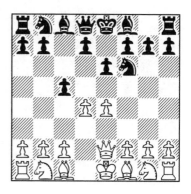

and:

(a1) 4 d5 d6 5 c4 exd5 6 cxd5 ♗e7 (6...g6 aims for a Benoni system with the queen misplaced on e2, so logical is 7 ♘c3 ♕e7 8 ♘f3 ♗g7 9 ♗g5 h6 10 ♗h4 0-0 11 0-0-0 g5 [or 11...♖e8!] 12 ♗g3 ♘h5 with standard counterplay) 7 ♘c3 0-0 8 ♘f3 ♘a6!? (8...♖e8; 8...♗g4) 9 ♕d1 ♘c7 10 a4 ♖b8 11 ♗d3 a6=.

(a2) 4 e5 ♘d5 5 c4 (5 ♘f3 cxd4 6 ♘xd4 d6 7 ♘f3 ♘c6∓) 5...♘b4!? (or 5...♘c7) 6 dxc5 (6 ♘f3 cxd4 7 ♘xd4 ♘8c6∓) 6...♗xc5 7 ♘f3 ♘8c6!? 8 ♘c3 (8 a3?! ♕a5 9 ♗d2? ♘c2+ 10 ♔d1 ♕a4 11 ♘c3 ♕b3-+) 8...♕a5! 9 a3 ♘d4 10 ♘xd4 ♗xd4 11 ♗f4 ♘c6 and e5 falls;

(b) 3 ♘f3 is arguably the main line. Rustemov's treatment was instructive in the following game: 3...d5 4 e5 (4 d3 is one line White was presumably not very interested in playing when he chose 2 ♕e2. Black's easiest solution is to develop by 4...♗e7 5 g3 0-0, but 5...♘c6 is also interesting, to meet 6 ♗g2 by 6...dxe4 7 dxe4 e5, and

6 e5 ♘d7 7 ♗g2 0-0 8 0-0 by 8...f6)
4...♘fd7 5 d3 (5 d4?! c5 6 c3 b6 –
Rustemov; 5 g3 b6 6 ♗g2 ♗c5!? 7 d3
♘c6 8 c3 a5 9 0-0 ♗a6 10 ♖e1 ♗e7 11
♕d1 ♘c5 12 ♗f1 d4! 13 c4 ♗b7∓
Troianescu-Cappello, Bari 1971)
5...c5 6 g3 ♘c6 7 ♗g2 ♗e7 (7...b5!?)

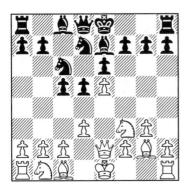

8 h4 (8 0-0 g5! – Rustemov; then
...g4 is threatened to win the e-pawn,
and ♗f4 is prevented, so 9 h3 h5 10
g4 hxg4 11 hxg4 ♕c7 12 ♖e1 f6! 13
exf6 ♘xf6∓ could follow, when Black
intends ...e5 and can answer 14 ♗xg5
by 14...♘xg4 15 ♗xe7 ♘xe7 [or
15...♘d4!? 16 ♕d1 ♔xe7∓] 16 ♘e5
♕xe5 17 ♕xe5 ♘xe5 18 ♖xe5 ♘g6 19
♖e1 ♘f4∓ with ...♗d7 and ...0-0-0)
8...h6 (or 8...b5) 9 c4 (Rustemov as-
sesses 9 ♗f4!? b5 10 c4 bxc4 11 dxc4
♗a6 12 ♘bd2 as unclear, although
the aggressive 12...♘b4! with the idea
13 0-0 (what else?) 13...g5! 14 ♗e3 d4
looks very strong) 9...dxc4 (9...0-0 is
less committal and probably equal)
10 dxc4 ♘d4 11 ♘xd4 (Rustemov
mentions 11 ♕e4, when 11...0-0! 12
♘xd4 cxd4 13 ♕xd4 is met by
13...♕a5+) 11...cxd4 12 ♗f4 (12 0-0
♕c7 13 ♖e1 g5!?) 12...♕b6 13 ♘d2 (13
0-0 g5 14 hxg5 hxg5 15 ♗c1 ♕c5∓; 13
b3 ♕a5+!? [or 13...♘c5] 14 ♘d2 ♗b4
15 0-0 ♗c3) 13...♘c5 (a sensible continuation, although 13...♕xb2 14 ♖b1

♕c2!? looks safe enough) 14 ♖b1 a5
15 h5 ♗d7 16 0-0 0-0 17 b3 (here
Rustemov offers 17 a3?! a4∓ and 17
♖fd1 ♖fd8∓) 17...♖fd8 18 a3 ♗c6 19
b4 ♗xg2 20 ♔xg2 ♘a4 (20...axb4!? 21
axb4 ♘a4 22 c5 ♘c3 23 ♕f3 ♕b5∓ or
24 ♖b3 ♖a4! – Rustemov) 21 c5 Fe-
dorov-Rustemov, Vilnius 1997. Black
was better after 21...♕c6+, but
Rustemov finds the stronger 21...♘c3!
22 ♕f3 (22 cxb6 ♘xe2) 22...♕b5∓;

(c) 3 f4 doesn't make much sense.
One game went 3...d5 4 e5 ♘g8!?
(4...♘fd7 5 ♘f3 c5) 5 ♘f3 ♘h6!? (or
5...c5) 6 ♘c3 c5 7 ♘d1 ♘c6 8 g3 ♘f5 9
c3 ♗e7 10 ♗h3 ♖b8 11 d3 b5 with a
queenside attack underway, Khou-
seinov-Villamayor, Bled 2002.

3...♘d5 4 ♘f3

(a) 4 d4 c5 transposes to 3 ♘f3 c5 4
e5 ♘d5; or there's 4...d6 'unclear' –
Rustemov;

(b) 4 c4 ♘f4 (or 4...♘b4 5 d4 c5= intending 6 a3 ♕a5!) 5 ♕e4 ♘g6 6 ♘f3
d6 (or 6...c5) 7 exd6 ♗xd6 8 d4 c5 9
♘c3 cxd4 10 ♘xd4 ♘d7!? 11 ♗e3
♘f6= Motwani-Nogueiras, Istanbul
2000;

(c) 4 g3 d6 5 d4 c5 6 c3?! cxd4 7
cxd4 b6! (7...♘c6 8 ♘f3 dxe5 9 dxe5
♗c5∓) 8 ♗g2 ♗a6∓ Arques Lopez-
Barria, Alicante 2000.

4...c5! 5 c4

Instead, 5 ♘c3 ♘c6! 6 ♘xd5 exd5 is
a very nice version of a Nimzowitsch
Sicilian Defence – 5 g3 ♘c6 6 ♗g2 d6
equalises on the spot.

5...♘b4!

Disrupting White's development.
The alternative was 5...♘c7 6 d4 cxd4
7 ♘xd4 d6!?.

6 d3 d5 7 ♕d1!

Best. 7 a3? ♕a5! 8 ♘c3 d4 9 ♖b1
dxc3 10 axb4 ♕a2 is awful.

7...dxc4

Black is slightly better after

7...♗e7.

8 dxc4 ♕xd1+ 9 ♔xd1 b6 10 a3 ♘4a6 11 ♘c3 ♗b7 12 ♗e2 ♘c6

and Black, intending ...0-0-0 and ...♘d4, has a nice advantage. The 2...♘f6 system guarantees an imbalance and looks like fun.

4.22 2...c5

A good reply: as I asked in PTF2: Who wants the queen on e2 in a Sicilian? I will look at just a small number of examples.

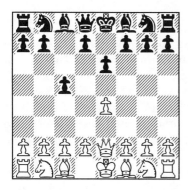

3 ♘f3

3 f4 ♘c6 4 ♘f3 ♗e7 5 ♘c3 d5 6 d3 (6 e5 ♘h6 intending to continue ...♘f5) 6...♘f6 7 e5 ♘d7 8 g3 b5! 9 ♗g2 ♕b6 10 0-0 b4 11 ♘d1 c4+! 12 ♗e3 (12 d4 c3! with the idea ...♗a6) 12...♗c5 13 ♔h1 ♗a6∓ Lendauf-Uhlmann, Graz 1991.

3...♘c6 4 g3 g6 5 ♗g2 ♗g7 6 0-0 ♘ge7 7 d3 e5

7...0-0 is a normal Sicilian: If White plays 8 ♘c3, Black has either 8...d6, with a standard position except for the strange and committal ♕e2; and if he plays 8 c3 Black can again play

8...d6 and, for example, 9 ♘bd2 h6 10 a4 e5!, transposing to 7...e5.

8 ♘bd2 0-0 9 ♘c4 d6 10 a4 h6 11 c3 ♗e6

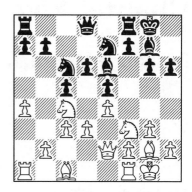

Black is well centralised and White has no breaks, whereas the prospects for ...d5 and/or kingside attack are good.

12 ♖d1 b6?!

Weakening. Instead, 12...f5! threatens ...f4 and 13 exf5 ♘xf5 clamps down on d4 while preparing the attack.

13 ♗d2 ♕c7!?

Better is 13...g5!.

14 b4!

14 ♖ab1?! d5!.

14...cxb4 15 cxb4 d5 16 exd5 ♘xd5 17 ♖ac1 ♘d4! 18 ♕e1?

18 ♘xd4 was better when 18...exd4 is equal.

18...♘xf3+!?

Correct was 18...♘b3! 19 ♖b1 ♘xd2 20 ♘cxd2 ♖fc8 with a solid advantage.

19 ♗xf3 ♖ac8 20 b5 ♕b8 21 ♕e2 ♖fd8 with double-edged play, Galego-Baches Garcia, Havana 2003.

Chapter Five

Exchange Variation

1 e4 e6 2 d4 d5 3 exd5

The Exchange Variation was probably the most popular variation of the French Defence in the late 19th century. It is not a particularly imaginative line.

3...exd5

The exchange of pawns has actually deterred some players from using the French Defence. With only one open file, they reason, both sides will mindlessly exchange their heavy pieces and a drawish position will ensue. But there is a huge hole in this reasoning: in most cases, neither side's rooks belong on the e-file. Why? Because there will be no points of penetration available for them along the file, e.g., squares like e2, e3 and e4 for White and e7, e6, and e5 for Black will customarily be covered 2 or 3 times by that side's pawns, knights, and bishops. Moreover, only one such defender is really necessary. So if, for example, White doubles or triples along the e-file while Black is blithely mounting a kingside pawn storm (backed by his rooks and queen), the second player has every chance of winning. Furthermore, Black can al-ways make the struggle imbalanced should he so choose. This has been pointed out and demonstrated by great players for at least 70 years.

Thus my comments from the first two editions and they still hold true. Although the Exchange Variation appeals to players who are trying to draw against stronger players, allow-ing equality on the third move as White may not be the way to go about that. Be aware that it's a strategy that has failed miserably throughout the years.

White's main moves are:

5.1 4 c4
5.2 4 ♘f3
5.3 4 ♗d3

He has other choices, but Black can always achieve an imbalance if he wants to:

(a) 4 ♘c3 ♗b4 is dealt with in Chapter 8, under the order 3 ♘c3 ♗b4 4 exd5;

(b) 4 c3 is slow: 4...♗d6 (or 4...♘c6; then 5 ♗b5 might look appealing, but c3 doesn't go well with this move, i.e. ♘c3 is preferable; compare the reversed positions in Chapter 8). Now if 5 ♗d3, 5...♘c6 transposes to 4 ♗d3 ♘c6 below. On 5 ♘f3, 5...♗g4 will often tranpose to 4 ♘f3, and 5...♘c6 6 ♘f3 ♗g4 is also possible;

(c) 4 ♗e3 is passive. Then 4...♘e7 intending ...♘f5 and 4...♗d6 5 ♘c3 ♘e7 are dynamic continuations; in practice, 4...♘f6 has also scored well;

(d) 4 ♕f3 has been played a bit more recently, but nearly every game develops independently and Black seems to get equality with 4...♘f6, 4...♗d6, 4...c6, or even 4...♘c6. A nice example of the latter was 4...♘c6 5 ♗b5 ♘f6 6 ♘e2 ♗g4 7 ♕c3 ♗d6! 8 ♗xc6+ bxc6 9 ♕xc6+ ♗d7, and Black has more than enough compensation: 10 ♕a6 ♘g4!? (10...0-0∓) 11 h3? ♕f6! 12 ♘bc3 (to stop ...♗b4+) 12...♕xf2+ 13 ♔d1 ♕xg2-+ Bykhovsky-Ulibin, Aaland-Stockholm 1997.

I like the straightforward 4...♗d6 5 c3 (5 ♗d3 ♘c6) 5...♘e7. A sequence which has come up more than once follows 4...♘f6 5 h3 (versus ...♗g4, which is often followed by ...♗h5-g6). Black has won several games from this position, for example, 5...c5 (or 5...♗d6 6 ♗d3 0-0 7 ♘e2 c5 8 dxc5 ♗xc5 9 0-0 ♘c6 10 ♗f4 ♖e8 11 ♘bc3 ♘e5 12 ♗xe5 ♖xe5 13 ♖ad1 ♗d7 14 ♘g3 ♕b6∓ Kos-Mohr, Ptuj 2000) 6 ♗b5+!? ♘c6 7 ♘e2 ♕b6! 8 ♕d3!? c4 9 ♕e3+ ♗e6 10 ♗a4 ♗d6∓ with a big lead in development, Hermann-Vaganian, Bundesliga 1992;

(e) After 4 ♗f4, Black has equalised with 4...♗f5, 4...c5, and:

(e1) 4...♘f6 5 ♗d3 c5 6 dxc5 (6 ♕e2+ ♗e7! 7 dxc5 0-0) 6...♗xc5 7 ♘f3 0-0 8 0-0 ♘c6 9 c3 ♖e8 10 ♘bd2 ♘e4= Meyers-Gleserov, Tzrkva 1990; or 10...♗g4!;

(e2) 4...♗d6 led to a nice example in Prie-Vaisman, Nimes 1990: 5 ♗xd6 ♕xd6 6 ♘c3 (6 c3 ♘f6 7 ♗d3 0-0 8 ♘e2 b6 9 0-0 c5 10 ♘d2 ♗g4!? 11 f3 ♗d7 12 ♕e1 ♖e8 13 ♕f2 ♘c6∓ Stefanova-Kindermann, Vienna 1996) 6...♗f5 7 ♗d3 ♗xd3 8 ♕xd3 ♘d7!? (8...♘c6=) 9 ♘f3 0-0-0 10 0-0-0 ♘gf6 11 h3 (White would lose material after 11 ♖he1 ♖he8 12 ♔b1 ♘e4! 13 ♘xe4?! dxe4 14 ♖xe4? ♘c5! 15 dxc5 ♕xd3 16 cxd3 ♖xe4) 11...♖he8 12 ♖de1 ♘e4! 13 ♘xe4? dxe4 14 ♖xe4 ♘c5 15 dxc5 ♕h6+ 16 ♔b1 (16 ♕e3 ♖xe4) 16...♖xd3 17 ♖xe8+ ♖d8 18 ♖xd8+ ♔xd8 19 ♘e5 ♕f4-+ Piroth-Apicella, Sautron 2003.

5.1 4 c4

This move has become one of White's main options. It can transpose to 4 ♘f3 and 5 c4, but also has independent significance. I will give two solutions.

4...♗b4+

A move this book helped to bring to attention. I think that it casts into doubt the value of 4 c4 as a practical weapon; in fact, Black has scored 53% with a clearly superior performance rating after many games. Also good is 4...♘f6, which is played about 10 times as often! Then White has:

(a) 5 ♘f3 ♗b4+ (or 5...♗g4) 6 ♘c3 (6 ♗d2 ♗xd2+ 7 ♘bxd2 tends to be bad in such positions because in the isolated pawn position following ...♗xd2 and ...dxc4, the exchange of bishops favours Black, e.g., 7...0-0 8 ♗e2 dxc4 9 ♘xc4 ♘bd7 10 0-0 ♘b6 11 ♘e3 ♗e6 12 ♘e5 ♕d6∓ Ellenbroek-Stellwagen, Wijk aan Zee 2001) 6...0-0 7 ♗e2 dxc4 8 0-0 (8 ♗xc4 ♗g4) 8...♗xc3!? 9 bxc3 ♗e6 10 ♖b1 ♘bd7! 11 ♗g5 ♘b6∓ Herrera-Campora, Argentina 1987;

(b) 5 ♘c3 ♗b4 6 cxd5 (6 a3 ♗xc3+ 7 bxc3 0-0 8 ♗d3 ♘c6 9 ♘e2 dxc4 10 ♗xc4 ♘a5=) 6...♘xd5 7 ♗d2 0-0 8 ♗d3 c5! 9 dxc5 ♘xc3 10 ♗xc3 ♗xc3+ 11 bxc3 ♘d7 12 c6 ♘c5! 13 ♗c2 ♖e8+ 14 ♘e2 ♕e7∓ Kuijf-Korchnoi, Tilburg 1992.

5 ♘c3 ♘e7

5...♘f6 has been played often with success and an appealing idea is 5...♕e7+!? 6 ♗e3 (6 ♕e2?! ♘c6 7 ♘f3 ♗g4) 6...♘f6, e.g., 7 ♗d3 ♗e6 8 c5 0-0 9 h3 b6∓ Perrin-Knott, USA 1857(!).

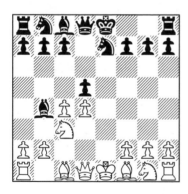

6 ♘f3

6 a3 ♗xc3+ 7 bxc3 0-0 8 ♘f3 ♘bc6= intending as always ...♘a5 and/or ...♗g4. Then 9 ♗d3!? dxc4 10 ♗xc4 ♘d5 11 ♗xd5 ♖e8+ 12 ♗e3 ♕xd5 13 h3 (13 0-0 ♗g4) 13...♕c4 14 ♕c2 b6∓ was the game Speck-Luther, Liechtenstein 1993.

6...0-0

6...♗g4! will usually transpose and pretty much amounts to the same thing. But I actually prefer this less common order because it puts immediate pressure on the centre. These useful early pins are characteristic of the Exchange French.

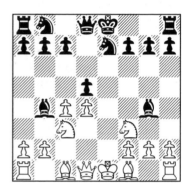

7 a3 (7 ♕a4+ ♘bc6 8 ♘e5 ♗e6=; 7 ♗e2 ♘bc6 8 a3 ♗xc3+ 9 bxc3 would transpose to this note, and here 7...dxc4 8 ♗xc4 0-0 9 0-0 ♘bc6 is the main line) 7...♗xc3+ 8 bxc3 ♘bc6 (8...0-0 is again the main line) 9 ♗g5 (9 a4 ♘a5∓; 9 cxd5 ♘xd5 10 ♗d2 ♕e7+ 11 ♕e2 ♗xf3 12 ♕xe7+ ♘cxe7 13 gxf3 ♘g6∓) 9...0-0! 10 ♗e2 (10 cxd5 ♕xd5 threatens capture on f3, hitting the g5 bishop) 10...f6 (10...♕d7 may be more accurate: 11 0-0 dxc4 12 ♗xc4 ♘d5 with the idea ...♘a5, ...b5 etc.) 11 ♗d2 ♘a5=. Black's control of the light squares compensates for the bishop pair: if 12 c5, 12...b6!; and 12 cxd5 ♕xd5 13 ♖b1 (13 0-0 ♘c4 14 ♖e1 ♖fe8 15 ♖b1 b5 16 a4 a6) 13...♘c4! plans ...b5.

7 a3?!

7 ♗e2 dxc4 8 ♗xc4 ♗g4 9 0-0 ♘bc6 is a typical position in which Black has pressure on the d-pawn and light squares. Several games have gone 10 ♗e3 ♘f5!? (10...♖b8!? 11 a3 ♗xc3 12 bxc3 ♘d5 13 ♗d2 ♘a5 14 ♗a2 b5 and

the light squares balance White's bishops) 11 ♕d3 ♘d6: 12 ♗d5 (12 ♗g5!? ♕c8 13 ♗d5 ♗f5!? 14 ♕d1 ♖e8=) 12...♗f5 13 ♕d1 (13 ♕e2 ♘a5 14 ♗g5 ♕c8 15 ♖fc1 ♖e8 16 ♕f1 c6 17 a3 ♗xc3 18 ♖xc3 ♗e6 19 ♗xe6 ♕xe6 20 b4 ♘ac4∓ Ashley-Remlinger, New York 1994) 13...♘e7 14 ♗b3 c6 15 ♘e5 ♔h8 16 ♖c1 f6 17 ♘d3 ♗xc3 18 bxc3 ♘d5 19 ♘f4 ♘xe3 20 fxe3 ♕e8∓ Waitzkin-Shaked, Mermaid Beach Club 1997.

7...♗xc3+ 8 bxc3 ♘bc6

9 ♗e2

9 c5 b6!∓, since 10 cxb6 axb6 gives Black the a-file and all the light squares, perhaps even with ...♗a6 next.

9...dxc4 10 ♗xc4 ♘d5 11 ♗d2 ♖e8+ 12 ♗e2 ♕e7∓ 13 c4 ♘b6

Or 13...♗f5!? with the idea 14 cxd5? ♗c2.

14 ♗e3 ♗g4 15 0-0 ♖ad8 16 d5 ♗xf3 17 gxf3 ♘e5 18 ♕b3 ♘bxc4! 19 ♗xc4 ♘xf3+ 20 ♔g2 ♕e4! with an overwhelming attack, Santo Roman-Shaked, Cannes 1997.

5.2 4 ♘f3

White's most common move; it is very natural but allows double-edged play because of the possibility of a ...♗g4 pin at some point. Black has:

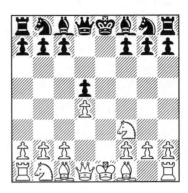

5.21 4...♗g4
5.22 4...♗d6

Of course, 4...♘f6 is fully playable (and a current favourite among grandmasters). I should point out that 5 c4 (a key white plan) then allows 5...♗b4+ 6 ♘c3 ♘c6, which is of particular interest because the light square theme after ...♗g4 can be effective.

5.21 4...♗g4

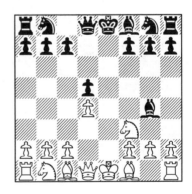

5 h3

(a) 5 ♗f4 ♗d6 6 ♗xd6?! ♕xd6 7 c3 ♕e7+ 8 ♗d2 ♘f6∓ Karolyi-Vaisser, Clichy 1991;

(b) 5 ♗e2 ♗d6 (5...♘c6 6 ♗f4 ♗d6 7 ♕d2 ♘f6 8 ♕e3+?! ♘e4! 9 ♘bd2 0-0

10 ♘xe4 dxe4 11 ♘e5 ♘b4 12 ♕d2 ♗xe2 13 ♕xe2 f6 14 ♕c4+ ♚h8∓ Omtvedt-Myreng, Norway 1982) 6 ♗g5 (6 0-0 ♘c6 7 c3 ♘ge7 8 ♕b3 a6 9 ♖e1 0-0 10 ♗g5 ♕d7= Malisauskas-Lputian, Moscow 1989) 6...♘e7 7 ♗h4 0-0 8 0-0 c6 9 c3 ♖e8 10 ♗g3 ♘f5 11 ♗xd6 ♘xd6∓ Haering-Hug, Wohlen 1993.

5...♗h5 6 ♕e2+!

This move took off after Kasparov used it in 1991. Harmless is 6 ♗e2 ♗d6 7 ♘e5 ♗xe2 8 ♕xe2 ♘e7 9 0-0 (9 ♕b5+ ♘bc6! 10 ♘xc6 bxc6 11 ♕d3 0-0=) 9...0-0 10 ♗f4 ♖e8 11 ♕g4 ♗xe5 12 ♗xe5 ♘g6 13 ♗g3 ♘d7 M.Gure-vich-Short, Manila 1990; Short as-sesses this as slightly better for Black.

6...♕e7

White wins a pawn after 6...♗e7? 7 ♕b5+ (7 g4 ♗g6 8 ♕b5+?! ♘c6 9 ♕xb7 ♘b4 10 ♗b5+ ♚f8 11 ♘e5 ♘f6∓) 7...♘c6 8 ♘e5 a6 9 ♘xc6!? (or 9 ♕a4±) 9...axb5 10 ♘xd8 ♗xd8 11 ♗xb5+.

7 ♗e3 ♘c6 8 ♘c3 0-0-0

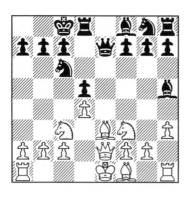

A position that has been played of-ten and is crucial for assessing 4...♗g4. The lines are very concrete.

9 g4

White does well to chase this bishop immediately and eliminate

some options for Black after 9 0-0-0 such as 9...f6, 9...h6, 9...f5, and 9...♕b4!?, e.g., 10 g4 ♗g6 11 ♘h4 (11 ♘e5?! ♘xe5 12 dxe5 d4 13 ♕d2 ♗e7!∓) 11...♕a5 12 ♘xg6 hxg6 13 ♕b5! ♗b4 (13...♘f6) 14 ♕xa5 ♘xa5 15 ♘b1 ♘f6 16 c3 ♗d6= Rutter-S.Williams, London 1993.

9...♗g6 10 0-0-0 ♘b4!?

A direct tactical solution that has barely been tried. It may be no better than the options, but leads to wonder-ful complications. Black has also played 10...♕e8 here, but I prefer 10...f6, covering e5 and allowing ...♗f7 after ♘h4. Black's main idea is ...♘a5: 11 ♗g2!? (11 ♘h4 ♗f7 12 a3 ♕d7!? clears the bishop on f8: 13 ♗g2 ♘a5!? 14 f4 ♘c4 15 ♖he1 ♘h6=, e.g., 16 ♕d3 ♗d6! 17 ♘xd5? ♕b5 18 b3 ♗xa3+ 19 ♚b1 ♖xd5! 20 ♕xc4 ♕xc4 21 bxc4 ♖a5∓; 11 a3 ♕e8!? 12 ♘d2 f5 13 ♗g2 ♘f6 14 ♖he1 ♕e6 15 g5!? ♘e4 16 ♘dxe4 fxe4=) 11...♕d7 12 a3 and 12...♘a5 looks natural, but Mitkov-Shirov, Batumi 1999 went 12...♘ge7 13 ♗f4 ♚b8 14 ♘a4!? ♘c8 (Shirov suggests 14...b6=) 15 ♘h4, when 15...♖e8 16 ♕d2 (16 ♕b5? ♗xc2) 16...♗f7 17 ♘f5 h5 looks equal.

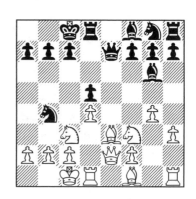

11 a3

This is supposed to be the refuta-tion.

(a) The natural 11 ♖d2 allows 11...f6!? (to cover e5; also, ...♗f7 in some lines strengthens c4 while protecting d5) 12 ♗g2! ♗f7 (another idea would be 12...♕d7 13 a3 ♘c6 14 ♘h4 ♗f7, e.g., 15 ♖e1 ♘a5 16 ♕f3 ♘c4 17 ♖de2 ♘e7!? 18 g5 ♘c6 19 gxf6 gxf6 20 ♕xf6 ♖g8 with dynamic compensation) 13 ♖e1 c6!? (13...♕d7=) 14 ♕d1 ♕c7 15 a3 ♘a6 16 ♖de2 ♗d6 17 ♕d2 ♘e7= (aiming for f4) 18 ♖d1 ♘g6 19 ♖ee1 ♘b8!? (19...♘f4∓) 20 ♗f1 ♘d7 21 ♘a4 ♖de8 ½-½ Mimon-Sanchez Jimenez, Spain 1993. Black still stands a little better;

(b) 11 ♘e1 ♘f6 12 a3 ♘c6 13 ♗g2 (13 ♘f3 ♘e4) 13...♘e4 14 ♘xe4 ♗xe4 15 f3 ♗g6 16 f4 ♗e4=, or here 16...♖e8 17 f5 ♕xe3+ 18 ♕xe3 ♖xe3 19 fxg6 hxg6 20 ♗xd5 ♘d8=.

11...♘xc2 12 ♗f4

This is Ulibin-Vilela, Santa Clara 1991. Instead of the tempting 12...♘a1?! 13 b4!, Black might have tried:

12...♘xa3!

which results in fascinating complications.

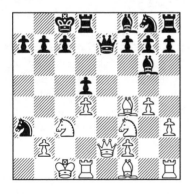

13 bxa3

13 ♕xe7 ♗xe7 14 bxa3 ♗xa3+ 15 ♔d2 ♘f6 transposes.

13...♕xa3+ 14 ♕b2 ♗b4 15 ♕xa3

Too slow is the alternative 15

♗d2?! h5! (15...♕a5!?) 16 ♗g2 ♘f6 17 g5 ♕xb2+ 18 ♔xb2 ♗xc3+ 19 ♗xc3 ♘e4 20 ♗e1 ♖he8∓.

15...♗xa3+ 16 ♔d2 ♘f6

Black has three pawns and enough play for the piece, for example:

17 ♘e5! ♗b4! 18 f3 c5 19 ♘xg6 hxg6 20 ♔c2 c4 21 ♗g2 b6

Planning ...♗b7-c6 followed by advancing the 3 connected passed pawns.

22 ♖b1!

22 ♗e5 ♔b7 23 f4 ♗xc3 24 ♔xc3 ♘e8! 25 f5 gxf5 26 gxf5 ♔c6∓.

22...♗xc3 23 ♔xc3 ♔b7 24 ♖he1 ♔c6

Riskier is 24...♖de8!? 25 ♗e5! ♔c6 26 f4 a5 27 g5 ♘d7 28 ♗xg7 ♖xe1 29 ♖xe1 ♖g8 30 ♗e5 b5, although the pawns are dangerous enough to hold the balance.

25 ♖e2

Now 25 ♗e5 a5 26 g5 ♘e8 achieves nothing.

25...♖de8 26 ♖eb2 ♖e7=

There follows ...♖he8, and the idea of ...♘h7, ...f6, ...g5 can be surprisingly effective. This is of course just sample analysis, but it includes several exact moves for White that let him escape from being overrun by the passed pawns. I think that the verdict is an objective one.

5.22 4...♗d6 5 c4

(a) 5 ♘c3 is rare because 5...c6 restricts the White knight, and 5...♘e7 is also fine;

(b) 5 ♗d3 ♘e7 (5...♘c6 might transpose to 4 ♗d3 ♘c6) 6 0-0 ♗g4 (or, again, 6...♘bc6) 7 ♗g5 (7 h3 ♗h5 8 c4 dxc4 9 ♗xc4 0-0 10 g4 ♗g6 11 ♘e5 c5!? 12 ♘xg6 ♘xg6 13 dxc5 ♗xc5 14 ♕xd8 ♖xd8 15 ♗g5 ♖d7= Thesing-Knaak, Bundesliga 1992; and here 11...♘bc6 would have been more confrontational) 7...♘bc6 8 c3 ♕d7 9 ♘bd2 f6 10 ♗h4 h5 11 b4 ♘d8 (or 11...0-0-0) Mokcsay-L.Portisch, Zalakaros 1991; Black's coming kingside pawn storm in this type of position will be seen again under 4 ♗d3.

5...c6

This has the advantage of reserving a later ...♘e7, when Black's knight will be better placed than White's in the event of cxd5. 5...♘f6 6 c5 ♗e7 is also played.

6 ♘c3

6 cxd5 cxd5 7 ♗d3 (7 ♘c3 ♘e7 transposes, and here 7 ♗g5 f6! only helps Black) 7...♘e7 8 ♗g5 h6 9 ♗h4 ♕b6!= Holubcik-Vavrak, Tatranske Zruby 2000.

6...♘e7

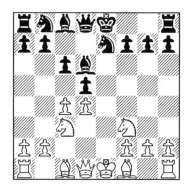

7 ♗d3

(a) 7 ♗e2 might transpose after 7...dxc4, but Black might also simply develop by ...0-0 and ...♗f5, in view of the passivity of White's bishop;

(b) 7 cxd5 cxd5 yields a static central pawn structure where knights are at least the equal of bishops. Thus White is ill-motivated to waste two tempi to win the d6 bishop by 8 ♘b5?! 0-0 (8...♘bc6) 9 ♘xd6 ♕xd6 10 ♗e2 ♗g4! 11 0-0 ♘bc6 (with the idea ...♘f5) 12 h3 ♗h5 13 b3? (but 13 ♗e3 f5! or 13 g4 ♗g6 14 ♘h4 f5! – Ren-

man) 13...♖fe8 14 ♗b2 ♘g6! 15 g4 (15 g3 ♕e6!; 15 ♗c1 ♖xe2!) 15...♘f4 16 ♘e5 ♗g6 17 ♗f3 ♘xh3+ 18 ♔h1 ♗e4-+ Johansson-Renman, Sweden 1982;

(c) 7 c5 tends to be harmless in these positions because it releases the pressure on the centre, e.g., 7...♗c7 8 ♗d3 (8 ♗g5 f6 9 ♗e3 0-0 10 ♗d3 ♗f5=) 8...0-0 (8...♗f5 is the more common move order, to force the kind of position that arises next) 9 0-0 h6 10 h3 (10 ♕c2 ♗g4! 11 ♘e5 ♗xe5 12 dxe5 ♘d7∓) 10...♗f5 (10...♗e6 would be more enterprising) 11 ♖e1 ♗xd3 12 ♕xd3 ♘d7 13 ♘h4!? (versus ...♘g6) 13...♖e8 14 ♗d2 ♘f8 15 b4 ♕d7 16 a4 ♘fg6 17 ♘xg6 ♘xg6= George-Hutchings, England 1986.

7...dxc4 8 ♗xc4 0-0 9 0-0

9 ♗e3?! ♘d7 10 ♕d2 ♘b6 11 ♗b3 ♘bd5 12 0-0-0 a5! 13 ♘xd5 ♘xd5∓ with the idea ...a4-a3, Jellison-J.Watson, Denver 1974.

9...♘d7 10 ♖e1

10 ♗g5 ♘b6 11 ♗b3 (11 ♗d3 f6!∓) 11...♔h8 (11...♗g4!? has a similar idea, e.g., 12 h3 ♗h5 13 g4 ♗g6 14 ♘e5 ♔h8! intending ...f6) 12 ♕d2 (12 ♗xe7 ♕xe7 13 ♖e1 ♕c7 14 d5 ♗g4=) 12...f6 (this plan is worth noting, since it has not been played in several recent games with this variation) 13 ♗f4 ♗b4!? (13...♗xf4∓) 14 a3 ♗a5 15 h3 (15 ♗a2 ♘bd5∓) 15...♘ed5 16 ♗g3 ♗e6 17 ♗a2 ♘a4 18 ♕e2 ♗xc3 19 ♕xe6 ♖e8 20 ♕f5 ♗xb2-+ Frederick-J.Watson, New York 1981.

10...♘b6 11 ♗b3 ♘bd5

11...♘ed5 12 ♗g5 f6 13 ♗h4 ♖e8 14 ♗g3 ♗xg3 15 hxg3 ♗e6 16 ♕d2 ½-½ was Neubauer-Borges Mateos, Santa Clara 2002.

12 h3 ♗f5

12...♕b6!? 13 ♗c2 f6 keeps things complicated.

13 ♘e4 ♗xe4 14 ♖xe4 ½-½ Leko-Varga, Budapest 1993.

I prefer Black here after 14...♕c7 and ...♖ad8, but it's a matter of taste.

5.3 4 ♗d3

Formerly the main move and certainly an important one. Here an old semi-arranged draw used to continue 4...♗d6 5 ♘e2 ♘e7 6 0-0 0-0 7 ♗f4 ♗f5 or something similar. I recommend lines which immediately break the symmetry. This section is mostly unchanged from earlier editions, as I see no major changes in the theory.

4...♘c6

One of the main reasons that 4 ♘f3 has been replacing 4 ♗d3 is the move 4...c5, against which White hasn't succeeded in finding any edge.

White's problem is that the bishop on d3 is not placed effectively for play against an isolated pawn. I will treat these lines briefly, since nothing much has occurred since the last edition:

(a) 5 ♕e2+ ♗e7 6 dxc5 ♘f6 7 ♘f3 0-0 8 0-0 ♗xc5 9 ♗g5 ♘c6 10 ♘bd2 h6 11 ♗h4 ♗g4 12 ♖fe1 g5! 13 ♗g3 ♘h5∓ Mantovani-King, Lugano 1989;

(b) 5 c3 ♘c6 6 ♘f3 (6 ♘e2 c4!? 7 ♗c2 ♗d6= with the idea ...♘ge7) 6...♗d6 7 ♗e3!? c4 and 8 ♗e2 ♗f5= or 8 ♗c2 ♗g4=;

(c) 5 ♘f3 ♘c6 6 ♕e2+ ♗e7 7 dxc5 ♘f6 8 h3?! 0-0 9 0-0 ♗xc5 10 c3 ♖e8 11 ♕c2 ♕d6! 12 ♘bd2? ♕g3! 13 ♗f5? (13 ♘g5!∓) 13...♖e2-+ Tatai-Korchnoi, Beersheva 1978;

(d) 5 dxc5 (the main move) 5...♗xc5 6 ♘f3 ♘f6 (or 6...♘e7) 7 0-0 0-0 8 ♘bd2 (8 ♗g5 ♘c6 9 ♘c3 ♗e6=) 8...♘c6 9 ♘b3 ♗b6 10 c3 ♗g4 11 ♗e2 ♕d6= Moldobayev-Orlov, Belgorod 1989.

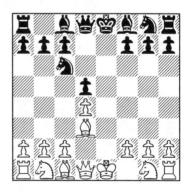

5 c3

5 ♘f3 ♗g4 6 c3 ♗d6 transposes. 5 ♘e2 is natural and can't be bad, but Black can play aggressively by 5...♗g4 (or 5...♗d6) and:

(a) 6 c3 ♗d6!? 7 ♕b3 ♘ge7 8 ♘a3!? (8 ♕xb7 ♖b8 9 ♕a6 0-0 10 0-0 ♖b6 11 ♕a4 ♘g6 followed by ...♕h4) 8...a6 9 f3 ♗f5! 10 ♗xf5 ♘xf5 11 0-0 0-0 12 ♕c2 ♕f6∓ Lau-J.Watson, Philadelphia 1978;

(b) 6 f3 ♗h5 7 c3 (7 ♘f4 ♗g6; 7 ♘g3 ♕h4 8 0-0 ♗d6 9 ♕e1+ ♔d7! 10 f4 ♖e8 planning ...♘f6-g4) 7...♗d6 8 ♗f4 (8 0-0 ♕f6!? or 8...♗g6 with the idea 9 f4 f5! and ...♘f6-e4) 8...♘ge7 9 0-0 ♗g6 10 ♗xd6 ♕xd6 11 f4?! (11 ♘a3 0-0-0 12 ♕d2 h5!? 13 ♘f4 ♗f5 14 ♗xf5+ ♘xf5 15 ♘d3 a6 16 ♘c2 h4= Lenic-Karer, Kranj 2001) 11...♕e6! 12 ♖f3 ♘f5 (12...♗h5!) 13 ♔f2 ♘d6 14 ♖e3 ♗e4 15 ♘g3 f5∓ Sollid-J.Watson, Gausdal 1981.

A particularly mischievous move is 5 ♗b5, which transposes into a Winawer with colours reversed (White has wasted a move)! As we show in the line 3 ♘c3 ♗b4 4 exd5 exd5, this is objectively equal, with chances for both sides (Black must be careful not to overextend).

5...♗d6 6 ♘f3

(a) 6 ♘e2 ♕h4! (6...♗g4 is often played; and Alekhine suggested 6...♕f6!?, for example, 7 0-0 ♘ge7 8 ♘d2 ♗f5 9 ♘f3 ♗xd3 10 ♕xd3 h6 planning ...0-0-0 and a kingside attack)

Here there are some fascinating ideas:

(a1) 7 ♘g3 ♘h6!? (7...♗g4!) 8 ♗xh6 ♕xh6 9 0-0 ♘e7∓ Westerinen-Kavalek, Solingen 1986;

(a2) 7 g3 with:

(a21) 7...♕h3 8 ♘f4 ♗xf4 9 ♗xf4 ♕g2?! (9...♘f6 10 ♕e2+ ♔d8 unclear) 10 ♕e2+! ♗e6 (10...♔d8 11 ♕f1) 11 ♕f1 ♕xf1+ 12 ♖xf1 0-0-0 13 ♘a3! ♗h3 14 ♖g1 ♖e8+ 15 ♔d2‡;

(a22) 7...♕h5 8 ♗f4 (8 ♘f4 ♕xd1+ 9 ♔xd1 ♘f6 10 ♖e1+ ♘e7∓ Apsenieks-Alekhine, Buenos Aires 1939, or 9...♗g4+=) 8...♗g4 (8...♗xf4 9 ♘xf4 ♕xd1+ 10 ♔xd1 ♗g4+= – McDonald). I called 8...♗g4 clearly better for Black, but Justin Horton points out the line 9 ♗xd6 cxd6 10 ♕b3!. Then 10...0-0-0 11 ♘f4 ♖e8+ 12 ♔d2 ♕h6! (with the idea ...♘f6-h5) is interesting but hardly a clear advantage for Black: 13 ♔c2! (13 ♕xd5? ♘f6 14 ♕b5 a6 15 ♕c4 ♗f3∓; 13 ♘a3? ♘f6! and 14 h4? ♘h5 or 14 ♔c2 ♗f3 15 ♖hf1 g5 16 ♘b5 gxf4 17 ♘xd6+ ♔c7 18 ♘xe8+ ♖xe8-+) 13...♘f6 14 ♘d2 ♔b8 15 h3 ♖c8! 16 ♕a4 ♗d7 unclear;

(a3) 7 ♘d2 ♗g4 (several readers and players have discussed this line, and some of the material is based upon that discussion; thanks to all) 8 ♕c2 (8 ♕b3 0-0-0 9 ♕xd5 ♘f6∓ – Alekhine) 8...♘f6 (8...0-0-0 9 ♘f1, and Black is better after either 9...♘f6 or 9...g6 10 ♗e3 ♘ge7 11 0-0-0 ♗f5 12 ♘eg3 ♗xd3 13 ♖xd3 h6∓ Alekhine-Winter, Nottingham 1936) 9 ♘f1 0-0 10 ♗e3 ♗h5 11 ♘eg3?! ♗xg3 12 ♘xg3 ♗g6 13 h3 ♖ae8 14 ♘f1 ♗xd3 15 ♕xd3 ♘e4∓ Ledwon-Bednarski, Poland 1975;

(b) 6 ♕f3 ♘f6!? (6...♗e6 is a solid alternative, or 6...♘ce7 7 ♗f4 ♘f6 8 ♘e2 ♗g4 9 ♕g3 ♗xe2 10 ♗xe2 ♗xf4 11 ♕xf4 0-0 12 ♗d3 ♘g6 13 ♗xg6 ♖e8+ 14 ♔d1 hxg6∓ Lazic-Kosten, Varallo 1991) 7 ♗g5 (7 h3 0-0 8 ♘e2 ♖e8 9 ♗g5 ♗e7 10 ♗e3 ♘e4! 11 ♗xe4 dxe4 12 ♕xe4 ♘b4!∓ Malanyuk-Psakhis, Moscow 1983) 7...♗g4 8 ♕xg4! (J.Horton's suggestion; 8 ♗xf6? ♗xf3 9 ♗xd8 ♗xg2-+; 8 ♕e3+?! ♔d7! 9 ♘e2 ♖e8∓) 8...♗xg4 9 ♗xd8 ♔xd8 (9...♖xd8 10 ♘f3 0-0 11 0-0=) 10 ♘f3 ♖e8+ 11 ♔f1 ♘f6 (11...g6 12 g3 ♔d7 13 ♘bd2 f5 14 ♔g2=) 12 g3 ♘e4 13 ♘bd2 f5 14 ♔g2 ♔d7 15 ♖ae1=.

6...♗g4

6...♘ge7 usually transposes.

7 0-0 ♘ge7

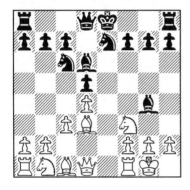

8 ♖e1

(a) 8 ♗g5 ♕d7 9 ♘bd2 f6 10 ♗e3 (10 ♗h4?! 0-0-0∓ intending ...♘f5 and, e.g., ...g5, ...h5-h4 is a position where Black's attack plays itself) 10...0-0-0 11 c4 (11 ♕a4 ♔b8 12 b4? ♗xf3 13 ♘xf3 ♘xd4∓ Trzaska-Koepf, Bundesliga 1988; 11 b4 ♖dg8 12 ♘b3 ♘d8! with the idea 13 ♘c5 ♕e8∓, when Black covers a4 and threatens the move ...♕h5) 11...♘b4!? (11...dxc4! 12 ♘xc4 ♔b8 13 ♘xd6 ♕xd6∓) 12 ♗e2 dxc4 13 ♘xc4 ♘bd5 14 ♕b3 ♗e6!? 15 ♖fc1 ♔b8 16 ♘fd2 ♘f4 17 ♗f3 ♗d5 18 ♘e4 ♘e2+!∓ Marcal-J.Watson, St Paul 1982;

(b) 8 h3!? ('inaccurate' – Psakhis) 8...♗h5 9 ♖e1 ♕d7 10 ♘bd2 0-0-0 (or 10...0-0!?, since 11 ♗xh7+? ♔xh7 12 ♘g5+ ♔g6 doesn't work) 11 ♘f1 (11 ♕c2!? ♖de8 12 b4 ♗g6 13 ♘b3 ♗xd3

14 ♕xd3 ♕f5=). What follows comes from a newsgroup discussion: 11...f6 12 ♘g3 ♗g6 13 ♕c2 (13 ♗f1 h5) 13...♗xd3 14 ♕xd3 h5!? (14...♗xg3! 15 fxg3 ♘f5 16 g4 ♘d6, analysis by C.Schulien) 15 ♘h4 g5! (15...♗xg3 16 fxg3 g5 17 ♘g6 Hagerty-Jeffrey, Parsippany 1996) 16 ♘hf5 (16 ♘g6 ♖h6 17 ♘xe7+ ♘xe7 18 h4 ♖g8 with good play) 16...♗xg3 17 ♘xe7+ ♘xe7 18 fxg3 g4 unclear – Mannien.

8...♕d7 9 ♘bd2

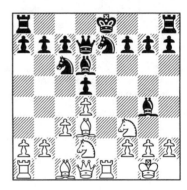

This one of the recurring positions of the French Exchange Variation.

9...0-0-0

An all-out move. Also perfectly good is 9...0-0 10 h3 ♗f5 11 ♘f1 ♖ae8 as in Tal-Korchnoi, USSR 1955, when White tried 12 ♗xf5!? (12 ♗g5= – ECO; but I think Black is slightly better here also, for example, 12...h6 13 ♗h4 ♘g6 14 ♗g3 ♘f4) 12...♕xf5 (12...♘xf5!?) 13 ♘e3 ♕d7 14 ♗d2 ♘d8 15 ♕c2 c6∓.

10 b4 ♘g6

10...♖de8 11 b5 ♘d8 12 ♕a4 ♔b8 13 ♗a3 f6 also worked well for Black in Kholmov-Psakhis, Kiev 1984.

11 ♘b3

11 b5!? ♘ce7 and Black is well off; a typical line was 12 ♕a4 ♔b8 13 ♗a3 (13 ♘e5 ♗xe5 14 dxe5 f6!) 13...♘f4 (13...♗xa3 14 ♕xa3 f6, e.g.,

15 ♖ab1?! ♖he8 16 ♖b4 ♘f4 17 ♖a4 ♘c8∓) 14 ♗f1 f6! 15 ♗c5 ♘c8∓ Z.Nik-olic-Barlov, Yugoslavia 1986.

11...♖de8

A position from Spielmann-Mar-oczy, Sliac 1932. It is easy for White to go wrong here, although equality seems the fair result. The obvious 12 ♗d2? fails to 12...♘h4 13 ♗e2 ♖xe2! 14 ♕xe2 ♗xf3 15 gxf3 ♕h3. A better line is 12 ♗e3! ♘h4!? 13 ♗e2 ♘f5 14 ♗d2 ♖xe2!? 15 ♕xe2 ♘h4 Havski-Vladimirov, USSR 1956. This is given as unclear in ECO. The only defense to ...♗xf3 and ...♕h3 is 16 b5!, when 16...♘b4!? (16...♗xf3? 17 bxc6 holds due to the counterattack) 17 ♘e5! (17 cxb4 ♗xf3 18 gxf3 ♕h3-+) 17...♗xe2 18 ♘xd7 ♘c2 19 ♖xe2 ♘xa1 20 ♘dc5 ♘xb3 21 axb3 ♘f5 leaves no advantage for either side.

Objectively, the Exchange Varia-tion is of course equal. But we have seen that there is ample leeway for the stronger player to outthink his opponent and win. This is all we can ask for from any opening.

Chapter Six

Tarrasch Variation: Introduction and 3...c5

1 e4 e6 2 d4 d5 3 ♘d2

With apologies for the digression, here are some general remarks that could be of particular importance to the readers of previous editions. After many years of modern practice with the Tarrasch Variation, I feel that theory has coalesced enough to come to some general conclusions. First, it will come as no surprise that 3 ♘d2 does not threaten the survival of the French Defence. The knight on d2 exerts no pressure on d5 and to some extent gets in the way of the development of White's other pieces. Leading players are using the Tarrasch Variation much less than 3 ♘c3 and only somewhat more often than 3 e5. On the other hand, it is equally clear that 3 ♘d2 is a solid continuation which, if handled well, does not expose White to great risk and gives some prospects for advantage. How does theory stand? It now seems to me that all of Black's most popular responses either equalise or stay within the bounds of a normal small edge for White; none, however, is clearly preferable. Since choosing a system (or two) against the Tarrasch

is among the most important decisions that a French player is faced with, let me briefly try to characterize the main options:

(a) 3...c5 4 exd5 exd5 has a long history of being safe, and it hovers near theoretical equality. Players like Bareev, Short, Vaganian and Dreev have been holding their own and reaching that equality in the line 5 ♗b5+ ♗d7 (or 5 ♘gf3 ♘f6 6 ♗b5+ ♗d7), but it offers few winning chances between opponents of equal strength and is hardly attractive to the average player;

(b) 3...dxe4 (also played via 3 ♘c3 dxe4) is popular among the world's leading players at the moment (compare the related lines in Chapter 14). This is also in the 'safe but dull' category;

(c) the variation from the previous two books, 3...♘f6 4 e5 ♘fd7, is still going strong, but I feel that the theory now runs too deeply to present in a repertoire. Not only are the lines forcing, but most readers will prefer something requiring less memorisation. I'm also not excited about repeating most of the same material from the previous edition, but those who wish to use 3...♘f6 can use it as a base from which to work.

One can also choose 3...♘c6 and 3...a6 to meet the Tarrasch, but they are marginal moves that have never become completely respectable. For this book, I have chosen two other systems. This chapter examines an ambitious variation from the previous editions, 3...c5 4 exd5 ♕xd5. There is still much to be discovered here. In the next chapter, a repertoire is offered with 3...♗e7, a fascinating move that is far from being understood, much less worked out. It is a leading defence at present and has thus far proven impervious to White's assaults.

1 e4 e6 2 d4 d5 3 ♘d2 c5

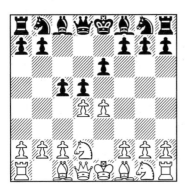

Black's philosophy here is to break up the centre immediately even at the cost of some time. This frustrates White's attempt to cramp Black (by e5), and in our main line leads to a Sicilian-like position in which Black hopes that his central majority will counteract White's his superior development. Those are essentially positional considerations but in practice the play can be rather sharp. White has two main replies:

6.1 4 ♘gf3
6.2 4 exd5

Others are relatively rare:

(a) 4 ♗b5+ ♘c6 5 exd5?! (5 ♘gf3 cxd4 6 ♘xd4 ♗d7 transposes to 4 ♘gf3) 5...♕xd5 6 ♘gf3 cxd4 7 ♗c4 Valenti-Huss, Lugano 1980. White is a full tempo down (♗b5-c4) on the main line. Most ambitious is 7...♕c5!? (7...♕d6) 8 ♕e2 e5 9 ♘g5 ♘h6 10 ♘ge4 ♕e7;

(b) 4 dxc5 ♗xc5 (more active than 4...♘f6 5 exd5 ♕xd5= Bronstein-Khasin, Kislovodsk 1968, with the idea 6 ♘b3 ♕xd1+ 7 ♔xd1 ♘a6!=) 5 ♗d3 (5 ♘b3 ♗b6 6 ♗b5+ ♘c6 7 exd5 exd5 with an ideally active isolated IQP position, since Black's bishop came to c5 in one move: 8 a4 ♘ge7 9 ♘e2 0-0 10 0-0 ♗g4∓ Bronstein-Makarichev, Reykjavik Open 1990) 5...♘f6 (or 5...♘c6) 6 ♕e2 (6 e5 ♘fd7 7 ♕g4 and 7...0-0 8 ♘gf3 ♕c7 or 7...♘xe5!? 8 ♕xg7 ♘xd3+ 9 cxd3 ♖f8 10 ♘gf3 ♘d7 11 ♕xh7 ♕f6 12 ♕h4 ♕g6 with compensation, Feldman-Botvinnik, Leningrad 1931) 6...♘c6 7 ♘gf3 0-0 and we have arrived at a position with Black a full tempo ahead of the corresponding line with 3...♗e7 4 ♗d3 c5 5 dxc5 etc. as described in the next chapter. This makes life easy:

(b1) 8 e5?! 8...♘g4 9 0-0 f6 10 ♘b3 (but 10 exf6 ♘xf6 is comfortable and at least equal; also possible is 10...♕xf6 11 ♘b3 ♗b6) 10...♗xf2+ 11 ♖xf2 ♘xf2 12 ♕xf2 fxe5∓ Landenbergue-Huss, Silvaplana 1993;

(b2) 8 0-0 ♕c7 (or 8...♗b6!) 9 e5 (9 c3 ♗b6) 9...♘g4 10 ♗xh7+ (10 ♘b3 ♗b6 11 ♗xh7+ ♔xh7 12 ♘g5+ ♔g8 13 ♕xg4 ♘xe5 14 ♕h5 ♕xc2) 10...♔xh7 11 ♘g5+ ♔g8 12 ♕xg4 ♕xe5 13 ♕h5 ♕f5∓;

(c) 4 c3 is played more often than it should be. Among several answers Black has 4...cxd4 (or 4...♞c6 5 ♞gf3 cxd4) 5 cxd4 ♞c6 6 ♞gf3 (6 exd5? ♛xd5 wins a pawn) 6...♛b6! (more pointed than 6...dxe4 7 ♞xe4 ♝e7 8 ♝d3 ♞f6=) 7 exd5 (7 ♛a4?! ♝d7 threatens ...♞b4 and ...♜c8: 8 ♝b5 dxe4 9 ♞xe4 a6∓ Suechting-Alekhine, Carlsbad 1911) 7...exd5 8 ♞b3 (8 ♛b3 ♛xb3 9 ♞xb3 ♞f6 10 a3 ♝d6 11 ♝d3 0-0 12 0-0 ♝g4∓ Hedenstroem-Nygren, Skelleftea 1999) 8...♝g4!∓ (only 8...♞f6 has been seen here) 9 ♝e2 ♞f6 10 0-0 ♝d6 11 h3 ♝xf3 12 ♝xf3 0-0 and as so often in these opposing d-pawn positions, the knights are better than White's bishops.

6.1 4 ♞gf3

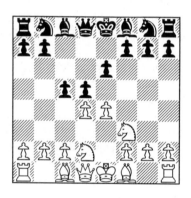

This is a common choice. White wishes to sidestep our main line, since now 4...♞c6 5 exd5 ♛xd5 6 ♝c4 ♛d6? loses its point after 7 ♞e4. But Black has two good answers:

4...cxd4

4...♞f6 is also fine:

a) 5 ♝b5+ ♝d7 6 ♝xd7+ ♞bxd7 7 e5 ♞e4 8 ♞xe4 dxe4 9 ♞g5 cxd4 10 ♛xd4 ♛a5+ 11 ♝d2 ♛xe5= Van der Wiel-P.Nikolic, Lucerne 1989;

b) 5 e5 ♞fd7 6 c3 ♞c6 7 ♝d3 ♝e7 transposes to 3 ♞d2 ♝e7 4 ♞gf3 ♞f6

5 e5 ♞fd7 (5...♞e4!?) 6 ♝d3 c5 7 c3 ♞c6, and here Black also has the popular options 7...g6 and 7...♛b6 8 0-0 g6;

c) 5 exd5 ♞xd5 (5...exd5 6 ♝b5+ ♝d7 7 ♝xd7+ ♞bxd7 8 0-0 ♝e7 9 dxc5 ♞xc5 10 ♞b3 ♞ce4 has held up well recently: 11 ♞bd4 ♛d7 and 11 ♞fd4 ♛d7 12 f3 ♞d6 13 ♞c5 ♛c7 14 ♞d3 0-0 15 ♔h1 ♜fe8 M.Pavlovic-Bukal, Saint Vincent 2002) 6 ♞b3 (6 c4 ♞f6 7 ♞b3, and best seems 7...♞a6!? – Psakhis; 6 ♞e4 can be met by 6...cxd4 7 ♞xd4 and 7...♝e7 or 7...a6 intending ...e5; Black also has 6...♞d7; finally, Black can answer 6 dxc5 by 6...♝xc5 7 ♞e4 ♝e7 8 c4 ♞b4!= or by 6...♞d7 7 c4 ♞5f6 8 ♞b3 ♛c7 9 ♝e3 ♞xc5=) 6...♞d7 (or 6...cxd4 7 ♞bxd4 ♝e7, e.g., 8 g3 0-0 9 ♝g2 ♞c6 10 ♞xc6 bxc6 11 0-0 ♝a6 12 ♜e1 ♝f6= Djuric-Uusi, Tallin 1981) 7 c4 (7 ♝g5 ♝e7 8 ♝xe7 ♛xe7 9 ♝b5 cxd4 10 ♛xd4 0-0 11 0-0-0 a6= Pavlovic-Short, Catalan Bay 2003) 7...♞5f6 8 dxc5 (8 ♝e2 ♝e7 9 0-0 0-0 10 ♝f4 b6 11 ♞e5 ♝b7 12 ♝f3 ♛c8= Arnason-Gulko, Groningen 1990) 8...♛c7 9 g3 ♞xc5 10 ♝g2 ♞xb3 11 ♛xb3 ♝d6= Belyavsky-P.Nikolic, Barcelona 1989.

5 ♞xd4

Here 5 exd5 ♛xd5 would be the main line of the chapter.

5...♞f6

5...♞c6 is often played as well. The most critical line is 6 ♝b5 (6 ♞xc6 bxc6 is solid; after 7 ♝d3 Black has several moves but I like 7...♞f6 8 ♛e2 [8 e5 ♞d7 transposes to the main line note to White's 8th] 8...♝e7 9 0-0 0-0 10 e5 ♞d7 11 ♞f3 ♝b7= with the idea ...♞c5 or ...c5) 6...♝d7 7 ♞xc6 bxc6 (or 7...♝xc6 8 ♝xc6+ bxc6 9 c4 ♝c5!? 10 ♛a4 ♞e7 11 exd5 exd5 12 ♞b3 ♝b6 13 0-0 0-0= Pixton-Gulko, Seattle 2003) 8 ♝d3 ♝d6 (no one has tried my suggestion 8...♕b8!? with the idea 9 ♕e2 ♗d6 10 ♘f3 ♘e7 11 e5 ♗c7) 9 ♕e2 (but the similar 9 0-0 ♕b8! 10 h3 ♘e7 was tried in Pert-Levitt, Telford 2003; Black has no problems, especially since 11 ♘f3 can be answered by 11...e5!) 9...♘e7 10 e5 (10 ♘f3 ♘g6!=) 10...♗c7! 11 0-0 ♘g6 12 ♘f3 f6 13 ♗xg6+ (13 exf6 ♕xf6 14 ♘g5 e5) 13...hxg6 14 ♗f4?! g5 15 ♗g3 f5!∓.

Let's return to the position after 5...♘f6:

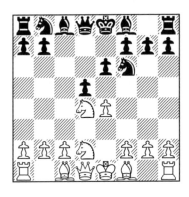

6 e5

The only dangerous move.

(a) 6 ♗b5+ ♗d7 7 ♗xd7+ ♘bxd7 8 exd5 ♘xd5 9 0-0 ♗e7 10 c4 ♘5f6 11 b3 ♘c5= Chiburdanidze-Luther, Graz 1991;

(b) 6 ♗d3 ♗c5 7 ♘4b3 dxe4 (7...♗b6!?) 8 ♘xc5 exd3 9 ♘xd3 0-0 10 0-0 ♘c6= Mi.Tseitlin-Teske, Polanica Zdroj 1988;

(c) 6 exd5 ♘xd5 (6...♕xd5!? 7 ♘b5 ♘a6 8 ♘c4 ♕xd1+ 9 ♔xd1 ♗c5 – Adams; this looks nice for Black, e.g., 10 ♘cd6+ ♔e7 11 ♘xc8+ ♖axc8 with the ideas ...♗xf2, ...♘g4 and ...♘b4) 7 ♘2f3 ♗e7 8 ♗d3 (8 ♗e2 a6!= planning ...♕c7 Eingorn-Dreev, Lucerne 1993) 8...♘d7 9 c4 ♘5f6= Scherzer-Remlinger, New York 1991.

6...♘fd7 7 ♘2f3

Not 7 f4? ♘xe5! 8 ♘xe6?! (8 fxe5 ♕h4+) 8...♗xe6 9 fxe5 ♘c6 10 ♘f3 ♗c5∓.

7...♘c6 8 ♗b5!?

8 ♘xc6 bxc6 9 ♗d3 ♗a6! 10 0-0 ♗xd3 11 ♕xd3 ♗e7 12 c4 0-0= Svidler-Dreev, Rostov 1993; and 8 ♗f4 ♕b6! is at least equal.

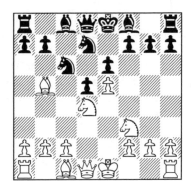

8...♕b6!

This is more straightforward than 8...♕c7!? 9 0-0 a6 (9...♗e7!?) 10 ♘xc6 bxc6 11 ♗a4 which has arisen in several games and seems very slightly in White's favour.

9 c3

(a) 9 ♗e3 ♘xd4 10 ♘xd4 ♗c5!? (or 10...a6 11 ♗xd7+ ♗xd7∓) 11 ♕g4 ♗xd4 12 ♗xd7+ ♗xd7 13 ♗xd4 ♕b4+!∓;

(b) 9 0-0 ♘xd4! (9...♗c5 has equalised in several games) 10 ♘xd4 ♗c5 11 ♗e3 transposes to note 'a'.

9...♗c5

9...♘xd4!? is still reasonable in view of 10 ♘xd4 (10 ♗xd7+ ♗xd7 11 ♘xd4 ♗c5 12 ♕g4 0-0-0!) 10...♗c5 11 ♗a4 (11 ♕a4 a6 12 ♗d3 0-0) 11...0-0 12 f4 f6! 13 exf6 ♘xf6 with a healthy counterattack.

After 9...♗c5, a possible line is 10 ♕a4 0-0! 11 ♗xc6 bxc6 12 ♕xc6 ♗xd4 13 ♘xd4 ♘xe5!∓, because 14 ♕xa8?? ♗a6 15 ♕xf8+ ♔xf8 is hopeless for White.

6.2 4 exd5 ♕xd5

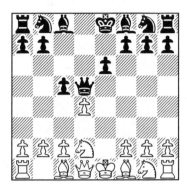

This line was obscure when I chose it for the first edition. Now 4...♕xd5 may well be the most popular line of the Tarrasch! Thus one can no longer expect any surprise value from the queen recapture; but on the bright side 4...♕xd5 has survived all challenges and the fact that so many of the world's top players use this system is an indication of its essential soundness. Black intends, by trading his c-pawn for White's d-pawn, to end up with an extra centre pawn. This is as if, in an Open Sicilian Defense, he had played ...d5 and replied to exd5 with a piece capture. As in the Sicilian, violent White attacks are possible, based on superior development, but Black's structural advantage can give him a long-term edge.

5 ♘gf3

The only serious alternative is 5 dxc5 ♗xc5 6 ♘gf3 ♘f6 and:

(a) 7 ♗d3 ♘c6 (7...0-0 8 ♕e2 ♘bd7 9 ♘e4 b6 10 ♘xc5 ♕xc5 11 ♗e3 ♕c7 12 ♗d4 ♗b7 13 0-0-0 ♘c5!= Kasparov-Anand, Reggio Emilia 1992) 8 ♕e2 ♘b4! 9 ♗b5+ ♗d7 10 ♗xd7+ ♘xd7 11 ♘e4 ♖c8 12 0-0 ♗e7= Chow-Remlinger, Chicago 1992;

(b) 7 ♗c4 ♕c6! 8 0-0 0-0 9 ♕e2 a6 10 ♘e5 ♕c7 11 ♘df3 b5 12 ♗d3 ♗b7=

Kudryashov-Petrosian, Moscow 1967. **5...cxd4 6 ♗c4 ♕d6**

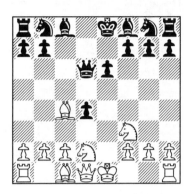

The trademark move of Black's system. The queen covers e5, prevents ♗f4, and keeps the back rank clear for rapid development; one might note that the older move 6...♕d8 did none of these things, although it sometimes transposed if ...♕c7 followed.

7 0-0

A common oversight is 7 ♘b3? ♕b4+ (8 ♘bd2 ♘c6 and White has lost time).

7 ♕e2!? has taken a leap popularity recently, especially since the main lines below have proven satisfactory for Black. White's main idea is to get a rook to d1 quickly in order to capture on d4 with more effect. The move ♘e4 can be useful, and the bishop on c4 won't necessarily lose a tempo if and when Black plays the move ...♕c7:

(a) 7...♘f6 8 ♘b3 ♘c6 9 ♗g5

(see following diagram)

This is an important position these days. Black's solutions are relatively unexplored; I particularly like the alternative idea in the recent game in 'a2':

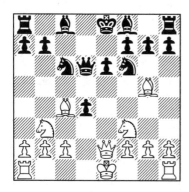

(a1) 9...a6!? 10 0-0-0 b5 11 ♗d3 ♗e7 is rather loose, but if Black gets ...♗b7 in he will be ideally active:

(a11) 12 ♔b1?! ♗b7 13 ♘fxd4 ♘xd4 14 ♘xd4 ♗d5! 15 ♘f3 0-0 16 h4 b4 17 ♘e5= Illescas Cordoba-Rustemov, Mondariz 2002;

(a12) 12 ♘bxd4 may be best, e.g., 12...♘xd4!? 13 ♘xd4 ♕d5 14 ♗xf6 ♗xf6 15 ♔b1 and 15...♗xb7 16 ♘xb5 or 15...♕c5 16 ♗e4 ♖a7 17 ♗c6+ with the idea 17...♗d7 18 ♘xe6!. Black should try 12...♗b7;

(a13) 12 ♖he1 ♗b7 (12...♕c7 13 ♘bxd4 ♘xd4 14 ♘xd4 ♗b7=) 13 ♘bxd4 ♘xd4 14 ♘xd4 ♗d5=;

(a2) 9...♕b4+! is a logical and apparently effective new move from Adams-Akopian, Enghien les Bains 2003: 10 ♗d2 (10 ♘fd2 ♗e7 11 0-0 0-0 12 a3 ♕b6) 10...♕b6 (now the queen won't be exposed down the d-file after 0-0-0) 11 0-0-0 ♗d7 12 ♗g5 ♗c5!? 13 ♔b1 (13 ♗xf6 gxf6 14 ♕e4 f5 15 ♕h4 ♗e7∓, e.g., 16 ♕h6 0-0-0 17 ♘bxd4 ♘xd4 18 ♘xd4 ♖hg8!? 19 ♕xh7 ♗f6!; 13 ♘e5 ♘xe5 14 ♕xe5 ♗e7=) 13...0-0-0?! (13...h6 14 ♗f4 0-0∓) 14 ♘e5! ♘xe5 15 ♕xe5 ♗d6 16 ♕e2 (16 ♕xd4 ♕xd4 17 ♘xd4 h6 18 ♗xf6 gxf6=) 16...h6=;

(a3) 9...♗e7!? (unpinning the e-pawn in the case of ...e5; Black's life

seems slightly difficult after this popular move) 10 0-0-0 e5 11 ♗b5! ♗g4 12 ♕xe5 ♕xe5 13 ♘xe5 ♗xd1 14 ♘xc6 ♗e2! 15 ♗xe2 bxc6 16 ♘xd4 unclear (Firman); White is an exchange down for a pawn but he has two bishops and will likely win another pawn, so I prefer his chances.

(b) For some reason, few players have paid much attention to the unique order 7...♘c6 8 ♘b3 (8 ♘e4 ♕c7 9 0-0 ♘f6 has proven solid in many games, e.g., 10 ♗g5 ♘xe4 11 ♕xe4 ♗d6 12 ♖fe1 0-0 13 ♘xd4!? ♗xh2+ 14 ♔h1 ♘xd4 15 ♕xd4 ♗d6 16 ♖ad1 ♗c5 17 ♕h4 ♗xf2!? 18 ♕xf2 ♕xc4 19 ♗f6! ♕g4 20 ♖d3 S.Pedersen-Ostenstad, Aars 1999, and Black should play 20...gxf6 21 ♖g3 ♕g6 with ...e5 next and a small material advantage), and now 8...a6!. In spite of Black's slow development I see nothing wrong with his position. White will have to waste time to regain the pawn and won't always succeed, e.g., 9 0-0 (9 ♗d2?! b5 10 ♗d3 ♘f6 11 0-0 ♗b7∓ Einvik-Lahlum, Gausdal 1994) 9...♘ge7!? (9...♘f6 10 ♗g5 ♕c7 11 ♖ad1 b5 12 ♗d3 Charbonneau-Sarkar, internet game 2001; and 12...♗e7 13 ♘bxd4 ♘xd4 14 ♘xd4 ♗b7 looks about equal, but there are many options here) 10 ♖d1 b5 11 ♗d3 e5 12 c3 f5 13 ♗c2 ♗e6 14 cxd4 e4 15 ♘g5 ♗c4 with ideas like ...♘b4-d3, ...♘d5, and ...h6/...g5 with ...♗g7. Given some recent White successes with 7 ♕e2, this is an idea worth noting.

7...♘f6

7...♘c6 8 ♘e4!? (8 ♘b3 usually transposes) 8...♕d8 is risky, but perhaps satisfactory. White can vary with 9 ♖e1 or even 9 c3!? dxc3 10 ♘xc3 with compensation.

8 ♘b3

Recently, Kasparov revived the old move 8 ♖e1, but it hasn't really caught on and I'm not sure why. One possible (but untested) solution might be 8...♘c6 (8...♗e7 9 ♘e4 ♘xe4!? 10 ♖xe4 ♘c6 11 ♘xd4 0-0 12 ♗f4 with advantage was Kasparov-Gelfand) 9 ♘e4 ♘xe4 (Rustemov recently tried 9...♕d8!? and achieved a draw) 10 ♖xe4 ♗d7 (to get ...0-0-0 in as fast as possible in some lines) 11 ♗f4 ♕c5 (11...♕b4 12 ♗b3 ♕b6 13 ♘xd4 0-0-0 14 ♗g5! ♖e8 15 ♗e3 ♗c5±) 12 ♗b3 ♗e7 13 ♘xd4 ♗f6=.

8...♘c6

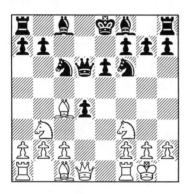

9 ♘bxd4

(a) 9 ♕e2!? risks losing a pawn:

(a1) 9...♗e7 10 ♖d1 e5 is solid: 11 ♗b5 ♗g4 12 ♘bd2 ♘d7 13 h3 ♗xf3 14 ♘xf3 0-0 15 c3 ♗f6 16 ♗e3 Lobron-Henley, Indonesia 1983; and now 16...♖fe8!?∓;

(a2) 9...a6 10 a4?! (10 ♖d1! b5 11 ♗d3 and 11...♗d7 12 c3 ♕c7= or 11...♕c7 12 a4 b4 13 ♗c4 ♗b7 14 ♘bxd4 ♘xd4 15 ♖xd4 ♗c5= Geller-Dolmatov, Moscow 1992) 10...♗e7 11 g3 (11 ♗g5?! e5 12 ♖fe1 ♗g4 13 h3 ♗xf3 14 ♕xf3 0-0∓ Siklosi-Brinck Claussen, Copenhagen 1988) 11...e5 12 ♘g5 0-0 13 f4 Di Lao-Terenzi, corr 1991, and now 13...♗g4! 14 ♘xf7 (14 ♕f2 e4!) 14...♗xe2 15 ♘xd6+ ♗xc4 16

♘xc4 e4∓ – analysis in CCYB#7;

(b) 9 ♖e1 ♗d7 (9...a6 10 a4 ♕c7 11 ♘bxd4 ♗d7 12 ♕e2 ♘xd4 13 ♘xd4 ♗c5 14 ♘b3 ♗d6= Lane-Levitt, British Ch 1987) 10 g3 ♗e7 11 ♗f4 ♕b4 12 ♕d3 ♖c8 (12...0-0 13 ♗c7 ♗d8! 14 a3 ♕e7= Winsnes-Lein, Gausdal 1990) 13 a4 0-0 14 a5 ♗d8 15 ♗d2 ♕d6 16 ♘bxd4 ♘xd4 17 ♘xd4 e5 18 ♘b5 ♕c5= Ljubojevic-P.Nikolic, Tilburg 1987.

9...♘xd4 10 ♘xd4

At this point, White can choose to go into an endgame with 10 ♕xd4

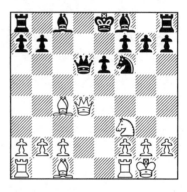

This option is obviously important but has grown less popular by the year. Essentially, White hopes that his slightly freer development (Black's c8 bishop is still restricted) will give him an edge, whereas Black counts upon his 4-3 kingside majority in conjunction with the c-file to equalise and perhaps lead to a long-term Sicilian-like advantage. Indeed, when 4...♕xd5 first hit the scene, Black managed to win several of these endings; later, players of White got their revenge by pressuring the queenside (e.g., by ♗e2-f3, ♗f4, and a4-a5 or ♘b3-a5). Now we know that the ending should be drawn, but also that either player can try for more if his opponent slips up, with White needing to be more careful. Little has essentially changed since the second edition, and Black has three reasonable moves: 10...a6, 10...♕xd4, and 10...♗d7. I believe that all three are playable; but to keep things clear I will limit myself to the latter, which develops quickly: 10...♗d7

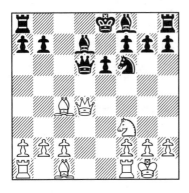

In this position, for what it's worth, Black has a higher performance rating than White! I will try to show correct play:

(a) 11 ♗e3 ♕xd4 (or 11...♖c8) 12 ♗xd4 ♖c8 13 ♘e5! ♗c5 (just for fun, Black can achieve equality by means of the bizarre line 13...♘g4!? 14 ♘xd7 ♖xc4 15 ♖ad1 ♗d6 16 ♗xg7 ♗xh2+ 17 ♔h1 ♖g8 18 ♘f6+ ♘xf6 19 ♗xf6 ♗c7 20 ♖d4! ♖g4!) 14 ♖ad1 ♔e7 (14...♗xd4 15 ♖xd4 ♔e7 16 ♖fd1 ♖hd8=) 15 ♘xd7 ♗xd4 16 ♖xd4 ♖hd8!? (16...♘xd7 17 ♖fd1 ♘e5 18 ♗b3 ♖hd8=) 17 ♖fd1 (17 ♘b6 ♖c6!) 17...♖xd7 18 ♖xd7+ ♘xd7 19 ♗b5 ♘e5 20 c3 a6 21 ♗e2 ♘c4= – Brodsky;

(b) 11 ♗e2 ♕xd4 12 ♘xd4 ♖c8 (12...♗c5=) 13 ♗f3 ♗c5 14 ♘b3 ♗b6 15 c3 (15 ♗xb7 ♖xc2) 15...♗c6=;

(c) 11 ♗f4 ♕xd4 12 ♘xd4 ♖c8 has been well tested:

(c1) 13 ♗b3 ♗c5 (White's bishop bites on granite; how awkward this

position has proven for him is indicated by the 200-point performance rating advantage that Black has here after more than 100 games! 13...♘e4!? was a creative solution in Eismont-Glek, Katowice Open 1993: 14 ♖fd1 ♘c5 15 ♖d2 ♗e7 16 c3 f6!? 17 ♗e3 e5 18 ♘e2 ♘xb3 19 axb3 a6 20 f4 ♗e6∓) 14 ♖ad1 0-0 15 ♖fe1 (15 h3 ♖fd8= 16 c3 ♔f8 17 ♗e3 h6 18 ♘c2?! ♘e4 19 ♗d4 ♗xd4 20 ♖xd4 ♘c5∓ Lindenann-Luther, Boblinger 2000) 15...♖fd8 16 c3 ♗e8 17 ♘c2 a5 18 a3 ♗c6= Ermenkov-Eingorn, St John 1988;

(c2) 13 ♗d3 ♘d5!? (13...♗c5 14 ♘b3 ♗e7 15 ♖fe1? ♘d5 16 ♗d2 ♘b4∓ Tagnon-Lane, France 1989) 14 ♗g3 ♗c5 15 ♘b3 ♗e7 16 c3 0-0= Wikman-Prystenski, corr 1990;

(c3) 13 ♗e2

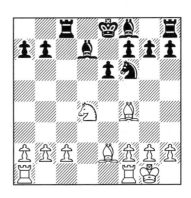

and both Black moves are instructive:

(c31) 13...♗c5 14 ♘b3 ♗b6 15 c4 (15 c3 0-0 16 ♗f3 ♗c6 17 ♗xc6 ♖xc6 18 ♖ad1 ♘d5 19 ♗g3 ♖fc8 ½-½ was the game Sedina-Naumkin, Tunis 2000) 15...♘e4!? 16 ♖ac1 ♔e7 17 ♗f3 ♗c6 18 ♗xe4 ♗xe4 19 ♖fe1 ♗c6 20 c5 ♗c7 21 ♗xc7 ♖xc7 ½-½ Vogt-Hug, Zurich 1999;

(c32) 13...♘d5 14 ♗g3 h5!? (14...♗c5 is common and equal, but this is more exciting; also of note is 14...g5!?, by which Black prepares a possible ...♘f4, as well as ...♗g7, e.g., 15 c3 ♘f4 16 ♖ad1!? ♘xe2+ 17 ♘xe2 f6 18 f4! ♗c5+ 19 ♗f2 gxf4= Jacoby-Weidemann, Bundesliga 1986) 15 c4 (15 h4 ♗c5 16 ♘b3 ♗b6 17 c3 ♘e7! 18 ♗d3 f6! 19 a4 a6 20 ♗d6 e5 21 a5 ♗a7 22 ♗e4 ♗e6∓ Acs-Shaked, Budapest 1997) 15...h4!? (15...♘b6! 16 b3 h4 17 ♗f4 f6) 16 cxd5 hxg3 17 hxg3 e5 18 ♘f3 ♗d6 with two bishops and activity for a pawn, Womacka-Glek, Cattolica 1993.

10 ♘xd4 a6

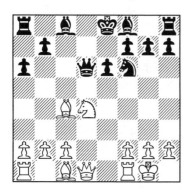

The main position of the 4...♕xd5 variation. Black prevents any tricks on b5 and prepares ...♕c7 and ...♗d6, to catch up on development. He also has the idea of developing the queen's bishop aggressively by ...b5 and ...♗b7. The analogies with the Sicilian continue, as ...a6 is part of the Najdorf, Scheveningen, Taimanov, and other Sicilian variations. From the diagram, White has tried a variety of plans:

6.21 11 ♗b3
6.22 11 c3
6.23 11 b3
6.24 11 ♖e1
Others are less critical:

(a) 11 ♗e3 ♕c7 12 ♗b3 (12 ♕e2 ♗d6 13 h3 b5 14 ♗b3 0-0= was Matanovic-Eliskases, Stockholm 1952) 12...♗d6 13 h3 (13 ♘f3? ♘g4∓; 13 g3 h5!? or 13...b6, which is often better than ...b5 in these positions because the b-pawn isn't subject to attack by a4) 13...0-0 14 c3 (14 ♕f3?? e5! 15 ♘f5 [15 ♘e2 e4] 15...e4 16 ♘h6+ ♔h8−+) 14...e5 (this tends to be safe when ♘c2-e3 is not handy) 15 ♘f3 e4 (15...h6!? intending ...♗f5) 16 ♘d4 ♕e7 17 ♘e2 ♖d8 18 ♕c2 ♗f5= Almasi-Luther, Kecskemet 1993;

(b) 11 a4 ♕c7 (11...♗d7 has also had excellent top-level results) and:

(b1) 12 ♗b3 ♗d6 13 ♘f3 b6 14 ♖e1 0-0 (14...♗b7 is probably more accurate, with a typical line being 15 h3 ♖d8 16 ♕e2 h6 17 c3 0-0) 15 c3 ♗b7 16 h3 ♖ad8= I.Dahl-Lahlum, Asker 1994.

(b2) 12 ♕e2 ♗d6 13 h3 (13 ♘f5 ♗xh2+ 14 ♔h1 ♔f8! 15 ♘g3 h5∓ Van der Wiel-Glek, Tilburg 1994) 13...0-0 14 ♗g5 (14 ♖d1 b6 15 ♗g5 ♗h2+ 16 ♔h1 ♗e5 − now that f4 is not possible − 17 ♖a3 ♗b7 18 ♖e3 ♗f4= Ljubojevic-Hübner, Wijk aan Zee 1988) 14...♘e4! (14...b6 is also fine, since 15 ♗xf6 gxf6 gives Black two bishops and the open g-file, a recurring theme) 15 ♗e3 (15 ♕xe4 ♕xc4∓ with two bishops and ...e5 in store) 15...b6 16 c3 ♗b7∓ Pleyer-Keitlinghaus, Bad Wörishofen 1997;

(c) 11 ♗d3 ♗d7 12 ♘f3 ♕c7 13 ♕e2 ♗d6 14 ♖e1 ♘d5 15 a3 (15 c4 ♘f4 16 ♗xf4 ♗xf4 17 g3 ♗h6 18 ♘e5 g6= with ...0-0 and ...♗g7 to come) 15...♘f4 16 ♗xf4 ♗xf4 17 g3 ♗h6!? 18 ♖ad1 ♖d8 19 ♘e5 g6 20 ♘xd7 was agreed drawn in Berelovich-Borovikov, Ukrainian Ch 2001 in view of the opposite-coloured bishops.

6.21 11 ♗b3

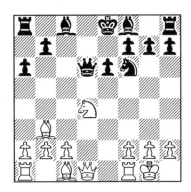

This takes the bishop off the exposed c4 square and waits one move before committing the white pieces to their posts.

11...♕c7 12 ♕f3

12 ♖e1 and 12 c3 transpose to 11 ♖e1 and 11 c3 below, respectively, whereas 12 a4 ♗d6 transposes to the note on 11 a4 above. 12 ♗g5 ♗d6 (or 12...♘e4! 13 ♗e3 ♘c5=, getting rid of the b3 bishop) 13 ♗xf6!? gxf6 14 ♕h5 (14 ♖e1? ♗xh2+ 15 ♔h1 h5!∓ Jansa-Hübner, Bundesliga 1989) 14...♕c5! (This idea pops up throughout the 10...a6 variation. Black will be better in an ending due to his two bishops unless White can use his developmental edge) 15 ♕h4! ♕g5!? 16 ♕e4 ♕f4 17 ♕xf4 ♗xf4 18 ♖ad1 ♗d7 19 g3 ♗c7=, but with slightly better practical chances for Black.

12...♗d6 13 h3

13 ♔h1 0-0 14 ♗g5 ♘d7!? (14...♗e5 15 ♖ad1 ♗d7= looks easier) 15 c3 ♘e5 16 ♕h5 ♘g6 17 ♗c2 h6!? 18 ♘f3 (18 ♗e3 ♘f4 19 ♕f3 Potkin-Rodriguez Guerrero, Linares 2002; and perhaps 19...♗d7 was best, to get developed) 18...b5 19 ♖ad1 ♗f4 20 ♗xf4 ♘xf4 21 ♕e5 ♕xe5 22 ♘xe5 ♗b7 23 f3 ♖fd8= Ivanchuk-Anand, Reggio Emilia 1992.

13...0-0

An important theme appears after

13...♗e5 14 c3 ♗d7 15 ♗g5!? (15 ♗e3 0-0=) 15...♗xd4! 16 cxd4 ♗c6 17 ♕e3 ♘d5= or slightly better, Ernst-Ornstein, Swedish Ch 1980.

14 ♗g5

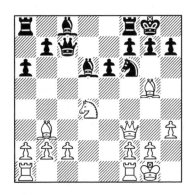

14...b5!?

Ornstein's bold gambit. Black can also equalise by 14...♘d7 15 c3 b5! 16 ♖ad1 (16 ♕xa8? ♗b7 17 ♕xf8+ ♘xf8 18 ♗d1 ♘g6∓ with the idea ...h6, ...♘h4 Ernst-Wiedenkeller, Swedish Ch 1989; 16 ♗c2 ♗b7 17 ♕h5 g6 18 ♕h4 ♗h2+ 19 ♔h1 ♗e5= Djurhuus-Lahlum, Bergen 2000; 16 ♖fe1 ♗b7 17 ♕h5 ♘c5 18 ♗c2 g6 19 ♕h4 ♖fe8 20 ♖e3 ♗d5= Asrian-Savchenko, Ohrid 2001) 16...♘c5 (16...♗b7 17 ♕g4 ♘c5 18 ♗f6 g6 19 ♖fe1 ♘xb3 20 axb3 ♖fe8 21 ♖d3 ♗h2+ 22 ♔h1 ♗f4= M.Adams-Levitt, London 1989) 17 ♗c2 ♗b7 18 ♕h5 ♗e4 19 ♗xe4 ♘xe4= Hellers-Hübner, Wijk aan Zee 1986.

15 ♗xf6

Not 15 ♕xa8? ♗b7 16 ♕xf8+ ♔xf8 because Black's attack continues.

15...gxf6 16 ♕xf6 ♗e5 17 ♕h4 ♗b7 18 c3 ♔h8 19 f4

Heretofore considered a kind of refutation, but Black has been given a new life recently. Instead, 19 ♗c2?! f5 20 ♖ae1 was Nolan-Spiegel, corr 1986; and Black should have played

20...♗h2+! 21 ♔h1 ♕g7 22 f3 ♗g3∓.
19...♖g8 20 ♖f2 ♗d6!

A creative idea of the strong correspondence player John Knudsen. 20...♗xd4?! 21 cxd4 ♖g6 22 f5! exf5 23 d5 was better for White in Yudasin-Ornstein, Trnava 1983.

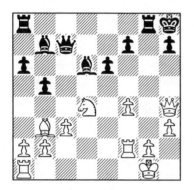

Here's some analysis, with themes that apply to the whole system:

(a) 21 a4 ♖g7 22 axb5? ♖ag8 23 ♕f6 ♗e7 24 ♕e5 ♕xe5 25 fxe5 ♗xg2 and there are no good defences against ...♗f3+ and ideas like ...♗g5-e3;

(b) 21 ♕f6+ ♖g7 22 ♖e1 (22 ♗xe6 ♗e7∓ 23 ♕h6?? ♖g6; 22 g4 ♗e7 23 ♕e5 ♕xe5 24 fxe5 ♗h4 25 ♖ff1 h5 26 ♘f3 ♗g3! 27 g5 ♖ag8∓) 22...♖ag8 23 ♖ee2 (23 g4 ♗e7 24 ♕e5 ♗d6 25 ♕e3!? ♗e7! 26 ♖d1? ♗h4 27 ♖e2 h5∓) 23...♗e7 24 ♕h6 b4! and White is very tied up, e.g., 25 ♖c2? ♕c5!-+ threatening ...♖g6 and answering 26 f5 with 26...♗g5;

(c) 21 ♗c2 ♖g7 22 ♖e1 ♖ag8 23 ♗e4 ♗c8! (preparing ...f5 and ...♗b7; 23...♗xe4 24 ♖xe4 b4!?= contemplates ...♕a5 or ...♕c4) 24 ♖ee2!? (24 ♕f6! ♗e7 25 ♕h6 f5 26 ♗c2 ♖g6 27 ♕h5 ♗c5=) 24...f5 25 ♗c2 ♕f7! (intending ...♗e7) 26 ♖f1 (26 ♗b3?? ♗e7 27 ♕h6 ♖g6) 26...♗b7 27 ♘f3 ♕c7! 28 ♗b3 ♗e4! and f4 is hard to defend, e.g., 29

♘e1 (29 ♘g5 ♗d3!) 29...♗e7 30 ♕h5 ♕c6.

6.22 11 c3

By protecting the knight on d4, White frees his queen to go to f3 or e2, and he awaits developments before committing his other pieces.
11...♕c7
Because 11 c3 is rather slow, 11...♗d7 comes under consideration, e.g., 12 ♕f3 ♕c7 13 ♗b3 ♗d6 14 h3 ♗h2+ (in the same vein, Remlinger suggests 14...0-0 15 ♗g5 ♗h2+ 16 ♔h1 ♗e5! 17 ♖ad1 h6 18 ♗h4 ♖ae8 intending ...♗c8, ...b5, and ...♗b7) 15 ♔h1 ♗e5 16 ♗e3 0-0 17 a4 Larsen-Seirawan, Mar del Plata 1982, and here I proposed 17...b6! 18 ♖ad1 ♖ad8= to be followed by ...♗c8-b7.

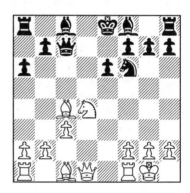

12 ♕e2

(a) 12 ♗d3 ♗d6 13 h3 b6!? (a less aggressive method is 13...♗d7 14 ♕f3 0-0 15 ♗g5 ♗h2+ 16 ♔h1 ♗e5= Tiviakov-Kramnik, USSR 1991) 14 ♕e2 ♗b7 15 a4!? 0-0 16 ♗g5 ♘d5 17 ♖fe1 (17 ♕h5 g6 18 ♕h6 ♗h2+ 19 ♔h1 ♗f4!=) 17...♗f4 (or 17...♘f4!?) 18 ♕g4 ♗xg5 19 ♕xg5 h6 20 ♕h4 ♘f6 21 ♖e3 ♖fd8! 22 ♖ae1 (22 ♖g3 ♔f8=) 22...♖d5! (threatening ...♖h5) and Black stood well in Maahs-Lahlum,

Hamburg 2002;

(b) 12 ♗b3 ♗d6 13 h3 0-0 (or 13...b6) and:

(b1) A standard tradeoff occurred after 14 ♗g5 ♗f4! 15 ♗xf6 gxf6 in Nunn-Speelman, London 1984, with Black's weaknesses compensated by his bishops and g-file: 16 ♕g4+ ♔h8 17 ♕h4 ♗g5 18 ♕h5 ♖g8= 19 ♘f3?! ♗f4 20 ♗c2 ♖g7 21 ♖ad1?! ♗d7∓ intending ...♗c6;

(b2) 14 ♖e1 b5 15 ♗g5 ♗b7 16 ♗c2 (16 ♗xf6 gxf6 17 ♕g4+ ♔h8 18 ♕h4 ♗h2+ 19 ♔h1 ♕f4!=) 16...♘d5 17 ♕h5 g6 18 ♕h4 ♗h2+ 19 ♔h1 ♗f4= M.Adams-Gulko, Groningen 1993.

12...♗d6 13 h3

The alternatives are instructive:

(a) 13 ♔h1 0-0 14 ♗g5 allows the trick 14...♘e4!=;

(b) 13 ♘f3 (watching e5 and often planning to go there) is often White's best idea in these lines. Here are two responses:

(b1) My second edition suggestion was 13...♗d7!? 14 ♗d3 (14 ♖e1 ♗c6 15 ♘e5 ♗e4!∓; 14 ♗g5? ♗c6 15 ♗xf6 gxf6 threatens ...♗xf3, which is hard to meet) 14...♗c6 15 h3 0-0-0 or here 15...0-0 16 ♗g5 ♘d5=;

(b2) 13...0-0 14 ♗g5 ♘d5 (on 14...b5 15 ♗d3 ♘d5, 16 a4± has to be dealt with) 15 ♖ad1 (probably more accurate would be 15 ♖fd1, leaving the idea of a4 open, or 15 ♗d3 with the idea ♕e4) 15...b5! 16 ♗d3 h6 17 ♗c1 Koehn-Lahlum, Goteborg 2000 (by transposition), when Black can equalise by simply 17...♗b7.

13...0-0 14 ♗g5

The most natural move, Others don't do much, e.g.,

(a) 14 ♗d3 ♗h2+ (14...b6!? transposes to the note on 12 ♗d3 above) 15 ♔h1 ♗f4 16 ♕f3 ♗xc1 17 ♖axc1 ♖e8 18 ♖fe1 ♕a5 19 a3 e5= Lansin-

Gurjatinski, USSR 1990;

(b) 14 ♖d1 e5! 15 ♘f3 (15 ♘c2!? b5 16 ♗b3 ♗b7 17 ♘e3) 15...b5 16 ♗b3 ♗b7 17 ♗g5 ♘e4 18 ♗h4 ♖ae8= Jovovic-Bohak, corr 1990.

14...♘e4 15 ♗h4!?

15 ♕xe4 ♕xc4 yields nothing after 16 ♗f4 ♗xf4 17 ♕xf4 ♗d7= Palac-Keitlinghaus, Prague 1990.

15...♘d2!? 16 ♕xd2 ♕xc4= Kosashvili-Holzke, Biel 1989.

In general, 11 c3 is a solid move that doesn't do more than equalise.

6.23 11 b3

This is one of White's better plans: he exerts pressure on the kingside via the long diagonal, protects his bishop on c4, and might in some cases expand on the queenside by ♗d3 and c4.

11...♕c7 12 ♗b2

Sometimes White prefers to delay the fianchetto by 12 ♕e2!?. This is a multipurpose move, keeping a queen out of f4 and contemplating attack by ♘f5 or c4, but keeping the idea ♘f3-e5 in reserve:

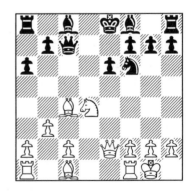

(a) 12...♗c5 13 ♗b2 0-0 14 ♘f3! (14 ♖ad1 b5 15 ♗d3 ♗b7 16 ♘f3 ♕f4! 17 ♘e5 ♕g5∓ Kotronias-Kindermann, Debrecen 1989) 14...b5 15 ♗d3 ♗b7

(15...♕f4!? 16 ♗e5 ♕g4 17 a4!) 16 ♘e5 (16 ♘g5?! ♕c6!) 16...♖ad8 17 a4 (17 ♖ad1 ♗a8! intends ...♕b7) 17...♗d4 18 ♗xd4 ♖xd4 19 axb5 axb5 20 ♖a7 ♕b8 21 ♖fa1 ♗e4 22 ♘f3 ♗xd3 ½-½ Ochsner-Brinck Claussen, Denmark 2000;

(b) 12...♗d6 13 ♘f5!? (13 ♗b2! ♗xh2+ 14 ♔h1 0-0 15 g3!? e5! 16 ♔xh2 exd4 17 ♗xd4=) 13...♗xh2+ 14 ♔h1 0-0 15 ♘xg7! (15 ♗b2? exf5 16 ♗xf6 gxf6 17 g3 Tavcar-Bohak, Bled 2001; and 17...♗xg3 looks good) 15...♗e5! (15...♕e5?! Rubin-Glek, corr 1989; 16 ♗h6! ♕xe2 17 ♗xe2 ♗e5= – Glek, but 18 ♖ad1±) 16 ♗h6 ♗xa1 17 ♖xa1 ♕c5 (17...♖d8 18 ♘h5 ♘xh5 19 ♕xh5 f6 20 ♕h4 ♕f7 21 ♗g5! ♖f8 22 ♗h6 ♖d8 23 ♗g5 ♖f8 ½-½ G.Perez-Pietra, email 2000) 18 ♖d1 b5 19 ♗e3 ♕e5 20 f4 Tsheshkovsky-Stirenkov, Belorechensk 1989; and instead of 20...♘e4 21 fxe5 ♘g3+ 22 ♔h2!±, Black might risk 20...♕c7.

12...♗d6

12...b5 13 ♗d3 ♗d6 transposes.

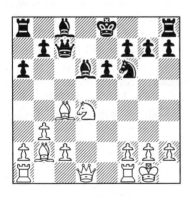

13 ♘f3

(a) 13 h3 b5 14 ♗d3 0-0 15 ♘f3?! ♗b7 16 ♕e2? Tal-Hübner, Brussels 1987; 16...♘h5! 17 ♖fe1 ♘f4 18 ♕e3 ♖ac8∓ with the idea 19 ♖ac1? ♗c5;

(b) 13 ♖e1 0-0 14 ♘f3 b5 15 ♗d3 ♗b7 16 a4 ♖fd8 17 ♕e2 ♗b4! 18 ♖f1

bxa4 19 ♖xa4 a5= Psakhis-Chernin, USSR Ch 1987.

13...b5 14 ♗d3 0-0

Or 14...♗b7 15 ♖e1 0-0 16 ♘e5 ♖ad8 17 ♕e2 ♘d5! 18 ♕g4 f5 19 ♕h4 ♘b4∓ Tiviakov-Psakhis, Rostov 1993.

15 ♖e1

Skrobek-Ornstein, Pamporovo 1981. This improves upon 15 ♗xf6?! gxf6 16 ♕e2 f5 – Ornstein, as well as 15 ♕e2 ♘d5!∓ Kaiszauri-Ornstein, Eksjo 1980, intending 16 ♗xh7+? ♔xh7 17 ♘g5+ ♔g8 18 ♕e4 (18 ♕h5 ♕xc2) 18...f5 19 ♕h4 ♘f6-+.

After 15 ♖e1, Ornstein suggests the ingenious manoeuvre 15...♗b7 16 ♗xf6?! (16 a4) 16...gxf6 17 ♗e4 ♖ad8 18 ♕e2 ♗c8!= The point is that White cannot safely prevent ...f5 and then ...♗b7, e.g. 19 h3 (19 c4 may be best) 19...f5 20 ♗d3 ♗b7 21 a4 (21 ♘e5 ♗b4!) 21...♗b4 22 ♖ed1 ♗c3∓.

6.24 11 ♖e1

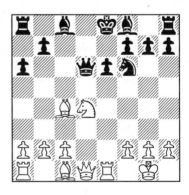

This direct move is by far the most popular among top players. 11 ♖e1 is the most active move and introduces ideas such as ♘f5 or sacrifices on e6. Theory has expanded dramatically since the second edition and this is a line that one should know intimately to get the most out of this 4...♕xd5 repertoire with 10...a6. I will therefore devote a great deal of analysis to it.

11...♕c7

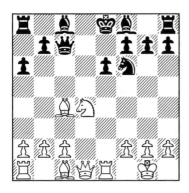

12 ♗b3

(a) 12 ♗d3?! used to be critical but is now considered solved: 12...♗d6 13 ♘f5 (the only ambitious try) 13...♗xh2+ 14 ♔h1 ♔f8 (14...h5? 15 g3± Shamkovich-Seirawan, US Ch 1980) 15 g3 (15 ♘xg7? h5!) 15...exf5 16 ♔xh2 (16 ♗f4 ♕c6+ 17 ♔xh2 ♗e6 18 c3 h5∓ Brindza-Bohak, corr 1989) 16...h5 17 ♗f4 ♕b6 18 ♔g2 ♗e6 19 f3 (19 c4 h4! 20 f3?? hxg3 21 ♗xg3 f4–+) 19...h4 20 ♖h1 ♘d5 21 ♕d2 h3+∓ Geller-Thesing, Dortmund 1992;

(b) 12 ♕e2 has two adequate replies:

(b1) 12...♗c5 13 c3, and although 13...0-0 isn't bad, the direct answer is 13...b5! 14 ♗b3 0-0 15 ♗g5 ♗b7!= – Speelman;

(b2) 12...♗d6 13 ♗g5!? (13 ♘f3 b5 14 ♗d3 ♗b7 15 ♘e5 0-0 16 ♗f4 ♘d5 17 ♗g3 ♘b4 18 ♖ad1 ♖ad8∓ Peters-Lakdawala, Los Angeles 2001) 13...0-0 14 g3 (14 ♗xf6 gxf6 15 ♗d3 ♗xh2+ 16 ♔h1 ♗f4= Emms-Knott, Millfield 2000) 14...♘e4! 15 ♕xe4 ♕xc4 16 ♗f4 ♗xf4 17 gxf4! (17 ♕xf4 f6∓ Van der Wiel-Nogueiras, Rotterdam 1989) 17...♗d7= Tal-Korchnoi, Brussels 1988.

12...♗d6

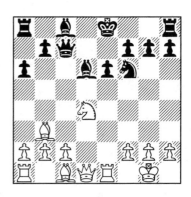

The ambitious move; everything else is slightly worse for Black.

13 ♘f5

This is the critical and most popular move, initiating amazing tactics. Others tend to lose the initiative:

(a) 13 h3!? 0-0 (13...♗f4 is also equal) 14 ♗g5 b5 15 ♗xf6 (15 c3 ♗b7 16 ♗c2 ♘d5!? 17 ♕g4 ♖fe8 18 ♕h4 g6 19 ♗e4 f5=) 15...gxf6 16 ♕h5 ♗b7, and 17 ♕h6 ♗e5! or 17 c3 ♔h8 18 ♕h6 ♖g8 19 ♕xf6+ ♖g7 20 f3 ♖ag8!= (intending ...e5 or ...♗e7 with attack), V.Akopian-Levitt, Groningen 1990;

(b) 13 g3!? 0-0!? (or 13...e5!, e.g., 14 ♗g5 ♗g4 15 f3 ♗h3) 14 ♗g5 b5!? (14...e5 is also thematic; then Furhoff-Backe, Sweden 2001 was drawn after 15 ♗xf6 gxf6 16 ♕f3! exd4 17 ♕xf6. White will get a perpetual check, which Black can force by 17...♕c6) 15 ♗xf6 gxf6 with astonishingly effective counterplay: 16 ♕d2!? (two other ideas are 16 ♕g4+ ♔h8 17 ♕f3 f5 18 ♕xa8 ♗b7 19 ♕xf8+ ♗xf8 20 ♖ad1 ♗a8! 21 f3!?; and 16 ♕f3 ♗e5! 17 ♕xa8 ♗b7 18 ♕xf8+ ♔xf8 19 c3, when 19...a5 20 ♖ac1 ♕b6 looks fully satisfactory for Black) 16...♗e5 17 c3 A.Ivanov-Brunner, Gausdal 1991; here 17...f5!? 18 ♕h6 ♗g7 19 ♕g5 ♔h8 is a reasonable continuation (but not 19...♗b7? 20 ♖xe6!).

13...♗xh2+ 14 ♔h1 0-0

14...♔f8?! was debated for several years until it was found that 15 ♕d4!? was strong, e.g., 15...exf5! 16 ♕xf6! h6! 17 ♕d4 ♗d6 18 ♗d2! threatening ♗c3 and ♗b4.

15 ♘xg7 ♖d8!

Gulko's move. Black cannot counter White's attack after 15...♔xg7? 16 ♕d4! (and even 16 ♕d2 is difficult).

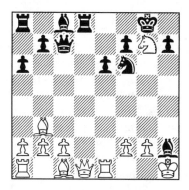

16 ♕f3

(a) Se.Ivanov mentions 16 ♘h5 ♖xd1 17 ♘xf6+ ♔h8 18 ♖xd1 ♗e5 19 ♗g5 ♕e7, but this must favour Black;

(b) 16 ♕e2?! (avoiding ...♗b7 with tempo) hasn't been decisively refuted (although see 'b2'), but isn't worth playing; 16...♔xg7 17 g3 ♗xg3 and:

(b1) 18 ♖g1? (after this White seems too exposed) 18...b5 19 ♖xg3+ ♔h8 20 ♗g5 ♗b7+ 21 ♔h2? (21 ♔g1 ♘e4! 22 ♗xd8 ♖xd8∓) 21...♘e4 22 ♕e3 ♖g8 and Black was winning in Kobalija-Kasimdzhanov, Wijk aan Zee 1998;

(b2) 18 fxg3 allows 3 good but only one possibly decisive move. The try for a kill is 18...♗d7! (18...♕c6+ gives some advantage, e.g., 19 ♔h2 h5!? 20 ♕e5 ♕b5! 21 ♗h6+ ♔g6∓ Mannion-Bryson, Scottish Ch 1993; 18...♕c5 19

♗f4 ♕h5+!? 20 ♕xh5 ♘xh5 21 ♗c7 ♖d7 22 ♗e5+ f6 23 g4 fxe5 24 gxh5 Efler-Grulich, corr 1999, and 24...♖d2∓) 19 ♗f4 (19 ♕e3 ♗c6+ 20 ♔g1 ♘e4! 21 ♕h6+ ♔g8 22 ♗f4 e5 or 22...♕e7) 19...♕a5! (I had HiArcs' help here; 19...♕c5 20 ♗e5 ♗c6+ 21 ♔h2 ♔g6 22 ♗xf6 has been analysed to a draw) 20 ♗e5 ♗c6+ 21 ♔g1 ♖d2! 22 ♕e3! (22 ♕g4+?? ♔f8 23 ♗xf6 ♕c5+; 22 ♗xf6+ ♔xf6 23 ♖f1+ ♔g7 24 ♕g4+ ♔h8 25 ♖f2 ♖g8-+) 22...♔g6 23 ♖e2 ♖ad8!-+.

16...♔xg7

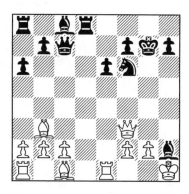

17 ♗h6+

17 g3? is complex but is now established as extremely good for Black. A few lines to illustrate this: 17...b5! 18 ♔xh2 (18 ♗f4? ♗b7 19 ♗xc7 ♗xf3+ 20 ♔xh2 ♘g4+ 21 ♔g1 ♖d2 22 ♖f1 ♖c8 23 ♗a5? ♖c5 0-1 Ye Jiangchuan-Dolmatov, Moscow 1992) 18...♗b7 19 ♕e2 (19 ♗h6+ ♔g6 and now a trick is 20 ♕f4 ♕c5! 21 ♖e5? ♕xe5!, and 20 ♗f4 ♕c8! 21 ♕e2 e5!∓ as given by Lahlum isn't much better; 19 ♕f4 ♕c6! 20 ♖g1 ♖d1! 21 ♗e3 ♖xa1 22 ♕g5+ ♔f8 23 ♕c5+ ♔e8 24 ♕xc6+ ♗xc6 25 ♖xa1 ♘g4+ 26 ♔h3 ♘xe3 27 fxe3 ♖d8∓ Kotronias-Chernin, Munich 1993) 19...♖d4! 20 f4 (20 ♗f4? ♖xf4; 20 f3?! ♖h4+ 21 ♔g2 ♘g4!; 20 ♗g5 ♘g4+ 21 ♔h3 ♕c6∓) 20...♖ad8∓,

e.g., 21 ♔h3 ♖e4 22 ♗e3 e5!.

17...♔g6 18 c3!

(a) 18 ♖ad1? ♖xd1 19 ♖xd1 e5! wins for Black, e.g., 20 ♔xh2 (20 g3 ♘g4 21 ♗c1 ♗f5 22 c3 e4-+ Radovanovic-Vakhidov, Chania 2000) 20...♘g4+ 21 ♔g1 ♔xh6 0-1 Zaw Win Lay-Khalifman, Bali 2000, in view of 22 ♗xf7 (22 ♕g3 ♗f5 23 ♖d4 ♔g5!-+) 22...e4 23 ♕h3+ ♔g7-+;

(b) 18 c4 tries to prevent ...♘d5, but then 18...e5! is similar to the main text and even better in variations where White would like to play ♗xe6 or where Black uses the d4 square. Black can also play 18...♘h5, when 19 ♗e3? f5 20 g4 (20 g3 b6 21 ♔xh2 ♗b7∓) 20...♘f6 21 gxf5+ exf5 22 ♕g2+ ♘g4 23 f3 ♗d7-+ was Gufeld-Ravi, Calcutta 1994.

18...e5!?

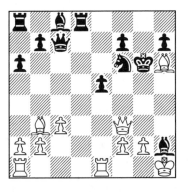

The most direct move and most promising, although 18...♘h5 may be okay as well. The game Adams-Dreev below (after 18...♘d5 19 ♖ad1) was given enormous publicity after it appeared in 1996, and has been given as the main line of this variation for many years (implying that the line was bad for Black). I found 18...e5 and decided that it was okay just a few weeks after becoming aware of Adams-Dreev, and yet it only recently

received serious attention. This illustrates the way that a single move in one top-level game (a move that would attract only mild notice if played by a lower grandmaster) can discourage even strong players from discovering obvious improvements.

There are alternatives to 18...e5:

(a) 18...♘d5?! is considered bad due to the aforementioned Adams-Dreev, Wijk aan Zee 1996: 19 ♖ad1! f5 20 ♗c1 ♗d6 21 ♗xd5 exd5 22 ♖xd5 ♗d7 23 ♕h3 ♗f8 24 ♖e3 ♔g7 25 ♖g3+ ♔h8 26 ♕h4 ♗e6 27 ♗f4 ♗e7 28 ♗xc7 1-0. Improvements for Black were long sought and not found, though they may be available;

(b) 18...♘h5 is a valid alternative and has now been played in at least 60 games. Since Black seems to end up with equality after either 18...e5 or 18...♘h5, this is a reasonable choice: 19 ♗c1 (19 ♗e3 f5! has won several games for Black, but the clever 19 ♖e4! seems to draw: 19...♔xh6 20 ♖h4 ♕e5! 21 ♖xh2 ♗d7 22 ♕xf7 ♗c6!? [22...♗e8 23 ♕f8+ ♕g7 24 ♕f4+ ♕g5 draws] 23 f4 ♕f5 24 ♕xf5 exf5 25 ♗f7 ♖d2 26 ♗xh5 Luther-Schlecht, Boblinger 2000, and now 26...♖ad8 was fully equal) and:

(b1) 19...f5 20 g4! (this probably doesn't yield much, but it is more interesting than 20 ♗xe6 ♘g7 21 ♗xc8 ♖axc8 22 g3 ♗xg3 23 fxg3 ♕c6= Womacka-Harikrishna, Pardubice 2002) 20...♘f4 (20...♘f6? 21 ♗xe6 ♔g7 22 ♕xf5 with attack; but 20...♗d7!? 21 gxh5+ ♔g7 22 ♕g2+ ♔h8 23 ♗g5 ♗e5 24 ♗xd8 ♕xd8 was dynamically equal in the game Blehm-S.Ivanov, Krynica 1997, one line being 25 ♗xe6!? ♕h4+ 26 ♔g1 ♗xe6 27 ♖xe5 ♗d7! with complications) 21 gxf5+ exf5 22 ♖g1+! ♔f6 23 ♗xf4 ♕xf4!? 24 ♕h5 ♗e6 25 ♗xe6

♗xe6 26 ♖ae1+ ♔d6 27 ♖g2. This position is unclear and most probably equal;

(b2) 19...♗f4 is also messy, but probably more reliable: 20 g4 ♘g3+ 21 fxg3 ♗xc1 22 ♖axc1 ♗d7 (this is clearer than 22...b6 23 ♕e3!?; instead, 23 ♗c2+ ♔g7 24 ♗e4 led to two draws) 23 ♕e3 ♗c6+ drawn, Winsnes-Sjodahl, Sweden 1994, a possible continuation being 24 ♔g1 ♖d2! 25 ♖c2 ♖ad8 26 ♖xd2 ♖xd2 27 ♕xd2 ♕xg3+ 28 ♔f1 ♕h3+ with repetition.

19 ♗c2+!

19 ♔xh2? ♘g4+ 20 ♔h1 (20 ♔g1 ♘xh6 21 ♕g3+ ♘g4 22 f3 ♕c5+ 23 ♔f1 ♗f5) 20...♔xh6 21 ♖e4 ♕c6–+ and White has no attack: 22 ♖ae1 ♕g6 23 ♗xf7 Forberg-Lahlum, Norway 2002; and the cutest win was 23...♕xe4! 24 ♖xe4 ♖d1+ 25 ♕xd1 ♘xf2+ etc.

19...e4

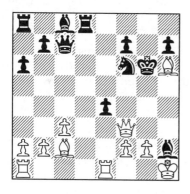

I have resisted the temptation to split up this 11 ♖e1 material at several points, but now it seems necessary:

6.241 20 ♗xe4+
6.242 20 g3
6.243 20 ♖xe4

6.241 20 ♗xe4 ♘xe4 21 ♖xe4 ♕c6!

Threatening ...♔xh6 and ...♗f5. Black is playing for the win. 21...♗d6 seems to lead to a pawn down but drawn opposite-coloured bishops ending after 22 ♖h4 ♕c5 23 ♖d1! ♗e6 24 ♗e3 ♕f5 25 ♖h6+ ♔g7 26 ♕xf5 ♗xf5 27 ♖hxd6 ♖xd6 28 ♖xd6 ♗e6 29 a4 ♖e8. Amazingly, after I had done all of this analysis, a game A.Olsson-Leer Salvesen, Stockholm 2002 was sent to me with exactly the same moves, indeed leading to a draw!

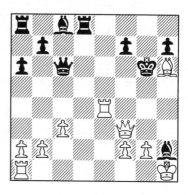

22 ♗e3!?

This may barely suffice, but White has a more promising choice:

(a) 22 ♔xh2? ♔xh6 23 ♕xf7 ♕xe4 24 ♕f6+ ♔h5 25 ♕xd8 ♗h3! 26 ♕a5+ b5 27 f3 ♕e7!∓;

(b) 22 ♖h4? ♕xf3 23 gxf3 ♗c7!? 24 ♖g1+ ♔f5 25 ♖h5+ ♔e6 26 ♖e1+ ♔d7∓ with the idea 27 ♗g5 ♖e8 28 ♖d1+ ♔c6;

(c) 22 ♕e3! leads to an interesting attack for a piece:

(c1) 22...♕b5 23 ♖h4 ♖e8 24 ♕d2 (24 a4!?, and 24...♕e5?! 25 ♕f3! ♕f5 26 ♔xh3 ♕xf3 27 gxf3 is difficult for Black, even if drawable, so much better is 24...♖xe3! 25 axb5 ♖e2 26 ♔xh2 ♖xb2 27 bxa6 ♖xa6 28 ♖xa6+ bxa6 29 ♗e3 ♗e6=) 24...♖e2 25 ♕d4!? (25 ♕d8 ♖e8 26 ♕d2=) 25...♕e5 26 ♕d1? (26 ♕d3+ ♗f5 27 ♖g4+ ♔f6 28 ♗g7+ ♔e7

29 ♗xe5 ♗xd3 30 ♗xh2 ♖xf2 31 ♖e1+ ♔f6 which is well within drawing bounds) 26...♗g3! 27 fxg3 ♕xg3 and Black has a very large advantage after 28 ♖h2 ♗g4 29 ♕g1 ♖d8! 30 ♖f1 ♖xb2;

(c2) 22...♕d5 looks like a forced draw (although you never know): 23 ♖h4 ♗d6 24 f4! (24 ♖e1 f6) 24...♗f5 25 ♕g3+ ♔f6 26 ♖e1 (26 c4 ♕d3; 26 ♗g5+ ♔e6 and not 27 ♖e1+? ♔d7, but 27 ♗xd8! ♖xd8 28 ♕g5, when Black's bishops may still give him a slight advantage after 28...f6 29 ♖h6 ♖f8) 26...♖g8 27 ♗g7+! (27 ♗g5+ ♔g7 28 ♗e7+ ♗g6) 27...♖xg7 28 ♖h6+ ♖g6 29 ♕h4+ ♔g7 30 ♖xh7+ ♔g8 31 ♖h8+ ♔g7 32 ♖h7+ with a draw by perpetual check.

22...f5

Not 22...♗c7?? 23 ♖g4+! ♗xg4 24 ♕xg4+ ♔f6 25 ♗g5+±.

23 ♖h4 ♕xf3 24 gxf3 ♗e5

Black has to be careful here, even being in possession of an extra piece: 24...♗d6? 25 ♖g1+ ♔f7 26 ♖xh7+ ♔e6 27 ♖e1±.

After 24...♗e5, White can stop Black from consolidating his material by 25 ♖g1+! (25 ♖e1? h5! 26 ♖g1+ ♔f7 27 ♖xh5 ♖h8) 25...♔f7 26 ♖xh7+ ♔e6 27 ♖h6+! (27 ♖e1 ♖d7 28 ♖h5 ♗f6! and while things are still not clear, Black will apparently be able to give up the f-pawn and retain his advantage) 27...♔d7 28 ♖d1+ ♔e8 29 ♖e1 ♔f7 30 ♖h7+ ♔g8 (30...♔f6 31 ♖h6+ achieves nothing) 31 ♖e7! ♗f6 32 ♖g1+ ♔h8 33 ♖f7 ♗e5 34 ♖e7 ♗f6 drawn.

6.242 20 g3!?

This was played recently and is extremely complicated. According to my analysis, it leads to a probable draw, but Black has some chances:

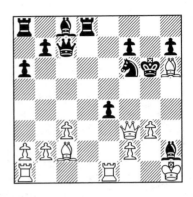

20...♖e8

This was suggested to me by Lahlum. It is good, but perhaps not the best way to get winning chances. Alternatives:

(a) 20...♘g4?? 21 ♖xe4! wins, although in Battaglini-Lahlum, Kecskemet 2003, Black survived after 21...♔h5 when White missed the instantly winning 22 ♕f6!;

(b) 20...♗xg3 is the critical move: 21 fxg3! (21 ♖g1 ♘g4! with 22 ♖xg3 ♔xh6, 22 ♕xe4+ ♔h5!!, or 22 ♗e3 f5 23 ♕xg3 ♕xg3 24 ♖xg3 h5 and Black consolidates his pawn with only slight compensation for White) and here one more split is necessary:

(b1) 21...♕d7? 22 g4! (22 ♗e3 ♕g4∓) 22...♘xg4 (22...♕xg4 23 ♗xe4+ ♘xe4 24 ♖g1 and regardless of the material Black's king is too exposed) 23 ♕f4! ♘f2+ 24 ♔g2!+− (analysis by Lahlum);

(b2) 21...♖e8! is the way to play for a win, but is difficult to analyse. One line would be 22 ♗f4 (22 ♕e3 ♕e5; 22 ♗e3 ♗g4 23 ♕f2 ♕e5) 22...♕e7 23 ♕e3 (23 ♔g1 ♗f5 24 ♕h1 ♘g4!) 23...♗f5 24 ♖ad1 (24 ♗g5? ♘g4) 24...♖ad8, and Black has the advantage, but it isn't a pawn's worth because the bishops count for something;

(b3) 21...♛e5 is the safe backup: 22 ♗f4 ♛f5 (or 22...♛e6 23 ♗xe4+ ♘xe4 24 ♖xe4 ♛g4) 23 ♗xe4 ♘xe4 24 ♛xe4 ♛xe4+ 25 ♖xe4 ♗f5 and the opposite-coloured bishops practically ensure a draw.

21 ♗f4 ♛c5!

21...♛b6!? 22 ♗e3! avoids various drawn bishops-of-opposite-colours endings, although it's hardly clear.

22 ♗e3!?

22 ♔xh2 ♗g4= is easy for Black, e.g., 23 ♛g2 ♔g7 24 ♔g1!? ♗f3 25 ♛h3 ♘g4! hitting f2 with ideas like ...♖ad8-d5-h5; then 26 ♗e3 ♛f5 27 ♗d4+ f6= is best play, when White has nothing special to do and ...♖ad8 follows.

22...♛d5!

22...♛b5 is playable but less accurate.

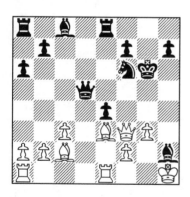

23 ♗d4!?

White should avoid 23 ♛f4?? ♛h5 as well as 23 ♖ad1?! ♛e5! intending 24 ♗d4? ♗g4 or 24 ♔xh2? ♗g4 25 ♛h1 ♛h5+ 26 ♔g1 ♛xh1+ 27 ♔xh1 ♗f3+ 28 ♔g1 ♖e5. Better is 23 ♛g2! ♛h5 24 ♛xh2 ♗h3!= (with the idea ...♘g4) 25 ♗d1! ♘g4 26 ♔g1 ♘xh2 27 ♗xh5+ ♔xh5 28 ♔xh2 ♗g4 and only Black has chances, although this is surely drawn.

After 23 ♗d4, a logical continua-

tion would be 23...♗f5 24 ♛f4 (24 ♛g2 ♘g4) 24...♘h5! 25 ♛e3 (25 ♛h4?? e3+) 25...♗xg3! 26 fxg3 ♗g4 27 ♔h2 f5 and Black looks solid enough; the bishops have their influence but don't fully compensate for the extra pawn.

6.243 20 ♖xe4

Probably the safest line.

20...♗f5

Black's only way to play for complications, although White can apparently bail out. Also leading to 'only' a draw for Black is 20...♘xe4 21 ♛xe4+ ♔xh6 22 ♛xh7+ ♔g5 with a perpetual check, in view of 23 g3? ♗xg3 24 ♛g7+ ♔h5 25 ♔g2 ♗h3+! 26 ♔xh3 f5! 27 ♛xg3 ♛xg3+ 28 ♔xg3 ♖d2∓.

21 ♖g4+!

Heading for a perpetual. Other moves seem to favour Black:

(a) 21 ♛e3 ♘xe4 22 ♗xe4 f6 23 ♗xf5+ ♔xf5 24 g3 ♗xg3 25 fxg3 ♛e5, and Black is simply an exchange up;

(b) 21 ♖c4!? ♛e5!? (21...♖xc2! 22 ♖xc7 ♗xc7 would be a winning try) 22 ♗xf5+ ♛xf5 23 ♛xf5+ ♔xf5, and not 24 ♔xh2?? ♘g4+ but 24 g3! ♖d3!=, a sample line going 25 ♗f4 ♘g4 26 ♖f1 ♖e8 27 ♖c5+ ♔f6 28 ♖g5 h5! 29 ♖xh5 ♗f3 30 ♖h4! ♔f5 31 ♖h5+ ♔f6=;

(c) 21 ♖ae1 is very messy, but I think that Black has good play, e.g., 21...♖d5!? 22 ♗f4 (22 ♖g4+? ♘xg4 23 ♗xf5+ ♔xh6 24 ♕h3+ ♔g7 25 ♕xg4+ ♔h8 26 ♕h3 ♖xf5 27 ♕xf5 ♕f4-+ with both ...♕h6 and ...♕xf2 in mind) 22...♗xf4 23 ♖xf4 ♕xf4! 24 ♕xf4 ♗xc2 25 ♖e3 (25 ♖e7 ♖ad8-+) 25...h5!∓; if 26 ♖g3+?, 26...♘g4 wins.

21...♘xg4 22 ♕xf5+

If instead 22 ♕xg4+? ♔xh6 23 ♕xf5 ♕e5! 24 ♕xh7+ ♔g5 and the attack is over.

22...♔xh6 23 ♕xh7+ ♔g5 24 ♕f5+ ♔h6=

This is all extremely long analysis and can doubtless be improved upon. Nevertheless, the fate of the whole 4...♕xd5 line with 10..a6 may be linked to the assessment of Black's 18th moves, so I think that this detailed look is justified and practically obligatory. My impression is that both 18...e5 and 18...♘h5 equalise, and in the former case White had better know some specifics or he can easily come out worse. In conclusion, Black's game is holding up against 11 ♖e1, which is the only serious try at refuting 10...a6 and thus 4...♕xd5.

Chapter Seven

Tarrasch Variation: 3...♗e7

1 e4 e6 2 d4 d5 3 ♘d2 ♗e7

Only a few years ago this lame-looking move was an obscure sideline. Stretching far into the past, Black attacked the centre by 3...♘f6 or 3...c5 followed by active development. Even 3...♘c6 and 3...dxe4 seem to have more to do with the position than 3...♗e7. It even looks like a beginner's idea, developing the bishop to a passive square before it knows where it wants to go and making no attempt to free Black's game or resolve the centre. But of late (mainly in the last five years), 3...♗e7 has become a hot main line. In fact, the move in many ways reflects the spirit of the times. It can be viewed as a sort of useful waiting move, and to some extent a prophylactic one. As we shall see, every logical move that White can now make commits him to a position in which Black can play a set-up that he might not have been able to reach via another third move. This is in line with the information-theoretic idea that one learns more about the opponent's intentions by doing less! Of course, any tempo used by Black will give White new opportunities as well.

This kind of interplay can only be demonstrated in practice. The most important moves are:

7.1 4 c3
7.2 4 e5
7.3 4 ♘gf3
7.4 4 ♗d3

White can also play 4 g3, a slow move that allows several answers, e.g., 4...♘f6 (the rarely-played 4...c5!? is likely to produce dynamic play beginning with 5 dxc5 ♘f6 6 e5 ♘fd7 7 ♘gf3 ♘c6 8 ♗b5 ♘xc5=) and:

(a) 5 ♗g2 0-0 6 ♘e2 c5 7 dxc5! (7 exd5?! exd5 8 c3 ♘c6 9 0-0 Baran-Bobrowska, Suwalki 1999, and one way to advantage is 9...♗g4! 10 f3 ♗f5∓) 7...dxe4 8 b4 (8 0-0 ♕d5!? 9 ♘c3 ♕xc5 10 ♘dxe4 ♘xe4 11 ♘xe4 ♕c7=) 8...a5 9 c3 axb4 10 cxb4 ♘c6 11 ♕b3 ♘d5 (or 11...♕d3 12 a3 e5∓) 12 ♗a3?! (12 0-0 f5) 12...♖xa3! 13 ♕xa3 ♘dxb4 14 ♗xe4 f5!∓ Oumnov-Stimpel, Bundesliga 1999, since 15 ♗xc6 runs into 15...♘d3+;

(b) 5 e5 ♘fd7 6 ♗g2 (6 f4 c5 7 c3 ♘c6 7 ♘df3 would be a standard 3

♘d2 ♘f6 variation which is fine for the second player. Black can also play 7...b6 8 ♘df3 cxd4 9 cxd4 a5 10 ♗d3 ♗a6= Rapp-Lenz, Hauenstein 1991) 6...c5 7 c3 ♘c6 8 ♘e2 ♕b6 (8...0-0 9 0-0 cxd4 10 cxd4 f5!? 11 f4!? ♘b6 12 ♘f3 a5 intending ...a4; this is a standard set-up in the 3 ♘d2 ♘f6 4 e5 ♘fd7 5 f4 Tarrasch) 9 ♘f3 cxd4 10 cxd4 f6 11 exf6 ♘xf6 12 0-0 0-0= intending ...♘e4.

7.1 4 c3

A fairly harmless move after which Black should be able to equalise easily, but he can also enter into complications should he choose to do so.
4...c5
This is a good move if Black wants positive chances. 4...dxe4 5 ♘xe4 is a kind of Rubinstein Variation that can't be too bad for Black, since the inclusion of c3 is not always appropriate; nevertheless the text is more exciting.

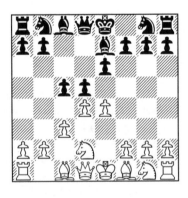

5 dxc5
(a) 5 exd5 exd5 (the easiest course, but 5...♕xd5 has also equalised after 6 dxc5 ♗xc5 7 ♘gf3 ♘f6; a simple answer to 6 ♘gf3 is 6...cxd4 7 ♗c4 ♕h5 8 cxd4 ♘f6=) 6 ♗b5+ (6 ♘gf3 ♘c6 7 dxc5 ♗xc5 8 ♘b3 ♗b6 is a nice

version of a 3 ♘d2 c5 Tarrasch line) 6...♘c6 (or 6...♗d7 7 ♗xd7+ ♘xd7 8 dxc5 ♘xc5=) 7 ♘gf3 ♕b6! and Black has already equalised, e.g., 8 ♕e2 c4! 9 ♗a4 ♘f6 10 0-0 ♗e6 11 ♘g5!? ♗f5! 12 ♖e1 (12 ♕e5 ♗d3 13 ♖e1 0-0∓) 12...0-0 13 ♘df3 ♗d6∓;
(b) 5 ♘gf3 ♘f6 (5...cxd4 6 ♘xd4 dxe4 7 ♘xe4 ♘f6) 6 exd5 exd5!? 7 dxc5 ♗xc5 8 ♘b3 ♗b6 9 ♗b5+ ♘c6 10 0-0 0-0 11 ♗g5 ♗g4=.
5...♗xc5

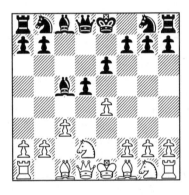

6 ♘b3
(a) 6 ♘gf3 ♘f6!? (6...♘c6 7 ♘b3 ♗b6 8 exd5 exd5= gives Black active play in an isolated queen's pawn position) 7 e5 (7 exd5 exd5 8 ♘b3 ♗b6) 7...♘fd7 (a safe move; 7...♕b6!? 8 ♘d4 ♘fd7 9 ♕g4!? was unclear in Onischuk-Morozevich, Bundesliga 1999; the best idea was probably just 9...g6, but the game got wild following 9...0-0!? 10 ♘2f3 ♘c6?! 11 ♗h6 g6 12 0-0-0 ♘dxe5 13 ♕f4! f6!? 14 ♗xf8?! ♗xf8 15 ♕xf6 ♘g4 16 ♕h4 e5 and Black had more than enough compensation) 8 ♘b3 ♗b6 9 ♘bd4 ♘c6 10 ♗b5 ♕c7= Vajda-Mkrtchian, Bled 2002, a critical line going 11 ♗f4 ♗xd4 12 ♘xd4 ♘dxe5 13 0-0 0-0 14 ♕e2 f6 15 ♖ae1 ♕b6=. But 6...♘c6 is probably easiest;
(b) 6 ♗d3 ♘f6 7 ♕e2 resembles one

of the main 3 ♘d2 ♗e7 4 ♗d3 c5 5 dxc5 lines, but White has committed to c3 rather early on. One idea for Black is 7...♘c6 8 ♘gf3 0-0!? 9 0-0 (9 e5 ♘g4! 10 0-0 f6=) 9...♗b6!? 10 e5 (10 b3 e5!) 10...♘d7 11 ♘b3 f6 12 ♕c2 (12 exf6 ♘xf6 13 ♗g5 ♕d6! with the idea 14 ♕c2? e5! 15 ♗xf6 ♕xf6 16 ♗xh7+ ♔h8∓) 12...♘dxe5 13 ♘xe5 fxe5 14 ♗xh7+ ♔h8 15 ♗g6 (15 ♕g6?? ♕h4) 15...e4 with at least equality.

6...♗b6 7 exd5

7 e5?! ♘c6 8 ♘f3 ♘ge7 9 ♗d3 ♘g6 10 ♕e2 ♕c7 11 ♗xg6 fxg6∓.

7...exd5 8 ♘f3

8 ♕e2+ ♘e7 9 ♗e3 ♗xe3 10 ♕xe3 0-0 11 ♗e2 ♘f5 12 ♕d2 ♖e8 13 ♘f3 ♕e7 14 ♘fd4 ♘xd4 15 ♘xd4 ♘c6 16 ♘xc6 bxc6 17 0-0 ½-½ Zatonskih-Shulman, Lindsborg 2002.

8...♘f6 9 ♗b5+ ♘c6 10 0-0 0-0 11 ♗g5 a6

Black can also play 11...♗g4, e.g., 12 ♗xf6 (12 ♕d3 ♕d6=) 12...♕xf6 13 ♕xd5 ♗xf3 14 ♕xf3 ♕xf3 15 gxf3 ♘e5 16 ♔g2 ♘g6=.

12 ♗e2 ♖e8= Langer-Atalik, Las Vegas 2001. Black can unpin by ...♕d6 or in some cases even ...h6 and ...g5.

7.2 4 e5

A fascinating and critical variation that prevents Black's knight from developing naturally to f6 (and e7 is already occupied). White's Advance Variation centre is subject to a serious attack (his knight on d2 is not ideally placed), but the idea of ♕g4 is difficult to meet and gives the struggle an added dimension.

4...c5

This is almost always played, but I think that the move 4...♘h6!? deserves serious consideration.

It brings out a piece, prevents ♕g4, prepares castling, and plans to develop the knight to f5 (or in some cases to f7 after the move ...f6). White will of course try to exploit the knight on the rim and consolidate his pawn wedge in the centre:

(a) 5 ♗d3 c5 (another plan is 5...b6 6 ♘df3 ♘f5 7 ♘e2 ♗a6) gives Black time for standard counterplay against d4, e.g., 6 c3 (6 dxc5 ♘d7 7 ♘b3 ♘xe5) 6...cxd4 (6...♘c6 7 ♘e2 cxd4 8 cxd4 ♘f5 9 ♘f3 0-0 10 0-0 f6) 7 cxd4 ♘c6 8 ♘gf3 (8 ♘df3 ♕a5+!? 9 ♗d2 ♕b6 or simply 8...♘f5) 8...♕b6 9 ♘b3 a5 10 a4 (10 ♗xh6 gxh6 11 a4 ♕b4+! 12 ♔e2 f6∓ opening lines for attack) 10...♗b4+ 11 ♔e2 (11 ♗d2 ♗xd2+ 12 ♘bxd2 ♘xd4) 11...♘f5 12 g4 ♘fe7 13 ♗e3 ♗d7 intending ...♖c8 and either

...h5 or ...0-0 and ...f6;

(b) 5 ♘gf3 0-0!? (a little committal; safer would be 5...♘f5, and very interesting is 5...♘d7 6 ♘b3 [6 ♗d3 c5=] 6...♘f5 7 ♗d3 a5!?; then we could see 8 a4 h5 intending ...b6, or something wild like 8 g4!? ♘h4 9 ♘xh4 ♗xh4 10 g5 ♗xg5 11 ♕g4 ♗xc1 12 ♕xg7 ♗xb2 13 ♕xh8+ ♘f8 14 ♖b1 ♗c3+ 15 ♔e2 ♕h4 with a pawn and plenty of play for the exchange!) 6 ♗d3 f6 7 ♘b3 ♘f7 8 exf6 ♗xf6 9 0-0 ♘c6 and ...e5 next, except after 10 ♗f4 g5!? 11 ♗g3 g4 12 ♘e5 ♗xe5 13 dxe5 ♘cxe5 14 ♕e2 ♕g5 when White definitely has compensation but this is probably only sufficient and not more;

(c) 5 ♘df3 (the most obvious move and the one played in most contests with 4...♘h6 thus far − everything above is analysis that I did a couple of years ago) 5...c5!? (ignoring the 'threat' of ♗xh6; or 5...♘f5 6 ♗d3 ♘c6!?, e.g., 7 c3 f6 8 exf6 ♗xf6 9 ♘e2 0-0 10 0-0?! e5! 11 dxe5 ♘xe5 12 ♘xe5 ♗xe5 13 ♗f4 ♗xf4 14 ♘xf4 c6 15 c4?! ½-½ Gajewski-Bartel, Laczna 2002; Black keeps the advantage with either 15...♘d6 or 15...♘h4! 16 g3 ♕g5) 6 ♗d3 (6 c3 ♘c6 7 dxc5 ♗xc5 8 ♗xh6 gxh6=; 6 ♗xh6!? gxh6 7 ♕d2 ♘c6 8 ♕xh6 ♕a5+!? 9 ♕d2 ♕xd2+ 10 ♔xd2 ♘xd4 11 ♘xd4 cxd4 12 ♘f3 0-0! 13 ♘xd4 f6 with compensation) 6...♘c6 7 ♗xh6 gxh6 8 ♕d2 (this looks more critical than 8 dxc5 ♗xc5 9 ♘h3 ♕c7 10 0-0 ♗d7!? 11 ♖e1 0-0-0 12 c3 f6! 13 ♕e2 ♘xe5 14 ♘xe5 fxe5 15 ♕xe5 ♗d6∓ Czarnota-Olszewski, Laczna 2002) 8...♕b6 9 0-0-0 ♗d7 with the idea 10 ♕xh6? c4! 11 ♕g7 (11 ♗xh7 ♘b4! with the idea of meeting 12 ♔b1 with 12...♗a4 13 ♖c1 c3) 11...0-0-0 12 ♗xh7 ♘b4 13 ♔b1 c3 14 b3 ♘xa2!−+.

5 ♕g4

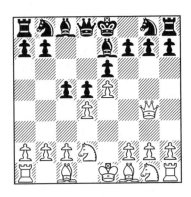

There are two other important moves here:

(a) 5 c3 is rather slow but Black still needs to play actively: 5...cxd4 (5...♘c6 6 ♘gf3?! cxd4 7 cxd4 ♕b6! is a favourable version of certain Advance Variation lines: 8 ♘b3 a5 9 a4 ♗b4+ 10 ♗d2 ♗xd2+ 11 ♔xd2 f6! 12 ♗b5 ♘ge7 13 ♖e1 0-0 14 exf6 gxf6 15 ♔e2 e5∓ Coratella-Glek, Porto San Giorgio 2001. But here 6 ♘df3! probably transposes to the main line) 6 cxd4 ♘c6 (6...♘h6!? 7 ♘df3 ♕b6 unclear) 7 ♘df3 (7 ♘b3 ♕b6 8 f4?! ♗d7 9 ♘f3 ♖c8 10 ♗d3 ♘b4 11 a4 ♘xd3+ 12 ♕xd3 ♖c4 with bishops and activity, Weisbuch-Genser, Halkidiki 2002)

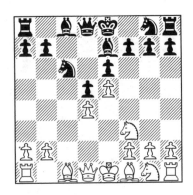

and now:

(a1) 7...♕b6! 8 ♗d3 (8 ♘e2 ♘h6!? 9 ♗xh6 gxh6 10 ♕d2 f6! 11 exf6 ♗xf6 12 0-0-0 0-0 with the idea 13 ♕xh6 e5 unclear; here 8...f6 might be a good option) 8...♗b4+! looks fully equal, with the idea 9 ♗d2 ♘xd4 10 ♘xd4 ♕xd4 11 ♕a4+ ♗d7 12 ♕xb4 ♕xd3 13 ♕xb7 ♖c8∓;

(a2) 7...♗b4+ 8 ♗d2 ♕a5 (or 8...♕b6, which transposes to 7...♕b6 above after 9 ♗d3?; best is 9 ♗xb4 ♕xb4+ 10 ♕d2 ♗d7! and not instead 11 ♕xb4?! ♘xb4 12 ♔d2 ♖c8, but 11 ♖c1! ♘h6!? 12 ♕xb4 ♘xb4 13 a3 ♘c6 14 ♗d3 f6, which is approximately equal)

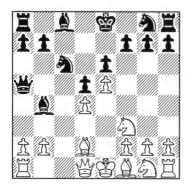

and now:

(a21) 9 ♗d3 f6!? 10 exf6 ♘xf6 11 a3 ♗xd2+ 12 ♕xd2 ♕xd2+ 13 ♔xd2 is equal, e.g., 13...0-0 14 ♘e2 ♗d7! 15 h3 ♘a5! or 13...♘g4 14 ♖f1 0-0;

(a22) 9 ♗xb4 ♕xb4+ 10 ♕xd2 ♗d7 is perhaps very slightly worse for Black, but here 9...♘xb4!? 10 ♘d2 ♘c6 is possible, e.g., 11 ♘gf3 ♕b4!? 12 ♕b3 ♘xd4 13 ♘xd4 ♕xd4 14 ♗b5+ ♔f8 15 ♕a3+ ♘e7 16 ♘f3 ♕b6 17 ♗d3 ♗d7 18 0-0 f6 unclear;

(a23) 9 ♘e2 ♗xd2+ 10 ♕xd2 ♕xd2+ 11 ♔xd2 f6 12 exf6 ♘xf6!? 13 ♘c3 0-0 (or 13...♘g4 14 ♗b5!? 0-0 15 ♖af1 ♗d7 16 h3 ♘h6=) 14 ♗b5 ♘e4+ 15 ♔e3 ♘e7!? 16 ♗d3 (16 ♘xe4? ♘f5+

17 ♔d3 dxe4+ 18 ♔xe4 ♘d6+) 16...♘d6 (16...♘f5+ 17 ♔e2 ♘fd6) 17 ♖hd1 ♘c4+!? 18 ♗xc4 dxc4 and Black looks okay;

(b) 5 dxc5 ♘c6 6 ♘gf3 (6 ♕g4 ♔f8 7 ♘gf3 transposes to the main line with 5 ♕g4 ♔f8) 6...♗xc5 7 ♘b3 ♗b6 8 ♗d3 f6! 9 ♕e2 (9 ♗b5 ♗d7 10 ♗xc6 bxc6=) 9...fxe5 10 ♘xe5 ♘f6 11 0-0 ♘xe5 12 ♕xe5 0-0 13 ♗g5 (Ftacnik analyses 13 ♕g5 e5! 14 ♕xe5 ♘g4 15 ♕h5 g6 16 ♗xg6 hxg6 17 ♕xg6+ ♔h8 18 h3 ♕f6 19 ♕xf6+ ♘xf6∓) 13...♗c7 14 ♕d4 h6 (better 14...e5! 15 ♕h4 h6∓) 15 ♗h4?! (15 ♗f4!) 15...e5 16 ♕c5 ♗e6∓ Adams-Morozevich, Dortmund 2001.

Now play splits into:

7.21 5...g6
7.22 5...♔f8

7.21 5...g6

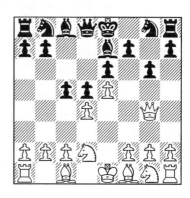

This hasn't been popular but strongly deserves consideration. It weakens the kingside somwhat but avoids moving the king. Whether the weaknesses can be exploited is another issue; I think that the benefits outweigh the problems.

6 dxc5

(a) 6 ♘df3 ♘c6 7 dxc5 ♗xc5! 8 ♗d3 f6!

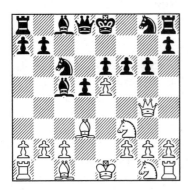

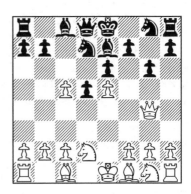

This position is highly relevant to the whole system, as it transposes to the line with 6 dxc5 ♘c6 7 ♘df3 ♗xc5:

(a1) 9 ♕h3 fxe5! (9...♔f7 may also suffice, e.g., 10 ♕g3 ♕c7 11 ♗f4 ♕b6) 10 ♗xg6+ ♔d7 11 ♗g5 (11 ♗f7 ♕f6!) 11...♘f6 12 ♗f7 ♗xf2+! 13 ♔e2! ♔d6! 14 ♖f1 ♖f8∓;

(a2) 9 ♕h4!? fxe5! (9...♘xe5 10 ♘xe5 fxe5 11 ♗xg6+ ♔d7 12 ♗g5 ♕b6 13 0-0-0 ♗d4! 14 c3 ♗xf2 with great complications) 10 ♗xg6+ ♔d7 11 ♕xd8+?! (11 ♗g5! ♕b6 12 0-0-0 ♗xf2 13 ♕h5 ♘ge7=) 11...♔xd8 12 ♘g5 (12 ♗h5 ♘f6 13 ♗g5 ♖f8 14 ♘e2 e4∓) 12...hxg6 13 ♘f7+ ♔e7 14 ♘xh8 ♔f6 and the knight does not escape, so Black stands better;

(b) 6 c3 ♘c6 7 ♘gf3?!, although played several times without penalty, is actually a mistake after 7...cxd4 (also good is 7...h5 8 ♕g3 h4 9 ♕h3 cxd4 10 cxd4 ♕b6) 8 cxd4 ♘h6! 9 ♕h3 ♘f5 10 ♗b5 ♕b6 11 ♗xc6+ bxc6 12 ♘b3 ♗a6∓.

6...♘d7

To get a knight to c5. 6...♘c6 is playable although White is a touch better: 7 ♘gf3 ♗xc5 8 ♘b3 ♗b6 9 ♗d3 ♕c7 10 ♗f4 ♘b4! 11 ♘fd4! ♘xd3+ 12 cxd3 ♗xd4 13 ♘xd4 ♕b6 14 ♘b3 ♕b4+ 15 ♔e2±.

7 ♘gf3

7 ♗b5 ♗xc5 and there's a crazy line following the natural 8 ♘gf3: 8...♗xf2+! 9 ♔xf2 ♕b6+ 10 ♘d4 ♘h6 11 ♕f4 g5! and Black stands well.

7...♘xc5 8 ♗e2

8 h4 h5!? 9 ♕f4 ♘h6 was unclear in Nykopp-Hoi, Reykjavik 1984.

8...♘h6 9 ♕h3 ♘f5 10 g4 ♘g7!

These knight fianchettoes are increasingly common in the French! As usual, Black has ideas of ...h5 and ...f5 or ...f6. Now Jaracz-Lputian, Istanbul 2003 continued 11 ♕h6 ♗f8 12 h4 ♗d7 13 ♖h3?! ♕c7 14 ♕f4 f5! 15 ♘d4? fxg4 16 ♖c3 ♘h5∓.

7.22 5...♔f8

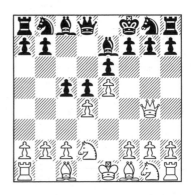

The most popular move, by which Black avoids weakening his position and bets that White's precarious centre and the awkward position of the queen will compensate him.

6 dxc5

(a) 6 ♘df3 ♘c6 7 dxc5 ♗xc5 8 ♗d3 f6 transposes to the 6 dxc5 ♘c6 7 ♘df3 line below, but Black also has 7...f6 8 ♗f4!? ♗xc5 9 ♗d3 ♕b6! 10 ♘h3! ♕b4+ 11 c3 ♕xb2 12 0-0 ♕xc3 13 ♗b5! fxe5 14 ♖fc1 ♕b4 15 ♖ab1 ♘f6!?, which led to an unclear, titanic struggle of material versus initiative in Pokorna-Matveeva, Bled 2002. Here 15...♗xf2+ 16 ♔xf2 ♕e4 17 ♗xc6 ♘f6 is a good option given by Shipov;

(b) 6 ♘gf3 h5!? (6...♘c6 7 dxc5 ♗xc5 again transposes to 6 dxc5) 7 ♕g3 h4 8 ♕f4 g5 9 ♕g4 ♘c6 10 dxc5 (10 ♘b3!? is worth thinking about. Then 10...c4 11 ♘c5 b6 12 ♘a4 ♘b4 13 ♔d1 f5! 14 exf6 ♗xf6 gives a lot of play, e.g., 15 ♗xg5 e5! 16 ♗xf6 ♕xf6 17 dxe5 ♗xg4 18 exf6 ♘xf6 19 a3! ♘c6 20 ♗e2 ♖e8 with complications) 10...♘h6 11 ♕h5 f5 12 exf6 ♗xf6 13 ♘b3 ♘f5 14 ♕g4 e5 15 ♕a4 e4 16 ♘g1 ♗d7 17 ♗b5!? (17 c3 had previously been played) 17...♖h7! 18 ♘h3 ♘cd4 19 ♗xd7 ♕xd7= Schaar-Andeer, email 2000;

(c) 6 c3 ♘c6 7 ♘b3?! (7 dxc5) 7...cxd4 8 cxd4 a5 (8...♘b4!?) 9 ♘f3? (9 ♗d2) 9...♘b4! 10 ♔d1 Rogovoi-Kashtanov, St Petersburg 1999; and simply 10...♕c7 11 ♘e1 ♗d7 intending ...♖c8 looks very strong;

(d) 6 ♘b3 is a straightforward and perhaps underrated move: 6...♘c6!? (6...cxd4 7 ♘f3 ♘c6 8 ♘bxd4±; 6...c4 7 ♘d2 f6 8 ♘gf3 ♘c6 may be best) 7 ♘xc5 ♘xe5 8 dxe5 ♗xc5 9 ♗d3 ♗d7 Wells-Pert, Southend 2002; and the natural 10 ♘f3 should yield a nice advantage if only because Black has little to show for his king position.

6...♘c6

6...h5!? has been played in many games and is still considered unclear, but I'm not convinced that Black gains by committing himself.

7 ♘gf3

Natural, but this is a juncture at which White has improvements:

(a) 7 ♕g3 is a good option: 7...♕c7!? 8 ♘gf3 (8 ♘df3 ♗xc5 9 ♗d3 ♘ge7=) 8...♗xc5 9 ♘b3!? (9 ♗d3! ♘b4 10 0-0± is a problem) 9...♗b6 10 ♗d2?! f6 11 ♗c3 fxe5 12 0-0-0 ♘f6! 13 ♘xe5 ♘e4 14 ♕f3+ ♔g8 15 ♘xc6 bxc6∓;

(b) 7 ♕e2!? also has good points: 7...♗xc5 8 ♘b3 ♗b6 9 ♘f3 f6 10 ♗e3! fxe5 11 ♗xb6 (better is 11 ♘xe5! ♘xe5 12 ♗xb6 axb6 13 ♕xe5 ♕f6 14 ♕d6+ ♔f7 15 c3±) 11...axb6 12 ♘xe5 ½-½ Andreev-Itkis, Alushta 2000; 12...♕f6 would follow with an equal game, since Black's centre becomes mobile;

(c) 7 ♘df3 f6 8 ♕g3 (8 ♗f4 ♗xc5 9 ♗d3 ♕b6!? was seen under the move order 6 ♘df3 ♘c6 7 dxc5) 8...♗xc5 9 ♗d3 fxe5 10 ♘xe5 ♘xe5 11 ♕xe5 ♘f6 12 ♘f3!? ♗xf2+ 13 ♔d1 (13 ♔e2!?) 13...♗c5 14 ♖f1 ♗d6 15 ♕e2 ♕c7 and White seemed short of compensation in the game V.Akopian-Pelletier, Aubervilliers 2002, although Black still had to resolve his king position.

7...h5!

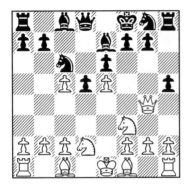

This move has been quite successful for Black and makes one wonder whether White does well to continually enter into this line instead of choosing a deviation earlier. His problem is that there is no safe place from which the queen cannot be attacked without giving up the centre. Black continually presses for the initiative and has thus far succeeded.

8 ♕f4

(a) 8 ♕a4!? ♕c7 9 ♕f4 (paradoxical, but now White has discouraged ...g5 by diverting Black's queen to c7) 9...f6 10 ♘h4 (10 ♘b3 ♘xe5 11 ♗e3 ♘h6 looks about equal) 10...♕xe5+ 11 ♕xe5 ♘xe5 12 f4 g5 13 fxe5 gxh4 14 ♘f3 ♗xc5 15 ♘xh4?! (The play has been forced to this point. Perhaps White could reinforce e5 with 15 ♗f4, but his advantage is small in any case) 15...♔g7 16 ♗f4? (16 ♘f3) 16...♗d4! 17 ♘f3 ♗xb2 18 ♖b1 ♗c3+∓ Liss-I.Botvinnik, Ramat Aviv 2000;

(b) 8 ♕g3 h4 9 ♕f4 g5! 10 ♕e3!? (The alternative is 10 ♕a4, when one of the stem games for this variation went 10...♗d7 11 ♗b5 a6 12 ♗xc6 ♗xc6 13 ♕d4 ♘h6 14 ♘b3 ♘f5 15 ♕d3 d4! 16 ♖g1 ♕c7 17 ♘fxd4 ♕xe5+ 18 ♗e3 ♕xh2 19 0-0-0 with dynamic equality, Adams-Morozevich, Sara-

jevo 1999. But there are many options along the way and White may want to return to this line) 10...♘h6 (threatening ...♘f5 with tempo) 11 ♗d3 ♘g4 12 ♕e2 ♕c7!? (12...♗xc5 13 ♘b3!? ♗xf2+ 14 ♔f1 ♗b6 15 ♗xg5 ♕c7 is fine for Black) and:

(b1) 13 ♘b3 ♖g8! 14 0-0 (14 ♗d2 ♘gxe5 15 0-0-0 ♘xd3+ 16 ♕xd3 b6! 17 cxb6 axb6 gave Black more than enough compensation with his two bishops and open lines on the queenside in P.Popovic-Del Rio Angelis, Halkidiki 2002) 14...♘gxe5 15 ♗d2 ♘xd3 16 ♕xd3 ♖g6 17 ♖fe1 g4 18 ♘fd4 ♘xd4 19 ♘xd4 ♗xc5 20 ♗f4 ♗d7∓ P.Popovic-Kosic, Yugoslavia 2002;

(b2) 13 ♘xg5! may the best try. It tries to keep Black's king exposed. Then 13...♕xe5?! is mentioned by McDonald along with the strong reply 14 ♘b3!, but I think that 13...♘gxe5! makes a better impression. Black can get his pawns moving after 14 ♘b3 ♘xd3+ 15 cxd3 a5! intending 16 a4 b6! 17 ♗e3 bxc5 18 ♖c1 f6 19 ♘f3 d4 20 ♗d2 ♕b6! etc.

8...g5! 9 ♕e3 ♘h6

So we have the same position as we did after 8 ♕g3 except that Black's pawn isn't on h4 (White went to f4 in one move). This makes the move 9...d4!? more plausible: 10 ♕e2 (10 ♕e4 g4! 11 ♘g1 f5! 12 exf6 ♘xf6 13 ♕d3 ♗xc5∓) 10...g4 11 ♘g1 ♗xc5 and Black has a space advantage. His problem is as usual the king. Play might go 12 h3! (12 ♘b3 ♕d5! 13 ♘xc5 ♕xc5 14 h3 ♘xe5 15 hxg4 ♘xg4 and Black is temporarily a pawn ahead) 12...g3!? (to keep lines closed) 13 f4 ♘b4 14 ♘e4 ♗e7 15 a3 ♕a5 16 c3!±.

10 ♗d3

10 ♘b3 ♘f5 11 ♕d2 g4 12 ♘fd4

♘fxd4 13 ♘xd4 ♘xe5 wins a key central pawn and should give adequate play.

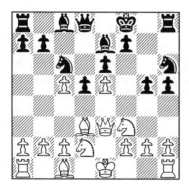

10...♘g4

Black has also tried 10...♕c7 on several occasions: 11 ♘b3 (Black's idea is to trade a flank for centre pawn after 11 ♘xg5?! ♘g4 12 ♕f4 ♕xe5+ 13 ♕xe5 ♘gxe5 14 ♘b3 ♘xd3+ 15 cxd3 ♖g8 and Black wins his pawn back) 11...g4?! (11...♘g4 looks best) 12 ♘fd4 ♕xe5 13 ♘xc6 ♕xe3+ and here Todorovic-Antic, Vrsac 2001 saw 14 fxe3! (14 ♗xe3 bxc6 15 ♘a5 ♗d7 16 0-0 e5 17 a3 f5! was more than satisfactory in Wang Yu-Kamble, Mumbai 2003) 14...bxc6 15 e4 (or 15 0-0!) 15...f6 (15...♗h4+!? 16 g3 ♗f6 – Antic) 16 ♗e3 with an extra pawn, although Black has almost enough central mobility to compensate.

11 ♕e2 ♗xc5 12 ♘b3!

12 0-0 ♘xf2! 13 ♖xf2 g4 14 ♘e1 ♕b6 15 ♘b3 ♗xf2+ 16 ♕xf2 ♕xf2+ 17 ♔xf2 ♘xe5 and Black's extra central pawns give him equal chances.

12...♗xf2+ 13 ♔d1

13 ♔f1 ♗b6 14 ♗xg5 ♕c7 15 h3 ♘gxe5 16 ♘xe5 ♘xe5 17 ♗f6 ♘xd3 18 ♗xh8 ♘f4 19 ♗e5 ♘xe2 20 ♗xc7 ♗xc7 21 ♔xe2 is assessed as slightly better for White by Antic, but this is

hard to believe because Black has the bishop pair, a pawn and a mobile centre in return for the exchange. We are following Blehm-Hausner, Ostrava 1999. At this point 13...♕b6 was promising, the likely course of play being 14 ♗xg5 ♗e3! 15 ♗xe3 ♕xe3, when Black actually wins a pawn, although 16 ♕xe3! ♘xe3+ 17 ♔d2 ♘xg2 18 ♖hg1 gives White some compensation, e.g., 18...♘f4 19 ♖af1! ♘xd3 20 cxd3 ♗d7 21 ♘c5 ♔e7∓.

To play 5...♔f8 one has to be willing to sacrifice a pawn for long-term compensation. There is generally a reward for doing so, but not always. In addition White seems to achieve small edges in some of the early sidelines. None of this is too worrisome but it makes me inclined to lean toward 5...g6 (I don't see a problem with it yet), and truly experimental types could look into 4...♘h6.

7.3 4 ♘gf3

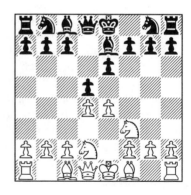

White develops naturally and leaves open the question of what to do with his bishop. In return, Black uses the commitment of White's knight as an inducement to switch strategies.

4...♘f6

Provoking the closing of the centre and a pawn chain struggle.

5 e5

The only try for advantage.

(a) 5 ♗d3 c5 is a subtle move order. Now 6 e5 ♘fd7 transposes to the main line, and White has nothing else particularly dangerous:

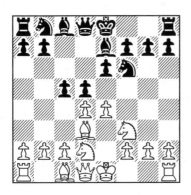

(a1) 6 dxc5 ♘c6 or 6...0-0 would transpose to 4 ♗d3 c5 5 dxc5 etc.; but Black has a nice solution in 6...dxe4 7 ♘xe4 ♘xe4 8 ♗xe4 ♕xd1+ 9 ♔xd1 ♗xc5=, a position dealt with in the next section via 4 ♗d3 c5 5 dxc5 ♘f6 6 ♘gf3 dxe4 etc.;

(a2) 6 exd5 ♕xd5 7 dxc5 transposes to the order 4 ♗d3 c5 5 dxc5 ♘f6 6 exd5 ♕xd5 7 ♘gf3 in the next section, and 6...exd5 is also fine: 7 dxc5 0-0 8 0-0 (8 b4 a5 9 c3 axb4 10 cxb4 ♘c6 11 ♖b1 ♖xa2=; 8 ♘b3 ♘bd7 [8...a5 is more interesting, but this will do] 9 ♗e3 ♕c7 10 0-0 ♘xc5=) 8...♗xc5. An isolated queen's pawn position arises in which Black has taken two tempi to capture on c5, but White's bishop is not ideally placed on d3. In Chow-J.Watson, Chicago 2003, play continued 9 ♘b3 ♗b6 10 h3 ♘c6 11 c3 ♖e8=;

(a3) 6 c3 cxd4 (6...♘c6 transposes to the main line after 7 e5 ♘d7) 7 cxd4 dxe4 8 ♘xe4 with an easy-to-play isolani position: 8...♘c6 (or 8...♘xe4!? 9 ♗xe4 ♘d7 10 0-0 0-0-0= De

la Paz-Arribas, Santa Clara 2001) 9 0-0 0-0 10 ♗e3 (10 ♕c2 ♘b4 11 ♘xf6+ gxf6! 12 ♕d1 ♘xd3 13 ♕xd3 ♔h8=) 10...♘b4 (or 10...♘d5=) 11 ♗b1 b6 12 ♘xf6+ (12 ♘g3 ♗b7 13 a3 ♘bd5 14 ♕d3 ♕d6∓ Kosintseva-Matveeva, Elista 2002) 12...♗xf6 13 ♗e4 ♘d5=;

(b) 5 exd5 exd5 is a comfortable Exchange Variation for Black, since White's knight gets in the way on d2: 6 ♗d3 0-0 7 0-0 ♗g4 8 c3 c5!? 9 dxc5 ♗xc5 10 ♘b3 ♗b6 11 ♖e1 (11 ♗g5 ♘c6 12 h3 ♗h5 13 ♖e1 ♕d6=) 11...♘c6 12 ♗e3?! ♖e8 13 ♗xb6 ♕xb6 14 ♗e2 a5! 15 ♖b1 ♗f5 16 ♗d3 ♖xe1+ 17 ♘xe1 ♘e4∓ was the game Akhmadeev-Rustemov, Moscow 1999; Black intends ...♘e5 and ...♖e8.

5...♘fd7

6 ♗d3

(a) 6 c4 has been played a bit but is easily met:

(a1) 6...c5 breaks up the centre, e.g., 7 cxd5 exd5 8 ♕b3 cxd4 9 ♕xd5 ♘c6 10 ♗b5!? ♘b4 11 ♕e4 a6 12 ♗xd7+ ♕xd7 13 a3 ♘c6 14 ♘b3 d3 15 0-0 0-0 and ...♖d8;

(a2) 6...0-0 asks White what he's up to: 7 cxd5 (7 ♗d3!? c5) 7...exd5 8 ♗d3 c5 9 ♕c2 h6 10 dxc5 (10 0-0 ♘c6∓) 10...♘xc5 11 0-0 ♘c6 and White has no good place for his important light-squared bishop.

(b) 6 c3 c5 7 a3!? is an interesting attempt that strongly resembles the a3-b4 ideas in the Advance Variation: 7...a5 (7...♘c6 8 b4 cxd4 9 cxd4 seems to fall in with White's plans, but Black has a clever change of plans in mind: 9...♘b6! 10 ♗d3 ♗d7 with queenside light square pressure, L.Cooper-Cobb, Newport 2001. One idea is ...a6, ...♘a7, and ...♗b5) 8 ♗b5?! (this doesn't work out well, but 8 ♗d3 b6 and ...♗a6 is one easy solution, and 8...a4!? is another way to fight for the light squares) 8...♕b6 9 ♕a4 0-0 10 0-0 ♘c6 11 ♖e1 (White has little to do) 11...f6 12 exf6 ♘xf6 13 ♗d3 ♗d7 14 ♕c2 cxd4 15 c4 h6 16 b3 ♖ac8 17 ♗b2 ♗d6∓ Rozentalis-S.Ivanov, Halkidiki 2002.

6...c5 7 c3 ♘c6 8 0-0

Other moves aren't of much interest here, and most of them can be met by a plan with ...f6, e.g., 8 b3?! f6 9 0-0 fxe5 (9...cxd4 10 cxd4 fxe5 11 ♘xe5 ♘dxe5 12 dxe5 ♘xe5 13 ♕h5+ ♘f7∓) 10 ♘xe5 ♘dxe5 11 dxe5 ♘xe5 12 ♕h5+ ♘f7 13 ♗xh7 Sutor-Vyoshin, Krakow 1999, and easiest was to get to the queenside by 13...♗f6 14 ♗b2 ♕a5 15 ♘f3 ♗d7 16 ♖fe1 0-0-0 17 ♕xf7 ♖xh7∓.

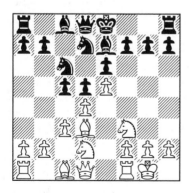

This position arose in the old days via 3 ♘d2 ♘f6 4 e5 ♘fd7 5 ♘gf3 c5 6 c3 ♘c6 7 ♗d3 ♗e7!? 8 0-0. Normally White would rather have his queen's knight go to f3 and his king's knight to e2, but it does take him one less tempo to arrange his knights this way and there are various attacking ideas that can stem from the ♘gf3 move. Furthermore, Black has committed his king's bishop on e7 whereas in the corresponding position he had 7...♕b6 8 0-0 g6 or 7...g6 Thus both sides have made small concessions from what they might ideally like and this tradeoff leads to unique play in fairly unexplored territory.

8...a5

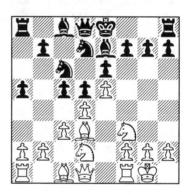

A subtle and multipurpose move that has become one of the main lines here, but no one knows what's best. Perhaps it shouldn't come as a surprise that the two moves receiving the most attention are 8...a5 and 8...g5, both flank moves that don't develop a piece or even prepare to develop one. These days centres are both protected and attacked from the wings.

Black has two other exciting approaches:

(a) It is worth mentioning the old line 8...♕b6!? 9 ♖e1 (9 dxc5! is the most critical move) and now an attractive mixing of systems is 9...g5! 10 ♘f1 (10 c4 g4 11 cxd5 exd5!∓, e.g., 12 e6 fxe6 13 ♘e5 ♘dxe5 14 dxe5 c4 15 ♗c2 ♗c5-+) 10...g4 11 dxc5 ♗xc5 12 ♘d4 ♘dxe5 13 ♗f4 ♘xd3 14 ♕xd3 ♘xd4 15 cxd4 ♗xd4 16 ♗e3 ♗xe3 17 ♘xe3 0-0 18 ♘xg4 f6 and Black has stood well in a couple of games (giving back the pawn via ...e5 is a theme);

(b) An older, likely better, and still hotly contested line is 8...g5!?, to chase the f3 knight away from defence of the centre and/or to grab space.

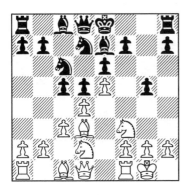

I won't attempt to cover all the dense theory of this variation, but here are a few lines that should indicate roughly where things stand:

(b1) 9 b4?! cxd4 10 cxd4 ♘xb4 11 ♗b1 b6 12 a3 ♘c6 13 ♘b3 ♗a6 14 ♖e1 ♗c4∓ Conquest-A.Summerscale, England 2001;

(b2) 9 h3 is one of the oldest moves, but Black seems fine after 9...h5 10 g4 hxg4 11 hxg4 ♕b6 12 ♕a4 ♕c7 (or 12...cxd4 13 cxd4 f6) 13 ♖e1 ♘b6 14 ♕d1 cxd4 15 cxd4 ♗d7 16 ♘b3 0-0-0! 17 ♔g2 f6 with good kingside prospects, Saltaev-Poldauf, Plovdiv 1988;

(b3) 9 ♔h1!? is the latest try: 9...h5 (9...♕b6!?) 10 dxc5 ♗xc5 (or 10...g4! 11 ♘d4 ♘dxe5!? 12 ♗b5 (Dembo);

then 12...♗xc5! 13 f4 ♗xd4 14 cxd4 ♘d7∓) 11 ♗b5 g4 12 ♗xc6 bxc6 13 ♘d4 Dembo-Goczo, Magyarorszag 2002. Dembo analyses 13...♘xe5 14 f4 ♗xd4!? 15 ♕a4 ♗b6 16 fxe5 'with attack on the king' but this doesn't look at all convincing;

(b4) 9 a3!? (another recent move) 9...cxd4 10 cxd4 ♕b6 (McDonald suggests 10...g4 11 ♘e1 f5!? 12 exf6 ♘xf6 13 ♘c2 ♗d7, which can fairly be described as 'unclear' after 14 f3 ♕b6) 11 ♘b3 g4 12 ♘e1?! (12 ♘g5! ♘f8!? threatens ...h6 and pretty much commits White to the unclear piece sacrifice 13 ♗c2! h6 14 ♘xf7 ♔xf7 15 ♕xg4 with considerable compensation and something like dynamic equality after 15...h5. Both this position and earlier alternatives need to be looked at) 12...♘xd4 13 ♘xd4 ♕xd4 14 ♘c2 ♕xe5 15 ♕xg4 h5 16 ♕h3 ♘c5 17 ♗b5+ ♗d7 and White lacked compensation for the pawn and centre in Hossain-Barsov, Dhaka 2003;

(b5) 9 dxc5 and now:

(b51) 9...♘dxe5 10 ♗b5 (10 ♘xe5 ♘xe5 11 ♗b5+ ♗d7 12 ♕e2 ♗xb5 13 ♕xb5+ ♕d7 14 ♕e2 ♘g6=) 10...♗d7 11 ♕e2 ♕c7 12 ♖e1 ♘g6 13 ♘b3 g4 14 ♘fd4 e5 with at least equality, Rublevsky-Volkov, Ohrid 2001;

(b52) 9...g4 10 ♘d4 ♘dxe5 11 ♘2b3 (11 ♗b5! – Dembo; but then 11...♗xc5 looks equal after, e.g., 12 ♖e1 ♗d7 13 ♗xc6 ♘xc6 14 ♕xg4 ♕f6 15 ♘2b3! ♗b6 16 ♗f4 0-0-0) 11...♘xd3 12 ♕xd3 e5 13 ♘xc6 bxc6 14 ♗h6 (14 f4 gxf3 15 ♕xf3 f6 16 ♕h5+ ♔d7 – Izoria) 14...f6 15 f4 gxf3 (15...e4!?) 16 ♕xf3 ♖g8 17 ♕h5+ ♖g6 18 ♗e3 ♕d7! 19 h3 (19 ♕xh7 ♕g4 20 g3 ♗f5= – Izoria) 19...♗d8= Gasanov-Izoria, Baku 2002.

9 ♖e1

Other moves are no better:

(a) 9 b3 a4! 10 bxa4 c4 (or 10...♕a5!) 11 ♗c2 ♕a5 12 ♘b1 (12 ♗b2 ♘b6) 12...h6! 13 ♗a3 ♘b6 14 h4?! (14 ♗xe7 ♘xe7 15 ♘a3=) 14...♗d7∓ Sulskis-Lputian, Las Vegas 2001;

(b) 9 ♕e2 cxd4 10 cxd4 ♘b6!? (10...g5!; 10...♕b6) 11 ♖d1 a4 12 ♘f1 ♘b4 13 ♗b1 ♘c4 14 ♘e3 b5= Van der Wiel-Korchnoi, Antwerp 1993.

9...cxd4

An experiment was 9...a4!? 10 dxc5 ♘xc5 11 ♗c2 f6 12 exf6 ♗xf6 13 ♘f1 0-0 14 ♘e3 a3! unclear, Ulibin-Shulman, Calcutta 1999.

10 cxd4 ♕b6

10...g5!? is a recent treatment: 11 g4?! (White stops ...g4, but as in several such cases, his kingside becomes vulnerable; better is 11 h3! h5 12 ♘f1! g4 13 hxg4 hxg4 14 ♘3h2, when 14...♘xd4 15 ♕xg4 and 14...♕b6 15 ♗e3 are both unclear) 11...h5 12 h3 hxg4 13 hxg4 ♕b6 14 ♕a4!? Gormally-McDonald, London 2001; and now Gormally suggests 14...♘f8! (14...f6!? McDonald) 15 ♘f1 ♗d7; then 16 ♗e3 (in view of 16 ♗b5? ♘xe5!; and 16 ♕d1 ♘xd4) 16...♕xb2 17 ♖ab1 ♘b4! gives Black an extra pawn and a seeming advantage.

11 ♕a4?!
This leads to a cute miniature. More critical moves are:

(a) 11 a3 g5! 12 h3 h5 13 ♘f1 (13 g4? hxg4 14 hxg4 ♘xd4) 13...g4 14 hxg4 hxg4 15 ♘3h2 ♕xd4 16 ♘xg4 ♘c5 (16...♗c5!?) 17 ♗c2 ♕xd1 18 ♖xd1 b6 19 ♗e3 ♗b7 (19...♘a6 20 ♘f6+ ♔d8!? 21 ♖ab1? ♗xf1! 22 ♔xf1 ♘xe5∓ Nisipeanu-Lputian, Batumi 1999) 20 ♖d2 0-0-0 21 ♖ad1 ♖dg8 22 ♘fh2 d4∓ Nouro-Gleizerov, Stockholm 1998;

(b) 11 ♕e2 g5! 12 h3 h5 13 ♘f1 ♘xd4!? (13...g4! 14 hxg4 hxg4 15 ♘3h2 ♕xd4) 14 ♘xd4 ♕xd4 15 ♘h2 g4! 16 hxg4 hxg4 17 ♘xg4 ♖g8 18 ♘h6 ♖g7= Rublevsky-Lputian, Montecatini Terme 2000;

(c) 11 ♘b1! (a nice attacking gambit) 11...♘xd4 12 ♘xd4 ♕xd4 13 ♘c3 ♗c5! (an aggressive replacement for the usual 13...♕b6) 14 ♘b5 (14 ♗e3 ♕h4 15 g3 ♕e7 16 ♘b5 0-0 17 ♕c2 b6!? 18 ♗xh7+ ♔h8 19 ♗xc5 ♘xc5 20 ♗d3 ♘xd3 21 ♕xd3 ♗a6, at least equal) 14...♕xf2+ 15 ♔h1 0-0 16 ♗g5 ♗b4!? 17 ♖e3 g6 (or 17...f5) 18 ♖f3 ♕xb2 19 ♗f4 ♘c5 20 ♗c2 ♗d7 21 ♘d6 ♗a4 22 ♗xa4 ♘xa4 23 ♖b3 ♕f2 24 ♖f3 ♕b2 ½-½ B.Vuckovic-Solak, Belgrade 2000.

11...g5 12 ♘b3?
Remarkably, this practically loses by force. But McDonald's excellent suggestion after 12 h3 h5 13 g4 is 13...♘f8! 'planning ...♗d7, ...♘g6, etc.'
12...g4 13 ♘fd2 ♕c7! 14 ♘f1?
But there's really no salvation. McDonald analyses 14 ♗b1! b5! 15 ♕xb5 ♗a6 16 ♕a4 ♘b6; also bad are 14 ♗f1 ♘b6 15 ♕b5 a4 16 ♘c5 ♘d7! 17 ♘xd7 ♗xd7-+; and 14 ♗e2 ♘b6 15 ♕b5 ♗d7!-+.
14...♘b6 15 ♕b5 a4 0-1
This was the game Kwiatkowski-Rendle, Hastings Challengers 2000. White resigned in view of 16 ♘c5 ♖a5.

7.4 4 ♗d3 c5 5 dxc5

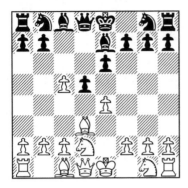

This is currently the main line of the 3...♗e7 variation at the top levels. White hopes the e7 bishop will move twice while he develops smoothly via ♕e2, ♘gf3, 0-0 and very often e5. Black does has the advantage of two centre pawns versus one, and it is often true that the bishop on d3 can be subject to tempo-winning attacks which allow Black to catch up in development. The main lines see a lot of dynamic pawn sacrifices for Black, but he also has calmer solutions.

5...♘f6

5...♘d7 is increasingly played and would be an ideal answer to this system, but I don't believe in the theoretical solutions to the rare sequence 6 exd5 (or 6 b4) 6...exd5 7 b4. One highly tactical line is 7...a5 8 a3! axb4 9 ♗b2 ♘xc5 10 ♗xg7 ♗f6 11 ♗b5+! ♗d7 12 ♗xd7+ ♘xd7 13 ♗xh8! (queried by commentators) 13...♗xh8 14 ♖a2 ♖xa3 and now I think that White can control the a-pawn after 15 ♖xa3! bxa3 16 ♘e2 and 16...♘c5 17 0-0 a2 18 c3 or 16...a2 17 c3 ♕a5 18 0-0. If the reader can answer the b4 idea, then I recommend 5...♘d7 as a good alternative.

6 ♕e2

This is definitely the most danger-

ous move for Black. The alternative tries seem rather timid in comparison:

(a) 6 exd5 ♕xd5 (6...exd5 is also equal, and is treated under the order 4 ♘gf3 ♘f6 5 ♗d3 c5 6 exd5 exd5) 7 ♘gf3 ♘bd7! (to put the knight on c5 rather the bishop or queen) 8 ♘b3 (8 0-0 ♘xc5 9 ♗c4 ♕d6 10 ♕e2 0-0 11 ♘e5 b6 12 ♘df3 ♘d5 13 ♖d1 ♗b7= Starostits-Drasko, Cutro 2002; 8 b4 a5 9 ♗c4 ♕h5 10 c3 ♘d5 11 ♗xd5 ♕xd5 12 ♕b3 ♗f6 13 ♖b1 ♘e5 14 0-0 ♘d3∓ Kholmov-Morozevich, Perm 1998) 8...♘xc5 9 ♘xc5 ♕xc5 10 0-0 0-0 11 ♗e3 ♕c7 12 ♗d4 b6 13 ♕e2 ♗b7 Bellia-Drasko, Italy 1999. This kind of position with 4 kingside pawns to 3 and a queenside minority tends to be favourable for Black unless White has a nice lead in development;

(b) 6 ♘gf3 allows Black to simplify by 6...dxe4 7 ♘xe4 ♘xe4 8 ♗xe4 ♕xd1+ 9 ♔xd1 ♗xc5 10 ♔e2 ♘d7=; again Black has the 4-3, 2-3 advantage, although White doesn't have any problems after the reply 11 ♗e3! (alternatively 11 ♖d1 ♘f6 12 ♗g5 ♗d7! 13 ♗xf6 gxf6) 11...♗xe3 12 ♔xe3 ♘c5 13 ♘d2 (13 ♖ad1?! ♘xe4 14 ♔xe4 b6 15 ♔e3 ♗b7 16 c4 ♔e7 17 ♖d4 ♖ad8 18 ♖hd1 ♖xd4 19 ♖xd4 ♖c8∓ Furhoff-Djurhuus, Sweden 2002, for example, 13...♘xe4 14 ♘xe4 ♔e7 (14...♗d7!?) 15 ♖hd1 b6 16 ♖d2 ♗b7 17 ♖ad1 ♖hd8 18 ♖xd8 ♖xd8 19 ♖xd8 ♔xd8 20 ♘d6 ♗xg2 21 ♘xf7+ ♔e7 22 ♘e5;

(c) 6 b4?! doesn't work this time due to 6...a5 7 c3 dxe4 8 ♘xe4 ♘xe4 9 ♗xe4 ♕xd1+ 10 ♔xd1 axb4 11 cxb4 11...f5!? (or 11...♗f6 12 ♖b1 ♖xa2) 12 ♗c2 (12 ♗f3 ♗f6 13 ♖b1 ♖xa2 14 ♗d2 0-0 with an early ...e5) 12...♘c6 13 ♗d2 ♗f6 14 ♖b1 ♘d4∓.

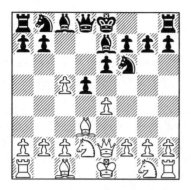

6 ♕e2 initiates one of the most hotly debated lines in the French Defence. I will examine one relatively calm solution and one that is well known but on the edge:

7.41 6...0-0
7.42 6...♘c6

7.41 6...0-0

I recommend the following lesser-known sequence as a first system and a sound way to avoid having to keep up with the latest nuances of theory.
7 ♘gf3

Others are easier to meet:

(a) 7 b4?! a5 8 c3 axb4 9 cxb4 ♘c6 10 ♖b1 ♖xa2∓ (or 10...b6! 11 cxb6 ♘xb4∓);

(b) 7 e5 ♘fd7 8 ♘b3 a5

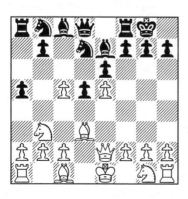

A position that is surprisingly easy for Black:

(b1) 9 c3 a4 10 ♘d4 ♘xc5 11 ♗c2 f5 12 exf6 ♗xf6 13 f4 (13 ♘gf3 e5!) 13...b6!? 14 ♘gf3 (14 ♕e3!? e5! 15 fxe5 ♗xe5 16 ♘gf3 ♗f4∓) 14...♗a6 15 ♕e3 ♕d7∓, e.g., 16 ♗d2 ♘c6 17 ♘xc6 ♕xc6 18 ♘d4 ♗xd4 19 ♕xd4 ♗c4!∓;

(b2) 9 a4 ♘a6!? 10 ♗xa6 ♖xa6 11 ♘f3 ♘xc5 12 ♘xc5 ♗xc5 13 0-0 ♖a8 14 c4 b6∓;

(b3) 9 ♕h5?! g6 10 ♕e2 ♘c6 and White is in trouble due to problems with the e-pawn;

(b31) 11 ♗h6 ♖e8 12 ♘f3 a4 13 ♘bd4?! (13 ♘bd2 a3 14 b3 ♘dxe5!) 13...♘dxe5! 14 ♘xe5 ♘xd4 etc.;

(b32) 11 ♘f3 a4 12 ♘bd2 (12 ♘bd4 ♘dxe5) 12...♕c7!∓ or 12...a3!?∓.
7...a5!?

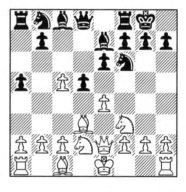

I think that this is the most effective of the move orders by which Black advances the a-pawn and prevents b4 in order to capture on c5 with a knight. ...a5 also anticipates White's move ♘b3 (to which ...a4 will be the reply) and opens up the two possibilities of ...♘a6 (hitting c5) or ...b6 and ...♗a6. The negative side of 7...a5 is of course that it doesn't develop a piece, but these flank pawn moves are increasingly acceptable in modern chess. In a similar vein, there are two little-known plans that deserve attention:

(a) 7...♘c6 8 0-0 (8 exd5!? exd5 9 ♘b3 a5! 10 a4 ♖e8 11 ♗e3 d4 12 0-0-0 dxe3 13 ♗xh7+ ♔xh7 14 ♖xd8 ♗xd8 15 fxe3 ♔g8! unclear) 8...♘d7!? (the point; compare our main line) 9 exd5 (9 ♘b3 ♘xc5 10 ♘xc5 ♗xc5) 9...exd5 10 ♘b3 ♘xc5 (10...a5!?) 11 ♘xc5 ♗xc5;

(b) 7...♘fd7 8 ♘b3 (8 b4 a5 9 c3 axb4 10 cxb4 ♘c6; 8 exd5 ♘xc5!? 9 dxe6 ♘xd3+ 10 ♕xd3 ♗xe6 11 ♕xd8 ♖xd8 12 0-0 ♘c6 with compensation in the form of activity and the two bishops) 8...a5 (or 8...♘xc5 9 ♘xc5 ♗xc5 10 0-0 ♘c6) 9 exd5 exd5 10 ♗e3 a4 11 ♘bd4 ♘xc5 12 0-0 a3 13 b3 ♘xd3 14 ♕xd3 ♘c6 with a reasonable position.

8 0-0

The most natural move but as usual there are serious alternatives here:

(a) 8 a4 ♘a6 9 e5 ♘d7 10 ♘b3 (10 0-0 ♘dxc5 11 ♗b5 ♘c7=; 10 ♗xa6 ♖xa6 gives up the powerful d3 bishop and should not be dangerous: 11 ♘b3 ♘xc5 12 ♘xc5 ♗xc5 13 ♗e3 b6=) 10...♘axc5 11 ♘xc5 ♘xc5 12 0-0 ♘xd3 (or 12...♗d7 13 ♗b5 ♗xb5 14 axb5 ♕c7 15 ♗f4 ♘e4) 13 ♕xd3 b6 14 ♖e1 ♗a6 15 ♕d1 ♖c8∓ P.Carlsson-Kruppa, Halkidiki 2002;

(b) 8 c3 ♘fd7 9 exd5 ♘xc5! 10 ♗b5!? exd5 11 0-0 ♘c6 (or 11...♘ba6 12 ♖e1 ♗f6 13 ♘d4 ♘c7 14 ♘2f3 ♗g4!? 15 h3 ♗h5 16 ♗e3 ♗xd4!? 17 ♗xd4 ♘5e6= – Radjabov) 12 ♘d4 Almasi-Radjabov, Pamplona 2001; and although 12...♗d7 equalised with time, Radjabov suggests 12...♘xd4! 13 cxd4 ♘e6 14 ♘f3 ♘c7 (I like 14...♗f6! 15 ♗e3 ♘c7 16 ♗d3 ♗g4=) 15 ♗d3 ♗g4 16 ♕e3! ♗d6 17 ♘e5 ♗e6 unclear;

(c) 8 e5 ♘fd7 9 ♘b3 a4 10 ♘bd4 ♘xc5=. After the bishop on d3 falls, Black has no problems.

8...♘a6

This seems to equalise rather easily. Black wants to play ...♘xc5 and capture the bishop on d3, but he leaves d7 free for the other knight in case of e5. In fact, it can go there immediately: 8...♘fd7 has been played several times with respectable results, e.g., 9 exd5 exd5 10 ♖e1 (10 ♘b3 a4 11 ♘bd4 ♘xc5 12 ♗f5 ♘c6= Grabarska-Mkrtchian, Warsaw 2001) 10...♘c6 11 ♗b5 (11 ♘b3 a4 12 ♘bd4 ♘xd4 13 ♘xd4 ♗xc5 14 ♗e3 ♖e8 15 c3 ♘e5 16 ♗b5 ♗d7 17 ♖ad1 ♘g4=) 11...♗f6 12 c3 ♘xc5 13 ♘b3 ♘e6!? (13...♘xb3 14 axb3 d4) 14 ♗e3 a4 15 ♘bd4 Lakos-H.Richards, Bled 2002; and 15...♘exd4 16 ♘xd4 ♘xd4 17 ♗xd4 ♗xd4 18 cxd4 ♕b6 was equal.

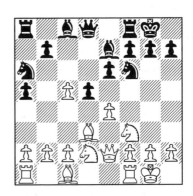

9 exd5

9 ♗xa6?! ♖xa6 doesn't help White (see the note to White's 10th); so the main alternative is 9 e5 ♘d7 (Black gets the move he's been wanting: ...♘xc5) 10 c3 (10 ♘d4 ♘dxc5 11 f4 ♕b6 12 ♘2f3 ♗d7∓ Kotronias-Barsov, Montreal 2002) 10...♘axc5 11 ♗c2 b6 12 ♖e1 Jens-Papa, Deizisau 2003; and a change of scene by 12...f6! seems indicated: (12...♗a6 13 ♕e3

f6!?) 13 exf6 ♗xf6=, due to Black's mobile centre and f-file.

9...exd5

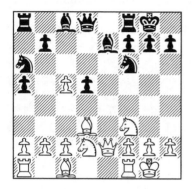

This is sound and well tested. 9...♕xd5 has been played a lot, but I'm not happy with the response 10 ♘c4! ♗xc5 11 c3 of P.Carlsson-Kjartansson, Hallsberg 2003.

10 ♖e1!

This untried move looks best, as it tries to either stop Black from capturing with the knight on c5 or to lure a rook to e8 where the bishop can attack it.

(a) 10 ♘b3 a4 (10...♘xc5 11 ♘xc5 ♗xc5=) 11 ♘bd4 ♘xc5 12 ♗b5 ♘fe4 (or 12...♗d7) 13 a3 ♗g4 14 h3 ♗h5 (14...♗xf3 15 ♕xf3 ♕b6!) 15 ♘f5 ♗f6 16 ♖d1 ♖a5 and Black was doing quite well in Womacka-Djurhuus, Gausdal 2002;

(b) 10 ♗b5 ♘xc5 11 ♖d1 ♕c7=;

(c) 10 ♗xa6 ♖xa6 leaves Black the two bishops and develops his rook actively, all for the sake of preventing a knight capture on c5. Black is probably already better, as in 11 ♘d4 ♖e8 12 ♕b5 ♕c7 13 ♘2f3 ♗d7!? (or 13...♗xc5∓; Black is active and better developed) 14 c6! ♗xc6 15 ♘xc6 Lenic-Erdos, Pula 2003; and even now 15...♕xc6! 16 ♕xc6 bxc6 is better for Black.

10...♖e8! 11 ♘b3 ♘xc5

A good alternative is 11...a4! 12 ♘bd4 ♘xc5 13 ♗b5 ♗d7 14 ♗xd7 (or 14 ♗e3=) 14...♕xd7 15 ♘e5?! ♕c8 and Black threatens ...♗d6 with good play.

After 11...♘c5, play might go 12 ♗g5 ♗d7 13 ♘xc5 ♗xc5 14 ♕d2 ♕b6= (another typical isolated pawn position in which Black has nice activity), when 15 ♗xf6 ♕xf6 16 c3 ♗g4= is a natural continuation.

7.42 6...♘c6 7 ♘gf3 ♘b4!?

For a second system I offer this often wild and tactical line championed by Morozevich. It has survived scrutiny for the last decade, so the likelihood of a refutation is remote. However, I do feel that a couple of lines are slightly but stably better for White. In them, White is a pawn up but Black has the bishop pair versus either the knight pair or a knight and bishop. One can argue that the bishop pair offers full compensation, and strong players including Morozevich are still playing 7...♘b4 without fear; nevertheless I don't feel that this system offers quite the positive chances that 6...0-0 and ...a5 does, so I will try to give a helpful repertoire without providing total detail.

Interestingly, 7...a5!? is also playable here and unrefuted. Briefly, the main line runs 8 0-0 (8 e5 ♘d7 9 0-0 ♘xc5 when the knight has gotten to c5 with no resistance) 8...0-0 9 c4 a4! 10 ♖d1 (10 cxd5 exd5 11 exd5 ♕xd5 frees Black's c8 bishop) 10...♗xc5 11 exd5 exd5 12 cxd5 ♘b4! 13 ♘e4 ♘xd3 14 ♘xf6+ (14 ♖xd3 ♘xe4 15 ♕xe4 ♖e8 16 ♕f4 ♕b6 when White had to give back the pawn by 17 ♗e3 with an unclear position which looked at least equal for Black after 17...♕xb2 18 ♖e1 ♕b4 19 ♕xb4 ♗xb4 20 ♖c1 ♗f5 Marinkovic-Drasko, Vrnjacka Banja 1999) 14...♕xf6 15 ♕xd3 ♗f5 and the bishops offer nice compensation: 16 ♕b5 b6 17 ♗g5 (17 ♗e3 ♖a5 18 ♕e2 ♗xe3 19 fxe3 a3 with near equality and a quick draw, Rublevsky-Pelletier, Poikovsky 2003) 17...♕g6 18 ♗e3 ♗xe3 19 ♘h4 ♕f6 20 ♘xf5 ♗xf2+ 21 ♔xf2 ♕xf5+ with approximate equality (soon drawn), Asrian-Lputian, Yerevan 2000.

8 ♘b3

Not necessarily best. Here are some options:

(a) 8 0-0 has become very popular and often yields a small positional edge.

As usual, Black must play sharply:
(a1) 8...♘xd3 9 cxd3 ♗xc5 10 ♘b3

♗e7 11 ♗g5 (11 e5 ♘d7 12 ♘fd4 0-0 13 ♗f4 ♘c5 14 ♕g4 ♔h8 15 ♘xc5 ♗xc5 16 ♘f3 ♗e7 17 ♖fe1 ♗d7 18 ♕h5 f6!= Svidler-Radjabov, Moscow 2002) 11...h6 12 ♗h4 ♗d7 13 e5 (13 ♗xf6 ♗xf6 14 exd5 ♗b5!∓; 13 ♖ac1 dxe4! 14 dxe4 ♕b6 15 ♖fd1 ♗a4 16 ♕c4 ♗xb3 17 axb3 0-0= Ponomariov-Morozevich, Istanbul 2000) 13...♘g8 14 ♗xe7 (14 ♗g3! h5 15 ♗f4 ♘h6 16 ♘fd4‡) 14...♘xe7 15 ♘c5 ♗c6 16 ♘d4 ♕b6 17 ♖fc1 0-0 18 a3 a5 19 ♖c3 ♖fc8 20 ♖ac1 ♗e8 21 ♕d2 ♖c7 22 ♖3c2 a4 was only very mildly better for White in Luther-Duppel, Boblinger 2000;

(a2) 8...0-0 9 e5 (9 ♘b3! a5 10 a4 b6 11 e5 ♘d7 12 c6 ♘xc6‡ Sadykov-Bhat, Oropesa del Mar 2001) 9...♘d7 10 ♘b3 a5 11 a4 ♘xd3 12 cxd3 ♘xc5 13 ♘xc5 ♗xc5 14 d4 (14 ♗e3 d4 15 ♗f4 ♕d5∓ Mrva-Kostenko, Istanbul 2000) 14...♗e7 15 ♗d2 b6= Heim-L.Johannessen, Bergen 2001;

(b) 8 e5 ♘d7 9 ♘b3 ♘xd3+ 10 ♕xd3!? (10 cxd3 ♘xc5 11 ♘xc5 ♗xc5 12 d4 ♗e7=) 10...a5! 11 ♗e3 (11 a4 b6! 12 cxb6 ♗a6 13 ♕e3 [13 ♕d1 ♕xb6] 13...0-0 14 ♘xa5 ♗c5 – McDonald; White is probably somewhat better after 15 ♘d4 ♕xb6 16 ♘ab3 ♗e7, although it's hard to find a positive plan) 11...a4 12 ♘bd2 0-0 13 0-0 ♘xc5 14 ♕d4 ♗d7 15 ♕g4 ♔h8 16 ♖ad1 ♖c8 17 c4 f5! Zagrebelny-Morozevich, Moscow 2003; Black is very active and stands better. Note that Morozevich is still willing to defend his system as this book is being written;

(c) 8 exd5 ♕xd5 9 ♘b3 ♗d7 10 0-0 (10 ♗c4 ♕e4=; 10 ♗e3! ♘xd3+ 11 ♕xd3 ♕xd3 12 cxd3 ♗b5 – Goloshchapov; a touch better for White, but not much) 10...♘xd3 11 ♕xd3 ♕xd3 12 cxd3 ♗b5 13 ♖d1 ♗a4! 14 d4 ♘d5!? with a blockade, Ganguly-Goloshchapov, Sangli 2000;

(d) 8 ♗b5+?! ♗d7 9 0-0!? ♘xc2 10 ♗xd7+ ♘xd7! (McDonald) gives Black a substantial advantage.

8...♘xd3+

A number of well-known world-class struggles stemmed from this move. Also seen is 8...a5!?, but 9 ♗b5+! (9 ♗g5 a4 10 ♘bd2 a3!? 11 b3 0-0 12 0-0 h6, when again 13 ♗e3± may be best) 9...♗d7 10 ♗xd7+ ♘xd7 Kanovsky-Jurek, Roznov 2002; and I think that 11 c3!? with the idea 11...♘a6 12 exd5 exd5 13 c6! bxc6 14 ♘bd4! and ♘f5 is very promising.

9 cxd3 a5

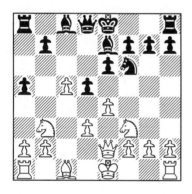

10 ♗g5

Objectively 10 a4 seems to yield some advantage but practice is a different matter: 10...b6!? 11 e5 ♘d7 12 c6 ♘c5 13 ♘bd4 ♗a6 14 ♘b5 (14 ♖a3 ♘e4!=) 14...♘b3 (14...d4 15 ♘fxd4! ♗xb5 16 ♘xb5 ♘xd3+ 17 ♔f1 favoured White in Barua-Ravi, New Delhi 2001) 15 ♖b1 ♗b4+ 16 ♔f1 0-0 17 d4 f6! 18 ♕e3?! (18 ♕d3! seems to improve, e.g., 18...♗xb5 19 axb5 a4 20 g3, and if 20...♘xc1?! 21 ♖xc1 ♕e8 22 exf6 gxf6 23 ♔g2±) 18...♗xb5+! 19 axb5 a4 20 g3 ♕e8! 21 ♕d3 (a crucial tempo down on the note to White's 18th) 21...♘xc1 22 ♖xc1 a3 23 b3 (23 bxa3 ♖xa3 24 ♕e2 ♕h5) 23...a2 24

♔g2 ♕g6! 25 ♕xg6 hxg6 and Black had the better chances (again White lacks a plan) in Adams-Morozevich, Wijk aan Zee 2000.

10...a4!?

10...0-0 is recommended by McDonald: 11 0-0 (11 e5?! ♘d7 12 ♗xe7 ♕xe7 13 d4 b6! 14 c6 ♗a6 15 ♕d2 ♘b8 16 ♖c1 ♖c8∓) 11...b6! 12 ♘e5 (12 e5) 12...dxe4 'with messy play, but Black looks fine', according to McDonald. Still, 13 ♘c6 exd3 14 ♕e3 ♕c7 15 ♘xe7+ ♕xe7 16 cxb6 probably favours White somewhat. The b-pawn is dangerous and d3 is vulnerable.

11 ♘bd2 h6

11...dxe4 12 dxe4 ♘d7 13 ♗xe7 ♕xe7 14 ♖c1 0-0 15 ♕e3! ♖a5 16 0-0 ♖xc5 17 ♕a3 b5 18 ♘e5! ♖e8 19 ♖xc5 ♕xc5 20 ♕xc5 ♘xc5 21 ♖c1 with an irritating pull, Almasi-Timman, Pamplona 1999.

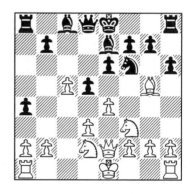

12 ♗xf6!?

12 ♗e3! ♕a5 13 0-0 ♗xc5 14 ♗xc5 ♕xc5 15 ♖fc1 ♕b6 16 e5 ♘g8 17 ♕e3 ♕xe3 18 fxe3 appeared to favour White in Navara-Duppel, Pardubice 2000; an interesting sequence.

12...♗xf6 13 e5

Black also gets counterplay after 13 exd5 a3! (13...0-0 14 dxe6 ♗xe6 15 ♘e4 a3 16 ♘xf6+ ♕xf6 17 ♘e5±) 14 d4 (14 d6 axb2 15 ♖b1 b6! 16 d4 bxc5

17 dxc5 ♖xa2 – Psakhis) 14...axb2 15 ♕b5+ ♕d7 16 ♕xb2 ♕xd5 17 ♕b3 'with the superior chances' – Psakhis; but 17...♕xb3 (or 17...0-0 18 0-0 ♗d7 19 ♕xd5 exd5 20 ♖fb1 ♖a7) 18 ♘xb3 ♗d7 (or 18...♖a4) 19 0-0 0-0 20 ♘e5 ♗b5 21 ♖fb1 ♖a4 and the two bishops fully compensate for the sacrificed pawn.

13...♗e7 14 ♕e3 ♕a5 15 ♖c1 b6!?

15...♗d7 16 0-0 0-0 17 ♖c2 ♖fc8 18 ♖fc1 ♖c7 19 d4 b6!? Pogonina-Matveeva, Elista 2002; yet another of those funny pawn-down two bishops lines if White plays 20 cxb6 ♖xc2 21 ♖xc2 ♕xb6; maybe it's enough, but

I'm not sure.

16 cxb6?!

16 c6 must be better; then 16...♕b5 17 ♖c2 ♗a6 18 ♔e2 has been suggested.

16...♗d8! 17 ♕c5 ♕xc5 18 ♖xc5 ♗xb6 19 ♖c2 0-0 20 ♘f1 ♗a6

with strong bishops and plenty of pressure, Godena-Morozevich, Istanbul 2000. The 7...♘b4 systems are still scoring well at the top levels, which says a lot; you should definitely consider them if you're a fan of the bishop pair. I prefer the 6...0-0/7...a5 plan and I like the fact that it's still relatively unexplored.

Chapter Eight

Winawer Variation: Fourth Move Alternatives

1 e4 e6 2 d4 d5 3 ♘c3 ♗b4

3...♗b4 is the Winawer Variation, one of the most fruitful and exciting openings in chess. Black puts pressure on e4 and prepares to double White's c-pawns with consequent positional pressure. It is one of the premier chess variations because it embraces so many types of closed manoeuvring positions and wide-open tactical ones, often both within the same game. For this edition, I have added an extra repertoire for the move 3...♘f6, hopefully an interesting one. But it's hard to match 3...♗b4 for complexity and excitement. After 3...♗b4, White's main move is 4 e5. Then White has to suffer through a counterattack on his centre and in most cases doubled pawns on c2 and c3. His rewards for this sacrifice are great in terms of both attacking chances and opportunities to dominate his opponent with his bishops, so 4 e5 continues to be easily the most popular choice. But some players prefer to avoid this kind of commitment and choose one of the alternatives in this chapter instead. Theory on and practice with these variations have

exploded and the well-prepared French player must know something about each:

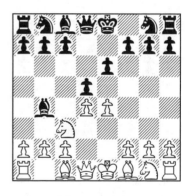

8.1 4 a3
8.2 4 ♕g4
8.3 4 ♗d2
8.4 4 ♘e2
8.5 4 ♗d3
8.6 4 exd5
8.7 4 ♕d3

8.1 4 a3 ♗xc3+

4...♗a5!? probably isn't objectively the best way to deviate, but might appeal to those who want original play and/or don't like 5...♘e7 of the next note. Here's just a sample of

what might happen: 5 b4 ♝b6 6 e5
♞e7 (6...a5?! 7 b5 c5? 8 ♞a4! cxd4 9
♕g4! ♚f8 10 ♞xb6 ♕xb6 11 a4!±
Mortensen-Fant, Copenhagen 2001) 7
♞a4 ♞f5 (7...0-0 is more flexible, e.g.,
...♞d7 and ...f6 or ...f5 might follow) 8
♞f3 0-0 9 ♝g5 f6 10 exf6 gxf6 11
♞xb6 axb6 12 ♝f4 ♞c6 13 b5 (13 ♝d3
e5!? 14 dxe5 fxe5 15 ♞xe5 ♞h4!? 16
♕h5 ♖xf4 17 ♕xh7+ ♚f8 18 ♕h6+
♚e8 19 ♞xc6 ♞xg2+ 20 ♚f1 ♕h4 with
a real mess) 13...♞ce7 intending
...♞g6 and perhaps ...e5. Probably
White gets an edge somewhere in this
line with perfect play (the two bishops must be worth something), but
that advantage will be small and
doesn't negate the value of this idea
for achieving a playable imbalance.

5 bxc3

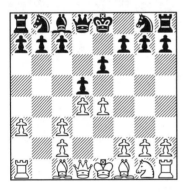

Used by Alekhine, Smyslov, and
Fischer, 4 a3 intends to prove that
White's doubled pawns are not as
important as the dark square vulner-
ability of Black's kingside. It has
never become very popular in top-
level play, however (even the above-
mentioned players mostly employed
other anti-Winawer systems), because White loses a tempo and Black
develops freely. Nevertheless, it is
extremely difficult to play against if
one is unprepared, and to play the

main lines well requires as much
study as any variation in this chapter.

5...dxe4

If one wants to avoid the prepara-
tion of a specialist in 4 a3, 5...♞e7 is a
good option, especially if you're willing to transpose:

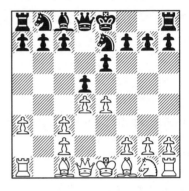

Then 6 e5 c5 is the main line of the
Winawer, and 6 ♕g4 0-0 (with the
idea ...e5) 7 e5 can be answered by
7...c5, which is another main line (7
♕g4 0-0 of Chapter 10); but Black
also has some original alternatives,
e.g. 7...♞d7 with the idea ...f5, securing the kingside before attacking via
...c5. Here are some other tries for
White:

(a) 6 ♝d3 c5 7 exd5 (7 dxc5 ♞d7=,
or 7...dxe4 and ...♕xd1+; 7 ♕g4 0-0 8
e5 is a main line, and instead, both
7...c4 and 7...♞bc6!? are interesting;
finally, after 7 ♞f3 c4 8 ♝e2, Black
has 8...♕a5!?= or 8...dxe4! 9 ♞g5 ♞d5
with the idea 10 ♝xc4 ♕c7 or 10...e3,
or here 10 ♞xe4 f5 11 ♝g5 ♕c7 12
♝h5+ g6 13 ♞f6+ ♞xf6 14 ♝xf6 0-0
15 ♝e5 ♕a5 with good play –
Wintzer) 7...exd5 8 dxc5 ♕a5 (or
8...♞d7 9 ♝e3 ♕c7 intending 10 ♕g4
♞xc5 11 ♕xg7 ♞xd3+ 12 cxd3 ♖g8=)
9 ♞e2 ♞d7 (a sequence that has occurred in several games) 10 ♖b1

♘xc5!? (10...a6! 11 0-0 ♘xc5 12 ♘d4 0-0) 11 ♗b5+ ♗d7 12 ♗xd7+ ♘xd7 13 ♖xb7 ♘c5 14 ♖b4 0-0 (White's extra pawn is balanced by his static weaknesses) 15 0-0 ♖ac8!? (15...♖fe8) 16 ♖h4 (16 c4 ♖fd8) 16...♘e4= Sariego-Arencibia, Bayamo 1990;

(b) 6 exd5 exd5 7 ♘f3 (7 ♗d3 0-0 8 ♘e2 ♗f5=) 7...♗g4 8 ♗e2 0-0 9 0-0 ♘g6 10 a4 ♘c6 11 h3 ♗f5 12 ♗a3 ♖e8 13 ♕d2 ♘a5 and White struggled with light square weaknesses, O.Pedersen-Tonning, Gausdal 1997;

(c) 6 ♘f3 dxe4 7 ♘g5 c5!? (7...0-0 8 ♘xe4 e5! 9 ♗g5?! exd4 10 cxd4 ♕d5!) 8 ♘xe4 cxd4 9 cxd4 ♘bc6 10 c3 e5 11 ♗c4 ♗f5!? (11...0-0 12 ♗g5?! exd4 13 cxd4 b5! 14 ♗a2 ♗f5) 12 ♘g3 (12 ♘g5 0-0∓) 12...exd4 13 0-0 0-0 14 ♗g5 Banas-Herzog, Keszthely 1981; when the light squares would again give Black the advantage after the continuation 14...♗e6! 15 ♗xe6 fxe6 16 cxd4 ♕d5.

After 5...dxe4, we will look at the main traditional move and a popular alternative:

8.11 6 f3
8.12 6 ♕g4

8.11 6 f3
The Winckelmann-Riemer Gambit, which has grown considerably in popularity since the second edition. The idea is to get something resembling the Blackmar-Diemer Gambit (1 d4 d5 2 e4 dxe4 3 ♘c3 ♘f6 4 f3) with Black's dark-squared bishop no longer available for defence. In the last edition I recommended 6...b6, which is reasonable but not very incisive. Since then I have successfully tested one lesser-known idea, and one solution that has been generally recommended also looks good:

8.111 6...♘d7
8.112 6...e5

8.111 6...♘d7
This is a very logical move because it gets out a piece, prepares central breaks (...c5 and ...e5), and doesn't commit to a fixed scheme of development. There is little theory about 6...♘d7, and I like it very much.

7 ♘h3
I think that this is best because White has few other choices that get a piece out effectively. Nevertheless, a knight on h3 is not ideally placed for a Blackmar-Diemer sort of position (it belongs on f3 watching over e5).

(a) 7 fxe4? ♕h4+ forces White's king to move;

(b) 7 ♗e3 ♘gf6 (or 7...exf3, since the bishop shouldn't be on e3 in an attacking system) 8 fxe4 ♘xe4 9 ♕g4 ♘df6 10 ♕xg7 ♖g8 11 ♕h6 ♖g6 12 ♕f4 ♘xc3∓;

(c) 7 a4 ♘gf6 8 ♗a3 c5!? (8...e3!?∓) 9 dxc5 ♘d5! 10 ♕d4 ♕h4+ 11 g3 ♕f6 12 fxe4 ♘xc3 and Black threatens ...♘xe4 while White's pawns are a mess.

7...♘gf6
Also good looks 7...exf3 8 ♕xf3 ♕h4+!? 9 g3 ♕f6, preventing ♕g3 and

asking the queen where it's going, e.g., 10 ♕e2 ♘e7 11 ♗g5 ♕f5 12 ♗g2 ♘f6 13 ♖f1 ♕a5∓.

8 fxe4 ♘xe4 9 ♕g4 ♘df6 10 ♕h4

Black's developmental advantage gets even bigger after 10 ♕xg7 ♖g8 11 ♕h6 ♘xc3 (or simply 11...c5 with the idea ...♕a5: 12 ♗b5+ ♔e7!? 13 0-0 ♕a5 14 ♗d3 ♕xc3 15 ♗xe4 ♘xe4 16 ♕xh7 ♕xd4+ 17 ♔h1 ♘f6) 12 ♗g5 ♖g6 13 ♕h4 ♘ce4 14 ♗xf6 ♘xf6∓.

10...♘xc3

Slower but still effective enough would be 10...c6!? 11 ♗d3 ♕a5 12 0-0 ♕xc3 13 ♖b1 (13 ♗e3 c5!) 13...♕d2 14 ♗xd2 ♕xd2 15 ♕g3 ♕h6∓.

11 ♗d3 ♘fe4 12 ♕f4 f5 13 ♗e3 0-0 14 0-0 ♕d6 15 ♕h4 ♗d7 and Black is two pawns up, Tahiri-J.Watson, Berlin 1997.

8.112 6...e5

This is the solution recommended by just about everyone. It frees the c8 bishop and therefore compels White to try to gain compensation quickly before Black develops.

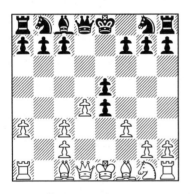

7 ♗e3

Black has a 200-point performance rating advantage after 6...e5, mainly because White has little to do. Again 7 fxe4? ♕h4+ is undesirable, and these alternatives don't help much:

(a) 7 ♗b5+ c6 8 ♗c4 ♕a5∓ (Pedersen), since 9 ♗d2 e3! wins;

(b) 7 a4 exd4 (7...♗e6 has been played several times and must be good as well) 8 cxd4 c5 puts the question to White's centre: 9 dxc5 (9 d5 ♘f6 10 ♗c4 0-0) 9...♕xd1+ 10 ♔xd1 ♗f5 (or 10...♘f6 11 ♗b2 ♘bd7 12 ♗b5 0-0 13 c6 bxc6 14 ♗xc6 ♖b8∓) 11 g4 ♗e6 12 ♗b2 f6!∓; White's pawns are extremely weak.

7...♘c6

Or 7...♗f5; or 7...exd4 8 cxd4?! (8 ♕xd4! ♕xd4!? 9 ♗xd4 f6 10 fxe4 ♘c6∓) 8...♘h6! 9 fxe4 (9 ♗xh6 ♕h4+ 10 g3 ♕xh6∓) 9...♕h4+ 10 ♔d2 ♕xe4 11 ♘f3 ♘f5 12 ♗b5+ ♘c6 13 ♖e1 0-0 with a decisive advantage, Grabarczyk-Gdanski, Lubniewice 1993.

8 ♗b5

Or 8 d5 ♘b8 9 ♗c4 ♘f6. After 8 ♗b5, Oparaugo-Cech, Passau 1997 went 8...♗d7 9 d5 ♘ce7 10 ♗xd7+ ♕xd7∓ (White hasn't developed and his pawn structure is damaged) 11 fxe4 ♘f6 12 ♕d3 ♕g4! 13 ♕b5+ ♘d7! 14 ♔f2 ♕xe4 15 c4 ♕f5+ 16 ♔g3 ♕xc2 17 ♖f1 ♘f5+ 18 ♖xf5 ♕xf5 19 ♕xb7 0-0 20 ♘f3 ♖ab8 21 ♕xa7 ♖b2 22 ♕xc7 ♘f6 0-1.

8.12 6 ♕g4 ♘f6 7 ♕xg7 ♖g8 8 ♕h6 ♘bd7

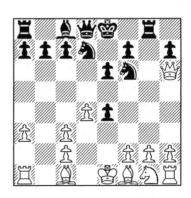

I think that this solution is the most fun. It takes some risks, especially in the main line below, so I will present some options along the way. 8...c5 is an established alternative that I gave in the previous edition, but I'll forego that and discuss similar lines with ...c5 below. After 8...♘bd7, White has:

8.121 9 f3
8.122 9 ♘h3
8.123 9 ♘e2

The latter move is the current favourite. The alternatives are less challenging, but they help to illustrate the basic themes:

(a) 9 ♗b2 is rarely seen anymore because of 9...♘b6! (or 9...c5 10 0-0-0 cxd4 11 cxd4 and one idea is 11...b5! 12 ♗xb5 ♖b8 13 c4 a6 14 ♗xd7+ ♗xd7 and White's king is exposed) 10 c4 (10 a4 ♗d7 11 a5 ♘a4 12 ♕c1 c5 13 ♘e2 ♕xa5 14 dxc5 ♕xc5 15 ♗a3 ♕e5 16 g3 ♖c8!∓ Quinteros-J.Watson Mexico 1976) 10...♘a4 11 0-0-0 ♗d7 12 f3 ♕e7 13 fxe4 (13 ♕e3 ♗c6 14 fxe4 ♗xe4!∓) 13...♘xe4 14 ♕e3 (14 ♕xh7? ♕g5+) 14...f5 15 ♘f3 c5! 16 ♖g1 0-0-0 17 ♕b3 ♘xb2 18 ♕xb2 cxd4 19 ♖xd4 ♗c6 20 ♖xd8+ ♖xd8 21 ♗e2? ♕c5 0-1 Foguelman-R.Byrne, Buenos Aires 1964;

(b) 9 h3 b6 (a legitimate but under-investigated move is 9...c5, e.g., 10 g4 ♕a5 11 ♗d2 ♕a4 12 g5 ♕c6! 13 ♗g2 cxd4 14 cxd4 ♖g6 15 ♕h4 h6 16 gxf6 ♖xg2∓) 10 g4 (10 g3 ♕e7 11 ♗g2 ♖g6 12 ♕h4 ♗a6!? is an idea of Amador Rodriguez; then 13 ♗xe4 loses the light squares, e.g., 13...♘xe4 14 ♕xe4 0-0-0 15 ♕a8+ ♘b8 16 ♕xa7 e5∓) 10...♗b7 11 ♗g2 (11 g5 ♖g6 12 ♕h4 and 12...♘g8!? 13 ♘e2 h6! 14 ♖g1! c5 15 ♘f4 ♖g7 16 ♘h5 ♖g6= or

12...♘d5!∓) 11...♕e7!? (a possible improvement is 11...c5 12 ♘e2 ♕c8!? thinking about both ...cxd4 and ...e3; again the light squares are weak after 13 ♗e3 ♗a6!) 12 g5 ♕f8! 13 ♕xf8+ (13 ♕h4 h6!) 13...♘xf8 14 h4 h6 15 f4 (15 ♘e2 ♘8h7∓) 15...0-0-0 16 ♘e2 ♘h5! 17 ♗e3 f5∓ intending ...♘g6 and ...♗a6, Vorotnikov-Uhlmann, Leningrad 1984. The sidelines look safer, however;

(c) 9 ♗g5 ♕e7!? (9...♖g6 10 ♕h4 c5 11 ♘e2 ♕a5 12 ♗d2 ♕a4 gave Black excellent play in Trnovec-Gyarmati, Balatonbereny 1997) 10 f3 ♘g4 11 ♗xe7 ♘xh6 12 ♗h4 ♘f5 13 ♗f2 Reissmann-Jolles, Dieren 1988, and easiest was 13...e3! 14 ♗g3 c5∓.

8.121 9 f3

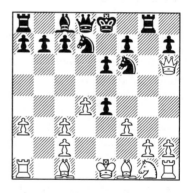

This is tricky move that forces Black to react in the centre:
9...c5

9...♖g6 was analysed briefly in the second edition but only played once that I know of. It still looks fine after 10 ♕h4 (10 ♕e3 b6! 11 fxe4 ♖g4 12 ♗d3 ♗b7=, e.g., 13 ♕e2 c5! threatening ...c4) 10...c5 11 fxe4 (else 11...♕a5) 11...♖g4 12 ♕h6 ♘xe4 (12...♖xe4+!?∓) 13 ♘e2 ♘df6∓.

10 ♗b2

(a) 10 ♕e3 and 10...♘d5 11 ♕xe4

♘xc3 12 ♕xh7 ♘f6 with advantage or 10...♕c7 11 fxe4 cxd4 12 cxd4 ♘xe4 (or just 12...♕xc2) with advantage;

(b) 10 fxe4 cxd4 11 cxd4 ♘xe4 with the idea of ...♕a5+, and if 12 ♕xh7?? ♘df6 13 ♕h4 ♕xd4.

10...♕a5!?

A cleaner and better solution appears to be 10...cxd4! 11 cxd4 ♕a5+ and 12 c3 b6 13 fxe4 ♗b7! or 12 ♕d2 ♕xd2+ 13 ♔xd2 b6.

11 0-0-0 b6 12 g3

Better is 12 fxe4 cxd4 13 cxd4 ♘xe4! 14 ♕xh7!? (14 d5 ♖g6 15 ♕e3 exd5∓) 14...♕g5+ 15 ♔b1 ♘df6 16 ♕h3 ♘d2+ (16...♘d5!?) 17 ♔a1 ♘xf1 18 ♖xf1 ♗b7 19 ♘f3 ♕xg2=.

After 12 g3, Temmink-Stull, corr 1983 went 12...♗b7 13 ♗g2 cxd4 14 cxd4 (14 ♖xd4 ♖c8) 14...♖c8 15 ♕e3 ♕a4 with the initiative.

8.122 9 ♘h3

This move is logical and very important, but has declined in popularity. White prepares ♗g5 or ♘g5 while leaving the bishop on f1 free to move.

9...b6

A good alternative is here is the continuation 9...c5 10 ♗e2 ♕a5 11 ♗d2

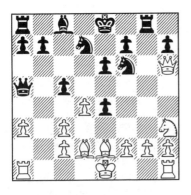

11...♖g6 (this line got a bad reputation from Ljubojevic-Korchnoi, Til-

burg 1986 after 11...♖xg2?! 12 ♘g5! cxd4 13 ♕g7!; but 11...cxd4 12 cxd4 ♕f5 intending ...b6, ...♗b7, ...0-0-0 is unclear – Ftacnik) 12 ♕h4 ♖xg2 13 ♘g5 cxd4 14 cxd4 ♕d5!? 15 ♗e3 ♕f5 16 ♔f1 ♖g4! launches a pretty attack: 17 ♗xg4 ♘xg4 18 ♕g3 h6 19 ♘h3 b6!? 20 ♘f4 ♗a6+ 21 ♔g2 0-0-0 22 ♖hd1 ♖g8 23 ♔h1 ♘gf6 24 ♕h4 ♗e2 25 ♖g1 ♗f3+ 26 ♘g2 ♖g4 27 ♕xh6 ♘g8 28 ♕h8 ♕g6 29 ♕h3 ♘e7 30 ♕h8+ ♔c7 31 d5 ♖xg2 0-1 Niedermaier-T.Martin, Bayern 1987.

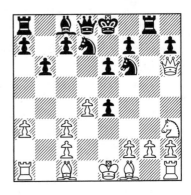

10 ♘g5!?

(a) 10 ♗g5 ♗b7 11 ♗b5 ♖g6 12 ♕h4 h6! 13 ♗xd7+ ♔xd7 14 ♗xf6 ♕xf6 15 ♕xf6= – Byr, although Black is quite active;

(b) 10 ♗e2 ♗b7 11 0-0 ♕e7. Now Lane-Tisdall, Gausdal 1987 saw Black develop a textbook attack: 12 a4 0-0-0 13 ♗a3 c5 14 ♕h4 ♕d6!? 15 ♖fd1!? (15 a5 e3 16 f3) 15...e3! 16 f3 ♖xg2+! 17 ♔xg2 ♖g8+ 18 ♘g5 h6 19 ♖g1? (19 dxc5! hxg5 20 cxd6 gxh4+ 21 ♔f1 ♘e5 unclear) 19...hxg5 20 ♕g3 ♕d5 21 ♔f1 ♘h5 22 ♕g2 ♘f4 23 ♕g3 ♘xe2 24 ♔xe2 ♕c4+ 0-1.

10...♖g6 11 ♕h4 ♗b7! 12 ♘xh7 ♘xh7 13 ♕xh7 ♕f6

This position has undergone quite a few tests; it seems to lead to a dynamic balance.

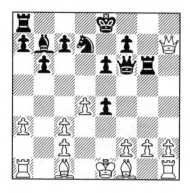

14 ♗e3

(a) 14 h4?! 0-0-0! 15 ♗g5 ♖h8 16 ♗xf6 ♖xh7 17 ♗e5 ♘xe5 18 dxe5 ♖g5∓ Degraeve-Djurhuus, Arnhem 1988;

(b) 14 ♕h3 0-0-0 15 ♕e3 ♕g7 16 ♗b2 ♘f6 17 0-0-0 ♘g4 18 ♕e1 ♕h6+ 19 ♔b1 ♕f4∓ Yeo-Knott, Birmingham 1999.

14...0-0-0 15 ♕h5 e5 16 ♖d1

Novotny-Kopecky, corr 1989 went 16 0-0-0, and now Black had several interesting ideas, e.g., 16...♕c6 and 16...♖h8 17 ♕e2 ♕e7! 18 ♔b2 c5 19 d5 with the idea 19...b5! or 19 dxe5 ♘xe5 intending ...b5, in both cases with attacking chances and a complex game ahead.

16...♖h8 17 ♕e2 ♕e7 18 ♕c4 f5

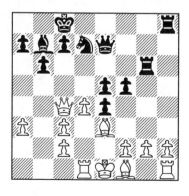

White's king is in the centre and

Black seems to have plenty for a pawn: 19 dxe5 ♘xe5 20 ♕b5 a6 21 ♕a4 ♘g4 22 ♕d4 ♖gg8 23 ♕b4 ♕h4!∓ 24 ♗d4 e3 25 ♗xe3 ♖e8 with a decisive attack, Leeuw-Mathews, IECC email 1999.

8.123 9 ♘e2

The old main line which is again receiving considerable attention of late. I suspect that it is the most effective move because it challenges Black to speculate. See his option in the next note, however.

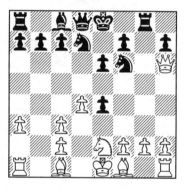

9...b6!?

A very interesting juncture. 9...b6 leads to fundamental and entertaining play, but if Black wants to avoid the somewhat speculative play that can follow from this move, he should seriously consider 9...c5. This is an attractive transpositional trick. Normally this position would be arrived at via 8...c5 9 ♘e2 ♘bd7, and in that case 9 ♘e2 is not the move that most tests Black. 9...c5 has in fact scored very well for the second player over the years. Black intends 10 ♘g3 ♕a5= or 10...♕c7=, and the try 10 a4 can be met simply by 10...b6 11 a5 ♗b7=. Lastly, 10 g3 b6 11 ♗g2 ♗b7 12 0-0 ♕e7 13 a4 ♘g4! was strong in Kir.Georgiev-Psakhis, Sarajevo 1986 due to 14 ♕xh7 0-0-0 15 ♕h5 f5!.

10 ♘g3!?

The currently popular choice: White protects g2, attacks e4, and prepares to complete his development. The main option is 10 ♗g5 ♕e7!?

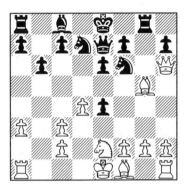

11 ♕h4 (11 ♘g3?? ♘g4 0-1 was I.Andersen-Matamoros Franco, Copenhagen 2002; 11 a4 ♗b7 12 ♘g3 of Zagorovsky-Kahn, corr 1980 seems well met by 12...♖g6 13 ♕h4 e5!, e.g., 14 ♘f5 ♕e6) 11...♗b7 12 ♘g3 (12 ♘f4 0-0-0 13 ♗e2 h6!, and 14 ♗xf6 ♕xf6 at least equalises, whereas 14 ♗xh6 ♖h8 is an extremely awkward pin for White) 12...h6!? (Black follows the the play in the famous game Fischer-Kovacevic, Rovinj-Zagreb 1970) 13 ♗d2 (13 ♕xh6? ♘g4! 14 ♗xe7 ♘xh6 15 ♗h4 ♖g4-+; 13 ♗xh6!? 0-0-0 unclear) 13...♖g4!? (Kovacevic played 13...0-0-0 14 ♗e2 ♘f8 and won, but the game is so overanalysed that 13...♖g4 is an appealing practical try. After Kovacevic's 14...♘f8, McDonald does much analytical work with 15 ♘h5 ♖xg2! to support my contention that Black is fine, but there have been whole articles about alternatives. My guess is that White has a small theoretical edge) 14 ♕xh6 0-0-0 15 c4!? (Finkel suggests 15 ♗g5! ♖g8

16 ♗h4! ♖8g6 17 ♕h8+ ♖g8 18 ♕h6=, but not here 16 ♗xf6 ♘xf6 17 ♗e2 ♖4g6 18 ♕e3 ♘d5 19 ♕d2 f5!) 15...♘g8!? (or 15...c5; both sides have a lot of options hereabouts) 16 ♕e3 f5 17 ♘h5!? e5 18 dxe5 ♘xe5 19 0-0-0?? (but the suggested 19 ♘f4 allows 19...♖xd2! and 20 ♕xd2 e3! 21 ♕xe3 ♖xf4! or 20 ♔xd2 ♕d6+ 21 ♔e2!? ♘xc4 22 ♕c3 ♗a6 23 ♔e1 ♕xf4 24 ♗xc4 ♗xc4 25 ♕xc4 ♖xg2 with an ongoing but unclear attack) 19...♘d3+!. Black is winning. Romero Holmes-Matamoros Franco, Elgoibar 1997 continued 20 cxd3 ♕xa3+ 21 ♔c2 exd3+ 22 ♗xd3 ♕a2+ 23 ♔c3 ♖xd3+! 24 ♕xd3 ♕a3+ 25 ♔c2 ♗e4 0-1.

10...♗b7

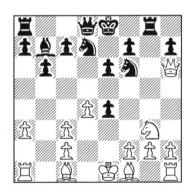

This long-known position has been the starting point for a number of relevant correspondence and email contests.

11 ♗e2

(a) 11 ♗b2 ♕e7 12 ♗e2 0-0-0 13 0-0-0 ♘g4! 14 ♗xg4 ♖xg4 15 ♕xh7 ♕g5+ 16 ♔b1 ♖h4 17 ♕xf7 ♖f8 18 ♕xe6 ♗d5∓ Lindinger-Sprotte, Germany 1999;

(b) 11 ♗g5 is probably equal, but has done horribly here. 11...♕e7 threatens ...♘g4, and 12 ♕h4 h6 13 ♗d2 0-0-0 has proven strong, e.g., 14

♗e2 e3 15 ♗xe3 ♗xg2 16 ♖g1 ♗b7 17 a4?! e5 18 a5 exd4 19 cxd4 ♕b4+ 20 ♗d2 ♕b2 21 ♖c1 ♘e4 22 ♗e3 ♕c3+ 23 ♔f1 ♘d2+∓ Benatar-Sukhov, IECG email 2000.

11...♕e7 12 a4

(a) 12 0-0 0-0-0 13 f3 ♖g6 14 ♕h4! exf3 (14...♖e8 15 fxe4 ♘xe4=) 15 ♗xf3 ♖dg8? (15...♗xf3! 16 ♖xf3 ♖dg8, perhaps still slightly better for White) 16 ♗xb7+? (16 ♗h5! wins the exchange) 16...♔xb7 17 a4 ♕d6!;

(b) 12 ♗g5 ♖g6 13 ♕h4 ♕d6! 14 ♗f4 e5 15 ♗e3 ♕c6∓ Zedekar-Spear, corr 1988.

12...0-0-0

Probably best. 12...♖g6!? 13 ♕h4 c5!? (13...0-0-0 is the old move) 14 0-0 e5!? 15 ♗b2 ♕e6 16 a5! bxa5 with complications, although White should have some advantage, De Waard-Lahlum, corr 2003.

13 0-0 ♘g4!? 14 ♗xg4

Or 14 ♕h3 f5 15 ♗f4 h5! (intending to advance further with ...h4) 16 a5 (16 ♘xh5? ♖h8) 16...h4 17 ♘h1 e5 18 dxe5 ♘dxe5 with promising attacking chances.

After 14 ♗xg4, Marez-D.Hardy, IECG email 2000 continued 14...♖xg4 15 ♗a3 ♕e8 (15...c5 is also playable, and if 16 ♕xh7?, 16...♕f6! 17 ♕h5 ♕g7! 18 h3 ♘f6 19 ♕e5 ♖d5-+) 16 a5 f5 (a key move in these lines) 17 axb6 axb6 18 ♗c1 ♕g6 19 h3 ♕xh6 20 ♗xh6 ♖g6 ½-½.

I think that the 8...♘bd7 variation is playable and exciting. However, there is massive theory attached to it, and the main lines with 9 ♘e2 b6 may not appeal to those who are nervous about sacrificing pawns. To them I would recommend looking into 9...c5 (less ambitious but solid) or even earlier deviations such as 5...♘e7.

8.2 4 ♕g4

The 'Blitz Variation'. White tries to save a tempo on 4 a3 by bringing his queen out immediately. The problem is that he hasn't bolstered his centre (as bxc3 did above), and Black can therefore counterattack more quickly in that sector. Although debate still rages about 4 ♕g4, I think that accurate play by Black makes it difficult for White to even equalise.

4...♘f6 5 ♕xg7 ♖g8 6 ♕h6 c5!

It turns out that this move is far better (not just a more accurate move order, as has been stated) than the immediate 6...♖g6 In the latter case, a critical line goes 7 ♕e3 c5 8 ♗d2! and 8...♘c6 9 ♘ge2 (see the notes below about how 6...c5 avoids this) or 8...♘g4!? 9 ♕d3 ♘c6 10 ♘ge2 (10 a3? c4 11 ♕h3 ♘xd4∓) 10...cxd4 11 ♘xd4 unclear. Current theory is fairly nice to White here. I have suggested 11...♕b6, but I don't think that it's been tested.

7 ♘ge2

This is supposed to be the best move and it is in fact the main line, because after 7...♖g6 8 ♕e3 we have transposed to a position that is also reached via 6...♖g6 7 ♕e3 c5 8 ♘ge2. If then 8...♘c6 9 ♗d2, we reach the traditional main line of 4 ♕g4. But we shall see that things aren't so easy. Here are White's alternatives:

(a) 7 ♗g5? ♖g6 8 ♕h4 cxd4 9 e5 ♖xg5! 10 exf6 ♕xf6 11 ♘ge2 ♘c6 12 a3 ♗a5 13 b4 ♘xb4! 14 0-0-0 ♘xc2! 15 ♘b1 ♗d7! 16 ♖d3 ♘e1 0-1 Crowl-Harris, corr 1938;

(b) 7 e5!? has been played a lot: 7...cxd4 8 a3 ♗f8 (also promising looks 8...♕a5!? 9 exf6 dxc3 10 ♖b1, and McDonald's idea 10...♘d7!?, since 11 axb4 ♕a2 is good, or 10...cxb2+ 11 axb4 bxc1♕+ 12 ♕xc1 ♕c7 with a positional advantage) 9 ♕xf6 (9 ♕h4 dxc3 10 exf6 ♘d7 11 ♗b5 cxb2 12 ♗xb2 ♕a5+) 9...♕xf6 10 exf6 dxc3∓

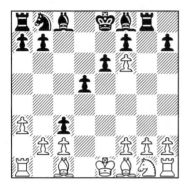

11 ♘e2 (11 bxc3 ♘d7 12 ♗b2 ♘xf6 13 c4 ♗g7∓ Y.Hernandez-S.Bjerke, Oropesa del Mar 1999) 11...♘d7 12 ♘xc3 ♗d6 13 g3 ♘xf6 14 ♗g2 (14 ♘b5 ♗b8 15 c4 a6 16 ♘c3 dxc4 17 ♗xc4 b5 18 ♗e2 ♗b7 19 0-0 h5 – McDonald) 14...♗d7 15 0-0 0-0-0 16 ♗e3 ♔b8 17 h3 ♗c6 (McDonald likes 17...♖c8) 18 ♖ad1 ♘d7 19 ♘e2 ♘b6 (19...♖c8) 20 ♗xb6 axb6 21 ♘d4 ½-½ Antoniewski-Shaked, Zagan 1997;

(c) 7 a3 is probably the best move. However, Black's position after 7...♖g6 8 ♕e3 (8 ♕h4?! ♕a5 9 ♗d2 cxd4 10 ♘b1 ♗xd2+ 11 ♘xd2 dxe4 12 0-0-0 ♕g5∓ A.Walters-R.Sample, corr 1966) 8...♗a5! is considered good.

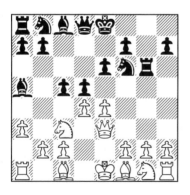

At this point, three bad mistakes that have happened over the board are: 9 e5? ♘g4 10 ♕d3 cxd4, 9 ♘f3? dxe4 10 ♘e5 cxd4 11 ♗b5+ ♔e7!, and 9 exd5? ♘xd5 10 ♕d3 cxd4 11 ♕xd4 e5! 12 ♕d3 ♖d6!. So White has:

(c1) 9 ♘h3 ♘xe4 (9...e5!?; 9...♘c6 10 ♗b5 dxe4∓) 10 b4 ♘xc3 11 ♕xc3 cxd4 12 ♕xd4 e5!∓ Plasman-Steenbekkers, Dieren 1998;

(c2) 9 ♘ge2 ♘c6 (or 9...cxd4 10 ♘xd4 ♘xe4) 10 ♗d2 cxd4 (10...♗b6!? 11 ♘xd5!? ♘g4∓) 11 ♘xd4 ♘g4 transposes to 9 ♗d2;

(c3) 9 ♗d2

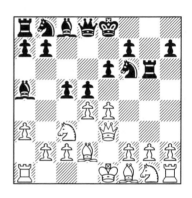

9...♘c6 (9...cxd4 10 ♕xd4 ♘c6 11 ♕d3 ♘xe4 12 ♘xe4 dxe4 13 ♕xd8+ ♗xd8 is 'only' equal) 10 ♘f3! (10 ♘ge2?! cxd4 11 ♘xd4 transposes, as (probably) does 10...♘g4; but 10...♗b6! is strong; 10 ♗b5!? cxd4 11 ♕xd4 ♗b6 12 ♕d3 ♘xe4 13 ♘xe4 dxe4 14 ♕xd8+ ♔xd8 15 ♗xc6 bxc6 16 g3 e5∓ with two bishops and light square play) 10...♘g4 11 ♕d3 cxd4 12 ♘xd4 (12 ♘b1?! dxe4 13 ♕xe4 f5! 14 ♕d3 e5) 12...♘xf2!? (12...♗b6 13 ♘xc6 ♗xf2+ 14 ♔d1 bxc6 is messy) 13 ♔xf2 ♗b6 14 ♗e3! (14 exd5 ♗xd4+ 15 ♗e3 ♕f6+ 16 ♔g1 ♘e5! 17 ♗xd4! ♘f3+ 18 ♔f2 ♘xd4+ 19 ♔e1 e5∓) 14...♕f6+ 15 ♘f3!? (15 ♔e1 ♘xd4∓) 15...♘e5! 16 ♕b5+! ♗d7 17 ♗xb6

♗xb5 18 ♗xb5+ ♔f8 19 ♗c5+ ♔g8 intending the moves ...♖xg2+ or ...dxe4 and ...♘g4+. In spite of the approximate material equality, Black stands better;

(d) 7 ♗d2? cedes the advantage immediately to 7...cxd4! (7...♖g6?! 8 ♕e3 is theory's main line) 8 e5 (8 ♘b5 ♘g4! 9 ♕xh7 ♗xd2+ 10 ♔xd2 ♘f6!) 8...dxc3 9 bxc3 ♕c7!∓.

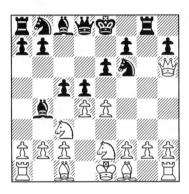

From the diagram, the normal move here has been 7...♖g6, when 8 ♕h4!? is a try to avoid the usual move 8 ♕e3. The latter can be met by 8...cxd4! (8...♘c6 9 ♗d2 is the main line of the 4 ♕g4 Winawer, considered dynamically equal) 9 ♘xd4 ♘xe4 and I don't see anything wrong with Black's position. This could be the first benefit of playing 6...c5 instead of 6...♖g6.

7...cxd4

Here's another benefit! Pederson says that 'it is obviously not favourable for [Black] to exchange so early on d4'. While that is a logical assertion because 7...cxd4 frees White's pieces, it happens that there are concrete tactical compensations. Interestingly, 7...♘c6!? also hasn't been sufficiently tested, the main line going 8 exd5 ♘xd4 9 ♘xd4 cxd4 10 a3 ♗f8 11 ♗b5+ and if nothing else,

11...♗e7!? 12 d6+ (what else?) 12...♕xd6 13 ♕xf6+ ♔xf6 14 ♘e4+ ♔g7 15 ♘xd6 ♗xd6 16 0-0 e5 is equal, whereas 11...♗d7 tries for more: after 12 ♗xd7+ of Polland-Rubinsky, corr 1983, 12...♔xd7!? 13 dxe6+ ♔e7 is an awfully speculative piece sacrifice for White. So 7...♘c6 may be much better than its reputation.

8 ♘xd4 e5!

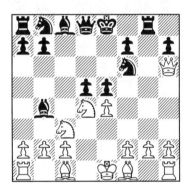

This looks very promising, e.g., 9 ♗b5+ ♗d7 10 ♗xd7+ ♘bxd7 11 ♘f5 d4 12 ♘g7+ (12 0-0 ♗f8−+) 12...♖xg7 13 ♕xg7 dxc3 14 0-0 cxb2 (or 14...♗f8∓) 15 ♗xb2 ♕e7!? (15...♕c7∓) 16 f4 ♘xe4 17 ♔h1 0-0-0 18 fxe5 ♗c5 19 h3 ♗f2 20 ♖fd1 ♗h4 21 ♖d4 ♘g3+ 22 ♔h2 ♘f5 23 ♖c4+ ♔b8 24 ♕xh7 ♘xe5 25 ♖e4 ♘f3+ 26 gxf3 ♖d2+ 27 ♔g1 ♕g5+ 0-1 Bartel-Szelag, Brzeg Dolny 2001. For all the lengthy arguments about the 4 ♕g4 main lines, it appears that 6...c5! avoids them completely and for several separate reasons resolves the variation favourably for Black.

8.3 4 ♗d2

Here again White's idea is ♕g4, and play will resemble 8.1 and 8.2. The main difference is that White develops more rapidly, but he forfeits any pretensions to holding his centre and in fact gambits a pawn. His reward is rapid development. 4 &d2 has some fascinating byways, and is quite as interesting as more popular options; I will treat it in some detail. It is notoriously difficult to avoid forcing drawing lines versus 4 &d2, so I'll give three unbalanced solutions with two based upon the same sequence.

4...dxe4

4...♘c6!? is also possible for original play: 5 ♕g4 (another idea was 5 a3 &xc3 6 &xc3 ♘f6 7 e5 ♘e4 8 &d3 ♘xc3 9 bxc3 ♕e7 followed by ...&d7, and ...0-0-0, Ljubojevic-U.Andersson, Palma de Mallorca 1971) 5...♘f6 6 ♕xg7 ♖g8 7 ♕h6 ♖g6! 8 ♕h4?! (8 ♕e3 dxe4 again transposes to the main line, and here 8...♘g4 is a good alternative) 8...♖g4 9 ♕h6 ♘xe4!? (9...♘xd4∓) 10 ♕xh7? (10 ♘f3 ♘xd2 11 ♕xd2 e5!) 10...♘xd2 11 ♔xd2 ♕g5+ 12 ♔e1 ♖e4+! 13 ♘ge2 ♘xd4∓ Petzold-Fuchs, Berlin 1965.

5 ♕g4

5 ♘xe4? ♕xd4∓, e.g., 6 &d3 &xd2+ 7 ♕xd2 ♕xb2 8 ♖d1 ♘d7.

5...♘f6 6 ♕xg7 ♖g8 7 ♕h6

And now:

8.31 7...♕xd4
8.32 7...♖g6

7...♘c6 has independent value if one is aiming for a draw. This can arise after 8 0-0-0 (8 ♘ge2!?) 8...♖g6 9 ♕h4, transposing to 7...♖g6 8 ♕h4 ♘c6 9 0-0-0 in 8.32.

8.31 7...♕xd4!

Fearlessly grabbing a pawn. Theory on this move has expanded considerably, and I think that it offers Black excellent chances for the advantage, thus calling 4 &d2 into some doubt.

8 0-0-0

White plays 8 ♘ge2!? fairly often, but Black has plenty of play after 8...♕e5 9 0-0-0 (or 9 &f4 ♕f5∓ – Keres; then 10 ♘g3 ♕g6 11 ♕xg6 &xc3+! 12 bxc3 ♖xg6 13 &xc7 ♘c6 offers Black some advantage, and Halldorsson-Schmitz, Reykjavik 2000 went 10 &xc7 ♕xf2+! 11 ♔xf2 ♘g4+ 12 ♔e1 ♘xh6 13 a3 &xc3+ 14 ♘xc3 f5 15 ♘b5 ♘a6∓ intending ...♘f7; without central breaks the bishop pair doesn't fully compensate for his extra pawn)

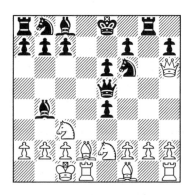

Here Black can play 9...&f8, which I won't deal with here, or choose between:

(a) 9...♖g6 10 ♕h4 ♖g4!? 11 ♕h3 ♘c6 12 f3 exf3 13 ♕xf3 a6 (13...&d7 is natural and good) 14 &f4 ♕a5 15

♗xc7!? ♕xc7 16 ♕xf6 ♗f8! 17 g3 ♗g7 18 ♕f2 ♗d7 19 ♘h3 ♖c4 and Black exerted queenside pressure in Mineur-Abenius, corr 1988;

(b) McDonald thinks that Black is doing well after 9...♘bd7! and that seems right, e.g., 10 ♘g3 (10 ♗f4 ♕f5 or 10...♕a5 are both good according to McDonald) 10...♘g4!? (or 10...♖g6 intending 11 ♕e3 ♗c5 or 11 ♕f4? ♗xc3 12 bxc3 ♕a5 13 ♔b2 e5 with a winning attack, Brouwers-Van Geemen, corr 1985) 11 ♕xh7 ♘df6 12 ♕h4 ♗e7 13 ♖e1?! ♘xf2 14 ♗f4 ♕a5 15 ♖g1 ♗d7 16 ♗e2? 0-0-0 and White's queen was embarrassed in Kasten-Kirwald, corr 1986.

After 8 0-0-0, Black has:

8.311 8...♘g4
8.312 8...♗f8

8.311 8...♘g4!?

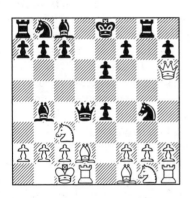

An obscure move that I've looked into and believe works. There have been almost no games with 8...♘g4 (two ended in mate 4 moves later!), but it seems to give full-fledged chances with oodles of non-forced play. At least it avoids drawish lines.
9 ♕h4!
Others are either disastrous or unpromising:

(a) 9 ♕f4? e5 10 ♕g3 ♕xf2 11 ♕h3 ♘c6 12 ♕xh7 ♘f6 13 ♕h6 ♗f8!? (also 13...♗g4-+) 14 ♕e3 ♘g4 (14...♗c5!-+) 15 ♕xe4 ♗f5 16 ♕a4 0-0-0 and Black's attack was too strong in Cross-Playa, Roque Saenz Pena 1997;

(b) 9 ♕xh7?? ♖h8 10 ♕xe4 (or 10 ♘ge2 ♕xd2+ 11 ♖xd2 ♖xh7 also winning) 10...♗xc3-+;

(c) 9 ♕h5 ♘xf2! (9...♘d7!? also looks good in view of 10 ♗e3 ♕e5 or 10 ♘b5 ♗xd2+ 11 ♖xd2 ♕b6 12 ♕xh7 ♘df6 13 ♕h4 ♗d7∓) and:

(c1) 10 ♘ge2? ♕f6 11 ♘b5 (11 ♕xh7 ♖g4! threatens ...♖h4 and guards the e-pawn: 12 ♕h5 ♗xc3 13 ♘xc3 ♕g6-+) 11...♗xd2+ 12 ♖xd2 ♖g5 13 ♘xc7+ ♔f8 14 ♕xh7 ♘xh1 15 ♘xa8 ♖f5-+);

(c2) 10 ♘b5! ♗xd2+ 11 ♖xd2 ♕e3 12 ♘xc7+ ♔f8 13 ♘xa8 ♘xh1 is messy, but I think that Black is always slightly better, e.g., 14 ♕xh7 (14 ♘h3 ♘c6) 14...♘f2 15 ♘e2 ♘c6 16 ♕h4 ♘e5! (16...♕g5!? 17 ♕xg5 ♖xg5∓) 17 ♘c7 ♗d7!∓ (17...♘c4 18 ♕d8+ ♔g7 19 ♕d4+ ♕xd4 20 ♖xd4 ♘e3 21 ♘g3 f5∓).

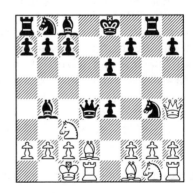

9...♘d7!?
Not necessarily best, this leads to dynamically balanced play. There are several alternatives, one of which is not 9...♕xf2?? 10 ♕d8+! ♔xd8 11

♗g5+ ♔e8 12 ♖d8 mate (as occurred in at least two games!). Instead there are:

(a) 9...♕f6 10 ♕g3

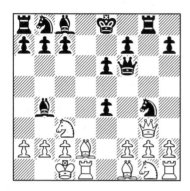

and:

(a1) 10...♗xc3 11 ♗xc3 e5! 12 ♘h3 (versus ...♕xf2) 12...♘c6 13 ♗b5 ♗d7 14 ♖he1 0-0-0 15 ♖xe4 ♕e6! 16 ♗c4 ♕h6+ (or 16...♕e7!? 17 ♖ee1! ♘f6 18 ♕f3 ♗g4 19 ♖xd8+ ♖xd8 20 ♕g3 ♗e6=) 17 ♗d2 ♕h5 with at least equality; Black is ready for ...f5;

(a2) 10...e3!? 11 ♗xe3 (11 fxe3 ♗d6=) 11...♗xc3 12 bxc3 ♕e7! is complex and hard to assess, but I think that White's strong bishop pair are more or less balanced out by his weaknesses.

(b) 9...♘xf2 is extremely complicated but looser than 9...♕f6 or 9...♘d7. A key line is 10 ♘b5 (10 ♘f3 ♗e7! 11 ♕xe7+ ♔xe7 12 ♘xd4 ♘xh1∓; probably 10 ♘xe4! ♗e7 11 ♕xf2 ♕xe4 12 ♘f3 ♘c6 13 ♗d3 is best) 10...♗e7! 11 ♘xc7+ ♔d7 12 ♕f4! ♘xd1!? (12...e5!? 13 ♕xf7 ♘xd1 14 ♘xa8 ♖f8 15 ♕b3 e3!?) 13 ♘xa8 e5 14 ♕xf7 ♖f8 seems to work out well enough, e.g., 15 ♗b5+ ♔d8 16 ♕b3! ♗e6!=.

10 ♘h3!

(a) 10 ♘b5 ♗xd2+ 11 ♖xd2 ♕b6 intending ...e3 looks fine;

(b) 10 ♗g5 ♕xf2! 11 ♘xe4 (11 ♕xg4 ♗xc3 12 bxc3 ♕c5 13 ♘h3 h6-+) 11...♕xh4 12 ♗xh4 ♗e7 (12...f5! 13 ♘g5 ♖xg5 14 ♗xg5 ♘f2∓ is also good) 13 ♗xe7 ♔xe7∓.

10...♕e5 11 ♔b1!

White correctly avoids 11 ♕xh7?! ♖h8 12 ♕xe4 ♗xc3 13 ♕xg4 ♗xb2+ 14 ♔b1 ♗a3 15 c3 ♘c5!∓.

11...♗e7 12 ♕xh7

12 ♕g3 ♕xg3 13 hxg3 allows 13...e3! 14 fxe3 ♗c5.

12...♘df6 13 ♕h4 e3! 14 fxe3 ♘d5 15 ♕e1!

Not 15 ♕h7? ♖h8; or 15 ♕g3? ♕xg3 16 hxg3 ♘xc3+ 17 ♗xc3 ♘xe3∓.

15...♘dxe3 16 ♗xe3 ♘xe3

The play has been pretty forcing thus far and this looks equal. It might continue 17 ♖d3 (17 ♖d2 ♗b4 18 ♖e2? ♗xc3 19 ♖xe3 ♗xe1 20 ♖xe5 ♗b4 leaves Black with two strong bishops) 17...♘c4 18 ♕xe5 ♘xe5 19 ♘b5!? ♗d8!=. I believe that the obscure move 8...♘g4 is fully playable, although the precise details have to be worked out.

8.312 8...♗f8 9 ♕h4

Worse is 9 ♕f4?! ♗d6 10 ♘ge2 ♗xf4 11 ♘xd4 ♗e5∓.

9...♖g4 10 ♕h3 ♕xf2

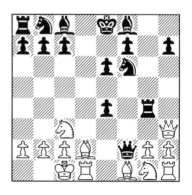

11 ♗e2

Hitting the rook and threatening ♖f1. Others are worse:

(a) 11 ♘b5? ♘a6 12 ♔b1 ♗d7 13 ♗e3 ♕f5 14 ♘d4 ♕g6∓ Boleslavsky-Bronstein, Moscow 1950;

(b) 11 ♗b5+? c6 12 ♖f1 ♕xg2 13 ♖xf6 cxb5∓ Mossung-Vrbata, Prague 1989;

(c) 11 ♗e3?! ♕h4! 12 ♕xh4 (12 g3 ♕xh3 13 ♘xh3 ♖g6 14 ♘f2 ♗d7 15 ♗g2 ♗c6 16 ♘cxe4 ♘xe4 17 ♗xe4 Jansen-Alger, email 1997; and best looks 17...f5 18 ♗xc6+ ♘xc6∓) 12...♖xh4 13 g3 (13 ♗g5? ♗h6) and here Black has the simple escape 13...♖h5!, when he'll remain a pawn up after the e-pawn falls (compare the main line).

11...♖h4

This was once considered a blunder, but is now the main line. I'm not sure if anyone has ever repeated 11...♕xg2!? of Redolfi-Idigoras, Mar del Plata 1956, but it looks promising: 12 ♗xg4 (12 ♘b5 ♘a6) 12...♕xg4 13 ♕xg4 ♘xg4 14 ♘xe4

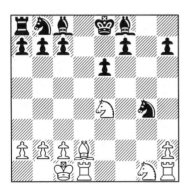

14...♗d7! (or 14...♘d7!?; Black has two bishops, material equality and the two unopposed central pawns that he gets in the main line, although his pieces aren't quite as well placed after 15 ♘f3 b6!? 16 ♖hg1 h5 17 h3 ♗b7 18 hxg4 ♗xe4 19 ♘g5

♗g6=) 15 h3 ♗c6 16 hxg4 ♗xe4 17 ♖h3 (17 ♖h4 ♘c6 18 g5 ♗g6∓) 17...♘d7∓ (or 17...♘c6∓). I don't know why 11...♕xg2 hasn't been touched in so many years, especially considering its similarity to lines that follow.

12 ♕xh4! ♖xh4 13 g3

The queen is trapped, but as compensation for losing the exchange Black will have the bishop pair and strong central pawns.

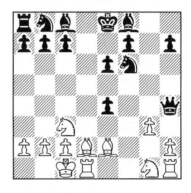

13...e3!?

This underrated pawn advance (threatening ...♕b4) has been around for a long time but has been overshadowed by the other trade-off of White's dark-squared bishop via 13...♕h6 14 ♗xh6 ♗xh6+ 15 ♔b1. Nevertheless, the latter position is justifiably popular for Black. Apart from the usual 15...e5 (about equal) and 15...♗d7 (unfathomable, but still doing well), a new move for Black is 15...a6!?. I like this modest-looking continuation, which plans to develop quickly by ...b5 and ....♗b7 while tossing ...b4 into the mix of ideas. Two sample games:

(a) 16 h4 b5 17 ♘h3 (17 g4 b4 18 ♘a4 ♗e3 19 g5 ♗d7 20 gxf6 ♗xa4 21 ♘h3 ♘d7∓) 17...b4 18 ♖df1 (18 ♘a4 ♗e3! 19 ♖hf1 ♔e7) 18...bxc3 19 ♖xf6 ♗g7 20 ♖ff1 f5 21 ♗h5+ ♔e7 22 g4?!

(but 22 b3 ♘d7∓) 22...cxb2 23 gxf5 exf5 and the central pair has survived with a three-pawn advantage, so White was effectively lost in the game Korepanov-Skomorokhin, Podolsk 1993;

(b) 16 ♘h3 is natural: 16...b5 17 ♖hf1 ♘bd7 18 g4 b4 19 g5 (19 ♘a4 ♘d5 20 g5 ♗f8 21 ♗h5 ♘e5 22 ♖de1 ♗d7 23 ♖xe4 ♘g6 24 c4 – forced, before or after ♗xg6 – 24...bxc3 25 ♘xc3 ♘xc3+ 26 bxc3 ♗c6 27 ♖g4 ♖b8+ 28 ♔c2 (28 ♔a1 ♗d6!∓) 28...♗a3 29 ♖b1 ♖xb1 30 ♔xb1 ♗d6!∓) 19...♗xg5 20 ♘xg5 bxc3 21 ♖f4 cxb2 22 ♗c4 (22 ♘xe4 ♘xe4 23 ♖xe4 ♖b8) 22...♗b7∓ Rantanen-Raisa, Tampere 1989, due to 23 ♘xf7? ♗d5!, winning material.

14 gxh4 exd2+ 15 ♔b1

Said to be best by nearly everyone. The obvious 15 ♔xd2 exposes the king to tempo-gaining attacks after 15...♗d7 (or 15...♗h6+ 16 ♔e1, and now 16...♔e7 17 ♘f3 ♗f4! with unclear prospects or 16...♗d7 17 ♘h3 ♗c6 18 ♖f1 ♘bd7 Hort-Nogueiras, Reggio Emilia 1986) 16 ♔c1 (16 ♘f3 ♗d6 17 ♔c1 ♗f4+ 18 ♔b1 ♘c6 19 ♖hf1 ♖d8 20 ♘g5 ♗e5 21 ♘ce4 ♘xe4 22 ♘xe4 ♔e7 and Black's central pawns are still dangerous) 16...♗c6!? (16...♘c6 17 ♘f3 0-0-0) 17 ♗b5 (17 ♗f3 ♗h6+ 18 ♔b1 ♘g4!? 19 ♘e4 ♘d7 20 ♗xg4 ♗xe4 21 ♗f3 ♘f6 22 ♖e1 0-0-0=) 17...♗h6+ 18 ♔b1 ♔e7 19 ♗xc6 ♘xc6 20 ♘h3 ♖g8 21 ♖hg1 ♖xg1 22 ♖xg1 ♗e3 23 ♖g3 ♗d4 24 ♘g5?! (24 ♘e2 ♗b6 25 ♔c1) 24...h6 25 ♘ge4 ♘xe4 26 ♘xe4 f5 (simplification tends to help Black in this line, because it frees his pawns to advance) 27 ♘d2 ♔f7!? 28 h5 ♗e5 29 ♖g2 ♗f6 30 c3 e5 31 ♔c2 e4 and Black's two passed pawns are beginning to dominate, D.Larsson-T.Karlsson, Vaxjo 1992.

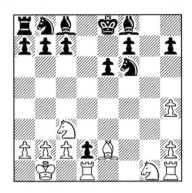

15...♗b4

I suggested this years back; Black is trying to isolate every White pawn! Whether that occurs or not, the essence of this position is Black's bishop pair and two passed central pawns versus White's temporary developmental edge.

A similar and potentially important idea would begin with 15...♗d7!, again using the ...♗b4 motif and counting upon the passed central pawns.

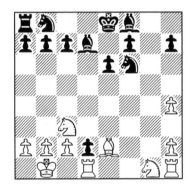

Some sample analysis:

(a) 16 ♖xd2?! ♗b4 17 ♖d3 (17 ♗f3 ♗xc3 18 bxc3 ♗c6) 17...♗xc3 18 bxc3 (18 ♖xc3 ♘e4 wins material) 18...♘e4 19 ♘h3 ♗b5 etc.;

(b) 16 a3 ♗c6 17 ♘f3 ♗h6! (17...♘bd7 18 ♖xd2 ♗h6 19 ♖dd1 ♔e7 is also fine) 18 ♗b5 ♔e7 19 ♗xc6 ♘xc6 20 ♘xd2 ♘g4! 21 ♘de4 ♘e3 22 ♖d2 ♘f5! and White's rooks lack squares; best is 23 ♖f2 ♗e3 24 ♖ff1 ♖g8 25 ♘d1 ♗b6, when one prefers Black;

(c) 16 ♘f3 ♗b4! 17 ♘xd2 ♗xc3 18 bxc3 ♘c6 19 ♖hg1 ♔e7 20 ♖g7 ♖g8! 21 ♖g5 h6 22 ♖xg8 ♘xg8 and again Black's pawns are the long-term factor, so White can hope for equality at best;

(d) 16 ♘b5 ♗xb5!? (or 16...♘a6 followed by ...♘e4) 17 ♗xb5+ c6 18 ♗d3 (18 ♗e2 ♘e4) 18...♘bd7 (18...♗h6 19 ♘f3 ♘g4! 20 ♖hg1 ♘f2∓) 19 ♖xd2 ♘e5 20 ♘e2 ♖d8 21 ♖f1 ♗h6 22 ♖dd1 ♔e7 leaves White looking for a plan.

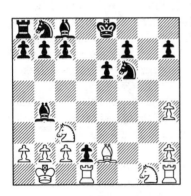

16 ♗f3

(a) 16 ♖xd2?? ♗xc3 17 bxc3 ♘e4−+;

(b) 16 ♘b5 ♗a5 (16...♘a6 17 c3 ♗c5 18 ♘f3 ♘e4) 17 ♘f3 ♘c6 intending ...e5, and answering 18 ♘xd2 by 18...♘a6 19 ♘c3 (19 ♘a3? ♗xd2 20 ♖xd2 ♘e4) 19...♗xc3 20 bxc3 e5 21 ♗f3 ♗e6! 22 ♗xc6+ bxc6 23 ♖de1 ♘d7.

16...♗xc3 17 bxc3 ♘bd7 18 ♖xd2 ♘e5 19 ♗g2 ♘c4 20 ♖e2 e5!?

Also interesting are 20...♗d7 and even 20...c6!?, e.g., 21 ♘h3 ♘d5 22 ♗xd5 cxd5 23 ♖g1 ♔f8 24 ♖f2 ♘d6.

After 20..e5, play might continue

21 ♔c1 ♗e6!? (or 21...c6 22 ♘f3 ♗g4) 22 ♗xb7 ♖b8 23 ♗c6+ ♔e7 24 ♘f3 ♔d6 25 ♗e4 (25 ♗a4 ♘d5 26 ♗b3 ♘xc3∓) 25...♗g4 with various threats and at least equal play.

8.32 7...♖g6

This is a solid move that forces White to commit at an early stage. It could serve as a backup if the 7...♕xd4 lines look shaky or intimidating.

8 ♕e3

The alternative is 8 ♕h4 when Black can apparently force a draw, but also has options:

(a) 8...♘c6 9 0-0-0 ♖g4 (9...♗xc3 10 ♗xc3 ♕d5!? lost a famous game between Keres and Botvinnik; 10...♕d6 is more interesting) 10 ♕h6 (10 ♕h3 ♖g6 intends ...e5; then 11 ♕e3?! ♕xd4 12 ♕xd4 ♘xd4 is considered good for Black, but so is 12 ♘b5 ♕xe3 13 ♗xe3 ♗a5∓) 10...♖g6 11 ♕h4 ♖g4 with a draw;

(b) 8...♕xd4 as a winning try has the problem 9 ♘f3 ♕c5 10 ♘xe4=;

(c) 8...♘bd7 is obscure but appealing, covering everything and aiming to develop rapidly and prepare ...0-0-0: 9 0-0-0 (9 ♘xe4 ♖g4 10 ♘xf6+ ♘xf6 11 ♕h6 is messy after 11...♗f8 12 ♕h3 ♕xd4 13 0-0-0! ♕xf2 14 ♘f3 ♗d6 and Black is temporarily a pawn up with ...♗d7 and ...0-0-0 planned) 9...♗xc3 10 ♗xc3 b6 11 ♗b5 ♗b7 12 ♘e2 (12 ♕h3 a6) 12...♘d5!? (simply 12...c6 13 ♗a4 b5 14 ♗b3 a5 looks effective; in several lines ...♖xg2 will follow) 13 ♕xh7 ♕f6 14 ♕h3 (14 ♗xd7+?? ♔xd7 and White's queen is trapped after 15 ♕h5 ♖g5 16 ♕h4 ♖h8) 14...0-0-0 15 ♗e1 Graf-Uhlmann, Wuerzburg 1992, and here 15...c6 16 ♗c4 ♖h8 gives compensation, e.g., 17 ♕a3 ♖xg2 18 ♕xa7

♖hxh2 19 ♖xh2 ♖xh2 and White has nothing on the queenside so Black is at least equal.

8...♘c6 9 ♘ge2

Minev gives the line 9 ♘xe4 ♘xe4 (9...♗xd2+ 10 ♘xd2 ♕xd4=) 10 ♕xe4 (10 ♗xb4? ♘xb4 11 ♕xe4 ♕xd4!) 10...♗xd2+ 11 ♔xd2 ♘xd4 (11...♕xd4+ 12 ♕xd4 ♘xd4 followed by ...e5 is equal) 12 ♖d1!. Then 12...c5 13 ♔c1 ♕a5 14 ♕e5?! (14 ♔b1 ♗d7=) 14...♕xa2! 15 ♗b5+ ♗d7 16 ♕h8+ (16 ♗xd7+ ♔xd7∓) 16...♔e7 17 ♕xa8 ♕a1+ 18 ♔d2 ♕a5+ 19 ♔c1 ♕xb5 gives more than enough for the exchange; Black is threatening ...♕c4.

9...♗xc3

A safe line which gives a reasonable game, as opposed to the theoretical 9...e5?! 10 dxe5 ♘g4 11 ♕f4 ♘cxe5?, when there's a huge hole in the traditional line 12 h3 ♗d6 13 ♕xe4 f5 14 ♕a4+! ♗d7, namely 15 ♘b5! and White is a pawn ahead with the better position.

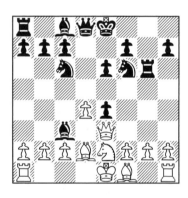

10 ♗xc3

(a) 10 ♕xc3 is also playable: 10...♘d5 11 ♕a3 (11 ♕c5!? ♕d7! 12 0-0-0 b6 13 ♕a3 ♗b7=) 11...♕f6! (tying White to the f-pawn; this is given as equal by the books, but it's not clear; here's some analysis:) 12 c4! ♘b6 13 ♕c3 ♗d7 14 ♗e3 0-0-0 15

0-0-0 ♘e7!? (15...♔b8 16 ♘f4 ♖gg8 17 ♗e2 ♘e7) 16 h4! ♗c6! 17 ♗g5 ♖xg5 18 hxg5 ♕xg5+ 19 ♕d2 (19 ♔b1 ♕f6 20 ♕b4 ♘f5) 19...e3! 20 ♕xe3 ♕xe3+ 21 fxe3 ♘xc4 22 ♖xh7 (22 ♖d3 ♘d5 23 ♖h3 ♘b4!) 22...♘xe3 23 ♖e1 ♘c2! 24 ♖d1 ♘e3=;

(b) 10 bxc3 e5!? 11 h3 (11 dxe5 ♘xe5 12 ♘f4 ♖g8 13 f3 ♕e7! 14 fxe4 ♘fg4 15 ♕e2 ♗e6=) 11...♗f5!= intending 12 g4 ♘d5.

10...♕d6!?

Another move is 10...♘e7, e.g., 11 ♘g3!? (but 11 ♘f4! looks better: 11...♖g8 12 0-0-0 ♕d6±) 11...♘ed5 12 ♕e2?! (12 ♕d2 h5! 13 h4? e3 14 ♕d3 ♕d6∓) 12...♘xc3 13 bxc3 ♕d5 14 ♕b5+ c6 (or 14...♗d7) 15 ♕b4 h5 16 ♗c4 ♕d8 17 ♖g1 h4 18 ♘f1 b5 19 ♗e2 ♘d5 20 ♕c5 ♕b6 with a nice advantage, Brendel-Poldauf, Tegel 2001.

11 ♘g3

At this point I'll give some sample moves. Instinctively White looks very slightly better, but that has to be proven. One old line is 11 0-0-0 ♘b4, but instead 11...♘g4! wins material after 12 ♕f4 ♕xf4+ 13 ♘xf4 ♘xf2 14 ♘xg6 ♘xd1 15 ♔xd1 hxg6.

11...♘b4 12 ♕e2

12 ♗b5+!? c6 13 ♗a4.

12...♗d7!? 13 ♘xe4 ♘xe4 14 ♕xe4 ♗c6 15 ♕e2 ♘d5 16 ♗d2 ♘f4 17

♗xf4 ♕xf4 and Black regains his pawn.

Unlike 7...♕xd4, 7...♗g6 plays only for equality; it is nevertheless a practical line that avoids much theory and yields a playable game.

8.4 4 ♘ge2

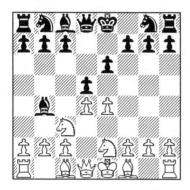

Still a popular alternative to 4 e5, mainly because White feels that this is a safe line. The avoidance of doubled c-pawns has its price, however, in that White confines his own development and allows his centre to be challenged quickly. Here I suggest the following:

8.41 4...♘c6
8.42 4...dxe4

Yet another solution is the recently revived 4...♘f6 5 e5 (5 ♗g5 dxe4 6 a3 ♗e7 7 ♘g3 0-0 with the idea 8 ♘cxe4 ♘xe4 9 ♗xe7 ♕xe7 10 ♘xe4 ♖d8) 5...♘fd7, e.g., 6 ♕d3 0-0 7 a3 ♗e7 8 ♕g3 ♔h8 9 ♗e3 c5 10 0-0-0 ♘c6 11 f4 b5! 12 ♘xb5 (12 dxc5 b4 13 axb4 ♘xb4 intending ...♕a5, ...♖b8 – Rustemov) 12...♖b8 13 ♘ec3 (13 ♘bc3 c4!) 13...c4!, and here R.Perez-Rustemov, Villa de Albox 2002 went 14 ♗e2?! f5 15 ♕f2 ♕a5 16 ♘d6 ♗a6 17 ♕e1 ♗xd6 18 exd6 ♘f6 19 ♗f3 ♕b6

with advantage. Rustemov analyses 14 f5 ♗a6! 15 ♘d6 ♗xd6 16 exd6 ♕b6 17 ♘a4 ♕a5 18 ♘c5 (18 ♘c3 ♖xb2! 19 ♔xb2 ♖b8+) 18...c3. This should favour Black, e.g., 19 bxc3 ♕xc3 20 ♘xa6 ♖b2 21 ♖d2 ♕xa3 and 22 ♖f2 ♖a2+ 23 ♔d2 ♖a1-+ or 22 ♖d3 ♕a1+ 23 ♔d2 ♕xa6∓.

8.41 4...♘c6

This was suggested in the first edition and has grown increasingly popular since. One theme of 4...♘c6 is that the b4 bishop can now react to a3 by ...♗a5-b6, putting pressure on d4. Another is to attack the centre by ...f6 after e5 is played.

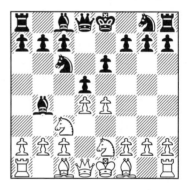

We look at:

8.411 5 e5
8.412 5 a3

(a) 5 exd5 exd5 just frees Black's bishop, for example, 6 g3 ♗g4! 7 ♗g2 ♘ge7 8 0-0 ♕d7 9 a3 ♗xc3 10 bxc3 ♘a5 11 ♖e1 0-0 12 f3 ♗f5∓ B.Jacobs-Remlinger, Philadelphia 1995;

(b) 5 ♕d3 dxe4 6 ♕xe4 ♘f6 7 ♕h4 ♘e7 (or 7...0-0, e.g., 8 ♗g5 ♗xc3+ 9 bxc3 e5 10 ♗xf6 ♕xf6 11 ♕xf6 gxf6 12 0-0-0 ♖d8∓) 8 ♗g5 ♘ed5 9 a3 ♗e7 is equal, Simon-Hofmair, Austrian Teams 1997.

8.411 5 e5

This has proven popular. Previously I argued that it is less flexible than 5 a3 ♗a5 6 e5 of 8.412, but then again White may not care for the bishop going to a5 and b6.

5...f6

Now 6 a3 ♗a5 transposes to 5 a3. But White has other approaches:

6 exf6

(a) 6 ♘f4 is similar to 5 a3 ♗a5 6 e5 f6 7 ♘f4, but here the bishop can come back to help the king: 6...fxe5 (6...g6!? 7 ♗b5 fxe5 8 ♘d3! ♗xc3+ 9 bxc3 e4 10 ♗xc6+ bxc6 11 ♘e5 ♗a6! is unclear but probably better for White, who has good attacking prospects) 7 ♕h5+ with:

(a1) 7...♔f8 8 dxe5 (8 ♘g6+? hxg6 9 ♕xh8 exd4 10 a3 ♗a5 11 b4 ♘xb4 12 axb4 ♗xb4 13 ♗a3 ♕e7-+) 8...d4 9 ♕f3!? ♘f6! (or 9...♔e8 10 ♕h5+ ♔f8=) 10 exf6 ♕xf6 11 ♗d2 dxc3 12 bxc3 ♗d6 13 ♗e2 e5 14 ♘h5 ♕xf3 15 ♗xf3 ♗f5=;

(a2) 7...g6 8 ♘xg6 ♘f6

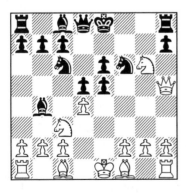

Black has just enough initiative to counteract his weaknesses:

(a21) 9 ♕h4!? exd4 10 ♘xh8 dxc3 11 b3 ♔e7 12 ♗b5 ♗d6 (12...♖b8! 13 ♗xc6 bxc6 14 ♕xf6+ ♔xf6 15 ♗g5+ ♔xg5 16 ♘f7+ ♔f6 17 ♘xd8 ♗d7) 13 ♗xc6 bxc6 14 ♕xf6+!? ♔xf6 15 ♗g5+

♔xg5 16 ♘f7+ ♔f6 17 ♘xd8 c5∓ 18 ♘c6 ♗d7 19 ♘a5 ♖b8 20 a3 (20 a4 c4) 20...♖b5 21 b4 cxb4 22 axb4 ♖xb4 23 ♔e2 ♗b5+ 24 ♔d1 0-1 Barczay-Dittmar, Oberwart 1995;

(a22) 9 ♕h6 ♘xd4 10 ♗d3! ♖g8! 11 ♘xe5 ♗d6=;

(a23) 9 ♕h3!? ♘xd4 10 ♗d3 e4! 11 ♘xh8 e5 12 ♕h4 exd3 13 ♗g5 ♗xc3+ 14 bxc3 ♘xc2+ and 15 ♔f1 ♘xa1 16 ♗xf6 ♕d7 17 ♕h5+ will draw by repetition. White can try for more by 15 ♔d1 ♗g4+ 16 f3 but he runs into 16...d4!! intending 17 ♗xf6? ♘e3+, so a wild line goes 17 fxg4 dxc3 18 ♕h6 ♘xa1 19 ♗xf6 ♕d4 20 ♕h5+ ♔d7 21 ♕f5+ ♔c6 22 ♗xe5 ♕a4+ 23 ♔e1 d2+ 24 ♔e2 ♕b5+ 25 ♔d1 c2+ 26 ♔xd2 ♖d8+ -+;

(b) 6 f4?! ♘h6 7 ♘d3 0-0 8 ♗e3 ♗d7 (or 8...♘f5) 9 a3 (9 g3 ♗e8 has the idea ...♗g6) 9...♗a5 10 ♘c1? (10 0-0-0 ♗e8!) 10...fxe5 11 fxe5 ♘f5 12 ♘b3 ♗b6 13 0-0-0 ♘xe5 14 ♕d2 ♘xe3 0-1 Brock-Hummel, Las Vegas 1999.

6...♕xf6!?

Quite as good seems 6...♘xf6, for example, 7 a3 ♗a5 (or 7...♗d6) 8 b4 ♗b6 9 ♘a4 e5! 10 b5 ♗a5+ 11 ♗d2 ♗xd2+ 12 ♕xd2 ♘e4∓ Ivanec-Kovacevic, Ljubljana 2001.

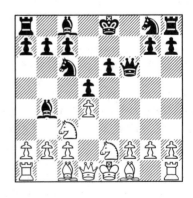

7 ♗f4

(a) 7 ♕d3 ♘ge7 8 ♗d2 0-0 9 f4 ♘f5

10 a3 ♗a5 11 ♗e3 ♘xe3 12 ♕xe3 ♗d7 13 g3 (13 0-0-0 ♘e7) 13...♘e7! 14 ♗g2 ♘f5 15 ♕f2 (15 ♕d3 ♗e8 16 0-0-0 ♗g6) 15...♖b6! 16 0-0-0!? (16 ♖d1 ♖ac8 17 b4, when the moves 17...a5 and 17...♘d6!? both favour Black) 16...♖ac8! 17 g4 ♘d6 18 ♕g3 ♘b5!? (18...c5 may be better) 19 g5 ♘xc3 20 ♕xc3 ♕e7!? 21 ♖he1 c5∓ Bhat-Hummel, Irvine 1997;

(b) 7 ♗e3 ♘ge7 8 a3 ♗a5 9 b4 ♗b6 10 ♘a4 0-0 11 ♘xb6 axb6∓ Rodina-Hacat, Ontario 2002; in most lines ...e5 follows.

7...♘ge7!

The game Guliev-Lieb, Berlin 1998 saw 7...♗a5 8 ♕d2 ♘ge7 9 0-0-0 0-0=.

After 7...♘ge7!, Herbrechtmeier-Lieb, Bundesliga 1988 continued 8 ♗xc7 0-0 9 f4 ♘f5 10 ♕d3 ♕e7?! (10...♘fxd4!∓) 11 ♗e5 ♘xe5 12 fxe5 ♕g5 with good play for the pawn.

8.412 5 a3 ♗a5

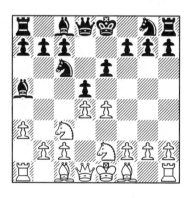

While we've now had a good deal of experience with 4...♘c6, the theory of this position is wide open. The play diverges here (with apologies for the mess):

8.4121 6 e5
8.4122 6 b4
8.4123 6 ♗e3

6 ♕d3 is far less challenging after 6...dxe4 7 ♕xe4 ♘f6 (or 7...♘ge7 8 ♗g5 ♕d5!? 9 ♕xd5 exd5=) 8 ♕h4 0-0!? (8...♘e7) 9 ♗g5 ♗xc3+ 10 bxc3 h6 (10...e5! 11 ♖d1 exd4 12 cxd4 ♖e8 13 ♗xf6 ♕xf6 14 ♕xf6 gxf6=) 11 ♗xf6 ♕xf6= Barczay-McCambridge, Dortmund 1982.

8.4121 6 e5 f6!?

Black plays the most challenging move. But it's not the only satisfactory one, e.g., 6...♗d7!? is an interesting semi-waiting move and 6...♘ge7 intends ...♘f5: 7 ♘g3 (7 b4 ♗b6 8 ♘a4 ♘f5 9 ♘xb6 axb6 10 c3 0-0 and ...f6) 7...0-0 8 ♗e2 ♗b6! 9 ♗e3 ♘f5?! (9...♘xd4! 10 ♗xd4 c5 11 ♗e3 d4 12 ♗d2 dxc3 13 ♗xc3 ♘d5=) 10 ♘xf5 exf5 11 ♘a4 f6 12 ♘xb6 axb6 13 f4 fxe5 14 dxe5 ♗e6 15 c3 ♘a5 16 0-0± Schramm-Kindermann, Dresden 1999.

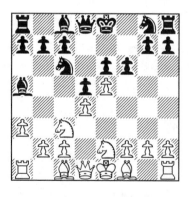

7 ♘f4

A direct attacking move. White has these options:

(a) 7 exf6?! ♕xf6 (or 7...♘xf6 and ...0-0 with some advantage) 8 ♗e3 ♘ge7 9 ♕d2 0-0 10 f4 ♘f5 11 ♗f2 ♘d6! 12 g3 ♗d7!? 13 ♗g2 ♗e8 14 0-0 ♗h5∓ Bolwerk-Pliester, Netherlands 2001;

(b) 7 f4 fxe5 (or 7...♘h6!) 8 fxe5

♘h6 9 ♗xh6 ♕h4+ 10 g3 ♕xh6 11 ♕d2 ♕xd2+ 12 ♔xd2 0-0∓ Medunova-Szymanski, Olomouc 2001;

(c) 7 b4 ♗b6 8 b5 ♘a5 9 ♘f4 fxe5! 10 ♕h5+ (10 dxe5 ♕g5) 10...g6 11 ♕xe5 (11 ♘xg6?! ♘f6 12 ♕h3 ♖g8 13 dxe5 ♖xg6 14 exf6 ♕xf6∓) 11...♕f6 12 ♕xf6 ♘xf6 13 ♗e3 c6 14 ♘a4 ♗c7 15 ♘c5 e5∓ Heyken-Kindermann, Dortmund 1993.

7...g6!?

A very interesting juncture; this position needs to be investigated more. Black's other options are 7...♕e7, 7...fxe5, and 7...♕d7, after which I gave 8 ♗b5 fxe5 9 ♕h5+ ♕f7 10 ♕xe5 ♘ge7 in the first edition, but here 10 ♗xc6+ is better.

8 ♗b5

8 exf6 ♕xf6 9 ♗b5 ♘ge7 10 0-0 0-0 with a balanced struggle in prospect.

8...fxe5 9 ♗xc6+

9 dxe5 ♘ge7 leads to a complex but balanced game, e.g., 10 0-0 0-0 11 b4 ♗b6 12 ♘d3 ♘d4 13 ♗a4 ♗d7 14 ♗g5 ♕e8=.

After 9 ♗xc6+, Olsson-Hector, Linkoping 2001 continued 9...bxc6 10 dxe5 c5 11 0-0 ♘e7 12 ♕g4 ♘f5 13 ♘d3 ♗b6 14 ♗g5 ♕d7 15 ♗f6 0-0=.

8.4122 6 b4 ♗b6

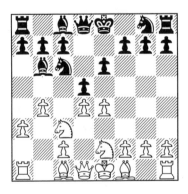

7 ♗b2

As usual, White has several options here:

(a) 7 e5 f6 8 b5 (8 ♘a4 fxe5 9 ♘xb6? axb6 10 dxe5 ♘xb4 Hoiberg-Antonsen, Aarhus 1997; 8 exf6 ♕xf6 9 ♗e3 ♘ge7∓) 8...♘a5 9 ♘a4 fxe5 10 ♘xb6 cxb6! 11 dxe5 ♕c7∓ Podesta-Giaccio, Buenos Aires 1995. Black has strong play along the c-file;

(b) 7 ♗e3 ♘f6 (7...dxe4 8 ♘xe4 e5!? 9 d5 ♗xe3) 8 e5 (8 f3?! dxe4 9 fxe4 e5!∓) 8...♘g4 with a complex position in which Black looks fine, e.g., 9 ♘f4 (9 ♗f4 f6∓) 9...♘xe3 10 fxe3 0-0 11 ♗d3 (11 ♗b5 f6 12 ♗xc6 bxc6 13 exf6 ♖xf6 14 0-0 e5) 11...♕g5 12 ♕h5 (12 0-0? ♘xe5) 12...♕xh5 13 ♘xh5 f6 14 exf6 g6!, playing for ...e5;

(c) 7 ♘a4 dxe4!?. Now White must take time to recover his pawn, and by angling for ...c6, Black will force White to exchange on b6 and then use his restraint of the centre to advantage.

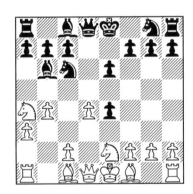

White has two important replies:

(c1) 8 ♗e3 ♘ce7! 9 c4 c6 10 ♘xb6 axb6 11 ♘c3 (11 ♘g3 ♘f6 12 ♗e2 ♘f5) 11...f5!? (11...♘f6=) 12 ♗e2 ♘f6 13 0-0 0-0 14 f3 b5!? (14...exf3 15 ♗xf3 ♘g6 16 ♕b3 ♕c7!=) 15 fxe4! (15 cxb5 ♘ed5) 15...bxc4 16 ♗xc4 fxe4 (16...♘xe4 17 ♘xe4 fxe4 18 ♖xf8+ ♕xf8=) 17 ♗g5 ♔h8! 18 ♗xf6?! (18

♗b3 ♘f5 19 ♘xe4 ♘xd4=) 18...gxf6 19 ♘xe4 ♘f5, winning the d-pawn;

(c2) 8 ♗b2 ♘f6! (8...♘ce7 9 c4 a5!?) 9 c4 a5 10 b5 (10 ♘xb6 cxb6=) 10...♘e7 11 c5 ♗a7 and Black's control of d5 ensures a decent game, because he can always play for ...e5 to free his queen's bishop: 12 ♕d2 (12 ♕b3 only temporarily stops ...e3: 12...♘ed5 13 ♘g3 0-0 14 ♗c4 c6 15 b6 ♗b8 16 0-0 e3!∓; 12 ♘g3 ♘ed5 13 ♗c4 e3!∓; 12 ♗c3 ♘ed5 13 ♗xa5 ♗xc5∓) 12...0-0 13 ♘g3 ♘ed5 (or 13...♗d7 14 ♗c4 c6) 14 ♗e2 c6! 15 b6 ♗b8 16 0-0 ♗f4∓ and ...e3.

7...♘ge7

7...♘f6 has also been played, but 7...♘h6 is the most interesting option:

(a) 8 ♘a4 ♕h4! 9 ♘xb6 axb6!? 10 e5 (10 ♘g3 dxe4 11 d5 exd5 12 ♗xg7 ♖g8 13 ♗xh6 ♕xh6 14 ♕xd5 ♖xa3!? 15 ♕xe4+ ♗e6∓) 10...f6 11 exf6 0-0 12 ♘g3 (12 g3 ♕e4 13 fxg7 ♖xf2!) 12...♕xf6 13 ♕d2 ♘e7= with the ideas ...♗d7, ...b5, ...♘hf5-d6;

(b) 8 ♕d3 0-0 9 ♘a4 ♕h4! 10 exd5 (10 ♘xb6 axb6 11 e5 f6 12 exf6 ♕xf6=) 10...exd5 11 ♕g3 ♕xg3!? (11...♘f5 12 ♕xh4 ♘xh4=) 12 hxg3 ♖e8=.

8 ♕d3

(a) 8 g3 e5! 9 exd5 ♘xd4 10 ♗g2 ♗g4∓ Volokitin-Stellwagen, Groningen 1999;

(b) 8 ♘a4 0-0 9 ♘g3 (9 ♘xb6 cxb6 10 ♘g3 f5!? 11 e5 ♘g6!, hitting f4 and thinking about ...f4-f3) 9...dxe4!? 10 ♘xb6 axb6 11 ♘xe4 ♘f5 12 c3 e5!? 13 d5 (13 b5 ♘a5 14 dxe5 ♕e7=) 13...♘ce7 14 c4 ♘d6 15 ♕e2!? f5 16 ♘xd6 cxd6 with mutual chances.

8...0-0 9 0-0-0

Not 9 g3? e5!.

9...a5! 10 b5 ♘a7

and Black will play ...c6 to open up the c-file.

8.4123 6 ♗e3 ♘f6!?

It's is not at all clear what is best here. This is the most popular move and has enjoyed success, but it is also more difficult to handle than the alternative of putting the knight on e7 instead.

(a) Here a neglected idea is 6...dxe4 7 b4 ♗b6 8 ♘xe4 ♘f6 9 ♘xf6+ ♕xf6 10 c4 a6 11 c5 ♗a7. This is quite interesting: White's d5 is weak and he should do something before Black occupies it and unravels his pieces, say, 12 ♘c3 0-0 13 ♕d2 (13 ♗d3!? ♖d8 14 ♘e4 ♕e7 15 ♘g5 h6 16 ♗h7+ ♔h8 17 ♗e4 ♘xd4! unclear) 13...e5!? 14 ♘d5 ♕d8 15 dxe5 ♘xe5 with counterplay, e.g., 16 0-0-0 c6 17 ♕c3 ♗g4! 18 f3 cxd5 19 ♕xe5 ♖e8 20 ♕d4 ♗d7=;

(b) The safest move is 6...♘ge7: 7 e5 (7 g3 e5! 8 ♗g2 ♗g4 9 f3 ♗h5 10 dxe5 dxe4 11 f4 ♘f5 [or 11...♘d5∓] 12 ♗c5 ♗f3 13 0-0 ½-½ Miladinovic-Atalik, Elista 1998; Black is slightly better after 13...♗xc3 14 ♕xd8+ ♖xd8 15 ♘xc3 ♗xg2 16 ♔xg2 e3)

7...0-0!? (Short's choice and not bad, but I prefer that Black take some initiative with 7...♘f5, e.g., 8 ♘f4 0-0 9 ♗b5 f6 10 exf6 ♕xf6! intending ...e5, and anticipating 11 ♗xc6 bxc6 12 b4? e5!; there's a lot to be analysed here) 8

♘g3 f6 9 f4? (9 exf6 ♖xf6 10 ♗d3 h6 aiming for ...e5 or ...♗xc3 and ...♘a5 etc.) 9...fxe5 (McDonald mentions the standard idea 9...♗d7 10 ♗d3 ♗e8 unclear) 10 fxe5 ♗d7 11 ♕g4!? (White has to get castled. Maybe he should try 11 ♕d2, when HiArcs anticipates 0-0-0 by 11...a6!? 12 0-0-0 ♘a7!, intending ...♘b5 or ...c5, e.g., 13 ♗d3 c5 14 dxc5 ♘ec6 15 b4 ♗c7 16 ♗g5 ♕e8∓) 11...♘f5!? (11...♗b6! would prepare this) 12 ♘xf5 exf5 13 ♕f3 (13 ♕f4 ♘e7 is unclear) 13...♗e6 14 ♗b5 ♗xc3+ 15 bxc3 f4 16 ♗f2 ♕d7! (threatening ...♘xe5!) 17 0-0? (17 ♗e2!; then maybe 17...♘e7 18 0-0 b6, playing for ...♘g6 and ...c5) 17...♘xd4 18 cxd4 ♕xb5∓ E.Berg-Short, Malmo 2002; Black is a pawn up and his bishop has better prospects than White's.

7 e5 ♘g4

Black has enjoyed much success here, but White may gain some edge by

8 ♘f4!

The alternatives are also significant:

(a) 8 ♗d2 f6 (8...0-0 9 f3 ♘h6 10 ♗xh6 ♕h4+ 11 g3 ♕xh6= Van Mil-B.Martin, Oakham 1994) 9 h3 ♘xf2! 10 ♔xf2 fxe5 with a strong attack for Black;

(b) 8 ♗f4 f6 9 ♘g3 (9 h3? fxe5)

and now there are two very tactical ideas:

(b1) 9...♘xf2!? 10 ♔xf2 ♗b6 11 ♔e1 ♗xd4 12 ♗b5?! (12 ♕h5+ g6 13 ♕h6 fxe5 14 ♗d2 ♕e7=) 12...0-0 13 exf6! (13 ♗xc6 fxe5 is good for Black) 13...♕xf6 14 ♖f1 ♗xc3+!? 15 bxc3 ♕xc3+ 16 ♗d2 ♕e5+ 17 ♗e2!? ♗d7 18 ♖b1 b6 19 ♖b3, when McDonald likes White, but Black plays for the central advance ...e5 by 19...♕d6 (or instead 19...♖xf1+ and ...♕d6);

(b2) 9...fxe5!? seems like a good alternative, since after 10 ♕xg4 exf4 White's best is probably to head for simplification by 11 ♕xg7 (11 ♘h5 ♗xc3+ 12 bxc3 g6; 11 ♕xf4 e5! 12 dxe5 ♖f8) 11...♖f8 12 ♘h5 (12 ♗e2 ♕e7 13 ♗h5+ ♔d8 14 ♕xe7+ ♔xe7 15 ♘ge2 ♗xc3+ 16 bxc3 ♔d6∓ and ...e5) 12...♕e7∓ or 12...♕f7!? 13 ♕g8+ ♔e7 14 ♕g5+ ♔d7∓;

(c) 8 b4 ♗b6 9 ♘a4 ♘xe3 (9...♕h4 has also been successful) 10 fxe3 f6 11 ♘f4 0-0 12 ♘xb6 axb6 13 exf6 ♕xf6 with a strong initiative, McDonald-B.Martin, London 1994;

(d) 8 ♗c1!? 0-0 9 h3 ♘h6 10 ♗xh6 gxh6 11 b4 ♗b6 12 ♘a4 f6 with good activity for Black, McDonald-B.Martin, London 1994.

8...♘xe3 9 fxe3 0-0!?

This move is certainly natural but

as far as I know untried. Practice has revealed some serious but not necessarily insoluble problems with the alternative 9...♕h4+ 10 g3 ♕h6 11 ♕d3!? (11 b4 ♗b6 12 ♘a4! also keeps some advantage) 11...♗d7 12 ♗g2 ♗b6 13 0-0-0± Illescas-Taddei, France 2000.

10 ♗d3!

Now 10 ♕f3? is pointless after 10...f6, and 10 g3 f6 11 exf6 ♕xf6 12 ♗g2 allows the interesting sequence 12...♗xc3+ 13 bxc3 g5!? (13...♗d7 14 0-0 ♕g5 15 ♕d3±) 14 ♘h3 ♗d7 15 ♕h5 h6 and I see nothing wrong with Black's position.

10...f5

With this move Black accedes to letting White's e-pawn survive, but he stops White's attack and retains play on the queenside.

11 0-0

11 b4 ♗b6 12 ♘a4 (12 0-0? ♘xd4) 12...♘xe5!? 13 dxe5 ♗xe3 14 ♕f3 ♗d4 wins a third pawn and leaves the situation unclear.

11...♗d7

White should have a small advantage here; play might continue 12 ♔h1 ♘e7 13 ♘ce2 (13 g4 c5!) 13...c6 14 b4 ♗c7 15 c4!? dxc4 16 ♗xc4 ♘d5 17 ♕d2 ♕e7±, but Black stands solidly enough and can contemplate ac-

tion on either wing. Given the nature of the play, however, I think that after 6 ♗e3, 6...♘ge7 promises more positive play than 6...♘f6.

This has been a long look at 4 ♘ge2 ♘c6. It's holding up very well in theoretical terms, and as an extra benefit it offers room for experimentation and development.

8.42 4...dxe4 5 a3 ♗e7 6 ♘xe4 ♘f6

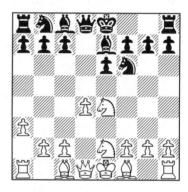

Some will like this clear solution. 6...♘f6 resembles the ...dxe4 lines of the Classical variation in Chapter 14, and those who are familiar with the order 3 ♘c3 dxe4 4 ♘xe4 ♘d7 5 ♘f3 ♘gf6 followed by ...♗e7 will realise that White has lost more than he has gained by comparison, since putting a knight on g3 or c3 in two moves can hardly be as good as having the knight on f3 in one.

7 ♘2g3

This has done the best recently. I don't think that any move is particularly dangerous versus natural play:

(a) 7 ♘xf6+ ♗xf6 8 ♗e3 (the slow 8 c3 can be met in several ways including the immediate 8...e5=. Also possible is 8...♘d7 with ...c5 or in some cases ...e5 next) 8...0-0 (8...c5!? 9 dxc5 ♕xd1+ 10 ♖xd1 ♗xb2= was Ambroz-Uhlmann, Trencianske Teplice 1979)

9 ♕d2 e5!? (9...a6!? 10 0-0-0 b5) 10
0-0-0 ♘c6= was Kurajica-Petrosian,
Zagreb 1970, when instead of the
strange 11 f3?, White could have
played 11 d5 ♘e7 12 ♘c3 ♘f5 13
♔b1=;

(b) 7 ♘g5?! c5 (7...e5=) 8 ♘f3 ♘c6 9
g3 cxd4?! (9...e5!∓) 10 ♘exd4 ♘xd4 11
♕xd4 ♕xd4 12 ♘xd4 Moreda-
Lageyre, Clermont Ferrand 2001; and
Black would still have some advantage after 12...♗d7 13 ♗g2 e5 14 ♘e2
0-0-0;

(c) 7 ♘2c3 ♘c6!? (7...0-0 8 ♗c4
♘c6= is easier) 8 ♗e3 (8 ♗b5 ♘xe4!?
9 ♗xc6+ bxc6 10 ♘xe4 ♗a6 is unclear) 8...0-0 (or 8...♘xe4 9 ♘xe4 e5=
– Euwe; then possible is 10 d5 ♘d4!?
11 ♗c4! ♘f5 12 ♗d2 ♘d6 13 ♘xd6+
cxd6 14 0-0 0-0 with ...f5 to come) 9
♕d2 (9 ♗e2 ♘xe4 10 ♘xe4 was
Lasker-Capablanca, Moscow 1935,
and Black missed the chance for
10...f5! 11 ♘c3 f4, picking up the d-
pawn at no cost) 9...a6!? 10 ♗e2! b5
11 ♗f3 ♗b7 12 g4?! ♘xe4 13 ♘xe4
Auwerswald-Fritz, corr 1989, and
best was 13...e5 14 d5 ♘d4!;

(d) 7 ♕d3 is a popular move in this
type of position, preparing quick castling on the queenside. Then 7...a6!?
and ...b5 is of interest, while 7...♘bd7
is a flexible move that has enjoyed
some success, e.g., 8 ♗f4 ♘xe4 9
♕xe4 ♘f6 10 ♕f3!? (10 ♕d3 0-0 11
0-0-0 ♗d7 with the idea ...♗c6, but
also ...b5/...a4/...b4) 10...0-0 11 g3?!
♗d7! 12 ♖g1?! (but 12 ♕xb7 ♖b8 13
♕xa7 ♖xb2 is depressing) 12...♗c6 13
♕b3 ♕d7 14 ♗g2 ♗xg2 15 ♖xg2 c5 16
f3!? ♕c6 17 c4 ♖ac8∓ McDonald-Pert,
Telford 2003.

7...0-0

Similar to the main line is 7...♘bd7
8 ♗d3 c5 9 dxc5 ♘xc5 10 ♘xc5 ♗xc5
11 0-0 ♕c7!? 12 ♕e2 ♗d7 intending

...♗c6 and perhaps ...0-0-0, Llaneza
Vega-Foisor, Istanbul 2003.

8 c3 ♘bd7

This is a rare but solid move, contemplating forthcoming breaks in the
centre.

9 ♗d3

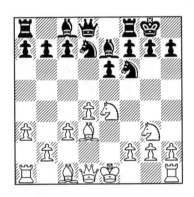

9...c5!

The break that corresponds to the
Classical Variation.

10 dxc5?

Better is 10 ♘xf6+ ♘xf6 11 dxc5
♗xc5= – Rogers. Then Black has a 4-
3 central pawn majority vs 3-2 on the
queenside, which is always an interesting imbalance.

**10...♘xe4 11 ♘xe4 f5! 12 ♘g3 ♘xc5
13 ♗c4 ♕xd1+ 14 ♔xd1 ♗d7∓**

Black intends ...♗a4+ and ...♖ad8,
while ...b5 and ...♘d3/b3 is another
plan, e.g., 15 ♗f4 b5 16 ♗a2 ♘d3 17
♗e3 f4 18 ♔c2 fxe3 19 ♔xd3 ♖xf2 and
Black is winning.

8.5 4 ♗d3

This lacks punch and is seldom
seen at the top levels any more. I haven't revised much here, but there
are people who play this regularly
and you still need to know some lines.

4...dxe4

4...c5 is also equal: 5 exd5 (5 a3
♗xc3+ 6 bxc3 c4 7 ♗e2 ♘f6 8 e5 ♘e4

9 ♗b2 ♘c6∓ Akhmedov-Fatullaev, Baku 2000) 5...exd5 6 dxc5 (6 ♘f3 c4! 7 ♗e2 ♘e7∓; 6 ♗b5+ ♘c6 7 ♘ge2 can be answered by 7...c4 or 7...♘ge7 8 a3 ♗xc3+ 9 ♘xc3 0-0= with the idea 10 dxc5?? d4) 6...♘c6 7 ♘f3 ♗xc5 8 0-0 ♘ge7 9 h3 0-0 10 a3 f6!? (a standard French idea, to support a knight on e5; but Black could also play simply by 10...a6 or 10...h6 11 ♗f4 ♗e6) 11 ♖e1 ♘e5!? 12 ♘xe5 fxe5 13 ♖xe5 ♕d6!? 14 ♖e2 (14 ♕h5 g6 15 ♕g5 ♗xf2+ 16 ♔h1 ♗h4!; 14 ♗e3!?) 14...♗xh3 15 ♘e4! ♕g6! 16 ♘g5 ♗f5∓ Sariego-Paneque, Pinar del Rio 1990.

5 ♗xe4

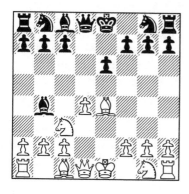

5...♘f6

A good alternative is the immediate 5...c5 (compare the main game), e.g., 6 a3 ♗xc3+ 7 bxc3 ♘f6 8 ♗f3 (8 ♗d3 ♕c7! 9 dxc5 ♘bd7 10 ♘e2 ♘xc5 11 f4 ♗d7 12 0-0 ♘a4!∓ intending ...♕c5+ and ...0-0 Bungo-E.Pedersen, corr 1986; or here 8...♘bd7 9 ♘f3 ♕c7! 10 0-0 c4 11 ♗e2 ♘d5∓ as in the game Barlov-Sahovic, Vrnjacka Banja 1984) 8...♘c6 (8...♕c7 is a useful way to avoid simplification, for example, 9 dxc5?! ♕xc5 10 ♕d4 Petkovic-Gavric, Yugoslavia 1991, and instead of 10...♕xd4 11 cxd4 ♘c6=, 10...♘bd7 11 ♗e3 ♕c7 would have given better chances for advantage) 9 ♘e2 e5 (or

9...0-0 10 0-0 cxd4! 11 cxd4 e5) 10 ♗g5 (10 ♕d3 cxd4 11 cxd4 exd4!∓, since White will have to play 12 ♗xc6+ and lose the light squares)

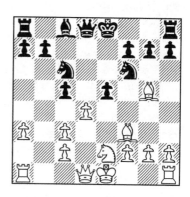

10...exd4 (or 10...cxd4 11 0-0!? dxc3 12 ♕xd8+ ♘xd8 13 ♘xc3 ♗e6=) 11 cxd4 (11 ♗xc6+ bxc6 12 cxd4 cxd4 13 ♕xd4 ♕a5+ 14 ♗d2 ♕d5= Hort-Pietzsch, Kecskemet 1964) 11...h6 12 ♗xf6 ♕xf6 13 c3?! (13 dxc5 0-0 14 0-0 ♖d8=) 13...0-0 14 0-0 ♖d8 15 ♕a4 cxd4! (this looks better than 15...♗d7!?∓ Ortega-Uhlmann, Polanica Zdroj 1967) 16 ♗xc6 bxc6 17 cxd4 (17 ♘xd4 c5!) 17...c5! 18 dxc5 ♗a6.

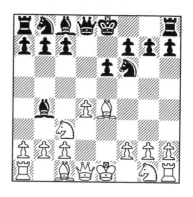

6 ♗f3

(a) 6 ♗d3 c5 7 ♘f3 is Djuric's specialty, although it seems harmless (others: 7 a3 ♗xc3+ 8 bxc3 ♕c7= with the idea ...c4; 7 dxc5 ♘bd7 8 ♗d2

♘xc5 9 ♗b5+ ♗d7 is perfectly good and even gives Black a lead in development) 7...0-0 (or 7...cxd4! 8 ♘xd4 e5 9 ♘de2 0-0 10 0-0 ♗g4 11 f3 Djuric-Drasko, Niksic 1996; 11...♗e6 12 a3 ♗e7 'looks very solid for Black' – Pedersen; I agree, and the kingside 4-3 majority may come in handy later) 8 0-0 (8 a3 ♗xc3+ 9 bxc3 Djuric-Prata, Lisbon 1999, and McDonald recommends 9...♘bd7 10 0-0 ♕c7) 8...♘c6 9 dxc5 ♗xc3 10 bxc3 e5 (10...♕a5) 11 ♘g5!? (11 ♗g5) 11...♕a5 12 ♗e3 ♕xc3 with complex and balanced play, Roitburd-S.Bjerke, Oropesa del Mar 2000;

(b) 6 ♗g5 is an innocuous line from the MacCutcheon French. Black can play, for example: 6...c5! (6...♘bd7 is also good) 7 ♘f3 (7 dxc5 ♕xd1+ 8 ♖xd1 ♘bd7 9 ♗f3 ♗xc3+ 10 bxc3 ♘xc5= intending 11 ♗e3 ♘fd7) 7...cxd4 8 ♘xd4 (8 ♗xf6 ♕xf6 9 ♕xd4 ♕xd4 10 ♘xd4 ♗xc3+ 11 bxc3 ♘d7∓) 8...♗xc3+ 9 bxc3 ♕a5 10 ♗xf6 ♕xc3+ 11 ♕d2 ♕xd2+! 12 ♔xd2 gxf6∓ Honfi-Lengyel, Budapest 1957.

6...c5 7 ♘ge2

7 a3 ♗xc3+ 8 bxc3 is 5...c5 above, and 7 ♗e3 is easily met by 7...cxd4 8 ♕xd4 ♕xd4 9 ♗xd4 ♘c6=, or by 7...♘d5 8 ♗d2 ♗xc3 9 bxc3 ♘c6.

7...♘c6

It seems that liquidating the centre is almost always reasonable in this line, e.g., 7...cxd4 8 ♕xd4 (8 ♘xd4?! e5 9 ♘db5 a6 10 ♕xd8+ ♔xd8) 8...♕xd4 9 ♘xd4 a6 10 0-0 ♘bd7 11 ♘a4!? 0-0 12 a3 ♗d6 13 c4 ♗c7 14 ♗g5 ♘e5!? 15 ♗e2!? (15 ♗xf6 gxf6 16 ♗e2 b6=) 15...♘e4 16 ♗e3 ♗d7 17 f3 ♗xa4 18 fxe4 ♖fd8 with a positional advantage (the e5 square), Grabarczyk-Gdanski, Polish Ch 1991.

8 ♗e3 cxd4 9 ♘xd4

Best may be 9 ♗xc6+!? bxc6 10 ♕xd4, when Black should probably opt for 10...♕xd4 11 ♗xd4 ♗a6=.

After 9 ♘xd4, the game Fichtl-Uhlmann, Zinnowitz 1966 went 9...♘e5 (9...♗xc3+ 10 bxc3 ♘e5=) 10 ♗e2 (10 0-0 ♘xf3+ 11 ♕xf3 ♗xc3 12 bxc3 0-0 13 c4 ♕c7 14 ♗g5 ♘d7 15 ♕e2 a6 16 ♖ad1 ♘c5 with a solid positional advantage, Kallio-Kristjansson, Gausdal 2003) 10...♘d5 11 ♗d2 ♘xc3 12 bxc3 ♗e7 13 0-0 0-0 14 f4 (14 ♖e1 ♕d5!?∓) 14...♘d7 15 ♗d3 ♘c5 16 ♕f3 ♗d7 17 ♖ae1 ♘xd3 (17...♕a5 is a good alternative, but Black wants the two bishops) 18 cxd3 ♕c7∓. Obviously White can't be worse after 4 ♗d3, but Black can make it complicated.

8.6 4 exd5

This is another version of the Exchange Variation (Chapter 5). One of the first lines played against the Winawer in the early part of the century, it has been somewhat revived by new and aggressive ideas. In our main line (Black's most ambitious strategy), White can get dangerous play by winning the two bishops at an early stage. The price he pays for this is surrender of the light squares, notably c4 and e4.

4...exd5

Now White has two main moves:

8.61 5 ♕f3
8.62 5 ♗d3

(a) 5 a3 ♗xc3+ 6 bxc3 ♘e7 7 ♘f3 (7 ♗d3 ♗f5=) 7...0-0 (or 7...♘bc6 8 ♗d3 ♗g4!) 8 ♗d3 ♗f5 9 0-0 ♘bc6 10 ♗f4 Treybal-Nimzowitsch, Carlsbad 1923; 10...♘a5∓ – Nimzowitsch, or instead 10...♕d7;

(b) 5 ♘f3 ♘e7 (a snippet from history is 5...♘c6 6 ♗d3?! ♗g4∓ Lasker-Botvinnik, Moscow 1936; 5...♗g4 6 h3

♗h5 is also good) 6 ♗d3 ♘bc6 7 h3 ♗f5 8 ♗xf5 ♘xf5 9 0-0 ♗xc3 10 bxc3 0-0 11 ♕d3 ♘d6∓ (light squares) Mannheimer-Nimzowitsch, Frankfurt 1930.

8.61 5 ♕f3

Used by Larsen in the old days, this prevents doubled pawns after a capture on c3 and intends 5...♘f6 6 ♗g5. But the White queen can be a target.

5...♕e7+

5...♘c6 is also fine, e.g., 6 ♗b5 ♘ge7 7 ♗f4 0-0 8 0-0-0 ♗e6 9 ♘ge2 a6 10 ♗d3 ♕d7 11 h3 (11 ♕h5 ♘f5 12 ♕h3 g6∓) 11...♗xc3! 12 bxc3 (12 ♘xc3 ♘xd4 13 ♗xh7+ ♔xh7 14 ♖xd4 c5) 12...♘a5 13 g4 ♘c4∓ Ghizdavu-Kapengut, Orebro 1966.

6 ♘ge2

(a) 6 ♗e3?! ♘f6 (6...♘c6 7 ♘ge2 is the main line) 7 ♗d3 (7 a3 ♗g4 8 ♕g3 ♗d6 9 ♕h4 ♗f4 10 ♘xd5 ♘xd5 11 ♕xg4 0-0∓) 7...c5! 8 ♔f1 ♗xc3 9 bxc3 c4 10 ♗f5 ♗xf5 11 ♕xf5 0-0∓ Mestrovic-Maric, Kraljevo 1967;

(b) 6 ♕e3 is passive: 6...♘c6 7 ♘f3 (7 ♗b5 ♗f5 8 ♕xe7+ ♘gxe7 9 ♗f4 ♗xc2 10 ♗xc7 ♖c8∓ Saharov-Antoshin, Sochi 1966) 7...♗f5 8 ♗d3 ♗xd3 9 cxd3 0-0-0 10 0-0 Ajala-I.Farago, Harrachov 1967, and 10...♕xe3! 11 ♗xe3 ♘ge7 12 a3 ♗d6 13 ♘b5 a6 14 ♘xd6+ ♖xd6∓; the knights are better than the bishop in this kind of position.

6...♘c6 7 ♗e3

Minev gives 7 ♕xd5 ♘f6 8 ♕c4 ♗e6 9 ♕d3 0-0-0 10 ♗e3. Then best seems 10...♘g4, e.g. 11 a3 ♘ce5! 12 ♕e4 f5 13 ♕f4 ♘g6∓.

7...♘f6 8 a3 ♗xc3+ 9 bxc3 ♘e4

with good play. Biyiasis-J.Watson, Vancouver 1977 went 10 ♕h5 ♗e6 11 f3 ♘d6 (11...♘f6 12 ♕h4 ♗f5 13 ♗g5 0-0-0 14 ♗xf6 gxf6 with a lot of

squares and good compensation) 12 ♗g5 (12 ♘g3?? ♗g4!) 12...♕d7 13 ♘f4 g6 14 ♕h4 ♘f5 15 ♕f2 h6 16 ♗f6 0-0 17 ♗d3 ♕d6∓.

8.62 5 ♗d3

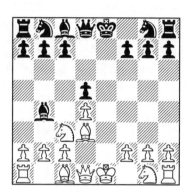

Developing logically. Now Black has a choice of 5 valid moves! I'll make two of them main lines:

8.621 5...♘c6
8.622 5...♘f6

Also playable are 5...c5 and 5...c6, whereas 5...♘e7 is similar to (and often transposes into) 5...♘c6.

8.621 5...♘c6

'The most precise equalizing line' – Psakhis.

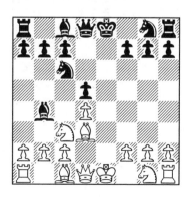

6 a3

Only this sharp move challenges Black:

(a) 6 ♘f3 ♗g4 7 ♗e2 (7 ♗e3 ♘f6 8 a3 ♗xc3+ 9 bxc3 ♘e4∓) 7...♘ge7 8 0-0 ♕d7 9 ♗g5 f6 10 ♗e3 0-0-0 11 h3 ♗e6!? 12 a3 ♗xc3 13 bxc3 g5! and Black's attack was well underway in G.Phillips-Barsov, Metz 2002;

(b) 6 ♘ge2 ♘ge7 (6...♕h4!? 7 ♗e3 ♘ge7 8 ♕d2 h6 9 a3 ♗xc3 10 ♕xc3 ♗f5 11 ♗f4 ♗xd3 12 ♕xd3 0-0-0= Czerniak-Ivkov, Eersel 1966) 7 0-0 (7 ♗g5 f6 8 ♗f4 ♗g4=) 7...♗g4 (or 7...♗f5=) 8 h3 (8 f3 ♗f5 9 a3 ♗xc3 10 bxc3 ♕d7 11 c4 ♗xd3 12 ♕xd3 dxc4 13 ♕xc4 0-0 14 ♗b2 ♘d5 15 ♕d3 b5! 16 ♖fe1 ♘a5!? with doubled-edged play, Sepman-Shchukin, St Petersburg 2000) 8...♗h5 9 a3 ♗d6 10 ♘b5 0-0 11 c3 ♖e8 12 ♕c2 ♗g6 13 ♘xd6 ♕xd6 14 ♗f4 ♕d7= O.Bernstein-Bronstein, Paris 1954.

6...♗xc3+

6...♗a5 has been used by Apicella and Uhlmann and is undoubtedly playable. The capture is thematic.

7 bxc3

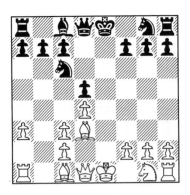

7...♗e6!?

I'm going to recommend this slightly offbeat but currently accepted move which maintains flexibility (sometimes bishops or queens are better developed before knights, as on move 3!). Then ♕h5 is met by ...♘f6, and Black can also play a quicker ...0-0-0 in several lines. 7...♘f6 has also been used to achieve equal chances.

More interesting is the older 7...♘ge7, which is still unresolved. Here's a fairly up-to-date example, with thanks to Neil McDonald: 8 ♕h5 ♗e6 9 ♘f3 ♕d7 10 ♘g5 0-0-0 11 0-0 (11 ♘xf7? ♕e8; 11 ♘xe6 ♕xe6+ 12 ♗e3 g6=) 11...♗g4! 12 ♕xf7 h6 13 f3 ♖df8 14 fxg4 (14 ♕xg7 ♗f5! 15 ♘f7 ♖hg8 16 ♘e5 ♖xg7 17 ♘xd7 ♖fg8! 18 ♗xf5 ♖xg2+ 19 ♔h1 ♘xf5 20 ♘f6 ♖8g7 21 ♘xd5 ♖xc2 with an unclear position – Knaak) 14...♖xf7 15 ♘xf7 ♖e8 16 g5 hxg5 (16...h5!) 17 ♗xg5 ♔b8 18 ♖ab1 ♗a8 19 ♖be1? (19 ♔h1 – McDonald) 19...a6 20 ♘e5 ♘xe5 21 dxe5 ♕c6∓ Brendel-Yusupov, Stockholm 2002.

8 ♕f3

(a) 8 ♖b1 gives Black time to make a useful move: 8...b6 (8...♘a5!?; 8...♕e7 9 ♘e2 0-0-0 10 0-0 ♘f6 11 ♖e1 ♖he8 12 ♘f4 ♕d6 13 ♘xe6 fxe6, with an unclear knights-v-bishops imbalance) 9 ♘e2 ♕d7 10 0-0 ♘ge7 11 ♘f4 ♗f5 12 ♘h5 0-0 13 h3 (13 ♗h6? ♗g4!∓) Nataf-Rustemov, Stockholm 2002; and although the game was shortly drawn after 13...♔h8, a more interesting move seems to be 13...♗g6!?, e.g., 14 ♕f3 ♘a5! 15 ♖e1 ♘c4!? (15...♖ae8 keeps more pieces on the board) 16 ♗xc4 dxc4 17 ♕f6!? ♗xh5 18 ♕xe7 ♕xe7 19 ♖xe7 c6 20 ♗f4 ♖fe8 21 ♖be1 f6=;

(b) 8 ♘f3 ♕d7 9 ♘g5 0-0-0 10 0-0 ♗f5=;

(c) 8 ♕h5 ♘f6 (8...♕e7 9 ♘e2 0-0-0=) 9 ♕h4 ♘e4 10 ♕xd8+ ♖xd8 11 ♘e2 0-0 12 ♗f4 ♘d6=.

8...♕d7

Or 8...♘ge7 9 ♘e2 ♕d7 10 ♘g3!? ♗g4 11 ♕e3 0-0 12 0-0 ♖ae8 Hausmann-S.Gross, Litomysl 1997; 13 f3! ♗e6=.

9 ♘e2

9 ♖b1 0-0-0 (9...♘a5!? is as usual a reasonable option) 10 ♘e2 ♘f6!? 11 ♗g5 (11 0-0 ♘e4!) 11...♗g4 12 ♕f4 (12 ♕g3 ♖he8) 12...♘h5 13 ♕d2 f6 14 ♗e3 g5 – compare the note to White's 11th.

9...0-0-0 10 0-0

10 ♕g3 f6 helps Black's kingside attack unless White moves quickly by 11 ♘f4 g5 (11...♘h6) 12 ♘xe6 ♕xe6+ 13 ♗e3 ♘ge7 14 0-0 h5 15 f4 h4 with unclear prospects.

10...♘f6 11 h3

11 ♗g5 ♗g4 12 ♕f4 ♘h5 13 ♕d2 f6 14 ♗e3 g5! intending ...♘g7 and ...♘f5 or ...h5.

11...♘e4!? 12 c4!

12 ♗xe4 dxe4 13 ♕xe4 ♖he8 with good light square pressure. After 12 c4, Pinol-Bartel, Balatonlelle 2002 went 12...♖he8! 13 cxd5? (13 ♗e3! f5 14 cxd5 ♗xd5 15 c4 ♗f7 16 ♖ab1 g5 17 ♖fe1 h5 is obscure) 13...♗xd5 14 c4?? (14 ♕h5! ♘f6 15 ♕g5 h6 16 ♕g3 g5! with initiative) 14...♘c3! 15 ♕f4 (15 cxd5 ♘xe2+ 16 ♗xe2 ♘xd4) 15...♘xe2+?! (15...♗e4!-+) 16 ♗xe2 ♖xe2 17 cxd5 ♕xd5∓.

8.622 5...♘f6

This has been played a lot recently and looks perfectly fine:

6 ♗g5

The most direct move. 6 ♘f3 comes out rather poorly after 6...♕e7+! 7 ♕e2 (7 ♗e3 ♘e4!∓) 7...♕xe2+ 8 ♔xe2 0-0 and Black may even be slightly better, e.g., 9 ♗f4 ♖e8+ 10 ♔d2 c5.

6...0-0

Also effective is the immediate 6...h6 (often transposing) 7 ♗h4 (7

♕e2+ ♗e6 8 ♗h4 g5! 9 ♗g3 c5!) 7...0-0 8 a3?! (8 ♘ge2 transposes to 6...0-0) 8...♖e8+ 9 ♘ge2 ♗xc3+ 10 bxc3 c5! 11 dxc5 ♘bd7 12 0-0 ♘xc5 13 ♘d4 g5! 14 ♗g3 ♘ce4∓.

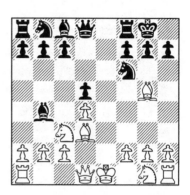

7 ♘ge2

Consistent with White's set-up. The options are worse:

(a) 7 a3?! ♗xc3+ 8 bxc3 ♕e8+! 9 ♘e2 (9 ♕e2 ♕c6 10 ♕d2 ♖e8+ 11 ♘e2 ♘e4 12 ♗xe4 ♖xe4 13 0-0 f6∓) 9...♘e4 10 ♗d2 (10 ♗f4 ♘xc3 11 ♕d2 ♘xe2 12 ♗xe2 ♕c6∓) 10...♘d7 11 0-0 ♘b6 12 ♘g3 (12 ♗f4 ♕c6=) 12...♕c6 13 ♕h5?! f5 14 ♗xe4 dxe4 15 f3 e3!-+ Druckenthaner-Kindermann, Austrian Teams 2002;

(b) 7 ♕d2? c5! is already better for Black: 8 a3 (8 dxc5 d4 9 0-0-0 dxc3 10 ♗xh7+ ♔xh7 11 ♕xd8 ♖xd8 12 ♖xd8 cxb2+ 13 ♔xb2 ♘bd7∓; 8 ♘f3 ♕e8+! 9 ♕e2 c4∓) 8...♗a5 9 ♘f3 ♕e8+ 10 ♗e3 c4 11 b4 cxd3 12 bxa5 dxc2 13 ♕xc2 ♘c6 14 0-0 ♗g4! 15 ♘d2 ♘xa5∓.

7...h6 8 ♗h4

8 ♗f4 c5!? 9 dxc5 ♘c6 10 0-0 ♗xc5 11 ♘a4 ♗d6 12 ♕d2 ♗e6=.

8...c5!?

8...c6 is solid, e.g., 9 0-0 ♘bd7 10 a3 ♗d6 11 ♗g3 ♘b6 12 ♗xd6 ♕xd6= Rechel-Eingorn, Metz 1998.

After 8...c5, Skripchenko-Barua, Groningen 1997 continued 9 dxc5

♘c6 10 0-0 ♗xc5 11 ♘xd5!? g5 12 ♘xf6+ ♕xf6 13 ♗g3 ♕xb2 14 ♖b1 ♕f6= ½-½.

8.7 4 ♕d3

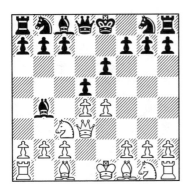

White covers e4 and would like to transfer the queen to pressure the kingside. In addition, he can prepare 0-0-0 by, say, ♗d2.

4...♘e7

White's main idea is 4...dxe4 5 ♕xe4 ♘f6 6 ♕h4, which may be fine for Black but isn't worth contesting. The text recognizes that the queen is not well placed on d3, and thus doesn't need to be forced to a better spot.

Another solution is 4...♘c6 5 e5 (5 ♘f3 ♘f6 6 e5 ♘e4 7 a3?! ♗xc3+ 8 bxc3 f6! 9 exf6 Jerez Perez-Romero Holmes, Cala Galdana 2001, and although 9...gxf6!? was fascinating and roughly balanced, 9...♕xf6 10 ♗e2 0-0 would have favoured Black, who can develop by ...b6, ...♗b7 and ...e5, while other plans such as ...a5/...♗a6 or ...♗d7-e8-g6/h5 are also possible) 5...f6 6 a3 ♗a5 7 b4 ♗b6 8 ♘f3 fxe5 9 dxe5 ♘ge7 10 ♗b2 (10 ♗g5 h6 11 ♗h4 0-0 12 ♗e2 ♕e8 13 b5 ♘f5! 14 bxc6 ♘xh4∓ Pascual Arevalo-Romero Holmes, Spain 1990) 10...0-0 (10...a6! 11 ♘a4 ♗a7∓) 11 ♘a4 ♗d7 12 ♘xb6

axb6= intending ...♘g6, Muench-Reimer, corr 1998.

5 ♗d2

Thematically preparing 0-0-0. Others:

(a) 5 ♘ge2 is the popular move.

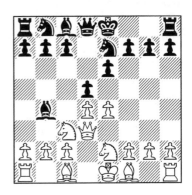

Now Black can play 5...♘bc6 (resembling 4 ♘e2 ♘c6), 5...b6, or:

(a1) 5...♘d7 6 a3 ♗a5 (or 6...dxe4 7 ♕xe4 ♘f6=) 7 b4 ♗b6 (White has stopped ...c5, but now has to face ...e5) 8 ♘g3 a5 9 ♖b1 axb4 10 axb4 0-0 11 ♗e2 (11 e5 f6 12 f4 fxe5 13 fxe5 ♘c6 14 ♘ce2 ♕h4 intending ...♘dxe5) 11...e5! 12 ♘xd5 ♘xd5 13 exd5 exd4 14 0-0 ♘e5∓ Chevallier-Luce, Torcy 1991;

(a2) 5...c5 6 ♗g5 (harmless is 6 dxc5 ♗xc5 7 exd5 exd5 8 ♗e3 ♗xe3 9 ♕xe3 0-0 10 0-0-0 ♘bc6 with good prospects on the queenside) 6...f6 7 ♗d2 ♘bc6!? (or 7...0-0!?, e.g., 8 a3 cxd4 9 axb4 dxc3 10 ♗xc3 e5=) 8 a3 ♗xc3 9 ♗xc3 Schmittdiel-Jolles, Groningen 1990. To counteract the bishops, Black should now win the centre by 9...cxd4 10 ♘xd4 e5 11 ♘xc6 bxc6=;

(b) 5 ♗g5 0-0 (5...f6 is also fine) 6 ♘f3 ♗xc3+ (6...f6 7 ♗d2 b6 8 0-0-0± – Vaganian; but here 7...c5! improves, with good play) 7 bxc3 f6 8 ♗d2 b6 9 ♕e3 ♗b7 10 ♗d3 (10 e5!? ♘f5 11 ♕f4

♘c6 – Vaganian) 10...dxe4 11 ♗xe4 ♘f5! 12 ♕e2 ♗xe4 13 ♕xe4 ♕d5∓ Smirin-Vaganian, Naberezhnye Chelny 1988.

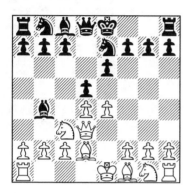

5...c5

5...b6 has been played in several games, but a more common order for this idea is 5...0-0 and:

(a) 6 0-0-0 c5 (or 6...b6 7 ♘h3 ♗a6 ½-½ Meszaros-Lahlum, Kecskemet 2003, due to 8 ♕f3 ♗xf1 9 ♖hxf1 ♗xc3 10 ♗xc3 dxe4 11 ♕xe4 ♕d5=; 9...♘bc6!?) 7 dxc5 ♘a6!? 8 a3 (8 ♕f3 ♘xc5 9 exd5 exd5 10 ♘xd5 ♗xd2+ 11 ♖xd2 ♘xd5 unclear) 8...♗xc5 9 ♗e3 ♕a5= Khemelnitsky-Shabalov, Philadelphia 1993;

(b) 6 a3 ♗xc3 7 ♗xc3 b6! 8 0-0-0 (8 ♘f3 a5 9 0-0-0 ♗a6=) 8...♗a6 9 ♕f3 (9 ♕e3 ♗xf1 10 ♖xf1 a5! 11 ♘f3 ♘bc6 12 ♗d2 b5!= Jerez Perez-Moskalenko, Barbera 1999) 9...♗xf1 10 ♖xf1 ♘bc6 11 ♘e2 a5 12 a4?! ♕d7! 13 ♘f4 dxe4 14 ♕xe4 ♘b4!∓ 0-1 Levitt-Nogueiras, Bled 2002.

6 dxc5 ♘bc6 7 0-0-0 0-0

7...♗xc5 is probably a more accurate move order.

8 ♘f3

White could try 8 exd5 exd5 9 ♘a4 ♗f5 10 ♕b3 when 10...♕a5! 11 ♗xb4 ♘xb4 12 c3 ♘a6 is about equal.

8...♗xc5 9 ♗e3

9...♗xe3+

More ambitious and at least equalising is 9...♕b6 10 ♗xc5 ♕xc5, since 11 exd5 exd5 12 ♘d4! (12 ♘xd5 ♘xd5 13 ♕xd5 ♕xf2 prepares ...♗e6 or ...♗g4) of Ribeiro-Russek Libni, Maringa 1991 can be met by 12...♗e6! with the idea 13 ♘xe6 fxe6 14 f3 ♘f5.

10 ♕xe3 ♕a5 11 ♗b5!? a6!?

Simpler is 11...♗d7=.

12 ♗a4!?

12 ♗xc6! bxc6 13 ♘d2! intending ♘b3 was worth thinking about.

12...b5 13 ♗b3 b4 14 ♘a4

Navinsek-Cebalo, Pula 2002. Although Black went on to win after 14...♗d7 15 ♕c5=, he might have done better by playing 14...dxe4 15 ♕xe4 ♘d5.

Chapter Nine

Winawer Variation: Fifth Move Alternatives

1 e4 e6 2 d4 d5 3 ♘c3 ♗b4 4 e5 c5

Our repertoire choice for Black is the traditional and natural 4...c5, attacking the centre. White's primary response to 4...c5 is 5 a3, so that after 5...♗xc3 6 bxc3, White's threatened d4 point is fortified and he has the bishop pair. White has several other 5th moves, and like the 4th-move options of the last chapter, one needs to know how to answer them. I have tried to stick to previous solutions, but with multiple answers and a lengthy new analysis of 5 ♗d2, which has provoked many emails and questions from readers who are not satisfied about what I presented in the last edition. In this position White has:

9.1 5 ♘f3
9.2 5 ♗d2
9.3 5 dxc5
9.4 5 ♕g4

9.1 5 ♘f3

This simple development isn't used much, mainly because White's centre isn't well supported. It is nevertheless perfectly sound.

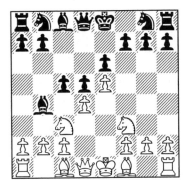

5...cxd4

This capture is an independent course. It is valid but not necessarily best because Black has some handy transpositional solutions, for example:

(a) After 5...♘e7, 6 a3 ♗xc3 transposes to the main line of Chapters 11 and 12, and 6 dxc5 is the 5 dxc5 ♘e7 line below. A unique line is 5...♘e7 6 a3 ♗a5!? 7 dxc5, when 7...♗xc3+ 8 bxc3 ♘d7 is a normal-looking 5 dxc5 line but with a3 in;

(b) 5...♘c6 is the most natural move, allowing some transpositions like 6 dxc5 (transposing to 5 dxc5) and 6 ♗d2 (see 5 ♗d2). White sometimes plays the harmless 6 &b5 (6 a3 &xc3+ 7 bxc3 ♘e7 and 7...♕a5 are also main-line Winawers) 6...♘ge7 (6...&d7 7 &xc6 &xc6= has also been played) 7 0-0 &d7 (threatening ...&xc3 and ...♘xe5) 8 &xc6 (8 ♘e2 ♘xe5 9 &xd7+ ♘xd7 10 c3 &a5 11 dxc5 e5!∓) 8...♘xc6 9 dxc5 &xc5 and White hasn't done anything except surrender the bishop pair.

6 ♕xd4

6 &b5+ &d7 is again unimpressive, and 6 ♘xd4 has several answers, the most popular being the double attack on c3 and e5 by 6...♕c7: 7 &b5+ &d7 (or 7...♘d7∓) 8 0-0! (a gambit that Black has declined in several games) 8...♘c6!? 9 ♕g4!? (9 &xc6 bxc6 10 ♕g4 &xc3 can lead to 11 ♕xg7 &xd4 12 ♕xh8 0-0-0 with an obvious advantage or 11 bxc3 ♕xe5 12 &a3 h5!? 13 ♕f3 ♕f6!? 14 ♕d3 ♘e7∓ Zavanelli-Livie, corr 1999) 9...&xc3! (9...♘xd4!? 10 &xd7+ ♔xd7) 10 &xc6 (10 ♕xg7 &xd4! 11 ♕xh8 0-0-0∓; 10 bxc3 ♕xe5 11 &f4 ♕f6∓) 10...&xc6 (10...bxc6 transposes to the note to move 9) 11 ♕xg7? (But 11 bxc3 ♕xe5 offers no compensation after 12 &f4 ♕f6 13 ♖fe1 h5 14 ♕g3 h4 15 ♕g4 ♘h6) 11...&xd4 12 ♕xh8 0-0-0 13 ♕xh7 &xe5 14 c3 ♘f6∓ 15 ♕h4 ♘e4 16 &e3 ♖h8 17 &h6 &g7 0-1 De Boer-Schaaps, corr 1987.

6...♘c6 7 &b5

7 ♕g4?! ♘ge7 is a position from 5 dxc5 below, but with White's c5 pawn gone!

7...♕a5 8 &d2

8 0-0 ♘ge7 (8...&xc3 9 &xc6+ bxc6=) 9 ♕g4 &xc3 10 &xc6+ bxc6 11 bxc3 &a6 12 ♖e1 ♕xc3∓ was seen in Arpi-Harikrishna, India 1999, with the idea of meeting 13 ♕xg7 with 13...♖g8 14 ♕f6 ♘f5∓.

8...♘ge7

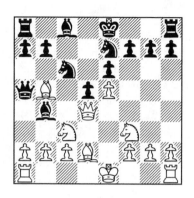

9 ♕g4

The alternatives are equal but also dull, which might encourage Black in the direction of 5...♘e7 or 5...♘c6:

(a) 9 a3 &xc3 10 &xc6+ ♘xc6 11 ♕xc3 ♕xc3 12 &xc3 0-0=, e.g., 13 0-0 a5!? (13...&d7 14 ♖ad1 b6 15 ♖fe1 ♖ac8=) 14 ♖ad1 &d7 15 ♖fe1 b5=;

(b) 9 &xc6+ bxc6 10 0-0 ♘f5 11 ♕f4 &a6 12 ♖fd1 0-0 13 a3 &xc3 14 &xc3 ♕c7= intending ...c5, and 15 g4?! ♘e7 is just weakening;

(c) 9 0-0 0-0 (9...&xc3!? 10 &xc6+ ♘xc6 11 ♕xc3 ♕xc3 12 &xc3 &d7 13 &d4= Hodgson-Saether, Stavanger 1989) 10 ♕d3 ♕c7 is logical, e.g., 11 &xc6 ♕xc6= or 11 a3 &a5!? 12 b4 &b6 13 ♘a4 ♘g6=.

9...0-0 10 &d3?!

More pointed but also more committal than 10 &xc6 bxc6 11 a3 &xc3 12 &xc3 ♕c7 13 0-0 c5=.

10...d4!?

10...♘g6! looks good: 11 0-0 (11 &xg6 fxg6!) 11...♘cxe5 12 ♘xe5 ♘xe5 13 &xh7+ ♔xh7 14 ♕h5+ ♔g8 15 ♕xe5 f6∓.

11 0-0?!

(a) 11 ♘b1 ♘xe5 12 &xh7+ ♔xh7 13 ♕h5+ ♔g8 14 ♕xe5 ♕xe5+ 15 ♘xe5 &c5∓ with the bishop pair;

(b) 11 ♕e4! ♘g6 12 ♘xd4 ♘cxe5 13 &e2=.

11...♘f5

11...dxc3 draws after 12 ♗xh7+ ♔xh7 13 ♕h5+ ♔g8 14 ♘g5 ♖d8=.

After 11...♘f5, Hodgson-Ravi, London 1987 continued 12 ♘e4 ♗xd2 13 ♘exd2 ♘xe5 14 ♘xe5 ♕xe5 15 ♘f3 ♕c5 16 ♖fe1 ♖d8!? 17 ♖ad1!? (17 ♗xf5 exf5 18 ♕xd4! ♕c7 19 ♕h4 ♗e6=), and here Myers suggests 17...h6 18 ♗xf5 (?!) 18...exf5 19 ♕f4, but now instead of his 19...♗e6, simply 19...♕xc2 20 ♖d2 (20 ♖xd4 ♗e6) 20...♕c5 21 ♘xd4 ♗d7 looks good.

9.2 5 ♗d2

This developing move prevents the doubling of White's c-pawns and prepares ♘b5, from where the knight can infiltrate to d6 or simply cover d4. After a spurt of great popularity, Black seems to have found good defensive resources. 5 ♗d2 is nevertheless critical and I give two solutions:

9.21 5...♘h6
9.22 5...♘e7

9.21 5...♘h6

I find this decentralising move, only just mentioned in PTF2, to hold forth the promise of original and complex play into what is a fairly thoroughly analysed variation.

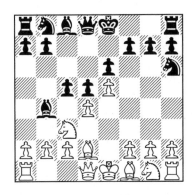

At the potential cost of allowing White to weaken his pawn structure, Black brings flexibility into his range of strategies, e.g., if White plays ♘b5-d6, Black can challenge that piece via ...f6 and ...♘f7. By not playing ...♘e7, Black's queen is free to move to the kingside, and can recapture on ...f6 if necessary. Even the move ...♘g4 can enter the picture (e.g. after dxc5), and one should note that White's standard sacrifice ♗xh7+ with ♘g5+ and ♕h5 is blocked by the knight. The most obvious negative is that White can at some point play ♗xh6, shattering Black's kingside pawn structure. As in other French variations with ...♘h6, the disadvantage to so doing is that White forfeits his dark-squared bishop and can easily become weak on the dark squares as a result (White's centre is constructed on dark squares for example). This normally wouldn't quite balance out Black's structural loss except that it will have cost White two moves to make this capture: ♗d2 and then ♗xh6. Let's see how this works out in practice:

9.211 6 ♘b5
9.212 6 ♗xh6
9.213 6 a3
9.214 6 ♗d3

Of these, 6 &d3 is considered the most important, perhaps incorrectly. In addition to these, White has three alternatives worthy of consideration:

(a) 6 f4 is less effective than after 6...♘e7: 6...cxd4 (or 6...0-0 7 ♘f3 cxd4 8 ♘b5 &c5 9 b4 &b6 10 &d3!? f6 11 ♕e2 ♘f7 12 ♘bxd4 Fernandez Romero-Del Barrio Gomez, Vila Real 2001; and Black should have played 12...fxe5! 13 fxe5 &xd4 14 ♘xd4 ♕h4+ 15 ♕f2 ♕xf2+ 16 ♔xf2 ♘xe5+∓) 7 ♘b5 &c5 8 b4 &e7 (available because e7 isn't occupied by a knight) 9 ♘f3 ♘c6 10 ♖b1 ♘f5 11 &d3 ♘h4!? (11...a6! 12 &xf5 axb5 13 &d3 ♖xa2) 12 0-0 (12 ♘xh4 &xh4+ 13 g3 &e7) 12...♘xf3+ 13 ♕xf3 a6 14 ♘d6+ &xd6 15 exd6 Willemze-Barsov, Vlissingen 2000; 15...♕xd6!∓;

(b) 6 ♘f3 ♘c6 (6...cxd4 7 ♘b5 &xd2+ 8 ♕xd2 0-0=) 7 a3 (7 &d3 transposes to 6 &d3) 7...&xc3!? 8 &xc3 cxd4 transposes to 6 a3;

(c) 6 dxc5

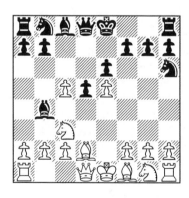

can transpose into other lines, but there are several unique ideas:

(c1) A safe solution is 6...♘d7 and 7 ♘f3 ♘g4! or 7 &b5 ♕c7 8 ♘f3 ♘g4 9 0-0 &xc5=;

(c2) 6...&xc5!? 7 &d3 (7 ♘f3?! ♘g4 8 &b5+ &d7 9 0-0 &xb5 10 ♘xb5 ♕b6∓; 7 &xh6 gxh6 8 ♕d2 ♘c6 with

the idea 9 ♕xh6 &xf2+! 10 ♔xf2 ♕b6+) 7...♘c6 (7...♕h4!?) 8 ♕h5 (8 &xh6 gxh6 9 ♕h5 ♕g5 10 ♕xg5 hxg5 11 ♘b5 ♔e7∓) 8...♘f5 9 &xf5?! exf5 10 ♘f3 d4 11 ♘a4 g6 12 ♕h3 &f8!∓;

(c3) 6...♘c6!? and now:

(c31) 7 &b5 (not the ideal square for this bishop) 7...0-0; this threatens ...♘xe5 and a plausible continuation is 8 &xc6 bxc6 9 &xh6 gxh6 10 ♕d4 ♖b8 11 ♘ge2 f6 12 a3 &a5 13 b4 &c7 14 ♕g4+ (14 exf6 e5=) 14...♔h8 15 ♕h3 fxe5 16 ♕xh6 a5!?=;

(c32) White can also lure the knight to g4 by 7 ♘f3 ♘g4 (7...&xc5) 8 &b5 &xc5! 9 0-0 ♕c7 10 ♕e2 &d7 unclear, e.g. 11 ♖ae1 0-0-0 12 h3 ♘h6 13 &xh6 gxh6 14 ♕d2 ♖dg8 15 ♕xh6 ♖g6 16 ♕f4 ♖hg8 17 ♘h4 ♖6g7 with compensation for the pawn, planning moves like ...f5 and ...&e7.

9.211 6 ♘b5 &xd2+ 7 ♕xd2 0-0

This is similar to 5...♘e7 6 ♘b5, but the knight on h6 has its advantages:

8 dxc5

(a) 8 f4 has at least two answers:

(a1) 8...a6! 9 ♘d6 cxd4 10 ♘f3 ♘c6 (10...f6!∓ is more accurate) 11 &d3 (11 ♘xd4 f6) 11...f6 (suggested by De la Villa Garcia) gives Black the advantage, e.g., 12 0-0 ♘g4!∓ with the idea 13 ♕e2 ♘e3 14 ♖f2 ♕b6;

(a2) 8...♘c6 9 ♘f3 f6 (9...a6!?) 10 c3 cxd4 11 cxd4 fxe5 12 fxe5 ♘f5= 13 &d3 ♕b6 14 0-0 &d7 15 g4? ♘fxd4 16 ♘fxd4 ♘xe5 17 ♔g2 ♘xd3 18 ♕xd3 e5-+ Perelshteyn-Shaked, Bloomington 1997;

(b) 8 ♘f3?! a6 9 ♘d6? cxd4 10 &d3 ♘c6 11 ♘xc8 ♖xc8 12 0-0 f6 13 ♖ae1 ♘f7 14 exf6 ♕xf6-+ Leiber-Shaked, Berlin 1997.

8...♘c6 9 ♘f3 b6!?

A very common theme, sacrificing

a pawn for activity.

10 ♕c3

10 cxb6 ♕xb6 11 0-0-0?! ♘g4 12 ♘bd4 ♘gxe5 13 ♘xc6 ♘xc6∓ A.Hunt-S.Williams, Witley 1999.

10...♗d7 11 ♗d3

Worse is 11 ♘d6!? bxc5 12 ♘b7 ♕b6 13 ♘xc5 ♘g4! 14 ♘xd7 ♕xf2+ 15 ♔d1 ♖fc8! – Kholmov.

11...bxc5 12 ♕xc5 ♘g4!∓

Kholmov-Nikitin, Moscow 1995.

9.212 6 ♗xh6 gxh6 7 a3

7 ♘f3 ♘c6, e.g., 8 ♗b5 ♗xc3+ 9 bxc3 ♕a5 10 ♗xc6+ bxc6 11 ♕d2 ♗a6 with plenty of play.

7...♗a5!?

The most interesting move, keeping the bishop that will attack White's dark squares. Black can also play 7...♗xc3+ 8 bxc3 ♕a5 9 ♕d2 ♘c6 10 ♘e2!? (10 ♘f3 ♗d7 11 ♗d3 0-0-0 is thematic, but also plausible is 10...b6, e.g., 11 ♗d3 ♗a6 12 0-0!? ♗xd3 13 cxd3 cxd4 14 ♕xh6 dxc3 15 ♕f6 ♖f8 16 ♘g5 ♘d4! 17 ♘xh7 ♖g8 18 ♘g5 ♖f8 19 ♘h7=) Frittchle-J.Watson, Los Angeles 1999, and most incisive was 10...b6!?, e.g., 11 dxc5 ♘xe5!? 12 ♕xh6 ♕xc5 13 ♕f6 ♘g6 14 ♘f4 ♖g8.

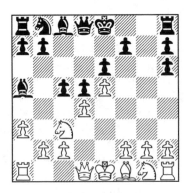

8 dxc5

(a) 8 ♕g4 cxd4 9 ♕xd4 ♗d7 10 ♘f3 ♘c6=;

(b) 8 ♘f3 ♕b6! is surprisingly strong, e.g. 9 ♖b1 (9 b4 cxb4 10 ♘b5 ♗d7 11 ♘d6+ ♔e7 12 ♗e2 bxa3+ 13 ♔f1 ♗b4) 9...♘c6 10 b4 (10 dxc5 ♗xc3+ 11 bxc3 ♕xc5) 10...cxb4 11 ♘b5 bxa3+ 12 c3 0-0 13 ♕d2 a2 14 ♖a1 ♔g7 15 ♕f4 ♕d8 16 ♔d2 f6∓.

8...♗xc3+ 9 bxc3 ♘d7

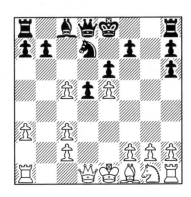

10 ♗b5

10 ♕d4 ♕a5 or 10 ♘f3 ♕a5 11 ♕d2 ♘xc5 12 c4 ♕xd2+ 13 ♘xd2 dxc4 14 ♘xc4 ♗d7 leave weaknesses on both sides.

10...♕a5 11 ♕d3 a6!? 12 ♗xd7+ ♗xd7

and Black seems to have good chances based upon the position of White's king: 13 a4 (13 ♘e2 ♕xc5 14 ♘g3 ♖c8; 13 ♕e3 ♖g8! 14 g3 d4! 15 ♕xd4 ♗c6 16 f3 ♖d8∓) 13...♖c8 14 ♕g3 ♖xc5 15 ♘e2 ♗b5 16 ♖a3 ♖c4!? 17 ♕g7 ♖f8 18 ♔d2 ♖e4 19 ♘g3 ♖d4+ 20 ♔c1 ♖xa4.

9.213 6 a3 ♗xc3

6...♗a5!? 7 dxc5 ♗c7?! (7...♘d7 8 b4 ♗c7) 8 f4? b6! 9 cxb6 ♗xb6 10 ♘f3 ♘g4 11 ♗b5+ ♗d7 12 ♗xd7+ ♘xd7 13 ♕e2 ♗f2+ 14 ♔f1 ♗b6 gave Black plenty of compensation in D.Fernandez-J.Watson, Chicago 1997; but 8 ♘f3! was strong since Black can't get enough pressure on e5.

7 ♗xc3

7 bxc3 ♘c6 8 ♘f3 ♘f5 9 ♗d3 ♕c7 10 0-0?! c4 11 ♗e2 ♗d7 12 ♘e1 0-0-0 13 g3 f6 14 f4 ♖df8 15 ♘g2 h6= Lobron-Hug, Beersheva 1985; an early game!

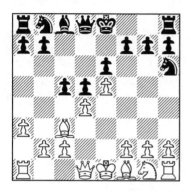

7...b6

(a) 7...♘c6 is the move analogous to 5...♘e7 lines except that White has a new idea after 8 ♘f3 cxd4 9 ♘xd4 ♘xe5: 10 ♕h5!? (10 ♘xe6 ♗xe6 11 ♗xe5 0-0= 12 ♗e2 – versus ...♘g4 – 12...♕g5 13 ♗g3 ♘f5 14 0-0 ♖ac8 intending 15 c3 d4! 16 cxd4 ♖fd8) 10...♘eg4!? 11 ♗b5+ ♔f8 12 f3 ♘f6 13 ♕e5 ♗d7 14 ♗d3 ♘e8 15 0-0 ♕b6 with the idea ...f6, when White has definite compensation for the pawn, but how much isn't clear;

(b) 7...cxd4 8 ♗xd4 (8 ♕xd4!? ♘c6 9 ♕f4 and a wild idea is 9...g5!? 10 ♕f3! d4 11 0-0-0 ♘f5 unclear) 8...♘c6 9 ♘f3 0-0 (9...♘f5 transposes to 5...♘e7) 10 ♗c5!? (10 ♗c3 ♕b6 11 ♗d3 ♘f5! 12 ♗xf5!? exf5 13 ♕xd5 ♗e6 with compensation) 10...♖e8 11 ♗d3 f6 12 ♕e2 ♘f7 (a handy move!) 13 ♗b5 (13 exf6 e5!) 13...♗d7 14 ♗xc6 ♗xc6 15 ♗d4 ♖c8= Quast-B.Schmidt, Bundesliga 1996.

8 b4

This is similar to the 5...♘e7 6 a3 lines.

(a) 8 ♘f3 0-0! is better than in the analogous 5...♘e7 line because after 9 ♗d3, 9...♗a6= can be played without ♗xh7+ being decisive.

(b) 8 ♗b5+ ♗d7 9 ♗d3 ♘c6 10 ♘f3 ♕c7!? with the idea 11 0-0? cxd4 12 ♘xd4 ♘xe5 13 ♘b5 ♕b8.

After 8 b4, A.Martin-Shaked, Schwarzach 1997 continued 8...♕c7 9 dxc5 (9 ♘f3 cxb4 10 ♗xb4 ♗a6!?) 9...bxc5 10 ♘f3?! cxb4 11 ♗xb4 a5! 12 ♗d2 ♘g4! 13 ♗b5+ ♗d7 14 ♕e2 ♗xb5 15 ♕xb5+ ♘d7 16 0-0 0-0 and the e-pawn falls.

9.214 6 ♗d3

You realise that a lot of lower players are following theory closely when this rather unnatural response to what is already a lesser-known line is chosen more frequently than any other. Why? Because Leko used it in the only 5...♘h6 game involving a world-class player. In fact, Pedersen's 3 ♘c3 book deals with no other move. That aside, the move does pose problems for Black because it activates an important piece. But it also allows a variety of responses that break up White's centre.

6...♘c6

6...cxd4 7 ♘b5 ♗xd2+ 8 ♕xd2 0-0 9 ♘xd4 has been considered slightly better for White. Black could still try 9...f6 10 ♘gf3 ♘f7 intending 11 exf6 ♕xf6 and ...e5, so maybe this should be looked at.

7 ♘f3

Now Black has a wide range of moves, several of them yielding satisfactory play.

7...f6

This seems neither better nor worse than other solutions:

(a) A very simple continuation is 7...♘xd4 8 ♘xd4 cxd4 9 ♘b5 (an alternative is 9 ♘e2 ♗xd2+ 10 ♕xd2 0-0 11 f4 f6) 9...♗xd2+ 10 ♕xd2 0-0 intending ...f6. Maybe I'm missing something because this doesn't seem to have been tried, but I can't see anything wrong with it, e.g., 11 ♘xd4 (11 0-0 f6 12 exf6 ♕xf6 13 f4? ♗d7) 11...f6 12 ♘f3 (12 f4 fxe5 13 fxe5 ♕h4+ 14 g3 ♕h5) 12...fxe5 13 ♘xe5 ♕f6 14 ♕e2 ♘f7 15 ♘xf7 ♖xf7=;

(b) 7...c4!? is more controversial and could be anti-positional, except that Black gets central play so quickly: 8 ♗f1! (8 ♗xh6?! gxh6 9 ♗e2 f6 10 exf6 ♕xf6 11 ♕d2 ♗d7∓; 8 ♗e2 ♘f5 9 ♘b1 ♗e7! 10 c3, and now R.Perez-Arencibia, Santa Clara 2002 went 10...b5!? 11 0-0 h5 12 b3 ♗d7 13 a4 ♘a5 14 bxc4 bxc4 15 ♗c1 ♘b3 16 ♖a2 ♘xc1 17 ♕xc1 ♖b8∓) 8...♘f5 9 ♘e2 ♗e7 10 c3 0-0 11 ♘g3 (11 g3 f6 12 exf6 ♗xf6∓; the main idea is ...e5) 11...f6 12 exf6 (12 ♘xf5? exf5 13 exf6 ♗xf6∓ – Kuzmin) 12...♗xf6 13 ♘xf5 exf5 14 ♗e2 ♖e8 15 0-0 ♗d7!? (15...♖e4!) 16 g3 h6∓ H.Hernandez-Marcel, Havana 1999.

8 exf6 ♕xf6 9 a3

9 dxc5 is called 'critical' by Pedersen. Then 9...0-0 10 0-0 ♗xc5 looks at least equal for Black. The position is reminiscent of the line in Chapter 15 with 2 ♘f3 d5 3 ♘c3 ♘f6 4 e5 ♘fd7 5 d4 c5 6 dxc5 ♘c6 7 ♗f4 ♗xc5 followed by ...f6, with several of Black's pieces on superior squares in the position before us. Sample lines: 11 ♗g5 (11 ♘g5 ♘f5 12 g4 ♘e5! 13 gxf5 ♘xd3 14 cxd3 ♕xf5 threatens ...h6, trapping the knight, and 15 ♘e2 h6 16 ♘g3 ♕xd3 17 ♘h3 e5 wins at least a third pawn with a nice attack) 11...♕f7 12 ♕d2 (12 ♘a4?! ♗d6 13 c4?! ♕h5!) 12...♘f5 13 ♖ae1! h6 (13...♗d7!?) 14 ♗f4 ♘h4! 15 ♘xh4 ♕xf4 16 ♕xf4 ♖xf4 17 ♘g6 ♖f6∓ and Black develops

by ...♗d7-e8.

9...♗xc3 10 bxc3

10 ♗xc3 cxd4 11 ♘xd4 0-0 12 0-0 ♘xd4 13 ♗xd4 e5.

10...c4!?

10...♘f7 is very solid, preparing ...e5, and 10...0-0 11 ♗g5 ♕f7 should also be considered.

11 ♗g5 ♕f7 12 ♗xh6!?

12 ♗e2 ♘f5 13 0-0 0-0 intending 14 ♕d2?! ♘d6!.

12...cxd3!?

12...gxh6 looks okay, followed by ...0-0-0, ...♗d7, and perhaps ...♗e8-g6.

After 12..cxd3, De la Villa Garcia-Al Modiahki, Ubeda 1998 went 13 ♗e3 dxc2 14 ♕xc2 0-0 15 0-0 ♗d7 16 a4 (slow) 16...b6 17 ♘e5? (17 ♖fe1) 17...♘xe5 18 dxe5 ♖fc8∓.

9.22 5...♘e7

This is the traditional line, where Black develops naturally. White usually chooses one of:

9.221 6 ♘b5
9.222 6 a3
9.223 6 f4

Alternatively:

(a) 6 dxc5 ♘bc6 7 ♕g4 0-0 transposes to 5 ♕g4. Black can also play 6...0-0 or 6...♘bc6 7 f4 0-0 8 ♘f3 f6, e.g., 9 ♗d3 ♗xc5 10 ♕e2 ♘b4 11 0-0-0 ♘xd3+ 12 ♕xd3 ♗d7 13 g4 ♘c6?! (13...f5! 14 h3 ♕b6) 14 ♘xd5?! (14 exf6 ♘b4 is unclear) 14...♗e8 15 ♘c3 ♕xd3 16 cxd3 ♘b4 17 ♘e1? (17 d4∓) 17...♗c6 18 ♘e4 ♘xd3+ 19 ♘xd3 ♗xe4 and Black went on to win in Areklett-S.Bjerke, Asker 2003;

(b) 6 ♘f3 cxd4 7 ♘b5 ♗xd2+ 8 ♕xd2 0-0 transposes to 6 ♘b5 ♗xd2+ 7 ♕xd2 0-0 8 ♘f3 cxd4. Black also has 6...♘bc6 7 dxc5 (7 ♘b5 ♗xd2+ 8

♕xd2 0-0 – see 6 ♘b5) 7...♘g6!? (7...0-0 8 ♗d3 f6=) 8 ♗b5 ♗xc5 9 0-0 ♗d7 10 ♖e1 a6 11 ♗d3 ♕b6! 12 ♕e2 ♘d4! 13 ♘xd4 ♗xd4∓ 14 ♗e3? ♗xe3 15 ♗xg6 Holms-Tosti, corr 1994, and among several winning moves is 15...hxg6 16 fxe3 ♕xb2 17 ♕d3 ♖c8–+.

9.221 6 ♘b5 ♗xd2+ 7 ♕xd2 0-0

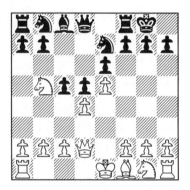

The main line. White's immediate concern is to resolve the central situation, and there is a wide choice of means:

9.2211 8 c3
9.2212 8 f4
9.2213 8 dxc5

(a) 8 ♘d6? cxd4 9 ♘f3 ♘bc6 (threatening ...♘e5) 10 ♘xc8 ♖xc8 11 ♗d3 f6∓;

(b) 8 ♘f3 a6 (8...cxd4 9 ♘bxd4 ♘bc6 can also arise via 6 ♘f3 cxd4 7 ♘b5 etc. The main line goes 10 ♗d3 ♘xd4 11 ♘xd4 f6 12 exf6 ♖xf6 13 ♕e3 ♕b6 14 0-0-0 ♘c6 15 c3 ♗d7 16 ♖he1 e5! 17 ♘xc6 bxc6= Kupper-Weinzetl, Brno 1991) 9 ♘c3 (9 ♘d6 cxd4 10 ♘xd4 ♘bc6 11 f4 f6 transposes to 6 f4) 9...cxd4!? 10 ♘xd4 ♘bc6 11 f4 ♘xd4 12 ♕xd4 ♘c6 13 ♕d2 f6 14 exf6 ♕xf6 15 g3 ♗d7 16 0-0-0?! (16

♗g2 ♗e8!?) 16...♗e8 17 ♗d3 ♘b4∓ Omari-Golz, Leipzig 1960.

9.2211 8 c3

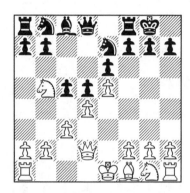

8...♘bc6!?
This is not the only move:

(a) 8...f6 9 exf6 ♖xf6 10 dxc5 ♘d7 11 b4 a5 12 f4!? (12 ♘f3 b6 13 cxb6 ♕xb6 14 ♗e2 axb4 15 cxb4 ♗a6=) 12...b6! 13 cxb6 ♕xb6 with dynamic play, Martinez-Arencibia, Cuba 1988;

(b) 8...a6 9 ♘a3 (9 ♘d6 cxd4 10 cxd4 ♘bc6 11 0-0-0 f6 12 f4 ♕b6 13 ♘f3 ♗d7 with the idea ...♘c8) 9...♘bc6 10 f4 (10 ♘f3 f6=) 10...cxd4 11 cxd4 ♘f5 12 ♘f3 f6 is equal.

9 f4
9 ♘f3 a6! 10 ♘a3 (10 ♘d6!? cxd4 11 cxd4 f6 12 ♘xc8 ♖xc8 13 exf6 ♖xf6 14 ♗d3 and now interesting is 14...♘g6! 15 ♗xg6 ♖xg6 16 0-0 ♕f6 17 ♔h1 ♖g4! 18 ♖ad1 ♖f4 19 ♕d3 g5!? 20 h3 h5 with a nice attack) 10...cxd4 11 cxd4 f6 12 exf6 ♖xf6 13 ♘c2 ♕d6 14 0-0-0 (14 ♗e2 e5 15 dxe5 ♘xe5∓) 14...♗d7 15 ♗d3 ♖af8 16 ♖de1 ♗e8 17 ♖hf1 ♘g6!∓ Strikovic-Ivkov, Cetinje 1991.

9...cxd4
Or 9...a6!? 10 ♘d6 cxd4 11 cxd4 f6=.

10 cxd4
10 ♘xd4 f6 11 exf6 ♖xf6 12 ♘xc6

♘xc6 13 0-0-0 ♗d7 14 ♘f3 ♗e8= with the idea of ...♗g6, Manolov-Spasov, Elenite 1992.

10...♘f5 11 ♘f3 f6 12 ♗d3

12 ♗e2 a6 13 ♘c3 fxe5 14 dxe5 ♕b6!.

12...a6 13 ♗xf5 axb5! 14 ♗d3 ♕a5!∓ Lilienthal-Mikenas, corr 1951.

9.2212 8 f4

A thematic strengthening of the centre, but Black gets great counter-play:

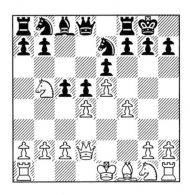

8...♘bc6

This seems easier than the well-known line 8...a6 9 ♘d6 cxd4 10 ♘f3 (10 ♘xc8 ♕xc8 11 ♘f3 ♘bc6 12 0-0-0 ♘f5∓). Now both 10...♘bc6 11 ♘xd4 f6 12 ♘xc8 ♕xc8 13 exf6 ♖xf6 14 0-0-0 and 10...f6 11 exf6 ♖xf6 12 ♘xc8 ♕xc8 13 0-0-0 ♘bc6 14 ♘xd4 reach the same position, slightly better for Black after 14...♘xd4 15 ♕xd4 ♘f5 16 ♕e5 ♕c5∓.

9 ♘f3

9 dxc5 f6 transposes to 8 dxc5, another nice line for Black.

9...a6 10 ♘d6

Now Black gets the advantage by 10...♘xd4! 11 ♘xd4 cxd4 12 ♕xd4 f6 13 exf6 ♖xf6 14 ♘xc8 ♖xc8, e.g., 15 c3 ♘c6 16 ♕d2 d4 17 ♗d3 dxc3 18 bxc3 e5∓.

9.2213 8 dxc5

White's idea is to overprotect e5 and clear d4 for a knight.

8...♘d7

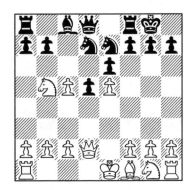

A good alternative is 8...♘bc6 9 f4 f6, when Remmelt Otten analyses 10 exf6 ♖xf6 11 ♘f3 b6 12 cxb6 ♕xb6 13 c3 ♖b8 14 b3? ♘g6 15 g3 e5 16 ♘xe5 ♘gxe5 17 fxe5 ♗g4. He says this is winning for Black, and it looks strong after 18 ♘d4 ♖e8 19 ♘xc6 ♕xc6 20 ♕d4 ♖f5 21 ♗d3 ♖fxe5+ 22 ♔d2 ♗f3∓ with the idea 23 ♖hf1? ♕h6+ 24 ♕f4 ♕xh2+.

9 f4

(a) 9 ♕c3 a6 10 ♘d6 ♕c7 and:

(a1) 11 b4? b6;

(a2) 11 ♘f3 ♕xc5 12 ♕xc5 ♘xc5=;

(a3) 11 0-0-0 ♕xc5 12 ♕xc5 ♘xc5 13 ♘f3 ♘c6 14 c4 dxc4 15 ♗xc4 b5 16 ♗d3 Holschuh-Lahlum, corr 1996-97, and Black could play 16...♘b4! 17 ♗b1 ♗b7!? 18 ♘xb7 ♘xb7, bring a rook to the c-file followed by ...♘d5 and ...♘c5;

(a4) 11 f4 ♕xc5 12 ♕xc5 ♘xc5 13 ♘f3 f6= Tradardi-Ottavi, Rome 1990.

(b) 9 ♘f3 ♘xc5 10 ♗d3 (10 0-0-0 ♘e4 11 ♕e1 ♗d7 12 ♘bd4 ♘c6 13 h4 f5 14 g3 ♕c7∓ Ciolac-Zysk, Vienna 1990) 10...♘c6 (10...♕b6!∓) 11 0-0 f6 12 ♖fe1 ♗d7∓ V.Knox-Levitt, British Ch 1993.

9...♘xc5 10 ♘d4 ♕b6

Also fine is 10...♘c6 11 ♘gf3 f6, e.g., 12 ♗d3? ♘xd4 13 ♘xd4 fxe5 14 fxe5 ♕h4+ 15 g3 ♕g4∓ Moen-Djurhuus, Norway 1989.

11 0-0-0 ♗d7 12 ♘gf3

Or 12 ♔b1 ♖ac8 13 ♖c1 ♘e4 14 ♕e3 ♘c6=.

On 12 ♘gf3, Sanz Alonzo-Sion Castro, Salamanca 1990 saw 12...♖fc8 13 ♕e3 ♘a4! 14 ♕b3 (14 ♕a3 ♖c7! – Nogueiras) 14...♕c5! 15 ♗d3 (15 ♔b1 b5!= or 15 ♕xb7 ♗c6 16 ♘xc6 ♘xc6 – Nogueiras) 15...b5 16 a3 ♖cb8 17 ♕b4 a5∓.

9.222 6 a3 ♗xc3 7 ♗xc3

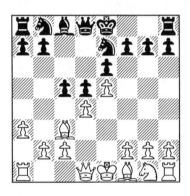

Here Black can choose between a drawish line (which might deter players of White from this line) or one with mutual chances:

7...♘bc6

Fully equalising, but with no prospects. 7...b6 is often played by stronger players and gives more winning chances for both sides, e.g.,

(a) 8 b4 ♕c7 9 ♘f3 cxb4!? 10 ♗xb4 a5 11 ♗d2 is the old main line, considered equal but unbalanced, e.g., 11...0-0 12 ♗d3 ♗a6= J.Friedman-Gulko, Philadelphia 1993;

(b) 8 ♘f3 is solid, e.g., 8...♗a6 (8...0-0 9 ♗d3 ♘g6!? has ideas of both

...♘f4 and ...♗a6 when White has already moved the king's bishop) 9 ♗xa6 ♘xa6 10 0-0 0-0 11 b4 ♘b8!? 12 ♕d3 cxd4 13 ♘xd4 ♘bc6 14 ♘e2!? (14 ♘xc6 ♘xc6 is not so easy because Black has the c-file) 14...♖c8 15 f4 h5 16 ♗e1 ♘f5 17 ♗f2 ♘ce7 18 c3 ♖c4 with active pieces, Cabrilo-Lputian, Cetinje 1991;

(c) 8 ♕g4 0-0 9 ♘f3 ♗a6 10 ♗xa6 ♘xa6 11 ♗d2 cxd4 (11...♕c7!?) 12 ♗g5!? ♕c7 13 ♗xe7 ♕xe7= De la Villa Garcia-Bareev, Leon 1995;

(d) 8 ♗b5+ ♗d7 9 ♗d3 ♘bc6 10 ♘f3 (10 f4!? cxd4 11 ♗d2 0-0 12 ♘f3 f6 13 ♕e2 Spassky-Mohr, Bundesliga 1988; this doesn't look very convincing after, e.g., 13...♗e8) 10...♘g6! (or 10...cxd4 11 ♗xd4 ♘xd4 12 ♘xd4 ♘g6=) 11 ♗xg6 fxg6 12 0-0 0-0 13 dxc5 bxc5 14 b4 ♕b6!∓ Leko-Bareev, Wijk aan Zee 1995.

8 ♘f3 cxd4 9 ♘xd4

9 ♗xd4 is also a little dull: 9...♘f5 (or 9...♘xd4 10 ♕xd4 ♘c6 11 ♕g4 0-0 12 ♗d3 f5= Balashov-Svistunov, Pinsk 1993; 12...f6 is perhaps more precise, but allows 13 ♕h5 and on the correct 13...g6, 14 ♗xg6 with a draw) 10 c3 ♗d7 11 ♗e2 ♖c8!? (11...♘fxd4 12 cxd4 ♕b6=) 12 0-0 0-0 13 ♕d2!? ♘fxd4 14 cxd4 ♘a5!= Savon-Hort, Skopje 1968.

9...♘xe5!

Otherwise Black is slightly worse.

10 ♘xe6 ♗xe6 11 ♗xe5 0-0 12 ♗d3

12 ♗e2 ♘c6 13 ♗g3 ♕f6 14 c3 d4! – Moles & Wicker.

12...♘c6 13 ♗g3

13 ♗c3 d4 14 ♗d2 ♘e5! 15 ♗xh7+? ♔xh7 16 ♕h5+ ♔g8 17 ♕xe5 ♖e8 18 ♕g3 ♗c4+ 19 ♔d1 ♖c8 with a huge attack as in the game Ljubojevic-Nogueiras, Wijk aan Zee 1987.

13...♕f6 14 ♖b1

14 0-0!? ♕xb2 15 ♖b1 ♕xa3 16

♖xb7 is an important try to stir things up, but offers insufficient play for the pawn: 16...♖fe8!? (or 16...♕c5! 17 ♕h5 h6 18 ♔h1 ♘b4 19 ♗e2 a5 20 ♖c7 ♕b6 21 c3 Hector-Sorensen, Berlin 1993; and now 21...♘a6! with the idea 22 ♗xa6 ♕xa6 or 22 ♖e7 ♖fe8 looks good) 17 ♕h5 (17 ♖e1? ♖e7!∓ was Tringov-Uhlmann, Skopje 1972) 17...h6 18 f4 ♖e7 19 ♖b3? (19 ♖xe7 ♕xe7 20 f5 ♗d7 21 f6 ♕e3+ 22 ♔h1 ♕g5) 19...♕c5+ 20 ♗f2 ♕d6 21 f5 ♗d7∓ as in the game Obukhovsky-Hasin, USSR 1973.

14...♗f5

This position offers little for either player, and also possible is 14...g6!?, e.g. 15 0-0 d4 16 ♗e4 (16 ♕d2) 16...♖ac8 and ...♖fd8.

15 0-0 ♖fe8

Or 15...♗xd3 16 ♕xd3 ♖ad8= Guedon-Naumkin, Cappelle la Grande 1993.

16 ♗xf5 ♕xf5 17 ♕d2

As usual this is drawn, but instead of the difficult 17...♖e6?! of Hector-Rowson, New York 1999, easier is 17...h6 18 ♖fe1 d4 ½-½ Raese-Franke, Bundesliga 1992.

9.2 2 3 6 f4 ♘f5!?

Somewhat ambitious. Others tries equalise quickly:

(a) 6...0-0 7 ♘f3 (7 dxc5 f6! 8 ♘f3 ♘c6) 7...♘bc6 8 dxc5 f6 transposes to 6 dxc5 ♘bc6 7 f4. Black can also play 7...f6 8 exf6 ♖xf6 9 dxc5 ♗xc5 10 ♗d3 ♘bc6 11 ♕e2 ♗d7 12 0-0-0 ♘b4 13 ♔b1 W.Watson-Knaak, Kecskemet 1987, and now 13...♘xd3! 14 cxd3 (14 ♕xd3 ♗e8!) 14...b5 intending the move ...b4;

(b) 6...cxd4 7 ♘b5 ♗xd2+ 8 ♕xd2 0-0 has been played in a number of contests and White has gotten nowhere, e.g., 9 ♘xd4 ♘bc6 10 ♘gf3

♘xd4 (or 10...f6 11 exf6 ♖xf6 12 ♗d3 ♘xd4 13 ♘xd4 ♕b6 14 c3 ♗d7 15 0-0 ♘c6=) 11 ♘xd4 ♗d7 12 ♗d3 ♕b6 13 ♘f3?! (13 c3 ♘c6=) 13...♗b5 (instead 13...♕xb2!? 14 0-0 ♕b6+ 15 ♔h1 f6 would be a reasonable winning try) 14 ♗xb5 ♕xb5 15 ♔f2!? ♖ac8 16 ♖hc1 h6!? ½-½ Gullaksen-Øgaard, Oslo 1998.

7 ♘f3

Mistaken is the try 7 ♘b5? a6! 8 ♗xb4 cxb4 9 ♘d6+ ♘xd6 10 exd6 ♕xd6∓ Santo Roman-Raicevic, Athens 1992.

7...♘c6

After 7...cxd4 8 ♘b5, 8...♘e3 9 ♕c1 ♗c5 10 b4 ♗e7 looks worth trying, as does 8...♗c5 9 b4 ♗e7 (9...♗b6 10 ♗d3 ♗d7 11 g4 a6!?) 10 ♘bxd4 ♘xd4 11 ♘xd4 ♘c6 12 ♘xc6 bxc6 13 ♗d3 ♖b8 14 ♕g4 g6 – McDonald.

8 dxc5 ♗xc5 9 ♗d3 ♘h4!? 10 ♕e2

McDonald gives 10 ♘xh4 ♕xh4+ 11 g3 ♕h3 12 ♗f1 ♕h6, when 13 f5 ♗e3 or 13 ♕f3 ♘d4 14 ♕d3 ♕h5 15 ♗g2 ♗d7 looks fine.

10...♘xf3+ 11 ♕xf3 ♘b4 12 0-0-0 ♗d7= Hebden-McDonald, British Ch 1989.

In spite of its popularity, 5 ♗d2 is a rather easy line to meet.

9.3 5 dxc5

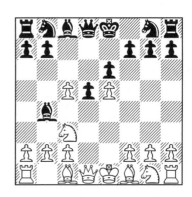

This cutting-edge move emphasizes piece play and is very dangerous. Of course the danger is on both sides! I will follow a main (very main) line, giving some options on moves 6 and 7, because Black can get these positions almost by force and secure good play thereby.

5...♘c6

In the last edition I gave 5...♘e7 emphasising ideas with ...♘d7 and ...♘xc5. Those are fine, but I'd rather devote space to the more forcing line that follows. A couple of thoughts on other moves:

(a) 5...♕c7 6 ♘f3 ♘c6 transposes to 6...♕c7 below, and here 6...♘d7 is also playable;

(b) 5...d4 6 a3 ♗a5 7 b4 dxc3 8 ♕g4 ♘e7 is underinvestigated and worth looking into.

6 ♘f3

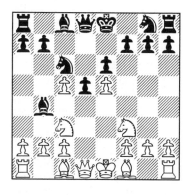

6 ♕g4 ♘ge7 transposes to 5 ♕g4, and 6 ♗f4? d4 7 a3 ♗a5 8 b4 ♘xb4! 9 axb4 ♗xb4 10 ♗b5+ ♗d7 11 ♕xd4 ♗xc3+ 12 ♕xc3 ♗xb5 is good for Black.

6...♘ge7

Two potentially significant alternatives:

(a) The logical move 6...♕c7 has been looked at more since the previous edition:

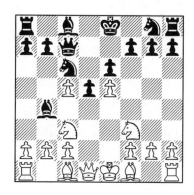

(a1) 7 ♗d2 ♘xe5 (or 7...♗xc5) 8 ♗b5+ ♗d7∓;

(a2) 7 ♗b5 ♘ge7 (7...♗d7 threatens ...♘xe5 and seems to equalise: 8 ♗xc6 ♗xc3+ 9 bxc3 ♗xc6 10 0-0 ♘e7) 8 0-0 0-0 9 ♘a4!? (9 ♖e1 ♗d7) 9...♘xe5 10 ♘xe5 ♕xe5 11 c3 ♗a5 12 f4!? ♕f6 13 ♗e3 ♘f5 14 ♗d4 ♘xd4 (14...♕e7!) 15 cxd4?! (15 ♕xd4 ♕e7) 15...a6 16 ♗e2 ♗d7 17 ♖c1 Gallagher-Carton, London 1986; 17...♗xa4! 18 ♕xa4 ♗d2∓;

(a3) 7 ♗f4 ♘ge7 8 ♗e2 (After 8 a3!? ♗xc3+ 9 bxc3, Black can choose between 9...f6, 9...♕a5, and 9...♘g6 10 ♗g3 h5!? with the idea 11 h4 ♘gxe5 12 ♘xe5 ♘xe5, which is now possible because White does not have ♕h5; 8 ♗d3 has been played, but should come up short after 8...d4 9 a3 ♗a5 10 b4 ♘xb4 11 axb4 ♗xb4 12 ♗b5+ ♗d7 13 ♕xd4 ♗xc3+ 14 ♕xc3 ♗xb5 15 ♘d4 ♗a6∓; 8 ♕d3 ♘g6!? 9 ♗g3 ♗xc5) 8...f6 9 exf6 ♕xf4 10 fxe7 ♗xc5 and Black's centre and two bishops compensate for the time it takes to recapture on e7;

(b) 6...d4 may be better than its reputation due to the line 7 a3 ♗a5 8 b4 dxc3 9 bxa5 ♕xd1+ 10 ♔xd1 ♘ge7 (10...a6!?) 11 ♗b5 (11 ♗d3 0-0 12 ♔e2 ♘xa5 13 ♖d1 ♘d5 14 ♗e4 ♗d7 15 ♗xd5 Soltis-Mednis, Cleveland 1975; perhaps this is better for Black: there could follow 15...exd5 16 ♖xd5 ♗f5!? 17 ♗f4 ♗xc2 18 ♖c1 ♗e4∓; 11 a6 bxa6 12 ♗d3 ♗b7 13 ♖b1 0-0-0=) 11...a6 12 ♗xc6+ ♘xc6 13 ♗e3 (13 ♔e2 ♗d7 14 ♔d3 ♘xa5 15 ♔xc3 ♗c6 should be fine, e.g., 16 ♗e3 ♗xf3 17 gxf3 ♘c6 18 f4 0-0-0=) 13...♗d7 14 ♖b1 ♘xa5 15 ♗d4 ♗c6 16 ♗xc3 ♗xf3+ 17 gxf3 ♘c6 18 ♔e2 0-0-0= Palliser-Knott, Scarborough 2001.

7 ♗d3

(a) 7 ♗d2 transposes to 5 ♗d2 ♘e7 6 ♘f3 ♘bc6 7 dxc5;

(b) 7 a3 ♗xc3+ 8 bxc3 ♘g6!? (8...♕a5 9 ♕d2 ♕xc5 10 a4 0-0 11 ♗a3 ♕a5=) 9 ♗b5 ♕a5 (9...♗d7 threatens ...♘xe5 and ...♕a5, so 10 ♗xc6 ♗xc6 11 0-0 f6!? 12 ♕d4 fxe5 13 ♘xe5 ♘xe5 14 ♕xe5 ♕f6 might follow) 10 ♗xc6+ bxc6 11 ♕d4 ♗a6 12 h4 ♕b5!? (12...♖b8 13 h5 ♘e7 and Black has a few more prospects) 13 c4! ♕a4!? (13...♕xc4! 14 ♕xc4 ♗xc4 15 h5 ♘f8 16 h6 g6 and the opposite-coloured bishops probably lead to a draw) 14 ♕c3 ♗xc4 15 h5 ♘e7 Tran Quoc Dung-Szymanski, Artek 1999; and 16 h6! gxh6 17 ♗xh6 ♘f5 would have been somewhat in White's favour.

7...d4

This begins a long forced sequence which ends with mutual chances. 7...♗xc5 has been played here with some success, but I don't fully trust it and probably White gets a small theoretical edge. More interesting and not fully tested is 7...♕c7 and:

(a) 8 ♗f4 d4 9 a3 dxc3 (9...♗xc3+ 10 bxc3 ♘d5∓) 10 axb4 cxb2 11 ♖b1 ♘xb4 (11...♘d5 12 ♗d2 ♘dxb4∓) 12 ♖xb2 ♘xd3+ 13 ♕xd3 ♘g6 14 ♗g3 ♕xc5∓ Paci-Taddei, Nancy 2003;

(b) 8 0-0 is the most critical move, gambiting a pawn: 8...♗xc3 9 bxc3 ♘xe5 10 ♘xe5 (10 ♗f4 ♘xf3+ 11 ♕xf3 e5 12 ♗b5+ ♔f8 13 ♗g3 ♕xc5 14 ♗a4 e4∓ Smagacz-Morkisz, Slask 1996) 10...♕xe5 11 ♕g4 ♗d7!? (11...0-0!, since 12 ♗xh7+ ♔xh7 13 ♕h4+ ♔g8 14 ♕xe7 ♕xc3 15 ♗f4 b6!? favours Black, but of course White doesn't have to play this way; ...f6 will be a useful move in any case) 12 ♖b1 ♗c6 13 ♕d4! Graf-Duebon, corr 1998, and 13...f6 14 f4 ♕c7 15 ♖e1 ♔f7 would have created some sort of balance.

8 a3 ♗a5 9 b4 ♘xb4 10 axb4 ♗xb4

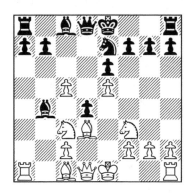

A position that has been debated for many years. I think that Black at least equalises and probably does more than that in several lines. He will also tend to pose more difficulties for his opponent than he himself has to suffer. This calls into question the value of 5 dxc5, both with 6 ♘f3/7 ♗d3, and in general. But the theoretical density of these lines is staggering.

11 0-0

Almost automatic, but occasionally other moves are tried:

(a) 11 ♗b5+ ♗d7 12 ♕xd4 ♗xc3+ 13 ♕xc3 ♗xb5∓ 14 ♘d4?! (14 ♗g5 ♕d5∓) 14...♗a6∓ according to older sources. Then 15 c6?! ♕d5! 16 cxb7 ♕xe5+ 17 ♗e3 ♗xb7 18 0-0 0-0 leaves Black on top;

(b) 11 ♘d2!? ♗xc3 12 ♖b1 ♕d5

(12...0-0 13 0-0 ♗xd2 14 ♗xd2 ♕c7!?) 13 0-0 ♗xd2 14 ♗xd2 resembles the main line, but Black hasn't had to spend a tempo on ...h6: 14...♗d7 15 ♖e1 ♗c6 16 ♗e4 ♕d7 17 ♖b3 Upton-Harley, England 1996, and here simply 17...♗xe4 18 ♖xe4 ♕d5 and ...0-0 leaves White with awful pawns.

11...♗xc3 12 ♖b1

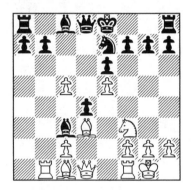

Now there are two main moves:

9.31 12...♕c7
9.32 12...h6

But what is possibly a very good third one is 12...♗d7!?. Of course White has a lot of ideas to play with and the 5 dxc5 experts don't seem worried, so I'm pretty sure that the following doesn't tell the whole story: 13 ♘g5 ♗c6 14 ♕h5 ('±' according to Pachman back in 1968! McDonald calls 14 ♘e4 'critical'; if nothing else, 14...♗xe4 15 ♗xe4 ♖b8 looks safe and sound. He gives 14...♕d5 15 ♘d6+ ♔f8 16 ♗e4 ♕xe5 17 f4 with various complications, although I think that Black is okay in those lines too) 14...g6 (14...♘g6 15 ♘xe6! fxe6 16 ♗xg6+) 15 ♕h6 (15 ♕h3 ♕c7 16 ♗f4 a5 17 ♗c4 ♘f5 ½-½ Gallagher-Shaked, Cannes 1997; Black is better) 15...♘f5 16 ♗xf5 (16 ♕h3 ♕c7∓

17 ♗f4 h5?! 18 ♘e4 0-0-0 19 ♘d6+ ♘xd6 20 cxd6 ♕a5 21 f3 ½-½ Palkovi-F.Portisch, Zalakaros 2000) 16...gxf5! (16...exf5 17 e6 ♕d5 18 exf7+ ♔d7 19 f3‡ was eventually drawn in Bokros-Hertneck, Austria 2001) 17 ♕g7 ♔d7! and Black is better, according to the post mortem by Shaked and Gallagher, an example being 18 ♘xf7 (18 ♘xh7 ♔c7 19 ♕xf7+ ♕d7) 18...♖g8 19 ♕xg8 ♖hxg8, for example, 20 f3 ♖g7 21 ♘d6 ♖ag8 22 g3 h5 23 ♗f4 h4 24 ♔f2 hxg3+ 25 hxg3 ♖h8 26 ♖h1 ♖gh7 27 ♖xh7+ ♖xh7-+.

9.31 12...♕c7

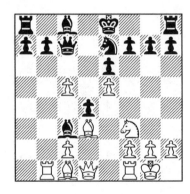

This has been played just a few times but I like it.

13 ♘g5!?

The only move used by strong players: White wants to play ♘e4-d6. But the alternatives are also noteworthy:

(a) 13 ♘xd4!? and now 13...♗xd4 14 ♗b5+ ♗d7 15 ♕xd4 ♗xb5 16 ♖xb5 ♖d8 17 ♕b2 ♖d7 yields some advantage, as does 13...♗d7, but 13...a6?! 14 ♗b5+! axb5 15 ♘xb5 ♕xe5 16 ♕f3 is less clear;

(b) 13 ♗d2 ♘d5 is solid; after 13...♕xc5 14 ♗xc3 dxc3 15 ♗b5+ ♘c6 16 ♗xc6+ ♕xc6 17 ♕d3 D.Myers-Katz, corr 1983, easiest is 17...b6!∓

with ...♗b7 to follow;

(c) 13 ♕e2 ♗d7 (13...h6 14 ♘d2 ♗xd2 15 ♗xd2 ♗d7 16 ♕e4 ♗c6 17 ♕xd4 0-0 18 ♕d6 ♖fc8 is unclear; but 13...♘c6 looks promising) 14 ♘g5 ♗c6 15 ♘e4 (15 ♕h5 g6; 15 ♘xh7 ♘d5 16 ♘g5 ♗b4!) 15...♗xe4 16 ♗xe4 ♘c6∓;

(d) 13 ♗f4!? hasn't been tried but I think it is the most challenging move other than 13 ♘g5: 13...♘g6 14 ♗xg6 hxg6 (14...fxg6 15 ♘xd4 0-0 isn't bad either) 15 ♘xd4 (15 ♘g5 f5!) 15...♕xc5 16 ♘b5 ♗xe5 17 ♗xe5 ♕xe5.

13...♕xe5 14 ♕h5 g6 15 ♕h6 ♘f5 16 ♗xf5 gxf5

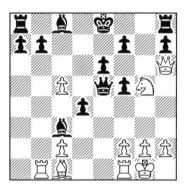

17 ♗f4

The crazy 17 ♘xf7!? might be used if the main line 17 ♗f4 isn't satisfactory: 17...♗xf7 18 ♕h5+ ♔e7 (18...♔f8 19 ♗h6+ ♔e7=) 19 ♗g5+ ♔d7! (19...♔f8=) 20 ♕f7+ ♔c6 21 ♗f6 ♕c7 22 ♕xc7+ ♔xc7 23 ♗xh8 ♔c6 24 ♖fd1 ♔xc5 and it's hard to believe that Black isn't better with his bishops and a-pawn, but White can go after the queen's pawn by 25 ♖d3 b5 26 ♖bd1 ♗b7 27 ♗xd4+ ♗xd4 28 ♖xd4 ♗d5 and Black has slightly better chances due to his ideal piece placement, but those will be hard to convert.

17...♕xc5!

17...♕xf4? 18 ♕g7 d3 19 ♕xf7+ ♔d8 20 ♖xb7 ♗xb7 1-0 Gallagher-Atanu, Sangli 2000.

18 ♕h5 ♕e7

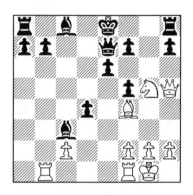

19 ♗e5

I'm not sure if 19 ♗d6 has been analysed, but Black seems okay after 19...♕f6!? 20 ♗e5 ♕xe5 21 ♕xf7+ ♔d8 22 ♘f3 ♕d5 23 ♕f6+ ♔c7 24 ♕xh8 b5! 25 ♕xh7+ ♔b6 and 26 ♖fd1 ♗b7 with good chances or 26 ♕g7 a5 27 ♖fd1 ♗b7 28 ♘xd4 ♖d8! 29 ♖xb5+ ♕xb5 30 ♕c7+! ♔xc7 31 ♘xb5+ ♔b6 32 ♘xc3 ♖xd1+ 33 ♘xd1 ♗e4∓.

19...h6 20 ♘xe6 ♗xe6 21 ♗xh8

and 'White is better but Black is clearly still in the game' – Gallagher. This is a fascinating position pitting Black's bishops and passed a-pawn against White's extra exchange and potential dark square play. I doubt that White is any better at all. Unfortunately, it took me 38 moves and numerous subvariations to arrive at equality, so I'll just get you started: 21...♗c4 22 ♖fc1 (22 ♕xf5 ♗xf1 23 ♔xf1 ♕e6! 24 ♕xe6+ fxe6 25 ♖xb7 a5∓) 22...♕e6! (the a-pawn is a factor in all of these positions; worse is 22...♗d2 23 ♖d1 ♗e2 24 ♕xf5! ♗xd1 25 ♖xd1 ♗c3 26 ♕f3 ♖b8 27 ♗f6 ♕e6 28 g3±) 23 ♖xb7 (23 ♕f3 ♕e4 24 ♕xe4+ fxe4 25 ♖xb7 a5) 23...♕e4!?

(Black can already draw by 23...0-0-0 24 ♖cb1 ♗a2 25 ♖b8+ ♔c7 26 ♖8b7+ ♔c8=) 24 ♕f3 ♕xf3 25 gxf3 ♗d5 26 ♖c7 ♗xf3 27 ♗f6 a5 and my analysis has 28 ♖b1! (and not 28 ♖e7+) leading to a dead draw.

9.32 12...h6
'!' Gallagher. The point is to stop ♘g5-e4.

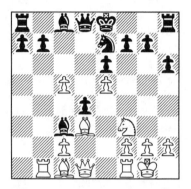

13 ♘d2
Much better than 13 ♘h4 ♕d5! 14 f4 ♗d7 15 f5 exf5 16 ♗xf5 Zinser-Ackerman, corr 1964; 16...♗xf5! 17 ♘xf5 ♘xf5 18 ♖xf5 0-0-0 19 ♕g4 ♕e6∓ – Moles & Wicker.
13...♗xd2
Black prevents ♘e4-d6.
14 ♗xd2 ♗d7!
There is a mass of analysis on 14...♕c7. I have no idea why, but theory says that White comes out with a small edge!
15 ♖xb7
Poorer is 15 ♕g4 ♗c6 16 ♖b4 ♕a5!? (or 16...♕d5 17 ♖xd4 ♕xe5 18 ♖e1 ♕f6 19 ♗c3, and here instead of 19...♕g5? 20 h4!, I recommended 19...0-0, intending 21 ♗a1 ♕g5 or 20 h4 ♘f5) 17 ♕xd4 ♖d8 18 ♕g4 (18 ♖a1 ♖xd4 19 ♖xa5 ♖xb4 20 ♗xb4 a6∓) 18...♕xc5 19 ♖e1 ½-½ Lima-McDonald, Hastings 1988; McDonald sug-

gests that he should probably have continued by 19...♘f5!, since 20 ♗xf5? ♖xd2 21 ♕xg7 ♕xf2+ mates.
15...♗c6 16 ♖b4
16 ♗b5?! ♕c8 (16...0-0!?∓) 17 ♗xc6+ ♘xc6 18 ♕b1 0-0 was drawn in Rubery-Harley, London 1996; McDonald analyses 19 ♖e1 ♖b8 20 ♖b3 ♕c7 21 ♕a1!? ♖xb3 22 cxb3 ♖b8∓.

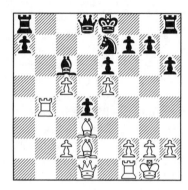

16...a5!
Actually, I don't really know if the fantastically convoluted lines after 16...♕d5 17 ♕g4 ♖d8 18 ♖e1 g5!? or even other orders beginning with 16...♕d5 are playable; but I only have space to present one alternative and the experts in this system seem to indicate that the advance 16...a5 is best.
17 ♖b6 ♕d5
Black's idea has been to lure the rook away from its attack on d4; in addition, the vital a-pawn gets rolling. Nevertheless, the tradeoff is double-edged: for one thing, the move ♖xc6 at the right moment can be devastating.
18 ♕g4 ♕xe5 19 ♖e1!
19 ♖fb1 is no longer considered correct, although it's not completely clear:
(a) 19...0-0?! 20 ♗f4 ♕f6 was drawn

in one game after 21 ♕g3, but winning the exchange was better: 21 ♗d6 ♗d5 (21...♖fc8? 22 ♗xe7 ♕xe7 23 ♖xc6 ♖xc6 24 ♕e4) 22 f4! (threatening ♗e5) 22...♘g6 23 ♗xf8 ♘xf8 24 c6±;

(b) 19...g5!? is plausible, but perhaps unnecessary, because:

(c) 19...h5! seems to solve all Black's problems after 20 ♕h4 f6!? (20...♕xc5! looks good, or perhaps 20...♕d5!?) 21 ♗xa5? (21 ♕h3! intends ♗c4, so 21...♕d5 22 ♖e1 ♔f7 might follow with complex play) 21...♕xc5∓ 22 ♖xc6?? ♘xc6–+ Van Mechelen-Meessen, Charleroi 2001.

19...♕xc5

This time 19...h5 might run into 20 ♖xe5 hxg4 21 ♖g5!? a4 (21...g6 22 ♖xg4 e5 23 c3!? f5 24 ♖xc6!) 22 ♖xg4 a3 23 ♖b1 ♖h5 24 ♖xd4, but that's certainly not clear, so 19...h5 deserves to be looked at.

20 ♖xc6! ♘xc6

20...♕xc6? 21 ♗e4 ♕c8 22 ♕xg7 ♖g8 23 ♕xd4 and the bishops are a terror, with ♗h7 a threat.

21 ♕xg7 ♔e7

Or 21...♖f8 22 ♗xh6 ♔e7.

22 ♗g6 ♖hf8

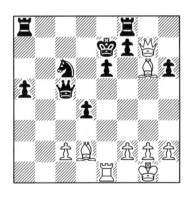

23 ♗xh6

Gallagher-Steenbekkers, Cappelle la Grande 2002. Here instead of

23...♕c3, Steenbekkers did some long analysis that indicates that 23...a4 leads to a draw, particularly in the line 24 h4 a3 25 ♗xf7 ♖xf7 26 ♗g5+ ♔e8 27 ♖xe6+ ♘e7 28 ♕g8+ ♖f8 29 ♕g6+ ♔d7 30 ♖xe7+ ♕xe7 31 ♗xe7 ♔xe7 and the a-pawn forces White into perpetual check.

The whole line with 5...♘c6 should serve Black well. Apart from the 3 choices on move 12, the options on moves 6 and 7 give one plenty of ideas to play with.

9.4 5 ♕g4

This aggressive queen sortie mobilises White's forces quickly at the inevitable cost of letting his central structure be compromised.

5...♘e7

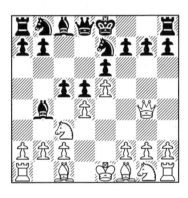

In this position White has two attacking ideas:

9.41 6 dxc5
9.42 6 ♘f3

Others are less effective:

(a) 6 a3?! ♕a5! 7 ♗d2!? (7 axb4 ♕xa1 8 ♔d1 cxd4 9 ♘b5 0-0!∓ Jansa-Korchnoi, Luhacovice 1969, due to 10 ♘c7 ♘a6! 11 ♘xa8 ♗d7; 7 ♘ge2 cxd4 8 axb4 ♕xa1 9 ♘b5 0-0! 10 ♘c7 ♘a6 11 ♘xa8 ♗d7 12 ♔d1 d3! 13 cxd3

♕a4+ 14 ♔d2 ♘xb4 0-1 Engholm-Freyer, corr 1968) 7...cxd4 8 axb4 ♕xa1+ 9 ♘d1 ♘bc6 (9...♘f5! – Moles) 10 ♘f3 ♗d7 11 ♕xg7 ♖g8 12 ♕xh7 a6∓ – Uhlmann;

(b) 6 ♕xg7 ♖g8 7 ♕h6 (7 ♕xh7? cxd4 8 a3 ♕a5–+, e.g., 9 ♖b1 dxc3 10 axb4 ♕a2) 7...cxd4 8 a3 ♗xc3+ 9 bxc3 ♕c7 10 ♘e2 (after 10 ♔d1, Tisdall suggests 10...♘d7! and I think that's the way to go. This position can be compared to the main-line Winawer with 7 ♕g4 ♕c7 8 ♕xg7 ♖g8 9 ♕xh7. In the position before us, crucially, White hasn't picked up the pawn on h7) 10...dxc3 11 f4 ♗d7 12 ♖b1 ♘bc6 13 ♘g3 (13 ♕xh7 d4 14 g3 0-0-0 15 ♕d3 J.Edwards-Mayo, corr 1986, and 15...♘a5 'preserves all the chances' – Edwards) 13...0-0-0 14 ♗d3 ♘d4 15 ♕h5 (15 ♗e3? ♖xg3! 16 hxg3 ♘df5∓; 15 0-0 ♘df5! 16 ♘xf5 ♘xf5 17 ♗xf5 ♕c5+! 18 ♔h1 exf5∓ – Uhlmann) 15...♕c5!∓ Sigurjonsson-Uhlmann, Hastings 1975/6.

9.41 6 dxc5

This can transpose from and is related to 5 dxc5. White attacks the bishop on b4.

6...♘bc6

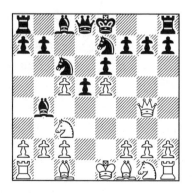

7 ♗d2

(a) 7 ♗b5 ♕a5 (or 7...0-0 8 ♗xc6 ♗xc3+ 9 bxc3 bxc6 intending ...♗a6) 8 ♗d2 (8 ♗xc6+ bxc6 9 ♗d2 ♘f5 10 ♘ge2 h5 11 ♕f4 ♕xc5 12 0-0 ♗a6= Yudasin-Lputian, Simferpol 1988) 8...0-0 9 ♗xc6 ♘xc6 10 ♘f3 ♕xc5 (10...f5! 11 exf6 ♖xf6∓) 11 0-0 f5 12 ♕f4 d4= Hebden-Raicevic, Vrnjacka Banja 1989;

(b) 7 ♘f3? d4! 8 ♗b5 ♕a5 (8...♔f8 is also promising) 9 ♗xc6+ bxc6 10 ♕xd4 (10 ♕xg7 ♖g8 11 ♕xh7 ♗xc3+ 12 ♔d1 ♖b8 13 ♘g5 ♗xb2–+) 10...♘f5 11 ♕c4 (11 ♕e4 ♗xc3+ 12 bxc3 ♕xc3+ 13 ♘d2 ♖b8!–+) 11...♗a6 12 ♕b3 ♕b5 13 ♔d1 ♕xc5 14 ♗d2 Banas-Prandstetter, Czechoslovakia 1978; 14...♕xf2! 15 ♕xb4 ♕xg2 16 ♖e1 ♕xf3+ 17 ♔c1 0-0-0∓.

7...0-0

Also played is 7...♘g6, which continues to score well and should be looked into if Black desires an alternative.

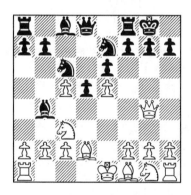

Now White has:

9.411 8 ♘f3
9.412 8 ♗d3

After 8 0-0-0, 8...b6!? has been played recently (8...f5 9 exf6 ♖xf6 10 ♗d3 ♕f8 11 ♘f3 ♗xc5 is given by Pedersen; it looks at least equal) 9 ♘f3 (9 cxb6 ♕xb6!? with open queenside lines; Pedersen mentions the move 9...axb6) 9...bxc5 10 ♗d3 ♘g6 11 ♕h5 and now Pedersen suggests 11...♕e8!, one idea being 12 ♘b5 c4! 13 ♘c7 ♗xd2+ 14 ♖xd2 ♕e7 15 ♘xa8 cxd3 etc.

9.411 8 ♘f3 f5

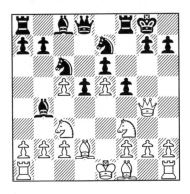

9 ♕h4

(a) 9 ♕h5 ♗d7 (or 9...d4) 10 a3 ♗xc5 11 ♗d3 ♘d4!∓;

(b) 9 exf6 ♖xf6 10 0-0-0 e5 11 ♕h5 ♖f5! 12 ♕h4 ♗xc3! 13 bxc3 (13 ♗xc3 ♖f4) 13...♕a5-+ Pietzsch-Uhlmann, Germany 1963;

(c) 9 ♕g3 ♘g6 10 ♗d3 d4 11 ♘b5 ♗xc5=.

9...d4

Or 9...♘g6! 10 ♕xd8 (10 ♕h3? ♘gxe5 11 ♘xe5 ♘xe5 12 ♕e3 ♘c6∓ Popovych-Mednis, US Ch 1972) 10...♖xd8 11 ♘a4 ♗d7∓.

10 ♘e2?! ♗xd2+ 11 ♘xd2 ♕d5!∓

Estrin-Rittner, corr 1966, which continued 12 ♘b3 ♘g6 13 ♕g3?! (13 ♕h3 – Schwarz; 13...a5!?) 13...f4 14 ♕f3 ♕xe5 15 0-0-0 ♕g5!∓.

9.412 8 ♗d3 ♗xc3!?

A move investigated by Tal Shaked and me. A couple of alternatives are:

(a) 8...♗xc5!? 9 ♘f3 ♘g6 10 ♕h5 ♘b4 gets rid of the bishop but keeps

White's centre intact, Van Perlo-Stigar, corr 1993;

(b) 8...f5!? 9 exf6 ♖xf6 10 ♕h5! g6 (10...h6 11 g4! is very dangerous) 11 ♕h4 was difficult for Black in Strenzewilk-J.Watson, Philadelphia 1996, but 11...♘f5! intending 12 ♗xf5 ♖xf5 would have been equal.

9 ♗xc3

9 bxc3 ♘xe5 10 ♗xh7+ ♔xh7 11 ♕h5+ ♔g8 12 ♕xe5 f6∓.

9...d4 10 0-0-0

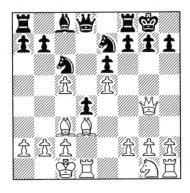

White's most obvious attempt to keep the initiative. Others in this position are:

(a) 10 ♗d2 ♘xe5 11 ♗xh7+ ♔xh7 12 ♕h5+ ♔g8 13 ♕xe5 f6 (a common theme; 13...♘c6!?) 14 ♕d6! e5 15 c3! ♘f5 16 ♕xd8 ♖xd8=;

(b) 10 ♖d1 dxc3!? 11 ♗xh7+ ♔xh7 12 ♖xd8 ♖xd8 13 ♕h3+ (the alternative 13 bxc3 ♖d5 14 ♘f3 ♔g8 favours Black) 13...♔g8 14 ♕xc3 ♘d5 is at least equal.

10...dxc3! 11 ♗xh7+ ♔xh7 12 ♖xd8 cxb2+ 13 ♔xb2 ♖xd8

I think that this favours Black, although it's close. He has the ideas of ...♘f5-h6. ...♘g6, and/or ...♗d7-e8 for defence, if necessary. On the positive side, there is an attack via ...♖d5 and ...b6. Here are some of the possible lines:

14 ♘f3 ♔g8 15 ♕h5

9.42 6 ♘f3

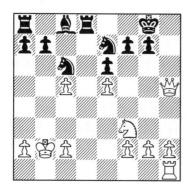

15...♘g6!?

This may or may not be the best move, but it sets up a tough defence. 15...♘f5 is also promising, e.g., 16 g4 (16 ♘g5 is met by 16...♘h6 17 ♘e4 ♖d5 or 16...♘xe5!? 17 ♕h7+ ♔f8 18 ♖e1 ♘g6) 16...♘h6 17 g5 ♘f5 18 g6 fxg6 19 ♕xg6 b6 (19...♗d7!?) 20 ♘g5 (20 ♖e1 ♘ce7 21 ♕h5 bxc5; 20 ♖g1 bxc5) 20...♘xe5 21 ♕h7+ ♔f8 22 ♖e1 (22 f4 ♘c4+ 23 ♔c3 ♘ce3) 22...♘f7 23 ♘xe6+ ♗xe6 24 ♖xe6 ♖d5! 25 c6 ♖c8∓. These are just sample analyses, but I think that Black stands well.

16 ♘g5!

16 ♖e1 ♖d5, and one of many possibilities would be 17 ♘g5 ♘cxe5 18 ♕h7+ ♔f8 19 h4 b6 20 h5 ♘c4+ 21 ♔c3 ♖xg5 22 hxg6 ♖xc5 23 ♕h8+ ♔e7 24 ♕xg7 ♘e5+ 25 ♔b3 ♘xg6-+.

After 16 ♘g5, play can go 16...♘cxe5 17 ♕h7+ ♔f8 18 h4 ♘g4! 19 h5 (19 ♕h5 ♖d4! 20 f3 ♘e3 21 g4 ♖d2-+) 19...♘f6 20 hxg6 ♘xh7 21 gxh7 ♔e7 22 h8♕ ♖xh8 23 ♖xh8 b6∓. This is all exciting stuff, and it's hard not to get the impression that Black is somewhat better throughout. The 5 ♕g4 ♘e7 6 dxc5 line is clearly a serious threat, but in the end it seems that White has to be careful not to come out worse.

Here White tries to hold the d4 square and develop quickly, but Black no longer has to worry about blitzkrieg attacks.

6...cxd4

This move has become increasingly popular. For reasons of space I won't analyse 6...♘bc6 from the last edition again, but it might be good to mention that 7 dxc5 transposes to the last section and that 7 a3 needn't be answered by 7...♗xc3+ with a Positional Winawer main line, but allows 7...♗a5!, when after 8 ♕xg7?! ♖g8 9 ♕xh7 cxd4 10 b4 I quoted a game with 10...♘xb4 11 axb4 ♗xb4 leading to equal and unclear play, but an interesting alternative was seen in Skripchenko-B.Socko, Cappelle la Grande 2000: 10...♗c7!? 11 ♘b5 a6 12 ♘bxd4 (12 ♘xc7+ ♕xc7 threatens ...♘xe5 and ...♘b4, e.g., 13 ♗b2 ♘xe5 14 ♘xd4 ♘c4 15 ♗xc4 ♕xc4 – McDonald) 12...♘xd4 13 ♘xd4 ♗xe5 14 c3 (McDonald gives both 14 ♗b2 ♕c7 15 0-0-0 ♗xd4 16 ♖xd4 e5 17 ♖d2 ♗f5 and 14 ♕d3 ♗f6 intending ...e5 and ...♗f5) 14...♕c7 15 ♗d2 ♗f6! 16 ♘e2 e5 17 ♘g3? e4! 18 ♕h6 ♗g5!-+.

7 ♘xd4 ♘g6

7...♕c7 seems fine. As far as I

know, the main move 8 ♗b5+ hasn't been answered by 8...♘d7!? since Grigorov-Lukov, Bulgaria 1976. Nevertheless, after 9 0-0 ♗xc3 (9...0-0 10 ♘xe6 fxe6 11 ♕xb4 ♘xe5= – Minev) 10 bxc3, Minev suggests 10...0-0!? when one idea is 11 ♗a3 ♘xe5∓.

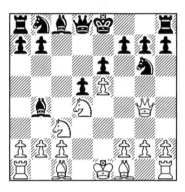

8 ♗d3

Others may not even equalise:

(a) 8 ♘f3?! ♗xc3+ 9 bxc3 ♕c7∓;

(b) 8 ♗b5+ ♗d7 9 0-0 0-0 (still better looks 9...♗xc3! 10 bxc3 ♕c7 11 ♗d2 0-0∓) 10 ♗xd7 (10 ♘xe6?? ♗xc3!–+; 10 ♗d3 ♘xe5 11 ♗xh7+ ♔xh7 12 ♕h5+ ♔g8 13 ♕xe5 ♘c6∓ Murey-Sigurjonsson, Brighton 1983) 10...♕xd7 11 ♘f3 ♘c6 12 ♕h5 f6 13 exf6 ♖xf6 14 ♗g5 ♖f5∓ Fernando Garcia-Matamoros, Seville 1992; or here 14...♗xc3! 15 bxc3 ♖f5∓;

(c) 8 ♗d2 0-0 9 ♘f3 ♘c6 10 0-0-0 f5! 11 exf6 ♕xf6 12 ♔b1 e5 13 ♕g3 ♘f4∓ Movsesian-Shaked, Zagan 1997.

8...0-0 9 ♗xg6

If White tries to maintain e5 by 9 ♘f3, Black has 9...♗xc3+ 10 bxc3 f5! with the idea 11 ♕h5 ♕c7 or 11 exf6 ♕xf6.

9...fxg6

By this recapture, Black activates his rook, but also prevents problems based upon ♘f3-g5.

10 0-0

10 ♗d2 ♗e7 (10...♗c5!?) 11 0-0 ♘c6 12 ♘f3 ♕b6 (12...♖f5!?∓ – Kinsman) 13 ♘d1 ♗d7 14 ♘e3 ♖ad8 15 b3 ♗c8 16 ♖ad1 ♕c7 17 ♕g3 b5! 18 ♗c1? d4! 19 ♘g4 h5 ½-½ Murey-Kinsman, Paris 1996; Black is practically winning after 20 ♘f6+ ♗xf6 21 exf6 ♕xg3, but he wanted to secure a norm.

10...♗e7 11 ♗e3

11 ♘f3 ♘c6 12 ♖e1 ♗d7 13 ♘e2 ♕b6 (threatening ...♘xe5) 14 ♗e3?! (14 ♘f4 ♕c5 15 c3 ♖f5∓) 14...♕xb2 15 ♖ab1 Hebden-Matamoros, London 1987, and easiest was 15...♕xa2! or even 15...♘xe5!.

11...♘c6 12 ♘xc6 bxc6 13 ♘a4 ♕c7 14 ♕d4 ♖f5! 15 f4

White might try 15 g4, but even 15...♖f7 16 f4 ♖b8! favours Black: 17 c3?! c5!∓.

After 15 f4, Murey-I.Farago, Seefeld 2002 went 15...g5! 16 g4 (16 fxg5 ♕xe5 17 ♖xf5 ♕xf5 18 ♖f1 e5! – Farago, although 18...♕xc2 seems easier) 16...c5! 17 ♕c3 (17 ♘xc5 ♖xf4!) 17...♖xf4! 18 ♖xf4 (18 ♗xf4 gxf4 19 ♖xf4 ♗b7 and ...d4 and ...♕c6 are coming – Farago) 18...gxf4 and Black stood clearly better.

Chapter Ten

Winawer Variation: Main Line with 7 ♕g4

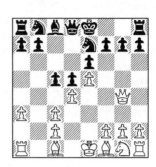

1 e4 e6 2 d4 d5 3 ♘c3 ♗b4 4 e5 c5 5 a3 ♗xc3+ 6 bxc3 ♘e7 7 ♕g4

This is the quintessential Winawer variation and the subject of ceaseless testing since Alexander's win over Botvinnik in 1946. It is as important today as ever, with many leading grandmasters using it as their anti-Winawer weapon. With 7 ♕g4, White is trying to exploit Black's lack of a dark square defender and provoke weaknesses on the kingside. Given his own structural disadvantage (the doubled c-pawns), the first player needs to utilise his bishop pair; his cramping e5 pawn makes the king-side a natural area to proceed on. As in many modern openings, however, both players (and especially Black) will frequently play on both sides of the board. What's more, whether and how White or Black should open the game varies from case to case. In the variations presented in this book (with 7 ♘f3 and 7 ♕g4 0-0), some kind of central action tends to be desirable for Black (...f6 or ...f5 and/or ...cxd4), to open lines for his pieces and establish aggressive posts for his knights. If he closes the position by

both ...c4 and ...f5, the bishops will come into their own. That is, White will be able to rearrange his forces at his leisure and then break through (e.g., by g4). In addition, White can sometimes benefit from the line-opening exf6 (in response to ...f6 or ...f5) and, less often, the move dxc5 can open lines for early rook and bishop action. Proper piece and pawn play is terribly complex and often paradoxical in this variation, which in general can only be understood by example.

7...0-0

A new system for this edition. I don't believe for a moment that 7...♕c7 deserves the negative and unsupported criticism that commentators regularly churn out (and I've looked at every new development for some years now). But addressing the enormous bulk of new theory would now take up too much of this book and anyway it's fun to present something fresh. The ideas behind 7...0-0 (apart from protecting g7, which is an important function!) will again become clear by example, and everything said above applies. I have drawn very heavily upon Kindermann and Dirr's definitive work *Franzoesisch Winawer* for material and will refer to its authors' contributions by 'K&D', or as 'Kindermann' for cases in which I saw his analysis separately.

After 7...0-0 White has:

10.1 8 ♘f3
10.2 8 ♗d3

Nothing else is dangerous, e.g.,

(a) 8 h4?! f5 9 exf6 ♖xf6 10 ♗g5 ♖f7 11 ♘f3 leaves Black effectively a tempo up on 8 ♘f3 f5 9 exf6 ♖xf6 10 ♗g5 ♖f7, a respectable line for Black. Thus 11...♕a5 (or 11...♘bc6) 12 ♗d2 ♘bc6 13 ♘e5 ♘xe5 14 dxe5 ♘c6 15 f4 ♕a4!∓ threatening ...♘xe5 and ...♕xc2, Durao-Ivanov, Cappelle la Grande 1995;

(b) 8 ♕h3 ♘bc6 9 ♗d3 ♘g6 10 ♘f3 c4 11 ♗xg6 fxg6 12 0-0 ♗d7. White has a normal 8 ♗d3 ♘bc6 line but he is committed to 0-0 and has his queen less than ideally placed on h3.

10.1 8 ♘f3

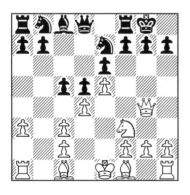

This natural move has lost in popularity as effective remedies have been found for Black, but in several cases it transposes into a 8 ♗d3 line and

that analysis is included in this section. I will show one entertaining solution to 8 ♘f3; it is also important because it solves a couple of the variations that could also arise after 8 ♗d3.

8...♘bc6

8...f5 9 exf6 ♖xf6 is also well known and considered satisfactory. Then a crazy line that seems to be holding up is 10 ♗g5 ♘d7!?, based upon 11 ♗xf6? ♘xf6 12 ♕f4 ♕a5 and the c-pawn can't be defended. The solid and respectable 10...♖f7 should also equalise according to K&D's book.

9 ♗d3 f5 10 exf6

(a) 10 ♕h3 contains some poison. The idea is not to open lines for Black on the kingside, at the same time developing and in some cases trying to get moves like g4 and ♖g1 in. Black's best-known answer is 10...♕a5 11 ♗d2 ♕a4, threatening ...c4 and ...♕xc2.

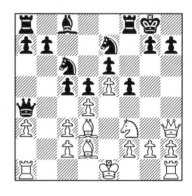

(a1) After 12 ♔d1?!, K&D give 12...cxd4!? 13 cxd4 ♘xd4 14 ♕h4 ♘ec6 15 ♗e3 ♘b5! with advantage, or 12...♗d7 13 g4 c4! 14 ♗e2 ♗e8!;

(a2) 12 dxc5 is the safest try: 12...♘g6 13 ♕g3 ♕g4 14 0-0 (14 ♖b1 h5!? 15 ♗g5 ♘gxe5 16 ♘xe5 ♘xe5 17 ♖b4 ♕xg3 18 hxg3 g6 – Mitkov) 14...♕xg3 15 hxg3 ♘cxe5 16 ♘xe5

♘xe5 17 ♖fe1 ♘xd3 18 cxd3 ♗d7 19 ♖ab1 b6!= Mitkov-Kasimdzhanov, Istanbul 2000;

(a3) 12 ♖g1!? (an ambitious pawn sacrifice) 12...c4 13 ♗e2 ♕xc2 14 ♖c1 ♕b2 15 g4 ♘a5 16 ♗d1 ♘b3 17 ♖c2 ♕xa3 18 ♗h6 (18 ♘g5!? h6 19 ♘f3 ♘xd2 20 ♔xd2 fxg4 21 ♖xg4 Velimirovic-Drasko, Niksic 1996, and K&D now improve upon 21...♘f5?! with 21...♔h8!, e.g., 22 ♖c1 b5 23 ♗c2 b4 24 ♖xg7 ♕xc3+ 25 ♔e2 ♔xg7 26 ♖g1+ ♔f7 27 ♕h5+ ♘g6!-+) 18...♘g6 (Polgar gives 18...gxh6 19 ♕xh6 ♘g6 as leading to perpetual check) 19 gxf5 ♖xf5 20 ♗e3 (K&D give 20 ♘h4 ♘xd4! 21 ♘xg6 ♘xc2+ 22 ♔f1 ♕a1, with a small advantage after great complications) 20...♗d7 21 ♘g5 ♘f8 22 f4 J.Polgar-Shaked, Hoogeveen 1998, and now 22...♕a1! (various) when Black stands better;

(b) 10 ♕g3 ♕a5 11 ♗d2 b6! (there are other solutions, e.g., 11...♕a4) 12 0-0 ♕a4 13 ♖fe1 (13 h3? c4 14 ♗e2 f4!∓ and ...♕c2) 13...♗d7 14 ♖a2 ½-½ Spassky-Ehlvest, Belfort 1988; K&D suggest 14...cxd4 15 cxd4 ♘xd4 16 ♗b4 ♘xf3+ 17 ♕xf3 ♖f7∓.

10...♖xf6

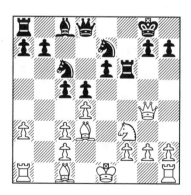

11 ♗g5

Natural and critical, but 11 ♕h5!? is also important: 11...h6 (11...g6 12 ♕g5

♕f8 is also played) 12 0-0 (12 ♘e5 ♘xe5 13 dxe5 ♖f8 14 0-0 c4 15 ♗e2 ♗d7∓ intending ...♗e8-g6, Vitolins-Zlotnik, Nabereznye Chelny 1988) 12...♗d7! (12...c4 13 ♗e2 ♕f8!? 14 ♗d2 ♗d7 15 ♕g4 ♘g6= Gallagher-Farago, Hastings 1990) 13 ♘e5 (13 ♖e1 c4 14 ♗e2 ♗e8 15 ♕h3 ♕a5 16 ♗d2 ♗g6∓ Lau-Vladimirov, Moscow 1989; Black doubles rooks, plays ...♗e4 and attacks) 13...♗e8 14 ♕g4 c4!? (14...♕a5∓) 15 ♗e2 ♘g6 (15...♕a5!? – K&D) 16 f4 unclear – K&D; then Black could play 16...♘cxe5 17 fxe5 ♖xf1+ 18 ♔xf1 ♗f7∓.

11...e5!

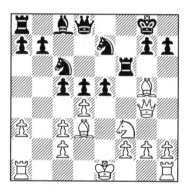

This surprising move commits Black to a material investment, but destroys White's centre and brings all the pieces into play.

12 ♕g3?!

This has been played most but in the end it doesn't work out well.

(a) 12 ♕h4 simplifies and is probably the safest move, even if Black retains some edge: 12...e4 13 ♗xf6 gxf6 14 ♕xf6 exd3 (14...♕f8 15 ♕xf8+ ♔xf8 16 dxc5! exf3 17 gxf3 ♗f5 18 ♖b1 b6 19 ♗xf5 ♘xf5 20 cxb6 axb6 21 ♖xb6 ♘ce7= – K&D; White has 4 extra pawns, but 6 weak ones!) 15 cxd3 cxd4! 16 ♘xd4 ♘xd4 17 ♕xd4 ♘c6 and instead of 19 ♕g3+ ♔h8 20 0-0

♗f5 (20...dxc3!? – K&D) of Vitolins-Dokhoian, Porz 1991, K&D suggest 18 ♕e3 d4 19 cxd4 ♗f5 20 0-0 ♕xd4 unclear, although it's hard not to prefer Black's pieces;

(b) 12 ♗xh7+ ♔xh7 13 ♕h5+ ♔g8 14 ♗xf6 gxf6 15 dxe5 ♕f8 is a position that has arisen many times.

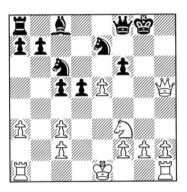

16 exf6 (16 0-0 ♕f7 17 ♕xf7+ ♔xf7 18 exf6 ♔xf6∓; 16 c4 d4 [here 16...dxc4!? is a good try] 17 exf6 ♕xf6 18 ♕xc5 d3 leads to unclear complications) 16...♕xf6 17 0-0 (17 ♕g5+ ♕g7 18 0-0-0 ♗g4 19 ♖d3 ♖f8 20 ♕xg7+ ♔xg7 Enders-Hübner, Bundesliga 1999) 17...♕xc3!? (17...♗f5 18 ♖ae1 ♔g7 19 ♘h4 ♖h8 20 ♘xf5+ ♕xf5 unclear – K&D; I like Black in all these positions, if only mildly) 18 ♘g5 ♕g7 19 ♖ae1 ♗f5 20 ♖e3 ♕g6 21 ♕h4 ♗xc2 22 g4!? – K&D; but the attack may not fully compensate White for his investment.

12...♖xf3!

Actually, this 'sacrifice' is forced in view of White's threats. It is nonetheless a good example of Black's dynamic chances in this line.

13 gxf3

13 ♕xf3 e4 14 ♗xe4 dxe4 15 ♕xe4 ♕d5! 16 ♕xd5+ ♘xd5 and Black's pieces are too active, e.g., 17 dxc5 ♗f5! 18 0-0-0 ♘xc3 19 ♖de1 ♖c8 20

♗e3 ♘a5 etc.

13...c4

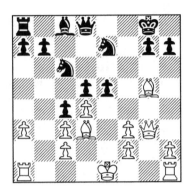

14 ♗e2

At least this keeps the bishops. Others:

(a) 14 ♗xe7?! ♕xe7 15 ♗e2 exd4 hardly improves, e.g., 16 ♔f1 ♗f5∓ Abramovic-Dokhoian, Belgrade 1988;

(b) 14 ♗xh7+?! ♔xh7 15 ♖g1 ♕f8 16 ♕h4+ ♔g8 17 ♗f6 ♘f5 18 ♕g5 exd4∓ Honfi-Portisch, Budapest 1958.

14...♕a5!

This has turned out to yield the clearest advantage because instead of grabbing material immediately it prepares ...♘f5. More players, including your author very recently, have more or less automatically picked the natural move 14...exd4

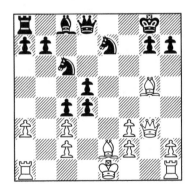

This leads to fascinating and instructive play with respect to typical exchange-down positions in the French pitting bishops versus knights. As far as I can see, Black always gets an advantage. I will point out a few problems with existing theory:

(a) 15 0-0 (the most direct move, but perhaps not best) 15...♗f5! 16 cxd4! (the main line in theory is 16 ♖fe1 dxc3, when White has no useful tactics, e.g., 17 ♗xc4? dxc4 18 ♖xe7 ♘xe7 19 ♖e1 and 19...h6 or 19...♕b8!? 20 ♖xe7 ♕xg3+ 21 fxg3 ♗xc2 22 ♖xb7 ♗d3 and Black's pawns were too strong in Szalanczy-Kindermann, Dortmund 1992) 16...♗xc2! (I found this move over the board, fortunately missing theory's 16...♘xd4, when White has two moves. The books give 17 ♗d1 ♗xc2 with a large advantage, although 18 ♕g4! then approximately equalises; my opponent was going to play still more actively by 17 ♖fe1!?, for example, 17...♘xc2 18 ♗xc4! ♘xe1 19 ♖xe1 dxc4 20 ♖xe7 with near equality due to the opposite-coloured bishops, a mistake being 20...♕d1+?! 21 ♔g2 ♗d3? 22 ♖xg7+! ♔h8 23 h4!, since 23...♔xg7 24 ♕e5+ leads to mate) 17 ♖fe1 ♘f5! 18 ♕g4 (18 ♗xd8 ♘xg3 19 fxg3 ♖xd8 and the d-pawn falls) 18...♕f8-+ 19 ♗f1 ♘fxd4 20 ♗g2 ♗f5 21 ♕g3 ♘c2 and Black was clearly winning in Rensch-J.Watson, Chicago 2003;

(b) 15 cxd4?! ♘xd4 16 ♗d1 (16 ♕e5 ♕a5+! 17 ♔d1 ♕c3 18 ♖c1 ♗f5-+ – Kindermann) 16...♕a5+ 17 ♗d2 c3 18 ♗e3 ♘df5∓ – Efimov;

(c) 15 ♗f6! ♕f8 16 ♗xd4 is the solidest position available to White, even if he has to play very accurately after 16...♘f5 17 ♕g5! (17 ♕f4 has been played twice, but Black has a solid advantage after 17...♘fxd4 18

♕xf8+ ♔xf8 19 cxd4 ♘xd4 and 20 ♗d1 c3! 21 0-0 ♗f5 or 20 ♔d2 ♗f5 21 ♗d1 ♖e8 22 ♖a2 of Nguyen Anh Dung-Galyas, Budapest 2000, when apart from the game's 22...b5, 22...♘b5! enforces ...c3 with a winning position, unless White opts for 23 c3 d4! 24 cxd4 c3+ 25 ♔c1 ♘xd4 etc.) 17...♘fxd4?! (17...♗e6! develops quickly and keeps options open; it favours Black somewhat after 18 ♖d1? ♕xa3 or 19 ♕d2!? ♖e8! or 18 ♗e3 d4! 19 cxd4 ♘fxd4 20 ♗d1 ♖e8 and moves like ...♘xf3+ or ...c3) 18 cxd4 ♗f5 19 c3 ♖e8 20 ♖a2! ♖e6 21 h4 of Maliutin-Piskov, Moscow 1989, which Kindermann justly assesses as unclear.

15 ♗d2

15 0-0 ♘f5 16 ♕g2 exd4 is worse still.

15...♘f5

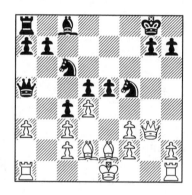

16 ♕g5

Not much better is the rather miserable-looking 16 ♕g2 when Black still has a big advantage after 16...exd4 17 cxd4 c3 18 ♗e3 ♘fxd4 19 ♗xd4 ♘xd4 20 ♗d3 ♗f5! 21 ♗xf5 ♖e8+.

16...exd4 17 cxd4 c3! 18 ♗e3 ♘cxd4 19 ♗xd4

Kindermann analyses 19 ♗d1 ♗d7 20 0-0 ♖e8∓ or 20...♖f8∓.

19...♘xd4 20 ♖g1 g6 21 ♕e5 ♕c5!
22 ♕e8+ ♕f8 23 ♕xf8+

23 ♖xg6+ hxg6 24 ♕xg6+ ♕g7 25 ♕e8+ ♔h7.

23...♔xf8∓

Roth-Kindermann, Vienna 1996; the game concluded 24 ♔d1 ♗f5 25 ♖c1 ♖e8 26 ♖e1 b5 (zugzwang!) 27 ♗d3 ♗xd3 28 ♖xe8+ ♔xe8 29 cxd3 c2+ 30 ♔e1 a5 31 f4 b4 32 axb4 axb4 33 ♔d2 ♘b3+ 34 ♔xc2 ♘xc1 35 ♔xc1 ♔d7 0-1.

10.2 8 ♗d3

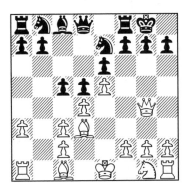

This has been the main move for a number of years (bishops before knights!). By attacking h7, White would like to get Black to make a weakening or at least committal move on the kingside, after which he can return to normal development. I'll examine two solutions:

10.21 8...♘bc6
10.22 8...f5

10.21 8...♘bc6

My preferred solution: it is both sound and offers plenty of chances. Again we look at two moves:

10.211 9 ♕h4
10.212 9 ♕h5

Here 9 ♘f3 f5 transposes back to (10.1) 8 ♘f3, but there is one more serious option with the line 9 ♗g5 ♕a5 10 ♘e2

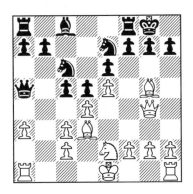

which leads to typically complex play which has never been fully resolved. Black has various ideas, but these two look the best:

(a) 10...cxd4 11 f4! dxc3 had a bad reputation but appears okay: 12 0-0 ♘g6 13 ♕h5 (13 ♖f3? ♘cxe5! 14 fxe5 ♘xe5 15 ♗xh7+ ♔xh7 16 ♕h5+ ♔g8 and Atlas gives 17 ♗f6! ♘xf3+ 18 gxf3, but misses 18...♕b6+ 19 ♔h1 e5–+) 13...♕c5+ 14 ♔h1 ♘ce7 15 ♖f3 f6!? 16 exf6 gxf6 17 ♖h3 ♖f7 18 ♗xf6 ♖xf6 19 ♕xh7+ ♔f8 20 ♖g3 ♕f2 21 h4!? (21 ♕h6+ ♔f7 22 ♕h7+=; 21 ♘g1 ♕xf4 22 ♖f1 ♕xf1 23 ♗xf1 ♖xf1 24 h4 ♔e8 25 h5 ♘f8 or 25...♘h4 Shaposhnikov-Riazantsev, Moscow 2000; I don't believe that White has enough for his material deficit). After 21 h4 (Hertneck-Uhlmann, Bundesliga 1992), K&D offer 21...e5!, which is equal after 22 h5 exf4! (K&D give the move 22...♘xf4, but it leaves the h-pawn too strong) 23 ♗xg6 fxg6 24 ♕h6+ ♔g8 25 ♕h7+ ♔f8 26 ♕h6+ etc.;

(b) 10...♘g6 11 0-0 (11 h4?! ♘xd4!) 11...♕a4 12 f4 c4 13 ♗xg6 fxg6 14 ♖a2 ♗d7 15 h4

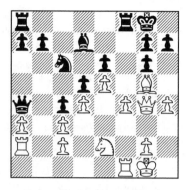

15...♖f5 16 h5 (16 ♘g3 ♕a5! 17 ♘xf5 gxf5 18 ♕g3 ♗e8! 19 ♗h6 ♕c7 with good play for the exchange, I.Almasi-Galyas, Budapest 2000) 16...gxh5 17 ♕xh5 h6 18 g4 ♖f7 19 ♔g2! ♗e8 20 ♕h3 hxg5 21 f5 is unclear and hard to assess, Koch-Apicella, Chambery 1994. White has a dangerous attack but I'm skeptical of its ultimate worth.

10.211 9 ♕h4

This is relatively rare and not terribly ambitious, but it's a sound move and important to know, particularly since the queens will come off and the second player needs be careful not to slip into passivity. The basics of a queenless middlegame are not otherwise explored in this chapter, so I'll give them a detailed look here.

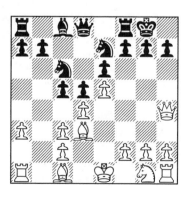

9...♘g6

Black has two other moves that look satisfactory:

(a) 9...♘f5!? 10 ♕xd8 ♖xd8 11 g4 (11 ♗xf5?! exf5 12 ♘e2 b6! 13 ♗g5 ♖d7 14 0-0-0 h6 15 ♗e3 ♗a6∓ S.Hall-Ludevid, email 1993) 11...♘fe7 12 ♗g5 (12 ♘f3± – K&D, but I like 12...♖f8!, preparing ...f6 preceded in some cases by ...c4, e.g., 13 dxc5 ♘g6 14 ♗xg6?! fxg6 with excellent play. White has better, of course, but Black seems okay in all lines) 12...♖d7!? (better seems either 12...♗d7 or 12...♖f8 13 ♘f3 c4 14 ♗e2 ♗d7 unclear; Black can always play for ...b5/...a5/...b4, but he can also play for ...f6, e.g., 15 h4 h6 16 ♗e3 ♔h7 17 g5!? ♘f5 18 gxh6 gxh6=) 13 ♘f3 ♖c7 (a clever reorganisation, but perhaps too exotic) 14 h4!? (14 0-0 ♗d7 15 ♖ab1±) 14...♗d7 15 h5 h6 16 ♗f4 and Black has made no progress although he eventually won in Resika-E.Lund, Budapest 2002;

(b) 9...f5!? is a suggestion of Kindermann, whose main line (mixed with just a few of my notes) runs 10 exf6 (10 ♘f3 ♕a5 [or just 10...♗d7] 11 ♗d2 c4!? 12 ♗e2 ♗d7) 10...♘f5

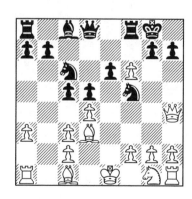

with:

(a) 11 ♗xf5 exf5 and the f-pawn is pinned, while 12 ♗g5 (12 dxc5 ♖xf6

13 ♘e2 ♕a5 14 0-0 ♕xc5 is unclear according to K&D) 12...♕a5 13 ♕g3 (13 ♘e2?! ♘xd4!) 13...f4! 14 ♗xf4 ♖xf6 15 ♘e2 ♘xd4! 16 ♘xd4 cxd4 is no fun for White;

(b) 11 f7+ ♔xf7 (to keep an eye on e5) 12 ♕xd8 (12 ♕h5+ ♔g8∓ – K&D) 12...♖xd8 13 ♘f3 (13 dxc5 e5 unclear; 13 g4 ♘fe7 14 ♘f3, and instead of K&D's 14...♔g8, 14...e5! 15 ♘xe5+ ♘xe5 16 dxe5 ♗xg4 seems very promising; 13 ♗g5 ♖e8 14 dxc5 e5 15 ♖b1 h6 16 ♗d2 ♖e7 17 ♘e2 ♗e6 18 0-0 ♖c8 unclear) 13...cxd4 14 ♗xf5 exf5 15 cxd4 ♖e8+ 16 ♔d1 'unclear'. Considering the importance of maintaining control of e5 and d4 and the dynamic necessities of opposite-coloured bishops, one is tempted to play 16...f4!?, to answer 17 ♗xf4 with 17...♗g4 and 17 h3 with 17...♗f5. But simply 16...h6 to prepare ...♖e4 also looks fine.

10 ♕xd8 ♖xd8

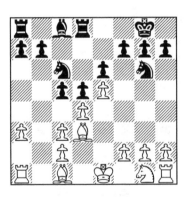

11 ♗g5

The most aggressive move and most testing, but it will lose time to ...f6.

(a) 11 ♘f3 cxd4 12 cxd4 f6! is analysed by Kindermann. Black should be fine, e.g., his main line runs 13 h4 fxe5 14 ♗xg6 e4!? 15 ♗xh7+ ♔xh7 16 ♘g5+ ♔g8 17 ♗e3 e5, when Black

must be at least equal;

(b) 11 ♗e3 ♗d7 (11...♘h4!? is an interesting HiArcs suggestion, when 12 g4 [12 ♔f1 ♘f5] 12...f6 13 f4?! fxe5 14 fxe5 ♖f8∓ is one of many ideas) 12 h4 ♘ge7 13 g4 cxd4 14 cxd4 ♘a5!? 15 h5 (15 ♗g5!? ♖e8 16 h5 'is little bit more accurate, but doesn't change estimation of position as equal' – Psakhis) 15...a6! (15...♗a4 16 ♗g5 ♖d7 17 h6 g6 was strategically complex in Bezgodov-Riazantsev, St Petersburg 2000; K&D like 18 f4!) 16 ♗g5 ♖e8 17 h6 g6 18 a4 (18 f4 ♗b5) 18...♖ac8! 19 ♘f3 ♘c4, intending ...b5 and on axb5, ...♗xb5. This is an abbreviated analysis of K&D's; they consider the position unclear.

11...♖f8 12 ♘f3

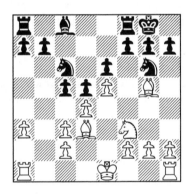

12...f6

Or 12...c4!? 13 ♗e2 f6 14 exf6 gxf6 15 ♗h6 Sutovsky-Drasko, Valle d'Aosta 2002; since White is going to play 0-0-0, Black should defend his d-pawn by 15...♖d8, e.g., 16 0-0-0 b5 – to protect c4 – 17 h4 e5 18 dxe5 fxe5 19 ♗g5 ♖d6 20 h5 ♘h8= with ...♘f7 and perhaps ...♗e6 next.

13 exf6 gxf6 14 ♗h6 ♖e8

This was the logical course in Mitkov-Gongora Montes, Merida 2002. After 15 0-0-0 the natural and sound move was 15...e5, and likewise after the game's 15...♗d7 16 h4, 16...e5 would have made sense, e.g., 17 dxe5 (17 c4?! cxd4 18 cxd5 ♘ce7 19 ♗c4 ♘f5!) 17...♘cxe5 18 ♘xe5 ♘xe5 19 ♗e2 ♗e6 20 ♗h5 ♖ed8 and White's bishops are balanced by his weak pawns.

10.212 9 ♕h5 ♘g6 10 ♘f3 ♕c7

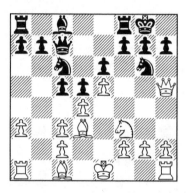

This introduces the Hertneck Variation, which has proven viable for over a decade now. The queen defends on the second rank against White's immediate threats and prepares ...c4, after which Black hopes to gain his usual kingside counterplay. I should mention that recently 10...♕e8!? has been played a few times, with several themes that are also found after 10...♕c7. One might find this a fun area for exploration.

After 10...♕c7, with apologies, I must split the material a final time:

10.2121 11 0-0
10.2122 11 ♗e3

However, others are both important and instructive:

(a) 11 ♘g5 is natural, but now we see why the queen is on c7: 11...h6 12 ♘xf7 ♕xf7 13 ♕xg6 (13 ♗xg6?? ♕xf2+ 14 ♔d1 cxd4-+) 13...♕xg6 (not

13...♕xf2+?? 14 ♔d1+-) 14 ♗xg6 cxd4 15 cxd4 ♘xd4 and:

(a1) 16 ♗e3 ♘f5 17 ♗c5 ♖d8 18 h4 (18 ♗xf5 exf5= due to the opposite-coloured bishops; 18 0-0 b6 19 ♗b4 ♗a6 20 ♗xf5 exf5 21 ♖fd1 ♔f7=) 18...b6 19 ♗b4 ♗d7 20 0-0-0 a5 21 ♗c3 ♖dc8= Baklan-Dgebuadze, Cappelle la Grande 2002;

(a2) 16 ♗d3 ♗d7 17 ♗b2 ♘f5 (17...♖f4 18 ♗c1 ♖f7 19 ♗b2 ♖f4 20 ♗c1 ½-½ Gelfand-Hübner, Wijk aan Zee 1992) 18 g3 a6 19 ♔d2 ♗b5 20 ♗xf5 ½-½ Vogt-Hertneck, Bad Lauterberg 1991;

(b) 11 h4 is the hot move now, but it seems quite manageable: 11...cxd4 (11...c4? 12 ♘g5 h6 13 ♗xg6 fxg6 14 ♕xg6 hxg5 15 hxg5 ♘xe5! 16 ♕h5 ♖f5 Skorchenko-Potkin, Ufa 2000; and here 16 ♕h8+! ♔f7 17 ♖g7 looks strong) 12 ♔d1 (12 ♘g5? h6 13 ♗xg6 fxg6 14 ♕xg6 hxg5 15 hxg5 ♕xe5+ 16 ♔d1 ♕f5) 12...dxc3 13 ♖h3 (13 ♘g5 h6 14 f4 ♘ce7!∓ – Kindermann) 13...b6!? (one of two good moves: true, 13...♘ce7?! 14 ♘g5 h6 15 ♘f3 f5 16 ♗xh6! led to a dangerous attack in Rowson-McDonald, Edinburgh 2003; but Rowson's 13...f6! looks very good, with 14 ♘g5 fxg5 15 hxg5 ♔f7 or 14 exf6 e5 15 fxg7 ♖f6! – McDonald) 14 ♘g5! (14 ♖g3?! ♘ce7! 15 ♘g5 h6∓ with the idea 16 ♘xf7?? ♖xf7 17 ♗xg6 ♘xg6 18 ♕xg6 ♖xf2-+) 14...h6 15 ♘f3 (15 ♘xf7?? ♕xf7 16 ♖f3 ♘f4!) 15...♘cxe5! 16 ♘xe5 ♕xe5 17 ♗xg6 ♕d4+ 18 ♗d3 ♕xf2 19 ♕e2 ♕g1+ 20 ♕e1 ♕xe1+ 21 ♔xe1 e5 22 ♖g3 ♔h8∓ – K&D; Black's central pawns are awesome;

(c) 11 a4 c4 (11...cxd4 12 0-0 dxc3 is also playable) 12 ♗xg6 fxg6 resembles the main line but White's bishop won't get to a3 so 11 a4 is a bit of a waste of time: 13 ♕g4 (13 ♕h3 ♕a5

14 ♗d2 ♗d7= is normal, but easier may be 13...♗d7!?, since 14 ♗a3 ♕a5 15 ♔d2 ♖f4 threatens d4 and 16 ♕g3 ♖f5 is very comfortable) 14 ♗d2 ♗d7 15 ♕g4 ♖f5 (15...♘e7 was balanced in J.Polgar-Gdanski, Budapest 1993) 16 h4 ♖af8 'unclear' according to K&D; compare the main lines;

(d) Similar is 11 ♗d2 c4 12 ♗xg6 fxg6 13 ♕g4 ♗d7 14 h4 ♖f5 15 ♘g5 ♖af8 16 h5 (16 f4 ♕b6 – Koponen) 16...♘xe5!? (16...gxh5! 17 ♕xh5 h6 18 g4 ♖xg5 19 ♗xg5 ♗e8 20 ♕h2 and 20...hxg5= or even the promising exchange sacrifice 20...♗g6!?) 17 ♕g3 ♖xf2 18 dxe5 ♖2f5 19 hxg6 ♕xe5+ 20 ♕xe5 ♖xe5+ 21 ♔d1 Wiesner-Gebhardt, Hessen 1992, and Black had to play 21...hxg6! with a messy equality.

10.2121 11 0-0 c4 12 ♗xg6

Not 12 ♘g5?? h6 13 ♘xf7 cxd3. 12 ♗e2 has been played many times but simply allows Black to free his game and gain activity after 12...f6 ('∓' – Knaak) 13 exf6 (13 a4 ♗d7 14 exf6 ♖xf6 15 ♘g5 h6 16 ♘h3 ♕a5∓ Shetty-L.Ravi, Indian Ch 1994) 13...♖xf6

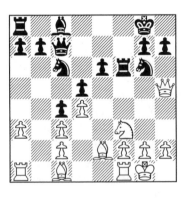

(a) 14 g3 ♗d7 (14...h6) 15 ♗e3?! (15 ♗g5 – Hertneck; 15...♖f5!∓) 15...♖af8 16 ♗g5 J.Polgar-Hertneck, Cologne TV 1991; and ECO gives 16...♗e8!∓;

(b) 14 ♗g5 ♘f4! 15 ♗xf4 ♕xf4 16 g3 (16 ♘g5 h6 17 ♕e8+ ♖f8 18 ♘xe6 ♖xe8 19 ♘xf4 ♖e4! 20 g3 g5 – K&D; this is at least equal) 16...♕d6 17 ♕g5 ♗d7= Oll-Dolmatov, Groningen 1993;

(c)14 ♗d1 ♗d7 15 ♖e1 ♖af8 16 ♖b1 h6∓ 17 ♔h1?! ♘ce7! and White was completely tied down in Kamsky-Yusupov, Belgrade 1991.

12...fxg6 13 ♕h3

13 ♕g4 is similar to the 11 ♗e3 main line, but after 13...♗d7!, White's best plan in that line is h4-h5, which has now lost its point without the rook on h1. The idea h4-h5 is also without value in the line 13...♕f7!? 14 ♘g5 ♕e8.

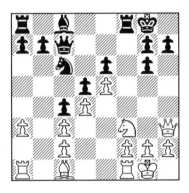

13...h6!?

Two other moves are simpler:

(a) 13...♕a5!? stops any a4 and ♗a3 plan, e.g., 14 ♗d2 ♗d7!? (14...♘e7 or 14...♕a4!? 15 ♖a2 ♗d7!?=, which relies upon the sequence 16 ♘g5?! h6 17 ♘xe6 ♕a5! 18 ♗xh6 ♖f7! 19 f4 ♕b6∓) 15 ♘g5 h6 16 ♘f3 ♖f7 17 ♕g4 g5=;

(b) 13...♗d7 is straightforward: 14 a4 ♕a5 15 ♗d2 ♖f5 16 ♘h4 ♖f7∓.

14 a4!

14 ♕g4 ♕f7 15 ♘e1!? (15 a4! ♕f5 16 ♕xf5 gxf5 17 h4 b6 is equal) 15...♗d7 16 ♕e2? (16 f4 ♕f5 or 16...g5!? 17 ♖f3 ♕g6 18 fxg5 ♖xf3 19 gxf3 h5! 20 ♕g2 ♘e7!=; the pawn is irrelevant) 16...g5 17 ♖b1 b6 18 ♗d2

♘e7 19 ♖d1 ♕g6 20 ♗c1 ♖f7 21 f3
♖af8∓ R.Rodriguez-De la Villa Garcia, Alcobendas 1993.

14...g5?

Loosening. Black's play should be pretty easy here, e.g., 14...♕f7 15 ♗a3 ♖d8 16 ♗d6 b6 17 ♕g4 ♕f5=. The opposite-coloured bishops are particularly drawish in these positions.

15 ♕g4!

Not 15 ♗a3?! ♖f4!, but 15 ♕g3!? preparing h4 is interesting: 15...♘e7! 16 ♗a3 ♘f5 17 ♕g4 ♖f7= 18 h4? ♘xh4 19 ♘xh4 ♖f4 – Koponen.

15...♕f7 16 h4!

Better than 16 ♗a3 ♕f5=.

16...gxh4 17 ♗xh6

Ashley-J.Watson, Seattle 2003. Now White will win a pawn with a nominal edge, but the opposite bishops and his own weak pawn structure will make a draw the correct result. The game continued 17...♘e7 (or 17...h3 18 g3 ♘e7±) 18 ♘xh4 ♘f5 19 ♗c1! ♘xh4 20 ♕xh4 ♕g6 21 ♗a3 ♖e8 22 ♖a2 ♗d7 23 ♗d6 ♕f5 (intending ...♔f7 and ...♖h8) 24 f4 ♕h7! 25 ♕g5 ♕f5 with an eventual draw after the exchange of queens. But Black's alternatives on moves 13 and 14 would have avoided this discomfort.

10.2122 11 ♗e3

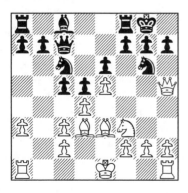

Protecting f2 and thus threatening ♘g5. There are over 200 games with this move in my largest database!

11...c4

11...♘ce7 is also played; one area to look at is the line 12 h4 ♗d7 13 ♕g4!? f5 14 ♕h3!, which has recently won two top-level games, including what I think is the stem game Nataf-Pelletier, Cap d'Agde 2002.

12 ♗xg6

(a) 12 ♘g5? h6 13 ♘xf7 cxd3 14 ♘xh6+ gxh6 15 ♕xg6+ ♕g7∓;

(b) 12 ♗e2 strongly resembles 12 0-0 c4 13 ♗e2. One example: 12...f6 13 h4!? ♗d7 14 g3 ♘ce7!? 15 ♕g4 f5 (15...fxe5! 16 h5 exd4 17 hxg6 dxe3 18 gxh7+ ♔h8 19 fxe3 e5∓) 16 ♕h3 h6 17 h5 ♘h8 18 ♘h4 ♗a4∓ Minasian-Apicella, Paris 1994.

12...fxg6 13 ♕g4

13 ♕h3 is like 11 0-0 c4 12 ♗xg6 fxg6 13 ♕h3 above except that the bishop on e3 is poorly placed. True, h4-h5 would have more point, but the queen on h3 is in the way and White's play is slow.

13...♗d7

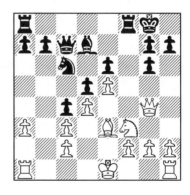

This may not be better but it is less worked out and contains a different set of dynamic possibilities than the more popular 13...♕f7. In that line most top-level games recently seem to demonstrate that Black (with very accurate move orders) can sacrifice the exchange and/or block the position to draw! That's not bad if you're willing to study and keep up, but of course it could change as theory charges into the 20+ move range. Here's a couple of exemplary recent games that illustrate the exchange sacrifice theme, one that is ubiquitous in modern French practice: 14 ♘g5 ♕e8 15 h4 h6 16 ♘h3 b5

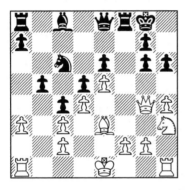

17 ♕e2 (an amazing game was 17 ♘f4 ♘e7 18 ♔d2 a5 19 ♕h3 ♗d7 20 ♖ab1 ♕f7 21 f3 ♖ab8 22 ♘e2 ♘c6 23 ♖b2 b4! 24 axb4 axb4 25 cxb4 c3+ 26 ♘xc3 ♘a5! 27 ♔e2 ♘c4 28 ♖b3 ♘xe3 29 ♔xe3 ♕f4+ 30 ♔d3 ♖fc8 31 ♕g4 ♖xc3+! 32 ♔xc3 ♖c8+ 33 ♔b2 ♕d2 34 ♖c1 ♔h7 Anand-Yusupov, Bastia 2002; White is the exchange and two pawns up(!), but apart from the structural issues moves like ...h5 and ...♗a4 are in the air; the game was eventually drawn) 17...a5 18 g4 ♗d7 19 h5 gxh5 20 ♖g1! ♘e7! 21 gxh5 ♔h7 22 ♕g4 ♘f5 23 ♔d2 ♕e7 24 ♕g6+ ♔h8 25 ♘f4 ♘h4 26 ♕g4 ♖xf4! (again! the light squares are often full compensation in such positions) 27 ♗xf4 ♖f8 28 ♖h1 ♘f5 29 ♗e3 ♗e8 30 f4 ♗f7 31 ♗f2 ♖b8 32 ♕h3 ♔h7 Leko-Z.Almasi, Budapest 2003. Black es-

sentially did nothing for the next 20 moves and a draw was agreed. Fascinating and possibly even useful as a weapon, but this is not what we're looking for as Black.

14 h4

14 ♘g5 h6 15 ♘h3 ♘e7 16 a4 ♖f5 17 ♘f4 ♔h7 18 h4 ♖af8= Stefansson-Hjartarson, Iceland 1994.

14...♖f5 15 h5

15 ♘g5 has been played often but with little effect:

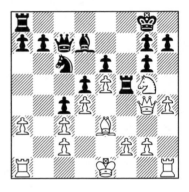

15...♖af8 (another good order is 15...♕a5 16 ♗d2 ♖af8, e.g., 17 0-0 ♘d8! 18 ♕e2 ♗a4 19 ♖ac1 ♖e8 20 g4 ♖ff8 21 ♔g2 ♘f7= Kovacevic-Sparic, Yugoslavia 1994; recently Dirr tried 15...h6 16 ♘h3 ♗e8 17 ♕e2 ♖f8 18 g4 with a position resembling the 13...♕f7 lines above, although I like the bishop on e8 better; the game went 18...♘e7 19 ♕d2 ♖c8!? 20 ♘f4 ♕d7 21 ♔e2 ♖c6! 22 ♖ag1 ♖b6 Nijboer-Dirr, Godesberg 2002 with complications in which Black looks better, although the game was drawn; 22...♖a6! was probably more accurate) 16 h5 (16 ♕e2 h6 17 ♘h3 ♕d8 18 g3 b5 19 ♕d2 ♕e7 20 ♔e2 a5 with good play, David-Enders, Godesberg 2000) 16...♕a5 (or 16...h6!? 17 hxg6 ♕a5 18 0-0 ♕xc3 19 ♘h7 ♖d8=) 17 ♗d2 h6 18 ♘h3 (18 ♘f3 g5∓ –

K&D) 18...gxh5 19 ♕g3 ♔h7∓ Lingnau-Kipper, Germany 1998.

15...gxh5 16 ♖xh5 ♖xh5!?

This was originally queried, but I feel that it's a good solution. Nevertheless, Black has an alternative in 16...♖af8, which is dicey but may suffice theoretically. Let me just mention a few ideas:

(a) 17 ♘g5 ♕a5! 18 ♗d2 ♖f4! 19 ♕h3 h6! 20 ♖xh6! gxh6 21 ♕xh6 ♖4f7!, and according to theory (extended by K&D), the game will be drawn or end in an unclear position on move 35!;

(b) 17 ♔d2!?

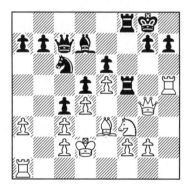

(b1) 17...♖xh5 18 ♕xh5 ♗e8 19 ♕h3 ♖xf3!? 20 ♕xf3 ♗g6 is a famous type of exchange sacrifice played several times right here. A brilliant conception, but nevertheless I don't fully trust this idea and in any case only White can win. Concretely, Black must deal with lines like 21 ♕h3 ♕d7 22 ♖b1 ♘d8 23 ♗g5 ♘f7 24 ♗h4 b6 25 ♖b4 ♘h6 26 g4 ♕f7 27 ♕g3 ♔h8 28 f3 ♕e8 29 a4 with nagging pressure, Makovsky-Raidna, email 2000;

(b2) Surprisingly I haven't seen 17...♗e8! mentioned, but I like it: 18 ♖h2 ♗g6!? (18...♕b6!? was played successfully by Hillarp Persson and is probably okay but needs more analy-

sis). Then play might go: 19 ♕g3!? (19 ♘h4 ♗h5= 20 ♕h3?! ♖xf2+ 21 ♗xf2 ♖xf2+ 22 ♔e1 ♖xc2 23 ♘f3! ♗g6 24 ♕xe6+ ♕f7 25 ♕c8+ ♕e8∓) 19...♖xf3 20 gxf3 ♕b6!;

(c) 17 ♖h3 ♗e8 (17...♕a5 18 ♔d2 ♗e8 transposes). Black's defence is not easy after 18 ♘g5 (18 ♔d2?! h5 19 ♕h4 ♖xf3 20 gxf3 ♘e7 21 a4 ♘f5 22 ♕g5 ♕e7 with a total bockade and awful white pawns, Rowson-Barsov, York 2000) 18...♕a5 19 ♔d2 and Black must again play an exchange sacrifice 19...♖xg5 20 ♕xg5 ♗g6 with compensation, but how much is not clear. It's better to leave one pair of rooks on if possible, so this position might be okay for Black. Nevertheless, 16...♖xh5 looks easier to me.

17 ♕xh5

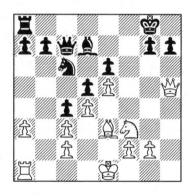

17...♗e8!?

As far as I know, this move hasn't been played or suggested; in fact it has been thought to be a serious mistake. The normal continuation is 17...♖f8, but this often depends upon the forementioned exchange sacrifice, e.g., 18 ♕h3 ♖xf3!? 19 ♕xf3 ♗e8 20 ♕h3 ♕d7±; compare the last note. White has begun to win this type of position.

18 ♕h3

K&D say that White has a clear

advantage now. But I doubt that there's anything wrong with

18...♘d8!

Black plans to play ...♗g6 next (without having to sacrifice an exchange!). Here's some analysis:

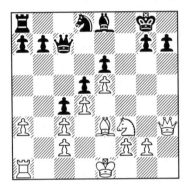

19 ♘g5

This is almost certainly the reason that no one has tried 17...♗e8, but it backfires. White has better alternatives:

(a) 19 ♗g5!? ♗f7 20 ♔d2! (20 ♗xd8 ♕xd8 21 ♔d2 ♕e7∓) 20...♕d7!? (to prepare ...♗g6) 21 ♖h1 ♗g6 22 ♘h4 ♕f7=;

(b) 19 ♔d2 also equalises, if only because the tactics work out to a draw: 19...♗g6 20 ♖h1 (20 ♘h4 ♕f7!, although the opposite-coloured bishops will leave few prospects) 20...♕b6!? (or again 20...♕f7; Black's plan might be expansion on the queenside; but 21 ♘g5!? ♕f5 leaves only an optical advantage, and 21...♕e8!? 22 ♘xh7 ♕a4! only draws after 23 ♘f6+! ♔f7 24 ♕h8! ♕xc2+ 25 ♔e1 with the idea 25...gxf6 26 exf6! ♕b1+) 21 ♘h4 ♗xc2!? 22 ♔xc2 ♕b3+ 23 ♔d2 ♕b2+ 24 ♔d1 ♕xc3!? (24...♕b3+=) 25 ♘f3 ♕d3+ 26 ♔e1 h6 (26...♕b1+=) 27 ♗xh6 gxh6 28 ♕g4+ ♔f8 29 ♖xh6 ♕b1+=.

19...h6 20 ♘xe6

20 ♘f3 ♗g6!∓.

20...♕a5!

White may still survive this position, but he's lost the chance for full equality:

21 ♗xh6!?

21 ♔d2? ♗d7 wins for Black, but 21 ♘xd8! ♕xc3+ 22 ♔e2 ♕xc2+ 23 ♔f1 ♖xd8 24 ♕e6+ seems to minimize the white disadvantage: 24...♔h7 (24...♗f7 25 ♕e7 ♖e8 26 ♕xb7 ♕c3∓) 25 ♕e7 ♕b2 26 ♖e1 ♕b6 27 e6! and 27...♕d6∓ will be hard to win, but Black must avoid 27...♗g6? 28 ♗xh6!.

21...♘xe6 22 ♕xe6+ ♗f7 23 ♕g4 ♕xc3+ 24 ♔e2

24 ♔d1 ♕xa1+ 25 ♔e2 ♗h5! 26 ♕xh5 ♕xd4 will win.

24...♕xc2+ 25 ♔e1 ♕h7 26 ♗c1 ♕h1+ 27 ♔d2 ♕f1!∓

Black is threatening both ...♕xf2+ and ...c3+ and will gain a large advantage.

If this analysis is correct, Black can be happy with the most critical lines of the Hertneck Variation.

10.22 8...f5

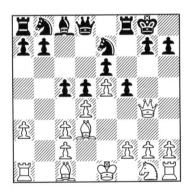

Rather than supply a complicated repertoire with this move, I'll recommend particular byways to simplify one's use of it. In particular, we'll use favourable transpositions from the

8...♘bc6 variation to help us.

9 exf6

(a) 9 ♕h3?! b6 (or 9...♕a5 10 ♗d2 ♘bc6 11 ♘f3 ♕a4=, transposing to 8 ♘f3 ♘bc6 9 ♗d3 f5 10 ♕h3 above) 10 ♘f3 ♕d7 (to protect e6 before playing ...♗a6) 11 0-0 ♗a6 12 a4 ♗xd3 13 cxd3 cxd4 14 ♘xd4 ♘bc6 15 ♘xc6 ♘xc6 16 ♗a3 ♖fc8 17 ♗d6 ♘d8∓ intending ...♘f7 – analysis by Kindermann and Dirr;

(b) 9 ♕g3 ♘bc6 10 ♘f3 transposes to 8 ♘f3 ♘bc6 9 ♗d3 f5 10 ♕g3.

9...♖xf6

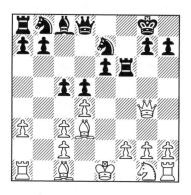

10 ♗g5

10 ♕h5 h6 11 ♘f3 (11 g4!? can be wild: 11...♘bc6 12 g5 g6! 13 ♕xh6 ♖f7 threatens ...♖h7, and 14 ♗xg6 ♖g7 15 ♗d3 e5! 16 dxe5 ♘xe5 17 ♕h4 ♘f5 18 ♕f4 ♘g6 19 ♕d2 ♘gh4∓ is analysis by Tischbierek; K&D continue 20 ♗e2 b6 21 ♘f3 ♗b7 22 ♘xh4 ♘xh4 23 ♖g1 ♕e7 with attack; it's also worth pointing out that 15...c4 16 ♗e2 ♖h7 17 ♕g6 ♖g7 was a draw) 11...c4!? (11...♘bc6 transposes to the 8...♘bc6 line again) 12 ♗e2 ♘bc6 13 ♗e3 ♗d7 14 g4?! ♕a5 15 ♗d2 ♘g6 16 g5 0-1 Zelcic-Dolmatov, Istanbul 2003. Unless it's a typo, White's resignation seems to be based on 16...♘f4! 17 ♕g4 (17 ♗xf4? ♕xc3+) 17...hxg5, which is very good for

Black although not resignable, e.g., 18 h4 (18 ♖g1? ♖af8 19 ♘xg5 ♘xe2 20 ♕xe2 e5!) 18...gxh4 19 ♖g1 ♘g6 20 ♘xh4 ♘ce7∓.

10...♖f7

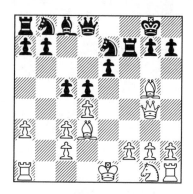

11 ♕h5

(a) 11 ♘f3 e5!? (11...♘bc6 is a well-known line satisfactory for Black, but the theory on it is immense) 12 ♗xh7+ ♔xh7 13 ♕h4+ (13 ♕h5+ ♔g8 14 ♘xe5 ♖f5 15 g4 ♖xg5 16 ♕xg5 cxd4 17 cxd4 ♘bc6∓ – K&D) 13...♔g8 14 ♘xe5 ♕e8 15 0-0 ♘bc6 16 ♘xf7 ♕xf7. This is Korchnoi's analysis, to which K&D add 17 ♗xe7! ♕xe7! 18 ♕xe7 ♘xe7 19 dxc5 ♗d7 20 ♖ab1 ♗c6 21 ♖fe1 ♔f7 with an unclear position. Although I tend to like Black's pieces in such lines, White's coherent kingside pawns make this one look equal;

(b) 11 ♕h4 h6 12 ♗xe7 ♖xe7!? (12...♕xe7 is considered equal) 13 ♘f3 (13 ♕g3 c4 14 ♗g6 ♗d7= with the ideas ...♗e8 and ...♘c6) 13...e5! 14 dxe5 (14 ♘xe5?? ♖xe5+) 14...♖xe5+ 15 ♔d2 ♕xh4 16 ♘xh4 ♘c6 (a position arrived at many times) 17 ♘g6 (17 ♖ae1 ♗d7 18 f4 ♖xe1 19 ♖xe1 ♖e8= Kwiatkowski-McDonald, Blackpool 1988) 17...♖e6! (17...♖e8 18 ♖ae1 ♗d7=) 18 c4 d4 19 f3 ♔f7 20 ♘f4 ♖e7 (20...♖f6 21 ♘d5 ♖d6 and ...♗e6; White's weak pawns give Black a small advantage) 21 ♖ab1 b6 22 ♗e4 ♗b7∓ Schreber-Knaus, email 2000.

11...g6

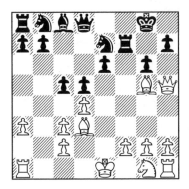

12 ♕d1

12 ♕h4 ♕a5! 13 ♗d2 (13 ♘e2? ♘bc6 threatens ...c4, but then 14 dxc5 e5∓ is not what White wants) 13...♘bc6 14 ♘f3 and a simple solution is 14...c4 15 ♗e2 ♘f5 16 ♕g5 ♗d7 with the idea 17 h4 ♖af8! 18 h5 h6!∓.

12...♕a5

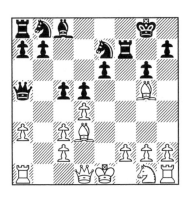

Kindermann's move, easier and more fun than the also-satisfactory line with 12...♘bc6 13 ♘f3 ♕f8.

13 ♗d2

Of course 13 ♘e2?? loses to 13...c4. But 13 ♕d2 is a logical positional attempt that has caused Black some real problems in the past. It still hasn't been fully worked out; but both

of these replies look good:

(a) 13...♘ec6 14 ♘f3, and 14...♘d7! is a new and paradoxical idea.

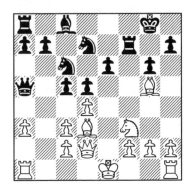

Although blocking off his own pieces, Black insists upon enforcing ...e5: 15 0-0 (15 h4 e5 16 dxe5 ♘dxe5 17 ♘xe5 ♘xe5 18 h5 ♗g4!∓; 15 ♗e2 tries to prevent ...e5 by indirectly covering d5, but after 15...♘f6, the threat of ...♘e4 practically forces White into 16 ♗xf6 ♖xf6, when 17 0-0? is met by 17...cxd4 and otherwise White is a bit stuck for a move; he might therefore try 17 dxc5 ♕xc5 18 0-0 e5 19 ♖ab1, but 19...a6!, stopping ♖b5, seems to retain some advantage) 15...cxd4! (15...e5 16 c4!? ♕xd2 17 ♘xd2 e4 18 cxd5 exd3 19 dxc6 bxc6 20 dxc5±) 16 cxd4 ♕xd2 17 ♗xd2 e5 (17...♖xf3!? 18 gxf3 ♘xd4 19 ♔g2 ♘e5 20 f4 ♘xd3 21 cxd3 ♘b3 22 ♖a2 ♗d7 ought to give Black enough for the exchange: a pawn and the opportunity to exploit White's isolated and weak pawns) 18 ♘xe5 (18 ♘g5!?) 18...♘dxe5 19 dxe5 ♘xe5 20 ♖fe1 (20 ♗e2 ♗f5=) 20...♘xd3 21 ♖e8+ ♖f8 22 ♖xf8+ ♔xf8 23 cxd3 ♗f5 24 ♖c1 ♖c8 25 ♖xc8+ ½-½ Leko-Ivanchuk, Monaco (rapid) 2002;

(b) Kindermann analyses 13...c4!, which has apparently not yet received tests but seems one of Black's most interesting responses to 13 ♕d2: 14 ♗e2 ♘f5 15 h4!? (15 ♘f3? ♘d6! 16 ♘e5 ♘e4∓; 15 ♗f4 ♘c6 and 16 ♘f3? ♘fxd4! or 16 ♘h3 e5!? 17 dxe5 ♘h4 18 0-0 ♗xh3 19 gxh3 ♖e8∓; 15 ♗f3 ♘c6 16 ♘e2 e5 17 dxe5 ♘xe5 18 ♗xd5 ♘d3+ 19 cxd3 ♕xd5 unclear – all from Kindermann) 15...♘c6 (maybe Black could try 15...h6!? 16 ♗f4 ♘c6 unclear, again threatening ...♘fxd4; then play might go 17 g3! ♗d7 18 ♘f3 ♖af8 19 0-0 b5!) 16 h5 e5 17 hxg6 hxg6 18 dxe5 ♘xe5 19 ♘f3 ♘xf3+ 20 ♗xf3 ♗e6=.

13...♘bc6 14 ♘f3 ♕c7!

Preparing ...e5. 14...c4 closes the centre; it has been played with varying success, but theoretically favours White slightly.

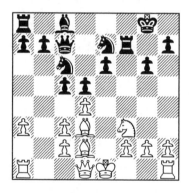

15 0-0

(a) 15 ♘g5 ♖f6 16 dxc5 (16 f4? cxd4∓) 16...e5 17 c4 e4 transposes to 'b';

(b) An important recent game went 15 dxc5 e5 16 ♘g5 ♖f8 17 c4 e4 18 cxd5! (18 ♗e2 ♕e5=) 18...exd3 19 d6 ♕d7 20 dxe7 ♕xe7+ 21 ♗e3 Pelletier-Lutz, Biel 2003; and Kindermann suggests 21...♖f5! 22 ♘f3 (22 h4 h6 23 ♘f3 ♗e6) 22...♗e6 23 0-0 ♗d5 24 ♘d2 ♖h5! 25 ♖e1 ♕h4 26 ♘e1 and 26...dxc2 27 ♕xc2 ♘e5 looks best, intending 28 f4 ♘c4.

15...e5

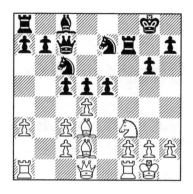

16 ♘g5

16 ♘xe5 ♘xe5 17 dxe5 ♕xe5 18 c4 ♗f5 (18...d4 also looks equal) 19 ♖e1 (19 ♗xf5 ♘xf5 20 ♖e1 ♕d4= Stefansson-Potkin, Pardubice 2000) 19...♕f6 20 ♕f3 ♗xd3 21 ♕xf6 ♖xf6 22 cxd3 ♘f5 23 ♖e5 dxc4 24 dxc4 ♖d6= Lutz-Kindermann, Porz 1997.

16...♖f8 17 c4 exd4! 18 ♖e1

18 cxd5 ♘e5 (18...♘xd5 19 ♗c4 ♘ce7 looks reasonable) 19 ♗e4 ♘g4! 20 g3 (20 f4 ♘f6!) 20...♘f6 21 ♗f4 ♕d7 (21...♕d8 22 d6 ♘ed5 23 ♗e5! with attack – Kindermann, although simplification via 23...♘xe4 24 ♘xe4 ♕e8!? 22 c4 h6 looks safe enough) 22 c4 h6 23 ♘e6 ♘xe4 24 ♘xf8 ♔xf8 25 ♗xh6+ ♔f7 'unclear' – Kindermann.

18...♗f5 19 cxd5 ♘xd5 20 ♗c4 ♖ad8

White has two bishops and will try to exploit the weakened kingside dark squares. Black has space and is centralised, so his prospects are good.

21 ♕f3 ♕d6 22 ♕b3!?

A dynamic balance arises after 22 ♗f4 ♕d7 23 g4!? h6! 24 gxf5 hxg5 25 ♗xg5 ♖xf5=. After 22 ♕b3, Hracek-Kindermann, Bad Homburg 1997 went 22...b6 23 ♘e4 ♗xe4 24 ♖xe4 ♘a5 25 ♗xa5 bxa5 26 ♖b1 ♔g7 27 ♕h3 ♖d7 (27...♘b6! 28 ♖e6 ♕d7 was worth a try) 28 ♖be1 ½-½.

Chapter Eleven

Winawer Variation: Positional Lines

1 e4 e6 2 d4 d5 3 ♘c3 ♗b4 4 e5 c5 5 a3 ♗xc3+ 6 bxc3 ♘e7

In this chapter, White chooses one of several positional continuations:

11.1 7 ♘f3
11.2 7 a4
11.3 7 h4

In contrast to our experience with 7 ♕g4, White keeps his pieces close to the centre and doesn't immediately try to get at Black's king (even with Black's king on the queenside, 7 h4 introduces a positional attack via h5-h6). To complement his centre, White has numerous ways to attack on both wings, e.g., h4-h5-h6, or a4 with ♗a3 and a5, or even dxc5 with ♘d4, hitting both sides of the board. For his part, Black can put pressure down the c-file, blockade the queenside by ...♗d7-a4 or ...♕a5-a4 (with or without ...c4), and at some point he usually attacks White's centre by ...f6. The extreme flexibility of both sides' strategies has produced fascinating strategic battles over many years. Arguably, the Positional Winawer has been one of the most intellectu-

ally fruitful openings not just of the French Defence but of modern chess. That said, we have probably seen less of an evolution of these lines in the past few years than since the time of Botvinnik. A decline in top-level interest has been partly due to a resurgence of 7 ♕g4, but also to the impression that the positional lines no longer offer as much challenge for Black. His strategies and concrete defensive schemes look very good at the moment, although this can of course change at any time. Aside from the above main moves above, White has these rare ones:

(a) 7 f4 cuts off the c1 bishop but is playable. One answer is 7...♕a5 (or 7...♘bc6 8 ♘f3 ♘f5) 8 ♕d2 (8 ♗d2 ♘bc6 9 ♘f3 cxd4 10 cxd4 ♕a4 11 ♗c3 b6= intending ...♗a6 – Korchnoi) 8...♗d7 (8...b6= intending ...♗a6) 9 a4 ♘bc6, e.g., 10 ♘f3 cxd4 11 cxd4 ♕xd2+ 12 ♔xd2 ♘f5 13 ♗b2 h5 14 a5 (versus ...♘a5) 14...a6 with queenside pressure after ...♖c8, ...♘a7, ...♗b5 etc.;

(b) 7 ♗d3!? is a bit committal but has been used by Short and should be taken seriously:

(b1) 7...♞bc6 8 ♕g4 (8 ♞f3 transposes to 7 ♞f3 ♞bc6 8 ♗d3) 8...♕a5 (8...c4 9 ♗e2 0-0 10 h4 f6! – Dvoretsky; then ECO gives 10 ♞f3 f5!? 11 ♕g3=) 9 ♗d2 c4 10 ♗e2 0-0 (10...♞f5 11 ♞f3 ♗d7 12 ♞g5 h6 13 ♕h5 ♖f8 14 ♞h7 and 14...♖h8= or 14...♖g8 15 g4 ♞fe7 unclear, Velimirovic-Timman, Sarajevo 1984) 11 h4 f6 12 f4 (otherwise Black breaks down the centre) 12...♕a4 13 ♗d1 ♕b5 (threatening ...♕b2) 14 ♗c1 ♕a5 15 ♗d2 and in Short-Shulman, Dhaka 1999 Black repeated by 15...♕b5 16 ♗c1 ♕a5 etc.; but 15...♕b6 would have been very interesting, since ...♕b2 is still a threat and now 16 ♗c1? fails to 16...fxe5 17 fxe5 ♞xe5!;

(b2) 7...♕a5 8 ♗d2 ♞bc6 (or 8...c4 9 ♗f1 ♕a4) 9 ♕g4!? c4 10 ♗e2 0-0 11 ♞f3 ♕a4 12 ♖a2 f6 13 exf6 ♖xf6=;

(b3) 7...♕c7 8 ♖b1 ♞bc6 9 ♕g4 Short-Poulton, Birmingham 2002, and as pointed out in CBM, Black should play simply 9...0-0! 10 ♕h5 (10 ♞f3 f5 11 exf6 ♖xf6 12 ♗g5 e5!∓) 10...♞g6 11 ♞f3 c4 12 ♗xg6 fxg6, practically a tempo up on the main line of our 7 ♕g4 0-0 chapter, since ♖b1 looks wasted;

(c) 7 ♞e2!? ♕c7! (my suggestion, stopping ♞f4) 8 ♖b1 (8 g3 b6! 9 ♗g2 ♗a6 10 0-0 ♞bc6∓) 8...b6 (8...♞d7 and ...♞b6 is promising, or simply 8...0-0) 9 ♞g3?! cxd4 10 cxd4 ♕c3+ 11 ♗d2?! (a strange pawn sacrifice) 11...♕xd4 12 f4 Spassky-Bruch, France 1994; and 12...0-0 is obvious and strong, with the idea ...♗a6.

11.1 7 ♞f3
The obvious move and still the most popular.
7...♞bc6
For this edition I give a different move order, in part just to infuse

some originality into the proposed lines and in part to more comfortably meet h4-h5 systems.

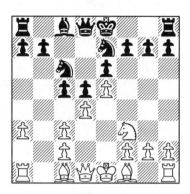

A look at the books will show that 7...♞bc6 is not the most common continuation, perhaps because it doesn't put any immediate questions to White (7...♕a5 attacks c3, for example, and 7...♗d7 has the idea of ...♗a4). It's very difficult to say in concrete, demonstrable terms what the advantages and disadvantages are of the various possible move orders here. For example, the commonly played moves 7...♕a5, 7...♗d7, 7...♕c7, and 7...b6 (even 7...h6 has been played at the top levels) can all be met by 3 to 5 legitimate strategies, each of which in turn can be answered by a new set of possible ideas that don't resolve themselves until well into the middlegame. This may seem true of many openings, but the difference here is the vague nature of the positions that result. Practically every type of strategic decision taken by either side is good in some positions and bad in very similar ones. On top of that, both sides have numerous possibilities for transposition (as well as whether to allow transpositions). It's interesting, for example, to see some general comments out of two recent books covering the Win-awer by first rate authors who understand these positions in depth. Neil McDonald finds himself 'rather puzzled as to the reason for' 7 a4, a move played by Smyslov, Fischer, Spassky and many others, and then offers as a possible justification for the move a rare manoeuvre that was employed by none of them! Pedersen on the other hand says that he prefers 7 a4 and considers 7 ♘f3 the easiest move to equalise against (suggesting 7...b6). Without trying to resolve the general question, I do like 7...b6 (a handy system to have at the ready), but it's not necessarily better than other solutions. Probably any of Black's 7th moves are ultimately playable (including 7...♗d7, given in the last edition). But none of them escape the necessity for solving original strategic problems over the board that aren't found (yet) in the theoretical books. The important thing is to be comfortable with the most common types of positions that arise and to be willing to compete in strategically dense battles. That said, there are certain specific positional and tactical traps that must be avoided, as with any opening. After 7...♘bc6, we look at:

11.11 8 ♗d3
11.12 8 ♗e2

Two very important moves, 8 h4 and 8 a4, are dealt with in the next two sections by transposition via 7 a4 (11.2) and 7 h4 (11.3). But the transposition involving 8 h4 is not a simple matter. If Black had chosen 7...♗d7 or 7...♕c7, for example, the move 8 h4 poses more difficulties than after 7...♘bc6, which is one good reason to

choose the latter move. I will try to include all the main h4-h5 systems under 7 h4, although the ideas are so popular and flexible that irregular ones sometimes pop up in other sections.

As usual there are some odds and ends which need to be considered before we look at the main lines:

(a) 8 g3 is rather slow and has several answers, e.g., 8...♕a5 (or 8...0-0 9 ♗g2 f6=) 9 ♗d2 ♕a4 (a traditional manoeuvre; or 9...cxd4 10 cxd4 ♕a4) 10 ♕b1 (10 dxc5?! ♘xe5! 11 ♘xe5 ♕e4+ 12 ♕e2 ♕xh1 13 ♕b5+ ♔f8) 10...c4 11 ♗g2 ♗d7 12 0-0 (12 ♕xb7?? ♖b8 13 ♕c7 ♕a6! 14 0-0 ♖b6 15 ♕d6 ♘f5 16 ♕c5 ♖b5) 12...0-0-0 13 ♘g5 ♖df8 14 f4 f6 15 ♘f3 fxe5 16 fxe5 h6 with good attacking chances since Black's king is secure;

(b) 8 ♖b1 ♕a5 (the alternative 8...♕c7 is also a natural continuation) 9 ♖b5 is supposed to be good, but after 9...♕c7! (the right square for the queen anyway) 10 ♖xc5? (10 ♗d3?! cxd4 11 cxd4 ♘xd4!) 10...a6 and ...b6 follows. B.Socko-Bartel, Warsaw 2001 went 9 ♕d2 c4 (9...0-0 keeps other options open) 10 h4, and Black should just play the natural 10...0-0 11 h5 h6 12 ♗e2 f6 13 exf6 ♖xf6=;

(c) 8 dxc5 leaves the valuable e-pawn up for grabs: 8...♕a5 (8...♘g6!? 9 ♗b5 ♕a5 10 ♗xc6+ bxc6 11 ♕d4 ♗a6 unclear) 9 ♗d2 ♘g6 10 c4 ♕xc5 11 cxd5 exd5 12 ♗e3 ♕a5+ 13 ♗d2 ♕c7∓.

11.11 8 ♗d3

This formerly rare move is being looked at more seriously these days. It can transpose to various other lines, but in this section we look at independent ideas involving the gain of tempo via ...c4.

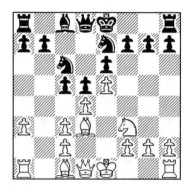

8...♕a5

Also fine is 8...c4 9 ♗f1 (rerouting the bishop rather than playing ♗e2/0-0/♖e1/♗f1 and then g3) 9...♕a5 (or 9...0-0 10 g3 h6 11 ♗g2 f6 12 exf6 ♖xf6=) 10 ♕d2 ♗d7 11 g3 h6 12 ♗h3 0-0-0 13 0-0 Rizsonkov-Papp, Szeged 1998; and 13...♖df8 intending ...f6 or ...f5 with ...g5 was one idea; but compare the main line.

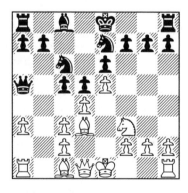

9 ♗d2

(a) 9 0-0 is generally not played because it allows the draw after 9...c4 10 ♗d3 ♕xc3 11 ♗d2 ♕b2 12 ♖b1 ♕xa3 13 ♖a1 etc. But Korchnoi and others have played for the win as Black by 9...c4 10 ♗e2 ♗d7!? (10...♕a4!? is another way to go, e.g., 11 ♘g5 h6 12 ♘h3 ♗d7 13 f4!? 0-0-0 14 ♗f3 f6 15 ♕e2 N.Rogers-Edelman,

USA 1987, and now 15...fxe5 16 fxe5 g5 looks right, intending either ...♗e8-g6 or ...♖df8 and ...♘f5) 11 a4 ♘c8 (Rogers and Edelman had another game with 11...f6 12 ♕d2 fxe5 13 ♘xe5 ♘xe5 14 dxe5 0-0 15 ♗a3 ♖f7=) 12 ♕d2 ♘b6 13 ♕g5 (or perhaps 13 ♕f4!? ♕xc3, e.g., 14 ♖a3 ♕xc2!? 15 ♗d1 ♕f5 16 ♕d2 f6 17 ♗c2 ♕h5 18 exf6 gxf6 19 a5 ♘c8 20 ♕f4 ♘8e7 21 ♕xf6 ♖f8 22 ♕g7 0-0-0 23 ♕xh7 ♕xh7 24 ♗xh7 ♖h8 25 ♗c2 ♖dg8 is extremely complicated, probably dynamically equal) 13...♖g8 14 ♖a3 ♘xa4 (14...h6 15 ♕h5 ♘xa4 16 g3 b5 17 ♗d2 ♕d8 18 ♖b1 ♕e7 19 ♖aa1 a6 20 ♘h4= Van der Sterren-Korchnoi, Wijk aan Zee 1978, assessed as equal by Short) 15 ♗d2 b5 16 ♖fa1 ♕d8 17 ♕h5 h6 18 ♘h4 ♕e7∓ Lovholt-Hoidahl, corr 2000;

(b) 9 ♕d2 is tame: 9...c4 10 ♗e2 ♕a4 (10...0-0 11 0-0 f6 12 exf6 ♖xf6 is safe and solid) 11 h4 (an instructive manoeuvre occurred in Posohov-Kurochkin, Kharkov 2002: 11 0-0 ♗d7 12 ♘e1 0-0-0 13 f4 f6 14 ♗g4!? f5 15 ♗d1 ♖dg8 16 ♔h1 h6 17 ♘f3 ♘d8! 18 ♖b1 ♘f7 19 ♘g1 g6 20 ♗e2 ♖g7 and Black followed with ...♖hg8 and ...g5 with strong pressure) 11...♗d7 12 h5 h6 13 ♘h4 ♘f5!? 14 ♘xf5 exf5 15 ♖g1?! ♘e7 16 g4 fxg4 17 ♗xg4 ♗xg4 18 ♖xg4 ♘f5 19 ♕e2 ♕d7 20 ♖f4 ♕e6 21 ♕f3 g6∓ as in Smyslov-Botvinnik, USSR Ch 1940.

9...c4 10 ♗f1

The slow 10 ♗e2 hasn't achieved much: 10...♗d7 (10...0-0!? with the idea ...f6 is also played) and:

(a) 11 0-0 f6 (11...0-0-0 12 ♘g5 ♖df8 is complex but also satisfactory, e.g., 13 f4 f5 14 exf6 gxf6 15 ♘h3 ♘f5 16 ♗g4 ♘ce7= Ljubisavljevic-Ugrinovic, Italy 1970; but Black also had 16...♘d6 17 ♘f2 f5! 18 ♗h3 ♘e4∓) 12

♖e1 (12 exf6 gxf6 13 ♘h4 0-0-0=)
12...fxe5 13 dxe5 (13 ♘xe5 ♘xe5 14
dxe5 0-0=) 13...0-0-0 (13...0-0 14 ♗f1
♖f5 15 g3 ♖af8 16 ♖e3 ♖5f7 17 ♗g2
♕c7 De Firmian-Gulko, Malmo 2001)
14 ♘d4!? ♘xe5 15 f4 ♘5c6 16 ♗g4
♘xd4 17 cxd4 Fillion-Rozentalis,
Quebec 2001; and best was 17...c3
intending ...♘f5;
  (b) 11 ♘g5 f5!? (11..h6 12 ♘h3 0-0
13 ♘f4 f6=) 12 exf6 gxf6 13 ♗h5+
♘g6 with the idea 14 ♘xh7?! ♔f7 15
♕g4 ♖ag8!∓.

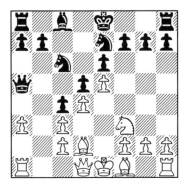

10...♗d7
  10...0-0 11 g3 f6 12 ♗h3 (12 exf6
♖xf6 13 ♗g2 ♗d7 14 0-0 ♖af8)
12...fxe5 13 ♘xe5 ♘xe5 14 dxe5 Ri-
cardi-J.Watson, Ubeda 1999, and now
14...♘f5!? 15 0-0 ♕c5 was best, e.g.,
16 ♗xf5 ♖xf5 17 ♗e3 ♕a5 18 ♗d4
♗d7∓.
11 g3 f6
  Or 11...f5= or 11...0-0-0, e.g., 12
♗h3 (12 ♘g5 ♖df8 13 ♗h3 h6 14 ♘f3
f6) 12...f5 13 exf6 gxf6 14 0-0 e5 15
♗xd7+ ♖xd7 16 ♘h4!? ♘g6! 17 ♘f5
h5 and at any rate Black chances are
not inferior.
  After 11...f6, G.Garcia-J.Watson,
Philadelphia 1998 continued 12
♗h3!? (simpler was 12 exf6 gxf6 13
♗g2 0-0-0 14 0-0 ♘f5=) 12...0-0-0 (or
12...fxe5 13 dxe5 0-0=) 13 0-0 ♘g6 14

exf6 gxf6 15 ♕e2 ♔b8 16 ♖fb1 ♖de8
17 ♗g2 ♕a4 (It was time for 17...e5∓)
18 ♖a2 ♖e7 19 ♖ab2 ♗e8=.

11.12 8 ♗e2

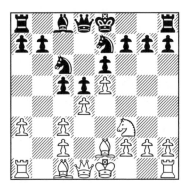

  This modest move, less dynamic
and threatening than 8 h4 or systems
with ♗d3, is still an important one
that reflects the desire to prop up the
centre quickly via 0-0 and moves like
♖e1.
8...♕a5
  Black tries to tie White to defence
of c3, and can also prepare the block-
ading move ...♕a4 in some situations.
This move order has always been
considered a little odd because White
doesn't have to defend the pawn on c3
immediately and apparently gets
more leeway to develop. One can also
argue that Black's deployment is less
effective when White hasn't yet committed to a4. But Black gains new
possibilities of blockade and White
often plays a4 at some point anyway.
  It's a little surprising that so few
players have made the simple developing move 8...0-0!? when White has
played the relatively passive ♗e2 and
not the attacking ♗d3. This directly
supports Black's standard idea of
playing ...f6. It's true that this forfeits
the option of ...0-0-0 and can expose

Black to an early kingside attack, but perhaps that attack is no worse than after 7 ♕g4 0-0? Just for fun, and to get used to the themes, here are a couple of ideas:

(a) 9 ♗d3 threatening ♗xh7+ is the move given by what little theory there is (e.g., Minev), although it does waste time, e.g., 9...f6 10 exf6 (10 ♗f4? fxe5 11 ♗xe5 ♘xe5 12 ♘xe5? ♕a5∓ with the idea 13 ♕d2 cxd4 14 cxd4 ♕xd2+ 15 ♔xd2 ♖xf2+) 10...♖xf6 11 ♗g5 ♖f7 12 0-0 (12 dxc5 e5) 12...c4 13 ♗e2 h6! (13...♕d6!?) 14 ♗h4 (14 ♗e3 ♕c7 15 ♕d2 ♗d7) 14...♕a5 15 ♕d2 ♗d7 16 ♖fe1 ♘f5;

(b) 9 0-0! f6!? (probably better is 9...♕a5 with a normal position, but also possible is 9...h6!? 10 ♖e1 f6 11 exf6 ♖xf6) 10 exf6 ♖xf6 11 ♗g5 ♖f7 12 ♖e1 ♕d6 13 ♕d2 ♗d7, probably ±. Presumably White has a move order that leads to advantage in these lines, but his edge would be a small one and can well be compared to the play that follows.

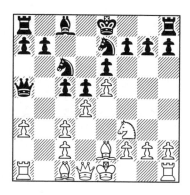

9 0-0!
The reason for the decline in the ...♘bc6/...♕a5 move order. White can also defend the pawn by:
(a) 9 ♕d2. This is usually played to prepare a4 and ♗a3, but here Black hasn't committed to ...♗d7 (see 11.3),

so a good answer is 9...b6! with the idea ...♗a6, e.g., 10 dxc5 (10 a4 ♗a6 11 ♗xa6 ♕xa6 12 dxc5 ♘g6!? 13 cxb6 axb6 14 ♕e3 0-0 with great pressure) 10...bxc5 11 c4 (11 0-0 ♗a6 12 c4 0-0) 11...♕xd2+ (11...♕a4) 12 ♗xd2 ♘g6 13 cxd5 exd5 14 c3! (14 ♗b5 ♗d7 15 ♗xc6 ♗xc6∓) 14...c4!? (14...♘gxe5 15 ♘xe5 ♘xe5 16 ♗e3) 15 ♗e3 0-0 16 ♖d1 ♗e6∓;

(b) 9 ♗d2 0-0 (two other moves of interest are 9...h6!? and 9...♕a4, the latter of which answers both 10 ♖b1 and 10 ♕b1 by 10...c4, and if 10 0-0, Black contests the light squares with 10...b6; lastly, the older 9...♗d7 10 0-0 c4 with ideas of ...0-0-0 and ...f6 is still respectable, but requires loads of study)

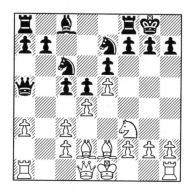

This position arises often and bears some analysis:
(b1) 10 c4 ♕c7 weakens White's centre, e.g., 11 cxd5 exd5 12 c3?! ♗g4 13 ♗e3 ♕a5 14 ♕d2 ♘f5;
(b2) One of the problems with an early ...0-0 tends to be 10 ♗d3 (threatening ♗xh7+), but here Black can defend by 10...♘g6 (or 10...h6 intending 11 0-0 c4 12 ♗e2 f6) 11 ♘g5 (11 c4? ♕c7; 11 0-0 c4 12 ♗e2 f6) 11...h6 12 ♘h3 c4 13 ♗e2 f6 14 ♗h5 ♘ge7 15 exf6 ♖xf6 with active pieces; ...♗d7-e8 is a good follow-up;

(b3) 10 0-0! c4!? (10...h6 11 c4 ♕c7 12 cxd5 exd5 13 dxc5 is better for White than in the last two examples, but Black should be able to defend after 13...♘xe5 14 ♘xe5 ♕xe5 15 ♖e1 ♕c7 16 ♗d3 ♗e6‡) and the play can be very instructive: 11 ♘g5 (11 a4 f6 12 exf6 ♖xf6 13 ♗g5 ♖f8 14 ♕d2 ♘f5= intending 15 ♖fe1?! ♘d6! and ...♘e4) 11...h6 12 ♘h3 f6 13 exf6 (13 f4 ♗d7 planning ...♗e8-g6 at some point, or just 13...fxe5 14 fxe5 ♖xf1+ 15 ♗xf1 ♗d7= and ...♖f8) 13...♖xf6 14 f4 (14 ♕e1 e5 15 dxe5 ♘xe5 16 ♘f4 ♗f5‡; 14 ♘f4 can be answered by 14...♗d7=, but more interesting is 14...e5!? 15 dxe5 ♘xe5 16 ♗e3 ♗d7 17 ♕d2 ♖af8 when neither side has a clear plan) 14...♗d7 15 ♗g4 ♖af8 16 ♕e2 ♘f5 (equal, but not necessarily best; 16...♘c8!? 17 ♘f2 ♘d6 is one idea, but most attractive is 16...♘d8!?, a multipurpose move that defends b7 and e6 and frees the bishop to go to a4 or to the kingside, e.g., 17 a4 ♗e8 18 ♖fb1 ♗g6 19 ♖b5 ♕a6) 17 ♘f2 (17 ♗xf5? exf5 and Black takes the e-file) 17...♕a4 (or 17...♗e8 18 ♗f3 ♘h4) 18 ♖fc1 ♘d6 19 ♗h5?! ♔h7 and White is out of effective ideas, since 20 ♘g4 is answered by ...♖f5 and 20 g4?? by 20...g6.

9...b6

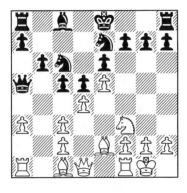

A move that has barely been tried or investigated, despite this position having arisen time and again. I think that it is logical to contest the light squares. Normally 9...♗d7 or 9...c4 are played. Of course, Black cannot grab the pawn in view of 9...♕xc3?? 10 ♗d2 ♕b2 11 ♖b1 ♕xa3 12 ♖b3 ♕a2 13 ♕c1 and ♖a3.

10 a4

White tries to give c4 added effect. With the queen out on a5, Black's game hangs on one tempo, but I don't think there's any real danger:

(a) 10 ♗d2 ♗a6 11 c4 (11 a4 ♗xe2 12 ♕xe2 0-0) 11...♕a4 12 cxd5 exd5! (12...♗xe2 13 ♕xe2 exd5 14 dxc5 bxc5 15 c4 ♕xc4 16 ♕xc4 dxc4 17 ♖fc1 ♖d8 is close to equality) 13 dxc5 bxc5 14 c4 (14 ♗xa6 ♕xa6 15 ♖e1 0-0=) 14...♕xd1 15 ♖fxd1 0-0 16 ♗d3 ♖ab8=;

(b) 10 c4 cxd4 (10...dxc4!? 11 dxc5 ♗a6! 12 cxb6 axb6 also looks good, but the d-pawn capture is more forcing) 11 cxd5 (11 ♘xd4 ♘xd4 12 ♕xd4 ♗a6 13 ♕g4 ♕c3! 14 ♗e3 0-0‡) 11...♕xd5 12 ♗b2 ♗b7 13 ♗xd4 ♖d8 (13...♘xd4 14 ♕xd4 ♕xd4 15 ♘xd4 0-0‡) 14 ♗b2 ♕c5 15 ♗d3 0-0‡.

10...♗a6 11 ♗xa6

11 ♗d2 ♗xe2 12 ♕xe2 0-0 13 c4?! ♕a6‡.

11...♕xa6 12 dxc5 bxc5 13 ♗a3

This is Babula-Trichkov, Czechoslovakia 1992. Black should retain a small advantage after 13...♕a5, e.g., 14 c4 ♖d8 15 cxd5 ♘xd5 (16 ♕e1 ♕xe1 17 ♖fxe1 ♘db4!). More direct if riskier would be 13...♕xa4!? 14 ♗xc5 ♕c4 15 ♗d4?! (better 15 ♗xe7! when 15...♔xe7!? 16 ♕d3! ♕xd3 17 cxd3 ♖hb8 gives only a tiny advantage at best, while 15...♘xe7 16 ♕d3 ♕c5!? 17 c4! equalises) 15...0-0 16 ♘d2!? (16 ♕d3? ♘xd4 17 cxd4 ♖fc8‡) 16...♕b5

17 ♖b1 (17 ♕g4 ♕b2! hits c2 and prepares ...♘f5) 17...♕a6 18 ♘b3 (18 ♕g4 ♕a4! 19 ♘b3 ♘xe5 20 ♕g3 ♘5g6) 18...♖fc8∓ with the idea ...♘f5 and meeting 19 ♘c5? by 19...♕c4! (20 ♕d3 ♘xe5).

Play in the manner of 9...b6 is experimental and will produce original situations with creative possibilities.

11.2 7 a4

This used to be the main line of the Positional Winawer, both preparing ♗a3 and preventing a blockade by either ...♗d7-a4 or ...♕a5-a4. It also provides a potential response to ...b6 systems, namely a5.

7...♕a5

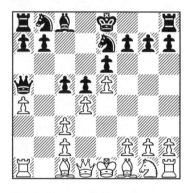

Black plays the most forcing move in order to make White commit either the queen or bishop to d2. Thus:

11.21 8 ♕d2
11.22 8 ♗d2

11.21 8 ♕d2

White plans to put his bishop on a3. This allows an endgame after ...cxd4/cxd4, when White hopes that possession of the two bishops will secure him an advantage. Practice has not confirmed this.

8...♘bc6

Another solid solution is 8...b6!? preparing ...♗a6, and:

(a) 9 ♖b1 ♗a6 10 ♗b5+ ♗xb5 11 axb5 a6 12 bxa6 ♘bc6 13 ♘e2 ♕xa6 14 0-0 0-0∓ Macieja-Gdanski, Poland 1992;

(b) 9 ♗a3 ♕xa4!? (playable, but risky; Black can play 9...♗a6! 10 ♗b4 cxb4 11 cxb4, when the queen is trapped but 11...♗xf1 12 bxa5 ♗xg2 13 f3 ♗xh1 14 axb6 axb6 15 ♔f2 ♘bc6 16 ♘e2 ♗xf3 17 ♔xf3 0-0∓ follows; material is even but Black is better coordinated and ...f6 is a potential move) 10 ♘f3 ♕c6 11 ♕g5 ♘g6 12 dxc5 bxc5 13 h4 h6 14 ♕g3 0-0 15 ♗d3 ♗a6!∓ (still with danger), I.Almasi-Blauert, Budapest 1993;

(c) 9 ♗b5+ ♗d7 10 ♗d3 ♘bc6 (here 10...♗xa4!? is a suggestion of Pedersen) 11 ♘f3 f6 (11...0-0 12 0-0 f6 13 exf6 ♖xf6=) 12 0-0? (12 exf6 gxf6 13 0-0 c4 14 ♗e2 0-0-0=) 12...fxe5 13 dxe5 0-0∓ Borkowski-Drasko, Polanica Zdroj 1988;

(d) 9 ♘f3 ♗a6 10 ♗d3 (10 ♗xa6 ♕xa6 11 ♕e2 ♕xe2+ 12 ♔xe2 ♘d7 13 a5 b5!? 14 ♗a3 a6∓ Pelitov-Uhlmann, Szombathely 1966) 10...♗xd3 11 cxd3 ♘bc6 (11...♘d7 12 0-0 ♖c8) 12 dxc5 bxc5 13 0-0 0-0 14 ♗a3 ♖fb8= Wiesmann-Holzke, Bundesliga 1990.

9 ♘f3 f6!?

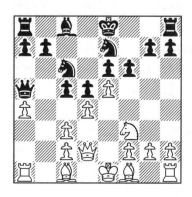

Korchnoi's move, given for some variety. I have covered the main move 9...♗d7 in some detail in previous editions and can only assure the reader that nothing has happened to change its assessment of full equality.

10 ♗d3?

This looks aggressive but doesn't work out. Black holds his own versus others:

(a) 10 ♗a3 fxe5 and:

(a1) 11 dxe5? ♕xa4! 12 ♗e2 b6 13 c4 ♘d8!? (13...♘a5 also opens a retreat for the queen while controlling c4, so 14 cxd5 exd5 15 0-0 ♘c4! becomes possible) 14 0-0?! (14 cxd5 exd5 15 c4∓) 14...♕d7 15 ♘g5 h6 16 ♘h3 0-0 17 ♖fd1 ♘dc6 18 ♗b2 ♗b7∓ Kuijpers-Korchnoi, Wijk aan Zee 1971;

(a2) 11 ♗xc5!? e4 12 ♘g1 (useless is 12 ♗b4 ♕c7 13 ♘g1 0-0! 14 f3 e5 15 fxe4 ♘xb4 16 cxb4 dxe4 17 ♘e2 ♘d5!∓)

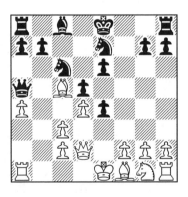

White has actually played this repeatedly, which says something about the favourable status of 9...f6! The first player exerts some dark square pressure but he is behind in development and outmanned in the centre: 12...♕c7 (or 12...0-0 13 ♗b5 ♖f7 14 ♘e2 a6 15 ♗xc6 ♘xc6 16 ♘g3 ♗d7 17 ♕e3 ♕c7∓ Zedtler-Schwertel, email 1998) 13 ♗e2 b6 14 ♗a3 0-0 15 c4 ♖f6

16 ♖b1 ♘f5 17 c3 ♘a5! 18 c5 ♗d7∓ 19 ♘h3 e3! 20 fxe3 ♘g3! 21 hxg3 ♕xg3+ 22 ♔d1 ♕xg2 23 ♕e1 ♗xa4+ 24 ♔c1 Brunner-Arnason, Gausdal 1988; here Black missed 24...♕e4! when White can resign;

(b) 10 exf6 gxf6 and:

(b1) 11 ♗b5 ♗d7 12 ♗a3 (12 0-0 cxd4 13 ♘xd4!? e5 14 ♘b3 ♕c7∓ Zude-Mueller, Germany 1989) 12...cxd4 13 cxd4 ♖g8 14 ♖g1!? ♕xd2+ 15 ♔xd2 ♘a5!? 16 ♗b4 ♘c4+ 17 ♗xc4 dxc4 18 ♗xe7 ♔xe7 19 ♔e3 ♗c6∓ with control of the light squares, Houtsonen-Eskola, Finland 1992;

(b2) 11 ♗a3 cxd4!? (11...c4) 12 cxd4 ♕xd2+ 13 ♔xd2

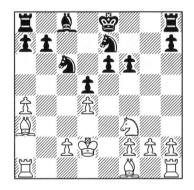

13...♘f5 ('=' – Uhlmann; another idea is 13...♗d7 14 ♗d3 ♔f7 15 ♗d6 ♘a5 16 ♖he1 ♖ac8=) 14 c3 ♖g8 15 g3 ♘a5 16 ♖b1 Pezdirc Praznik-Zelic, corr 1978; play on both sides has been logical, but now instead of 16...♗d7?, Black had 16...♗d7! 17 ♗d3 ♔f7! 18 ♖he1 ♖ae8 19 ♖b4 ♘d6 20 ♔c2 h6=;

(b3) 11 dxc5 e5 is a standard structure in these positions. The chances are equal, e.g., 12 c4! (12 ♗e2!? ♗e6 13 0-0 0-0-0 14 ♖e1 ♖hg8 15 ♔h1 ♕xc5 16 ♗f1 ♘f5 17 ♗a3 ♕a5 18 ♗b4 ♕c7∓ Schmittdiel-Karwatt, Wiesbaden 1988) 12...d4 13 ♖xa5 ♘xa5 14 ♗d2 ♘ec6 15 ♖b1 a6!? (15...♗f5! 16

♖b5 a6 17 ♖xa5 ♗xc2 is a remarkable position which seems in some sort of balance) 16 ♖b6 0-0 17 ♔d1 ♗g4 18 h3 ♗h5 19 g4 ♗g6= Kuijpers-Pytel, Wijk aan Zee 1974.

10...fxe5 11 dxe5 0-0

11...c4 12 ♗e2 ♘g6 13 0-0 0-0, and disaster followed 14 ♗a3? ♖f5 15 g4 ♖f4 16 h3 h6 17 ♔h1 ♖f7 18 ♗d1 ♘cxe5 19 ♘xe5 ♘xe5 20 f4 ♕xa4 0-1 C.Carlson-Fawbush, corr 1971.

12 0-0 ♖xf3!

These days this is almost a routine exchange sacrifice, although with the bishop and rook out of play and the queen over on the queenside, it still takes some nerve to play it!

13 gxf3 c4 14 ♗e2 ♘xe5

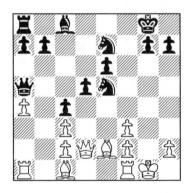

Black has a pawn for the exchange and White has six isolated pawns!

15 ♗a3

15 f4 ♘5g6 16 ♗h5 ♗d7!?, and a possible line is 17 ♗a3 ♕c7 18 ♗xe7 ♘xe7 19 ♗g4 ♖f8 20 ♖fe1 ♖f6∓, when White is at loss for a move.

After 15 ♗a3, Felgaer-Korchnoi, Bled 2002 continued 15...♘f5 16 f4 ♘g6 17 ♗g4 ♘gh4 18 ♗b4 ♕c7 19 a5 ♕f7 20 f3 ♗d7 21 ♖ae1 ♕g6 22 ♔h1 ♗c6 23 ♕f2 d4 24 ♗xf5 ♘xf5 25 cxd4 ♗d5 26 c3 ♕h5 27 ♖e5 ♕h6 28 ♖e4 ♕h3 29 ♖g1 b6 30 ♕g2 ♕h5 31 a6 ♖c8 32 ♗d6 g6 33 ♗e5 ♘h4 0-1.

11.22 8 ♗d2

White abandons the idea of ♗a3 (although ♗c1-a3 can occur later), but keeps the kingside dark squares covered and gives solid support to the weak c3 square.

8...♘bc6 9 ♘f3

(a) 9 ♕g4 compares poorly with the main 7 ♕g4 line because the move a4 is practically wasted; play might go 9...0-0 (a cute game went 9...♗d7 10 ♕xg7 0-0-0 11 ♕xf7? ♕b6! 12 ♗d3 ♖df8 13 ♕h5 c4 14 ♗f1 ♘xd4! 15 0-0-0 ♘xc2! Rebej-Spitzenberger, corr 1965, due to 16 ♔xc2 ♕b3+ 17 ♔c1 ♗xa4) 10 ♘f3 f6 (or 10...f5 11 ♕h5 ♕b6!? 12 dxc5 ♕c7∓) 11 exf6 ♖xf6 12 ♕h5 ♗d7 13 ♗d3 h6 14 0-0 c4 15 ♗e2 ♗e8 16 ♕h4 ♗g6∓;

(b) 9 ♘e2 ♕c7. Now that the bishop can't come to a3, this is an ideal spot for the queen. It also ties White to defence of d4. Myreng-Glueck, St Paul 1982 went 10 ♗f4 ♘g6 11 ♗g3 ♕a5 12 ♕d2 f6= (or 12...0-0! and ...f6).

9...♗d7

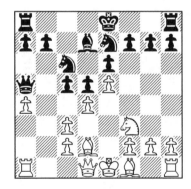

Here White normally plays:

11.221 10 ♗b5
11.222 10 ♗e2

None of the many other 10th moves is as critical:

(a) 10 ♘g5?! intends ♕h5, but abandons the centre: 10...h6 11 ♕h5 (11 ♘h3? ♕c7! hits d4: 12 ♗c1!? cxd4 13 cxd4 ♘b4! 14 c4 dxc4 15 ♗e2 ♘d3+! 16 ♗xd3 cxd3 17 ♕xd3 ♗c6∓ Milton-J.Watson, San Diego 1986; 12 ♕g4 ♘f5 13 ♗d3 cxd4 14 cxd4 ♘xe5!∓ – Suetin) 11...g6 12 ♕h3 cxd4 13 cxd4 ♕b6! 14 c3 ♕b2 15 ♖d1 ♘a5∓;

(b) 10 ♕b1 ♕c7 11 ♗d3 c4 12 ♗e2 f6 13 ♗f4?! ♘g6 14 ♗g3 fxe5 15 dxe5 ♕a5 16 0-0!? Schoneberg-Tischbierek, Leipzig 1986, and easiest was 16...b6!∓;

(c) 10 c4 ♕c7 11 cxd5 exd5 (11...♘xd5=) 12 dxc5?! (12 c3 0-0 intending ...cxd4 and ...♗g4) 12...0-0 13 ♗e2 ♘xe5 14 0-0 ♘xf3+ 15 ♗xf3 ♕xc5∓ Dubinin-Boleslavsky, USSR 1947;

(d) 10 h4 doesn't mix well with a4: 10...f6 (or 10...0-0-0! 11 h5 h6) 11 h5 fxe5 12 ♘xe5 (12 h6 gxh6 13 ♘xe5 ♘xe5 14 dxe5 0-0-0 15 ♖xh6 ♕c7 and ...♘f5) 12...♘xe5 13 dxe5 ♕c7 14 f4 0-0-0 15 ♕g4 h6!= Pirttimaki-Farago, Helsinki 1983;

(e) 10 ♖b1

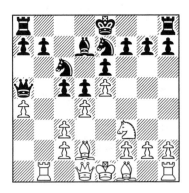

10...♕c7 (10...0-0-0!? 11 ♖b5 ♕xa4 with the idea 12 ♖xc5? b6 13 ♖b5 ♘xe5!; better is 12 ♕b1 ♘a5 13 ♖b2! ♕c6 14 ♖a2 ♕c7 Enders-Piersig, Germany 1985, and now 15 dxc5 is

best, but 15...♘g6 gives Black no problems, e.g., 16 c4!? ♘c6 17 ♕a1 d4!∓) 11 ♗e2 (11 ♗b5 is well met by 11...a6 intending 12 ♗e2 f6 or 12 ♗xc6 ♘xc6; compare 10 ♗b5) 11...f6 12 ♗f4?! ♘g6 13 ♗g3 fxe5 14 ♗b5? cxd4 15 cxd4 ♕a5+ 16 ♘d2 exd4 17 ♗d6 ♕d8 18 h4 ♕f6∓ Hirsig-Jurek, Bad Ragaz 1993;

(f) 10 g3 0-0-0 (safest looks 10...0-0 11 ♗h3?! [11 ♗g2 f6=] 11...f6 12 exf6 ♖xf6∓) 11 ♗h3 (11 ♗g2 f6 12 c4 ♕a6!? 13 cxd5 ♘xd5= with many options for both sides) 11...f5! 12 ♗g2 (12 exf6 gxf6 13 0-0 e5 14 ♗xd7+ ♖xd7 15 c4 ♕c7∓ Doda-Raicevic, Banovici 1979) 12...h6 13 h4 ♕c7 14 ♗c1 (14 0-0 ♘a5 15 dxc5 ♘c4 16 ♖e1∓) 14...cxd4 15 cxd4 ♘b4 16 ♔d2 ♗e8!? 17 ♗a3 ♘bc6 18 ♗d6 ♖xd6! 19 exd6 ♕xd6 20 ♔c1 (20 c3 f4 21 g4 h5 22 g5 ♗g6) 20...f4! with a strong attack, Kavalek-Hort, Montreal 1979;

(g) 10 ♗d3 is a tempo down on some 10 ♗e2 lines after 10...c4 11 ♗e2 f6 12 0-0 fxe5 13 ♘xe5 (13 dxe5 0-0! 14 ♖e1 ♘g6 15 ♗f1 ♖f5) 13...♘xe5 14 dxe5 0-0 15 f4 ♗e8 16 ♗g4 ♕b6+ 17 ♔h1 ♗g6 18 ♕b1 ♕c6! 19 ♕b5 ♕c8! 20 ♖a2 ♗e4∓ S.Nikolic-Ivkov, Sarajevo 1967.

11.221 10 ♗b5

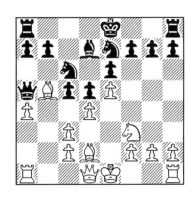

White tries to provoke ...a6, hoping that it will be a weakness.

10...a6

Anyway! I'm not really sure that any logical move isn't good here, for example, 10...c4 11 0-0 f6. But a particularly sound alternative is 10...♕c7 11 0-0 0-0

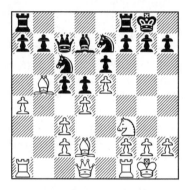

with these continuations:

(a) 12 ♗d3 f6 13 exf6 ♖xf6 14 ♗g5 (14 dxc5!? ♖af8 15 c4 ♖xf3! 16 gxf3 ♘e5 with plenty of compensation) 14...♖ff8 (14...♖f7! 15 ♖e1 c4 16 ♗f1 ♖af8) 15 ♖e1! c4 16 ♗f1 ♘g6 (16...♘f5!? would anticipate 17 ♘e5 ♘xe5 18 ♖xe5 ♘d6! intending ...♘f7 or ...♘e4) 17 g3 Roiz Baztan-Carrasco Martinez, Spain 1994; now 17...h6! 18 ♗c1 ♖f6=;

(b) 12 ♗c1 b6 13 ♗a3 ♘a5! 14 dxc5 (14 ♗xd7 ♕xd7 15 dxc5 ♖fc8! 16 cxb6 axb6 – Knaak) 14...♗xb5 15 cxb6 axb6 16 axb5 ♖fc8 17 ♗b4 ♘c4= Nunn-Yusupov, Belgrade 1991;

(c) 12 dxc5 ♘xe5 13 ♗f4 ♘xf3+ 14 ♕xf3 ♕c8 15 ♗d6 ♖e8 16 ♗d3 ♘f5 17 ♗xf5 ½-½ Zelcic-Psakhis, Bled 2002;

(d) 12 ♖e1, the most flexible move. Black has two good responses:

(d1) 12...b6 13 ♗d3 h6 14 ♕c1 c4 15 ♗f1 f6 16 g3 fxe5 17 ♘xe5 ♘xe5 18 ♖xe5 ♘c6 (or 18...♘g6 19 ♖e3!? e5∓ as in the game Hellsten-Wiedenkeller,

Borlange 1992) 19 ♖e1 e5 20 ♗g2 e4 21 ♕d1?! (21 ♗xh6! gxh6 22 ♕xh6 ♗f5 23 g4 ♗h7!? 24 ♕g5+ ♔h8 25 ♕xd5 ♖f4!? unclear) 21...♖ae8 22 f3 exf3 23 ♖xe8 ♖xe8 24 ♗xf3 ♕f7 25 ♗g2 ♕f2+ 26 ♔h1 ♗f7∓ and White's weak pawns hurt him in Kindermann-Zugzwang, Lippstadt 1998;

(d2) 12...h6 13 ♗f4 (13 ♗c1 a6 14 ♗xc6 ♗xc6 intending 15 ♗a3 ♗xa4 16 ♗xc5 ♗b5=) 13...♘g6 14 ♗g3 ♘ce7 15 ♗d3 c4 16 ♗xg6 (16 ♗e2 ♘f5 17 ♕d2 ♘xg3 18 hxg3 f6 19 exf6 ♖xf6 20 ♘h2! ♖af8 21 f4 ♘e7 22 ♘g4 ♖f5= Nunn-Yusupov, Belgrade 1991) 16...fxg6!∓ 17 h4 ♖f7 18 ♕b1 ♔h7 19 ♕b4 ♘f5 20 ♗h2 ♖af8∓ Byrne-Vaganian, Moscow 1975.

11 ♗xc6

Probably best, in view of:

(a) 11 ♗e2 (extremely popular, on the theory that ...a6 would be a weakness by comparison with 10 ♗e2, but it hasn't proven so) 11...f6 12 c4 ♕c7 13 cxd5 (13 exf6 gxf6 14 c3 Morris-Klein, New York 1991; 14...dxc4 15 ♗xc4 cxd4 16 cxd4 ♘xd4!?) 13...♘xd5 14 c4 ♘de7 (14...♘db4!?) 15 exf6 gxf6

16 dxc5 (16 d5!? exd5 17 cxd5 ♘xd5 18 ♕b3 ♗e6∓ 19 0-0 ♕g7?! 20 ♗c4 0-0-0 21 ♖fe1 ♖hg8 22 g3 ♕f7 unclear, Chandler-Kummerow, Solingen

2000; Black can probably improve) 16...0-0-0 17 ♗c3 e5 18 ♕d6 ♗f5!? (18...♘f5 looks more accurate: 19 ♕xc7+ ♔xc7 with compensation, Tischbierek-Poldauf, Germany 1991; compare 10 ♗e2) 19 ♕xc7+ (19 ♕xf6!? ♖hf8 20 ♕h6 ♘g6 – Pelletier) 19...♔xc7 20 ♖c1 (20 0-0 ♗d3 – Pelletier) 20...♘g6!? 21 g3 ♘f8± intending ...♘e6xc5, Short-Pelletier, Leon 2001;

(b) 11 ♗d3 c4 12 ♗e2 f6 13 0-0?! (13 exf6 gxf6 14 0-0 e5=) Dineley-Levitt, Swansea 1995, and instead of 13...♕c7!?, the standard 13...fxe5! was good: 14 ♘xe5 ♘xe5 15 dxe5 0-0 16 ♕b1! ♕c7 17 f4 ♘f5∓;

(c) 11 c4!? ♕c7 12 cxd5 ♘xd5 (12...axb5? 13 d6!) 13 ♗xc6 ♕xc6 (13...♗xc6! with a healthy advantage, e.g., 14 0-0 ♖d8!? 15 c3 ♘e7 16 ♗e3 0-0∓) 14 0-0 cxd4 (14...0-0 looks a little better) 15 ♘xd4 ♕c7= Casella-Shulman, Connecticut 2002.

11...♘xc6
Here both recaptures look fine as long as Black is careful; thus 11...♗xc6 and:

(a) 12 ♘g5 h6 (12...0-0 13 ♕h5 h6) 13 ♕h5 g6 14 ♕h3 ♕c7 15 0-0? cxd4 16 cxd4 ♗xa4∓ Berzinsh-Kahn, Berlin 1994;

(b) 12 c4?! ♕c7 13 cxd5 ♗xd5

(13...♘xd5 is also good) 14 0-0 ♖d8∓ C.Lopez-Celis, Buenos Aires 1996 (or 14...cxd4 15 ♗b4 ♘f5∓);

(c) 12 0-0 h6 (12...♕c7!? 13 dxc5 ♕a5! is a cute idea that seems to equalise immediately) 13 dxc5 (13 ♕c1 c4 14 ♕a3 ♕c7 15 ♖fe1 0-0-0!? 16 h4 ♖dg8 17 a5 ♕d8 18 ♕c1!? ♘f5= Suetin-Misiano, Biel 1997; 13 ♕e1 ♕c7 14 dxc5 ♕d7! 15 ♘d4 ♗xa4 16 f4 ♗c6!? 17 ♕g3 ♘f5! 18 ♕h3 g6 19 g4 ½-½ Gashimov-Guseinov, Baku 2000) 13...♕xc5 14 ♘d4 0-0 15 ♕g4 ♔h7 16 ♖fe1 ♗d7 17 ♖ab1 ♕c7 18 ♖e3 Kovalov-Tischbierek, Bundesliga 1991, and apart from 18...♘f5 19 ♘xf5 exf5, which was drawish, Black might try 18...♘g6 19 ♘f3 (19 f4 ♗xa4) 19...f6 20 exf6 ♖xf6∓.

12 0-0
12 ♘g5?! h6 13 ♕h5 0-0!? (13...♖f8 14 ♘f3 0-0-0 15 0-0 c4 16 ♖a2 Sherzer-Filatov, Philadelphia 1993; and now 16...♘e7!=, tying White to the a-pawn) 14 ♘f3! (14 ♘h3 ♗e8 15 ♕g4 f5!) 14...♗e8 15 ♕g4 f5 16 exf6 ♖xf6 17 c4 ♕b6 18 cxd5 exd5 19 dxc5 ♕xc5∓.

12...0-0
12...♕c7 13 ♖e1 ♘a5 14 dxc5 ♘c4 equalised in El Taher-Shulman, Pardubice 1999.

13 ♖e1 ♕c7 14 dxc5
Black answers just about any move with ...♘a5.

14...♘a5 15 ♗e3
15 ♘d4 ♘c4!? (this is natural, but 15...♕xc5 might cover the kingside better, e.g., 16 ♕g4?! f5) 16 ♗g5! ♖ae8? (16...♕xc5 17 ♕g4 ♔h8 with an unclear White attack; Black threatens ...♘xe5!) 17 ♘b3! ♘xe5 18 ♗f4 f6 19 ♕d4±, winning on the dark squares, Wedberg-Spielmann, Stockholm 2002.

After 15 ♗e3, Cabrilo-Shulman,

Belgrade 1998 went 15...♘c4 16 ♕b1!? ♖ab8?! (16...♘xe3! 17 ♖xe3 ♖ab8 would have quashed worries on the kingside) 17 ♗d4 b6 18 cxb6 ♘xb6 19 ♕d1 ♘xa4 20 ♖e3 ♕b7 21 ♘d2 h6 ½-½. Again White has some real attacking chances to compensate for his weaknesses, and 22 c4 is also an option.

11.222 10 ♗e2

This is still the most challenging move.

10...f6

A central attack that has discouraged White from 10 ♗e2, and yet many things remain unclear. In my opinion, a related move order that has been tried recently is very significant: 10...0-0-0! ('!' for reasons given below) 11 0-0 f6, to reduce White's options in the main lines. For example, 11 c4 ♕c7 12 cxd5 ♘xd5 13 c4 ♘de7 transposes to a main line but avoids ideas like dxc5 and a5 (14 dxc5? at once allows 14...♘xe5).

An independent test of this move order would be 10...0-0-0 11 ♘g5, e.g., 11...♖df8 12 ♗h5 (12 f4 f6 13 ♘f3 fxe5 14 fxe5 h6 15 0-0 g5 with good counterplay) 12...g6 (12...♗e8!? also looks okay) 13 ♗g4?! h5! 14 ♗e2 (14 ♗h3 ♕b6! with the idea 15 ♗e3 ♕b2 or 15

dxc5 ♕xc5∓) 14...♕c7 15 ♗c1 ♘f5 16 ♗a3 cxd4! 17 ♗xf8 ♖xf8 18 cxd4 ♘fxd4∓.

11 c4

This is aggressive but loosening. Here are typical examples of other moves:

(a) 11 0-0 c4 (or 11...0-0-0, e.g., 12 ♕c1!? ♕c7 13 ♕a3 c4 14 ♖fe1 ♘g6 15 exf6 gxf6 16 ♗h6 ♖hg8 17 ♕c1 e5∓ intending ...♗f5-e4 Marfia-J.Watson, Columbus 1977) 12 ♖e1 fxe5 13 dxe5 0-0 14 ♗f1 ♖f5! 15 g3 ♖af8∓ Pein-Plaskett, British Ch 1987;

(b) 11 exf6 gxf6 and 12 c4 will transpose. Others:

(b1) 12 0-0 c4 (a creative strategic battle followed 12...0-0-0 13 ♕c1 c4 14 ♖e1 ♖de8!? [14...e5] 15 ♗f1 ♘d8 16 ♗f4 ♘f5 17 ♖b1 ♘f7! 18 ♖b4 ♘7d6 19 g3 Ricardi-Dominguez Gonzalez, Malaga 1999; then a good move was 19...h5!= and the knights coordinate to defend and attack) 13 ♘h4 0-0-0 (a typical pawn sacrifice is 13...♘g6!? 14 ♗h5 0-0-0 15 ♗xg6 hxg6 16 ♘xg6 ♖hg8 17 ♘f4 e5 18 ♘e2 ♖g7 19 ♘g3 ♖h8 with attack) 14 g3 (14 ♗h5 ♘g6!) 14...e5 (14...♘g6!∓) 15 f4 exd4 16 cxd4 ♕c7 17 c3 ♘f5 18 ♘g2 ♘a5 19 ♗f3 ♘b3 20 ♖a2 ♕a5= Spassky-Shaked, Hoogeveen 1998;

(b2) 12 ♘h4!? 0-0-0 13 ♗h5 ♕c7! 14 ♗e3?! ♘g6! 15 ♗xg6 hxg6 16 ♘xg6 ♖xh2 17 ♖g1 ♖h7∓ Gold-J.Watson, New York 1978;

(c) 11 ♖b1!? is Wedberg's active move, important to know but no longer feared: 11...♕c7! (safest) 12 ♗f4 (12 exf6 gxf6 13 dxc5 e5 with typical central play: 14 c4 ♗e6 15 cxd5 ♗xd5 16 0-0 0-0-0 17 ♕c1 ♖hg8 18 g3 ♘f5 19 c3 Poretti-Weber, email 2000; and by 19...♗e4!? 20 ♖b5 ♗d3! 21 ♗xd3 ♖xd3 the light squares and White's shattered pawns must give

Black at least a satisfactory game)
12...♘g6 13 ♗g3 fxe5

(c1) 14 ♗b5 cxd4 15 cxd4 ♕a5+ 16
♔f1 0-0 17 ♗xc6 ♗xc6 18 ♘g5!? (18
♘xe5 ♘xe5 19 ♗xe5 ♕xa4) 18...h6 19
♘xe6 ♖f6 20 ♘c5 exd4 21 ♕xd4 b6–+
and ...♕xa4. Weinzettl-Dueckstein,
Nendeln 1986;
(c2) 14 0-0 cxd4 (14...♕c8!? seems
good enough: 15 dxe5 0-0 and 16 c4
♘ce7! 17 ♕d2 ♗c6∓ Maki-Ogaard,
Oslo 1983 or 16 ♕d2 ♘ce7∓) 15 cxd4
0-0 16 ♗b5 (16 dxe5 ♘f4 17 c4!? d4!∓)
16...♘f4 (a safe alternative is 16...♕c8
17 dxe5 ♘ce7) 17 ♗xc6 (17 ♘xe5
♘xe5 18 dxe5 ♗xb5 19 ♖xb5 Karell-
D.Myers, corr 1990; 19...♖f7! – Myers)
17...♗xc6 18 ♘xe5 ♗xa4 19 ♖b4 (a
much-tested position: 19 ♕g4 h5!
wins; 19 ♕d2 ♘h5 is strong; 19 ♖b2
♖ac8!∓ with the idea 20 ♕d2 ♕c3)
19...♕xc2! (This seems clearer than
19...♗c6 20 ♘d3 ♕a5 21 ♗xf4 ♖xf4
22 ♘xf4 ♕xb4 23 ♘xe6 ♖e8∓ Ivanov-
Hanauer, corr 1996) 20 ♖xa4 (20 ♕g4
h5) 20...♘e2+ 21 ♔h1 ♕xd1 22 ♖xd1
♘c3∓ 23 ♖da1 ♘xa4 24 ♖xa4 ♖fc8 25
h3 a5 26 ♘d7 b5 27 ♖a1 ♖c2 28 ♘c5
a4–+ Bickel-Hund, corr 1983.
Notice that in all of these lines
Black plays ...0-0-0, indicating that
the order 10...0-0-0 (instead of 10...f6)
probably won't create insoluble prob-

lems in these situations.
11...♕c7 12 exf6
12 cxd5 ♘xd5 13 c4 is more accurate, preventing ...♘f4.
12...gxf6 13 cxd5
13 ♗c3 0-0-0! 14 dxc5 d4! and 15
♗xd4 ♗e8 or 15 ♘xd4 ♗e8∓.
13...♘xd5

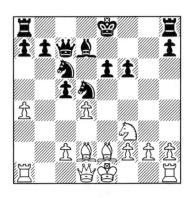

14 c4
(a) 14 dxc5 is perhaps the best:
14...0-0-0 (14...♘f4?! 15 0-0 ♘xe2+ 16
♕xe2 e5 17 a5! ♗g4 18 ♗c3±; 14...e5
15 a5 a6 16 c4 ♘de7 17 ♕b1!? 0-0-0
18 0-0 ♗g4 19 ♖d1 ♗xf3 20 ♗xf3 ♘d4
21 ♖a3±) 15 a5! (15 0-0 e5 16 c4
♘db4! 17 ♗xb4 ♘xb4 18 ♕d6 ♖hf8 19
♕xc7+ ♔xc7 20 ♖fd1 ♘a6∓ McCrory-
J.Watson, Denver 1976) 15...a6!?
(15...♗e8!? 16 a6 ♘c3 17 axb7+ ♔b8
18 ♗xc3! ♖xd1+ 19 ♖xd1±) 16 c4 (or
16 0-0 e5 17 ♖b1 ♗g4 18 ♘h4)
16...♘de7 17 ♗c3 e5 18 0-0±. Black
has in fact done well from this kind of
position, and these lines are certainly
playable, but I don't trust them to
fully equalise. This might be a good
reason to play 10...0-0-0, which
avoids such play;
(b) 14 c3 0-0-0 15 0-0 ♖hg8 16 ♖e1
e5!? (or 16...♘f4 17 ♗xf4 ♕xf4∓
Mann-Flugge, corr 1983) 17 c4 (17
dxe5 ♗h3 unclear – Korchnoi)
17...♗h3! 18 ♗f1 ♘b6 (18...♘f4!? 19

♗xf4 exf4 20 d5 ♗g4! has occurred in two games and equalises) 19 d5 ♘xc4! 20 dxc6 ♕xc6 21 g3 ♗xf1 22 ♖xf1 e4∓ 23 ♕c2 (23 ♕b3?! ♕d5 24 ♖ac1 Spassky-Korchnoi, Belgrade 1977; 24...♘e5! 25 ♖xc5+ ♕xc5 26 ♖c1 ♕xc1+ 27 ♗xc1 ♘xf3+∓) 23...♕d5 24 ♗f4 exf3 25 ♖fc1? (25 ♖ac1 ♘e5=) 25...♘e5 26 ♕f5+ ♖d7 27 ♕xf6 ♘d3∓ Mazi-Farago, Bled 1992.

14...♘de7

Black can also play 14...♘db4 and 14...♘f4! (e.g., 15 ♗xf4 ♕xf4 16 d5 ♘b4! 17 dxe6 ♗xe6 18 0-0 ♗d7! 19 g3 ♕c7 20 ♕b3 0-0-0∓ Spraggett-J.Watson, Columbus 1977), but White can avoid both by the 12 cxd5 move order.

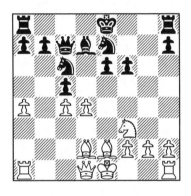

15 ♗c3

(a) 15 d5!? exd5 16 cxd5 ♘xd5 17 ♕c2 Ratsch-Raderer, corr 1982; 17...♘cb4!? 18 ♕e4+ ♔d8! 19 ♖d1 ♖e8 20 ♕c4 ♔c8 and White is a pawn down and tied up (21 0-0?? ♘b6);

(b) 15 dxc5!? is similar to the last note. Black has done well in practice, but the a5 idea is still irritating: 15...0-0-0 16 a5 a6 (16...♖hg8 17 0-0 e5 18 a6!) 17 0-0 (17 ♗c3 e5 18 ♕b3 ♖hg8 [18...♘f5 19 ♕b6!] 19 g3 ♗g4 20 ♕b2 ♘f5! with good play and the idea 21 h3? ♘xg3!!-+ 0-1 Mauro-Pieretti, corr 1999, due to 22 fxg3 e4!-+) 17...e5 18 ♕b1!? ♗g4 19 ♖d1 f5 20

♗c3‡.

15...0-0-0 16 d5

16 0-0 ♗e8! 17 d5 ♖f8 18 ♕c2 exd5 19 ♕xh7 ♗g6∓ – Korchnoi.

16...exd5 17 ♗xf6

17 cxd5 ♗e6 18 dxe6?! (18 ♗xf6 ♗xd5 19 ♕c1 ♖hf8∓) 18...♖xd1+ 19 ♖xd1 ♕f4! 20 0-0 ♖g8∓ Ekstrom-Belyavsky, Stockholm 1986.

17...♖hg8

17...♖hf8 has also been played with the idea 18 ♗h4 ♕a5+!.

18 cxd5

And now 18...♗e6! 19 0-0 ♗xd5! (improving upon two games with 19...♖xd5?! 20 ♕c2) 20 ♕c1? (20 ♕c2?? ♕f4!; best is 20 ♕d3 ♖g6 21 ♗xe7 ♕xe7∓) 20...♖df8!∓ 21 ♕c3? ♕f4 22 ♗xe7 ♖xg2+! 23 ♔xg2 ♕g4+ 24 ♔h1 ♖xf3 25 ♕xc5 ♗e4-+.

11.3 7 h4

An ultra-modern way of playing it: White will grab space on the kingside and worry about his development later. He also preserves some leeway as to where to put his pieces, depending upon how Black replies. Before turning to h4 proper, an important move order that I have put here to group similar ideas (which can of course transpose) is 7 ♘f3 ♘bc6 8 h4 (the less common 7 h4 ♘bc6 8 ♘f3 transposes). In both move orders, White waits to see how Black responds, e.g., after 7 h4, he may think that 7...♘bc6 requires 8 ♘f3, whereas after 7...♗d7 he might play 8 h5. Even after 7...♕c7 White can forge ahead with 8 h5!? cxd4 9 cxd4 ♕c3+ 10 ♗d2 ♕xd4 11 ♘f3 ♕e4+ 12 ♗e2, a gambit whose reputation is not bad. Then White threatens ♖h4, but he can also play for 0-0 and ♗d3. Likewise, after 7 ♘f3, White may plan to answer 7...♗d7 or 7...♕c7 with 8 a4 (for example), but prefer to answer 7...♘bc6 with 8 h4, which is the position we are looking at (see the diagram).

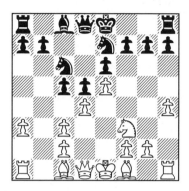

I will present two unusual solutions:

(a) As far as I know, 8...f6!? is not suggested in the major sources, yet it seems fully playable. After 9 h5 (9 exf6 gxf6 is inconsistent and must be fine for Black; now both 9 ♗b5 ♕a5 and 9 ♗e2 fxe5 10 dxe5 ♕c7 are also unattractive) 9...fxe5, play might continue:

(a1) 10 h6 exd4!? (10...g6 11 dxe5 ♕a5 – among others – 12 ♗d2 ♗d7 is also possible) 11 hxg7 ♖g8 12 cxd4 (12 ♖xh7?!, and 12...e5 is playable, e.g., 13 cxd4 cxd4 14 ♘g5 ♗f5 15 ♖h8 ♔d7!; but 12...♕a5! threatens to get castled, while 13 ♘g5 e5! 14 ♕h5+ ♔d8∓ threatens ...♕xc3+, ...♗f5 etc.) 12...cxd4 (or 12...♖xg7 13 ♗h6 ♖g4!? intending 14 dxc5 e5) 13 ♘xd4 (13 ♖xh7 e5) 13...♖xg7 14 ♕h5+ ♖f7 15 ♘f3 ♘g6 16 ♘g5 ♕f6!;

(a2) 10 ♘xe5 ♘xe5 11 dxe5 ♕c7 12 f4 ♗d7 (12...♘f5 13 ♖h3!?) 13 ♗e2 0-0-0 14 0-0 g6! 15 ♗e3 (15 h6? ♘f5) 15...♖hg8 (15...gxh5! 16 ♗xh5 ♘f5∓) 16 ♗g4 gxh5 17 ♗h3! ♖g3∓ Fontaine-Bergez, Clichy 1998;

(b) 8...♕a5 9 ♗d2 f6!?

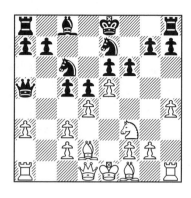

I like this very direct move. Just about everything has been played in this popular position, among them 9...♗d7, 9...c4, 9...♕c7, 9...b6, and 9...cxd4 10 cxd4 ♕a4 (transposing to one of our main lines below after 11 h5!?). After 9...f6!? then:

(b1) 10 c4 ♕c7 11 cxd5 ♘xd5 12 c4 ♘de7 13 exf6 gxf6 14 dxc5 e5 15 ♗c3 Reis Luis-Dias, Lisbon 1999, and now 15...♗e6! 16 ♕d6 ♕c8! intending ...0-0 and ...♖d8 or a variety of ideas such as ...♘g6-f4, or ...♗g4 and ...♘f5-d4; 10 h5 fxe5 11 h6 gxh6! 12 ♘xe5 ♘xe5 13 dxe5 ♗d7 14 ♖xh6 0-0-0 15 ♕h5 ♘g6 16 ♖xh7?! ♖xh7 17 ♕xh7 ♘xe5 18 ♕g7 ♘c6 19 ♗d3 c4 20 ♗g6 e5∓ Pulkkinen-Manninen, Finnish Teams 1989; White's pieces are tied up and his king has nowhere to go.

(b2) 10 exf6 gxf6 11 ♘h2! (an ingenious try, planning simply ♘g4 to pressure Black's kingside; 11 a4 ♕c7 '!∓' with the idea ...e5 is given by Shirov, and 11...♗d7! is a good alternative) 11...♕a4! 12 ♖b1 c4 13 ♕h5+ ♔d8 14 ♘g4 (14 ♖c1 ♖f8!? 15 ♘g4 ♕xa3!? 16 ♕h6!? ♘f5 17 ♕xh7 ♗d7=) Shirov-Plaskett, Reykjavik 1992; and now instead of 14...e5?, Shirov gives 14...♕xc2! 15 ♖c1 ♕e4+ 16 ♗e3 ♕f5! 17 ♕xf5 ♘xf5 18 ♘xf6 ♘xe3 19 fxe3 ♔e7 20 ♘g4 b5∓ (perhaps 20...h5 21

♘h2 e5∓ is better). Overall this is a fun line that seems dynamically balanced.

Returning to 7 h4:

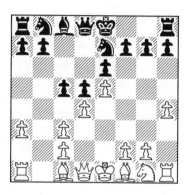

7...♘bc6 8 h5 ♛a5

8...h6 is another standard answer, when again there are some unique sequences like: 9 ♛g4 ♘f5 19 ♗d3 0-0 11 ♘e2 c4 12 ♗xf5 exf5 13 ♛g3 ♔h7=, and 9 ♘f3 ♗d7!? 10 ♗d3 ♛c7 11 0-0 c4 12 ♗e2 f5!, avoiding 12...f6 13 ♗f4!.

9 ♗d2

And now I recommend two systems, beginning with:

11.31 9...♗d7
11.32 9...cxd4

11.31 9...♗d7

Black emphasises quick development.

10 ♘f3

10 h6 is the more common order: 10...gxh6 11 ♘f3 0-0-0 etc. Here 11 ♖xh6 is possible, but then 11...♛c7!? 12 ♘f3 ♘f5 13 ♖h3 cxd4 14 g4 dxc3∓ is good. 11 ♖b1!? allows a draw by 11...♛xa3 12 ♖a1 ♛b2 13 ♖b1 ♛a3, and Black can also play 11...0-0-0, because 12 ♖b5?! ♛a4! 13 ♖xc5 b6 wins the exchange (unless 14 ♖b5 ♘xd4 15 ♖b2 ♘dc6∓ follows).

10...0-0-0

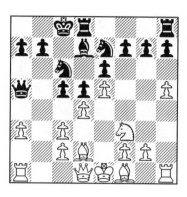

11 h6

11 ♖b1 h6!? 12 ♖b5 ♛xa3 13 ♛b1 can lead to 13...c4 14 ♖xb7 ♛a6 15 ♖b2 ♔c7 16 ♖a2 ♖b8 17 ♛a1 ♛b5 18 ♗c1 ♛b1= Wang Zili-Reefat, Calcutta 2001; or to the crazy 13...♘xd4!?, when 14 cxd4 ♗xb5 15 ♗xb5 a6 16 ♗d3 ♘c6 17 dxc5 ♛xc5 is hard to assess; ...f6, ...b5, and ...♘a5-c4 are all possibilities; and 14 ♘xd4! ♗xb5 15 ♘xb5 ♛a4 with the idea 16 ♘d6+ ♖xd6 17 exd6 ♘f5 is also highly unclear.

11...gxh6! 12 ♗d3

(a) 12 ♖xh6 ♖dg8! has done well (12...♘g8!? resembled our main line in Berndt-Wegener, Graz 2002, although White has many more options), e.g., 13 g3 (13 ♖b1 ♛c7 14 ♖h4 ♘f5 15 ♖f4 f6 16 exf6 e5! 17 dxe5 ♘xe5 18 ♘xe5 ♛xe5+ 19 ♛e2 ♛xf6∓ Kotter-Kindermann, Germany 2001) 13...♘f5 14 ♖h5 ♗e8 15 ♗d3 f6 16 ♗xf5 ♗xh5 17 ♗xe6+ ♔b8 18 ♗xg8 ♖xg8 19 exf6 ♖f8∓ Vujadinovic-Karabalis, email 1999;

(b) 12 a4 ♘g8! has historical value: 13 ♗b5 ♘ce7? (13...c4= or 13...♛c7=) 14 dxc5 a6 15 c4 ♛c7 16 cxd5 ♘xd5 17 c4± Drimer-Uhlmann, Raach 1969; a game that no one seemed to notice for 30 years!

12...c4 13 &e2 &g8!

Another brilliant Uhlmann idea (we saw the precursor above), retreating for positional reasons. With an obvious move like 13...&f5 or 13...&hg8, Black won't get in the break ...f6, which is the move needed to contest the key central area.

14 a4

14 &f1 wasn't much better after 14...f6 15 &e1 fxe5 16 &xe5 (16 dxe5!? &f8 17 g3 Tischbierek-Uhlmann, Baden-Baden 1992; and now 17...&c7 gives Black the advantage – Uhlmann, with the idea 18 &f4 &ce7 19 &d4 &g6) 16...&xe5 17 dxe5 &e7 18 &xh6 &hg8 19 &f3 &e8! 20 a4 &g6∓ Short-Psakhis, Isle of Man 1999.

14...&f8

14...f6 may be just as good or better in view of White's next idea, but with 14...&f8, Black hopes to gain a tempo by not ceding h6 yet.

15 &c1!? f6 16 &a3 &f7 17 &f4 &ge7 18 exf6 &xf6 19 &xh6

19 &e5!? wasn't much of an improvement in Sedlak-Kristjansson, Budapest 2002: 19...&xe5 20 dxe5?! (20 &xe5 &c6 21 &xc6 &xc6∓) 20...&f5 (or 20...&g6! 21 &h4 &g7 22 &f3 &f5) 21 &xh6 &g6 22 &b4 &c7 23 &d6; and although 23...&xd6

should have given Black the edge, 23...&hf8! (or 23...&g8 24 &xh7 &xe5) 24 &xc7+ &xc7 25 &xh7 &xe5 would have secured Black a permanent structural advantage.

After 19 &xh6, Hector-Hillarp Persson, York 1999 continued 19...&g8 20 &f1 &f5 21 &d2 &fg6 22 g3 e5 23 &xh7?! (but 23 &xe5 &xe5 24 dxe5 &xg3! or 23 dxe5 &xg3 24 fxg3 &xg3+ 25 &f2 &b6+ leaves Black much better – Pedersen) 23...e4 24 &e5 &xe5 25 dxe5 e3! 26 &xe3 &xe3+ 27 fxe3 &xg3 28 &f2 &b6 29 &f1 &xe3 30 a5 &g2+! 31 &xg2 &g6+ 0-1.

11.32 9...cxd4 10 cxd4 &a4

A sound second system for Black. I will deal with the main line in less detail than 9...&d7.

11 &f3

(a) 11 c3 is better played when the move &f3 isn't in, because in this kind of position White wants to play &e2, defending c3 and leaving open the moves f4 and &f4. Black has no real trouble after 11...&xd1+ 12 &xd1 h6 13 g4!? (13 &d3 &d7 14 &b1 b6 15 &e2 &a5 16 g4 &c4= Dowden-Wang, Wanganui 2003) 13...&d7 14 f4 &c8 15 &d3 &a5 16 &b1 b6= Shaked-Remlinger, Los Angeles 1993;

(b) 11 &c3 b6 is easy for Black, e.g.,

12 h6 gxh6 13 ♕d3 (13 ♘f3 ♗a6 14 ♗xa6 ♕xa6 15 ♕e2 ♕xe2+ 16 ♔xe2 ♖c8 17 ♔d3 ♖g8 18 ♖ag1 ♖g6= Pritchett-Rogers, Blackpool 1988) 13...a5 14 ♕d2 ♘f5 15 ♖b1!? ♘cxd4 16 ♔d1 Short-Korchnoi, Wijk aan Zee 1987, and now 16...♗a6!∓.

11...♘xd4

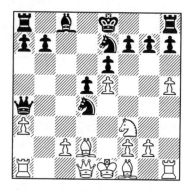

12 ♗d3

This is a gambit made famous by Kasparov. I don't think that it prevents Black from equalising, however, and he can sometimes do better than that.

12...♘ec6

The main move by far, but what I suggested in the last edition still deserves tests: 12...♘ef5!? 13 ♖b1 (13 h6 gxh6 14 g4!? and 14...♘e7 unclear or even 14...♘xf3+ 15 ♕xf3 ♘d4 16 ♕f6 ♖g8, e.g., 17 ♖xh6 ♘xc2+ 18 ♗xc2 ♕xc2 19 ♗b4 ♕e4+ with perpetual check; 13 ♗b4 ♘xf3+ 14 ♕xf3 a5) 13...♘c6 (13...a5!?) 14 ♔f1 b6 15 ♕e2! ♗d7 16 h6 Dominguez-Harikrishna, Oropesa del Mar 1999, and 16...♘xh6!? 17 ♗xh6 gxh6 should give Black at least equal chances.

13 ♔f1 ♘f5 14 ♔g1

An attempted improvement upon 14 ♗xf5 exf5 15 h6 ♖g8 16 ♗g5 ♗e6= Hellers-Gulko, Biel 1993.

14...♕g4 15 ♕e2 f6 16 h6! fxe5 17 hxg7 ♖g8 18 ♖xh7 e4 19 ♘g5 ♕xe2 20 ♗xe2 ♖xg7 21 ♖h8+

'?' – McDonald, who gives instead 21 ♖xg7 ♘xg7 22 c4 'with sustained pressure'. Fair enough, but is Black actually worse? I doubt it, for example, 22...♔e7 23 ♖d1 (23 ♗c3 ♘f5 24 ♖d1 d4 25 ♗b2 e3) 23...♘f5 24 ♗c1! ♘cd4 25 ♗g4 dxc4! 26 ♘xe4 e5 27 ♗g5+ ♔f7 (with the idea 28 ♗f6? ♘g3), and it's hard to choose between White's bishop pair and Black's outpost and extra pawn. A verdict of equality seems fair.

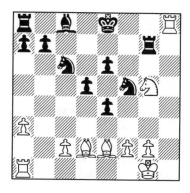

21...♔e7!?

McDonald annotates: '21...♔d7! heading for the queenside. Black seems clearly better, e.g., 22 f4 – to stop the threat of 22...e3! cutting off the defence of the knight – 22...♔c7! 23 ♘xe6+?! ♗xe6 24 ♖xa8', and here he likes 25...♘h4, but I think that simply 24...♘fd4! gives a clear edge.

After 21...♔e7, Fedorov-Gulko, Las Vegas USA 1999 went 22 f4, and Fedorov suggests 22...e5! 23 ♗g4 e3 24 ♗e1 ♘d6!; it would be odd if Black weren't at least equal in that case. Thus the 9...cxd4 and 10...♕a4 line looks like another good solution to 7 h4.

Chapter Twelve

Winawer Variation:
Black Plays 6...♛c7

This chapter was guest written by Hans Olav Lahlum, an expert in and great enthusiast of the 6...♛c7 Winawer. It describes a variation that was included in the second edition but not originally intended for this one. Since Black has the options of the main 6...♘e7 Winawer lines and the Classical 3...♘f6 lines, I had decided to forego an update of the early queen development. However, players from all over the world have expressed interest in the 6...♛c7 repertoire from *Play the French 2*, so when Hans Olav offered to write up a survey of the 6...♛c7 system using those lines I was happy to agree. He not only has extensive experience in the lines recommended, but has a sharp critical eye. The following is the result of his work, with editing and a few suggestions on my part.

1 e4 e6 2 d4 d5 3 ♘c3 ♝b4 4 e5 c5 5 a3 ♝xc3+ 6 bxc3 ♛c7

First popularized in the 1940s by World Champion Mikhail Botvinnik and then in the 1960s by Edmar Mednis and Jan Hein Donner, 6...♛c7 might now be characterised as a 'Scandinavian' variation, since it has been played by a number of young players from Norway and Sweden in recent years. Among others, Danish GM Curt Hansen, Swedish IM Emanuel Berg, and Norwegian GMs Rune Djurhuus and Leif Erlend Johannessen have all been successful with 6...♛c7 in numerous games.

Black's main point when playing 6...♛c7 is to avoid the critical 6...♘e7 variations involving 7 ♛g4 followed by 8 ♛xg7, because now 7 ♛g4 f5 protects the g7-pawn with the queen and also wins a tempo on White's queen. For his part, Black hopes to exert pressure down the c-file and immediately threatens 7...cxd4 8 cxd4 ♛c3+. When he plays ...f5 Black naturally loses the thematic French idea of ...f6 with play along the f-file. By delaying ...♘e7, Black might also gain time for exchanging his troublesome light-squared bishop by ...b6 and ...♝a6, which incidentally deprives White of his bishop pair and removes his best kingside attacker. On the minus side, of course, he delays the development of his kingside. In addition, Black has exchanged his dark-squared bishop and can be vulnerable on the kingside to attacking strokes like ♘g5 and/or ♕h5. He will often find it effective to castle long or leave his king in the centre in order to launch a kingside pawn storm. Thus White has to take into account each of these possible king placements. Black's king's position will also influence whether he closes the queenside with ...c4 or opens it up with ...cxd4; often Black remains flexible by postponing both decisions as long as possible. Piece exchanges will usually favour Black, since White has better possibilities for a kingside attack while Black's better structure will favour him in the endgame. Finally it's worth mentioning that because the centre commonly remains closed, flank attacks are critical for both players.

White's main alternatives are:

12.1 7 ♕g4 (going for an immediate kingside attack)
12.2 7 ♘f3 (settling for piece development)

Other moves are played much less:
(a) 7 ♘e2?! leaves the knight on a less active square and deprives the f1-bishop of its natural development. Then 7...♘e7 intending 8...b6 is normal, but directly 7...b6!?, to get in ...♗a6 as soon as possible, might be even better. One example is 8 g3 ♗a6 9 ♗g2 ♘c6 (9...♗xe2 and 9...cxd4 are also attractive) 10 0-0 cxd4 11 cxd4 ♗xe2 12 ♕xe2 ♘xd4−+ Raddatz-Leer Salvesen, Hamburg 1999;
(b) 7 ♗b2?! also seems too slow to challenge Black: 7...♘e7 (7...b6 is also interesting, as 8 ♕g4?! f5 9 ♗b5+?! ♔f8! followed by ...c4 and ...a6 traps White's bishop at b5 – Bjerke) 8 ♘f3

♘bc6 (8...b6 intending 9...♗a6 is also sound) 9 ♗e2 ♗d7 10 0-0 0-0 11 ♘h4 A.Geller-Peterson, USSR 1967, after which Korchnoi gives 11...♘g6 12 ♘xg6 hxg6=. 11...f6!? tries for more and is probably better;
(c) 7 h4?! is too ambitious: 7...cxd4!? (or 7...♘e7) 8 cxd4 ♕c3+ 9 ♗d2 ♕xd4 10 ♘f3 ♕b6 11 ♗d3 ♘c6 12 h5 f6 13 h6 g6 14 exf6 ♘xf6 15 ♖b1 ♕c7 and Black consolidated in Van Delft-L.E.Johannessen, Guarapuava 1995.

12.1 7 ♕g4 f5

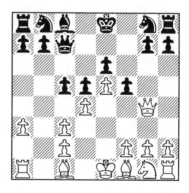

Now White has:

12.11 8 ♕g3
12.12 8 ♕h5+

8 exf6?! ♘xf6 9 ♕g3 has been played by GM Alexei Shirov, but that's the most positive thing that can be said about it: 9...♕a5! 10 ♗d2 0-0 ('∓' – Pedersen) has the idea 11 c4? ♕xd2+! 12 ♔xd2 ♘e4+ −+. Instead, 11 ♕h4 ♕a4! 12 ♖a2?! (12 ♘f3 ♘c6∓) 12...e5! was −+ in Mork-Djurhuus, Bergen 2000.

12.11 8 ♕g3
This might be called the traditional main line, keeping up pressure

against g7 and hoping for a kingside attack.

8...cxd4

Safer than 8...♘e7!? – compare PTF2.

9 cxd4 ♘e7

9...♕xc2?! 10 ♗d2 ♕c7 11 ♖c1 ♘c6 12 ♗b5 gave too much pressure for a pawn in Layton-Kimber, corr 1965.

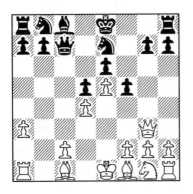

10 ♗d2

Practically forcing Black to commit his king. 10 ♕xg7?? ♖g8 11 ♕xh7 ♕c3+ loses, but after 10 ♗d2 Black has to reckon with 11 ♕xg7. One alternative is particularly important:

(a) 10 h4?! ♕xc2!? 11 ♗d2 ♘bc6 12 ♘e2 0-0 13 h5?! f4! is already better for Black, Kniazer-Wrichselbaumer, Amsterdam 1954;

(b) 10 ♗e2!? probably works tactically after 10...♕xc2 11 ♗d2; but Black should play as in the main line by 10...0-0 11 ♘h3 b6 12 ♘f4 ♕d7 13 0-0 ♗a6;

(c) 10 c3 0-0 11 ♘h3 (11 ♘e2!? transposes into 10 ♘e2 0-0 11 c3; 11 ♗e2 b6 intending 12...♗a6 – Moles; 11 h4 b6 12 h5 ♗a6 13 ♗xa6 ♘xa6 14 ♘h3 ♖ac8= Firnhaber-Kaiser, corr 1987) 11...♘g6!? 12 ♗d2 b6 13 ♗d3 ♗a6 14 ♗xa6 ♘xa6 15 0-0 ♖fc8 16 ♘g5 ♘f8= Pfeifer-Kacirek, Klatovy 1997;

(d) 10 ♘e2!? 0-0 11 c3 has scored very well in practical play; this idea might become important because ultimately 10 ♗d2 seems fine for Black. By omitting ♗d3 White hopes to save a tempo on the main line, as he did after 11...b6 12 ♘f4 ♕d7 13 h4 ♗a6 14 ♗xa6 ♘xa6 15 h5 in Laursen-B.Lundberg, corr 1986 and after 13 a4 ♗a6 14 ♗b5+!? ♗xb5 15 axb5 a5 16 ♗a3 ♖e8 17 h4 ♖a7 18 h5 in Ernst-Nordahl, Gausdal 1994. Of course neither line gives White a decisive advantage. Instead, Black can play 11...♘bc6 (with the idea ...♘a5), and now:

(d1) 12 ♘f4 ♘a5 13 ♖b1 ♘c4 14 h4 (or just 14 ♗e2 intending 0-0) of Doggers-Westerman, Utrecht 2000 gave White a pleasant advantage.

(d2) 12 a4 ♘a5 13 ♗a3 ♘c4 14 ♗xe7 ♕xe7 15 ♘f4 with an edge, Kruppa-Feigin, Nikolaev 1995;

(d3) What is probably the most critical line was tested in Sax-Lahlum, Hamburg 2002, which went 12 h4!? ♘a5 13 ♗g5 (Tiemann's 13 ♖b1 ♗d7 14 h5 ♗a4 15 ♗g5 is also interesting) 13...♖f7 14 ♘f4 (14 h5!?) 14...♗d7 (or 14...♕b6 15 ♗e2 ♘c4 16 ♗h5 g6 17 ♗e2± Pavlovic-Dgebuadze, Ubeda 1997; this attacking manoeuvre is worth noting, especially with a Black rook on f7: White spends two tempi to force ...g6 because h5 will then be very powerful) 15 ♗e2 ♖c8 16 ♖h3?! (16 ♗h5 g6 17 ♗e2 ♕xc3 and here White has some compensation) 16...♕b6 17 ♖c1?! ♕b2 18 ♖d1, when 18...♗a4! would have forced White to give up an exchange for insufficient compensation.

Although 10 ♘e2!? can hardly refute this variation, it seems at the moment to be White's best bid for an advantage and is the only move

against which Black has not (yet) demonstrated how to equalise.
10...0-0

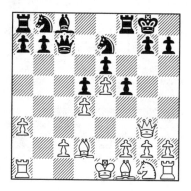

11 ♗d3

After the seldom-played 11 ♘h3!?, 11...♛xc2?! 12 ♖c1 gives White at least adequate compensation, but 11...♘bc6 12 c3 ♘g6 13 ♗e2 ♗d7 14 0-0 ♘ce7 was solid and at worst ± in A.Fischer-S.Meyer, Hessen 1992. Also natural is 11...♘g6!? planning 12 ♗e2 ♘bc6 and otherwise ...b6 and ....♗a6.

11...b6 12 ♘e2

12 h4?! ♗a6 was Ernst-Djurhuus, Gausdal 1994, and Ernst gives 13 ♘e2 (13 h5? ♗xd3 14 cxd3 ♘bc6 15 ♘e2 f4! 16 ♛g4 ♘xd4∓) 13...♗xd3 14 cxd3 ♘bc6 15 ♖c1 ♛d7=.

12...♗a6 13 ♘f4

(a) 13 ♗b4?! ♖c8 14 ♘f4 ♛d7 might transpose to 14 ♗b4?!, which seems better for Black. An attractive alternative is 13...♗xd3 14 cxd3 ♘bc6: 15 ♗d6 ♛d7 16 0-0 ♖f7 (or 16...♖fc8) 17 ♗xe7 (White avoids a bad bishop versus good knight ending; not 17 a4? f4!∓ Gabrielsen-Djurhuus, Oslo 1994) 17...♖xe7 18 ♖fc1 ♖c8 19 ♛e3 (19 ♖c3? ♘xd4! 20 ♖xc8+ ♛xc8 21 ♘xd4 ♛c3 Schleiffer-Just, corr 1987) 19...♛e8 20 ♖a2 ♖ec7 21 ♖ac2 ♛d7 22 f3 ♘d8∓ due to Black's better pawn

structure, Koch-Schnicke, corr 1990;

(b) The slow 13 0-0?! was Gullaksen-Djurhuus, Alta 1996: 13...♗xd3 14 ♛xd3 ♖c8 15 ♖fc1 ♛c4 16 ♛xc4 ♖xc4 17 a4 ♘bc6 18 c3 ♘a5∓. This example illustrates that White has to do something in the middlegame so as not to end up in a worse ending.

13...♛d7

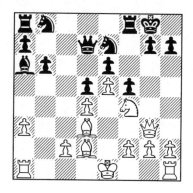

14 h4

(a) 14 ♗b4?! ♖f7? 15 ♘h5! with an attack was the old main line, which now seems refuted by GM Grigory Kaidanov's 14...♖c8!, coolly pointing out that Black's rook is not needed to defend the kingside: 15 ♛g5 (15 ♘h5 ♘g6 or 15...♗xd3 followed by the move 16...♘bc6; 15 ♛h4?! ♘ec6 [or 15...♗xd3 16 cxd3 ♘ec6] 16 ♖d1?! J.Berg-Djurhuus, Alta 1996, and I see nothing wrong with 16...♘xd4!; 15 h4 ♗xd3 16 ♛xd3 ♖c4 17 ♗d2 ♘bc6 18 ♘e2 ♖c8 with the initiative, Zaw Htun-Villamayor, Vung Tau 2000; 15 0-0 ♗xd3 16 ♛xd3 ♖c4 with counterplay as in the main line) 15...♘ec6! 16 ♘h5 ♛f7 17 ♖d1?! (17 ♗xa6 ♘xa6 18 c3 ♘axb4 19 axb4 h6 20 ♛h4 a5! opens up the queenside to Black's advantage – Watson) 17...♘xd4! 18 ♘f6+ ♔h8 19 ♘xh7 ♘xc2+-+ Shaked-Kaidanov, San Francisco 1995;

(b) 14 0-0 ♗xd3 15 cxd3 (15 ♛xd3

215

♘bc6 16 h4 ♖ac8 17 h5 ♘d8 18 g3 ♖c4 19 ♔g2 ♘ec6= Leko-C.Hansen, Groningen 1995) 15...♘bc6 (15...♖c8) 16 ♗e3 ♔h8 (not necessary because Black can always meet ♘h5 by ...♘g6; 16...♖fc8!?) 17 ♖ac1 Mednis-Foldi, Varna 1958, with a position similar to the main line. Moles' 17...♖ac8 18 h4 ♘d8 looks = since White has to watch out for queenside;

(c) 14 ♘h5?! ♘g6 15 ♗xa6 ♘xa6 16 h4 threatens 17 ♘f6+ gxf6 18 h5 with some attack, but then 16...♔h8! preparing 17...♖ac8, 17...♕a4 or 17...f4 – Watson;

(d) 14 ♗xa6 ♘xa6 15 ♕d3 (15 h4 ♖f7?! 16 h5 ♖c8 17 c3 ♖c4 18 h6 g6 19 ♘e2 ♘b8 20 ♗g5 ♕c8= as in Zezulkin-Matlak, Czech Republic 2003. 15...♖ac8 intending 16 c3 ♖c4 looks more pointed. In general, ...♖f7 should be played only when it is absolutely necessary to defend the kingside) 15...♘b8 16 h4 ♖c8 is the main line. Instead, Reshevsky-Botvinnik, Moscow 1948 went 16...♘bc6 17 ♖h3 (17 h5 ♖ac8 18 ♔e2 ♘d8 19 ♖ac1 O.Karlsson-Hylen, corr 1973, and again 19...♖c4∓ seems best) 19...♖ac8 18 ♖g3 ♔h8?! (18...♘d8; compare 15...♘bc6 in the main line) 19 h5 ♖f7 20 h6 g6 21 ♖c1 ♖ff8=.

14...♗xd3 15 ♕xd3

This loses a tempo for the kingside attack, but 15 cxd3?! is seldom played as it destroys White's pawn structure and gives Black a queenside pawn majority, e.g., 15...♘bc6 16 ♗e3 ♘a5 17 h5 ♖ac8 18 h6 g6 19 0-0 ♔h8 20 ♖ab1 ♘g8 21 ♗d2 ♘c6 22 ♘e2 ♘d8 23 ♖fc1 ♘f7= Smyslov-Botvinnik, Moscow 1957.

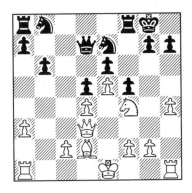

15...♖c8!

I consider this better than the natural and often-played 15...♘bc6?! (this position can also be reached after 14 ♗xa6 ♘xa6 15 ♕d3 ♘b8 16 h4 ♘bc6) because Black can increase the pressure against d4 by playing ...♖c4 before ...♘c6. One prominent example with 15...♘bc6?! was 16 ♖h3 ♖ac8 17 ♖g3 ♖f7?! (Kasparov gives 17...♘d8! 18 ♘h5 ♘g6 as unclear; one line is 19 ♘xg7 ♔xg7 20 h5 ♘f7 21 ♔e2 ♕d8 22 ♖h1 ♖h8 23 c3 ♕e7) 18 h5?! (18 ♔f1! ♘d8 19 ♔g1± – Kasparov) ♘d8 19 c3 ♖f8?! (19...♕a4∓ – Kasparov) 20 ♔f1 ♖c4 21 ♔g1 ♘f7 22 a4 ♖fc8 with balanced chances, Kasparov-Short, Novgorod 1997. Short later preferred 15...♖c8.

16 ♖h3

16 h5 ♖c4 17 h6 g6 18 ♕g3 ♘bc6 19 c3 ♔h8 20 ♕h4 ♖f8 21 0-0 ♘a5 22 ♖fb1 ♘g8= Teichmeister-Halldorsson, corr 2000. The primitive h5-h6 sel-

dom gives White anything unless he can infiltrate the dark squares after ...g6.

16...♗c4 17 ♖g3

17 ♘h5?! (threatening ♗h6) 17...♛e8?! (17...♘bc6!? intending 18 ♗h6? ♖xd4 or 18...♘bc6!? with the idea 19 ♘xe6?! ♛c8) 18 ♘f4 ♛d7?! Sebastian-Lahlum, Hamburg 2001 transposes back to the main line.

17...♘bc6 18 c3

18 ♘e2?! ♔h8 19 h5 ♖c8 20 ♔f1 ♘d8 21 c3 ♘f7 22 ♔g1 ♘c6 23 ♔h1 ♘a5 24 ♖g1 (not a convincing manoeuvre) 24...♖a4 25 ♖h3 ♘c4 26 ♗f4, and now both ways of taking the a-pawn would have been ∓, Michiels-Wintzer, Amsterdam 2001. Black's queenside play advanced steadily while White failed to demonstrate anything on the kingside.

18...♖f8

The more subtle 18...♔h8 also has done well in several games, e.g., 19 ♛e2 ♘a5 20 ♛d1 ♖c6 21 ♔f1 ♘c4 22 ♗c1 b5 23 ♘h5!? (23 ♘d3 ♛e8 with about even chances – Psakhis) 23...♘g6 24 ♘xg7 ♔xg7 25 h5 ♖h8 26 ♗g5 ♔f8 27 ♗f6 ♖g8 28 hxg6 ♖xg6 29 ♖h3 ♖a6 Svidler-Cu.Hansen, Esbjerg 2000; best was 30 ♛h5 ♔g8 31 ♛xg6 hxg6 32 ♖h8+ ♔f7 33 ♖h7+!= – Psakhis.

19 ♔f1

19 ♔e2?! ♖f7 20 ♘h5 ♘g6 21 ♖h1?! ♛e7! 22 ♖xg6 hxg6 23 ♘f4 of D.Hersvik-Lahlum, Bergen 2003 was a creative kingside attack, but 23...b5! planning 24 ♘xg6 ♛xa3 would have given White insufficient compensation for the exchange.

19...♖f7 20 ♖e1

20 ♔g1 ♘a5 21 a4 ♛c6 22 ♖a3 ♔f8 23 ♛b1 ♘b7 ½-½ Teran Alvarez-Short, Lanzarote 2003. Black would have to run risks to try to win.

20...♛c8

This is the game Konstantinopolsky-Olle Smith, corr 1955, given as ∓ by Watson. That might be overblown, but Black is in control. The game went 21 ♛f3?! ♘a5 22 ♛h5? ♘b3 23 ♗e3 ♖xc3 24 ♖d1 ♘a5 25 ♛h6?! ♘g6! 26 ♖xg6 hxg6 27 ♛g5 ♘c4-+, but for unknown reasons Black forced a draw a few moves later.

As shown above, the old main line with 8 ♛g3 often ends with a balance of power: White has chances on the kingside and Black on the queenside, but both have difficulties making anything out of their position because they have to keep some pieces defending the other wing. If Black watches out for dramatic kingside breakthroughs, he will in any case avoiding losing. This main line is demanding for both players but seems sound for Black; hence White's most critical continuation might be the still rarely-played 10 ♘e2!?.

12.12 8 ♛h5+

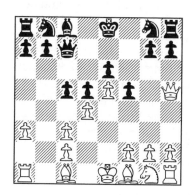

This might be called the modern main line. White is using tempi with his queen to provoke a weakening of Black's kingside.

8...g6

This is an important decision: Black weakens his kingside and the dark squares, but wins tempi for active counterplay on the queenside. More sound but less dynamic is 8...♕f7, when White has three alternatives:

(a) 9 ♕xf7+ ♔xf7 10 ♘f3 (10 ♖b1 cxd4 11 cxd4 ♘e7 12 ♗d2 b6 13 ♘f3 h6 intending 14...♗a6 didn't give White any lasting advantage in Jakic-Haba, Bibinje 2001; 10 dxc5!? ♘d7 11 c4 Sutovsky-Komarov, Vondroll 1996, and 11...♘xe5 13 cxd5 exd5 seems ±; 10 c4 cxd4 11 cxd5 exd5, and now Uhlmann gave 12 ♘f3 ♘c6 13 ♗b2 ♘ge7 14 0-0-0 h6, but Gullaksen's 12 f4! safeguards e5 and is at least a ± after 12...♘c6 13 ♘f3) 10...cxd4 11 cxd4 (11 ♘xd4?! ♗d7 12 f4 ♘e7 13 ♖b1 b6 14 c4 ♖c8! was = or even ∓ in Kindermann-Yusupov, Munich 1990) 11...h6 12 c4 ♘e7 13 c5 (otherwise 13...dxc4 followed by b6) 13...♘bc6= Vogt-Bodo Schmidt, Bundesliga 1993;

(b) I.Berg gives 8...♕f7 as "?!" due to 9 ♗b5+! ♗d7 10 ♕xf7+ ♔xf7 11 ♖b1±. White might very well be ±, but I am not sure about 11...♗xb5 12 ♖xb5 b6 13 dxc5 ♘d7 14 cxb6 axb6 15 ♘f3 h6 with compensation. Black can also limit White's advantage by 9...♘c6 10 ♕xf7+ ♔xf7 11 ♘f3 ♘ge7 12 ♖b1 h6, planning ...♗d7 or even ...a6. Thus White has no clear road to an advantage after 9 ♗b5+; in practice he only has a very slight plus score with a high drawing rate. Black plays without much margin for error, however, and must be careful not to open the position for White's bishop pair;

(c) 9 ♕d1 is playable: 9...b6 10 a4!? (10 ♘f3 ♗a6 11 dxc5 ♗xf1 12 ♖xf1 bxc5 13 c4 ♘e7= Csabo Horvath-

Uhlmann, Dresden 1988) 10...♗a6 11 ♗xa6 ♘xa6 12 ♘h3 h6 (or 12...♘e7, as 13 ♘g5 ♕g6 is not really a threat) 13 ♘f4 ♘e7 14 ♕e2 c4 15 ♗a3 (15 a5!? ♖b8) 15...♘c6, at best ±, Gullaksen-Lahlum, Copenhagen 1998.

9 ♕d1

This seems paradoxical, but although other moves might be underrated White has no better square for the queen:

(a) 9 ♕h3 ♘c6 (9...cxd4!? 10 cxd4 ♕xc2 planning ...♘c6, but White has compensation) 10 ♘f3 (10 ♘e2 ♗d7 11 g4?! fxg4 12 ♕xg4 0-0-0 was at worst = in Fletzer-Casaldi, Venice 1948) ♗d7 11 ♗e2 0-0-0 (11...♘ge7; 11...h6) 12 0-0 h6 13 a4 ♘ge7 14 ♗a3 g5 15 ♘d2 ♘g6 unclear, Boleslavsky-Bondarevsky, USSR 1954;

(b) 9 ♕f3 ♗d7!? (9...cxd4!? 10 cxd4 ♕xc2 has scored well in a few games, e.g., 11 ♘e2 ♘c6 12 h4 h6 13 ♕e3 ♘ge7 and Black converted her extra pawn, Polovnikova-Zielinska, Zagan 1997) 10 h4 ♘c6 11 ♘e2 0-0-0 12 h5 ♘ge7 13 ♗g5 ♖de8= Westerinen-D.Madsen, Gausdal 1991.

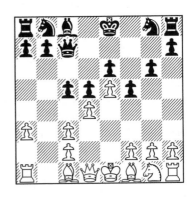

9...♗d7

(a) 9...cxd4?! 10 cxd4 ♕c3+ 11 ♗d2 ♕xd4 12 ♘f3 might be better than it looks, but White gets (too) much development for a pawn;

(b) 9...♘c6!? was given by Watson and still seems sound after 10 a4 cxd4 11 cxd4 ♘b4 or 10 ♘f3 ♗d7 11 dxc5 h6! 12 ♖b1 ♘ge7= from Spassky-Portisch, Mexico 1980. More critical than 10 a4 is 10 h4!? ♘ge7? (Fyllingen gives 10...h6!; then 11 ♘f3 ♘ge7 is complex and at worst ⩱) 11 h5 ♗d7 12 hxg6 ♘xg6 13 ♗g5 (13 ♘f3 might be even better) 13...cxd4 14 cxd4 ♕a5+ 15 ♕d2 ♕xd2+ 16 ♔xd2 ♘xd4 17 ♗f6 0-0 18 ♖b1 Gullaksen-Lahlum, Porsgrunn 1999.

10 ♘f3
(a) Against 10 h4, 10...h6 is most natural, but Black also has 10...cxd4!?, when Watson's analysis goes 11 cxd4 (11 h5? dxc3 with the idea 12 hxg6 hxg6 13 ♖xh8 ♕xe5+) 11...♕c3+ 12 ♗d2 ♕xd4 13 ♘f3 (13 ♘e2 ♕c4 14 h4 ♘e7∓ Kreiman-Shaked, US Junior 1996) 13...♕e4+ 14 ♗e2?! ♗b5∓;
(b) 10 a4 cxd4 (Watson suggests both 10...h6 planning ...♘ge7 and 10...♘c6 with the idea 11 ♘f3 cxd4 12 cxd4 ♘b4 or 11 ♗a3?! cxd4 12 cxd4 ♕a5+) 11 cxd4 ♕c3+ 12 ♗d2 ♕xd4 13 ♘f3 ♕e4+ 14 ♗e2 ♘c6 15 0-0 ♘d4 yielding only just compensation, T.Pähtz-Uhlmann, Dresden 1988.
10...♗a4!?
This original but flexible bishop

move establishes pressure against c2. Black has two principle strategies: he can either play ...c4, castle long, and attack on the kingside; or castle short or leave the king in the centre to attack down the c-file. Instead, 10...cxd4 11 cxd4 ♗a4 can be played but Black can keep that option open.

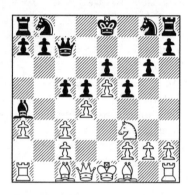

11 ♖b1!?
This is 'most critical and probably best' according to E.Berg. I will use it as the main line here, although five other alternatives have been played and three of them might be as good as 11 ♖b1:
(a) 11 c4?! ♘e7 12 ♗e2 (12 dxc5 ♘d7 13 ♗e2 ♘xc5 14 0-0 0-0-0 15 ♗d2?! ♘e4 16 cxd5 ♖xd5 17 ♕c1 ♘xd2 18 ♘xd2 ♖xe5∓ Ariel-Matlak, Groningen 1998) 12...♘bc6 13 0-0 h6 14 cxd5 ♘xd5 15 ♕d3? (15 dxc5!, but Black still has an active position after 15...0-0-0 and seems fine) 15...cxd4 16 ♕c4?! b5! 17 ♕d3 ♕b6 18 ♘h4 ♔f7 19 ♖e1 ♕c5 20 ♕g3 ♘ce7 0-1 Richardson-Kujala, corr 1993;
(b) 11 ♗d3 cxd4! (or Watson's 11...♘d7, e.g., 12 0-0 c4!? 13 ♗e2 h6 14 g4!? fxg4 15 ♘h4 ♘f8 16 ♗xg4 0-0-0 17 ♔h1 g5, Anka-Koczka, Budapest 1991) 12 cxd4 ♕c3+ 13 ♗d2 ♕xd3! 14 cxd3 ♗xd1 15 ♔xd1 ♘c6 16 ♖b1 (16 h4 h6! 17 ♔e2 ♘ge7 18 a4

♔f8 19 ♖hb1 ♖b8 20 a5 ♔g7 21 ♖b2 b6!∓ Stefansson-Short, Reykjavik 2000) 16...b6 17 ♖c1 ♔d7 18 h4 h6 19 ♔e2 ♘ge7 20 ♖c2 ♖ac8 21 ♖hc1 ♘d8∓ J.Polgar-Morovic, Buenos Aires 1992;

(c) 11 ♗d2!? is also critical: 11...♘d7 (11...cxd4? 12 cxd4! ♕xc2?? 13 ♗b5+! or 12...♗xc2? 13 ♗b5+ ♘d7 14 ♖c1 ♖c8 15 ♕e2 ♕d8 16 ♘g5!; 11...♘c6 12 ♗d3 h6 13 h4 ♘ge7 14 ♕c1 0-0-0 15 ♖h3 ♖h7 16 ♔f1 ♖dh8 17 ♔g1 c4= Zhao-E.Berg, Athens 2001) 12 ♗d3 ♘e7 (12...h6 – Tiemann) 13 0-0 h6 14 h4 ♔f7!? 15 ♖b1 ♖ac8 16 ♖b2 ♘b6 17 ♕c1 ♔g7 18 ♗e3 c4∓ F.Andersson-A.Olsson, Hallstahammar 2002;

(d) 11 ♖a2!? overprotects c2 and removes ...♕c3+ threats. On the minus side, the rook is less active at a2 than on b1, e.g., 11...♘d7 (or 11...h6, but not 11...♘e7? 12 ♗h6! ♘d7 13 ♗d3 cxd4 14 cxd4 ♕c3+ 15 ♕d2! Gullaksen-Lahlum, Asker 2000)

(d1) 12 h4 h6 13 ♗e3 (13 ♗f4? ♘gf6! – planning 14...♘e4 – 14 ♗xh6 ♖xh6 15 exf6 ♘xf6 16 ♗d3 c4 17 ♕c1 ♕g7 18 ♗e2 ♘e4 19 ♕b2 g5!∓ Stokke-L.E.Johannessen, Bergen 2002) 0-0-0 14 ♕c1 ♔b8 15 ♖h3 ♖c8 16 ♗d3 ♔a8 17 ♔f1 c4 (closing off the queenside and planning ...g5) 18 ♗e2 ♘b6 19 ♘g1 ♕g7 20 ♖g3 ♘e7 21 ♘h3

♖cg8=/∓ Gullaksen-Leer Salvesen, Asker 2000;

(d2) Critical is 12 ♗d3!: 12...h6 (12...c4?! 13 ♗e2 h6 Gdanski-Matlak, Cappelle la Grande 1999, 14 ♘h4 ♘e7 15 g4 – E.Berg; 12...cxd4? 13 cxd4 ♕c3+?! 14 ♔e2! – Watson, or here 13...♗b5 14 0-0! ♗xd3 15 cxd3±) 13 0-0 c4 14 ♗e2 0-0-0 (14...♘e7 – E.Berg) 15 h4 (15 g4!? fxg4 16 ♘h4) 15...♘e7 16 g3 ♘c6 17 ♔g2 ♖dg8 18 ♖h1 ♘d8 19 ♗e3 ♘f7 with a promising position Wedberg-E.Berg, Sweden 2002;

(e) 11 dxc5!? tries to open up the queenside; it has been heavily debated among young Polish stars recently:

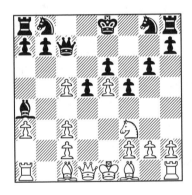

11...♘d7 (11...♕xc5!? 12 ♗d2 ♘c6 13 ♗d3 0-0-0 14 0-0 h6 15 ♕b1 g5 16 ♘d4 ♕e7 17 ♘xc6 ♗xc6 looks solid, Dworakowska-Kadziolka, Brzeg 2001) 12 ♕d4 (12 ♗e3?! ♘xc5 13 ♖b1 ♘e4 14 ♕d4 ♗d7 15 ♕b4 b6 16 c4 ♘e7 17 ♗e2 ♖c8∓ Carlsen-A.Olsson, Stockholm 2003) 12...♘xc5 and:

(e1) 13 ♗d3!? h6 14 0-0 (or 14 h4 b6 15 0-0 0-0-0 16 ♗f4 ♕h7 17 ♖fb1 ♘e7 18 ♔f1 ♘c6 19 ♕e3 ♘e4 and Black evetually won in Dworakowska-M.Socko, Ostrow 2002) 14...♘e7 (14...b6!?) 15 ♗e3 b6 16 ♕h4± Chandler-Kinsman, England 1998;

(e2) 13 ♗e3 b6 14 ♗d3 h6 15 0-0
(Berg gives 15 h4 ♘e7= and 15 ♕h4!?
♘xd3+ 16 cxd3 ♕xc3+ 17 ♔e2 ♗b5 18
♕d4 'with compensation') 15...g5 16
♕b4 ♗d7 17 c4 ♘e7 18 a4 0-0 19 h3=
Macieja-E.Berg, Pardubice 2002.

11...♘d7
White's point is 11...cxd4?! 12 ♖b4!
(E.Berg) or even 12 ♘xd4!? ♕xc3+ 13
♕d2 ♕xd2+ 14 ♗xd2 with a strong
initiative.
12 ♗e2
White later turned to 12 dxc5!?
opening queenside lines: 12...♘xc5 13
♗e3 b6 (13...♘e4? 14 ♕d4 ♘xc3? 15
♗d2! ♘xb1 16 ♕xa4+ ♔d8 17 ♕b4
♘xa3 18 ♕f8+ –+ Groszpeter-Atanu,
Paks 2000) 14 ♕d4 ♘e7 (14...♗xc2?
15 ♗b5+ ♔e7 16 ♖b2 ♗e4 17 ♘h4) 15
♗d3 h6 16 0-0?! (16 ♕h4!? ♘e4 17 0-0
0-0-0 looks =) 16...g5! 17 c4 0-0 18
♖fe1 f4 19 ♗d2 (19 cxd5? fxe3 20 d6
♕d7 21 dxe7 ♖xf3!–+ – E.Berg)
19...♘xd3 20 cxd3 ♘f5 21 ♕c3 dxc4
22 ♖e4 ♕d7!∓ Wedberg-E.Berg,
Malmo 2002.
12...h6 13 dxc5!?
13 0-0 c4?! (Black should be fine if
he remains flexible with 13...♘e7 –
Watson) 14 ♘h4! ♘e7 15 f4 0-0-0 16
♗e3 ♕a5 17 ♕d2± Velimirovic-Moro-
vic, Vrsac 1985.
After 13 dxc5!?, Timman-Shaked,

Merillville 1997 went 13...♘xc5 14
♖b4 ♗d7 15 0-0 ♘e4 16 ♗d3!? ♘e7 17
♘d4 (Timman mentions 17 c4, but
17...a5 intending ...dxc4 and 17...♘c6
are good) 17...♘xc3 18 ♕e1 ♘a2 19
♖b3 ♘xc1 20 ♕xc1, and now 20...b6?!
21 ♗b5 ♔f7 22 a4 ♖ad8 23 ♖e1 a6 24
♗xd7 ♖xd7 25 ♕b2 ♖b8 26 ♖h3 ♘g8
27 ♖c3 gave White a strong initiative.
Critical is 20...♕xe5! (as suggested by
Timman), e.g., 21 ♘f3! (21 c3?! ♕c7!
22 f4 0-0 23 ♕e3 [or 23 ♖e1 b6]
23...♖ac8 24 ♘xe6 ♗xe6 25 ♕xe6+
♖f7) 21...♕f6 (or 21...♕d6 22 ♕b2 0-0
23 ♖xb7 ♖ab8 – Lie; 21...♕c7? 22
♕b2±, since 22...0-0 23 ♖xb7 ♕d6? 24
♕e5! wins – Tallaksen) 22 ♖xb7 ♗c6
23 ♗b5 ♗xb5. White still has to prove
that he has compensation. Thus we
can conclude (for now) that in the
modern main line with 7 ♕g4 f5 8
♕h5+ g6 9 ♕d1 ♗d7 10 ♘f3 ♗a4!?
White has many possibilities that
have not been tested properly on a
top level but he also lacks a clear way
to any advantage. Black, having a
flexible position, should be fine as
long as he is not afraid to play the
typical closed positions; those
demand much patience and accuracy
from both players. White's bishop
pair is not much of an advantage and
Black's better pawn structure often
gives him the last laugh (if there is
one).

12.2 7 ♘f3 b6!?
7...♘e7 transposes a Winawer with
6...♘e7 7 ♘f3 ♕c7. With 7...b6, Black
claims that it is worth some lost
tempi to exchange the light-squared
bishops by 8...♗a6. Recommended by
Watson in the last edition, this line
still seems satisfactory for Black. The
similar 6...♘e7 7 ♘f3 b6 has remain-
ed popular in recent years, and it is

not clear that ...♘e7 is more useful than ...♕c7.

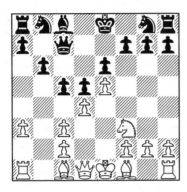

8 a4

This flank attack tries for a5 before Black can complete his development.

(a) 8 ♗d3?! falls in with Black's plans: 8...♗a6 9 0-0 ♗xd3 (9...♘e7 10 dxc5 bxc5 11 ♖e1 ♗xd3 12 cxd3 0-0 13 ♗g5 ♘bc6 14 ♕a4 h6 15 ♗e3 ♘xe5 16 ♘xe5 ♕xe5 17 ♗xc5 ♕c7= De Firmian-E.Berg, Gausdal 2003) 10 cxd3 (10 ♕xd3 might be better, but 10...♘e7 retained the advantage after 11 a4 h6 12 ♗a3 0-0 13 ♘h4 ♘bc6 Blazek-Heyken, Pardubice 1996, and 11 c4 dxc4 12 ♕xc4 ♘d7 13 dxc5 0-0 14 ♕e2 ♘xc5 15 a4 ♖fd8 Sakhatova-Couche, Cappelle la Grande 1995) 10...♘e7. Here Black is equal, e.g., 11 a4 ♘d7 12 ♗a3 0-0 13 ♖c1 ♖fe8 14 c4 ♖ac8 15 cxd5 ♘xd5 Kaminski-Gdanski, Warsaw 1995, or 11 dxc5 bxc5 12 a4 0-0 13 ♗g5 h6 14 ♗xe7 ½-½ Biolek-Matlak, Czech Republic 1994, or 11 ♖e1 ♘bc6 12 ♕a4 0-0 13 dxc5 bxc5 14 ♕g4 ♕a5 Ketola-Lehtivaara, Finland 1996;

(b) 8 h4?! appears overambitious: 8...♘e7 9 h5 h6 10 ♗d3 ♗a6 11 0-0 ♗xd3 12 ♕xd3 ♘d7 13 a4 ♖c8 14 ♗a3 0-0 and Black is better, Riemsdijk-Matlak, Moscow 1994;

(c) A more popular and disturbing attack on Black's strategy is 8 ♗b5+!? ♗d7 9 ♗d3 (9 a4 ♗xb5 transposes into 9 ♗b5+), when 9...♘c6 was discussed in the second edition, but here we concentrate upon 9...♗a4, as recommended by Watson. It has been much discussed since. Black will sometimes play ...c4 followed by ...0-0-0, with the idea of attacking the centre via ...f6. Of course the problem with this strategy is that regardless of the king position White can take command on the kingside, as Black's pieces can be bound up on the queenside. So Black often pursues the alternative strategy of playing ...cxd4 for a direct attack down the c-file.

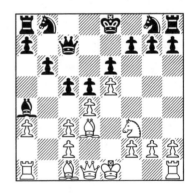

(c1) 10 h4?! ♘e7 11 h5 h6 12 ♖h4 ♘d7 13 dxc5 b5! 14 ♕e2 a6 15 ♖g4 ♔f8 16 ♖b1 ♖c8∓ Wedberg-Djurhuus, Munkebo 1998 due to Black's better structure;

(c2) 10 dxc5!? is a new and critical idea from the German GM Roland Schmaltz, avoiding the c4 blockade and keeping the queenside open. Schmaltz-Leer Salvesen, Amsterdam 2000, continued 10...bxc5 (10...♕xc5?! 11 0-0 ♕xc3 12 ♖b1 ♘c6 13 ♕e2 ♕c5 14 ♗e3 with too much initiative for the pawn, Trescher-Lahlum, Kecskemet 2003; but L.E.Johannessen's 10...b5 (!) planning ...♘d7 and ...♘xc5 may be best – compare Wedberg-Djurhuus above) 11 c4 ♘e7?! (better is 11...d4 12 0-0 ♘c6 or 11...dxc4 12 ♗xc4 ♘bc6) 12 0-0 (12 cxd5 might be more accurate) 12...♘bc6 13 cxd5 ♘xd5 14 ♖e1 ♖d8 15 ♕e2 ♘d4 16 ♘xd4 cxd4 17 ♕e4 ♕c5 18 c4 ♘e7 19 ♕g4 0-0 with some initiative for White;

(c3) 10 ♘g5!? (suggested by Richard Beale and Watson) is worth examining; White sacrifices his centre and development, but may get good attacking chances;

(c4) 10 0-0 and:

(c41) Here Watson recommended 10...c4!? 11 ♗e2 ♘e7 with the point of 12 ♘h4 ♘g6!; then 13 ♗g5 h6 14 ♘xg6 fxg6 15 ♗h4 ♘c6 16 f4 0-0 17 g4 ♘e7 18 ♕d2 ♖f7 19 ♖f2 ♖af8 20 ♗f1 ♕d8 with the idea of ...g5 and ...♘g6! was = equal in the game Djurhuus-L.E.Johannessen, Oslo 1999. White also has 12 ♘e1 (12 g3 h6 13 ♘h4 ♘bc6 14 f4 g6 15 g4 h5 16 gxh5 0-0-0= A.Horvath-L.E.Johannessen, Oropesa del Mar 1998; Watson also gave 12 ♘g5 h6 13 ♘h3 ♘bc6 14 f4 0-0-0=) 12...♘d7 (12...f6 13 ♗h5+ ♘g6 – Watson, but 14 exf6 gxf6 15 f4! is critical) and Black retains the possibility of castling on either wing;

(c42) 10...♘d7 11 ♘g5 (11 ♖e1 ♘e7 planning ...h6 and ...0-0-0 – Watson) 11...c4 (11...h6 – Watson) and 12 ♗e2 h6 or 12 ♕h5 ♘f8 13 ♗e2 ♗xc2;

(c43) 10...♘e7 11 h4 (11 ♖e1 h6 12 h4 ♘d7 13 ♖b1 a6 soon gave Black an advantage in Walek-Matlak, Pardubice 1996, while 12 ♖b1 ♘d7 13 ♗e3 a6 14 ♘h4 b5 15 ♖b2 0-0-0!? 16 dxc5 ♘c6 was Bruzon – L.E.Johannessen, Linares 2002) 11...h6 12 h5 ♘d7 13 ♘h4 with the idea of f4-f5. This is Timman's recent aggressive plan, but it seems that Black can successfully

control the f5-square and get counterplay: 13...0-0-0 14 f4 c4 15 ♗e2 g6 16 hxg5 fxg6 17 ♗g4 ♘f8 18 ♗f3 ♘f5= Rudolf-Enders, Schwerin 1997.

8...♗a6 9 ♗xa6

Misplacing Black's knight at a6 since exchanging bishops is unavoidable anyway. 9 ♗b5+?! is less threatening after 9...♗xb5 10 axb5 a5! (Moles' 10...♘e7 11 0-0 a5 12 dxc5 bxc5 13 c4 ♘d7! is fully satisfactory) 11 c4!? (11 bxa6 gives White nothing here, e.g., 11...♖xa6 12 ♖xa6 ♘xa6 13 0-0 ♘e7 14 ♕e2 ♘b8 15 ♗a3 0-0, and 16 ♕b5?! ♘d7 17 ♖b1 ♖a8∓ Elseth-Lahlum, Porsgrunn 2003, or 16 c4!? dxc4 17 ♕xc4 ♖c8 18 dxc5 bxc5 19 ♖b1 ♘d7= R.Smith-A.Dowden, New Zealand 2001) 11...dxc4 12 ♘g5 (12 ♕e2 ♘e7 13 ♕xc4 ♘d7 14 0-0 ♖c8=) 12...♕b7! (Epelman's move)13 f3 ♘e7 14 ♘e4 0-0 15 ♗a3 ♘d7 16 ♘d6, and now Watson's 17...♕d5!? seems ∓.

9...♘xa6

10 ♕e2

(a) 10 0-0 ♘e7 11 ♘g5 (11 ♕e2 ♘b8 12 c4 dxc4 13 dxc5 0-0 14 ♕xc4 ♘d7 15 ♗a3 ♖fc8 16 ♖fe1 ♘xc5= Timmermans-Jetzl, Graz 1997) 11...h6 12 ♘h3 Ree-Bouwmeester, Amsterdam 1968; 12...cxd4 13 cxd4 ♖c8∓ – Watson;

(b) 10 c4 ♘e7 11 cxd5 ♘xd5 12 0-0

Play the French

cxd4 13 ♘xd4 0-0 (13...♕xe5? 14 ♖e1 ♘c3 15 ♕d2) 14 ♖e1 ♘ab4 and Black's active knights gave him at least equality in the game Golubev-Haba, Chemnitz 1998;

(c) 10 ♕d3 (White's queen is usually worse placed here than on e2 as Black can get in ...c4 or ...♘xe5 with tempo in some lines) 10...♘b8 (10...c4!?) 11 0-0 ♘d7 (11...♘e7 12 a5 bxa5 13 ♗a3 ♘d7 14 dxc5 ♘c6 15 c4 ♘dxe5! 16 ♘xe5 ♘xe5 17 ♕g3 0-0 18 ♗b2 f6 19 ♗c3 ♕xc5 20 cxd5 ♖ac8 21 ♗xe5 fxe5 22 dxe6 ♖fe8 23 ♕a3 ♕xa3 24 ♖xa3 ♖c5 ½-½ Bareiss-De Waard, corr 1998; Moles also gives 17 ♕d4?! ♘xc4 18 ♕xg7 0-0-0) 12 a5 (12 ♗a3 ♘e7 13 ♘d2 0-0 14 f4 ♖fe8 15 ♘f3 h6 16 ♖fc1 ♖ac8∓ due to the c-file, Zoughani-L.E.Johannessen, Patras 1999) 12...♖c8!? 13 axb6 axb6 14 dxc5 bxc5 15 ♖e1 ♘e7 16 h4 Suetin-Donner, Havana 1968, when Moles' 16...h6! looks ∓ as White has no kingside attack;

(d) 10 a5!? is more critical, the obvious answer being 10...bxa5 with play similar to the main line, e.g., 11 ♕d3 ♘b8 12 ♕b5+ ♘d7 13 ♗a3 ♘e7 14 ♗xc5 ♕c6 15 ♕xc6 ♘xc6 16 ♗d6 f6= A.Horvath-E.Berg, Oropesa del Mar 1999. Others are 10...♕b7!? intending 11 axb6 axb6 12 ♕e2 ♘e7 13 ♕b5+ ♘c6 – Watson; and the more ambitious 10...cxd4!? 11 cxd4 (11 axb6 ♕xc3+ 12 ♗d2 ♕c4 intending 13 b7 ♖b8 14 ♕e2 ♖xb7!) 11...♕c4 12 axb6 axb6, at least =.

10...♘b8
Preparing to reactivate the knight to a more active square at c6 or d7. 10...c4?! is less flexible but playable.
11 a5!?
The only critical try; Black is fine if given time to consolidate with 11 0-0 ♘e7 and:

(a) 12 c4 dxc4 13 dxc5 bxc5 14 ♕xc4 ♘d7 15 ♖e1 0-0 16 ♗g5 ♘g6 17 ♕e4 ♖ab8 was complex but probably about balanced in Bakre-E.Berg, Athens 2001;

(b) 12 dxc5 bxc5 13 c4 d4!? 14 ♘g5 ♘bc6 15 ♕h5 ♘g6 with mutual chances, Bobras-B.Socko, Warsaw 2002;

(c) 12 ♗a3 ♘d7 13 c4 0-0 14 ♖fe1 ♖fe8 15 dxc5?! ♘xc5∓ El Faher-Djurhuus, Cairo 1999;

(d) 12 a5 bxa5 13 ♗a3 ♘d7 14 dxc5!? a6 15 c4 ♘xc5 16 cxd5 ♘xd5 17 ♘g5 0-0 18 ♗xc5 ♕xc5= Arutunian-E.Berg, Pardubice 2002. Compare 12 0-0 ♘e7 in the main line below.
11...bxa5
Watson's 11...♘d7 12 axb6 ♘xb6 planning ...♘c4 looks =. But 11...bxa5 is sharper and as far as I can see works well for Black.

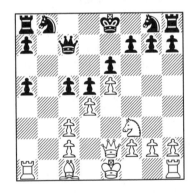

12 ♗a3
Consequent. 12 0-0 ♘e7 13 ♗a3 ♘d7 14 c4 (14 dxc5!? a6! 15 c4 ♘xc5 16 cxd5 ♘xd5 17 ♘g5 0-0 18 ♗xc5 ♕xc5 19 ♕d3 ♘f6 20 exf6 ½-½ was the game Sarbok-E.Berg, Gausdal 2003) 14...0-0 15 cxd5 ♘xd5= Ivkov-Donner, Bamberg 1968.
12...♘d7!?
12...♘e7!? 13 ♗xc5 ♘d7 14 ♕b5 ♖b8 15 ♕a4 ♕c6 16 ♕xa5 (16 ♕xc6 ♘xc6 17 ♗d6= Carlson-Davis, corr

1976) 16...♘xc5 'unclear' – Moles; this is solid but less ambitious.

13 dxc5 ♘e7

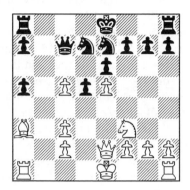

14 c6!

Otherwise 14...♘ec6!, when Black is in control. White needs to open the a3-f8 diagonal to get an attack.

14...♕xc6 15 0-0 ♕xc3 16 ♖fd1

16 ♗d6?! ♘f5 17 ♕b5 ♘xd6 18 exd6 ♕c5 19 ♕xc5 ♘xc5 20 ♖xa5 ♘e4 21 ♖fa1 ♘xd6 22 ♖xa7 ♖xa7 23 ♖xa7 0-0∓ Benassi-Ooorebeek, corr 1997.

16...♘c6 17 ♗d6

Otherwise Black can close off the diagonal a3-f8 with 17...♘b4 and then castle.

17...♕c4 18 ♕e3 ♕e4

18...h6!? to prevent 19 ♕g5 is an untested move which might work.

19 ♕b3

19 ♕c3 ♕c4 20 ♕e3 ♕e4 21 ♕c3 ♕c4= was von Bahr-Lahlum, Gothenburg 2002, when White played on with 22 ♕d2?! f6!? (22...h6!) 23 ♖a3!? ♘cxe5 24 ♘xe5 ♘xe5 25 ♕xa5 ♕c6 26 ♗xe5 fxe5 27 ♖c3 ♕d6 28 ♕b5+ ♕d7 29 ♕c5 ♖f8∓.

19...♘b6 20 c4! ♕xc4 21 ♕a3

21 ♕b2?! ♖c8 22 ♕d2 h6 23 ♖dc1 ♕a6 24 ♕f4 ♘e7 25 ♖xc8+ ♘bxc8 26 ♕g4 0-0 27 ♖c1? ♘xd6 0-1 Scheske-N.Stewart, Wittlich 1997.

21...♕a6

22 ♖ac1

Thus far the famous game Tal-Donner, Wijk aan Zee 1968, which for decades frightened Black players away from this variation. White stormed through in classical Tal fashion after 22...♖c8?! 23 ♘d2! (planning ♘b3-c5) 23...f6? (Moles gives 23...♘d4! 24 ♖xc8+ ♕xc8 25 ♕xa5 ♕d7, and 25...♕c2!? as suggested by Evans looks even better. Moles also gives 24 ♔h1 ♔d7, when 25 ♗c5!? ♘e2 26 ♖b1 might be best, but White's compensation looks airy. But this is just an extra possibility, as Black can improve earlier on.) 24 exf6 gxf6 25 ♕f3 ♔d7 26 ♕xf6 ♖he8 27 ♘e4!. However, Black keeps his pawns without losing his king after 22...♘c4! 23 ♕a4 ♖c8 – Shamkovich, who gives 24 ♘d4? ♘b2! 25 ♖xc6 ♖xc6-+. Instead 24 ♖c2 f6! 25 ♖dc1 ♔f7 was tested in two correspondence games of the Nordic Cup 1997, Pelle Larsen proved it insufficent for White after 26 h4? ♖hd8 27 ♖c3 ♔g8 0-1 Kontuilainen-P.Larsen and 26 exf6 gxf6 27 ♗g3 ♖he8 28 ♖xc4? (desperation, as Black was about to evacuate his king) 28...dxc4 29 ♖xc4 ♘e7 30 ♕c2 ♕xc4 31 ♘e5+ fxe5 32 ♕xh7+ ♔f8 0-1 Szalai-P.Larsen. 24 ♘d2!? might be best, but still Black held the advantage all the way through Seydoux-Dieu, corr 1998: 24...♘xd6 25 exd6 ♕b7 26 ♘b3 0-0 27 ♘c5 ♕a8 28 d7 ♖cd8 29 ♘xe6 fxe6 30 ♖xc6 ♕b7 31 ♖xe6 ♕xd7 32 ♕xd7 ♖xd7 33 ♖a6 d4 34 ♖xa5 d3 ½-½.

Many sources give the Tal-Donner game as the way to play for White against 6...♕c7 7 ♘f3 b6, but without quoting Moles' analysis or testing whether the pawn sacrifices were correct. It seems they are not. Although the last word almost certainly hasn't been written about these sharp variations, correct play from both sides seems to result in a black advantage. White undoubtedly gets some attacking chances, but 2 or 3 pawns is a lot to invest and the queenside is a risky area for White to operate in since Black has natural advantages on that side of the board. Hence after 7 ♘f3 b6 White will have to settle for one of the equalizing lines or try to explore some new territory, probably by risking a double-edged dxc5!? at some stage.

I have devoted a great deal of time to study of this particularly demanding variation, and my conclusion is that Black is fine from a theoretical point of view.

Chapter Thirteen

Classical Variation: 4 e5

1 e4 e6 2 d4 d5 3 ♘c3 ♘f6

This is the Classical Variation of the French Defence. It is similar in pawn structure to the Advance Variation as well as those lines of the Tarrasch variations that include the moves ...♘f6 and e5.

4 e5

In the next chapter we consider 4 ♗g5. 4 ♗d3 is seldom played due to 4...c5 and:

(a) 5 exd5 cxd4 (5...exd5=) 6 ♗b5+ ♗d7 7 ♗xd7+ (7 ♕xd4 ♗xb5 8 ♘xb5 ♘xd5 9 ♘e2 ♘c6 10 ♕a4 ♗c5!∓; 10...a6 11 ♘bd4 ♘b6 12 ♘xc6 ♘xa4 13 ♘xd8 ♖xd8= − Steinitz) 7...♕xd7 (7...♘bxd7!? 8 dxe6 dxc3 9 exd7+ ♕xd7∓) 8 dxe6 ♕xe6+ (8...fxe6!? 9 ♘ce2 ♘c6 10 ♘f3 ♗c5∓) 9 ♘ce2 ♘c6 10 ♘f3 ♗b4+ 11 ♗d2 0-0-0= Lasker-Marshall, New York (2) 1907;

(b) 5 ♘f3 cxd4 (5...♘c6=) 6 ♘xd4 e5 (6...♗b4!?; 6...♘c6 7 ♗b5 ♗d7 8 exd5 exd5 9 0-0 ♗e7 10 ♗e3 0-0= Lasker-Bogoljubow, Zurich 1934) 7 ♘f3 d4 8 ♘e2 ♗g4, just a shade better for Black after 9 0-0 (9 ♘xe5?? ♕a5+) 9...♘c6.

4...♘fd7

Now White has:

13.1 5 ♘f3
13.2 5 ♘ce2
13.3 5 f4

The only other interesting move is 5 ♕g4!? c5 (5...b6!?) and the centre is breaking up so White must try to get ♘b5-d6 in, or perhaps dxc5 at the right moment: 6 ♘f3 (6 ♘b5 cxd4 7 ♗f4 ♕a5+ 8 ♗d2 ♕b6∓) 6...cxd4 7 ♘b5 (7 ♕xd4 ♘c6 8 ♕f4 a6! intending ...♕c7) 7...♘c6 8 ♘d6+ ♗xd6 9 ♕xg7 ♗xe5 10 ♘xe5 ♕f6 11 ♕xf6 ♘xf6 12 ♘xc6?! (12 ♗f4! and 12...♔e7 13 ♗g3 ♘e4= or 12...♘d7 13 ♗b5 ♘cxe5 14 ♗xe5 ♖g8 15 g3 a6 16 ♗xd7+ ♗xd7 17 ♗xd4 ♔e7=) 12...bxc6 13 ♗f4 c5! 14 ♗e5 ♔e7 15 b4 cxb4 16 ♗xd4 ♖g8 17 ♗c5+ ♔d7 18 ♗xb4 a5 19 ♗a3 ♗a6∓.

13.1 5 ♘f3

Aiming for piece play instead of pawn expansion; it is played frequently but considered fairly harmless.

5...c5 6 ♘e2

Now we have reached the position from 5 ♘ce2 c5 6 ♘f3. 6 dxc5 transposes to 1 e4 e6 2 ♘f3 d5 3 ♘c3 ♘f6 4 e5 ♘fd7 5 d4 c5 6 dxc5, which is in the Odds and Ends chapter via 2 ♘f3 d5 3 ♘c3.

6...♘c6

6...cxd4 7 ♘exd4 ♘c6 is also reasonable, e.g., 8 ♘xc6 bxc6 9 ♗d3 ♘c5 10 ♗e2 ♗e7 11 0-0 0-0 12 ♗e3 ♖b8= Jimenez Chacon-Hamdouchi, Dos Hermanas 1998.

7 c3 cxd4

7...♗e7 is a flexible option: 8 a3! (8 ♘g3?! ♕b6 9 ♗e2 cxd4 10 cxd4 ♗b4+ 11 ♔f1 f6∓; 8 ♘f4 cxd4 9 cxd4 ♕b6 10 ♗e2? Yudkovsky-Coello, Cannes 1997, and Black should play 10...g5! 11 ♘h5 g4 12 ♘g5 ♗b4+ 13 ♔f1 ♕xd4∓) 8...a5 9 ♘f4 ♕b6 10 h4 a4=.

8 cxd4 f6

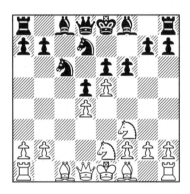

9 ♘f4

9 exf6 ♘xf6 10 ♘c3 ♗d6 is comfortable for Black (compare a 3 ♘d2 ♘f6 Tarrasch; here White is committed too early to ♘c3):

(a) 11 ♗b5 0-0 12 0-0 ♕c7 (or 12...♕b6!) 13 h3 ♗d7 14 ♖e1 ♖ae8 15 ♗e3 a6 16 ♗f1 Lau-Gleizerov, Dresden 1994, and here 16...e5! was strong;

(b) 11 ♗e2 0-0 12 0-0 h6 (12...♕b6!) 13 h3!? ♗d7 14 ♗e3 Hort-Knaak, Bundesliga 1996; now 14...♗e8! 15 ♖e1 ♗g6 was promising;

(c) 11 ♗d3 0-0 12 ♗g5 ♕e8!?

(12...♕b6!) 13 ♕d2? ♘h5? (13...e5!∓) 14 ♘e2? (14 ♕c2; 14 0-0 ♘f4) 14...e5 15 ♘xe5 (15 dxe5? ♗b4 16 ♘c3 ♖xf3! 17 gxf3 d4 18 f4 dxc3 19 bxc3 ♘xe5! 20 fxe5 ♕xe5+ –+ McDonald) 15...♘xd4 16 ♘xd4 ♕xe5+ 17 ♗e3 ♘f4∓ Nijboer-Glek, Wijk aan Zee 1999.

9...♗b4+ 10 ♗d2 ♕e7

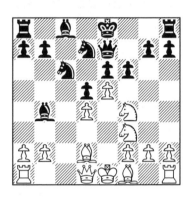

11 ♗xb4

11 exf6?! ♘xf6∓ 12 ♗d3 0-0 13 0-0 ♘e4 14 ♗e3 ♗d6 15 g3 ♕f6 16 ♗xe4 dxe4 17 ♘d2 ♗xf4 18 gxf4 ♗d7! 19 ♘xe4 ♕g6+ 20 ♘g3 ♘e7! 21 ♖c1 ♗c6 with light square domination, Tate-Shulman, Sioux Falls 2001.

After 11 ♗xb4, Shirov-Ivanchuk, Tilburg 1993 continued 11...♕xb4+ 12 ♕d2 ♔e7! 13 exf6+ gxf6 14 ♕xb4+ ♘xb4 15 ♔d2 ♘b6 16 a3 ♘c6 17 ♗b5 ♗d7!? (17...♘a5! 18 ♖ae1 ♘ac4+ 19 ♔c1 ♔f7= with the idea ...a6) 18 ♗xc6 ♗xc6 19 ♖he1 ♗d7 20 b3 ♔d6 21 ♖e3 and White had a small advantage. As a whole, however, 5 ♘f3 is rather easy to play against.

13.2 5 ♘ce2

This is considered the optimal order to get to the main f4 lines, but that is not so clear. Before we get to how Black can throw a wrench (spanner!) in the works, let's take a close look at 5 f4. That is the move used in the next section (13.3), but I'm going discuss it here first for early deviations in the context of ♘ce2 systems. The move order issues examined here and in the next few notes are of great importance and will repay study: 5 f4 c5 6 ♘f3 (6 dxc5 and other non-transpositional moves not leading to ♘ce2 systems are given in 13.3) 6...♘c6 7 ♘e2

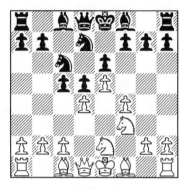

This can also arise after 5 ♘ce2 c5 6 f4 ♘c6 7 ♘f3, as well as from 3 ♘d2 ♘f6 4 e5 ♘fd7 5 f4 c5 6 ♘df3 ♘c6 7 ♘e2. Although it is appearing regularly, books tend to either treat lightly or even ignore this position. Black has several ways to respond. 7...♕b6 returns the game to normal channels after 8 c3. And 7...b5!? has been played quite a bit recently, although it seems more logical once White has played g3. A problem for Black, not necessarily insoluble, is 8 a3 ♖b8 9 c3 a5 (9...b4 10 dxc5! bxc3 11 b4 a5 12 ♘ed4) 10 dxc5 ♘xc5 11 ♗e3!? with the idea 11...♘e4? 12 ♘g3±.

But it's not so easy for White. Two other nontranspositional moves are playable, with one that I find particularly attractive:

(a) 7...cxd4; McDonald thinks that this is dubious, yet it has a long his-

tory. Perhaps White is a little better, but Black has many possibilities, for example, 8 ♘exd4 ♗c5 (or 8...♘xd4 9 ♘xd4 ♕b6 10 c3 ♗c5 11 ♗e2 0-0) 9 c3 ♕b6 10 b4!? (10 ♗e2 0-0!? 11 ♗d3! g6 12 ♗c2 ♘xd4 13 cxd4 ♗b4+ 14 ♔f2 f6±) 10...♘xd4 11 ♘xd4 ♗xd4 12 ♕xd4 ♕xd4 13 cxd4 ♘b6 14 ♗d3 (14 a4 ♗d7 15 a5 ♘c4=) 14...♗d7 15 ♗d2 ♖c8 (15...a6 16 0-0 ♗b5!?) 16 ♔e2 a6 17 ♖hc1 0-0 18 g4 ♘a4 with the idea ...♗b5, was Niedermaier-B.Schneider, Bundesliga 1986. Neither side played perfectly, of course, but at least we see some ideas;

(b) 7...♗e7!? is an interesting waiting move, not committing to ...♕b6, ...cxd4, or ...b5. I quite like it.

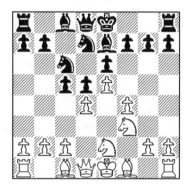

White has to show his cards:

(b1) 8 ♗e3 ♕b6 forces White to lose a crucial tempo defending his b-pawn, which isn't so easy – compare main lines;

(b2) 8 g3 ♕b6 gives White the option of entering a main line by means of 9 c3 (also from the 3 ♘d2 ♘f6 Tarrasch Variation), but with g3 already in, which isn't always his plan in the 5 ♘ce2 lines. An independent and logical plan for Black would be 8...0-0 9 ♗g2 b6!? intending 10 0-0 ♗a6. In fact, even the immediate 8...b6 is worth thinking about;

(b3) 8 c3 is the key move. It allows Black to transpose into a main line by 8...♕b6 or he can go his own way by 8...0-0, e.g., 9 a3 (9 g3 allows another known position after 9...♕b6, but Black can also play a standard anti-f4 plan by 9...f5 and queenside expansion; or choose an aggressive strategy by 9...a5!? 10 ♗g2 b5!? having in mind ...♗a6 and ...b4) 9...a5 10 g3 cxd4 (alternatives are 10...b6!? and 10...a4!? 11 ♗h3) 11 cxd4 (11 ♘exd4 ♘c5= intends moves like ...♗d7 and ...a4) 11...f6!? (11...f5 12 ♗g2?! a4 13 0-0 ♘b6 wins key queenside squares) 12 ♗h3 fxe5 13 dxe5 (13 ♗xe6+ ♔h8 is messy, but the first point is 14 dxe5?! ♘dxe5!) 13...♕b6!? (13...♘c5! with the idea ...a4) 14 ♘c3? (for better or worse, correct was the risky 14 ♗xe6+ ♔h8 15 ♗xd5) 14...♘dxe5!? (14...♘c5 ties White down completely, since 15 ♘d4 ♘xd4 16 ♕xd4 ♕a6 threatens ...♘b3 and ...♘d3+) 15 fxe5 ♘xe5 16 ♗g2 ♗d7 17 ♖f1 ♘c4 with a strong attack for the piece. Bologan-M.Gurevich, Cap d'Agde 2002 went 18 ♖b1 ♗f6 19 ♕d3 ♖ac8 20 ♘g5 ♗xg5 21 ♗xg5 ♖xf1+ 22 ♗xf1 ♖f8 23 ♕e2 ♖f5! 24 ♗f4 g5 25 ♘xd5 exd5 26 ♗b8 ♖f8 0-1.

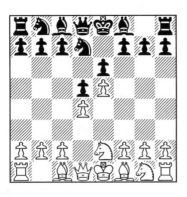

5...c5 6 c3

6 ♘f3 transposes into 5 ♘f3 c5 6

♘e2 above. 6 f4! may well be the best move order, because of the issues raised in the note to 6...♘c6 below.

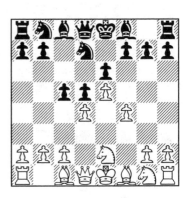

Now 6...♘c6 7 ♘f3 is the last note, but 7 c3! will transpose to our main line without having to deal with the 7...f6 variation below. And 6...cxd4 7 ♘xd4 ♘c6 8 ♘gf3 also transposes to the last note, but not to Black's best line. Nevertheless, I think that Black has other good opportunities to deviate at this point. Here are a some ideas:

(a) 6...♕b6 7 ♘f3 (7 c3 ♗e7 8 ♘f3 0-0 transposes) 7...♗e7 is a sort of waiting game: 8 c3 0-0 with the idea 9 dxc5 ♘xc5 10 ♘ed4 ♘c6 11 ♗e2 ♘e4=;

(b) 6...♗e7 is a similar idea, when White might try 7 ♘f3 0-0 8 c3 (8 ♗e3 ♕b6), leading to 8...f6!? (or 8...♕b6) 9 ♗e3 fxe5 10 fxe5 ♕b6 11 ♕d2 ♘c6 with mixed prospects, e.g., 12 0-0-0 (12 ♘f4? cxd4 13 ♘xd4 ♖xf4! 14 ♗xf4 ♘xd4 15 ♕xd4 ♕xb2 16 ♖d1 ♕xa2∓) 12...♕a5 13 ♔b1 cxd4 14 cxd4 ♘b6! 15 ♕xa5 ♘xa5 16 b3 ♗d7= intending ...♘c6 and ...a5-a4;

(c) 6...♕a5+!? 7 c3 (7 ♗d2 ♕b6 8 ♗c3 ♘c6 9 ♘f3 cxd4!? 10 ♘exd4 ♗b4 is promising) 7...b5!? (risky but perhaps okay; 7...♘c6 is of course an option) 8 ♘f3 (8 dxc5 b4 9 a3 ♗xc5 10

♗d2 ♛b6=) 8...b4 9 ♗d2 ♞c6 10 cxb4 cxb4 with the idea 11 a3!? ♗e7! 12 axb4 ♞xb4 etc. The interesting thing is that if any of these moves is satisfactory for Black, White has no order that gets him to the main lines by force without legitimate options for Black.

6...♞c6

Assuming that Black has achieved this exact position after all the move order jockeying implicit in the last two notes, he actually has a significant move that seems to equalise at this point: 6...cxd4 7 cxd4 f6!:

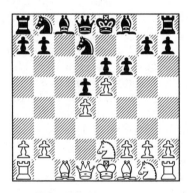

(a) Black's development is fast after 8 exf6 ♞xf6 9 ♞f3 ♗d6 (9...♞c6 10 ♞c3 transposes to 13.1, the note to 9 ♞f4, which was fine for Black) 10 g3 ♞c6 11 ♗g2 0-0 12 0-0 ♛b6 13 ♖b1 ♗d7 14 ♗f4 ♞e4 with good activity in Bologan-Glek, Bundesliga 1992;

(b) 8 f4 fxe5 9 dxe5 (9 fxe5 ♗b4+ 10 ♔f2 0-0+ 11 ♞f3 ♞c6 with initiative and ideas of sacrificing on e5) 9...♞c6 10 ♞f3 ♗b4+ 11 ♞c3 (11 ♗d2 ♞c5) 11...♞c5 12 ♗e3 Shirov-Ivanchuk, Tilburg 1993, and a straightforward path was 12...♞e4 13 ♛c2 (13 ♖c1 ♛a5 14 ♗d2 0-0) 13...♛a5 14 ♖c1 ♛xa2∓;

(c) 8 ♞f4 ♗b4+ 9 ♗d2 ♛b6 10 ♗xb4 (10 exf6 ♞xf6 11 ♛a4+ ♞c6∓;

10 ♖c1 0-0 11 ♗xb4 ♛xb4+ 12 ♛d2 ♛e7 unclear – Atalik; 10 ♛h5+ g6 11 ♞xg6 ♗xd2+ 12 ♔xd2 ♛xb2+ 13 ♔e3 ♛xa1 14 ♞xh8+ ♔d8 and Black is at least okay) 10...♛xb4+ 11 ♛d2 ♛xd2+ 12 ♔xd2 ♔e7

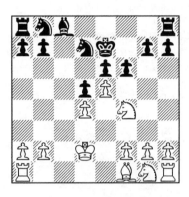

13 exf6+ (the most commonly played move; 13 ♞f3 fxe5 14 ♞xe5 ♞xe5 15 dxe5 ♞c6 16 ♞d3 ♗d7 [or 16...b6 17 ♖c1 ♗b7=] 17 f4 ♗e8 18 ♖c1 ♖f8 19 g3 is '±' according to theory, but then 19...♗g6!, e.g., 20 ♞c5 ♖fc8!? 21 ♞xb7 [21 ♗b5 ♞b4!] 21...♞b4! and White loses the c-file) 13...gxf6 14 ♖e1 (14 ♞f3?! ♔d6; 14 ♞ge2 ♞c6 15 ♞d3 e5) 14...♞b6 and now two important moves:

(c1) 15 ♗d3?! allows Black to force things in the centre by 15...♞c6 16 ♞f3 ♔d6! 17 ♞h5 ♖f8! (17...e5 18 ♞xf6 e4 19 ♞g5 ♔c7 is unclear) 18 ♗xh7 (18 ♖e2 e5 19 ♞xf6 e4 20 ♞xe4+ dxe4 21 ♗xe4 ♗g4∓) 18...e5 (18...♖h8!? is messy) 19 dxe5+ (19 ♞g3 e4 20 ♞h4 ♞xd4 21 f3 ♖h8! 22 ♞hf5+ ♗xf5 23 ♞xf5+ ♔e5 and Black's king was a monster in Bezgodov-Sakaev, Russia Ch 1999) 19...fxe5 20 ♔c1 (20 ♖hf1 ♗g4∓; 20 ♞g3 ♗g4!∓) 20...♗g4 21 ♞g3 ♗xf3 22 gxf3 ♞d4-+ Arakhamia Grant-Gleizerov, Port Erin 2001;

(c2) 15 ♞f3 ♔d6 (15...♞c6 16 ♗b5

♗d7 17 ♗xc6 bxc6 18 ♖e2 favoured White in Anand-Bareev, Shenyang 2000) and here White must find something better than transposing into the previous note by 16 ♘h5 (16 ♗b5 a6 17 ♗d3 ♘c6 is no improvement) 16...♖f8 17 ♗d3 ♘c6.

7 f4 ♛b6

For 7...♗e7, compare 6 f4 ♗e7, although delaying ...♘c6 there allowed a queen on b6 to cover e6 for the ...f6 break.

8 ♘f3 f6

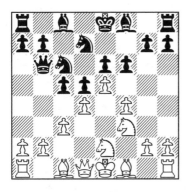

Finally the main line position of the 5 ♘ce2 variation has been reached. Black wants to blast open the centre, sacrificially if necessary, whereas White knows that if he can hold on to his space advantage without compromising his pawns or creating weaknesses, he must stand better. A particularly fascinating thing about this position, which has been around for years, is that White has begun to neglect his development entirely in order to expand on the flanks. Thus one will see a3 and b4 as well as h4-h5 in order to clamp down on both wings. In the end I believe that Black, with superior development, has sufficient resources to achieve dynamic equality. In any case, the play will seldom become

drawish! At this point there is a vitally important fork in the road:

13.21 9 g3
13.22 9 a3

(a) 9 ♛b3 is normally answered by 9...cxd4 10 ♛xb6 ♘xb6=; a fun alternative is 9...♛c7 (what's the queen doing on b3?): 10 g3 cxd4 (10...fxe5 11 fxe5 cxd4 12 cxd4 ♗b4+ 13 ♗d2 ♗xd2+ 14 ♘xd2 0-0) 11 cxd4 ♗b4+ 12 ♔f2 0-0 13 ♔g2 ♗a5 (13...fxe5!? 14 fxe5 ♗e7 15 ♗e3 ♘b6∓ 16 ♘f4 ♘a5 17 ♛d1 ♘ac4) 14 ♗e3 ♗b6 15 ♖c1 ♛b8 16 exf6 ♘xf6 17 ♘e5 ♗d7 18 ♘xd7 ♘xd7= B.Lalic-Dizdar, Porec 1998;

(b) 9 ♘g3? is better after the move a3: 9...cxd4 10 cxd4 ♗b4+ 11 ♔e2 (this is the only move) 11...g5! 12 exf6 g4 13 f7+ ♔e7 14 ♘d2 ♘xd4+ 15 ♔e1 ♛c7;

(c) 9 exf6 ♘xf6 10 g3 ♗d6 11 ♗g2 0-0 12 0-0 cxd4 13 cxd4 e5!? (13...♗d7 14 b3 ♘e4∓) 14 fxe5 ♘xe5 15 ♘xe5 ♗xe5 16 ♔h1 ♗c7 17 ♘c3= Aseev-Pesiakov, St Petersburg 1999;

(d) 9 h4 is playable but probably a move too early: 9...cxd4 (9...♗e7 10 h5? fxe5 11 fxe5 cxd4 12 cxd4 0-0∓) 10 cxd4 fxe5 11 fxe5 ♗b4+ 12 ♘c3 0-0 13 a3 ♗e7 14 ♗e2? ♖xf3! 15 gxf3 ♛xd4∓ Mahdi-Weinzettl, Mureck 2001.

13.21 9 g3 cxd4
and the play splits a last time:

13.211 10 ♘exd4
13.212 10 cxd4

13.211 10 ♘exd4
This has become the key line of late, following some White improvements.

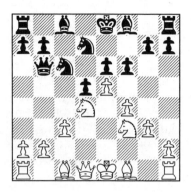

10...fxe5

The only solution that I see working here apart from my main line is the immediate 10...♘xd4 11 cxd4 ♗b4+ (without ...fxe5) 12 ♗d2 (12 ♔f2 0-0 13 ♗e3 fxe5 14 fxe5 ♗e7 15 b3 ♖f7 16 h4 K.Schmidt-Merker, corr 1987; and the same idea of 16...♘f8 17 ♗d3 ♗d7 and ...♗e8 or ...♗b5 works fine) 12...fxe5 13 fxe5 0-0. This sidesteps the ♔f2-g2 idea and equalises effortlessly after 14 ♗xb4 ♕xb4+ 15 ♕d2 ♕xd2+ 16 ♘xd2 ♘b8! 17 ♗e2 ♘c6 18 ♘f3 ♗d7, e.g., 19 0-0 ♗e8 20 ♖ad1 h6 21 h3 ♗g6.

11 fxe5

11 ♘xe6 is normally queried although none of the given solutions is clear: 11...♘f6 (11...♘e7?! 12 ♘xf8 ♖xf8 13 ♕e2!; 11...e4 12 ♘fd4! ♘f6 13 a4! and 13...♗d7 ends in equality, but more interesting is 13...♘xd4 14 ♘xd4 ♗c5 15 ♗b5+ ♗d7 16 ♗xd7+ ♔xd7=) 12 fxe5 (12 ♘xf8 ♗g4 13 ♗e2 ♗xf3 14 ♗xf3 ♖xf8=) 12...♗xe6! 13 exf6 0-0-0 with good compensation, e.g., 14 ♕e2 ♖e8! 15 ♗e3 ♗c5 16 ♗xc5 ♕xc5 and White has problems: 17 fxg7 ♖hg8∓ 18 0-0-0 ♗g4 19 ♕d3 Strobel-Piasecki, Baden 1993; now 19...♕f2!∓.

11...♘c5!

A move played by Luther that gives Black his full share of the play. With other moves Black won't equalise:

(a) 11...♘dxe5? 12 ♘xe5 ♘xe5 13 ♕h5+;

(b) 11...♘xd4 12 cxd4 ♗b4+ 13 ♔f2 0-0 14 ♔g2 ♗e7 15 ♗d3 ♖f7 16 h4 ♘f8 17 ♘g5 ♗xg5 18 hxg5 g6 19 ♖h4± or better, as occurred in two games;

(c) 11...♗c5? 12 ♘xe6 ♘dxe5 13 ♘xc5! ♕xc5 14 ♘xe5 ♘xe5 15 ♕h5+ ♘g6 16 ♕e2+!± with ♗e3 and ♗e2 – Pedersen.

12 ♗h3

I don't know of other games, so here's some analysis:

(a) 12 ♘xc6 bxc6 13 ♕c2 (13 ♘d4 g6! 14 ♖b1 [14 ♗e2 ♗g7] 14...♗g7 15 ♗f4 0-0 16 ♗e2 ♘e4 17 0-0 c5 18 ♘f3 ♗b7∓) 13...♗e7! 14 ♗e3 0-0 15 ♗e2 ♗a6 16 b4 ♘d3+ 17 ♔d2 c5!;

(b) 12 ♗b5 ♗e7 13 0-0 0-0 14 ♗g5 h6 15 ♗xe7 ♘xe7 16 a4 a6 17 a5 ♕c7=.

12...♗e7!

12...♕a6!? 13 ♗f1 ♕b6= draws.

13 0-0 0-0 14 ♕e2

14 ♔h1 ♘xd4 15 ♕xd4 ♕c7∓.

14...♘xd4 15 ♘xd4

Or 15 cxd4 ♘e4∓. After 15 ♘xd4, Atlas-Luther, Moerbisch 2001 went 15...♖xf1+ 16 ♔xf1 ♗d7 17 ♔g2 ♔h8

(17...♖f8!? 18 ♗e3 a5=) 18 ♗e3 ♕c7 19 ♗g1 ♖f8 20 ♖e1 with equality.

13.212 10 cxd4

This move is so associated with miniature disasters for White that some people are surprised to find that it's theoretically playable, if only equal. I won't spend too much time showing brilliancies by Black.

10...♗b4+

I think that this move order is more flexible and therefore preferable to the exchange of f- for e-pawn first. But often they transpose and there are some nuances: 10...fxe5

(a) 11 dxe5? ♗b4+ 12 ♗d2 ♕e3! is winning: 13 ♗g2 (13 ♕b3! ♕e4!) 13...0-0 14 ♔f1? (14 a3 ♘c5!; 14 ♕b3! ♕xb3 15 axb3 ♘c5∓) 14...♗xd2 15 ♕xd2 ♕xd2 16 ♘xd2 ♘dxe5-+;

(b) 11 fxe5 ♗b4+ 12 ♘c3 0-0 13 ♗f4 (this is the good defensive move that White doesn't have if Black omits the exchange on e5; compare the main line; not 13 a3? ♖xf3!∓) 13...♗e7 (threatening b2 and also ...g5 in many cases) 14 ♕d2? (14 ♗h3? ♕xb2 15 ♗xe6+ ♔h8 16 ♖c1 ♖xf4! 17 gxf4 ♘xd4-+ – Sisniega; 14 ♘a4 is equal after 14...♕a5+ 15 ♘c3 ♕b6 16 ♘a4 ♕a5+= etc.; for 14 a3!, compare the main line; White has some advan-

tage) 14...g5! 15 ♘xg5 ♗xg5 16 ♗xg5 ♘xd4 17 ♗g2 ♘xe5-+ Dolmatov-Bareev, Elista 1997.

11 ♘c3

11 ♗d2 has lost countless games after 11...fxe5 12 fxe5 0-0 13 ♗g2 ♘dxe5! 14 dxe5 ♘xe5, e.g., 15 ♘ed4 (15 ♘f4 ♕e3+ 16 ♔f1 ♗xd2-+) 15...♘d3+ (15...♘c4 also wins) 16 ♔e2 ♘xb2 17 ♕b3 ♕a6+ 18 ♔f2 ♗xd2 19 ♕xb2 ♕d3-+ was Hamann-Uhlmann, Halle 1963.

11...0-0

Now there's no ♗f4 defence, so White's task is much harder.

12 a3!

(a) 12 exf6 ♘xf6 13 ♗g2 (13 a3= – Bondarevski; 13...♗e7∓) 13...♘e4 14 ♕d3 e5! 15 0-0 (15 fxe5 ♗g4∓) 15...♘xc3 16 bxc3 e4-+ Grischuk-Mraz, corr 1986;

(b) 12 ♗h3? is often played, but is only good after 12 a3 ♗e7. Here it has lost numerous contests in the manner of 12...fxe5 13 ♗xe6+ ♔h8 14 fxe5 ♘dxe5! 15 ♗xd5 ♘xf3+ 16 ♗xf3 ♘xd4-+ Chevalier-Lempereur, Paris 1994.

12...♗e7

Possible is 12...♗xc3+ 13 bxc3 fxe5 14 fxe5 ♕c7 intending ...♘b6 with light square pressure.

13 ♗h3!

Without ♗f4, the threat of 13...fxe5 14 fxe5? ♖xf3 is difficult to meet:

(a) 13 ♗d3?! fxe5 14 dxe5 (14 fxe5 ♘xd4 15 ♘xd4 ♘xe5 with more than enough compensation, even after the mild 16 ♖f1! ♗d7! 17 ♗b1 ♗c5∓) 14...♘c5 15 ♗c2 ♖d8∓;

(b) 13 ♘a4 ♕c7 14 ♗d3 fxe5 (14...a6!?) 15 fxe5? ♖xf3! 16 ♕xf3 ♘xd4 17 ♕d1 (or 17 ♕e3 ♘xe5!) 17...♘xe5 18 0-0 ♘xd3 19 ♕xd3 e5∓;

(c) 13 exf6 ♘xf6 14 ♗d3 a6 15 ♗c2 ♗d7 16 0-0 ♗e8!∓ with the idea of ...♗h5.

13...fxe5

13...♔h8!? isn't bad, e.g., 14 ♘a4 (14 ♗xe6? ♘dxe5!; 14 0-0) 14...♕a6! 15 ♗f1 b5 16 ♘c3 fxe5 17 ♗xb5 ♕b6 18 ♗xc6 (18 fxe5 ♖xf3! 19 ♗xc6 ♘xe5!! 20 ♗xa8 ♘d3+ 21 ♔e2 ♕xd4-+ Knaak) 18...♕xc6 19 fxe5 ♗a6!, was Sznapik-Knaak, Bratislava 1983; Black has a small edge after 20 ♗f4 ♖ab8.

14 ♗xe6+

14 fxe5? ♖xf3 15 ♕xf3 ♘xd4-+.

14...♔h8 15 ♘xd5

15 dxe5 ♘dxe5.

15...♕d8 16 ♗xd7

16 ♘xe7 ♕xe7 17 d5 e4 18 ♘g5 ♘c5! 19 ♗xc8 (19 0-0! ♗xe6 20 dxe6 ♘xe6 21 ♘xe4 ♘xf4= – Yudasin and Ivanov; or 19...♘xe6) 19...♘d3+ 20 ♔f1 ♖axc8 21 dxc6 ♕xg5 22 cxb7 ♖b8 23 ♔g2 ♕f6 24 ♕e2 ♖xb7 unclear, Lukin-Se.Ivanov, USSR 1984.

16...♗xd7 17 dxe5 ♗g4

With activity and the light squares, Black is probably a little better despite the two pawn deficit. Smagin-Dimitrov, Prilep 1992 continued 18 0-0 ♗c5+ 19 ♗e3 ♗xe3+ 20 ♘xe3 ♕b6 21 ♕d2 ♗xf3 22 ♖xf3 ♘d4 23 ♖ff1 (23 ♖af1 ♘xf3+ 24 ♖xf3 unclear – Smagin) 23...♘b3 24 ♕f2 ♘xa1 25 ♖xa1 ♖ae8 26 ♖c1 g5!∓.

13.22 9 a3 ♗e7

10 h4

The modern move. Alternatives:

(a) 10 b4 cxd4 and:

(a1) 11 ♘exd4?! fxe5! 12 fxe5?! (12 ♘xe6! ♘f6 planning 13 ♘xg7+ ♔f8 14 b5 ♘e4!? 15 ♕c2 ♘d8 16 ♘h5 ♕h6∓ – Pedersen) 12...♘dxe5 13 ♘xe5 ♘xe5 14 ♕h5+ ♘g6 15 ♗d3 0-0 16 ♗xg6 hxg6 17 ♕xg6 ♗f6 18 ♗e3 e5 0-1 F.Meyer-Pedersen, Germany 1999;

(a2) 11 cxd4 0-0 12 ♖b1 a5 (12...♘a5!? 13 ♘c3 ♘c4 is unclear; 12...♖f7!? 13 ♕d3 ♘f8= with the idea ...♗d7, ...♖c8) 13 b5 a4 was Shirov-Gurevich, Munich 1993; 14 exf6 ♘xf6 15 ♘c3 ♘d8 16 ♗d3 ♘f7 unclear (Shirov);

(b) 10 ♘g3 is easily met by 10...0-0 11 ♗d3 fxe5 12 fxe5 (12 dxe5 c4 13 ♗c2 ♘c5∓) 12...cxd4 13 cxd4 g6!∓ and 14...♘xd4 or 14...♖xf3 next, since ♗xh7+/♕h5 ideas are eliminated.

10...0-0 11 ♖h3!

The star move for this variation. 11 b4 cxd4 12 cxd4 a5 (12...♖f7=) 13 b5!? (13 bxa5 ♕xa5+ 14 ♗d2 ♕b6∓) 13...♕xb5!? (13...♘d8=) 14 ♘c3 ♕b6 15 ♖b1 ♕d8 16 ♗d3 gave White some attack in Bauer-Bareev, Enghien les Bains 2003; 16...h6 17 ♘b5 ♖a6!? (17...f5) 18 ♗c2 f5 19 g4 ♘b6 20 gxf5 exf5∓.

11...a5

A legitimate alternative is 11...cxd4 12 cxd4 ♘a5 13 b4 ♘c4 14 ♘c3 (14 ♘g3 a5 15 ♗d3 f5) 14...a5 15 b5 ♖f7! with the standard plan ...♖f7, ...♘f8, ...♗d7; I used to play this way in the Tarrasch 3...♘f6 variation with 5 f4.

12 b3 ♕c7

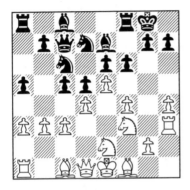

13 ♘eg1!

An ingenious retreat: White undevelops his pieces just to hold the centre and play prophylactically. A pretty game followed 13 ♕c2?! b6! 14 ♗d2 ♗a6 15 a4?! ♖ac8 16 f5? fxe5 17 fxe6 e4! 18 exd7 ♕xd7 (winning) 19 ♘e5 ♘xe5 20 dxe5 ♕xh3! 21 gxh3 ♗xh4+ 22 ♔d1 ♖xf1+ 23 ♗e1 ♖xe1+ 0-1 Jamrich-H.Schneider Zinner, Budapest 2001.

13...a4

Anand recommends 13...b6, which he thinks is fine based upon the mistaken combinative try 14 ♗d3 (14 ♗e3 ♗a6 15 ♗xa6 ♖xa6= – Anand) 14...♗a6 15 ♗xh7+? ♔xh7 16 ♘g5+ fxg5 17 hxg5+ ♔g8 18 ♕h5 (18 g6 ♖f5-+) 18...♗xg5! 19 fxg5 ♖f1+ 20 ♔d2 ♖af8 21 ♕h7+ ♔f7-+.

14 b4 fxe5 15 fxe5 ♘dxe5!? 16 dxe5 ♘xe5 17 ♘xe5 ♕xe5+ 18 ♕e2 ♗xh4+!?

Generally condemned. Black could also play 18...♕c7 followed by ...e5

(hitting h3) and/or ...♗f6. This isn't easy to assess because Black has the centre and White's king is exposed. Of course it's only two pawns and if White can develop he's winning. Oddly enough, HiArcs already likes Black. There might follow something like 19 ♗g5!? (19 ♘f3 cxb4 or 19...e5; 19 ♕h5 cxb4 20 axb4 g6 21 ♕h6 e5 22 ♖g3 ♖xf1+! 23 ♔xf1 ♕c4+ 24 ♘e2 ♗g4∓) 19...♗xg5 20 hxg5 e5 21 ♖f3 (21 ♖e3 e4 22 ♖d1 cxb4 23 cxb4 ♗e6 24 ♘h3 ♖ad8 and ...♕e5 with a strong attack) 21...♗f5 22 ♕f2!? cxb4 23 cxb4 e4 24 ♕g3 ♖ac8!. This shows that the assumption that White was better throughout this game should at least be questioned.

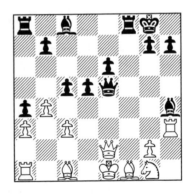

19 ♔d1

Not 19 ♖xh4? ♕g3+.

19...♕f6?

After this Black is doomed. There have been various statements (with little analysis) about the ending after 19...♕xe2+! 20 ♗xe2 ♗f2 (actually 20...♗f6 has some good points, e.g., 21 bxc5 ♖a5 22 ♗e3 ♗xc3 23 ♖b1 d4 or 23...e5; maybe this is better?). Positions so deep into the opening seldom determine its validity, and Black has had better options on the last few moves, so I won't take too serious a look here. But to me chances seem about balanced. Since 21 ♘f3? e5 looks bad, White's has 21 ♖h1 (Kavalek) 21...e5 (or 21...cxb4) 22 bxc5 ♖a5!; or Anand's 21 ♗e3 e5 22 ♗xf2 ♖xf2 23 ♖g3 and 'White has a comfortable edge in the ending'. This strikes me as unclear, one plausible continuation being 23...b6 24 ♔e1 (24 ♘h3 ♖f6 25 ♖g5 ♖f5 26 ♗b5 ♖a7!) 24...♖f6 (24...♖f4!?) 25 ♖e3 ♖e6 and White may be slightly better but this would have to be proven.

After 19...♕f6, Anand-Shirov, Tehran 2000 continued 20 ♘f3! (Kavalek analyses the alternative 20 ♖f3 ♕e7 21 ♗e3 d4 to White's advantage, but 21...b6! is better) 20...♕xc3 (there isn't anything better) 21 ♗b2 ♕b3+ 22 ♔c1 e5 23 ♖xh4 (23 ♘d2! ♗xh3 24 ♘xb3±) 23...♗f5 24 ♕d1 e4 25 ♕xb3 axb3 26 ♘d2 e3 27 ♘f3 (27 ♘xb3±) 27...♖ae8 28 ♔d1 c4 29 ♗e2 and White's two extra pieces decide.

13.3 5 f4 c5

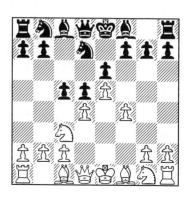

6 ♘f3

Here we look at lines not involving ♘ce2.

6 dxc5 ♘c6 7 a3 is an old line: 7...♗xc5 8 ♕g4 0-0 9 ♘f3 ♘d4 10 ♗d3 f5 11 ♕h3 ♘xf3+ 12 ♕xf3 ♗b6 13 ♘e2 ♘c5∓ Tarrasch-Spielmann, Nuremberg 1906) 7 ♕g4 0-0 8 ♗d3 f5 9

♕h3 ♗xg1! (this is an original idea; 9...♘c6=) 10 ♖xg1 ♘c5 11 ♗d2 ♘c6!? 12 ♘b5?! ♕b6 13 0-0-0 ♗d7 14 ♘d6 ♘a4! 15 ♗b5 ♘d4 16 ♗e3 ♘e2+! 17 ♗xe2 ♕xb2+ 18 ♔d2 ♕b4+ 19 ♔c1 ♘c3∓ Fischer-Benko, Curaçao 1962.

6...♘c6

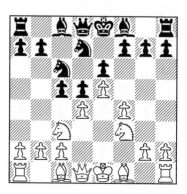

6...cxd4 7 ♘xd4 ♗b4!? is definitely worthy of consideration; I don't know of any examples.

7 ♗e3

For 7 ♘e2, see 13.2 5 ♘ce2. Others are barely touched upon (if at all) in the books:

(a) 7 ♗d3?! cxd4 8 ♘e2 ♕b6 9 0-0 f6! 10 exf6 ♘xf6 11 ♔h1 ♗c5 12 a3 a5 13 b3 0-0 14 ♗b2 g6? (14...♘g4! 15 ♕e1 e5! 16 ♘xe5 ♘cxe5 17 fxe5 ♖xf1+ 18 ♕xf1 ♘xe5∓) 15 ♕e1 ♗d7?! (15...♘h5∓) 16 ♕h4 unclear, Abdel Aziem-Peng Zhaoqin, Cairo 2002;

(b) 7 a3? meets the fate of any slow move: 7...cxd4 8 ♘xd4 ♘dxe5! with the idea 9 fxe5 ♕h4+;

(c) 7 ♗b5 a6!? (7...cxd4 8 ♘xd4 ♘xd4 9 ♕xd4 a6 10 ♗xd7+ ♗xd7 11 0-0 ♖c8 12 ♗e3 ♗c5=) 8 ♗xc6 bxc6 9 0-0 (9 ♘e2 cxd4 10 ♘fxd4 c5 11 ♘f3 ♗e7 12 0-0 ♘b6!? 13 c3 0-0 14 ♕c2 a5!∓ Varga-Lehmann, Hungary 1999) 9...cxd4 10 ♘xd4 c5 11 ♘f3 ♗e7∓ Megibow-Cotton, Concord 1995; the bishop pair counts for something;

(d) 7 dxc5 ♗xc5 8 ♗d3 a6!? (8...f6! 9 exf6 ♘xf6 10 ♕e2 0-0 11 ♘e5 ♕c7∓) 9 ♕e2 ♕c7 10 ♗d2 b5 11 a3 ♖b8= Boleslavsky-Pachman, Saltjobaden1948.

7...cxd4

This exchange is in line with my philosophy for a second system: to give the reader a solid and extremely well-established variation that will always be playable.

8 ♘xd4 ♗c5

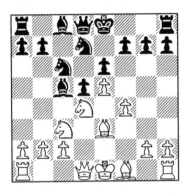

9 ♕d2

Preparing 0-0-0. Nothing else is considered sharp enough:

(a) 9 g3 ♕b6 10 ♘a4 ♕a5+ 11 c3 ♗xd4 12 ♗xd4 ♘xd4 13 ♕xd4 b6= 14 ♕b4!? ♕xb4 15 cxb4 f6 16 ♗b5? fxe5 17 fxe5 0-0∓ Antal-Hoang Thanh Trang, Budapest 2002;

(b) 9 ♗e2 ♕b6!? (usually arrived at by 8...♕b6 9 ♗e2 ♗c5) 10 ♘a4 ♕a5+ 11 c3 ♘xd4 12 ♗xd4 ♗xd4 13 ♕xd4 0-0 14 0-0 b6 15 ♗d1 ♗a6!? 16 b4 ♕b5 17 ♖f3 ♕c4= Vera-Borges Mateos, Havana 1987;

(c) 9 ♘a4? ♗xd4 10 ♗xd4 ♘dxe5! 11 ♗e2 (11 ♗xe5 ♘xe5 12 fxe5 ♕h4+ 13 g3 ♕xa4∓) 11...♘g6 12 0-0 ♘xd4 13 ♕xd4 0-0∓ Redmon-Marechal, Glenalmond 1996;

(d) 9 ♗b5 0-0 10 ♘xc6 bxc6 11 ♗xc5 ♘xc5 12 ♗xc6 (or 12 ♕d4 ♕b6 13 b4 cxb5 14 bxc5 ♕a5= Suetin)

12...♖b8 13 ♕d4 ♕a5= Laplaza-Rogemont, corr 1992.

9...0-0

It's an indication of Black's flexibility in this line that he has still another option here in 9...♗xd4 10 ♗xd4 ♘xd4 11 ♕xd4 ♕b6

This plan has beeen around for years and is still popular right now among the chess elite; in particular, Korchnoi and Bareev have championed it. The basic idea is that in the ending, a kingside advance by White tends to be harmless, so that despite White's better bishop Black will have time to develop rapidly on the queenside using the open c-file to level the chances. The interesting endgame it produces tends to lead to a draw with accurate play by Black; but that can be a problem for both sides. After all, White will also have limited prospects against a strong player or one who knows the ideas well. Thus 9...♗xd4 trades safety for complexity.

From the diagram, searching for genuine winning chances, White has been offering a pawn by 12 ♕d2!? ♕xb2 (12...♘c5 13 0-0-0 ♗d7 is also playable) 13 ♖b1 ♕a3 14 ♘b5 ♕xa2 15 ♘d6+ ♔e7 but for the moment Bareev has demonstrated in two top-level games that Black's two pawns are as important as White's attack.

After 9...0-0, White can choose between two strategies:

13.31 10 g3
13.32 10 0-0-0

The alternative 10 ♗e2 gives Black the choice of playing for a simplified game by 10...♘dxe5!? 11 ♘xc6 (11 fxe5 ♘xd4 with the idea 12 ♗xd4 ♕h4+) 11...♗xe3 12 ♘xd8 ♗xd2+ 13 ♔xd2 ♘c4+! 14 ♗xc4 dxc4 15 ♘xf7 ♖xf7 16 ♔e3 b6 17 ♖hd1 ♗a6!=, intending ...e5 and on fxe5, ...♖e8. Or he can play for more with the 'normal' 10...a6 11 0-0 ♘xd4 12 ♗xd4 ♕b6 13 ♗xc5 ♕xc5+ 14 ♔h1 b5 15 ♗d3 ♘b6 16 b3 ♗b7= Rayner-C.Daly, Debrecen 1992, when 17 ♘e2?! was answered by 17...♘c4!∓.

13.31 10 g3

This is a semi-waiting move in the sense that White wants to see what Black is doing before committing his king's bishop or king. White's bishop may go to g2 or h3, a drawback being the loss of control over c4.

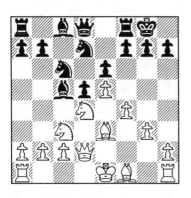

10...a6

The direct plan with 10...♗xd4 11 ♗xd4 ♘xd4 12 ♕xd4 ♘b8! intending ...♘c6 is also satisfactory. Black can play along the c-file after ...♗d7 and ...♖c8 and may also think about ...f6, for example, 13 0-0-0 ♘c6 14 ♕f2 ♗d7 15 ♔b1 ♕a5 16 ♗d3 ♖fc8 17 ♕e1 (17 a3!? b5!?) 17...♘b4 18 a3 ♘xd3 19 ♖xd3 ♖c4 20 ♕d2 ♖ac8 21 ♘e2 ♕xd2 22 ♖xd2 ♖e4 23 ♘c3 Anand-Shirov, Leon 2001; and although Black shouldn't have serious problems with other moves, it seems to me that 23...♖e3! 24 ♖hd1 (24 ♘e2 f6) 24...♖c4 is a good set-up. Black may play for ...f6 after, say, ...♔f8 and/or ...♗c6.

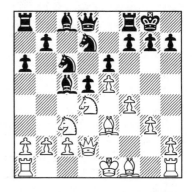

11 ♘ce2

White logically reinforces d4. Nevertheless, it takes pressure off of d5 and e4. Options are:

(a) 11 ♗g2 ♘xd4 (11...♘a5!? 12 b3 b5=) 12 ♗xd4 b5 13 ♘e2 ♕c7 14 ♗xc5 ♘xc5 15 ♘d4 ♗b7 16 0-0 ♘e4= Kuczynski-Gunnarsson, Ohrid 2001; when Black gets this move in he's normally okay;

(b) 11 ♗h3 ♘xd4 12 ♗xd4 ♕c7 (both 12...b5 13 0-0 ♕b6 14 ♘e2 b4 and Leitao's more active suggestion 13...a5!? 14 ♘xb5 ♗a6 15 a4 ♗xb5 16 axb5 ♕b6 are unclear) 13 0-0-0 (13 ♗xc5 ♘xc5 14 0-0 b5 15 ♕d4 b4! 16 ♕xb4 ♖b8 17 ♕a3 ♕b6 18 ♔h1 d4!=) 13...b5 14 ♖he1 Paehtz-Lomineishvili, Leon 2001; and 14...b4! 15 ♘a4!? ♗xd4 16 ♕xd4 a5 17 f5 ♖e8 18 fxe6 fxe6 would be equal.

11...♛b6

In this particular instance, I think 11...♛e7 makes sense, since after 12 ♝h3 Black's defence of e6 gives him leeway to contest the light squares:

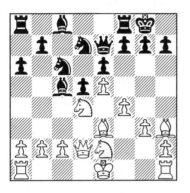

12...f5!?, a unique idea that I like. It challenges White to capture en passant and lose central control for the sake of free play; otherwise, any plan with g4 grants Black f-file play: 13 0-0 (13 exf6 ♞xf6 threatens ...♞e4, and Black gets easy play after 14 ♝g2 e5 15 ♞xc6 bxc6 16 ♝xc5 ♛xc5 17 fxe5 ♞g4; 13 0-0-0 ♞xd4 14 ♞xd4 ♞b6 15 b3?! ♝d7 with the speedier attack) 13...♞xd4 14 ♞xd4 and a sample line is 14...♝a7 (with the idea ...♞c5) 15 ♖ac1! ♞c5 16 c4 ♞e4 17 ♛e2 ♝d7 18 ♖fd1 ♝xd4 19 ♝xd4 dxc4 20 ♛xc4 ♖ac8 21 ♛b3 ♝c6 22 ♝b6 ♝d5=.

12 c3

12 0-0-0 f6!.

12...a5

Here too 12...f6 looks quite reasonable, since 13 exf6 ♞xf6 14 ♝g2 ♝d7 discourages 15 0-0 due to 15...♞g4.

After 12...a5, Ermolaev-Sumets, Lviv 2002 continued 13 ♝h3 a4 14 ♔f2 ♛d8 15 ♔g2 ♝b6 16 b4 ♝c7!? 17 ♞b5 ♝b8 18 ♞ed4 ♞b6 19 ♛d3 ♞c4 20 ♝f2 ♝d7=.

13.32 10 0-0-0 a6

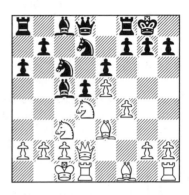

Preparing ...b5 with an advance on the queenside. My first instinct in this type of position was that White, with more central space and good pieces, probably stands slightly better. But White's goals on the kingside are hard to achieve and Black has White's king as a target for his queenside expansion. Moreover, in some cases a well-timed simplification will equalise on the spot. Statistically, in fact, Black has done remarkably well from this position in terms of both raw results and performance rating.

11 h4

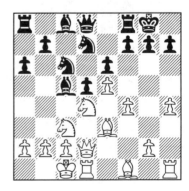

A critical point. With this move White demonstrates his intention to attack on the kingside, perhaps via

♖h3, a move that incidentally defends along the third rank. White can choose also to play positionally, which usually entails strengthening the d4 point and/or neutralising Black's ideas on the queenside, as shown by:

(a) 11 ♔b1 (this will often transpose to 11 h4 lines, but sometimes White switches plans) 11...♘xd4 12 ♗xd4

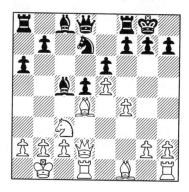

12...b5 (after 12...♕c7, it's important to note that 13 h4 b5 transposes to one of the main lines below with 11 h4 ♘xd4 12 ♗xd4 ♕c7 13 ♔b1 b5; instead White can play 13 ♕f2 b5 14 ♗d3 b4 15 ♘e2 a5 16 ♕h4 g6 17 ♖hf1 ♗a6 Zahariev-I.Ivanisevic, Chania 2000; then Black is way ahead of the lines with 11 ♕f2 and can follow up by ...♖fc8 and even ...♘f8 if needed – ChessPublishing) 13 ♕e3 (13 h4 transposes to 11 h4 ♘xd4 12 ♗xd4 b5 13 ♔b1) 13...♕c7 (13...♕e7 could be considered – Pedersen) 14 Íd3 Íxd4 (14...b4 15 ♕h3!) 15 ♕xd4 ♗b7! (This is a fashionable treatment of such lines; Black wants to develop quickly and tie White's pieces to e4 by placing a knight on c5 before pushing his queenside pawns. Still, after 15...♕c5 16 ♘e2 b4 17 ♖he1 ♖e8 18 ♕xc5!? ♘xc5 19 ♘d4 Libiszewski-Buhmann, Pula 2003, 19...♗d7! doesn't look bad)

16 ♖he1 ♘c5 17 ♘e2 ♖ac8!? (17...♖fc8 looks better, because a later ...b4 and ...a5 will be more effective) 18 ♕e3 ♘e4 19 ♘d4 (19 ♗xe4 dxe4 empowers the bishop, e.g., 20 ♖d2 f6! 21 exf6 ♖xf6 22 ♖ed1 ♗d5=) 19...♕e7!? (19...b4!?) 20 ♘f3!? (I prefer White a bit here, because Black isn't well set up for ...b4 and ...a5) 20...♕b4 21 ♔a1 ♕e7 22 ♘g5 d4!? 23 ♕h3 ♘xg5 24 fxg5 g6 25 ♕g4± J.Polgar-Luther, Ohrid 2001. White intends h4-h5, although things are still complex and Black went on to win;

(b) 11 ♕f2 was recently played by Kramnik. The idea is to launch a kingside attack by ♗d3 and ♕h4. Here are two responses:

(b1) 11...♗b4!? meets the threat 12 ♘xc6 and tries to force White's knight to a worse square. It may well equalise, e.g., 12 ♘ce2 (uninspiring is 12 ♘xc6 bxc6 13 ♘e2 ♖b8=; and a mistake is 12 ♘a4? ♕a5) 12...♘a5 (heading for c4; 12...♕a5!?) 13 c3 ♗e7 14 ♘g3 b5 15 ♗d3 ♗b7 16 ♕c2 h6 17 ♔b1 ♘c4 18 ♗f2 ♘c5=. These moves are hardly forced, but the general idea is that White has a difficult time attacking;

(b2) 11...♘xd4 12 ♗xd4 should probably be played in a non-standard manner, because otherwise White remains somewhat better: 12...♕c7 (for example, 12...♕e7 would keep an eye on h4 and should be considered; then the move ...f6 is also appropriate in some lines) 13 ♗d3 ♗xd4!? (13...b5?! 14 ♕h4 h6 15 ♘e2 f6?! 16 ♕g4!± was the game Kramnik-Radjabov, Linares 2003; 13...f6!? might be playable, with the idea 14 exf6 ♖xf6! 15 f5!? b5) 14 ♕xd4 ♘c5 (14...b5) 15 f5! ♘xd3+ 16 ♖xd3 with a nice advantage; this is the sort of position White wants;

(c) Nijboer has specialised in the relatively unexplored 11 ♘b3. A couple of his recent games went 11...b6 12 ♘e2 a5!? (12...♕e7 13 ♘ed4 ♘xd4 14 ♘xd4 f6 15 exf6 ♘xf6 16 ♗d3 ♗b7 17 ♘f3 Nijboer-Arizmendi Martinez, Bled 2002; and Nijboer recommends 17...♘h5 with complications, apparently dynamically equal ones) 13 ♘ed4 ♘xd4 14 ♘xd4 ♗a6 15 ♔b1 ♕c7 16 ♗d3 (16 ♗xa6 ♖xa6 17 g4!?) 16...a4 17 ♕e2 ♗xd3 18 cxd3 Nijboer-Stellwagen, Wijk aan Zee 2003; and simply 18...a3 was equal.

11...♘xd4

11...♕c7 has led to very similar games, and is better played later (see below). One early example went 12 ♖h3 (12 h5!± or even 12 g4 ♘xd4 13

♗xd4 b5 14 g5!?±) 12...♘xd4 13 ♗xd4 b5= 14 ♕e3!? ♗b7 15 ♗d3 f6! 16 exf6 ♖xf6∓ Mokry-Bareev, Trnava 1989.

12 ♗xd4 b5

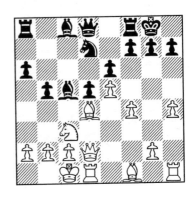

13 ♖h3!?

This has been very popular, but recently White has been looking at other courses as well:

(a) 13 h5 looks scary, but gives Black a critical tempo for his own attack, e.g., 13...b4 (13...♕c7 is often arrived at by a move order with an earlier ...♕c7; when White commits to h6 it usually doesn't achieve much, e.g., 14 h6 g6 15 ♔b1 and 15...♗b7 16 ♗xc5 ♘xc5= or 15...♗b7 16 ♗xc5 ♘xc5=)

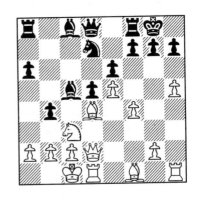

This leads to a typical and major decision. Does White want to block the queenside and simplify, or to concentrate upon the centre at the cost of allowing Black's queenside pawns to advance? We have:

(a1) 14 ♘e2 15 ♕e3 ♕c7 16 ♔b1 (16 ♗xc5 ♘xc5 17 ♘d4 ♗a6 18 f5 – McDonald; 18...♘e4! with the idea 19 fxe6 ♕xe5 or 19 ♕f4 exf5=) 16...♗a6 17 ♗xc5 ♘xc5 18 ♘g3?! ♖fc8 19 ♖c1 a4! 20 ♗xa6 ♖xa6 and both ...a3 and ...b3 are serious worries for White, Topalov-Morozevich, Sarajevo 1999;

(a2) 14 ♘a4 ♗xd4 15 ♕xd4 a5 (15...f6!? 16 h6 g6 and Black's king seems secure while White's centre is becoming loose) 16 ♗b5 (to stop ...♗a6; this same manoeuvre is tried in the main line) 16...♖b8 17 ♗d3 and a recent game Olenin-Zvjaginsev, Togliatti 2003 went 17...♗b7 18 ♔b1 ♗c6 19 ♘c5 ♗b5 20 ♘xd7 ♕xd7 21 g4!? ♖fc8 22 f5 ♗xd3 23 cxd3? b3! 24 a3 ♖c2∓;

(b) 13 ♗xc5 ♘xc5 14 ♕d4 ♕c7 15 a3 (15 f5 ♗b7 16 f6?! – committing too quickly – 16...gxf6 17 exf6 ♔h8∓ A.Ivanov-Glek, USSR 1987) 15...♗d7 16 f5 ♖fc8! 17 f6?! (the same problem) 17...gxf6 (17...♘e4!) 18 exf6 Apicella-M.Gurevich, Clichy 2001; 18...♘e4!;

(c) 13 ♔b1!? is a subtle move order that has recently come into prominence. 13...♕c7

reached by other orders, e.g., 11 ♔b1 ♘xd4 12 ♗xd4 ♕c7 13 h4 b5. Now both of White's moves are critical:

(c1) 14 ♖h3 (Anand gives this '?!') 14...b4!? (as usual, 14...♗b7 is an option, especially in view of 15 h5 b4 16 ♘a4 ♗xd4 17 ♕xd4 ♕a5 18 b3 ♗c6!∓) 15 ♘a4 ♗xd4 16 ♕xd4 ♖b8!? (or 16...a5 17 c3 ♗a6!) 17 ♖e3 a5 18 f5?! (18 h5 ♗b7 19 f5 ♖bc8 20 ♗d3 ♗a6! with initiative) Anand-Buhmann, Stuttgart 2002; and Anand gives 18...exf5! 19 ♕xd5 ♗b7! 20 ♕xd7 ♖bd8 21 e6 ♖xd7 22 exd7 ♗c6 23 ♘c5 ♖d8 24 ♗c4 ♔f8 25 ♖de1 ♗e4 26 ♘xe4 fxe4 27 ♗b5 f5∓;

(c2) 14 h5! b4 15 ♘a4 ♗xd4 16 ♕xd4 a5 (16...f6!) 17 h6 (17 ♗b5 ♖b8 18 h6 g6 19 c4 bxc3 20 ♘xc3 f6!=) 17...g6 18 ♖c1! ♕c6 19 b3 ♗a6 20 ♗xa6 ♕xa6 21 c3 bxc3 22 ♖xc3± Khamatgaleev-Kosic, Patras 2002.

13...b4

One last time 13...♕c7 14 ♔b1 transposes, this time to note 'c' 13 ♔b1 above. An important alternative, currently popular, is 13...♗b7 Although move order is certainly important, this may be one of those variations where a knowledge of basic ideas (like the difference between ...b4 and ...♗b7 lines) is more helpful that memorising exact orders.

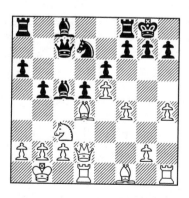

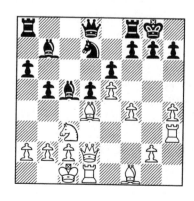

An important position is often

Here are some examples of play after 13...♗b7:

(a) 14 f5?! is premature: 14...exf5 15 ♘xd5 ♗xd5 16 ♗xc5 ♘xc5 17 ♕xd5 ♕b6 18 ♕d6 ♕a7! 19 ♖f3 ♘e6 20 ♕a3 f4 21 ♖d6?! ♕g1 22 ♕d3 ♖ac8 and everything is going Black's way, Van der Weide-Stellwagen, Leeuwarden 2001;

(b) 14 ♖g3!? b4 15 ♘a4 ♗xd4 16 ♕xd4 ♕a5 17 b3 ♗c6 18 ♘b2 (18 f5!? – Pedersen) 18...♘c5 19 ♗d3 ♖fd8∓ was Dutreeuw-M.Gurevich, Brussels 1995;

(c) 14 g4 (a popular move) 14...b4 15 ♘e2 a5 16 g5 ♕b6 17 ♔b1 ♗a6 18 ♖e3 (18 h5, and instead of 18...♖ac8?! 19 g6! Coco-Daconto, corr 1997, Black should play 18...♖fc8!, as follows...) 18...♖fc8! 19 ♗g2 (19 h5 a4 20 g6 hxg6 21 hxg6 fxg6 22 ♖g3 ♘f8)

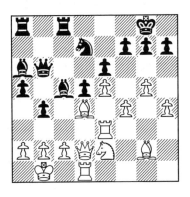

19...♗xe2! 20 ♖xe2 a4 21 f5 b3 22 cxb3 axb3 23 a3 ♗xd4 24 ♕xd4 ♖c5!? 25 h5 ♖ac8 26 ♕d3 ♖c2∓ Borriss-Korchnoi, Panormo 2001;

(d) 14 ♔b1?! has been played a lot, but Black's attack is better than usual, e.g., 14...b4 15 ♘e2 a5 16 ♕e3 ♕c7 17 ♖g3!? ♗a6∓ 18 ♗xc5? ♘xc5 19 f5 f6?! (19...♘e4!–+) 20 fxe6? (20 exf6 ♖xf6 21 ♘f4 d4!) 20...fxe5 21 ♖f3 d4–+ Aagaard-Stellwagen, Wijk aan Zee 2001.

14 ♘a4

14 ♘e2 is rather slow in the face of 14...a5 15 ♕e3 (15 h5 ♗a6 16 h6 g6 17 g4 ♕b6 18 ♔b1 a4 19 ♖e3?! ♗c4 20 c3?! ♗xa2+! 21 ♔xa2 b3+ 22 ♔b1 a3 with a huge attack, Adriano-C.Jones, corr 2003) 15...♕c7. Then 16 ♗xc5?! ♘xc5 17 ♘d4 a4 18 ♔b1 a3! 19 b3 ♗a6 20 ♗xa6 ♖xa6 favoured Black, J.Polgar-Shirov, Prague 1999.

14...♗xd4 15 ♕xd4 a5

Black will simplify and White's attack is not yet underway. There are two exciting alternatives, one fully satisfactory:

(a) 15...f6 16 ♕xb4 fxe5 17 ♕d6! ♕f6 18 f5!; this is Kasparov's ingenious move. A playable line is that given by Ron Langeveld in ChessPub (with some additions from me): 18...♖e8! 19 ♖b3 (19 fxe6 ♕f4+ 20 ♔b1 ♕xa4 21 exd7 ♗xd7 22 ♖a3! ♕g4 23 ♕xd5+ ♗e6‡; 19 ♕c6 ♖b8 20 fxe6?! ♕f4+ 21 ♔b1 ♘f6 22 ♖f3 ♕g4∓; 19 ♘c3!? ♔h8! 20 fxe6 ♕h6+ 21 ♔b1 ♘f6 22 g4!? ♘xg4 23 ♘xd5 ♗xe6∓) 19...♕xh4 20 fxe6 ♕xa4 21 ♖b4 (21 ♕xd5 ♘c5!!) 21...♕xb4!? 22 ♕xb4 ♘f6 with a small edge for White;

(b) 15...♕a5! seems fine for Black, the main line being 16 b3 ♗b7!? (or 16...f6! 17 exf6 ♘xf6=) 17 c3! (17 ♖g3 ♗c6 18 ♘b2 ♘c5!) 17...♖fc8 18 ♔b2 bxc3+ 19 ♖xc3 ♖xc3 20 ♕xc3 Nijboer-Luther, Leuwaarden 1992; and after 20...♕d8 21 ♖c1?! (21 g3! ♖c8 with a tiny edge for White) 21...♖c8 22 ♕b4, Langeveld suggests 22...♖xc1! 23 ♔xc1 ♗c6! 24 ♗xa6 ♕xh4∓.

16 ♗b5!?

This is considered best, to prevent 16...♗a6. 16 c4!? ♗b7! is easier than 16...bxc3 17 ♖xc3!? ♕xh4 18 g3 ♕d8 19 ♔b1 with some play for the pawn, Nijboer-Korchnoi, Arnhem 1999.

16...♖b8

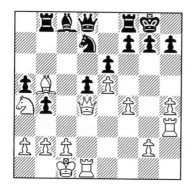

17 ♗d3!

White's loss of tempo is supposed to be worth prevention of ...♗a6. The alternatives lack punch, e.g., 17 ♗e2 ♗b7 18 ♔b1 ♗c6 19 ♘c5 ♗b5 (19...♘xc5 20 ♕xc5 ♖c8 21 ♕d4 f6=) 20 ♗d3 ♘xc5 21 ♕xc5 ♕d7= De la Riva Aguado-Glek, Saint Vincent 1999.

17...f6!

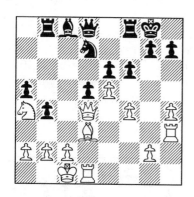

A rare but effective solution in this well-known position, recommended by Pedersen. It also seems that

17...♕c7 equalises in both theory and practice, e.g., 18 ♖e1 ♕c6 19 b3 ♗a6 20 ♗xa6 ♕xa6 21 h5 (21 ♖g3!? ♔h8 – Pedersen) 21...♖fc8 22 f5 ♕c6 23 ♖e2 ♘c5= Sedlak-Antic, Subotica 2000.

18 exf6

18 b3?! fxe5 19 fxe5 ♕c7 20 ♖e1 ♕c6 21 h5 ♗a6∓ Garofalo-Latronico, email 2000.

18...♕xf6 19 ♕xf6

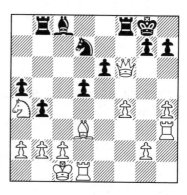

19...♘xf6

A recent test of 17...f6 by Shirov went 19...♖xf6 20 ♖e3 ♖xf4 21 ♖xe6 ♘f6 22 ♖d6 ♗g4 23 ♖e1 ♗h5 24 ♘b6 ♗f7 25 ♘d7 ♘xd7 26 ♖xd7 ♖xh4 27 ♖ee7?! (27 ♖a7=) 27...♖f8 28 ♗f5 ♖h6 29 ♗g4 ♖f6∓ Langheinrich-Shirov, Cologne 2003.

After 19...♘xf6, Pedersen's analysis goes 20 ♖f3 ♘e4 21 ♗xe4 dxe4=. White has nothing after 22 ♖e3 (although not 22 ♖ff1? ♗a6 or 22 ♖f2 e5!) 22...♖xf4 23 g3 ♖f8 24 ♖xe4 ♖b5!=. Black's idea is to cover c5 and e5 while preparing ...♖d5 or ...e5, freeing his bishop.

Chapter Fourteen

Classical Variation:
4 ♗g5 (4...dxe4 5 ♘xe4 ♗e7)

1 e4 e6 2 d4 d5 3 ♘c3 ♘f6 4 ♗g5 dxe4 5 ♘xe4 ♗e7

This system, called the Burn Variation, is comparable to the Rubinstein Variation (3...dxe4 4 ♘xe4 ♘bd7 and 5...♘gf6) except that the opposition of White's bishop on g5 and Black's on e7 will almost inevitably lead to an exchange. 5...♘bd7 is also popular at this point, instead of 5...♗e7. The disadvantage of any ...dxe4 system is that it leaves White with space and better control of the centre. The advantage of the variation we see here is that Black will normally get the two bishops and is constantly threatening to equalise in the centre with ...c5 or ...e5. Although essentially a solid line, it tends to be more double-edged than the other two ...dxe4 systems, and thus enjoys great popularity in contemporary play.

6 ♗xf6

It's remarkable that the two main (and best) recent books covering these lines, by Jacobs and Pedersen, don't mention natural alternatives at this point, nor many deviations from main lines in the moves to follow. Through the years, White has tried a number of other approaches, some quite often:

(a) 6 ♗d3? is a mistake that was made by several top-class players in the early part of the 20th century, but not established as weak until later: 6...♘xe4 7 ♗xe7 ♘xf2!? (or 7...♕xe7! 8 ♗xe4 ♕b4+ 9 c3 ♕xb2 10 ♘e2 c6 11 0-0 ♘d7 12 ♗c2 ♕a3 13 ♕d3 ♘f6 and White lacked compensation, Leonhardt-Swiderski, Vienna 1908) 8 ♗xd8 ♘xd1 9 ♗xc7 ♘xb2 10 ♗e2 ♘a4! 11 ♗d6 Barasz-Balla, Gyor 1906, and here 11...♗d7! 12 ♖b1 ♗c6 was good;

(b) 6 ♘g3

and:

(b1) After 6...0-0, 7 ♘f3 is natural and likely to be met by ...♘bd7. Instead, Djurhuus-U.Andersson, Malmö 1995 took an interesting positional course after 7 ♗d3 c5 8 dxc5 ♘bd7 9 ♗xf6 ♘xf6!? 10 ♕e2 ♕a5+ 11 c3 ♕xc5 12 ♘f3 ♗d7 13 0-0 ♖ad8 14 ♖fe1 ♗c8!? 15 ♖ad1 ♕c7 16 ♘e4 ♖d5!?=;

(b2) 6...c5 7 dxc5 (7 ♘f3 ♘bd7 8 ♗c4 0-0 9 0-0 a6! 10 dxc5 ♘xc5 11 ♕e2?! b5 12 ♗b3 ♘xb3 13 axb3 ♕c7 14 ♖fe1 ♗b7∓ Van Gompel-De Bock, Vlissingen 1995) 7...♕a5+ 8 ♕d2 ♕xc5 9 ♘f3 ♘bd7 10 0-0-0 b6 11 ♗e3 ♕d5 12 ♕xd5 ♘xd5= Gesos-Van den Doel, Agios Kyrikos 2000;

(c) 6 ♘xf6+ allows Black to develop quickly and achieve an equalizing central break. An older example: 6...♗xf6 7 ♗xf6 ♕xf6 8 c3 0-0 9 ♗d3 ♘c6 10 ♘f3 e5 11 dxe5 ♘xe5 12 ♘xe5 ♕xe5+ 13 ♕e2 ♕xe2+ 14 ♗xe2 ♗e6 15 0-0 ♖fd8 16 ♖fd1 ♖xd1+ 17 ♗xd1 ♖d8∓ Thomas-Tartakower, Hastings 1945 – see also note (a) to White's seventh move.

(d) 6 ♘c3 has been tried surprisingly often. A simple solution is 6...0-0 7 ♘f3 ♘bd7 8 ♗e2 c5 9 0-0 b6 10 ♕d2 ♗b7 11 ♖ad1 ♘d5= Botvinnik-Rauzer, Odessa 1929.

6...♗xf6

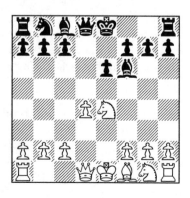

There are roughly 3000 games from this position in my database, with players of all strengths represented. Recently it has become an extremely popular opening at the highest levels. Of the leading contemporary players, Bareev and Mikhail Gurevich have employed it most consistently over the years, but Shirov, Khalifman, Korchnoi and Short have been exponents, and a number of others such as Kramnik, Dreev, Ehlvest, Psakhis and (many others) have played it from time to time.

7 ♘f3

Again, others have often been seen:

(a) 7 ♘xf6+ ♕xf6 8 ♘f3 0-0 (8...c5 also equalises) and now:

(a1) 9 ♕d2 is a simplifying line that offers few positive prospects, e.g., 9...♖d8 10 0-0-0 c5 11 ♕c3 b6 12 ♗b5 ♗a6!? 13 ♕c4 ♗xb5 14 ♕xb5 ♘d7 15 ♕e2 ♖ac8∓ ½-½ Anand-Bareev, Paris 1992;

(a2) 9 c3 ♘d7 (or 9...b6 10 g3 ♘d7 11 ♗g2 e5! 12 ♘xe5 ♘xe5 13 dxe5 ♕xe5+ 14 ♕e2 ♕xe2+ 15 ♔xe2 ♗a6+∓ was Szamoskozi-Jakab, Paks 1995) 10 ♗d3 (10 ♗e2 e5 11 dxe5 ♘xe5 12 ♘xe5 ♕xe5= Capablanca-Alekhine, New York 1927) 10...e5 11 0-0 exd4 12 ♘xd4!? ♘e5 13 ♗e4 ♖d8 14 ♕c2 g6 15 ♖fd1 ½-½ Oll-Kindermann, Debrecen 1990;

(a3) 9 ♗d3 ♘c6!? (or 9...c5 10 0-0 cxd4 11 ♘xd4 ♖d8= Gashimov-Radjabov, Baku 1998) 10 c3 e5 11 dxe5 ♘xe5 12 ♘xe5 ♕xe5+ 13 ♕e2 ♕xe2+ 14 ♔xe2 ♖e8+ 15 ♔d2 ♗e6= Yurchenko-Moiseenko, Kaluga 1996;

(b) 7 c3 ♘d7 and:

(b1) 8 f4!? 0-0 9 ♘f3 b6 10 ♗d3 ♗b7 11 0-0 c5 12 dxc5 ♘xc5 13 ♘xc5 bxc5= Boll-Dreev, Tilburg 1993;

(b2) 8 ♕c2 e5 9 dxe5?! (9 0-0-0! – Bareev, when 9...exd4 10 ♘xf6+ ♘xf6 11 ♖xd4 ♕e7 12 ♘f3 0-0 looks equal)

9...♘xe5 10 f4 (Knaak gives the interesting line 10 ♗b5+ c6 11 ♖d1 ♕e7 12 ♘d6+ ♔f8 13 ♗e2 ♗e6∓, which seems true, e.g., 14 b3 ♖d8 15 ♘e4 ♗f5!) 10...♘g6 11 g3 0-0 12 ♗d3 (12 ♗g2 ♖e8) 12...♕d5 and Black is slightly better: 13 a3? (13 ♘xf6+? gxf6–+ with the idea 14 0-0-0 ♕xh1 15 ♗e4 ♗f5!; 13 ♘e2!∓) 13...♘xf4! 14 ♘xf6+ gxf6 15 ♗xh7+ ♔g7–+ Topalov-Bareev, Linares 1994;

(b3) 8 ♘f3 0-0 9 ♕c2 (9 ♗e2 e5 10 d5 ♗e7 and ...f5) 9...e5= 10 0-0-0 (10 d5 ♗e7 11 0-0-0 has arisen more than once and 11...f5!? is curiously untried:, e.g., 12 d6! ♗xd6 13 ♘xd6 cxd6 14 ♖xd6 e4! 15 ♘d4 ♕e7 16 ♖e6 ♕g5+ 17 ♔b1 ♘b6 with satisfactory play) 10...exd4 11 ♘xd4 (11 ♘xf6+?! ♕xf6 12 ♖xd4 ♘c5 and Black is already better, Ljubojevic-Dreev, Linares 1995) 11...♗xd4!? 12 ♖xd4 ♕e7 13 h4 ♘e5 14 ♘g5 g6= Glek-Lputian, Dortmund 1992.

7...♘d7

I use this move as the first repertoire line because it prepares the ideas of ...e5 and ...c5 without delay. Nevertheless, 7...0-0 is flexible with respect to minor piece development and is in fact more popular.

This has turned out to be a solid position for Black. Here's a mini-repertoire of critical ideas:

(a) 8 c3 ♘d7 9 ♕c2 (9 ♗d3 e5) 9...e5 transposes to 7 c3;

(b) 8 ♕d3 (to target h7 and play 0-0-0 quickly) 8...♘d7 9 0-0-0 b6 10 h4 ♗b7 11 ♘fg5 (11 ♘eg5 g6 12 ♕e3 h6 13 ♘e4 ♗g7 14 ♗d3 c5!, or here M.Gurevich's 12...c5!? 13 dxc5 ♕e7) 11...♗xe4!? 12 ♕xe4 ♗xg5+ 13 hxg5 ♕xg5+ 14 ♔b1 ♘f6 15 ♕c6 Milos-Shirov, Las Vegas 1999, when White had only limited compensation for the pawn;

(c) 8 ♗c4; as Pedersen points out, many of the top players think that this is the drawback to 7...0-0, because that move doesn't contribute towards stopping the d5 break (as ...b6 does) or enforce ...c5, (as ...♘d7 does). But I have grown fonder of 7...0-0 since I realised that Black can now switch plans by 8...♘c6!? 9 c3 e5 Then the only challenging move is 10 d5, when both moves of Black's moves are valid:

(c1) 10...♘a5 11 ♗d3 b6 12 h4, and Jacobs suggests 12...♘b7! intending ...♘d6, e.g., 13 ♘xf6+ ♕xf6 14 ♕c2 g6 15 h5 ♘c5=;

(c2) 10...♘e7!? 11 ♘xf6+ gxf6 has done reasonably well for Black, the current main line going 12 ♘h4 ♘g6 13 ♕h5 ♕d7! (intending ...♕g4) 14 h3

♕a4! 15 b3 ♕a5 16 0-0 Shirov-V.Akopian, Kallithea 2002; and here Shirov suggests 16...♔g7 17 b4 ♕a3 18 ♗b3 a5 with complications;

(d) 8 ♕d2 is the most common move, when 8...♘d7 transposes to our 7...♘d7 main line, or Black can play 8...♗e7 9 0-0-0. In the latter case, 9...♕d5!? (9...♘d7 again transposes to 7...♘d7 8 ♕d2 0-0 9 0-0-0 ♗e7 below) 10 ♘c3 ♕a5 is independent: 11 a3!? (11 ♘e5 ♗b4 12 ♘c4 ♗xc3 13 ♘xa5 ♗xd2+ 14 ♖xd2 b6 15 ♘c4 ♗b7= was the game Ehlvest-Khalifman, Japfa 2000) 11...♘d7 and:

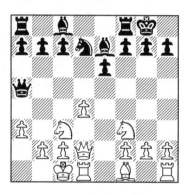

(d1) 12 ♗c4 c6 13 ♖he1 b5 14 ♗b3 Landa-Baklan, Halkidiki 2002; and Baklan suggests 14...b4 15 ♘a2 ♖b8 16 ♔b1 ♖d8 'with counterplay';

(d2) 12 ♔b1 ♕b6 (or 12...c6!? – Knaak; both sides have numerous options here) 13 ♕e3 ♘f6 14 ♘e5 Ponomariov-Ivanchuk, and here Knaak suggests the simple 14...♘d5! 15 ♕f3 (15 ♘xd5 exd5 frees Black's bishops) 15...♘xc3+ 16 ♕xc3 c5, which should be fine for Black, e.g., 17 dxc5 (17 ♗e2 cxd4 18 ♖xd4 ♗c5=) 17...♕xc5 18 ♕xc5 ♗xc5 19 f3! (19 f4 b6 20 ♗b5 ♗b7∓) 19...a6! 20 ♗e2 b5 21 ♘d7 ♗xd7 22 ♖xd7 ♖fd8 23 ♖hd1 ♗b6=.

I have dwelled upon 7...0-0 because it is a good alternative for anyone

who mistrusts something in the 7...♘d7 lines.

8 ♕d2

A very important choice. 8 ♕d2 is perhaps the best move since it leaves Black few ways to exploit his early ...♘d7 and usually merges with a line that could arise after 7...0-0. There are many other moves, however, several of them leading to highly critical play:

(a) 8 ♕e2!? 0-0 9 0-0-0 b6 10 h4!? ♗b7 11 h5 c5! (breaking up the centre based upon a tactic) 12 h6 g6 13 dxc5?! (13 ♘xf6+ ♕xf6 14 ♖h3 cxd4 15 ♘xd4=) 13...♗xe4 14 ♕xe4 ♘xc5 15 ♕b4 (15 ♖xd8 ♘xe4∓) 15...♕c7 16 ♗e2 J.Polgar-Bareev, Cannes 2001, and Black launched an attack aided by the opposite-coloured bishops: 16...b5! 17 ♔b1 a5! 18 ♕g4 ♘a4 19 ♘d4 ♖fc8 20 ♖d2?! (already there is no good defence, but better was 20 c3 b4 21 ♗b5 bxc3! 22 ♗xa4 ♖ab8∓) 20...♘xb2! 21 ♘xb5 ♖ab8! 22 ♔c1 (22 ♘xc7 ♘d3+) 22...♕e5-+;

(b) 8 ♗c4 is by far the most important option to 8 ♕d2 because White wants to support d5 in some variations, especially after ...c5. Now 8...0-0 transposes to certain passive 7...0-0 lines that are unappealing. But Black has the alternative 8...a6!?:

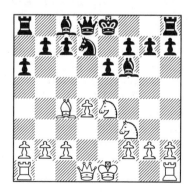

A dynamic and ambitious idea on which M.Gurevich has taken out a patent. Black wants to develop his bishop aggressively even at the cost of some looseness: Play normally continues 9 ♕e2 (9 a4 0-0 10 ♕d2 b6 11 0-0-0 b5! – McDonald; 9 0-0 b5 10 ♗d3 ♗b7=, e.g., 11 c3 ♗e7!? 12 a4 0-0! 13 axb5 axb5 14 ♖xa8 ♕xa8 15 ♗xb5 ♗xe4 16 ♗xd7 ♖d8 17 ♗b5 c5∓; the key in these lines is to stay dynamic) 9...b5 (9...0-0 is safer: 10 0-0-0 b5 11 ♗b3 ♗b7 12 d5 exd5 13 ♗xd5 c6 14 ♗b3 ♕c7 15 ♖he1 Lutz-Dizdar, Frohnleiten 2002; and here 15...c5 is similar to our main line, e.g., 16 ♗d5 ♗xd5 17 ♖xd5 ♗e7=; no better was 15 ♘d6 ♘c5= Anand-Radjabov, Dubai (rapid) 2002)

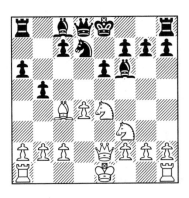

Now there's a significant division:
(b1) 10 ♗d3 ♗b7 11 ♘xf6+ ♕xf6 12 ♗e4 ♗xe4 13 ♕xe4 0-0 14 0-0 ♕e7 15 a4 ♘b6 16 axb5 axb5 17 ♕c6 b4 ½-½ Timman-M.Gurevich, Wijk aan Zee 2002; Black can soon play ...♕d6;

(b2) 10 ♗b3 0-0 11 0-0-0 (11 0-0 c5 12 dxc5 ♗b7 13 ♖fd1 ♗xe4 14 ♕xe4 ♘xc5= Van den Doel-Komarov, Clermont-Ferrand 2003; 11 ♖d1 ♗b7 12 0-0 c5 13 c3 ½-½ Milos-Bareev, Shenyang 2000) 11...♗b7 12 d5!? exd5 13 ♗xd5 c6 14 ♗b3 ♕c7 15 ♖he1 c5 16 ♗d5 ♗xd5 17 ♖xd5 ♗e7 18 ♔b1 Van

den Doel-Mullon, Clermont-Ferrand 2003; and Black might have kept up some pressure by 18...♖fe8!;

(b3) 10 ♗d5!? ♖b8 11 0-0-0 0-0 (11...♖b6!?) 12 ♗c6! ♖b6 13 d5 exd5 14 ♗xd5 c6 15 ♗b3 c5! (15...a5!? 16 c3 a4 17 ♗c2 ♕c7‡) 16 ♗d5 (16 ♘xc5? ♗xb2+! and 17 ♔xb2 ♕f6+ or 17 ♔b1 ♗f6 18 ♘xd7 ♗xd7 19 ♘e5 ♗xe5 20 ♕xe5 ♕c8∓ Goloshchapov-M.Gurevich, Wijk aan Zee 2001) 16...♕c7 17 ♖he1 ♗d8! (with the idea ...♘f6) 18 ♘eg5 (18 ♕e3 c4 19 ♘fg5 ♗xg5 20 ♕xg5 ♘f6 21 g3 ½-½ Shirov-M.Gurevich, New Delhi 2001) 18...♗xg5+ 19 ♘xg5 ♘f6 20 ♕e5?! ½-½ Svidler-M.Gurevich, Esbjerg 2000; in fact, 20...♕xe5 21 ♖xe5 ♘xd5 22 ♖exd5 ♗b7 23 ♖xc5 ♗xg2! is quite appealing. When the world's leading players make no progress against a variation, it's a good indication that Black's play is sound;

(c) The natural 8 ♗d3 can be answered with 8...c5!, when 9 dxc5 (9 ♘d6+? ♔e7 will actually win material for Black; 9 ♘xf6+ ♕xf6 10 0-0 cxd4 11 ♖e1 0-0 12 ♘xd4 ♖d8 with an easy game, Kindermann-Nikolaczuk, Dortmund 1986) 9...♘xc5! was Alekhine's idea in 1927! If 10 ♘xc5 (10 ♘xf6+ ♕xf6 11 0-0?! ♕xb2∓ Yates-Alekhine, Kecskemet 1927), 10...♕a5+ 11 c3 ♕xc5 frees Black's game and keeps the two bishops;

(d) 8 ♘xf6+ is tame:
(d1) 8...♘xf6 9 ♗b5+ (9 ♘e5 0-0 10 ♗d3 c5! 11 dxc5 ♕a5+ 12 c3 ♕xc5 13 ♕e2 b6= Standke-Krueger, Germany 1995) 9...♗d7 10 ♗xd7+ ♕xd7 11 ♕e2 0-0 12 0-0 ♖fd8= Efimov-M.Gurevich, Saint Vincent 2003;

(d2) 8...♕xf6 9 ♕d2 (trying to anticipate and perhaps clamp down on ...c5 and ...e5; 9 ♗c4 0-0 10 ♕e2 a6!? 11 0-0-0 b5 12 ♗d3 ♗b7=; 9 ♗d3 c5

10 0-0 cxd4 11 ♖e1 ♘c5 12 ♗b5+ ♗d7 13 ♗xd7+ ½-½ Sigurjonsson-Pachman, Munich 1979) 9...c5! (9...0-0 10 ♕e3!) 10 0-0-0 cxd4 11 ♕xd4 ♕xd4 12 ♖xd4 e5 13 ♖d2 f6=.

We return to the main line after 8 ♕d2:

8...0-0

In my database this main line position, also arising from 7...0-0 8 ♕d2 ♘d7, has scored 51% for Black with only a miniscule edge in performance rating for White. It continues to offer reasonably active play while keeping risks to a minimum.

It's definitely worth it to briefly compare a couple of the older moves in this position, one of which difficult yet instructive, the other of which is doing well again:

(a) 8...♗e7, to retain the bishop pair, has had a poor reputation ever since Fischer-Benko, Curacao 1962, but Benko's recent notes illustrate how even a passive-looking and underdeveloped position can be playable when one has the bishop pair: 9 0-0-0 ♘f6 10 ♗d3 0-0 11 ♘xf6+ ♗xf6 12 ♕f4 c5 (queried, but Black needs activity) 13 dxc5 ♕a5 14 ♕c4 ♗e7 15 h4 ♕xc5 16 ♕e4 f5 17 ♕e2 b5! 18 ♘g5 (18 ♗xb5 ♖b8 19 ♗c4 ♗f6 20 ♗b3 a5 is unclear – Benko) 18...♗f6! 19 ♘xe6!? (19 ♕h5 h6 20 ♕g6 hxg5 21 hxg5 ♗xb2+ 22 ♔xb2 ♕b4+ 23 ♔c1 ♕f4+ 24 ♖d2 ♕d4 25 ♕h7+ ♔f7 is given as unclear by Benko) 19...♗xe6? (19...♗xb2+! 20 ♔xb2 ♕b4+ 21 ♔c1 ♕a3+ 22 ♔d2 ♕a5+ with perpetual check – Benko) 20 ♕xe6+ ♔h8 21 ♔b1 ♕xf2 22 ♕xf5 ♕xf5 23 ♗xf5±, a game Fischer went on to win after further mistakes by Black. But the opening was not to blame;

(b) 8...b6 is another old move, quite popular in the early days of the French Defence. It scored overwhelmingly for White up to about 1985, but has served Black well since and remains a viable alternative to 8...0-0:

(b1) 9 ♗b5 0-0 10 ♗c6 ♖b8 11 0-0-0 ♗b7 12 ♗xb7 (12 d5!? ♘c5 13 ♕f4 ♘xe4 14 ♕xe4 ♗xc6 15 dxc6 ♕c8 16 ♘e5 ♕a6 17 ♔b1 ♗xe5 18 ♕xe5 ♕c4=) 12...♖xb7 13 d5 ♘c5 14 ♘xf6+ ♕xf6 15 ♖he1 ♖d8 16 ♕e3 ♖bb8 17 dxe6 ♘xe6= Balcerak-Atalik, Cappelle la Grande 2003;

(b2) 9 0-0-0 ♗b7 10 ♕f4 (10 ♗d3 ♗e7 11 ♕f4 ♘f6 12 h4 ♗xe4 13 ♗xe4 ♘xe4 14 ♕xe4 ♕d5 15 ♖he1 (15 ♕xd5 exd5 16 ♖he1 f6=) 15...♕xe4 16 ♖xe4 Solovjov-Grishina, St Petersburg 2001; and best was 16...♖d8! 17 c4 c6 18 ♘e5 ♖c8=) 10...♕e7!? 11 ♗c4 0-0-0!? (11...0-0!=) 12 ♖he1 ♘f8 13 g3 ♘g6 14 ♕e3± Vallejo Pons-Korchnoi, Biel 2002.

9 0-0-0

9 ♕c3, similar to Kasparov's idea 9 0-0-0 ♗e7 10 ♕c3, hasn't been tried as far as I know. Again Black can break up the centre, e.g., 9...c5! 10 ♘xf6+ (10 ♘xc5 ♘xc5 11 ♕xc5 b6 12 ♕c6 ♖b8 13 ♕a4 ♗b7 14 ♖d1 ♗xf3 15 gxf3 ♕d5∓) 10...♕xf6 11 0-0-0 ♖d8 12 ♗d3 b6 (12...cxd4 is also playable) 13 ♗e4 ♖b8 14 ♖he1 ♗b7 (14...h6=) 15 ♗xb7 ♖xb7=.

9 0-0-0 introduces the main position for this chapter. Black has a choice:

14.1 9...♗e7
14.2 9...b6

14.1 9...♗e7

9...♗e7 has been a favourite weapon of Bareev's for years. Black courageously retains his two bishops at the cost of time. This does strengthen the support for ...c5 and makes way for ...♘f6; but White also gains in that the time spent makes it more likely that a kingside attack will yield results. Thus this may be seen as a somewhat riskier and more ambitious strategy than developing move 9...b6 of the next section. Although it occasionally suffers a tactical reverse, the two bishops often have their say and Black actually has an excellent performance rating with 9...♗e7.

10 ♗c4

I make this the main line because of its importance rather than its frequency of use. Black's problem now is that the move ...c5 is generally answered by d5. In fact, a complete solution to 10 ♗c4 could be taken as a general sign of the system's worth.

Nevertheless, of the alternatives that follow, 10 ♗d3 and 10 ♕c3 are particularly important to take into account:

(a) 10 ♕f4!? c5!? 11 dxc5 ♕a5 12 ♔b1 ♘xc5=;

(b) 10 ♔b1 b6!? (or 10...c5 11 dxc5 ♕c7) 11 ♗c4 ♘f6 12 ♘xf6+ ♗xf6 13 ♕e3 (13 d5 b5 14 ♗b3 c5! and now 15 dxe6 c4 or 15 dxc6 ♕b6=) 13...♗b7 14 ♖he1 ♕e7 15 g4!? ♖ad8 16 ♘e5 c5= Stefansson-Bareev, Yerevan 1996;

(c) 10 ♗d3 is a solid move that aims for an attack that Black musn't underestimate:

(c1) 10...b6 11 ♘eg5! h6?! (11...♘f6 is solid and natural) 12 ♗h7+ ♔h8 13 ♗e4!! hxg5 (13...♗xg5! 14 ♘xg5 ♖b8 and 15 ♘f3 ♘f6 16 ♗d3 ♗b7= or 15 h4 ♘f6= – Polgar) 14 g4! (14 ♗xa8 g4 and ...♗g5 if the knight moves) 14...♖b8 15 h4 g6 (I doubt that there's a sufficient defence, e.g., 15...gxh4 16 g5 f5 17 ♕f4! looks very strong) 16 hxg5+ ♔g7 17 ♕f4! ♗b7 18 ♖h7+! ♔xh7 19 ♕h2+ ♔g8 20 ♖h1 ♗xg5+ 21 ♘xg5 ♕xg5+ 22 f4 ♕xf4+ 23 ♕xf4 ♗xe4 24 ♕xe4 1-0 J.Polgar-Berkes, Budapest 2003. A superb game, whatever its theoretical significance;

(c2) 10...c5! 11 dxc5 ♕c7 12 ♕e2 (12 ♖he1 ♘xc5 13 ♘xc5 ♗xc5=) 12...b6!? (12...♘xc5=) 13 c6!? ♕xc6 (13...♘b8!) 14 ♘eg5 ♗xg5+ 15 ♘xg5 ♘f6= Fressinet-Radjabov, Halkidiki 2002. Another critical sequence here would be 11 ♘xc5 ♘xc5 12 dxc5 ♕d5 13 ♔b1 ♕xc5 14 h4 a5!? intending ...a4 and/or ...b5;

(d) 10 ♕c3!? is Kasparov's invention, designed to meet Bareev's favourite 9...♗e7 when the two met in Sarajevo 2000. It tries to clamp down on both ...c5 and ...e5. Although this poses serious problems, Black has a couple of ideas that seem satisfactory.

For example, since White has no threats, a move like 10...a5 is plausible, with ideas of expansion on the queenside as well as ...♘b6-d5. Othewise:

(d1) 10...♘f6 was Bareev's response: 11 ♘xf6+ ♗xf6 12 ♗d3 ♕d6 13 ♔b1 ♖d8 14 h4 a5 15 ♕e1! (preventing ...♕b4 from forcing the exchange of queens) 15...♗d7?! (risky but playable seems 15...c5 16 dxc5 ♕xc5, when and 17 ♕e4 ♕b4! saves the day while 17 ♘g5 h6 18 ♘e4 ♕e5 19 ♘xf6+ ♕xf6 20 g4! ♗d7 holds, even if it must favour White) 16 ♘g5 h6 17 ♗h7+ ♔f8 18 ♘e4 ♕e7 19 ♘xf6 ♕xf6 20 ♗e4 and White was distinctly better;

(d2) Even with the queen on c3, 10...c5! looks good. The most interesting line in that case would be 11 ♗b5 (recommended by McDonald; 11 dxc5 ♕c7 is fine for Black; 11 d5 exd5 12 ♖xd5 ♕c7∓ plans ...♘b6 followed by ...♗e6) 11...♕c7!. This introduces the kind of long-term positional pawn sacrifice that is common these days. Here even the exchange of queens leaves Black's bishop pair worth more than the pawn in a continuation like 12 ♗xd7 ♗xd7 13 ♘xc5 (13 dxc5 ♗c6 14 ♘d6 b6∓) 13...♗c6 14 ♘d3 ♖ac8! 15 ♘de5 ♗d5 16 ♕xc7 ♖xc7

17 a3 (17 ♔b1 ♖fc8 18 ♖d2 f6 19 ♘d3 g5!, restricting the knights and preparing the simple minority attack with ...b5-b4, ...a5-a4) 17...♗b3 18 ♖d2 ♖fc8 19 c3 b5 20 ♘d3 a5 with a powerful minority attack, for example, 21 ♔b1 b4 22 axb4 axb4 23 ♘xb4 ♗xb4 24 cxb4 ♖a8! and wins, since ...♖ca7 follows.

Returning to 10 ♗c4:

10...a6!?

An aggressive move resembling several other lines in this chapter, but retaining the two bishops.

(a) 10...♘f6 11 ♘xf6 12 ♖he1 favours White due to his space and better development. This sort of position is hardly that bad, however, because White's major break with d5 would tend to free both of Black's bishops. In Yermolinsky-Bareev, Lucerne 1997, the play became sharp instead after 12...♖b8!? 13 ♘e5 b5! 14 ♗d3! (14 ♘c6 ♕d6 15 ♘xb8 bxc4 threatens ...c5) 14...♖b6!? (14...♗b7) 15 ♕e3 and White was still somewhat better;

(b) An alternative is 10...c5, which is double-edged yet holding up well:

(b1) 11 dxc5 ♕c7 12 ♖he1 ♘xc5 13 ♘xc5 ♕xc5 14 ♗d3 ♗f6 15 ♕e2 g6 16 h4 ♖d8 17 ♗b5 ♗xb2+ ½-½ Almasi-Dizdar, Makarska Tucepi 1995;

(b2) 11 d5!? exd5 12 ♗xd5 ♕c7

with the idea ...♘b6 – Timman; one would think that White's centralised pieces and control of d5 were vital, but the two bishops seem to hold their own.

(b3) the widely-recommended move is 11 ♗b5!, but 11...♕c7! 12 ♗xd7 ♗xd7 looks fine, e.g. 13 ♘xc5 ♗c6 14 ♘d3 ♖ac8! 15 ♘de5 ♗d5 with compensation, or 13 dxc5?! ♗c6∓ with the idea 14 ♘d6 b6!∓;

(b4) 11 ♖he1 cxd4 12 ♘xd4 (12 ♕xd4 ♘b6 13 ♗b3 ♕xd4 14 ♖xd4! ♗d7 15 ♘e5 ♗c6 16 ♘xc6 bxc6 17 c3 c5 18 ♖dd1 c4=) 12...♘b6 13 ♗b3 ♗d7 14 ♕f4 a5 15 ♕g3!? (this is probably too ambitious, but 15 a3 a4 16 ♗a2 ♖a5! covers a lot of key squares) 15...a4 16 ♗xe6 fxe6 17 ♘xe6 ♗xe6 18 ♖xd8 ♗xd8 (I like Black's bishop pair) 19 ♘d6 ♗d5 (McDonald analyses 19...♗xa2!?, which seems very good for Black after 20 b3 axb3 21 cxb3 h6, e.g., 22 ♘xb7 ♗g5+ 23 ♔d1 ♖a3-+) 20 ♖e8 Fressinet-Radjabov, Pamplona 2001, and here Radjabov gives 20...♗c7 with advantage.

11 ♗b3

11 ♖he1 b5 12 ♗d3 ♗b7 equalises easily, e.g., 13 ♔b1 ♗d5! (13...c5=) 14 ♕f4 c5.

11...a5!

Suddenly changing plans based upon the bishop's position. Black threatens ...a4. Also good enough is 11...c6: 12 ♕f4 b5 13 h4 (13 ♘e5 ♕c7) 13...♖a7 14 ♘eg5 ♘f6= Khalifman-Bareev, Belgrade 1993.

12 ♗c4

Alternatives are 12 a3 a4 13 ♗a2 ♘f6, and 12 a4 ♘b6!?, targeting a4.

12...c6 13 ♔b1 ♕c7 14 h4!? ½-½

Anand-Bareev, Wijk aan Zee 2003. Here 14...b5 15 ♗d3 ♗b7 could follow, when Black is well enough developed to resist any attack.

14.2 9...b6 10 ♗c4

10 ♕f4 ♗b7 11 h4 c5 12 ♗b5!? cxd4 13 ♗xd7 ♗xe4 14 ♕xe4 ♕xd7 15 g4 (15 ♘xd4 ♕a4 16 ♔b1 ♖fd8 17 c3 ♖ac8∓) 15...g6 16 g5 ♗g7 17 h5 ♖fd8 18 hxg6 hxg6 19 ♕h4 ♕d5 Gallagher-Eliet, Clermont-Ferrand 2003, and White seems to lack any compensation whatsoever.

10...♗b7!?

Black should certainly consider Dreev's slow move 10...c6 to stabilise the centre and prevent d5. Then if White tries to eliminate Black's bishop pair by 11 ♘d6 ♕c7 12 ♘xc8 ♖fxc8, he has only encouraged Black to attack on the queenside. Better is 11 ♘xf6+ ♕xf6 12 ♖he1 h6 13 ♕e3 ♗b7 with ...c5 shortly.

11 d5!?

An ambitious move, and the only try for a serious advantage. Others allow Black to consolidate:

(a) 11 ♖he1 ♗d5!? (Probably okay, but 11...♗xe4! 12 ♖xe4 c6 would be safe and solid; ...b5, ...a5, and ...♘b6 could follow) 12 ♗d3 (12 ♗xd5 exd5 13 ♘g3 Vallejo Pons-Radjabov, Leon 2001; 13...g6!= 14 ♘e5 ♘xe5 15 dxe5 ♗g7 16 ♕xd5 ♕g5+ 17 ♔b1 ♖ad8=; 12 ♕d3 c6 13 ♗b3 ♗xb3 14 ♕xb3 ♕c7=) 12...c5!? 13 c4 ♗b7!? (or 13...♗c6, when 14 ♘eg5 h6! looks fine and otherwise the bishop is slightly better placed) 14 dxc5 bxc5 15 ♘xf6+ and White got a small but lasting edge after 15...♕xf6?! in Hübner-Short, Novi Sad 1990; but there seems nothing wrong with the active 15...♘xf6! intending ...♗xf3 or ...♕b6, e.g., 16 ♘e5 (16 ♕f4 ♕a5; 16 ♘g5 ♕c7) 16...♕e7 17 g4!? ♖fd8 18 ♕c2 g6 19 g5 (19 f4 ♖d4!) 19...♘d7=;

(b) 11 ♕f4 ♗d5 (11...♕e7!?) 12 ♗d3 ♗e7!? (12...c5! with the idea 13 c4 ♗c6 14 dxc5 bxc5∓) 13 c4 ♗b7 14 g4!? ♘f6 15 ♘xf6+ ♗xf6 16 ♗e4 ♗xe4 17 ♕xe4 ♕e7 18 h4 ♕b4! 19 ♕c2 ♕d6 20 ♕e4 ♕b4= Bologan-M.Gurevich, Belfort 1998.

11...b5!?

Also satisfactory is 11...e5 (Hübner) 12 g4!? (12 ♖he1 a6!=) 12...a6 13 g5 ♗e7 – McDonald.

12 ♗b3

12 dxe6? bxc4∓; 12 ♗xb5 exd5 13 ♘xf6+ ♘xf6 14 ♖he1 c5.

12...c5!

The '!' is partly for ingenuity. Safer options are 12...♘b6 13 ♘xf6+ ♕xf6 14 dxe6 fxe6= and 12...exd5 13 ♗xd5 c6 14 ♗b3 c5 15 ♗d5 (15 ♕xd7 ♗xe4 16 ♕xb5 ♕c7) 15...♖b8 unclear – M.Gurevich; compare the game.

13 ♘d6!

White loses after 13 dxe6? ♗xe4 14 exf7+ ♔h8 15 ♕xd7 ♕xd7 16 ♖xd7 c4 and lacks enough compensation after 13 ♘xf6+?! ♘xf6 14 dxe6 ♗xf3 15 exf7+ ♔h8 16 ♕xd8 ♖axd8 17 ♖xd8 ♖xd8 18 gxf3 c4.

13...♗xd5 14 ♗xd5 exd5 15 ♕xd5 ♘b6! 16 ♕e4

16 ♕xc5? ♘a4 is awful, as is 16 ♕c6? ♗xb2+ 17 ♔xb2 ♕f6+. But a serious alternative is 16 ♕f5!? as played in Almasi-Tukmakov, Pula 2001. Because of the number of earlier paths to equality, I'm not going to

analyse this deeply but I think that it's equal. Here's one line of many: 16...g6 (16...♘a4 also seems fine, e.g., 17 ♘e5 ♕e7 18 ♖he1 ♖ad8! 19 ♘c6 ♕xd6 20 ♖xd6 ♗xb2+ 21 ♔b1 ♖xd6∓) 17 ♕f4 and now easiest was 17...♘a4! 18 c3 (18 ♘c4 bxc4 19 ♖xd8 ♗xb2+ 20 ♔b1 ♖axd8 21 ♕xc4 ♖b8=) 18...♗g7 19 ♖he1 (19 ♘e5 ♕c7) 19...♕a5=.

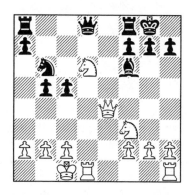

16...♘a4

16...♕d7!? is also fully equal. After 16...♘a4, Van den Doel-M.Gurevich, Hoogeveen 1999 went 17 ♘e5 ♕b6?! (17...♕a5! 18 f4 c4 19 ♔b1 ♘xb2! 20 ♔xb2 ♕b4+=) 18 ♕d5 (18 ♘dxf7? ♕e6-+) 18...♖ad8 19 f4! (19 ♘exf7? ♗xb2+ 20 ♔d2 ♕a5+ -+) 19...c4 20 ♔b1 ♕c7 21 ♖he1 (21 ♘xb5 ♖xd5 22 ♘xc7 ♖xd1+ 23 ♖xd1 ♖b8) with a small edge for White.

In this chapter we have seen just about every possible type of idea stemming from the 4...dxe4 and 6...♗xf6 system. There are a lot of options for Black at almost every move, so this can be a particularly flexible and practical system. Both sides can steer away from tactical play if they wish, so one should be willing to play somewhat quieter positions than are produced, for example, by the Winawer Variation.

Chapter Fifteen

Odds and Ends

1 e4 e6

In this chapter I will briefly discuss White's irregular second and third moves. I've had relatively little feedback on these moves so I will mainly redo what was in the second edition in order to conserve space for the rest of the book. One advantage of the French Defence is that most of White's moves other than 2 d4 are harmless. Of what follows, only 2 ♘f3 d5 3 ♘c3 presents a serious challenge to Black. The main White third move after 1 e4 e6 2 d4 d5 is 3 ♗e3 (a gambit). I will organise as follows:

15.1 2 b3
15.2 2 ♘f3
15.3 2 d4 d5 3 ♗e3

It's worth mentioning that Black generally has two or more good answers in addition to the one I've presented.

Here are some rare second moves:
(a) 2 e5 c5 (2...d6 3 exd6 ♗xd6 4 d4 ♘c6 5 ♘f3 ♘ge7 6 ♗d3 e5=; 2...d5 3 ♘f3 c5 4 b4 is given under the order 2 ♘f3 d5 3 e5 etc.) 3 f4 ♘c6 4 ♘f3 ♘h6 (4...d6=) 5 g3 (Steinitz-Mason, Vienna

1892) 5...♘f5 6 ♗g2 d6=;
(b) 2 ♗b5 c6 3 ♗a4 d5 4 ♕e2 ♕a5! 5 ♗b3 ♘f6 6 e5 ♘fd7 7 c3 c5 8 d3 ♘c6 9 f4 ♘d4! 10 ♕d1 ♘xb3 11 ♕xb3 c4! 12 dxc4 ♘c5∓ Wahls-Vaisser, Berlin 1988;
(c) 2 f4 d5 3 e5 (3 ♘c3, and 3...d4 4 ♘e2 c5= or 3...dxe4 4 ♘xe4 c5 5 ♘f3 ♘c6 6 ♗b5 ♗d7 7 ♕e2 ♘h6 8 0-0 ♗e7 9 d3 0-0=) 3...c5 4 ♘f3 ♘c6 5 c3 (5 c4 d4 6 d3 ♘h6=) 5...d4 (or 5...♘h6 intending 6 d4 ♕b6) 6 d3 ♘h6= Weiss-Maroczy, Budapest 1895;
(d) 2 c4 d5 (2...c5 is a Sicilian Defence) 3 exd5 (3 cxd5 exd5 4 ♕a4+ ♗d7 5 ♕b3 ♘c6! 6 ♕xd5 ♘f6 7 ♕c4 ♗e6 8 ♕a4 ♗c5∓ – ECO) 3...exd5 4 cxd5 (4 d4 is an Exchange Variation) 4...♘f6 5 ♘c3 (5 ♗b5+ ♘bd7 6 ♘c3 ♗e7 7 ♘ge2 0-0 8 0-0 a6 9 ♗xd7 ♕xd7 10 ♘f4 b5 11 ♕f3 ♗b7 12 a3 a5∓ Grob-Johner, Zurich 1941) 5...♘xd5 6 ♗c4 ♘b4! 7 ♘f3 ♘d3+ 8 ♔f1 ♗e7 9 ♕e2 ♘xc1 10 ♖xc1 0-0∓ Velimirovic-P.Nikolic, Novi Sad 1984;
(e) 2 g3 d5 3 ♘c3 (3 ♗g2 c5= or 3...dxe4 4 ♘c3 ♗d7!= and ...♗c6, or 3...♘f6 4 e5 ♘fd7 5 d4 c5 6 c3 ♕b6 7 ♘f3 ♘c6 8 0-0 ♗e7= intending ...0-0, ...f6 – ECO) 3...dxe4 (3...♘f6 4 e5

♘fd7 5 f4 c5 6 ♘f3 ♘c6 7 ♗g2, and 7...♗e7 or 7...a6 8 a4 ♗e7 9 0-0 0-0 10 d3 ♘d4 11 ♘e2 ♘xf3+ 12 ♗xf3 f6= Vavra-Totsky, Leonid 1995) 4 ♘xe4 ♘f6 (4...♗d7 5 ♘f3 ♗c6 6 ♕e2 ♘f6= Bartsch-Reefschlaeger, Bundesliga 1981) 5 ♘xf6+ ♕xf6 6 ♗g2 ♗c5 7 ♕f3 ♕e7! 8 ♘e2 e5∓ Suttles-Uhlmann, Palma de Mallorca 1970;

(f) 2 ♘e2 d5 3 exd5 exd5 4 ♘g3 ♘f6 (4...♕h4!? – ECO) 5 d4 ♗d6 6 ♗d3 0-0 7 0-0 ♖e8= Tartakower-Fine, Kemeri 1937;

(g) 2 ♘c3 d5 tranposes to the main line after 3 d4, or to 2 ♘f3 below after 3 ♘f3, or to note 'e' after 3 g3.

15.1 2 b3

A safe move, but b3 and e4 do not mix very well.

2...b6

Trying to force White to defend e4. Perfectly good is the normal 2...d5 3 ♗b2 (3 exd5 exd5 simply frees Black's pieces) 3...♘f6 (3...dxe4 is fine, but there's a fair amount of theory) and:

(a) 4 exd5 exd5 (4...♕xd5 5 ♘c3 ♕a5=) 5 ♘f3 (5 ♕e2+ ♗e6 6 ♕b5+ ♘bd7 7 ♕xb7 ♗c5! with strong compensation, one point being 8 ♗xf6 ♕xf6! 9 ♕xa8+ ♔e7 10 ♕xh8 ♕xf2+ 11 ♔d1 ♕xf1 mate) 5...♗e7 (5...♗c5 6 d4 ♗b4+! 7 c3 ♗d6 8 ♗e2 0-0 9 0-0

♗f5= Sandmann-Rausch, Bundesliga 1989) 6 ♗e2 0-0 7 0-0 ♗f5 8 ♖e1 c5 9 d4 ♘c6 10 ♘bd2 ♖c8∓ (c-file and activity) Castro-Petrosian, Biel 1976.

(b) 4 e5 ♘fd7 5 f4 c5 6 ♘f3 (6 ♘c3 ♘c6 7 ♘f3 a6 8 g3 b5= Tartakower-Alekhine, Kemeri 1937) 6...b6!? (or 6...♗e7 7 ♗e2 ♘c6=) 7 d4 ♗a6 8 ♗xa6 ♘xa6 9 ♕e2 ♘b4 10 0-0 ♗e7 11 ♔h1 ♖c8 12 ♘a3 0-0 13 c3 ♘c6 14 ♘c2 cxd4 15 ♘fxd4 ♘c5 16 ♖f3 ♘xd4 17 cxd4 ♘e4 and Black dominates the light squares, E.Hummel-Archangelsky, Wijk aan Zee 2000.

3 ♗b2 ♗b7 4 ♘c3

The e-pawn is awkward to defend: 4 ♕e2 ♘f6 5 ♘c3 c5 with the idea ...♘c6 is equal, as is 4 d3 d5.

4...c5

Or 4...d5 5 exd5 exd5 6 d4 ♘f6=.

5 ♘f3 ♘c6 6 d4 cxd4 7 ♘xd4 ♘xd4 8 ♕xd4 ♘f6

Black shouldn't delay his development with moves like ...a6 and ...d6.

9 f3?!

9 ♗e2 ♗c5 10 ♕d3 0-0=.

9...♗c5 10 ♕d2 0-0 11 ♘a4 ♗e7

Bury-J.Watson, Leominster 1977. Black has the idea 12 0-0-0 ♘xe4! and is better developed.

15.2 2 ♘f3 d5

and now:

15.21 3 ♘c3
15.22 3 e5

15.21 3 ♘c3 ♘f6

3...d4 is also fully satisfactory.

4 e5

4 ♕e2 ♗e7 achieves nothing, and 4 exd5 exd5 5 d4 is an inferior type of Exchange Variation: 5...♗b4 (5...c6 and; 5...♗e7 are equal) 6 a3 ♗xc3+ 7 bxc3 ♗g4 (7...0-0! 8 ♗e2 ♖e8 avoids 8 ♕e2+) 8 ♗e2 (8 ♕e2+! ♕e7 9 ♕xe7+

♔xe7 10 ♘e5 ♗f5 11 ♗d3!) 8...0-0 9 0-0 ♘e4 (or 9...♘bd7!?∓ with the idea ...♘b6) 10 ♗b2 ♘d7 11 c4 Bibiloni-Bosco, Buenos Aires 1993; and very strong was 11...dxc4! 12 ♗xc4 (12 c3 ♘b6) 12...♗xf3 13 gxf3 (13 ♕xf3 ♘d2) 13...♘d6 14 ♗b3 ♕h4∓.

4...♘fd7 5 d4 c5

Black can also wait for White to commit by 5...♗e7, e.g., 6 ♗d3 (6 ♘e2 c5 7 c3 ♘c6 8 ♘f4 – Minev, but 8...cxd4 9 cxd4 ♕b6 threatens ...g5 and then ...♗b4+) 6...c5 7 0-0 (7 dxc5 ♘xc5=) 7...♘c6 8 ♗e3? (8 dxc5 ♘xc5=) 8...cxd4 9 ♗xd4 ♘xd4 10 ♘xd4 ♘xe5 11 ♗b5+ ♗d7 12 ♖e1 ♘c6∓ Fleger-Sermier, Biel 1993.

6 dxc5

(a) 6 ♘e2 transposes to Chapter 13, 5 ♘f3;

(b) 6 ♗b5 has more than one answer, but the most important is 6...♘c6! 7 0-0 cxd4 8 ♘xd4 ♘dxe5! (8...♕c7 9 ♗f4!) 9 f4 (9 ♗f4 ♗d7 10 ♖e1 ♘g6∓; 9 ♖e1 ♗d6! 10 f4! ♘d7 11 ♘xd5 ♘xd4 12 ♕xd4 0-0 13 ♘e3 ♕c7∓; 9 ♕h5?! ♗d6 10 ♗g5 ♕c7∓) 9...a6! 10 ♗a4 ♘d7! 11 f5 (11 ♘xd5?? ♘xd4 12 ♕xd4 b5–+) 11...♘xd4 12 ♗xd7+ ♗xd7 13 ♕xd4 ♖c8∓ was D.Schneider-J.Watson, Chicago 1992.

6...♘c6 7 ♗f4

7 ♗g5 ♗e7 8 ♗xe7 ♕xe7 9 ♗b5

♘xc5 10 0-0 0-0 11 ♖e1 ♗d7= Gelashvili-Radjabov, Halkidiki 2002.

7...♗xc5 8 ♗d3 f6 9 exf6

White cannot maintain the pawn on e5:

(a) 9 ♗b5? fxe5 10 ♘xe5 (10 ♗xe5 0-0! 11 ♗g3 d4! 12 ♗xc6 dxc3 13 ♗xd7 cxb2 14 ♖b1 ♗b4+ 15 ♔e2 ♗xd7–+) 10...♘dxe5 11 ♗xe5 ♗xf2+! 12 ♔xf2 0-0+ and ...♘xe5;

(b) 9 ♕e2 fxe5 10 ♘xe5 ♘dxe5 11 ♗xe5 ♘xe5 12 ♕xe5 0-0 13 0-0 ♕f6 (or 13...♕h4!? 14 g3 ♕d4) 14 ♕xf6 ♖xf6∓ with two bishops and the mobile centre, e.g., 15 g3 ♗d7 16 ♔g2 g5! 17 ♖ae1 ♖af8 18 f3 ♗c6∓.

9...♘xf6 10 0-0 0-0

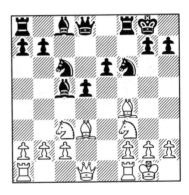

A key position for this variation. White's control of e5 and the e-file are balanced by Black's central majority and f-file pressure. Unquestionably White has the harder time of it in practice. We have:

15.211 11 ♗g3
15.212 11 ♘e5

Others:

(a) 11 ♕e2 ♘h5! (or 11...♗d7 12 ♖ad1 a6= 13 ♘a4?! ♗a7 14 c4?? e5!∓ 15 cxd5 ♘d4! 16 ♘xd4 ♗xd4–+ Rigo-Gulko, Rome 1988) 12 ♗g5 ♘f4! 13 ♕d2 ♕c7 14 ♘b5 ♕b8 15 c4? (15 ♗xf4

♖xf4 16 ♖ae1 ♗d7∓) 15...♘xd3 16 ♕xd3 ♘e5 17 ♘xe5 ♕xe5 18 ♗h4 a6! 19 ♘c3 ♕f4∓ Larsen-Spassky, Stockholm 1969;

(b) 11 ♘e2 ♕e7 (or 11...♘h5= 12 ♗g5 ♕d6) 12 ♘e5 ♘xe5 13 ♗xe5 ♘g4 14 ♗g3 ♕f6! hitting b2 and f2 and giving White problems;

(c) 11 ♕d2 ♕e8 (objectively 11...a6 is probably as good e.g., 12 ♖ae1 ♘h5 13 ♗g5 ♕c7 14 ♗h4 ♘f4 15 ♗g3 ♗d6 16 ♗xf4 ♗xf4 17 ♕d1 ♗d7∓ Rigo-H.Meyer, Delmenhorst 1986) 12 ♖ae1 (12 ♘b5 ♘h5 13 ♗d6 [13 ♘c7? ♕d8] 13...♗xd6 14 ♘xd6 ♕e7 15 ♘xc8 ♖axc8 with the ideas ...e5, ...♘b4 – Nunn) 12...♗d7 13 a3!? (13 ♘e5= Nunn; 13...♘xe5 14 ♗xe5 ♕h5∓) 13...♕h5 14 b4 ♗b6 15 ♗d6!? ♘g4! with a powerful attack, Rigo-Klinger, Vienna 1986;

(d) 11 ♘a4 ♗d6 12 ♗xd6 ♕xd6 13 c4 ♗d7 14 ♘c3 ♖ac8=.

15.211 11 ♗g3

This is very natural and considered a safe option. But remarkably it seems almost impossible for White to even equalise.

11...♘h5! 12 ♗h4

(a) 12 ♕e2 ♘xg3 13 hxg3 ♗d7 (13...♕f6!?∓) 14 ♘a4 ♗d6 15 c4 ♘b4! 16 ♘c3 ♖c8∓;

(b) 12 ♗e5? ♘xe5 13 ♘xe5 ♘f4 14 ♘e2 ♕g5 15 ♘xf4 ♕xe5 16 g3 ♕g5 17 ♕c1 e5!∓.

(c) 12 ♗h4 ♕c7! 13 ♘b5 ♕d7! 14 ♘g5 (14 ♖e1 ♘f4 15 ♘g5 h6! 16 ♘h7 ♖f7∓) 14...g6 15 c3 (15 ♖e1 ♘f4 16 ♗g3 e5∓) 15...e5 (15...♘f4 16 ♗c2 a6 17 ♘a3 b5∓) 16 ♗c2 ♖f4!? 17 ♗g3 (17 g3 ♖xh4! 18 gxh4 ♘f4∓) 17...♘xg3 18 hxg3 ♖g4 19 ♘e6!? (19 ♘f3 e4!? 20 ♘fd4 a6 21 ♘a3 ♕d6∓) 19...♕xe6 20 ♘c7 ♕d6! 21 ♘xa8 e4∓ 22 b4 ♕xg3 23 ♕xd5+ ♔h8 24 ♕xe4 ♘e5-+.

15.212 11 ♘e5 ♗d7

The traditional move. I analysed 11...♕e8!? in the last edition, and A.Bennett-J.Watson, Seattle 2003 took an interesting course after 11...a6!? (I like this move) 12 ♕e2 ♕e8 (12...♘xe5 13 ♗xe5 b5!? 14 ♖ae1 ♖a7!? 15 ♔h1 ♖af7! 16 f4 ♗b7 and ...d4) 13 ♘xc6 (13 ♘a4?? ♘d4) 13...bxc6 14 ♘a4 ♗a7 15 ♗d6, and although Black eventually mobilised his central pawns and won after 15...♖f7=, I might have tried my original intention 15...c5!? 16 ♘xc5 (16 b3 c4) 16...e5! 17 ♗xf8 (17 ♘xa6 e4 18 ♗b5 ♕g6!?) 17...♕xf8 18 ♘xa6 ♕d6 with a fascinating attack.

12 ♘xc6

There are several options, none impressive:

(a) 12 a3 a6 (12...♘xe5 13 ♗xe5 ♕b6 14 ♕e2 ♗d6∓) 13 ♘xc6 ♗xc6 14 ♕e2 ♕e7! 15 ♖ae1 ♖ae8 16 ♗e5 ♘d7! 17 ♕h5 ♖f5!! 18 ♗xf5 exf5 19 ♔h1 (19 ♗g3 ♕xe1) 19...♘xe5 20 f4 ♕f7∓;

(b) 12 ♕f3!? can be answered by 12...♗d4! 13 ♘xc6 ♗xc6 14 ♖ae1 e5! 15 ♗xe5 ♗xe5 16 ♖xe5 d4 17 ♗c4+ ♔h8 18 ♘d5 ♖c8! 19 ♕b3 b5-+;

(c) 12 ♕e2 ♕e7 13 ♖ae1 ♖ae8 14 a3 (14 ♗g3 is recommended by Baker; then some interesting play can follow 14...a6!? 15 a3 b5!, e.g., 16 ♘d1 ♘xe5

17 ♗xe5 ♗c6 18 c3 ♘e4!? 19 ♘e3 ♕g5!? 20 f4 ♕g6) 14...a6 15 ♔h1 (15 ♗g3 ♘xe5 16 ♕xe5!? ♗c6 17 b4 ♗a7 with the idea ...♗b8 and a small advantage, Drozdov-Hoang Than Trang, Budapest 1994) 15...♗d4! 16 ♘xd7 ♕xd7 17 ♗d2 e5∓ Ljubojevic-Petrosian, Las Palmas 1973.

12...♗xc6 13 ♕e2

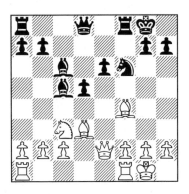

13...♕e7

Or 13...♘e4!? 14 g3 (14 ♗e3?! ♗xe3 15 ♕xe3!? d4 16 ♕e2 dxc3 17 ♗xe4 cxb2 18 ♖ab1 ♕f6 19 c4 ♖ab8!∓ Bellon-Speelman, Amsterdam 1978) 14...♘xf2 15 ♖xf2 ♗xf2+ 16 ♔xf2 Vogt-Farago, Kecskemet 1979, and now 16...g5! 17 ♕xe6+ ♔g7 unclear – Vogt; but this seems to favour Black, e.g., 18 ♕g4 ♔h8!? 19 ♕h5 ♕e7 20 ♖e1 ♕g7 with advantage.

14 ♖ae1 ♖ae8 15 ♗e5!?

15 ♗g3 a6 16 a3 ♕f7!? 17 b4 ♗d4 18 ♗e5 ♗xe5 19 ♕xe5 ♘d7 20 ♕g3 e5∓ Spassky-Petrosian, Moscow 1966.

15...♘d7 16 ♘b5

16 ♕h5 g6! 17 ♗xg6 ♘xe5 18 ♗xe8 ♖f5! 19 ♖xe5 ♖xh5 20 ♗xh5 ♗d6 21 ♖e2 ♕h4 22 h3 ♕xh5 23 ♖xe6 ♗b4–+.

16...a6!?

16...♘xe5!? 17 ♕xe5 ♖xf2! 18 ♖xf2 ♗xf2+ 19 ♔xf2 ♗xb5 20 ♗xb5 ♕c5+ 21 ♖e3 ♕xb5∓, but Black probably can't win this.

After 16...a6, Shilov-Ulibin, Barlinek 2001 went 17 ♘d4 ♘xe5 18 ♕xe5 ♗d7 19 f4 ♗d6 20 ♕h5? (20 ♕e3 e5 21 fxe5 ♗xe5 22 ♔h1!=) 20...g6 21 ♕g4 e5! 22 ♕g3 and one win was Bangiev's 22...e4 23 ♗e2 ♕f6.

15.22 3 e5 c5 4 b4!?

This is the French Wing Gambit, trying to win the centre by diverting Black's c-pawn. It has never attracted much attention from strong players and in my opinion it is suspect. Some passive alternatives:

(a) 4 d3 ♘c6 5 c3 (5 ♗e2 ♕c7 6 ♗f4 f6) 5...f6 6 d4!? and Black is a tempo ahead of the Advance Variation: 6...♗d7!? (6...fxe5; 6...♕b6!) 7 g3 ♖c8 8 ♗g2 cxd4 9 cxd4 ♗b4+ 10 ♗d2 ♕b6 11 a3? ♗xd2+ 12 ♕xd2 ♘a5–+ Hamadto-Rahman, Dubai 1986;

(b) 4 g3 ♘c6 5 ♗g2 g5!? 6 h3 ♗g7 7 ♕e2 h6 (7...♕c7!∓) 8 0-0 ♕c7 9 ♖e1 ♘ge7 10 ♘a3 a6 11 c3 c4! 12 b3 b5∓ with the idea ...♘g6 Gatica-Levitt, New York 1994.

4...cxb4

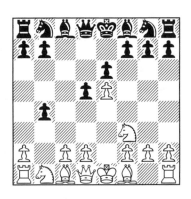

5 a3

5 d4 is also played:

(a) 5...♗d7 (Harding gives this '!') 6 a3 (6 ♗d3 has several answers, e.g., 6...♕b6 intending ...♗b5 or 6...♘e7 7 a3 ♘bc6 8 axb4 ♘xb4∓ Barendregt-Bronstein, Hamburg 1965) 6...♕a5!? 7 ♗d3 ♗b5 ('This is a hard line for White to play' – Harding) 8 0-0 (8 axb4? ♕xa1 9 ♗xb5+ ♘c6 10 ♗d2 ♕b2 11 c3 a5∓ Day-Hübner, Jerusalem 1967) 8...♕xd3 9 ♕xd3 ♕a6! 10 ♕b3 ♘c6 11 ♕b2 ♕b6!? 12 ♖d1 Vedder-Poulton, Gausdal 1990; and here 12...f6 was one of several moves, still a pawn up;

(b) 5...♘c6 6 a3 and:

(b1) 6...bxa3 7 c3 ♘ge7 (7...f6 8 ♗d3 ♕c7) 8 ♗xa3 ♘g6!? 9 ♗xf8 (9 h4 ♗e7 10 h5 ♘h4 11 h6 ♘xf3+ 12 ♕xf3 g6∓) 9...♘xf8 10 ♗d3 f6 11 ♘a3 fxe5 12 ♘xe5 ♘xe5 13 dxe5 ♘g6!? 14 ♕h5 0-0 15 0-0 (15 ♗xg6 hxg6 16 ♕xg6 ♕c7) 15...♗d7 16 f4 ♖c8∓ Bosch-Blees, Dieren 1988;

(b2) 6...f6 7 axb4, and 7...♗xb4+ 8 c3 ♗a5 intending ...♗c7 or 7...fxe5 8 ♘xe5 ♘xe5 9 dxe5 ♕c7 (9...♗xb4+ 10 c3 ♗c5∓) 10 ♕d4 ♘e7∓.

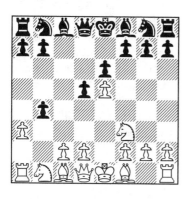

5...♘c6

5...d4!? was given in the last edition but is too worked out now.

5...♘h6!? is a clever idea played in C.B.Baker-Harding, corr 1986: 6 axb4 ♗xb4 7 c3 ♗e7 (the point: ...♘h6 developed, but left e7 free for the bishop) 8 d4 ♘f5 9 ♘a3 (Harding prefers 9 ♗d3) 9...♗d7!? (9...♘c6 10 ♗d3

f6!∓) 10 ♗d3 ♘c6 11 g4 ♘h4 12 ♘xh4 ♗xa3?! (12...♗xh4∓) 13 ♗xa3 ♕xh4 14 ♖b1 with some compensation.

6 axb4 ♗xb4 7 c3 ♗e7

7...♗a5 8 d4 f6 is also good, but requires more accurate play, as Harding has shown.

8 d4

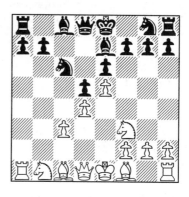

8...f6!

Or the creative 8...♘h6! 9 ♗xh6!? (9 ♗d3 ♘f5) 9...gxh6 10 ♗d3 f6! 11 ♕c2 fxe5 12 dxe5 ♕c7∓ 13 0-0 ♗c5! 14 ♖a4 ♗d7 15 ♗g6+ ♔e7! 16 ♗xh7 ♘xe5∓ Lanzani-Vezzosi, Chianciano Terme 1990.

9 ♗d3 fxe5 10 ♘xe5

10 dxe5 ♕c7 11 0-0 ♘xe5 12 ♘xe5 ♕xe5 13 ♗b5+ ♔f7!∓ Hamed-Garma, Novi Sad 1990.

After 10 ♘xe5, Reindermann-Glek, Groningen 1992 continued 10...♘f6 11 ♗g5 ♘xe5 12 dxe5 ♘e4! 13 ♗xe7 ♕xe7 14 ♗xe4 dxe4 15 ♕d4 0-0 16 ♕xe4 (16 ♖xa7 ♖xa7 17 ♕xa7 ♕g5∓) was the game Buturin-Glek, Belgorod 1989) 16...♗d7! 17 ♕e3 (17 ♕xb7 ♕c5!) 17...♗b5 18 ♘d2 ♕c7 19 f4 ♖ad8∓ intending ...♖d3.

15.3 2 d4 d5 3 ♗e3

This is called the 'Alapin-Diemer Gambit' by Harding. The idea after 3...dxe4 is to get into a sort of Blackmar-Diemer Gambit (1 d4 d5 2 e4 dxe4 3 f3, or 2 ♘c3 ♘f6 3 e4 dxe4 4 f3), normally playing f3 early on. The drawback to this strategy is that the bishop on e3 would be poorly placed in a Blackmar-Diemer (an opening of marginal soundness anyway). Nevertheless the line has its defenders and White with the extra tempo can get away with more in the opening than Black. The only other serious 3rd move options are:

(a) 3 ♗d3 (An innocuous move that seeks to avoid risk) and:

(a1) 3...c5 4 c3 ♘c6 (4...cxd4 5 exd5 exd5 6 cxd4 ♘c6 7 ♗e3 ♗b4+ 8 ♘c3 ♘ge7 9 a3 ♗xc3+ 10 bxc3 ♗f5= Maroja-Kovacevic, Zadar 2000) 5 ♘e2 cxd4 6 cxd4 ♘b4!? 7 ♗b5+ ♗d7 8 ♗xd7+ ♕xd7 9 e5 ♘e7 10 ♘bc3 ♘f5 11 a3 ♘c6 (a sort of Advance Variation with the light-squared bishops off) 12 b4 ♗e7 13 0-0 ♖c8 14 ♕d3 f6 15 g4 ♘h4 16 f4 f5! 17 h3 fxg4 18 hxg4 h5! 19 gxh5 ♘f5∓ Bluvshtein-Degraeve, Montreal 2002;

(a2) 3...dxe4 4 ♗xe4 ♘f6

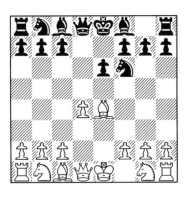

and now:

(a21) 5 ♗g5 c5! 6 ♗xf6 (6 c3 cxd4 7 cxd4 ♕b6! 8 ♗xf6 ♕xb2 9 ♘d2 gxf6) 6...♕xf6 7 ♘f3 ♘c6 8 c3 cxd4 9 ♗xc6+ bxc6 10 cxd4 ♖b8 11 ♕d2 c5∓;

(a22) 5 ♗d3 c5! 6 ♘f3 (6 dxc5 ♗xc5

7 ♘f3 ♘c6 8 0-0 0-0 9 ♘c3 ♘b4!∓ Rivera-P.Hummel, Oropesa del Mar 1998) 6...♘c6 7 c3 ♗e7 (7...cxd4=) 8 dxc5 ♗xc5= Tartakower-Trifunovic, Saltsjobaden 1948;

(a23) 5 ♗f3! (at least this is active) 5...c5 6 ♘e2 (6 c3 ♘c6 7 ♘e2 cxd4 8 cxd4 ♗e7 9 ♘bc3 0-0 10 0-0 ♕b6=) 6...♘c6 7 ♗e3 cxd4 (7...e5!? 8 ♗xc6+ bxc6 9 dxe5 ♕xd1+ 10 ♔xd1 ♘g4= Suechting-Alapin, Barmen 1905) 8 ♗xc6+?! (8 ♘xd4 ♘e5!?) 8...bxc6 9 ♕xd4 ♕xd4 10 ♗xd4 c5! 11 ♗xf6 gxf6∓ with open lines and two bishops that compensate for Black's weaknesses: 12 ♘bc3 ♖g8 13 ♘e4 ♗e7 14 0-0 ♗b7 15 f3 0-0-0 16 ♖ad1 f5! 17 ♘4g3 c4∓ Bezgodov-Hanley, Hoogeveen 2002;

(b) 3 c4?! dxe4 is a dubious gambit, e.g., 4 ♘c3 ♘f6 (or 4...f5 5 f3 ♘f6 6 fxe4 fxe4∓) 5 ♗g5 (5 f3 c5 6 d5 exd5 7 cxd5 exf3 8 ♘xf3 ♗d6∓ – ECO) 5...♗e7 6 f3 ♘c6! 7 d5 (7 ♘ge2 exf3∓) 7...exd5 8 ♗xf6 (8 cxd5 ♘xd5∓) 8...♗xf6 9 cxd5 ♘d4 10 ♘xe4 0-0∓;

(c) 3 f3 c5 (3...♘f6 4 e5 ♘fd7 5 f4 c5=) 4 ♗e3 ♘c6 5 c3 dxe4 6 fxe4 ♘f6 7 e5 ♘d5 8 ♗f2 cxd4 9 cxd4 Stanka-Lalic, Oberwart 2001; and one path was 9...♗b4+ 10 ♘d2 f6 11 exf6 ♘xf6 12 ♘gf3 (12 a3 ♗xd2+ 13 ♕xd2 ♘e4∓) 12...♘e4∓.

3...dxe4 4 ♘d2!

4 f3 ♘h6!? threatens ...♘f5 (or 4...♘f6 5 ♘c3 and 5...♘d5 6 ♘xd5 exd5 7 ♕d2 ♗d6∓ or 5...♗b4 6 a3 ♘d5! – Minev) 5 ♕d2 (5 ♗xh6 ♕h4+ is good for Black; 5 fxe4? ♕h4+ 6 ♗f2 ♕xe4+∓) 5...♘f5 6 ♗f2 c5!∓ with the idea 7 dxc5? ♕xd2+ 8 ♔xd2 e3+! 9 ♗xe3 ♘xe3 10 ♔xe3 ♗xc5+∓.

4...♘f6 5 c3!

(a) 5 f3?! ♘d5! 6 ♕e2 ♘xe3 7 ♕xe3 exf3 8 ♘gxf3 ♗e7 or 8...g6, and White lacks compensation;

(b) 5 ♗c4 ♘c6 6 ♘e2 e5 7 c3 exd4 8 ♘xd4 ♘e5 9 ♕b3 ♗d6∓ Edvardson-J.Watson, Gausdal 1980.

5...b6!?

This has been the most frequent move; also reasonable is getting the bishop pair by 5...♘d5 6 ♘xe4 ♘xe3 7 fxe3 g6=.

6 g3

White doesn't get his pawn back after 6 ♕c2 ♗b7 7 ♘e2 ♕d5 8 g3 ♗d6 9 ♗g2 ♕f5∓.

6...♗b7 7 ♗g2 c5!?

7...♘bd7 8 ♕c2 ♗e7 9 ♘xe4 ♘xe4 10 ♗xe4 ♗xe4 11 ♕xe4 0-0= Mieses-Mason, Monte Carlo 1903.

After 7...c5, play might go 8 dxc5! ♗xc5 9 ♗xc5 bxc5 10 ♕c2 ♕d5 11 ♘e2 ♘bd7 12 c4 ♕e5 13 0-0-0 ♖b8! (targeting b2 and preparing ...e3; 13...0-0 14 ♘c3=) 14 ♘c3 e3! 15 ♘de4 ♗xe4 16 ♘xe4 ♘xe4 17 ♗xe4 ♘f6! 18 ♗c6+ ♔e7 and Black is still a pawn up with open lines, e.g., 19 ♖he1 ♕c7 20 ♗f3 exf2 21 ♕xf2 ♖hd8∓.

Index of Variations

3 Advance Variation: 5...♛b6

1 e4 e6 2 d4 d5 3 e5 c5 4 c3 ♘c6 5 ♘f3 ♛b6

4 King's Indian Attack

1 e4 e6

4.1 2 d3 d5 3 ♘d2 *57*
  4.11 3...♘f6 4 ♘gf3 *58*
    4.111 4...♘c6 *59*
    4.112 4...♗c5 *61*
    4.113 4...b6 *63*
  4.12 3...c5 4 ♘gf3 ♘c6 5 g3 ♗d6 6 ♗d2 ♘ge7 7 0-0 0-0 *65*
    4.121 8 ♖e1 *66*
    4.122 8 ♘h4 *68*
4.2 2 ♕e2 *68*

  4.21 2...♘f6 *69*
  4.22 2...c5 *71*

5 Exchange Variation

1 e4 e6 2 d4 d5 3 exd5 exd5

5.1 4 c4 *73*
5.2 4 ♘f3 *75*
  5.21 4...♗g4 *75*
  5.22 4...♗d6 *77*
5.3 4 ♗d3 *79*

6 Tarrasch Variation: Introduction and 3...c5

1 e4 e6 2 d4 d5 3 ♘d2 c5

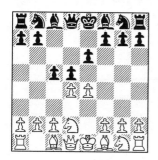

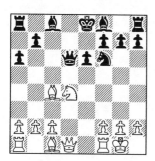

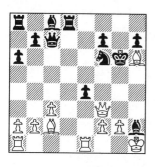

7 Tarrasch Variation: 3...♗e7
1 e4 e6 2 d4 d5 3 ♘d2 ♗e7

7.1 4 c3 *104*
7.2 4 e5 c5 5 ♕g4 *105*
  7.21 5...g6 *107*
  7.22 5...♔f8 *108*
7.3 4 ♘gf3 *111*
7.4 4 ♗d3 c5 5 dxc5 ♘f6 6 ♕e2 *116*
  7.41 6...0-0 *117*
  7.42 6...♘c6 *119*

8 Winawer Variation: Fourth Move Alternatives
1 e4 e6 2 d4 d5 3 ♘c3 ♗b4

8.1 4 a3 ♗xc3+ 5 bxc3 dxe4 *123*
  8.11 6 f3 *125*
    8.111 6...♘d7 *125*
    8.112 6...e5 *126*
  8.12 6 ♕g4 ♘f6 7 ♕xg7 ♖g8 8 ♕h6 ♘bd7 *126*
    8.121 9 f3 *127*
    8.122 9 ♘h3 *128*
    8.123 9 ♘e2 *129*
8.2 4 ♕g4 *131*
8.3 4 ♗d2 dxe4 5 ♕g4 ♘f6 6 ♕xg7 ♖g8 7 ♕h6 *133*
  8.31 7...♕xd4 0-0-0 *134*

9 Winawer Variation: Fifth Move Alternatives
1 e4 e6 2 d4 d5 3 ♘c3 ♗b4 4 e5 c5

10 Winawer Variation: Main Line with 7 ♕g4

1 e4 e6 2 d4 d5 3 ♘c3 ♗b4 4 e5 c5 5 a3 ♗xc3+ 6 bxc3 ♘e7 7 ♕g4 0-0

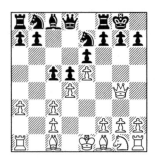

11 Winawer Variation: Positional Lines

1 e4 e6 2 d4 d5 3 ♘c3 ♗b4 4 e5 c5 5 a3 ♗xc3+ 6 bxc3 ♘e7

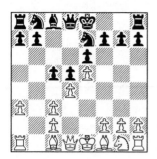

12 Winawer Variation: Black Plays 6...♕c7

1 e4 e6 2 d4 d5 3 ♘c3 ♗b4 4 e5 c5 5 a3 ♗xc3+ 6 bxc3 ♕c7

13 Classical Variation: 4 e5
1 e4 e6 2 d4 d5 3 ♘c3 ♘f6 4 e5 ♘fd7

14 Classical Variation: 4 ♗g5 (4...dxe4 5 ♘xe4 ♗e7)
1 e4 e6 2 d4 d5 3 ♘c3 ♘f6 4 ♗g5 dxe4 5 ♘xe4 ♗e7 6 ♗xf6 ♗xf6 7 ♘f3 ♘d7 8 ♕d2 0-0 9 0-0-0

15 Odds and Ends
1 e4 e6